1920 • The Retirement Act creates the first federal civil service pension system.
• The Nineteenth Amendment gives women the right to vote.
1921 • The Budget and Accounting Act establishes (1) the Bureau of the Budget in the Department of the Treasury and (2) the General Accounting Office as an agency of the Congress.
1922 • Max Weber's structural definition of bureaucracy is published posthumously.
1923 • The Classification Act brings position classification to Washington-based federal employees and establishes the principle of equal pay for equal work.
1924 • Hawthorne studies begin at the Hawthorne Works of the Western Electric Company in Chicago; they will last until 1932 and lead to new thinking about the relationship of work environment to productivity.
1926 • Leonard D. White's *Introduction to the Study of Public Administration* is the first text in public administration.
• Mary Parker Follett, in calling for "power with" as opposed to "power over," anticipates the movement toward more participatory management styles.
1929 • The University of Southern California establishes the first independent professional school of public administration.
• Stock market crashes; Great Depression begins.
1930 • Durham County, South Carolina, is first to install county-manager form of county government.
1933 • President Franklin D. Roosevelt's New Deal begins.
• Francis Perkins, the first woman in a president's cabinet, is appointed Secretary of Labor.
• The Tennessee Valley Authority (TVA) is established by Congress as an independent public corporation.
1935 • The National Labor Relations (Wagner) Act establishes the right of private sector employees to organize and bargain collectively.
• Social Security program created.
1936 • J. Donald Kingsley and William E. Mosher's *Public Personnel Administration* becomes the first text in this field.
• John Maynard Keynes publishes his *General Theory of Employment, Interest, and Money,* which calls for using a government's fiscal and monetary policies to positively influence a capitalistic economy.
• E. Pendleton Herring in *Public Adminstration and the Public Interest* asserts that bureaucrats, by default, must often be the arbiters of the public interest.
1937 • The Brownlow Committee's report says that the "President needs help" and calls for the reorganization of the executive branch.
• Luther Gulick calls attention to the various functional elements of the work of an executive with his mne-monic device POSDCORB.
1938 • The Fair Labor Standards Act provides for minimum wages, overtime pay, and limits on child labor.

• Chester I. Barnard's *tive* foreshadows thinking about org
1939 • American Society founded.
• The Reorganization Act enables the creation of the Executive Office of the President and the transfer of the Bureau of the Budget from the Treasury to the White House.
• The Hatch Act is passed to inhibit political activities by federal employees.
• The federal government first requires the states to have merit systems for employees in programs aided by federal funds.
1940 • *Public Administration Review* first published.
1941 • James Burnham's *The Managerial Revolution* asserts that as the control of large organizations passes from the hands of the owners into the hands of professional administrators, the society's new governing class will be the possessors not of wealth but of technical expertise.
• Japanese attack on Pearl Harbor brings the United States into World War II.
1943 • Abraham Maslow's "needs hierarchy" first appears in *Psychological Review.*
• Withholding for federal income tax begins as a temporary wartime measure.
1944 • J. Donald Kingsley's *Representative Bureaucracy* develops the concept that all social groups have a right to participate in their governing institutions in proportion to their numbers in the population.
1945 • With the dropping of the atomic bomb and the end of World War II, the suddenly public Manhattan Project marks the federal government's first major involvement with science in a policymaking role.
• Paul Appleby leads the postwar attack on the politics/administration dichotomy by insisting in *Big Democracy* that apolitical governmental processes went against the grain of the American experience.
1946 • The Employment Act creates the Council of Economic Advisors and asserts that it is the policy of the federal government to maintain full employment.
• The Administrative Procedure Act standarized many federal government administrative practices across agencies.
• Herbert A. Simon's "The Proverbs of Administration" attacks the principles approach to management for being inconsistent and often inapplicable.
1947 • President Harry S. Truman announces his doctrine.
1949 • The First Hoover Commission recommends increased managerial capacity in the Executive Office of the President.
• The National Security Act creates the Department of Defense.
1951 • David Truman's *The Governmental Process* calls for viewing interest groups as the real determinant of, and focal point of study on, public policy.
• Kurt Lewin proposes a general model of organizational change consisting of three phases, "unfreezing, change, refreezing" in his *Field Theory in Social Science.*

Introducing Public Administration

SECOND EDITION

Jay M. Shafritz
Graduate School of Public and International Affairs
University of Pittsburgh

E. W. Russell
Public Sector Research Unit
Victoria University of Technology

LONGMAN

An imprint of Addison Wesley Longman, Inc.

New York • Reading, Massachusetts • Menlo Park, California • Harlow, England
Don Mills, Ontario • Sydney • Mexico City • Madrid • Amsterdam

Editor-in-Chief: Priscilla McGeehon
Acquisitions Editor: Eric Stano
Supplements Editor: Mark Toews
Marketing Manager: Megan Galvin-Fak
Full Service Production Manager: Patti Brecht
Project Coordination, Text Design, and
    Electronic Page Makeup: Pre-Press Company, Inc.
Cover Design Manager: Nancy Danahy
Cover Designer: Kay Petronio
Photo Researcher: Mira Schachne
Senior Print Buyer: Hugh Crawford
Printer and Binder: The Maple-Vail Book Manufacturing Group
Cover Printer: Coral Graphic Services, Inc.

Library of Congress Cataloging-in-Publication Data

Shafritz, Jay M.
    Introducing public administration / Jay M. Shafritz, E. W. Russell.
        p.   cm.
    Includes bibliographical references and index.
    ISBN 0-321-04483-5
    1. Public administration.   I. Russell, E. W. (Edward W.)
    II. Title.
  JF1351.S448   1999
  351—dc21   99-34820
                                                                CIP

Please visit our website at http://www.awlonline.com

ISBN 0-321-04483-5

12345678910—MA—02010099

Brief Contents

Detailed Contents

Preface

The Method to This Madness!

With college, university, and public libraries bulging from tens of thousands of new books published each year and the ever-increasing concern for the wholesale destruction of forests to make paper, the would-be authors of today should have a definite reason for bringing a new book into the world.

It's madness, just madness, we were assured by some of our academic colleagues, to attempt a new public administration text. There already were too many! But as Hamlet happily said, "Though this be madness, yet there is method in it." We saw a need—or as they say in advertising—a niche in the market. Almost all of the widely used public administration texts seem to be written primarily for graduate students. This was to be expected since the field has long been dominated by professional graduate school programs.

However, the last two decades have seen a flowering of undergraduate public administration majors, minors, and individual course offerings. With this fact—with this market—in mind, we sought to create a text that would bridge both worlds, one that would be informal enough to be accessible to undergraduates yet comprehensive enough for beginning graduate students. It is now up to you, dear reader, to decide if we succeeded.

Each chapter starts with a story—what we call a keynote—that highlights a major aspect of the subject. These accounts deal with a rich variety of topics: from the Oklahoma City bombing, the space shuttle disaster, and the mutiny on the *Bounty* to Robert McNamara's angst over the Vietnam War. All of these keynotes have significant public policy and public management implications that are developed further in the text.

The material in each chapter is then presented in an order that should not surprise anyone familiar with public administration. We have made every effort to keep the tone lively so that students as well as their professors might take some pleasure in reviewing the material. When a word appears in **boldface** in the text, it is defined at the bottom of its page. The Key Concepts at the end of each chapter supplement rather than duplicate these boldfaced definitions.

Readers will also find a list of recommended books and a separate list of related web sites at the end of each chapter. These have been included as guides to further information on chapter topics for any interested reader—student or instructor.

Every effort has been made to keep the material as current as possible. Thus there is extensive coverage of the reinventing government movement, privatization, and contracting out. Because American public administration is being increasingly influenced by practices in other countries, such as managerialism in Britain, a comparative perspective has been added wherever appropriate.

For this second edition, we made many important changes. Among them are:

- Expanded photo captions that better relate the pictures to the content of their chapters
- A list of related web sites at the back of each chapter
- A list of recommended books (fully annotated) for additional reading at the back of each chapter
- Figures and tables have been updated and additional graphic presentations created
- An expanded section on government regulation (Chapter 1)
- Expanded coverage on public policymaking (Chapter 2)
- Expanded coverage of the machinery of government including new sections on metropolitan government and voluntarism and philanthropy (Chapter 3)
- A major updating and expansion of the intergovernmental relations of welfare reform (Chapter 4)
- Expanded coverage of the influence of Herbert A. Simon on organization theory (Chapter 5)
- A new keynote—Organization Development in Hollywood: From *The Sands of Iwo Jima* to *G.I. Jane*—to show how management can be learned from the movies (Chapter 6)
- Expanded coverage of the Government Performance and Results Act (Chapter 7)
- Expanded coverage of benchmarking and the strategic planning requirements of state and federal agenies (Chapter 8)
- A refocused keynote on transformational leadership at the U.S. Postal Service (Chapter 9)
- An updating of trends on reinventing public personnel administration (Chapter 10)
- An updating on equal employment opportunity and affirmative action policies (Chapter 11)
- The latest U.S. Supreme Court decisions on sexual harassment and disabilities discrimination (Chapter 11)
- The keynote on the Orange County, California, bankruptcy is brought up to date (Chapter 12)
- Updated coverage on the auditing activities of the U.S. General Accounting Office (Chapter 13)
- A new section on the ethics of lying about sex and how this led to President Clinton's impeachment (Chapter 14)

There are no traditional footnotes in this book. Generally, if a work or author is referred to in a chapter, the corresponding full citation will be found in that chapter's bibliography. The major exceptions are works or statements so famous and existing in so many formats—such as the *Bible* and Shakespeare's plays—that further bibliographic information was deemed unnecessary. Most long quotations are kept in boxes, separate from the main body and rhythm of the text. This informal format was used very successfully through four editions of the Shafritz et al. text, *Personnel Management in Government* (New York: Marcel Dekker, 1978–1992).

Sometimes it was too awkward to incorporate a reference to a citation in the body of the text. These "fugitive" quotations have their sources identified in an appendix.

No book is born without debts. We are happy to acknowledge the helpful suggestions of David H. Rosenbloom of the American University; Albert C. Hyde of the Brookings Institution; Elizabeth Hecker of Boise State University; Carol Edlund of California State University-Hayward; Geert Bouckaert of the Catholic University of Leuven in Belgium; Larry Terry and Jennifer Alexander of Cleveland State University; Richard Wandling of Eastern Illinois University; Barbara Yarnold of Florida International University; John Sacco of George Mason University; Gashaw W. Lake of Kentucky State University; Jerry McCaffery of the Naval Postgraduate School; Michael L. Vasu of North Carolina State University; Christopher A. Simon of Oregon State University; Beverly Cigler of Penn State/Harrisburg; Jeffrey K. Guiler of Robert Morris College; Peter Foot of the Royal Naval College, Greenwich, United Kingdom; Marc Holzer of Rutgers/Newark; Katherine Naff of San Francisco State University; Curtis R. Berry of Shippensburg University; Kenneth Warren of St. Louis University; Norma Riccucci and Frank J. Thompson of the State University of New York at Albany; Harry A. Bailey of Temple University; Ari Halachmi of Tennessee State University; William H. Stewart of the University of Alabama; Daniel Martin of the University of Baltimore; Kathy Boyd of the University of Colorado at Denver; Kenneth L. Nichols of the University of Maine; Gary S. Marshall of the University of Nebraska at Omaha; Gordon P. Whittaker of the University of North Carolina; Breena Coates, Donald Goldstein, Lawrence Howard, Kevin Kearns, Jerome McKinney, Rowan Miranda, Lou Picard, and Harvey L. White of the University of Pittsburgh; Jean Wahl Harris of the University of Scranton; Sharon Ridgeway of the University of Southwest Louisiana; David H. Davis of trhe University of Toledo; J. Steven Ott of the University of Utah; and Frank Bryan of the University of Vermont; Richard Crockett of Western Illinois University.

Finally, a note of special thanks to Ann Ostroski and Peter Dzewaltowski, both of the University of Pittsburgh, for their efforts on behalf of this second edition. We also acknowledge the permission of Marc Holzer, Editor-in-Chief of *Public Voices*, to reprint in a slightly altered form (as the keynote to Chapter 6) the article "Organization Development in Hollywood War Movies," originally written by Jay M. Shafritz and Peter Foot. We also thank Dr. Foot of the Joint Services Command and Staff College of the United Kingdom's Ministry of Defense for allowing us to seamlessly meld this material into the text.

This has been a collaboration by two friends at opposite ends of the world—Melbourne, Australia, and Pittsburgh, Pennsylvania. While we could hardly have been farther apart physically, we are kindred academic spirits. Despite the fact that we were bred in differing administrative cultures, we were totally in accord on what we wanted to say. Being curious souls, we would be pleased to hear the opinions of our readers on this effort. Feel free to write to either of us. Please direct correspondence to Jay Shafritz, Graduate School of Public and International Affairs, Pittsburgh, PA, or E. W. Russell, Victoria University of Technology, Melbourne, Australia. Given sufficient encouragement, we would be happy to continue revising this text until we get it right.

Jay M. Shafritz
E. W. Russell

1

Defining Public Administration

Keynote: The Heroes of Oklahoma City

Rhonda Griffin thought her computer was exploding. So she quickly covered her face with her hands and saved her life by instinctively rolling her office chair backward. Upon uncovering her eyes, her first thought was "Oh my God, the computer has blown the ceiling down." But the floor beneath her desk was missing. So was the desk. She saw in the space where she had been sitting "a huge concrete slab dangling, held only by a piece of rebar." She instantly realized that a malfunctioning computer was the least of her problems.

The explosion that destroyed Rhonda Griffin's Department of Housing and Urban Development office in the Alfred P. Murrah Federal Building in Oklahoma City was caused by a homemade bomb containing more than two tons of fertilizer and fuel oil. It was packed into a Ryder rental truck and parked in front of the nine-story building housing 16 federal agencies, from the Agriculture Department to the Veterans Administration.

At 9:02 on the morning of April 19, 1995, just after more than 500 federal government employees had arrived for the day's business, the bomb was detonated, with devastating effect. A shock wave moving at 7,000 miles per hour suddenly disintegrated fully a third of the building, blew out windows for blocks around, and hurled burning automobiles to the roofs of buildings across the street. More than 200 survivors were treated at area hospitals; exactly 168 nonsurvivors were murdered by this cowardly act of terrorism. The dead included federal employees, citizens seeking government services, and 15 children who were in the day-care center housed in the second floor of the building. Perhaps the most poignant news photo of the tragedy was that of firefighter Chris Fields carrying the broken body of the soon to die Baylee Almon, who had celebrated her first birthday the day before.

Throughout the nation, citizens were shocked by how one bomb could vaporize so much of such a large building, dismayed by the enormity of the suffering, and disgusted that Americans could do this to their innocent fellow citizens. They stayed glued to their television sets to learn of each new development in both the dramatic rescue and the ensuing criminal investigation.

The villains of this story are the twisted souls who thought such mass murder was an appropriate way to demonstrate their grievances against the federal government. But there were heroes, too. Immediately after the blast, scores of people, many still anonymous, came from the streets to help victims. One such volunteer, Rebecca Anderson, a 37-year-old nurse, died after being hit by falling concrete. The only other rescuer to die was Michael Loudenslager, a 48-year-old General Services Administration employee who was unharmed by the initial blast. After pulling several colleagues from the rubble, he went back into the collapsing building, apparently headed for the day-care center. He was not seen again until three days later, when he was found under a concrete block near a stairwell. Jackhammers were needed to free his lifeless body.

For two weeks the nation, indeed the world, watched on live television as the professional rescue teams brought out the stranded, the wounded, the dying, and the dead. The Oklahoma City Fire Department rescued almost all of the survivors. When firefighter Clinton Greenwood climbed up the aerial ladder of Truck 5 to rescue several people stranded on a high open ledge, they hesitated to climb on the fragile-looking top of the ladder. One man broke the silence and asked Greenwood if the extremely extended ladder could hold the weight of more than one person. Greenwood responded: "This is state-of-the-art equipment. The city paid big bucks for this truck. This is your taxpayer's dollars at work." Thus reassured, the man climbed on and afterward told Greenwood he would "never gripe about high taxes again." But there were few moments of levity in the rescue operation. There were too many dead and mangled bodies, too many grief-stricken families, and too many orphans too young to even understand the full meaning of their loss. Thirty children were made orphans; another 219 lost one parent.

Although the victims were all in Oklahoma City, it was the whole nation that cried with their families. This was not just another office building. As a federal building, it belonged to all citizens. The people who worked there were working for all Americans. So the barbarous attack wounded the entire country. All the more so because of where it occurred—in the heartland of the nation. If one couldn't feel safe

The Alfred P. Murrah Federal Building (above) in Oklahoma City after being bombed on April 19, 1995. For this crime a federal district court sentenced Timothy McVeigh to death. He is now awaiting execution, pending appeal, in a federal prison. His accomplice, Terry Nichols, was sentenced to life without possibility of parole, plus 48 years. They were sentenced not only for murder, but for what the judge in both trials, Richard Matsch, called "a crime against the Constitution of the United States" in that the people and the offices destroyed were engaged in the constitutional functions of providing for a common defense, establishing justice, promoting the general welfare, and ensuring domestic tranquility. (Right) Two of the "lucky" victims—they survived ●

from such attacks smack in the geographic middle of the country, where was it possible to feel safe? In the days right after the blast the news media put forth much banal talk about America's "loss of innocence" along with the increasing body count on the loss of the innocents.

While no one would be found alive in the rubble after the first day, that was impossible to know at the time. Beginning at 1:00 A.M. on the second day, the first of ten out-of-state rescue teams arrived to help. These teams, deployed by the Federal Emergency Management Agency, included two dozen search dogs. These dogs are trained to bark when they find something alive and whine when they find a body. The dogs spent most of their time whining.

While it is less dramatic, recovering a body at a disaster site is often just as dangerous as rescuing a survivor. The Murrah Federal Building, damaged beyond repair, was a hazard to anyone even near it. So less than a month after the story began, the world's attention was called to Oklahoma City once again as strategically placed explosives reduced the building to one immense dusty heap. Only now would it be safe to recover the body of the last victim.

The heroic efforts of the rescuers in Oklahoma City received massive publicity. The stories many of the survivors told of the bravery and daring of the rescue teams were heartrending. The news media heralded their heroism (many literally risked their lives), dedication (they worked round the clock), and self-sacrifice (they left home at a moment's notice). But one point was largely missed in all the news reports. All these highly trained search and rescue professionals were public employees. They and the administrative apparatus that sustains their organizations are part of the government. They are representative of the bureaucrats that so many people—even some who were then lauding them as heroes—had often described as overpaid and inefficient.

These everyday heroes got so much attention after the Oklahoma City bombing because they were doing wholesale what they did retail on a daily basis. It is a common, if not everyday, occurrence when a firefighter rescues a child from a burning building. But carry an injured baby from what the FBI called the worst terrorist attack ever committed in the United States and you get on the cover of *Newsweek*. The point is not to diminish the heroism evident in Oklahoma City but to merely assert that it is not unusual.

Citizens the world over complain about their governments. But once disaster strikes—whether caused by nature or criminals—they expect instant service. When there is an earthquake in California, when the Mississippi River floods, or when a Gulf Coast hurricane wreaks havoc, volunteers come running. But only those with special training can usually save someone from a raging torrent that was once a gentle stream or a cage of twisted metal that was once a car. And the lasting help that disaster victims need—from social services to low-interest loans for rebuilding—is generally only available from government. Suddenly these "bureaucrats" are angels of mercy. When danger lurks, they become our modern versions of medieval knights in shining armor. Call 911 in most U.S. cities and within minutes you'll have a career public servant at your door ready to risk his or her life for you and yours. On more than half the days of any given year, a police officer or firefighter in the United States will die in the line of duty.

In response to the death of a police officer murdered on the job, Mayor Ed Rendell of Philadelphia said: "Last night I just thought about how tough it is to be a policeman or a fireman, because no matter how tough it is for us in our jobs and whatever—the pressures we operate under—none of us leave the house in the morning [not knowing] whether we're coming back at night."

To be sure, there are heroes in Oklahoma City. But there are heroes in your city, too. Most of them are invisible to you. Modern public service allows vast scope for heroism. Throughout history, classic heroes used their special skills for the public good usually by performing feats of military prowess and physical bravery. And some societies recognized other kinds of heroes, too. For example, Michelangelo, who became one of the greatest heroes of Renaissance Italy, was known only for his prowess with a chisel and a paintbrush. Today traditional heroes—police officers and firefighters—are joined by great numbers of quiet unsung heroes—public works department engineers who provide safe drinking water, highway department drivers who work all night clearing snow in a blizzard, and public health officials who keep diseases from becoming epidemics. These virtually invisible heroes often hold our lives in their hands no less than their uniformed coworkers. More than that, they make modern life, civilization as we know it, possible.

Then there are those public employees who do not deal with life and death issues. Their concerns are instead with quality of life. They are, for example, the teach-

TABLE 1.1   Annual Police Officer and Firefighter Deaths in the Line of Duty

Year	Police Officer Deaths	Firefighter Deaths
1989	145	111
1990	132	103
1991	123	105
1992	129	79
1993	129	74
1994	140	104
1995	131	96

SOURCE: *Statistical Abstract of the United States* (1997); National Fire Data Center.

ers who inspire students to excel, the social workers who find a loving home for a suddenly orphaned child, the economic development officers who bring hundreds of new jobs into a community, and the public managers who reinvent programs so that costs can be cut and taxes lowered. While not called upon to be physically brave, they are nonetheless often heroic. The public service has a large variety of heroes. Some are just more visible than others.

The Definitions of Public Administration

There is a scene in Edmond Rostand's play *Cyrano de Bergerac* in which the hero's big nose is purposely insulted by someone wishing to provoke him into a duel. But the challenger's insult of "rather large" is so commonplace that Cyrano then lectures him on "the great many things" he might have said if he'd had "some tinge of letters, or of wit." Defining public administration poses a similar challenge—even without the ensuing swordplay.

The authors of this book believe that nothing is more important to an introduction to public administration than the most expansive possible definition. How else to explore its richness and subtlety? How else to savor its historical significance, universal application, and present development? How else to gain an appreciation for the later technical chapters? Nevertheless, the discussion that follows is inherently incomplete. Public administration is so vast that there is no way to encompass it all with only one definition. So we have written eighteen of them and clustered them into four categories: (1) political, (2) legal, (3) managerial, and (4) occupational. This quartet of definitions essentially expands upon the trio—political, managerial, and legal—established by **David H. Rosenbloom.** But even with such an array of definitions the authors are in the uncomfortable position of Cyrano's challenger. We would have said even more if we'd only had the wit!

David H. Rosenbloom (1943–) The leading authority on the constitutional aspects of public employment. His paradigm of public administration as the intersection of management, politics, and law has become the standard way the subject is analyzed and taught.

Political Definitions of Public Administration

Public administration cannot exist outside of its political context. It is this context that makes it public—that makes it different from private or business administration. Consequently, our first definitions of public administration focus on its political nature.

Public Administration Is What Government Does   It is a White House chef preparing the menu of a state dinner for a visiting **chief of state**, a Department of Agriculture inspector examining beef at a slaughterhouse, and a Food and Drug Administration scientist determining the number of rodent hairs that food processors can safely and legally leave in chocolate, popcorn, and peanut butter. It is a firefighter rescuing a child from a disintegrating building, a meter reader attaching a ticket to your automobile for overlong parking, and a state prison official injecting deadly fluids into the veins of a condemned criminal. It is an astronomer exploring the furthest reaches of outer space, a physician searching for cancer in the colon of the president of the United States, and a sewer crawler seeking to discover what has clogged up a municipal drain pipe. It is giving **food stamps** to the poor, mortgage interest deductions to homeowners, and tax-free earnings on **municipal bonds** to the rich.

Throughout the world, government employees do things that affect the daily lives of their fellow citizens. These things range from the heroic (as we saw in Oklahoma City) to the mundane. Usually these efforts are beneficial. Too often they are not. Most of the time in most countries public administrators tend to the public's business; for example, they build bridges and highways, collect garbage, put out fires, plow snow where it is cold, kill mosquitoes where it is hot, and provide essential social services for the less fortunate. But in other lands public employees may torture the innocent and murder children. When **Amnesty International** publishes its annual report on the states that brutalize and violate the civil rights of its citizens, who do you think does all this brutalizing and violating? None other than the local public administrators. Of course such nefarious activities are usually orga-

---

chief of state The ceremonial head of a government, such as a king, queen, or president. This is in contrast to the chief executive of a government, such as a prime minister, chancellor, or president. The American presidency combines in one office, one person, the roles of chief of state and chief executive.

food stamps A welfare program designed to improve the nutrition of the poor. Administered by the Department of Agriculture and state and local welfare organizations, the program provides coupons (stamps) that can be exchanged for food at many grocery stores.

municipal bonds The debt instruments of subnational governments in the United States. Because the interest on municipal bonds is exempt from federal taxes (state and local exemptions may vary), such bonds allow jurisdictions to borrow money at lower than commercial market interest rates. The buyers of the bonds find them an attractive investment because their high marginal tax rates make a tax-free investment more advantageous than a taxable one paying even higher interest.

Amnesty International A worldwide organization that seeks to gain the release of political and religious prisoners by publicizing their plight and lobbying governments. It has been especially effective in exposing cases of government-sanctioned torture. In 1972 the organization was awarded the Nobel Peace Prize.

Box 1.1

How the Inherent Criminality of Some Public Administrators Is Hidden by Political Language

In our time, political speech and writing are largely the defense of the indefensible. Thus political language has to consist largely of euphemism, question-begging, and sheer cloudy vagueness. Defenseless villages are bombarded from the air, the inhabitants driven out into the countryside, the cattle machine-gunned, the huts set on fire with incendiary bullets: this is called pacification. Millions of peasants are robbed of their farms and sent trudging along the roads with no more than they can carry; this is called transfer of population or rectification of frontiers. People are imprisoned for years without trial, or shot in the back of the neck, or sent to die of scurvy in Arctic lumber camps; this is called elimination of unreliable elements. Such phraseology is needed if one wants to name things without calling up mental pictures of them. . . .

Political language . . . is designed to make lies sound truthful and murder resepctable, and to give an appearance of solidity to pure wind.

SOURCE: George Orwell, "Politics and the English Language," in *Shooting an Elephant and Other Essays* (New York: Harcourt Brace, 1946).

nized within some innocuous sounding program having to do with "population control" or "internal security." Thus modern public relations seeks to put a kindly face on ancient atrocities.

As a profession, public administration has developed values and ethical standards. But as an activity, it has no values. It merely reflects the cultural norms, beliefs, and power realities of its society. It is simply government doing whatever government does—in whatever political and cultural context it happens to exist. **Dwight Waldo,** writing in 1955, was the first to insist that analysts "see administration in terms of its environment" because "it enables us to understand differences in administration between different societies which would be inexplicable if we were limited to viewing administration analytically in terms of the universals of administration itself." So essentially similar administrative acts can be performed differently in different cultures. Thus a routine customs inspection in one state parallels the solicitation of a bribe by a corrupt customs official in another. The same act that is performed honestly in one state (because of a culture that supports honesty) may be performed corruptly in another (where the culture supports corruption by government officials).

Public administration is the totality of the working day activities of all the world's bureaucrats—whether they are legal or illegal, competent or incompetent, decent or despicable. British scientist J. B. S. Haldane wrote that "the universe is

---

Dwight Waldo (1913–) The preeminent historian of the academic field of public administration.

not only queerer than we suppose, but queerer than we *can* suppose." Things are much the same with public administration. It is not only far vaster in scope than most people suppose, it is so extensive and pervasive in modern life that not even the most imaginative of us can imagine it all.

Public Administration Is Both Direct and Indirect   It is direct when government employees provide services to the public as varied as mortgage insurance, mail delivery, and electricity. It is indirect when government pays private contractors to provide goods or services to citizens. For example, **NASA** operates the space shuttle, but the shuttle itself was built by private corporations. The security guards and cleaning staffs of many government buildings are employees of private companies. Does this put them outside the realm of public administration? Not at all. Remember that a government agency must hire, evaluate, and hold all employees and contractors accountable for the quality of their performance—whether they are cleaning toilets or building rockets.

Governments have used private contractors since ancient times. For example, the executioner who once operated and maintained the guillotine in France was an independent contractor who earned a fee per head chopped off—literal severance pay. The current trend toward greater **privatization** of government functions, which began most notably in the 1980s during the Reagan administration in the United States and the Thatcher administration in the United Kingdom, is now worldwide. This trend has been reinforced by the growth of the nonprofit sector, which receives much of its funding from government contracts—especially for social services and research. By 1995, 40 percent of the budget of private nonprofit organizations providing human services was derived from government. According to former New York Governor Mario Cuomo, government funds account for two out of every three dollars spent by Catholic Charities USA, a national network of some 1,400 social service organizations. By comparison, Lutheran Social Ministries obtains 54 percent of its funding from government sources, and the Salvation Army obtains 15 percent from such sources. Thus we may conclude that privatization has not necessarily reduced the total amount of public administration in the world; it has simply forced it to take different forms.

Public Administration Is a Phase in the Public Policymaking Cycle   Public policymaking never ends. Government perpetually suffers from a problem similar to that faced by Shakespeare's Hamlet, the indecisive prince of Denmark who struggled with whether "to be or not to be." Governments are in a constant flurry over whether to do or not to do. And whatever they do or do not do is public policy. All such decisions (including decisions not to make a decision) are made by those who control political power and implemented by the administrative officers of the bureaucracy.

NASA (National Aeronautics and Space Administration) The federal agency created by the National Aeronautics and Space Act of 1958 to conduct research on problems of flight and to explore outer space.

privatization The process of returning to the private sector property (such as public lands) or functions (such as trash collection, fire protection) previously owned or performed by government.

Thus public policy and public administration are two sides of the same coin. One decides, the other does. They cannot be separate because one side cannot exist without the other. But because policymaking is a continuous process, it cannot end with **implementation**. Whenever government does something, critics will suggest ways to do it better. This feedback can be informal—from citizen complaints to journalistic investigations—or it can take the form of an agency or legislative program evaluation. In any case, new decisions must be made even if the decision is to avoid making a decision.

Public Administration Is Implementing the Public Interest   The public interest is the universal label in which political actors wrap the policies and programs that they advocate. Would any **lobby**, public manager, legislator, or chief executive ever propose a program that was not "in the public interest"? Hardly! Because the public interest is generally taken to mean a commonly accepted good, the phrase is used both to further policies that are indeed for the common good and to obscure policies that may not be so commonly accepted as good. A considerable body of literature has developed about this phrase, because it represents an important philosophic point that, if successfully defined, could provide considerable guidance for politicians and public administrators alike. **Walter Lippmann** wrote that "the public interest may be presumed to be what men would choose if they saw clearly, thought rationally, acted disinterestedly and benevolently." Clear eyes and rational minds are common enough. Finding leaders who are disinterested and benevolent is the hard part.

In the early twentieth century, **E. Pendleton Herring** examined the problems posed by the dramatic increase in the scope of the administrative discretion of government. He accepted that laws passed by legislatures are necessarily the products of legislative compromise; thus they are often so vague that they need further definition. The bureaucrat, by default, then has the task of giving defining detail to the general principles embodied in a statute by issuing supplemental rules and regulations. "Upon the shoulders of the bureaucrat has been placed in large part the burden of

---

implementation Putting a government program into effect; the total process of translating a legal mandate into appropriate program directives and structures that provide services or create goods.

lobby Any individual, group, or organization that seeks to influence legislation or administrative action. Lobbies can be trade associations, individual corporations, good-government public interest groups, or other levels of government. The term arose from the use of the lobbies, or corridors, of legislative halls as places to meet with and persuade legislators to vote a certain way. Many lobbies provide legislators with reliable first-hand information of considerable value. However, some lobbies have given the practice an undesirable connotation, because they often contribute money to political campaigns and offer special favors to officials in the expectation of favorable treatment on some issue in the future.

Walter Lippmann (1889–1974) A journalist who went beyond being the preeminent political pundit of his time to being a political philosopher who wrote pioneering analyses of public opinion and foreign policy.

E. Pendleton Herring (1903–) One of the most influential of the pre-World War II scholars of public administration. His *Group Representation Before Congress* (1929) was one of the pioneering works in the study of pressure groups. His *Public Administration and the Public Interest* (1936) remains a major analysis of the relations between government agencies and their formal and informal constituencies.

reconciling group differences and making effective and workable the economic and social compromises arrived at through the legislative process." In effect, it becomes the job of the anonymous administrator to define the public interest.

Herring's discussion of the public interest and the critical roles played by bureaucrats and interest groups in public policy formulation correctly anticipated many of the critical issues still being grappled with in schools of public policy and administration today. Herring is a significant voice in what political science calls group theory, a school of thought that views government as representing various group interests and negotiating policy outcomes among them. According to Herring, the most basic task of a bureaucrat has been to establish working relationships with the various special interests so that their concerns can be more efficiently brokered.

The role that Herring would have public administrators play is that of **Edmund Burke's** trustee, a representative who exercises personal judgment and doesn't just follow the exact orders of a legislature or the perceived opinion of a constituency. In his classic 1774 "Speech to the Electors of Bristol" Burke told the voters: "Your representative owes you, not his industry only, but his judgment; and he betrays, instead of serving you, if he sacrifices it to your opinion." Few would argue with the desirability of using good judgment in the furtherance of the public interest. However, some would argue that the interest-group broker role that Herring espouses for high-level public administrators is inherently undemocratic.

Public Administration Is Doing Collectively That Which Cannot Be So Well Done Individually

This is Abraham Lincoln's understanding of the "legitimate object of government, . . . to do for a community of people, whatever they need to have done, but cannot do, at all, or cannot, so well do, for themselves—in their separate, and individual capacities." Thus public administration is the mature manifestation of the community spirit. What started as voluntary service (such as fire protection or care for the poor) became institutionalized as people indicated a preference (via elections) to pay taxes so that once voluntary activities could become government functions.

Twentieth-century communications have brought about a "revolution of rising expectations" whereby the people of traditionally poor countries realize just how poor they are relative to industrialized states. Similarly, the citizens of these rich states benefit from programs that they increasingly resent paying for. Senator Ernest Hollings of South Carolina often tells this story of a veteran returning from Korea who went to college on the **GI Bill**; bought his house with a Federal Housing Administration loan; started a business with a Small Business Administration loan; got electricity from Tennessee Valley Authority and, later, clean water from an Environmental Protection Agency project. His parents, on Social Security, retired to a farm, got electricity from Rural Electrification Administration and had their soil tested by the U.S. Department of Agriculture. When his father became ill, the family was

---

Edmund Burke (1729–1797) The British political philosopher and member of parliament who is often referred to as the father of modern conservative thought.

GI Bill The American Servicemen's Readjustment Act of 1944. It provided low-interest, no-down-payment home mortgages and education benefits that allowed a whole generation of working-class veterans to go to college and advance into the middle class.

saved from financial ruin by Medicare and a life was saved with a drug developed through the National Institutes of Health. His kids participated in the school lunch program, learned physics from teachers trained in a National Science Foundation program, and went to college with guaranteed student loans. He drove to work on the Interstate and moored his boat in a channel dredged by the Army Corps of Engineers. When floods hit, he took **Amtrak** to Washington to apply for disaster relief, and spent some time in the Smithsonian Institution museums. Then one day he got mad; he sent his congressman an angry letter. "Get the government off my back," he wrote. "I'm tired of paying taxes for all those programs created for ungrateful people!"

But we all want—indeed expect—government employees to literally pull our backs out of the rubble when disaster strikes, as it did in Oklahoma City. Volunteers could do the easy tasks, such as driving the walking wounded to local hospitals, but only the highly trained public service professionals could do the real rescue work. Their organizations—the police and fire departments—were created, in Lincoln's words, to be available to do what the citizens "cannot do, at all, or cannot, so well do, for themselves."

Legal Definitions of Public Administration

Because public administration is what a state does, it is both created and bound by an instrument of the law. Indeed, in many communities, such as those of continental Europe, it is an academic subject that has never escaped from the faculties of law. While public administration in the United States is not a "legal" subject, its foundations are always legal.

Public Administration Is Law in Action   Public administration is inherently the execution of a **public law**. Every application of a general law is necessarily an act of administration. Administration cannot exist without this legal foundation. In the United States, the Constitution of 1787 as amended is the law of the land. All legislation must conform to it—or at the very least not violate it in a manner obvious to the U.S. Supreme Court. The law that creates an agency or program is known as its enabling legislation—the law that legally "enables" a program to exist. In theory, no government administrator can do anything if it is not provided for in the legislation or in the rules and regulations that the legislation allows the agency to promulgate. And how much government money can the president of the United States spend on his own without the approval of the Congress? Not a penny! Everything the president does, if it involves spending public money, must have a basis in legislation. This is often difficult for people in less democratic regimes to understand. Tip O'Neill, the former **Speaker** of the U.S. House of Representatives, wrote in a memoir: "I must have met Deng Xiaoping of China a half-dozen times, and every

---

Amtrak The National Railroad Passenger Corporation, the federally subsidized corporation created in 1970 to operate intercity rail passenger service.

public law A legislative act that deals with the citizenry as a whole; a statute that applies to all. This is in contrast to a private law, which affects only one person or group.

speaker The presiding officer of a legislature such as a House of Representatives or a House of Commons, elected by its members. Thomas P. "Tip" O'Neill was Speaker from 1977 to 1987.

time he would ask, 'The President has to go to you for his money?'" O'Neill always answered this question the same way: "Yes, and the President better not forget it." And the same is true of governors and mayors who must go to their respective legislative bodies for appropriations.

While many books have been written about the implementation of this or that government program, there is ultimately only one thing that government is in essence capable of implementing—that is the law. Of course the law is often in turmoil. The legislative basis of programs, or specific agency rules and regulations, are constantly being challenged in court by those who oppose as well as those who support the program involved. The opposition wants the enabling legislation declared unconstitutional and the program destroyed while supporters often want the program administered even more generously. Ever since the **New Deal,** a pattern has emerged with controversial legislation. After its passage, opponents challenge its legality in court, hoping that the judicial branch will overturn it. In effect, there is a new final phase to the legislative process, a **judicial review** to see if the new law is constitutional.

Public Administration Is Regulation   It is government telling citizens and businesses what they may and may not do. Regulation is one of the oldest functions of government. The Code of Hammurabi in ancient Babylonia provided that "the mason who builds a house which falls down and kills the inmate shall be put to death." While not exactly a modern building code, this nevertheless proved an effective means of regulating the soundness of housing.

Modern day regulation is so pervasive and so commonplace that we see it every day and accept it without thinking. Consider the simple act of going to McDonald's to buy a hamburger or a salad. You leave your house or apartment, which has been built according to local building codes—regulation. You get into your car, which has many safety features required by the federal government—regulation. You drive to an intersection and stop at a red light—regulation. Once at McDonald's, you notice a sticker on the door from the local public health agency indicating that the establishment has been inspected and found free of insect and rodent infestation—regulation. On the wall is a framed certificate from the local municipality indicating that the property is licensed to operate as a business—regulation. Then you give your order to a person whose minimum wages and maximum working hours are set by legislation—regulation—whose supervisor is required by guidelines issued by the Equal Employment Opportunity Commission to maintain a workplace free of sexual harassment—regulation—and whose wages are reduced by mandatory deductions for income tax and Social Security—regulation. If after your meal you feel the need to visit one of the rest rooms, you will find one oversized toilet stall designed for the physically handicapped—regulation.

Our lives are constantly governed, or interfered with, by regulation. We are not officially born until we have a birth certificate—regulation. We must attend school

---

New Deal The domestic programs and policies of the administration of President Franklin D. Roosevelt (1933–1945).

judicial review Any court's power to review executive actions, legislative acts, or decisions of lower courts (or quasi-judicial entities, such as arbitration panels) to either confirm or overturn them.

Box 1.2

Why Regulation Came to the Meatpacking Industry

There was never the least attention paid to what was cut up for sausage. . . . There would be meat that had tumbled out on the floor, in the dirt and sawdust, where the workers had tramped and spit uncounted billions of consumption germs. There would be meat stored in great piles in rooms; and the water from leaky roofs would drip over it, and thousands of rats would race about on it. It was too dark in these storage places to see well, but a man could run his hand over these piles of meat and sweep off handfuls of the dried dung of rats. These rats were nuisances, and the packers would put poisoned bread out for them, they would die, and then rats, bread, and meat would go into the hoppers together. This is no fairy story and no joke; the meat would be shoveled into carts and the man who did the shoveling would not trouble to lift out a rat even when he saw one—there were things that went into the sausage in comparison with which a poisoned rat was a tidbit. There was no place for the men to wash their hands before they ate their dinner, and so they made a practice of washing them in the water that was to be ladled into the sausage. There were the butt-ends of smoked meat, and the scraps of corned beef, and all the odds and ends of the waste of the plants, that would be dumped into old barrels in the cellar and left there. Under the system of rigid economy which the packers enforced, there were some jobs that it only paid to do once in a long time, and among these was the cleaning out of the waste barrels. Every spring they did it; and in the barrels would be dirt and rust and old nails and stale water—and cart load after cart load of it would be taken up and dumped into the hoppers with fresh meat, and sent out to the public's breakfast.

SOURCE: Upton Sinclair, *The Jungle* (1906). This novel caused such a sensation that President Theodore Roosevelt authorized an investigation of the meatpackers. This led to the Pure Food and Drug Act of 1906, which provided for federal inspection.

up to a certain age—regulation. We cannot engage in many occupations without a license from the state—regulation. Finally, we cannot be declared legally dead without a death certificate—regulation. And it doesn't end here. We can be buried only in government-approved cemeteries and our estate taxes must be paid—regulation.

As a general rule of thumb, the more crowded and economically developed a place is, the more regulations. Society needs rules so that people don't inadvertently bump into each other's cars, live in houses that fall down because they are structurally unsound, or get food poisoning from meat that was not wholesome. Why? Because things such as these were common problems before government regulations—at least in the developed world—made them relatively rare.

This is the reason why so many people die in traffic accidents in China. According to Thomas L. Friedman, in 1997, seventy thousand people suffered death by automobile; that's 630 deaths per 100,000 cars. By comparison the U.S. had 21 deaths per 100,000. The discrepancy is caused by the fact that mass driving is so new in China that drivers are inexperienced and new roads lack regulations about passing, notices of intersections or hills to come, and all manner of traffic regulating signs and lights.

Regulation has its origin in legislation. But since legislation can never be totally comprehensive on any subject, rules are typically needed to address the details that have not been specified in the written law. Thus rulemaking authority is necessarily exercised by administrative agencies; it is a power that has the full force of law. Agencies begin with some form of legislative mandate and translate their interpretation of that mandate into policy decisions, specifications of regulations, and statements of penalties and enforcement provisions. The exact process to be followed in formulating regulations is only briefly described in the federal Administration Procedure Act (APA). The APA does distinguish between rulemaking that requires a hearing and rulemaking that requires only notice and the opportunity for public comment. Whether the formal or informal procedure is to be used is determined by the enabling statute: the Supreme Court's decision in *United States v. Florida East Coast Railway* (1973) held that formal rulemaking need only be followed when the enabling statute expressly requires an agency hearing prior to rule formulation. The APA also requires that rules be published 30 days before their effective date and that agencies afford any interested party the right to petition for issuance, amendment, or repeal of a rule. In effect, while the APA establishes a process of notice and time for comment, it accords administrative rulemakers the same prerogatives as legislatures in enacting statutes. There is, of course, the additional requirement that the rule enacted be consistent with the enabling statute directing the rulemaking.

All new federal rules must be pubished in the *Federal Register*, the daily publication (begun in 1935) that is the medium for making available to the public the forthcoming rules and regulations of federal agencies—as well as other legal documents of the executive branch, such as presidential proclamations and executive orders. Of course any controversial proposed rules will quickly find their way into the mainstream press as well. All the states have similar rulemaking procedures involving the publication of proposed rules, mechanisms for receiving comments, and final action.

Public Administration Is the King's Largesse

It is whatever goods, services, or honors the ruling authority decides to bestow. This was the earliest meaning of public administration. Since everything was owned by the crown, whatever was granted to the nobles and peasants was a gift. In the modern world this version of public administration can be seen in traditional monarchies and dictatorships, where hospitals, schools, parks, and such are touted as something given by the autocrat to a grateful people. The last vestige of this kingly largesse in **representative government** can be seen on the plaques often attached to public buildings and bridges indicating that the edifice was built during the tenure

---

representative government A governing system in which a legislature freely chosen by the people exercises substantial power on their behalf.

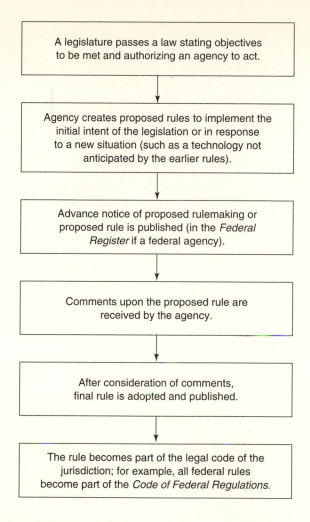

Figure 1.1   The Rulemaking Process

of Mayor Smith or Governor Jones. Of course, whenever representative governments grow corrupt, largesse as an operating mode of public administration reasserts itself. Then citizens may only get public services such as police protection and welfare benefits if they are deserving in the eyes of the rulers.

The traditional big city **political machine** lasted only as long as there was largesse to distribute. For example, in Cambridge, Massachusetts, during the Great

---

political machine Historically, an informal organization that controlled the formal processes of a government through corruption, patronage, intimidation, and service to its constituents. A political machine usually centered on a single politician—a boss—who commanded loyalty through largesse, fear, or affection. The phrase is usually pejorative, because the machine works to achieve political control through those who run the machine, rather than through the popular will.

Box 1.3

Modern Presidential Largesse "Is in the Details"

In 1995 Harold Ickes, the White House Deputy Chief of Staff, wrote the following memo to Donna Shalala, the Secretary of Health and Human Services, complaining that the president's largesse to the people wasn't being recognized in a grant for a grade school sex education program:

> The President was somewhat mystified as to why there was no mention of him in the October 3, 1995, article in the *Arkansas Democrat Gazette* entitled "Sex Can Wait Plan Gets $200,000 Grant: Federal Aid to Benefit 16 School Districts." According to the article, the money comes from the Office of Adolescent Pregnancy Programs, which apparently is part of the Department of Health and Human Services.
>
> Obviously, not every announcement will specifically refer to the President, but all federal departments are being urged to make sure that announcements of grants and other programs refer to the President

SOURCE: "Re-election Is in the Details," *Harper's* magazine, January 1996.

Depression, Democratic party **ward heelers** were authorized to distribute up to 50 "snow buttons" each time there was a major snowstorm. Each button entitled the holder to a day's work shoveling snow for the city. This was a highly prized benefit sought by unemployed men in each **ward**. While certainly at the low end of the **patronage** food chain, this largesse bought the ward heeler loyalty that translated into votes for the party. Snow buttons are a relic of the past. So are political machines, because welfare benefits as a matter of right, as an entitlement, have made them superfluous. Thus the comprehensive public services of the **welfare state** have driven out the informal welfare system of the machines. Without largesse the political machines cannot hold the loyalty of their audience.

Public Administration Is Theft   There are those who believe that a government should do little more than provide police and military protection; other than that, it should not interfere—either for good or ill—in the lives of its citizens. A major in-

---

ward heeler A local political functionary; someone who is involved with, but insignificant in, party affairs. A heeler is not worthy of much respect. The term comes from the way a dog is brought to heel by its master; ward heelers are known by their obedience to their masters.

ward A subdivision of a city, often used as a legislative district for city council elections, as an administrative division for public services or as a unit for the organization of political parties. A ward is often further divided into precincts.

patronage The power of elected and appointed officials to make partisan appointments to office or to confer contracts, honors, or other benefits on their political supporters.

welfare state A governing system in which it is a public policy that government will strive to provide a universal minimum floor of economic and social benefits for all of its citizens.

tellectual force advocating such **libertarianism** was Ayn Rand, the **objectivist** philosopher who attacked welfare state notions of selflessness and sacrifice for a common good in novels such as *The Fountainhead* (1943) and *Atlas Shrugged* (1957). In *Capitalism: The Unknown Ideal* (1966) she wrote: "The only proper function of the government of a free country is to act as an agency which protects the individual's rights, i.e., which protects the individual from physical violence." Such **reactionary** attitudes are an extreme form of **conservatism**. Political conservatives are most often found among those who have, or have the potential to have, wealth and property. They naturally resist change, because they have something to lose. Economist John Kenneth Galbraith offers a brief quantitative analysis of this phenomenon: "It is a simple matter of arithmetic that change *may* be costly to the man who has something: it cannot be so to the man who has nothing."

Conservatives are continuously fearful of public policies involving redistribution, such as domestic policies and programs whose goal is to shift wealth or benefits from one segment of the population to another. The welfare state is founded on this notion of redistribution. The basic mechanism for redistribution is taxation. However, the laws themselves can sometimes redistribute benefits. For example, **tax loopholes** benefit one group of taxpayers at the expense of others; and civil rights legislation, through equal employment opportunity mandates, gives economic benefits to one segment of the population at the theoretical expense of another. Redistribution is one leg of Theodore J. Lowi's three-part classification of all domestic public policies into distribution, regulation, or redistribution. Obviously, redistribution is more popular with some classes of society than with others. As **Alexis de Tocqueville** wrote in 1835: "Countries . . . when lawmaking falls exclusively to the lot of the poor cannot hope for much economy in public expenditure; expenses will always be considerable, either because taxes cannot touch those who vote for them or because they are assessed in a way to prevent that." Playwright George Bernard Shaw put it more succinctly: "A government which robs Peter to pay Paul can always depend on the support of Paul."

And just who is the government's chief robber in this Robin Hood game? None other than your local public administrator! This is why so many citizens with their assets at risk consider thieving the underlying occupation of the public administrator. It is a long-standing legal maxim that government regulation that goes too far

---

libertarianism A political doctrine holding that a government should do little more than provide police and military protection; other than that, it should not interfere—for either good or ill—in the lives of its citizens.

objectivist One who believes that reason and logic is the only means to knowledge, that self-interest determines ethics, and that capitalism should prevail in society.

reactionary A person who supports outmoded ideas of the past. The term is a derogatory reference to political malcontents who yearn for a previous status quo.

conservatism Adherence to a political disposition that prefers the status quo and accepts change only in moderation.

tax loophole An inconsistency in the tax laws, intentional or unintentional, that allows the avoidance of some taxes.

Alexis de Tocqueville (1805–1859) The French historian who visited the United States in the early 1830s and went home to write *Democracy in America* (1835), a landmark description of American governance and a classic analysis of American political culture.

amounts to a taking. This conservative attitude is strikingly similar to the famous invective issued in 1851 by anarchist **Pierre-Joseph Proudhon** against all governments: "To be governed is to be watched over, inspected, spied on, directed, legislated at, regulated, docketed, indoctrinated, preached at, controlled, assessed, weighed, censored, ordered about, by men who have neither the right nor the knowledge nor the virtue."

Proudhon was wrong about at least one thing. Public administrators *do* have the right under law to do what they do. The major exception to this occurs when they cross the line from metaphorical to actual thievery. Just as the fictional British secret agent James Bond had a "license to kill," government employees in some countries consider their jobs a license to steal—usually by soliciting bribes. This is extremely common in developing countries where bureaucrats are not paid reasonable wages and have almost no choice but to engage in petty corruption. Often an informal system of fees evolves that tells the citizen, for example, how much is expected to "fix" a parking ticket or to speed up a building permit.

Managerial Definitions of Public Administration

Public administration is so much a branch of management that many graduate schools of management (or business or administration) are divided into public and private—and now increasingly nonprofit—programs. Its legal basis allows public administration to exist, but without its management aspect, not much of the public's business would get done.

Public Administration Is the Executive Function in Government   In democratic states, whether they are republics or constitutional monarchies, it is government agencies putting into practice legislative acts that represent the will of the people. According to **Alexander Hamilton** writing in *The Federalist*, No. 72: "The administration of government . . . in its most usual, and perhaps most precise signification . . . is limited to executive details, and falls peculiarly within the province of the executive department." In dictatorial regimes similar agencies do the bidding of the people who hold power. But the process is far more interactive and dynamic than any separation of powers diagram would suggest. While the executive, legislative, and judicial branches are separate and distinct in the United States, all sides struggle to influence the others. A president, governor, or mayor is constantly recommending new programs to the Congress, state legislature, or city council. Modern government executives at all levels do not meekly sit back and merely "execute" the will of the legislature. They actively compete to influence that will and to fight for the enactment of programs they are anxious to implement. Because this can lead to dramatic and highly publicized confrontations, the impression is often given that

---

Pierre-Joseph Proudhon (1809–1865) The French journalist who is considered the intellectual father of anarchism.

Alexander Hamilton (1755–1804) George Washington's aide and secretary during the Revolutionary War. A supporter of a strong national government, he signed the U.S. Constitution and co-authored the Federalist Papers to help get it ratified in his native New York. When Washington became president, he made Hamilton secretary of the treasury.

Box 1.4

Saint Augustine Distinguishes Between Public Administration and Organized Crime—Is It Just a Matter of Size?

What are kingdoms but gangs of criminals on a large scale? What are criminal gangs but petty kingdoms? A gang is a group of men under the command of a leader, bound by a compact of association, in which the plunder is divided according to an agreed convention.

If this villainy wins so many recruits from the ranks of the demoralized that it acquires territory, establishes a base, captures cities and subdues peoples, it then openly arrogates to itself the title of kingdom. . . . It was a witty and a truthful rejoinder, which was given by a captured pirate to Alexander the Great. The king asked the fellow, "What is your idea, in infesting the sea?" And the pirate answered, with uninhibited insolence, "The same as yours, in infesting the earth! But because I do it with a tiny craft, I'm called a pirate; because you have a mighty navy, you're called an emperor."

SOURCE: Saint Augustine, *Concerning the City of God Against the Pagans* (London: Penguin Books, 1972). Charlie Chaplin summed all this up in one of his last films, *Monsieur Verdoux* (1947). Convicted of murdering a woman for her money, his character complains: "One murder makes a villain. Millions a hero. Numbers sanctify."

---

this is what executives do—fight for new legislation, fight for the annual budget, and fight for or against various interest groups. The reality is far less dramatic and more mundane. Most of what an executive does is to manage existing programs, to run the bureaucracy. This work is virtually invisible to the public except when something goes wrong and the media circus begins.

Public Administration Is a Management Specialty   Management refers both to the people responsible for running an organization and to the running process itself—the use of numerous resources (such as employees and machines) to accomplish an organizational goal. Top managers make the big decisions and are responsible for the overall success of the organization. In government the top managers are always the political leaders of society whether they gain power by election, appointment, or assassination. When a new president comes into office in the United States, he or she may appoint persons into approximately 3,000 jobs as the top managers who will be responsible for implementing policy. These appointees, while functioning as top managers with significant management responsibilities, are seldom professional managers and seldom think of themselves as management experts. They tend to be simply old friends, political party loyalists, campaign contributors, and representatives of interest groups.

Consequently, the public administrators of a jurisdiction (the actual management specialists) are to be found in the vast area of middle management—the group responsible for the execution and interpretation of top management policies and for the day-to-day operation of the various organizational units. These individuals often have advanced degrees in general fields such as public administration or business administration or technical fields such as public health or social work. These are the people who have made the management of government programs their life's work. They typically have supervisory or first level managers, those responsible for the final implementation of policies by rank-and-file employees, reporting to them. These middle managers, despite their disparity in functions and technical backgrounds, largely constitute the management specialty of public administration. They spend their working lives fighting as officers in the administrative wars started by their political leaders.

Public Administration Is Mickey Mouse   This otherwise innocent cartoon rodent has lent his name as a pejorative term for many aspects of governmental administration. When Walt Disney's famous mouse made it big in the 1930s, he appeared in a variety of cartoon shorts that had him building something (such as a house or boat) that would later fall apart, or generally going to a great deal of trouble for little result. So Mickey gradually gave his name to anything requiring considerable effort for slight results, including many of the Mickey Mouse requirements of bureaucracy. The term is also applied to policies or regulations felt to be needless, inane, silly, or mildly offensive. For example, President Ronald Reagan used the term to good effect when he complained in 1982 that "The United States government's program for arriving at a budget is about the most irresponsible Mickey Mouse arrangement that any government body has ever practiced."

Mickey Mouse is often used to mean *red tape*, the symbol of excessive formality and attention to routine. This has its origins in the red ribbon with which clerks bound official documents in the nineteenth century. The ribbon has disappeared, but the practices it represents linger on. Herbert Kaufman found that the term "is applied to a bewildering variety of organizational practices and features." Organizations create and retain such seemingly rigid "practices and features" because they promote efficiency and equity on the whole—even though this may not be true in many individual cases. After all, "one person's 'red tape' may be another's treasured procedural safeguard." Kaufman concluded that "red tape turns out to be at the core of our institutions rather than an excrescence on them."

Public Administration Is Art, Not Science—or Vice Versa   Some people have a gift for administration. We have all met such natural administrators. They are not only perpetually organized but have a knack for getting people to harmoniously work together. The administrative art is judgment, panache, and common sense. But the artist is useless without tools—without the technical skills (the science) that allow for the digestion and transference of information. Nothing is more pointless than to argue whether the practice of public administration is more art or science. It is inherently both. Of course, the more science you have, the better artist you'll be. But "book learnin'" won't make you an artist if you don't possess an element of the gift in the first place.

At the beginning of the American Civil War, Henry Wager Halleck was perhaps the most knowledgeable northerner on the art and science of war. His textbook, *El-*

ements of Military Art and Science, and translations of foreign military texts were used at West Point, where he taught. He was nicknamed "Old Brains," and much was expected when he was given a field command. But while he knew all the science, he just didn't have the art to be a leader in actual battle. Although he ended up as the **chief of staff** of the U.S. Army, he is on nobody's list of great generals. By contrast, Ulysses S. Grant, the winning general of the Civil War, dismissed books on tactics as "nothing more than common sense." He wrote in his 1885 *Memoirs* that he didn't believe his officers "ever discovered that I had never studied the tactics that I used."

So which are you likely to be? "Old Brains" Halleck, all science and no art, good at **staff** work but incapable of command? Or a Grant, all art and no science, the archetypal line officer? Just because you have a master's or even a doctorate in public administration or a related field doesn't mean that you can function as a high level administrator. Being highly educated does not always equate with being professionally able. If your goal is to make it as a city manager or agency administrator, you may wish to avoid staff jobs. Get out there and run something. Gradually prove with progressively more responsible jobs that you are an artist, that you can cope with and thrive among the usual administrative chaos.

It is the same in all professions. You prepare yourself by doing smaller versions of the big thing you really want to do. Organizational theorist Antony Jay wrote of the advice traditionally given to aspiring actors: if you want to be a leading actor you must only play leading parts—"much better to play Hamlet in Denver than **Laertes** on Broadway." You thus learn "to lead a big organization by leading smaller ones." But lead you must! When selection committees are seeking a manager for a major agency, those with only staff experience are not as likely to make the short list of finalists. Appointing authorities may not have heard of the historical Halleck, but they have all seen a Halleck—and don't want to see one in the administrative structure of their group.

Occupational Definitions of Public Administration

One of the joys of public service occupations is the frequent opportunity to participate in analyses and evaluations of public programs. However, not all public sector workers seek to engage in the public debate over policies, laws, and management practices. But all of them are interested in their jobs. So let's look at public administration—as an occupation.

Public Administration Is an Occupational Category
It is whatever the public employees of the world do. It ranges from brain surgery to street sweeping. Most of the people in this broad occupational category do not even think of themselves as public administrators. They identify with their specific

---

chief of staff An army's highest ranking officer.

staff Specialists who assist line managers in carrying out their duties. Generally, staff units do not have the power of decision, command, or control of operations. Rather, they make recommendations (which may or may not be adopted) to executives and line managers.

Laertes A supporting role in Shakespeare's *Hamlet;* Laertes and Hamlet have the big sword fight in the final act.

A public administrator at work: NASA astronaut Bruce McCandless II on the first untethered space walk in 1984. To make him a better astronaut, NASA had him take graduate courses in public administration. In 1978 he enrolled at the University of Houston in the very course for which this textbook is designed. His instructor was one of this text's coauthors. McCandless earned the highest possible grades and Professor Shafritz predicted he would go far.

professions (physician, engineer, or architect) and trades (carpenter, electrician, or plumber). While it is true that they may not be administrators in the sense of being managers, they are nevertheless, whether they realize it or not, ministering (in the sense of providing services) to the public. In 1996 the United States had more than eighteen million civilians working for its local, state, and federal governments. And only the smallest portion of them would define their work as public administration. They simply see themselves as police officers, social workers, or forest rangers; but they are also, unavoidably, public administrators.

In 1995 Richard Klausner became the director of the federal government's National Cancer Institute. He then defiantly told the *New York Times*, "I am not an administrator." He asserted that he was "a scientist and a physician." But the *Times* was not fooled by Dr. Klausner. Its lengthy profile of him was headlined: "New Administrator is 'Not an Administrator.'" Administrators, even if they, like Dr. Klausner, are in denial, are still administrators.

Public Administration Is an Essay Contest   People in bureaucratic careers tend to rise or fall on how well they can write. In a game of shuffling paper, the person whose memorandum ends up on top wins. It is a legendary truism in the U.S. State Department that nobody who's good writes their own memos. If you are considered talented enough, your boss will want you to write his or her memos. Because you're

Box 1.5

Why Thomas Jefferson—and Not John Adams—Wrote the Declaration of Independence

The committee met, discussed the subject, and then appointed Mr. Jefferson and me to make the draught, I suppose because we were the two first on the list.

The sub-committee met. Jefferson proposed to me to make the draught. I said, "I will not."

"You should do it," he said.

"Oh! No."

"Why will you not? You ought to do it.

"I will not."

"Why?"

"Reasons enough," I said.

"What can be your reasons?"

"Reason first—You are a Virginian, and a Virginian ought to appear at the head of this business. Reason second—I am obnoxious, suspected, and unpopular. You are very much otherwise. Reason third—You can write ten times better than I can."

"Well," said Jefferson, "if you are decided, I will do as well as I can."

SOURCE: John Adams, July 1776 letter quoted in *Eyewitness to America*, ed. David Colbert (New York: Pantheon Books, 1997).

too busy writing the boss's memos, you find a younger talent to write yours. Then when your boss gets the big new job, you go along—with an appropriate promotion. And of course you pull along the person who's been writing for you. Remember that Thomas Jefferson was offered the job of writing the Declaration of Independence because of his reputation as a fine stylist. And his eventual elevation to president came because he made the most of this writing opportunity. When General Douglas MacArthur was head of the U.S. Army in the 1930s, a young captain (later a major) wrote the general's reports and speeches. Coworkers knew that Dwight D. Eisenhower was an officer who was going places because he could write.

Oral presentation skills are also essential; but since more people can talk than write a good game, writing is more decisive in determining whose ideas get advanced. All organizations place great value on the person who can write succinctly in times of stress. That is the person who will be turned to when an important opportunity comes up. This is why public administration is an essay contest; because your writing reputation creates your administrative persona of winner or loser. According to a U.S. Department of State report, the Foreign Service "has prized drafting ability above almost all other skills. We emphasize this skill in recruitment and reward it generously in our promotion system. The prize jobs in the service are the reporting jobs." Donald P. Warwick in his analysis of the State Department's bureaucracy found that "following the classic model of the gentleman generalist, the Foreign Service exalts graceful prose and the well-turned phrase." Other agencies with fewer "gentlemen" are equally anxious to reward "graceful prose."

Public Administration Is Idealism in Action   Many people enter public service careers because they are idealists; they believe in and seek to advance noble principles. "Noble" is the key word here because traditionally the nobility had public service obligations. They were the warrior class, so it was their obligation to heroically protect the weak and less fortunate, to accept the notion of **noblesse oblige**. Gradually, their duties expanded from military affairs to the whole realm of public affairs. High-level government service, which was once the prerogative of the wellborn, the financially well-off, and the well-connected, is now also open to those who were born with talent but without money or connections.

Idealism draws people into public administration because it provides them with worthwhile—and exciting—things to do with their lives. Nowhere else can someone without private wealth achieve such vast power so quickly. Even the children of the very wealthy—such as the Kennedys and Rockefellers—tend to enter public service for the same reasons other people do—because it's fun, it offers ego gratification, and, most importantly, because it satisfies their dual desires to do good works and exercise power. When someone asked the multimillionaire presidential candidate John F. Kennedy why he wanted to be president, he candidly replied, "Because that is where the power is."

The idealism associated with public administration goes far beyond the individual. The goal is the mystical one of building "a city upon a hill," an ideal political community thoroughly fit for others to observe as an example. This phrase comes from John Winthrop, governor of the Massachusetts Bay Colony. In 1630 he wrote: "For we must consider that we shall be as a city upon a hill. The eyes of all people are upon us." This is a famous statement in Massachusetts history and both Presidents Kennedy and Reagan favored using it in speeches. It also illustrates how the nondenominational religious elements of public administration allow participants to gain satisfaction by becoming involved with a cause greater than themselves.

According to an old story, a supervisor asks three bricklayers what they are doing. The first says: "I'm just putting one brick upon another." The second says: "I'm building this here wall." The third says: "I'm creating a cathedral." They are all doing the identical job but this last worker is emotionally caught up in a great and noble enterprise. We cannot necessarily presume that the third bricklayer will do a better job, but he'll feel better about it. And because he feels better about it, it is more likely that he'll do a better job. His idealism is no different than the emotional high available to individuals engaged in any number of projects to improve their communities. A neighborhood free from crime or a city with safe drinking water for all are goals every bit as worthy as building a cathedral.

Ironically, Woodrow Wilson, the closest thing to a patron saint that American public administration has, is also the archetypal idealist in world politics. In 1919,

---

noblesse oblige A French term meaning nobility obliges; the notion that the nobles (or those of the upper class) have a special obligation to serve society.

during his futile effort to gain his country's support for the **League of Nations**, he told a Sioux Falls, South Dakota, audience that "Sometimes people call me an idealist. Well, that is the way I know I am an American. America, my fellow citizens— I do not say it in disparagement of any other great people—America is the only idealistic nation in the world."

It is strange how these idealists in government who only want to do good for their fellow citizens are considered not much better than thieves and social parasites by others—usually not by those who need government help but by those **rugged individualists** who don't. Many who seek careers in public service believe that government is a legitimate vehicle for solving social problems—and they want to be driving that vehicle when the problem gets solved. What's the good of doing good if you can't have fun doing it? This attitude is similar to that of the sixteenth-century Spanish conquistador Bernal Diaz del Castillo, whom Samuel Eliot Morison quotes as saying: "We came here [to the Americas] to serve God and also to get rich." Today's public administration idealists know that getting rich in terms of money is unlikely; the riches they seek are those of the joys of experience, the sense of personal satisfaction, and of building "a city upon a hill."

Public Administration Is an Academic Field   It is the study of the art and science of management applied to the public sector. But it traditionally goes far beyond the concerns of management and incorporates as its subject matter all of the political, social, cultural, and legal environments that affect the running of public institutions. As a field of study, it is inherently cross-disciplinary because it encompasses so much of political science, sociology, business administration, psychology, law, anthropology, medicine, forestry, and so on. Indeed, it can be argued that because public administration borrows so much from other fields, what is left as its core is hardly worthy of being considered a legitimate academic field at all. Yet there is a center about which the parts of public administration have coalesced (see Figure 1.2).

American public administration as a field of study traditionally traces its origin to an 1887 *Political Science Quarterly* article by **Woodrow Wilson**. In "The Study of Administration" Wilson attempted nothing less than to refocus the newly emerging field of political science. Rather than be concerned with the "lasting maxims of political wisdom," he argued that political science should concentrate on the more generally neglected details of how governments are administered. This was necessary because "It is getting harder to *run* a constitution than to frame one."

League of Nations The world order organization that preceded the United Nations. It was first called for by President Woodrow Wilson in a 1918 address to Congress. However, the United States never joined it because both the Congress and the country were in an isolationist mood after World War I.

rugged individualists Those who staunchly believe that citizens should take care of their own economic needs and not be dependent on government for the necessities of life. Rugged individualists also tend to oppose paternalistic government welfare programs out of concern that the poor will have their character undermined. This philosophy was most associated with Presidents Hoover and Reagan.

Woodrow Wilson (1856–1924) Before Wilson became president of the United States (1913–1921), he was a professor of history and political science who rose to be president of Princeton University (1902–1910) and governor of New Jersey (1911–1913).

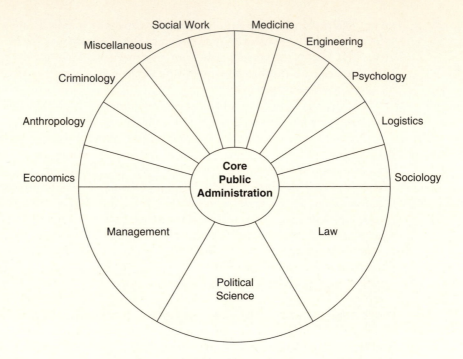

Figure 1.2   The Interdisciplinary Nature of Public Administration

Wilson wanted the study of public administration to focus not only on the problems of personnel management, as many other reformers of the time had advocated, but also on organization and management in general. The reform movement of the time had a reform agenda that did not go beyond the abolition of the **spoils system** and the installation of a **merit system**. Wilson regarded civil service reform "as but a prelude to a fuller administrative reform." He sought to push the concerns of public administration into investigations of the "organization and methods of our government offices" with a view toward determining "first, what government can properly and successfully do, and secondly, how it can do these proper things with the utmost possible efficiency and at the least possible cost either of money or energy." He was concerned with overall organizational efficiency and economy—that is, productivity in its most simplistic formulation. What could be more current—then or now?

In his essay, Wilson also proclaimed the existence of a major distinction between politics and administration. This was a common and necessary political tactic of the reform movement because arguments that public appointments should be

---

spoils system The widespread practice of awarding government jobs to political supporters as opposed to awarding them on the basis of merit.

merit system A public sector concept of staffing that implies that no test of party membership is involved in the selection, promotion, or retention of government employees and that a constant effort is made to select the best qualified individuals available for appointment and advancement.

Woodrow Wilson thinking about public administration. In 1885 Wilson, having not yet completed his doctoral program at Johns Hopkins University, began his teaching career at the newly founded Bryn Mawr College for Women. While reportedly a lecturer of genius, he resented having to teach women. As he told an associate, such an activity "relaxes one's mental muscle." In 1887 he summed up his life by saying, "thirty-one years old and nothing done!" In retrospect Wilson seems to be like many another ambitious academic seemingly stuck in a post that did not do justice to talent. And he chose as the way out the now traditional road to high academic fame, fortune, and position: he wrote and published and was saved! And what happend to the young Wilson who plaintively wrote in 1888, "I have for a long time been hungry for a class of men"? Shortly thereafter he took up an appointment at Wesleyan University in Connecticut. From there he went to Princeton, made good, and became president of that university. In later life he found a job in Washington.

based on fitness and merit, rather than partisanship, necessarily had to assert that "politics" was out of place in public service. As Wilson said, "Although politics sets the tasks for administration, it should not be suffered to manipulate its offices." In reinforcing what became known as the "politics-administration dichotomy," Wilson was really referring to "partisan" politics. While this subtlety was lost on many, Wilson's main themes—that public administration should be premised on a science of management and separate from traditional politics—fell on fertile intellectual ground. The ideas of this then-obscure professor eventually became the dogma of academic public administration.

However, if Wilson had not become president, his now seminal article would have continued to enjoy the obscurity its verbosity warrants. The article's significant influence came only after World War II—more than half a century after it was published. Administrative historian Paul van Riper found that none of the early public administration scholars, Wilson's contemporaries, cited the article in their otherwise heavily referenced works. "In reality, any connection between Wilson's essay and the later development of the discipline is pure fantasy! An examination of major political and social science works of the period between 1890 and World War I shows no citation whatever of the essay." So how did it get rediscovered and become required reading for generations of students? According to a historical analysis by Daniel W. Martin "The simple answer is . . . the glowing reprint of Wilson's article in the December 1941 *Political Science Quarterly*. It was a masterwork of public relations, complete with a photostatic copy of Wilson's tentative letter of submission." Thereafter, Wilson's essay, cited only modestly in the interwar period, grew to its current influence.

While Woodrow Wilson and many others of the **progressive movement** called for a "science of administration," new intellectual fields evolve amorphously. It is difficult to trace the exact moment of their conception. What is certain is that the first real American public administration text is *Introduction to the Study of Public Administration* by **Leonard White**, published in 1926.

While Woodrow Wilson provided the rationale for public administration to be an academic discipline and professional management specialty, it remained for White to most clearly articulate its preliminary objectives. In his pioneering text, he noted four critical assumptions that formed the basis for the study of public administration:

1. Administration is a unitary process that can be studied uniformly, at the federal, state, and local levels.
2. The basis for study is management, not law.
3. Administration is still art but the ideal of transformation to science is both feasible and worthwhile.
4. Administration "has become, and will continue to be the heart of the problem of modern government."

White's text was remarkable both for its influence over four decades (the fourth and last edition was published in 1955) and for its restraint in not taking a prescriptive cookbook approach to public administration. He recognized that public administration was above all a field of study that had to stay close to reality—the reality of its largely untrained practitioner base that still professed great belief in the art of administration. Even more interesting, his work avoided the potential pitfall of the politics-administration dichotomy. Defining public administration as emphasizing the managerial phase, he left unanswered "the question to what extent the administration itself participates in formulating the purposes of the state."

As an independent academic field, public administration has always been controversial. First, it was the stepchild of political science. And in many colleges, the field is still represented by a few courses within the political science curriculum. Later, schools of business or management began to offer it as one of a variety of administrative specialties. In recent decades, independent departments and graduate schools of public administration have been created. But as the field of public

---

progressive movement While the term has its origins in religious concepts that argued for the infinite improvability of the human condition, by the end of the nineteenth century it had come to refer to a political and cultural movement that focused on reforming industrialized societies to provide for greater democratic participation by the individual in government, and the application of science and specialized knowledge and skills to the improvement of life.

Leonard D. White (1891–1958) The University of Chicago professor who wrote the first public administration text in 1926. He is the author of the standard administrative histories of the U.S. government in the nineteenth century. Overall White is one of the most significant voices in the development of public administration as an academic discipline.

Box 1.6

The Voice of a Founding Father

The science of administration is the latest fruit of that study of the science of politics which was begun some twenty-two hundred years ago. . . .

Why was it so late in coming? Why did it wait until this too busy century of ours to demand attention for itself? Administration is the most obvious part of government; it is government in action; it is the executive, the operative, the most visible side of government, and is of course as old as government itself. It is government in action and one might very naturally expect to find that government in action had arrested the attention and provoked the scrutiny of writers of politics very early in the history of systematic thought.

But such was not the case. No one wrote systematically of administration as a branch of the science of government until the present century had passed its first youth. . . . Up to our own day all the political writers whom we now read had thought, argued, dogmatized only about the *constitution* of government. . . . The central field of controversy was that great field of theory in which monarchy rode tilt against democracy, in which oligarchy would have built for itself strongholds of privilege, and in which tyranny sought opportunity to make good its claim to receive submission from all competitors. Amidst this high warfare of principles, administration could command no pause for its own consideration. The question was always: Who shall make law, and what shall that law be? The other question, how law should be administered with enlightenment, with equity, with speed, and without friction, was put aside as "practical detail" which clerks could arrange after doctors had agreed upon principles. . . .

The field of administration is a field of business. It is removed from the hurry and strife of politics; it at most points stands apart even from the debatable ground of constitutional study. It is a part of political life only as the methods of the counting-house are a part of the life of society; only as machinery is part of the manufactured product. But it is, at the same time, raised very far above the dull level of mere technical detail by the fact that through its greater principles it is directly connected with the lasting maxims of political wisdom, the permanent truths of political progress.

The object of administrative study is to rescue executive methods from the confusion and costliness of empirical experiment and set them upon foundations laid deep in stable principle.

It is for this reason that we must regard civil service reform in its present stages as but a prelude to a fuller administrative reform. We are now rectifying methods of appointment; we must go on to adjust executive functions more fitly and to prescribe better methods of executive organization and action. Civil service reform is thus but a moral preparation for what is to follow. It is clearing the moral atmosphere of official life by establishing the sanctity of public office as a public trust, and, by making the service unpartisan, it is opening the way for making it businesslike. . . .

Box 1.6

Continued

> Most important to be observed is the truth already so much and so fortunately insisted upon by our civil-service reformers; namely, that administration lies ouside the proper sphere of politics. Administrative questions are not political questions. Although politics sets the tasks for administration, it should not be suffered to manipulate its offices.

SOURCE: Woodrow Wilson, "The Study of Administration," *Political Science Quarterly*, June 1887.

---

administration matured, its constituent elements began to intellectually fly away. The public policy analyst increasingly identified with the mathematical rigor of political science methodologists. Public finance has been claimed by the economists. The core management elements have drifted toward the field of public management. Increasingly, the field seems to be less a discipline than a holding company for disparate intellectual components. This is hardly new. In 1975 Dwight Waldo was decrying that "public administration is suffering from an identity crisis, having enormously expanded its periphery without retaining or creating a unifying center." A quarter century later, this crisis shows no signs of abating.

In answer to the question "Is public administration a legitimate academic field?" honest people of differing views will argue both pro and con. We side with Waldo and assert that, whatever its problems with unity, public administration is most decidedly a legitimate field. We also contend that the growth and frisky independence of its elements is both healthy and intellectually invigorating. An academic field without controversy must necessarily be in decline. Thus public administration is very healthy indeed.

Public Administration Is a Profession   It is the application of its unique arts and sciences to the problems of society. But is it a profession such as law, medicine, engineering, or architecture? The case for public administration's status as a profession can be made by applying to it the test of professionalism. Does it possess the three core features common to traditional professions?

1. A body of academic and practical knowledge that is applied to the service of society.
2. A standard of success theoretically measured by serving the needs of society rather than seeking purely personal gain.
3. A system of control over the professional practice that regulates the education of new members and maintains both a code of ethics and appropriate sanctions.

Public administration amply meets all three of these criteria even though, unlike law or medicine, it cannot control entry to practice through licenses and examinations. However, public administration acts like these long-established professions by drawing upon different fields of specialization to solve problems and prepare new practitioners. While public administration is not a pure social science, as some would have it, it is fully equal to these more traditional fields of study. Perhaps it supercedes many in one respect. Society's original professionals were clergy because they professed the word of God. Such people were said to have a "calling." Why? Because God was said to have called them. Public administration with its idealistic notions of building "a city upon a hill" is closer to this original religious conception of professionalism than many other professions today.

The Evolution of Public Administration

There was nothing preordained about the preceding discussion of definitions. It is a product of the life experiences of the authors. It could have been written in a radically different framework and accomplished essentially the same task. Similarly, public administration itself did not have to evolve the way it did. As with any evolutionary process, there were a seemingly infinite number of possible outcomes. Biologist Stephen Jay Gould in his book about the Burgess Shale, a fossil-rich limestone quarry in the Canadian Rockies, shows how animal evolution had any number of starts and stops. According to Gould, no "handicapper, given Burgess evidence as known today, would have granted very favorable odds" that the vertebrate creatures from which humans evolved would have survived. The most disturbing thing about this kind of natural selection, according to Gould, is the random nature of it—that so much of evolutionary history takes on the character of a lottery.

So it has been with public administration. The administrative institutions that we presently have could so easily have been radically different. How humans learned to approach the practice and definition of public administration could so easily have taken a surprising turn. For example, if the Greeks had insisted that administration was household management on a grand scale, they might have developed it as a female occupation. And it might have been copied that way by the Romans who adopted so much else of Greek science and culture. If the classical world developed the notion that men were fit only for war and physical toil, women might have evolved a beneficent administrative matriarchy. And there is a third possibility—rule by eunuchs. No joke!

For over two thousand years and into the twentieth century, eunuchs—males with their external sex organs amputated—were the public administrators of choice. Why? Because their missing parts meant that they could be trusted—first with the ruler's wives and concubines; then with other administrative chores. Eunuchs proved to be particularly effective and loyal administrators. As slaves usually long removed from any family, they knew that the only way to thrive was to do well by the only people who could enrich and protect them. The eunuchs formed a kind of civil service system. Entrance was typically limited to captured slave boys from the edge of the empire who were castrated by the thousands. While a large percentage died from the crude surgery, the survivors were put into service as court eunuchs. There they could work their way up to the highest level of administrative responsibility. Eunuchs grew to be the servant class most trusted by the rulers of ancient Syria, Persia, China, and Rome. In an era rife with nepotism (hiring of relatives), they were immune from such influences. While Christian Byzantium made extensive use of eunuchs in government posts, Western Christendom did not.

The last of the traditional bureaucrat-eunuchs were still to be seen in imperial China and the Ottoman Empire early in this century. Thus for most of recorded history eunuchs were a "normal" means by which states managed their affairs. The advantages they offered, absolute loyalty and disinterestedness, are not to be sneered at. Fortunately today there are ways to instill high standards of ethics in government officials other than sending castration technicians to visit the bureaucrats of Washington, **Whitehall**, and the **Kremlin**.

The Core Content

But even if public administration had evolved along radically different lines, it would have had to come out about where it is concerning its core content. While there is no agreement on all the details, there is broad general agreement about the subject matter. Thus all public administration introductory texts have chapters very similar to the ones that follow. What differs is the method of presentation. But there is almost universal agreement that organization theory, bureaucratic behavior, personnel management, public finance and budgeting, policy analysis, program evaluation, and administrative ethics, among other topics, are essential to a basic understanding of the field. This essential information is all here.

It is an underlying premise of this book that public administration cannot be properly understood without an appreciation of its political dynamics. All of the actors in the public administration world must accept their political fate—they cannot pretend either to themselves or to the public that they operate as a public sector counterpart to industrial management. And the political nature of public administration must be faced maturely. Just as the first step in arresting alcoholism is to have the alcoholic admit that he or she is an alcoholic and will always be an alcoholic even after he or she stops drinking, the first step toward putting public administration operations on a more realistic footing is for public managers to admit that public sector administration is an inherently political process.

Public administration is increasingly a cross-governmental field. Yet too many of the comprehensive texts available for introductory courses in the United States are decidedly parochial in that they focus on the national government. This is an incongruous situation when it is realized that a relatively small percentage of American public administrators work for the federal government. While the United States has one federal government, it has more than 80,000 units of state, county, metropolitan, and local governments led by administrators as esteemed as governors and as unnoticed as the executive director of a mosquito abatement district. Most pub-

---

Whitehall That area of London between Trafalgar and Parliament Squares in which government buildings have historically (since the time of Henry VIII) been concentrated. Thus it has come to refer to the most senior members of the British civil service.
Kremlin The Moscow citadel in which are located the main offices of the Russian government.

lic administration students in the United States will go into state and local government or are foreign nationals who expect to return home with readily applicable skills. Still others will work in nonprofit organizations. The end of the Cold War has only encouraged an ever-increasing worldwide market for Western-oriented public administration. Thus to a large extent this text takes a unified approach—appropriate for U.S. students at all levels (federal, state, and local) but generic enough to be truly useful to students of other countries and cultures.

Most of the content of introductory public administration texts can be universally applicable. There exists a unified whole (public administration in general) which is greater than the sum of its parts (public administration in each jurisdiction). The core concept of the unified approach to introducing public administration is to write the material in such a manner that it can be readily applied to the differing political systems within the American federal system and throughout the rest of the world. Indeed, no public administration textbook can be comprehensive today if it is not cross-governmental in the most expansive sense. National administration figures from the president on down hardly ever make a major speech without some reference to government policies and practices in Asia, Europe, and elsewhere. This is just the latest evidence of how imperative it is that American students of public administration develop a greater international perspective.

This will not be a "how-to-do-it" book written for people who want to be public administration experts in ten easy lessons. It will be a "what-is-it" book written for people who seek or are engaged in managerial careers in the public sector and are in need of a basic introduction to, or a review of, public sector administrative machinations. The "nuts and bolts" of administrative processes vary considerably from jurisdiction to jurisdiction. Because of differing laws and customs, it would be futile to present the "one right way" for any given procedure. Instead, the procedural chapters (on personnel, budgeting, strategic management, etc.) concentrate on the historical evolution, essential theory, and future trends of their subjects. With this information, diligent readers will have the kind of conceptual foundation that will allow them to rapidly digest and master the procedural nuts and bolts that differ with every jurisdiction.

The Cycles of Administrative Reform

The longshoreman philosopher Eric Hoffer wrote that "the nature of a society is largely determined by the direction in which talent and ambition flow—by the tilt of the social landscape." Public administration has certainly been tilted about in recent decades. When John F. Kennedy in his 1961 inaugural address told Americans to "ask what you can do for your country," millions responded by aspiring to public service careers—many of which were made possible by the Great Society programs of the ensuing Johnson administration. This idealistic surge came to a screeching halt with the unpopularity of the Vietnam War and the scandal of Watergate. And when Ronald Reagan was twice elected while effectively running against the federal bureaucracy, there seemed to be little hope for a resurgence of interest in public administration. In his first inaugural address in 1981, Reagan asserted that "government is not the solution to our problem. Government is the

TABLE 1.2 Twentieth Century U.S. Presidential Administrations Classified as Conservative or Reform Based on Domestic Policies

Reform	Conservative
Theodore Roosevelt (1901–1909)	
William Howard Taft (1909–1913)	
Woodrow Wilson (1913–1921)	
	Warren G. Harding (1921–1923)
	Calvin Coolidge (1923–1929)
	Herbert Hoover (1929–1933)
Franklin D. Roosevelt (1933–1945)	
Harry S. Truman (1945–1953)	
	Dwight D. Eisenhower (1953–1961)
John F. Kennedy (1961–1963)	
Lyndon B. Johnson (1963–1969)	
Richard M. Nixon (1969–1974)	
	Gerald R. Ford (1974–1977)
	Jimmy Carter (1977–1981)
	Ronald Reagan (1981–1989)
	George Bush (1989–1993)
Bill Clinton (1993–)	

SOURCE: Developed from data in Arthur M. Schlesinger Jr., *The Cycles of American History* (Boston: Houghton-Mifflin, 1986). Schlesinger's 30-year cycles of reform began in 1901, 1933, 1961, and 1993.

problem." Who wants to join up to be part of the problem? The 1992 election of Bill Clinton as president was expected to create renewed interest in government careers. In his inaugural address Clinton called on citizens to have the "courage to reinvent America." But vast deficits, a growing public distrust of government, and the 1994 midterm election that gave the Republicans control of the congress for the first time in more than four decades made it impossible for the Clinton administration to expand federal programs. Indeed, his reinventing effort has focused on downsizing the bureaucracy. In this he and the Congress found common ground—in principle if not in all the details.

Historian Arthur Schlesinger Jr. has asserted that American history fluctuates in 30-year cycles between periods of conservative (with few administrative initiatives) and liberal (with relatively more administrative initiatives) politics. "Reform in the United States tends to come in bursts. The model is the Hundred Days of Franklin D. Roosevelt. Finally the rush of innovation begins to choke the body politic, which demands time for digestion."

Clinton became president almost 30 years after Kennedy. So maybe the recent increased enrollments in public administration courses are due to Clinton's efforts to echo Kennedy's call to public service, maybe it is just time for a new "Schlesinger cycle," or maybe people are more interested in careers that offer satisfactions other than money. But something else is happening on the other side of the political spectrum that is equally important. The Republicans of the 1990s, in the best managerial tradition, have sought to reinvent government in terms of greater efficiency and more bang for the buck, and even to redefine the role of government in society. Their search for a redefinition has massive implications for public administration. The smaller public sector that they seek means fewer direct jobs in public administration but more indirect ones. The locus of jobs will shift. Fewer state prison guards; but more private prison guards. Fewer teachers in public schools, but more private school teachers. But whether jobs are formally public or ostensibly private, they are still public service operations. Regardless of whether the left-of-center Democrats or the right-of-center Republicans prevail, it is certain that public administration is a growing field. We just never know which way it will grow.

It's an Adventure!

The U.S. Navy once used this recruiting slogan: "It's not just a job, it's an adventure." So it is with public administration. A public service career is often the most exciting thing individuals can do with their lives. Walter Lippmann often observed that "the joys of private life" are much overrated. "For the truth is that public life, once a man [or woman] has been infected with its excitement and importance, is something that few ever get over." Whether one comes to a capital to expand government or to contract it, it is a worthy personal quest, a great personal adventure—and equally worthy and adventurous if you serve in a national capital, a state capital, a city hall, or a neighborhood association. Public service, like adventures, come in all sizes.

Many of you would not be holding this book if you were not engaged in or contemplating a public service career. Consider what follows not so much as a guidebook—the field is too vast to be encompassed in one or even a hundred books—but as a reconnaissance. Herein is the lay of the land that you will encounter in a public administration adventure. Learn how to tinker with the machinery of government, discover the ancient secrets of modern strategic management, review the arcane rules of public personnel administration, buy into the politics of the budgetary process, and finally, examine how ethical it all is. Public administration not only has a cast of millions, it's a show that's been playing for more than 5,000 years. The goal of the authors has been to make your journey in the sometimes wild and woolly public sector more successful by giving necessary historical perspectives on this strange world and by alerting you to the dangers and opportunities that lie ahead. You, as the adventurer, must make the most of them. Enjoy the trip!

Summary

Public administration can be defined from political, legal, managerial, and occupation perspectives. However defined, its vast scope encompasses whatever governments do. Public administration cannot exist outside of its political context. It is this context that makes it public—that makes it different from private or business administration. Public administration is what a state does. It is created by and bound by the law and is an instrument of the law. It is inherently the execution of public laws. Every application of a general law is necessarily an act of administration. Its legal basis allows public administration to exist, but without its management aspect, not much of the public's business would get done.

Public administration as an academic field is the study of the art and science of management applied to the public sector. But it traditionally goes far beyond the concerns of management and incorporates as its subject matter all of the political, social, cultural, and legal environments that affect the running of public institutions. It is inherently cross-disciplinary, encompassing so much of other fields—from political science and sociology to business administration and law. American public administration as a field of study is traditionally traced to Woodrow Wilson's 1887 article "A Study of Administration." The discipline of public administration, after developing as part of political science, emerged as an independent field in the second half of the twentieth century.

As a profession, public administration offers significant opportunities for idealism in the pursuit of public service—and even heroism, as we saw in Oklahoma City. Concerns for an increasingly effective or more expansive public service ebb and flow with the changing political philosophies of differing administrations. But the provision of public services—whether by career public servants or by contracted private sector employees—remains the very essence of public administration.

Key Concepts

administration   The management and direction of the affairs of governments and institutions; a collective term for all policymaking officials of a government; the execution and implementation of public policy.

executive branch   The part of a government responsible for applying or administering the law. Thus a president, governor, or mayor and the supporting bureaucracies are the executive branches of their respective jurisdictions.

management   A word that refers both to the people responsible for running an organization and to the running process itself; the use of numerous resources (such as employees and machines) to accomplish an organizational goal.

professional   A member of an occupation requiring specialized knowledge that can be gained only after intensive preparation. Professional occupations tend to possess three features: a body of academic and practical knowledge that is applied to the service of society, a standard of success theoretically measured by serving the needs of society rather than seeking purely personal gain, and a system of control over the professional practice.

public administration   Whatever governments do for good or ill. It is public administration's political context that makes it public—that distinguishes it from private or business administration.

public interest   The universal label in which political actors wrap the policies and programs that they advocate.

public policy   Decision making by government. Governments are constantly concerned about what they should or should not do. And whatever they do or do not do is public policy.

red tape   The ribbon that was once used to bind government documents; the term now stands as the symbol of excessive official formality and overattention to prescribed routines.

regulation   The totality of government controls on the social and economic activities of its citizens; the rulemaking process of those administrative agencies charged with the official interpretation of laws.

Bibliography

Cuomo, Mario. (1995). *Reason to Believe*. New York: Simon and Schuster.

Edelman, Murray. (1964). *The Symbolic Uses of Politics*. Urbana: University of Illinois Press.

Friedman, Thomas L. (1998). "Desperado Democracies," *New York Times* (July 14).

Galbraith, John Kenneth. (1956). *American Capitalism*. Boston: Houghton Mifflin.

Gould, Stephen Jay. (1989). *Wonderful Life: The Burgess Shale and the Nature of History*. New York: Norton.

Haldane, J. B. S. (1928). *Possible Worlds and Other Essays*. New York: Harper.

Halleck, Henry W. (1863). *Elements of Military Art and Science*, 3rd ed. New York: Appleton.

Herring, E. Pendleton. (1936). *Public Administration and the Public Interest*. New York: McGraw-Hill.

Hoffer, Eric. (1967). *The Temper of Our Time*. New York: Harper and Row.

Irving, Clive, ed. (1995). *In Their Name: Dedicated to the Brave and the Innocent—Oklahoma City, April 1995*. New York: Random House.

Jay, Antony. (1967). *Management and Machiavelli*. New York: Holt, Rinehart and Winston.

Kaufman, Herbert. (1977). *Red Tape: Its Origins, Uses, and Abuses*. Washington: Brookings Institution.

Lippmann, Walter. (1955). *The Public Philosophy*. Boston: Little, Brown.

Lowi, Theodore J. (1969). *The End of Liberalism*. New York: Norton.

Martin, Daniel W. (1988). "The Fading Legacy of Woodrow Wilson," *Public Administration Review* 48 (March-April).

Morison, Samuel Eliot. (1974). *The European Discovery of America: The Southern Voyages*. New York: Oxford University Press.

O'Neill, Tip. (1994). *All Politics Is Local and Other Rules of the Game*. New York: Times Books.

Rosenbloom, David H. (1990). *Public Administration*, 2nd ed. New York: Random House.

Rossiter, Clinton, and James Lare, eds. (1963). *The Essential Lippmann: A Political Philosophy for Liberal Democracy*. New York: Random House.

Schlesinger, Arthur, Jr. (1986). *The Cycles of American History*. Boston: Houghton-Mifflin.

Shaw, George Bernard. (1944). *Everybody's Political What's What?* New York: Dodd, Mead.

Tocqueville, Alexis de. (1835; translation 1899). *Democracy in America*. New York: Appleton.

U.S. Department of State. (1970). *Diplomacy for the 70s*. Washington: U.S. Department of State.

Van Riper, Paul. (1983). "The American Administrative State: Wilson and the Founders—An Unorthodox View." *Public Administration Review* 43 (November-December).

Waldo, Dwight. (1955). *The Study of Administration*. New York: Random House.

———. (1975). "Education for Public Administration in the Seventies." *In American Public Administration: Past, Present, Future*, ed. Frederick C. Mosher. University: University of Alabama Press.

Warwick, Donald P. (1975). *A Theory of Public Bureaucracy: Politics, Personality, and Organization in the State Department*. Cambridge: Harvard University Press.

Wilson, Woodrow. (1887). "The Study of Administration," *Political Science Quarterly* 2 (June); reprinted 50 (December 1941).

Winthrop, Robert C. (1971). *Life and Letters of John Winthrop*. New York: Da Capo Press.

Recommended Books

Lynn, Naomi B., and Aaron Wildavsky, eds. (1990). *Public Administration: The State of the Discipline*. Chatham, NJ: Chatham House. A collection of articles assessing the knowledge base of the academic field of public administration as it entered the last decade of the twentieth century.

Rosenbloom, David H., and Rosemary O'Leary. (1987). *Public Administration and Law*, 2nd ed. New York: Marcel Dekker. An extensive explanation of how the legal system—the courts—influence administrative values, decision making, organizational structures, policy implementation, and program evaluation.

Shafritz, Jay M., editor in chief. (1998). *International Encyclopedia of Public Policy and Administration*. Boulder, CO: Westview Press. Nine hundred articles defining and analyzing every aspect of public administration; the first place to go to look up a concept, practice, theory, or issue in the field.

Waldo, Dwight. (1984). *The Administrative State: A Study of the Political Theory of Amercian Public Administration*, 2nd ed. New York: Holmes and

Meier. The classic work on the philosophy of public administration (originally published in 1948) wherein the prevailing "gospel of efficiency" is rejected and administrative value neutrality is denied.

Related Web Sites

American Political Science Association
http://www.apsanet.org/
Amercian Society for Public Administration
http://www.aspanet.org/
Amnesty International
http://www.amnesty.org/
Association for Public Policy Analysis and Managment
http://qsilver.queensu.ca/appam/
Council on Licensure, Enforcement and Regulation
http://www.csg.org/clear.html
Federal government laws and regulations
http://fedlaw.gsa.gov/

National Association of Schools of Public Affairs and Administration
http://www.naspaa.org
National Emergency Management Association
http://www.csg.org/nemaweb
Oklahoma City bombing
http://www.cnn.com/US/OKC/bombing.html
Woodrow Wilson
http://www.whitehouse.gov/WH/glimpse/presidents/html/ww28.html

2

The Political and Cultural Environment of Public Policy and Its Administration

Keynote: Were the *Challenger* Astronauts Killed by Fog?

What Is Public Policy?

Public Policymaking in a Republic • Executive Powers

The Policymaking Process

Agenda Setting • Decision Making • Implementation • Evaluation • Feedback

Power—The External Perspective

Pluralism • Group Theory

Power—The Internal Perspective

Organizational Goals • Internal Power Relationships

The Cultures of Public Organizations

The Outside Cultural Environment • The Inside Cultural Environment • Professional Socialization • Symbolic Management

---

Keynote: Were the *Challenger* Astronauts Killed by Fog?

In 1961 President John F. Kennedy told a joint session of Congress "that this nation should commit itself to achieving the goal, before this decade is out, of landing a man on the moon and returning him safely to the earth." As with much grand policymaking, this was easy enough to say. Few believed that the National Aeronautics and Space Administration (NASA), the federal agency created in 1958 to beat the Soviet Union in the Cold War space race, could achieve this "man on the moon" goal in the allotted time.

When the race started, it seemed that the Soviets were decidedly ahead of the United States in rocketry. The problem of getting to the moon was generally agreed to be technically feasible; the question of who would win would be decided by which side could better apply and manage its resources. This was the American advantage. Both sides had the technical expertise. Both sides gave their space programs virtually unlimited money. The Americans won because they had managers—public administrators—who were not necessarily more capable as individuals but decidedly more capable within their political, organizational, and cultural environment.

NASA not only won the space race but became the national exemplar of managerial excellence. At least until a clear day in January 1986 when the space shuttle *Challenger* blasted off into the Florida skies to become a now-classic example of managerial incompetence. The shuttle, with six astronauts and New Hampshire schoolteacher Christa McAuliffe aboard, blew up 73 seconds after liftoff because an O-ring seal on one of the booster rockets failed. Yet this was not a complete surprise to anyone who followed the shuttle program in the news media. It was widely reported that such seals nearly failed on earlier shuttle flights. They were most likely to fail when the outside air temperature was close to freezing, as it was on the day of the *Challenger* launch.

The problem seems so obvious now. NASA managers had more information than they could adequately process. So while the skies were sunny when the *Challenger* last "slipped the surly bonds of Earth," it can be said that the crew truly died from the fog—caused by a blinding array of information that led to a faulty decision by public administrators.

The "fog of war" is the wonderfully descriptive phrase for the confusion and uncertainty that is inherent in combat. Prussian General Karl von Clausewitz originated this meteorological metaphor in his 1832 classic on military strategy, *On War*. It is as if a literal fog descends upon the battlefield and blinds the combatants to what the enemy and even other elements of their own forces are doing. In the days of black powder, the fog was almost as literal as it was proverbial.

Today, wherever far-flung or large-scale operations have to be coordinated, whether military or managerial, fog or uncertainty is always a possibility. The field of management information systems has grown up in recent decades to reduce the inevitable fog to manageable proportions. But the reduction mechanisms themselves—computer data and memorandums in a seemingly endless stream—often create more problems than the fog they were designed to dispel.

And sometimes the fog is made all the more blinding by political considerations. It was not just that NASA had developed an organizational culture that inhibited bad news from getting to the top in a timely manner, those who decided to launch that day were under the most exquisitely subtle of political pressures as well. If the shuttle had kept its schedule on that ill-fated day, it would have returned in time for Ms. McAuliffe—who had been selected in a highly publicized national search—to sit in the balcony of the Chamber of the House of Representatives as President Ronald Reagan pointed her out during his State of the Union speech as an inspiration to the nation and all those desirous of winning lotteries.

Of course, as soon as the accident occurred all those responsible went into deep denial. Top NASA managers denied having heard of O-ring problems. The White

House denied it put any pressure on NASA that would compromise safety. To sort out the denials and gather the facts, the Presidential Commission on the Space Shuttle *Challenger* Accident was promptly appointed. Six months later it reported that the failure of the O-ring seals were the physical cause of the *Challenger* explosion. But it also declared that the "decision to launch the *Challenger* was flawed." It further concluded that "if the decision makers had known all the facts, it is highly unlikely that they would have decided to launch." In essence, the commission found that the NASA managers responsible for the launch decision were ignorant—because they were blinded by the fog of competing information.

The Commission's report also absolved managers of succumbing to political pressures to prove that shuttle flights were routine and routinely on schedule. It simply denied that there were any political pressures. This was only polite. It certainly would have been unusual for a Presidential Commission to criticize the president who appointed it. But denial fooled no one and only made them look foolish. According to Barbara Romzek and Melvin Dubnick writing in *Public Administration Review*, political "pressures existed and came from a variety of sources outside of NASA, including the White House." Charles Peters of *The Washington Monthly* reported that "top NASA officials didn't want to hear the bad news (about the O-rings) because they were determined to launch the next day so that President Reagan could point to this accomplishment in his State of the Union Message. They had even written a suggested insert for the speech."

Good managers with the facts before them can make good decisions. But otherwise good managers with an overwhelming volume of data to digest often become unable to make timely or wise decisions; they are reduced to incompetence by the efforts to make them more competent. We live in a contradictory world when the fog does not come in, as poet Carl Sandburg suggests, "on little cat feet," but rides on the crest of an endless wave of computer printouts. The *Challenger* disaster leads an infinite list of things gone wrong despite the best efforts of highly talented and otherwise able individuals—people who have banded together to create an organization that as a whole is less talented than the sum of its very talented human parts.

And just how did NASA respond to this problem of perceived incompetence? A few weeks after the *Challenger* disaster, NASA awarded bonuses to dozens of its top managers for the excellent work they had done. The media made a big joke of this by pointing out the incongruity of giving $10,000 bonuses to members of a team that couldn't "shuttle straight." NASA managers promptly complained that they shouldn't all be punished for the screw-ups of a few. True, the O-ring failed, but the other 30,000 parts of the shuttle worked just fine!

Of course they missed the point. Judgments about competence and incompetence rightly are determined by the work of the entire organization. If even a slight percentage of the work is bad, it can cause disaster or color the public's perception of it. This is the perception problem of the U.S. Postal Service. Practically all of the mail gets delivered on time. But because we all remember a check that was lost five years ago or a letter that arrived two weeks late, we perceive the Postal Service to be far more incompetent than it really is.

The 1969 moon landing was such an awesome feat of technical and managerial wizardry that it made even the most intractable problems seem soluble by government.

A NASA space shuttle launch. The odds are excellent that your congressional district is represented in this picture. NASA, in order to gain as much political support for the shuttle program as possible, made a concerted effort to ensure that shuttle components were built in (meaning shuttle jobs existed in) at least 300 of the 435 congressional districts •

Clausewitz contemplating the O-rings on the space shuttle •

After all, if we could go to the moon, we could do anything! This attitude gave rise to the moon-ghetto metaphor, a phrase that is often used for the contrast between the great managerial task of putting a man on the moon and the government's perennial but often futile efforts at solving the economic and social problems of America's urban ghettos. It is often posed as a question: If we can go to the moon, why can't we solve the problems of the ghetto? It's a good question.

But even the best-run organization, of which NASA is still an example, can be befuddled by fog. As with real weather, this kind of fog is a sometime thing. It can be disrupted by more effective management information systems, by supportive organizational cultures, and by determined top managers. The best managers will use a bout of fog as a learning experience—as an opportunity to change their information system, organization culture, and decisional processes so this particular bad weather can never happen again. That is exactly what NASA has proceeded to do. There may be accidents in the future—that is an inherent problem with experimental technology. But it seems safe to predict that there will never be another O-ring accident, nor one caused by the same kind of external political pressures or internal miscommunications.

Box 2.1

Journalist David Brinkley on the Moon-Ghetto Metaphor

We evolved a little cliché in the sixties which led people to say, in relation to almost every social problem we had, "If we can land man on the moon, why can't we . . . ?" and you fill in the blank. It's been applied to almost everything: curing cancer, clearing slums. Hundreds of problems had that little recipe applied. It has a kind of superficial charm, but I don't believe it really holds up because the problems are not really comparable. When we decided to land a man on the moon, we knew precisely what it was we wanted to do, we knew pretty well how to do it, the objective was clear, the methods were reasonably clear and, because it was government, the financing was freely available. There was no question of profit or loss. So the space objective was achieved. . . .

In the case of poverty, the goal is obviously to eliminate poverty, but we don't know how to do it. . . . People are fond of saying the problem with poor people is they don't have any money. Well, that's nice. That's cute. But there's more to it than that. If we gave them money, some people would wind up with a lot of it and some people would soon wind up, again, with none of it. Compared to the problems we have to solve on earth, flying to the moon is child's play.

SOURCE: Quoted in Peter Joseph, *Good Times: An Oral History of America in the Nineteen Sixties* (New York: William Morrow, 1974), pp. 386–387.

What Is Public Policy?

In the beginning there was chaos. Then came policy. "Let there be light" (Genesis, 1:3) was a policy decision. Policy creates orderly structures and a sense of direction. Public administration cannot exist in a policy vacuum. It must have administrative structures that are directed by leaders who wish to do something—if only to maintain the **status quo**. Thus all of public administration is inherently an instrument of policy—whether that instrument plays well, poorly, or not at all.

Any policy is a decision. A public policy is whatever a government decides to do or not to do. It is what a government does in response to a political issue. A public program consists of all those activities designed to implement the public policy: often this calls for the creation of organizations, public agencies, and bureaus, which in turn need to create more policies that give guidance to the organization's employees on how to obtain the overall public policy.

---

status quo The existing state of affairs. This term is often used to describe policies designed to maintain the existing distribution of power.

Policy is hierarchical. The broadest, most overarching policy is made at the top. Then increasingly more focused policies must be made at every level on down. For example, the president of the United States sits at the top of the foreign policymaking pyramid. Dozens of layers below him sit thousands of clerks in the **visa** sections of hundreds of embassies and consulates making policy—that is, making decisions—on who may legally enter the United States. To be sure, policy at the bottom is heavily impacted by laws and regulations. But to the extent that these low-level officials, what Michael Lipsky calls **street-level bureaucrats**, have any discretion at all, they are making policy. And if you are on the receiving end of that policy, whether as a visa applicant or a motorist receiving a traffic citation from a police officer, the policy is as real to you as if it were coming from higher levels in the policymaking hierarchy.

Public Policymaking in a Republic

It is the sovereign who makes legitimate policy in a political community. In a traditional society, the sovereign (meaning the monarch) is the sovereign (meaning the boss). In the United States, the people are sovereign and government is considered their agent. In a 1916 speech, President Woodrow Wilson rhetorically asked: "Just what is it that America stands for? If she stands for one thing more than another, it is for the sovereignty of self-governing people." This kind of sovereignty is generally referred to as a democracy.

But democracy is not a simple concept. It started, like so many things having to do with government, with the Greeks. Their democracy consisted of rule by an elite group of male citizens, whose well-being was maintained by politically suppressed women and a large slave population. Not a desirable situation if you were a woman and worse if you were a slave. The development of popular or universal democracy in the eighteenth century led to revolutionary conceptions of democracy that called for the placing of all power in the hands of the people—at first just white males. The problem remained of constructing a state that could exercise that power not just in the name of, but for all of the people. This is what President Abraham Lincoln, a man with strong antislavery credentials, was concerned about in his 1863 Gettysburg Address: " . . . that this government of the people, by the people, for the people, shall not perish from the earth."

The modern problem with "the people" is that so many nasty individuals have done too many despicable things in their name. Because the term democracy often has been used by totalitarian regimes and their "people's democracies," one person's democratic regime is too often another's totalitarian despotism. So modern democracy, like the modern contact lens, is in the eye of the beholder. By being used to describe such a large range of institutional possibilities, the term democracy has tended to lose its meaning—but not its vitality—in political debate.

---

visa A document, usually in the form of a stamp in a passport, which allows a citizen of one nation to visit another.

street-level bureaucrats Those public officials who are literally closest to the people by being in almost constant contact with them. Examples are police officers, welfare case workers, and teachers.

The **founders** of the United States were rightly suspicious of the so-called "pure" democracy of the free male citizens of ancient Athens. As **Aristotle** had warned, time and again throughout history these pure democracies had been captured by **demagogues** and had degenerated into dictatorial tyrannies. John Adams wrote in an 1814 letter: "Remember, democracy never lasts long. It soon wastes, exhausts, and murders itself. There never was a democracy yet that did not commit suicide." This well-justified fear of "the mob" led the founders to create a **republic**, a form of government one step removed from democracy, that presumably protects the people from their own passions. The frustration of coming to grips with the concept and the reality of democracy is illustrated by Winston Churchill's 1947 remark in the House of Commons: "No one pretends that democracy is perfect or all wise. Indeed, it has been said that democracy is the worst form of government except all those other forms that have been tried from time to time."

While the founders specifically wanted a governing structure that was insulated from a pure democracy, they also wanted a governing arrangement that, unlike the city states of ancient Greece, could function over a large area. As James Madison wrote in *The Federalist*, No. 14: "In a democracy the people meet and exercise the government in person; in a republic, they assemble and administer it by their representatives and agents. A democracy, consequently, will be confined to a small spot. A republic may be extended over a large region." Yet the founders all knew that many republics in history, such as the Roman republic, had been replaced by despots. Consequently, when Benjamin Franklin was asked what sort of government had been hatched at the **Constitutional Convention of 1787** he replied, "a republic, if you can keep it." He knew that "keeping it" was far from certain.

In a republic the legislature, whether parliament or **Congress**, is supreme. After all it has the greatest number of enumerated powers and the executive and judicial

---

founders An imprecise phrase for all of those individuals who played a major role in declaring U.S. independence from Britain, fighting the Revolutionary War, and writing and adopting the U.S. Constitution.

Aristotle (384–322 B.C.) The Greek philosopher who originated much of the study of logic, science, and politics. For several years, Aristotle, who was a student of Plato, served as the tutor of the boy who would become Alexander the Great.

demagogue A political leader accused of seeking or gaining power through the use of arguments designed to appeal to a mass public's sentiments, even though critics may consider those arguments exaggerated or spurious. The term is loaded and is never considered a compliment except as an indirect way of referring to a politician's rhetorical powers. The term, derived from the Greek *demagogos,* meaning a leader of the people, is one of the most time-honored epithets thrown at successful opposition politicians.

republic A Latin word meaning the public thing; the state and its institutions; that form of government in which sovereignty resides in the people who elect agents to represent them in political decision making. The United States is a republic.

Constitutional Convention of 1787 The meeting in Philadelphia, May 25 to September 18, at which 55 delegates from the various states designed the U.S. Constitution. The convention was called to revise the Articles of Confederation. Instead, the convention, presided over by George Washington, discarded the articles and designed an entirely new framework for American governance.

Congress The legislative branch of the U.S. government. The Congress was created by Article I, Section 1, of the Constitution, which provides that "all legislative powers herein granted shall be vested in a Congress of the United States, which shall consist of a Senate and House of Representatives."

branches must enforce its laws. As Madison wrote in *The Federalist*, No. 51: "In republican government, the legislative authority necessarily predominates." President Franklin D. Roosevelt in a press conference on July 23, 1937, put it another way: "It is the duty of the President to propose and it is the privilege of the Congress to dispose." Yet this system was perverted from World War II until very recently. Because of the necessities of both hot and cold wars, the president has been unusually strong vis-à-vis the Congress. With the end of the Cold War and without the need to rally behind a wartime leader, the power relationship seems to be returning to its "normal" condition. At the very least, Congress is reasserting its traditional dominance.

Executive Powers

Many political executives, whether mayors, governors, or presidents, have tried—often for sound cause relating to the public good—to take more policymaking power unto themselves than may be constitutionally warranted. Just how far can an executive deviate from the legislative will or the letter of the constitution in a republican government? This is usually a function of the political strength of the executive as evidenced by a large electoral mandate, control by the executive's party in the legislature, or public opinion poll ratings. Strong executives are able to put into place more of the policies they espouse. But just how much strength should an executive ideally have or be allowed to have? Fortunately, we can answer this question with the help of three famous statements on executive power, all made by past presidents of the United States—and all equally applicable to any political executive, whether president, governor, or mayor, in any constitutional system. They are (1) the restricted view, (2) the prerogative theory, and (3) the stewardship theory.

The Restricted View   This is the limited (or literalist) view of presidential power espoused by President **William Howard Taft**. He, as an archconservative, held that "the president can exercise no power which cannot be fairly and reasonably traced to some specific grant of power or justly implied and included within such express grant as proper and necessary to its exercise." Furthermore (and directly contrary to President Theodore Roosevelt's stewardship view that follows), "there is no undefined residuum of power which he can exercise because it seems to be in the public interest." Taft viewed the president as the agent of the Congress—in no way a free agent. In a constitutional sense, Taft was a **strict constructionist**. He was disdainful of those who asserted the presence of a "residuum of power" when he clearly saw none. As an administrator, he felt his political hands were tied by the constraints of his office. And he was happy in his bondage. Today he remains a role model for all those public managers who would instantly solve public problems

---

William Howard Taft (1857–1930) The only person to be both president of the United States (1909–1913) and chief justice of the Supreme Court (1921–1930). Taft, at 321 pounds, also holds the record as the largest of all presidents.

strict constructionist One who believes the U.S. Constitution should be interpreted narrowly and literally. A loose constructionist, in contrast, believes that the Constitution should be interpreted liberally in order to reflect changing times.

with new public policy if only they had the power. Not having it, they sit back, survey the poor conditions in their administrative realm and feel quite strongly that they too are a victim of "the system."

The Prerogative Theory   This theory of executive power was espoused by President Abraham Lincoln and supported by **John Locke** in his *Second Treatise of Government* (1690). Under certain conditions, they believed that the chief executive possessed extraordinary power to preserve the nation: "Many things there are which the law can by no means provide for; and those must necessarily be left to the discretion of him that has the executive power in his hands." This power, as Lincoln saw it, might not only exceed constitutional bounds but act against the Constitution. A president, according to this view, could at least for a short while even assume dictatorial powers. Lincoln explained this theory in an 1864 letter:

> [T]hat my oath to preserve the Constitution to the best of my ability imposed upon me the duty of preserving, by every indispensable means, that government—that nation, of which that Constitution was the organic law. Was it possible to lose the nation and yet preserve the Constitution? By general law, life and limb must be protected, yet often a limb must be amputated to save a life; but a life is never wisely given to save a limb. I felt that measures otherwise unconstitutional might become lawful by becoming indispensable to the preservation of the Constitution through the preservation of the nation.

Lincoln's attitude was commendable enough in the middle of a civil war. However, when recent presidents have sought extraordinary powers even with claims of national security and **executive privilege**, they have been "checked" by the Supreme Court. A notable example occurred during the midst of the Korean War. President Harry S. Truman issued an executive order directing the Secretary of Commerce to take possession of and operate the nation's steel mills because of a labor dispute that threatened to disrupt war production. In response, the Supreme Court held in *Youngstown Sheet and Tube Co. v. Sawyer* (1952) that the president exceeded his constitutional powers. Two decades later the Court in *United States v. Nixon* (1974) rejected President Richard M. Nixon's claim that the Constitution provided the president with an absolute and unreviewable executive privilege—specifically, the right not to respond to a **subpoena** in connection with a judicial trial. The court

---

John Locke (1632–1704) The English physician and philosopher whose writings on the nature of governance were a profound influence on the founding fathers. It is often argued that the first part of the Declaration of Independence, which establishes the essential philosophic rationale for the break with England, is Thomas Jefferson's restatement of John Locke's most basic themes.

executive privilege The presidential claim that the executive branch may withhold information from the Congress or its committees and the courts to preserve confidential communications within the executive branch or to secure the national interest. Although the Constitution does not explicitly grant the executive a privilege to withhold information from the Congress, presidents have from the beginning of the Republic claimed it.

subpoena A written order issued by a judicial officer requiring a specified person to appear in a designated court at a specified time, either to serve as a witness in a case under the jurisdiction of that court or to bring material to that court.

held that "neither the doctrine of separation of powers, nor the need for confidentiality of high-level communications, without more, can sustain an absolute, unqualified, presidential immunity from judicial process under all circumstances." The Court allowed there was a limited executive privilege that might pertain in the areas of military, diplomatic, or security affairs, and where confidentiality was related to the president's ability to carry out his constitutional mandates. This was the decision that forced Nixon to give the Watergate **special prosecutor** tape recordings of criminal activities in **Oval Office** meetings, and, in effect, forced Nixon to resign as president in 1974.

The prerogative approach is not a theory for all seasons. Since it is applicable only in times of extraordinary national emergency, presidents have been able to "get away with it" only during wartime when the Congress has been compliant (as it was during the Civil War) or kept ignorant (as it was during the Vietnam War). The important thing to remember is that this theory of executive power is quietly reserved to support the efforts of a leader who sees the nation through in a time of crisis; or alternately, it lurks in the hands of an unprincipled opportunist or demagogue to stifle republican institutions.

The Stewardship Theory   This is President Theodore Roosevelt's view that the president, because he represents and holds in trust the interests of all the people, should be free to take any actions in the public interest that are not specifically forbidden by the Constitution or statutory law. Although he only articulated this doctrine in his autobiography, published in 1913 after he left office, Roosevelt certainly lived it. For example, he sent the U.S. Navy's battleships on an around-the-world training cruise without congressional permission; he then told Congress that if they wanted the ships back, they would have to appropriate funds to buy fuel for the return journey. Roosevelt believed strongly that "every executive officer . . . was a steward of the people bound actively and affirmatively to do all he could for the people." Roosevelt felt, in sum, that he was free to do as he pleased in that twilight zone lying between the prohibitions of the law and the duties required by specific constitutional or statutory enactments. The most glaring example of this attitude was the dismemberment of the Isthmus of Panama from Colombia to create a government that would be more cooperative in the American effort to build a canal. According to David McCullough in his history of the creation of the Panama Canal, when Roosevelt met with his cabinet to report what had happened, he asked his attorney general to construct a defense. The attorney general is reported to have remarked, "Oh, Mr. President, do not let so great an achievement suffer from any taint of legality."

---

special prosecutor A prosecutor appointed to consider the evidence in a case and, if necessary, to undertake the prosecution of a case that presents a possible conflict of interest for the jurisdiction's regular prosecutor.

Oval Office The oval-shaped White House office of the president of the United States. Although the office itself was built in the 1930s as part of an expansion of the West Wing of the White House, the term did not come into general usage until the Nixon administration. Until then, the president's office was just called the president's office.

Nevertheless, no executive, whether king or president, can afford to stray too far from the legislative will. Charles I of England tried it and got his head chopped off by Parliament in 1649. Ever since, the monarchs of England have been more respectful of the elected representatives of the people. Richard Nixon, no less a miscreant than Charles I in the eyes of some of his legislative opponents, was fortunate to live in more genteel times. He, for his Watergate-related crimes, was merely forced to resign in the face of certain **impeachment** by the Congress.

These three models of executive leadership are all still very much with us. Of course, the prerogative approach of Lincoln and Locke is not much in evidence except in despotic regimes. Only Boris Yeltsin comes to mind as a prerogatist in the grand manner, stretching his constitutional powers as the Soviet Union disintegrated in 1991. The more common situation at all political and organizational levels is illustrated by the two ends of a continuum with a literalist (a Taft) at one end and a steward (a Teddy Roosevelt) at the other. The choice for leaders then is to be inactive in terms of policy initiation—basically to just maintain what is, or to be **proactive** in terms of policy—and to be at the forefront of continuous change and reform. Or to be where most political and administrative executives are—somewhere in between. That is, they are proactive only on a limited number of issues.

The Policymaking Process

Because public policymaking involves so many aspects, so many players, and so many issues, it is difficult to grasp it as one single thing. Of course, it is not a tangible thing; it is a never-ending intangible process. This process can be illustrated by the public policymaking cycle (see Figure 2.1), a conceptual model that views the public policy process as moving through a succession of stages: (1) agenda setting (or the identification of a policy issue), (2) policy decision or nondecision, (3) implementation, (4) program evaluation or impact analysis, and finally (5) feedback, which leads to revision or termination. Thus the process comes full circle—which is why it is called a "cycle." A review of this process will show that public administration is both at the heart of the process and a feature of every aspect of it.

Agenda Setting

Agenda setting is the process by which ideas or issues bubble up through the various political channels to wind up for consideration by a political institution such as a legislature or court. We have already mentioned the two greatest sources of

---

impeachment A quasi-judicial process for removing public officials from office. Impeachment is the beginning of the process by which the president, vice president, federal judges, and all civil officials of the United States may be removed from office if convicted of the charges brought against them. Officials may be impeached for treason, bribery, and other high crimes and misdemeanors. The U.S. House of Representatives has the sole authority to bring charges of impeachment (by a simple majority vote), and the Senate has the sole authority to try impeachment charges. An official may be removed from office only upon conviction, which requires a two-thirds vote of the Senate.
proactive An administrative style that encourages taking risks on behalf of one's clients or one's moral values; the opposite of a reactive style.

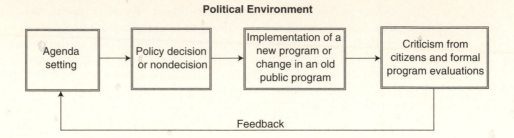

Figure 2.1 The Public Policymaking Cycle

agenda items—the executive and the legislators. Their constituents expect that they will seek the enactment into law of the policies that they advocated in their campaigns for elective office. Additionally, the administrative agencies of a government often generate legislative proposals. Sometimes, these are incorporated into the executive's legislative recommendations.

The agenda-setting process often makes extensive use of the mass media to take a relatively unknown or unsupported issue and, through publicity, expand the numbers of people who care about the issue so that an institution, whether it be city hall or the Congress, is forced to take some action. One example can be traced back to 1955, when Rosa Parks, an African American woman, was arrested for refusing to take a seat in the back of a bus in Montgomery, Alabama. This confrontation sparked the modern civil rights movement. Dr. Martin Luther King Jr. would later use the tactics of nonviolent confrontation with southern segregational policies to arouse sufficient sympathy and support in the rest of the nation, which would lead to the passage of landmark civil rights legislation in Congress. When these nonviolent demonstrators turned violent, it was all the better—because it made better TV and thus ensured a bigger audience for the message of the cause. Starting in the 1980s, pro-life (meaning antiabortion) groups used demonstrators in front of medical offices providing abortion services to arouse the national consciousness about this issue. These, too, often became spontaneously violent and thus made for better TV. The lesson is clear. "Nonviolent" demonstrators that turn violent or at least contentious once the TV news cameras arrive are more likely to get on the six o'clock news. These approaches to placing issues on the public policy agenda are called pseudo-events by historian Daniel Boorstin because they are "nonspontaneous, planted, or manufactured 'news,' whose main purpose is to gain publicity for the person or cause which arranged the 'event.'"

Agendas are often set by public policy entrepreneurs, political actors who take a political issue and run with it. Thus certain senators might make particular issues their own by sheer force of expertise that, if respected, "forces" colleagues to take cues on the matter from them. Or a staffer might become such an expert on an issue that he or she can heavily influence legislation dealing with it. Thus a public policy entrepreneur can be anyone in the political environment whose expertise and actions can affect an issue.

Agenda setting, which is usually confined to professional politicians, is a game that anybody can play. A federal judge could rule that a state prison is unconstitutionally overcrowded and thus force the state's legislature to deal with the issue by appropriating funds for new prisons. A citizens' group could grow so excited about an issue that they organize themselves to gather enough signatures of registered voters to put the issue as a proposition on the ballot of the next election. A public interest law firm could challenge the legality of an agency's action and force the courts to ascertain its constitutionality. Or an interest group could get thousands of its members to write (or e-mail) letters to their legislative representatives demanding action on a controversy. While there are only a few places—such as a legislature, court, or regulatory commission—where agendas can be formally enacted, there are infinite numbers of sources from which agenda items spring. And like hope, they spring eternally.

The issue-attention cycle is a model developed by **Anthony Downs** that attempts to explain how many policy problems evolve on the political agenda. The cycle is premised on the notion that the public's attention rarely remains focused on any one issue, regardless of the objective nature of the problem. The cycle consists of five steps:

1. The preproblem stage (an undesirable social condition exists, but has not captured public attention);

2. Alarmed discovery and euphoric enthusiasm (a dramatic event catalyzes the public attention, accompanied by an enthusiasm to solve the problem);

3. Recognition of the cost of change (the public gradually realizes the difficulty of implementing meaningful change);

4. Decline of public interest (people become discouraged or bored or a new issue claims attention); and

5. The postproblem stage (although the issue has not been solved, it has been dropped from the nation's agenda).

Decision Making

Public policymaking is the totality of the processes by which a government decides to deal or not to deal with a particular problem or concern. It is a never-ending process. Nineteenth-century British statesman Lord Salisbury is usually credited with first remarking: "There is no such thing as a fixed policy, because policy like all organic entities is always in the making."

There are two distinct and opposite theories seeking to explain the mechanisms that produce policy decisions or nondecisions. The first might be called the rational

---

Anthony Downs (1930–) The economist and policy analyst who is generally credited with establishing the intellectual framework for public choice economics in his *An Economic Theory of Democracy* (1957). His classic book on bureaucracy, *Inside Bureaucracy* (1967), sought to justify bureaucratic government on economic grounds and to develop laws and propositions that would aid in predicting the behavior of bureaus and bureaucrats.

decision making approach and it generally has been attributed to **Harold D. Lasswell**. In his book *The Future of Political Science*, he posited seven significant phases for every decision:

1. The intelligence phase, involving an influx of information;
2. The promoting or recommending phase, involving activities designed to influence the outcome;
3. The prescribing phase, involving the articulation of norms;
4. The invoking phase, involving establishing correspondence between prescriptions and concrete circumstances;
5. The application phase, in which the prescription is executed;
6. The appraisal phase, assessing intent in relation to effect; and
7. The terminating phase, treating expectations (rights) established while the prescription was in force.

A rejection of this approach was urged by **Charles E. Lindblom**, the leading proponent of the second theory of policy decision making—the incremental approach. In his most famous article, "The Science of Muddling Through," Lindblom took a hard look at the rational models of the decisional processes of government. He rejected the notion that most decisions are made by rational (total information) processes. Instead, he saw such decisions—indeed, the whole policymaking process—as dependent upon small incremental decisions that tend to be made in response to short-term political conditions. Lindblom's thesis essentially held that decision making was controlled infinitely more by events and circumstances than by the will of those in policymaking positions. Disjointed incrementalism as a policy course was in reality the only truly feasible route, since incrementalism "concentrated the policymaker's analysis on familiar, better-known experiences, sharply reduced the number of different alternative policies to be explored, and sharply reduced the number and complexity of factors to be analyzed." Moreover, Lindblom argued that incrementalism was more consistent with the pluralistic nature of American democracy where individuals are free to combine to pursue common interests, whose contention "often can assure a more comprehensive regard for the values of the whole society than any attempt at intellectual comprehensiveness."

The rational and incremental models, often viewed as two ends of a continuum, are useful intellectual tools for conceptualizing the decision making process. But in reality they are not much more than mind games for **policy wonks**. The real world of political executives and harried legislators is not an intellectual arena so much as

---

Harold D. Lasswell, (1902–1978) One of the most influential and prolific of social scientists. While he made major contributions to the fields of communications, psychology (he pioneered the application of Freudian theory to politics), political science, sociology, and law, his most lasting legacy is probably his pioneering work in developing the concept and methodology of the policy sciences.

Charles E. Lindblom, (1917–) The Yale University political scientist who since the 1950s has been asserting that incrementalism is the most viable approach to understanding how public policies are made.

policy wonk A compulsive analyst of public policy processes. Wonk is slang for a student who is a grind or a nerd.

it is a bare knuckles political arena. Decisions in the political arena are influenced far more by the perception of a situation than by any rational concept of objective reality. It is far more than the differences between a pessimist seeing a glass half empty while the optimist sees the same glass as half full. One actor in the decisional drama may view a program as absolutely essential for the national interest while another actor is equally certain that it is nothing more than an example of petty bureaucrats wasting the taxpayers' money.

Policymakers bring two kinds of intelligence to bear on their thinking. First is their mental ability to cope with complicated problems. Second is the information they have on and the experience they have with the issue at hand. Both kinds of intelligence are then filtered through their ideological predispositions and personal biases before an attitude toward any given problem is set. Thus political decisions are seldom made on the objective merits of a case because a case only has merit in the eyes of a political decision maker if he or she is intelligent enough to see it and, equally important, is ideologically and politically predisposed to support it.

At the end of the day the policy processes of government are not only about equity or justice; they are fundamentally about power. But once power is exerted, once a law is enacted, once a program is created, these power brokers—whether democrats or autocrats—turn to their public administrators to make their wishes, to make their power, a reality. Without the administrators of the state to do their bidding, the power brokers are quite literally broke.

Implementation

Implementation is the process of putting a government program into effect; it is the total process of translating a legal mandate, whether an executive order or an enacted **statute**, into appropriate program directives and structures that provide services or create goods. Implementation, the doing part of public administration, is an inherently political process. Architects often say that "God is in the details." So is implementation. Its essence is in the details. A law is passed but the process of putting it into effect requires countless small decisions that necessarily alter it. According to President Carter's National Security Adviser Zbigniew Brzezinski, "policy makers are overwhelmed by events and information . . . a great deal of decision making is done through implementation by the bureaucracy, which often distorts it." "Distort" is a harsh word. It implies intentional change. But most administrative implementators act in good faith. There is seldom intentional distortion. However, there is substantial friction. This concept has been well expressed by Clausewitz, who holds that no matter how well planned a large operation is, the reality of delays, misunderstandings, etc., will make its inevitable execution less than ideal. While military in origin, friction has become a generally recognized phenomenon in all aspects of the administration of public and **international affairs**.

---

statute A law passed by a legislature; legislative-made as opposed to judge-made law.
international affairs A term that is loosely used as a synonym for international politics. It can include almost anything that is not exclusively domestic in nature.

TABLE 2.1   The Polis Model

Policy analysts have long been critical of the "either/or" nature of the rational versus the incremental approaches to decision making. A model advocated by Deborah Stone holds that the political community, the polis, is better able to deal with the ambiguity of less-than-perfect information—information often "spun" by "spin doctors"—than with the look at hard facts approach of the rational model. While rational analysis does not lend itself to the inconsistencies of real life, the polis model assumes them. Stone's comparison of the two models is below. Note how the polis model is so much more congenial and digestible to the public.

Rational-Analytic Model	Polis Model
State goals/objectives explicitly and precisely.	State goals ambiguously and possibly keep some goals secret or hidden.
Adhere to the same goal throughout the analysis and decision-making process.	Be prepared to shift goals and redefine goals as the political situation dictates.
Try to imagine and consider as many alternatives as possible.	Keep undesirable alternatives off the agenda by not mentioning them. Make your preferred alternative appear to be the only feasible or possible one.
	Focus on one part of the causal chain and ignore others that would require politically difficult or costly policy actions.
Define each alternative clearly as a distinct course of action.	Use rhetorical devices to blend alternatives; don't appear to make a clear decision that could trigger strong opposition.
Evaluate the costs and benefits of each course of action as accurately and completely as possible.	Select from the infinite range of consequences only those whose costs and benefits will make your preferred course of action look "best."
Choose the course of action that will maximize total welfare as defined by your objective.	Choose the course of action that hurts powerful constituents the least but portray your decision as creating maximum social good for a broad public.

SOURCE: Table adapted from Deborah Stone, *Policy Paradox: The Art of Political Decision Making* (New York: W. W. Norton & Co., 1997)

While implementation is obviously at the heart of public administration, it has only recently been self-consciously studied. The first major analysis of implementation as a new focus for public administration was Jeffrey Pressman and Aaron Wildavsky's 1973 study of federal programs in the city of Oakland, California. The unabridged title of their work tells part of the story in itself: *Implementation: How Great Expectations in Washington Are Dashed in Oakland; Or, Why It's Amazing that Federal Programs Work At All; This being a Saga of the Economic Development Administration as Told by Two Sympathetic Observers Who Seek to Build*

Box 2.2

Seven Reasons for Incrementalism

Why is emphasis on alternatives closely related to existing reality an aid to rational calculation? First, the consequences of alternatives that bear a remote relation to existing reality are generally more difficult to predict.

Second, . . . people cannot accurately foresee their own wants. . . . To be sure, they can exclude many unwanted alternatives without actually testing them. . . . But it is much more difficult to know which of the remaining alternatives is preferable. . . .

Third, because an individual has many goals, some of which conflict with one another . . . a marginal adjustment will bring about a gain in goal attainment. This is incrementalism in individual action, and the logic applies equally to social action.

Fourth, incrementalism is an aid to verifying the results of one's choices. This is in keeping with the principle of isolating a single variable. Results after one has acted can be compared with conditions before the change, and the relation of the particular choice to the particular changes is more easily determined.

Fifth, incrementalism helps to ensure control. Incremental change gives prescribed superiors an opportunity to issue rather detailed instructions or to check in detail the actions of their subordinates. As a general matter, the larger the increments of change, the more difficult it is for prescribed superiors to check on their subordinates or even to give instructions that are any more than a blank check.

Sixth, incrementalism is reversible. When mistakes are made, they can more easily be repaired.

Seventh, incrementalism permits both the survival and the continual alteration of the operating organization. The attempt to secure abrupt change by prescription usually fails because the operating organization, with its own codes and norms, resists sudden, large-scale change.

SOURCE: Robert A. Dahl and Charles E. Lindblom, *Politics, Economics and Welfare* (Chicago: University of Chicago Press, 1953).

Morals on a Foundation of Ruined Hopes. What Pressman and Wildavsky related in their landmark book seems almost simplistic—that policy planning and analysis were not taking into account the difficulties of execution or "implementation." The goal of their book was to consider how a closer nexus between policy and implementation could be achieved. A direct result of this book was a spate of works explaining how policy analysis can accomplish this objective—an objective, it is fair to say, that has yet to be comprehensively implemented.

Pressman and Wildavsky define implementation as "a process of interaction between the setting of goals and actions geared to achieving them" as well as "an ability to forge subsequent links in the causal chain so as to obtain the desired results."

This definition usefully calls attention to the interaction between setting goals and carrying them out. This helps clarify that implementation is political in a very fundamental sense in that the activities that go on under its banner shape **who gets what**, when, and how from government. Like lawmakers, administrators and those with whom they interact during the implementation process exert power over program objectives and influence program inputs and outcomes. Implementation involves administrators, interest groups, and other actors with diverse values, mobilizing power resources, forming coalitions, consciously plotting strategies, and generally engaging in strategic behavior designed to ensure that their point of view prevails. The terrain may be different from that found in Congress or other legislatures, but the basic staples of the political process are very much present.

Never forget that the goal of program implementation is necessarily the creation of the myriad details of everyday administrative life. Policy analyst Charles O. Jones maintains that implementation consists of "those activities directed toward putting a program into effect." This involves the "translation of program language into acceptable and feasible directives" as well as creating appropriate organizational structures and routines. A major virtue of Jones's definition is that it explicitly points to the role of routine and other aspects of organizational structure in implementation. In order to conserve time and energy, as well as to promote the equal treatment of clients, organizations develop **standard operating procedures**. These procedures plus other informal **decision rules** greatly simplify choices for administrators. Decisions can be made almost without thinking. Any effort to comprehend how implementation processes affect program outcomes cannot, then, ignore the collective impact of countless procedures and simple decision rules. Implementation is always a mix of the consciously strategic with the daily routine.

Evaluation

Any evaluation is an assessment. A program evaluation is the systematic examination of activities undertaken by government to make a determination about their effects, both for the short term and the long range. Program evaluation is distinguished from management evaluation (also called organization evaluation) because the latter is limited to a program's internal administrative procedures. While program evaluations use management and organizational data, the main thrust is necessarily on overall program objectives and impact. Thus a program is less concerned with the management of a police department than with that department's overall effect on crime; less concerned with a welfare agency's internal administration than with its effectiveness in dealing with clients.

---

who gets what This is the very definition of politics provided by the title of Harold Lasswell's classic 1936 book, *Politics: Who Gets What, When, How.*

standard operating procedures The established routines by which organizations accomplish their objectives.

decision rule Any directive established to make decisions in the face of uncertainty. For example, a payroll office might be given a decision rule to deduct one hour's pay from an employee's wages for each lateness that exceeds ten minutes but is less than one hour.

The concepts of **efficiency** and **effectiveness** are the standard criteria against which programs are pitted by evaluation. In addition, these concepts helped to forge a workable distinction between **audits** and evaluations. Audits, primarily financial accounting audits, were traditionally geared to control—to ensure that every dime of public funds is accounted for and that every regulation is complied with. This law-enforcement style of management is being increasingly displaced by program evaluation—a far more comprehensive management tool. We still expect programs to be administered efficiently, just as we expect complete fiscal accountability for funds and receipts. But efficiency is not enough. A work unit could be terribly efficient while working toward the wrong goals. Because of this, evaluations, if they are themselves to be effective, must also deal with the questions of effectiveness and relevance. It is not unreasonable to demand that programs have an effect on problems, and the right problems at that. Simply put, the most basic objective of a program evaluation is to assay the impact of a program on its target problem.

Program evaluations, while usually undertaken by the executive and legislative branches of government, are sometimes even done by the courts in response to petitions by client groups. While the three regular branches of government are heavily involved in evaluation, so too is the so-called "fourth branch of government"—the press. It conducts evaluations with every exposé of a mismanaged agency. Many a journalistic career has been made by breaking the "big story" of government ineptness and corruption. Bob Woodward and Carl Bernstein, the *Washington Post* reporters who exposed the Watergate scandal (see Chapter 14) are now the classic examples of intrepid journalists hot on the trail of public **malfeasance**. Not only did they get rich with a best-selling book (*All the President's Men*) but leading movie stars (Robert Redford and Dustin Hoffman) played them in the film of the same name. So in the furthest reaches of the minds of ambitious journalists digging through a government agency's dull files to get the story—to do the evaluation—is always the pleasant question: If I get this right and the story is "big," who will play me in the movie? However, accurate or not, journalistic evaluations often tend to be too superficial to serve as instruments of reform, although they do serve to provide impetus for full-scale evaluation efforts by others.

Feedback

The public policy cycle comes full circle when evaluative information creates new agenda items for subsequent decisions. This is called feedback because the new in-

---

efficiency Competence as well as speed in performance. Americans have historically been suspicious of a too-efficient government, feeling that a truly efficient administration of public affairs could eventually eat into political liberties.

effectiveness The extent to which an organization accomplishes some predetermined goal or objective; more recently, the overall performance of an organization from the viewpoint of some strategic constituency.

audit The final phase of the government budgetary process, which reviews the operations of an agency, especially its financial transactions, to determine whether the agency has spent its money in accordance with the law, in the most efficient manner, and with desired results.

malfeasance The performance of a consciously unlawful act on the part of a public official.

formation feeds back into its original source. Note how everything about this cycle is impacted by politics. This is because the whole process takes place in a political environment, as in Figure 2.1.

Feedback is effective to the extent that it is noisy. The people who set the goals and make the decisions must hear it. Sometimes feedback is heard as a complaint about slow service or poor quality products. Sometimes it is the silent noise of the citizens voting to **throw the rascals out**. And sometimes it is an exploding rocket ship, as in the *Challenger* disaster. The earlier quiet voices of NASA were not noisy enough for top management to hear. But NASA managers at all levels were soon blasted out of their complacency.

Power—The External Perspective

The administrators of public agencies often seem to live in a fairy tale world. Like the "old woman who lived in a shoe" who "had so many children she didn't know what to do," they have so many claims upon their scant resources that they often don't know how to cope with the incessant daily demands. But unlike the old woman, they don't have the option to whip "them all soundly and put them to bed." All too often they are in the position of Old Mother Hubbard, who "went to the cupboard to fetch her poor dog a bone" only to find that "the cupboard was bare." However, constituents do not want to hear that the cupboard is bare. Too often they dwell in a never-never land of endless resources. But days of surplus resources are over. Like Humpty Dumpty and his "great fall," neither "all the king's horses" nor "all the king's men" will ever put the good old days back "together again."

Fairy tales can help explain the world—the environment—to both children and administrators. For a more sophisticated environmental analysis, we need a less allegorical example from the social sciences. One of the best ways to visualize and understand an administrator's environment is to do a force field analysis of the pressures that bear upon any agency. Field theory originated in physics. It was borrowed by psychology to explain how an individual's behavior at any given time is the result of his or her personality interacting with the psychological forces in the environment. Organizational analysts refocused field theory from the individual to the group, the group that made up an organization. By systematically examining all of the forces—all of the powers—in the organization's field (meaning environment)—thus a force field analysis—they were better able to understand why the organization acted the way it did. Those wishing to understand why a government or an agency does seemingly irrational or contradictory things use a force field analysis to arrive at an explanation. For example, the federal government has a variety of laws and programs designed to prevent people from smoking tobacco. It forbids cigarette advertising on television and demands health warnings on tobacco products. But at the same time it encourages the growing of tobacco by American farmers and the sale of tobacco overseas by American companies. Thus the federal government is both for and against the use of tobacco at the same time.

---

throw the rascals out An oft-heard campaign slogan of the party not in power. Sometimes all it really means is that it is time for a change of rascals.

This contradictory policy seems silly on the surface. But the forces of good health work their will on the system to curtail tobacco use at the same time that the forces of commerce work their will on the system to encourage profit from tobacco—and the latter were here first. The obnoxious weed was introduced to Europe by none other than Christopher Columbus. For hundreds of years tobacco has been a major part of the economic foundation of colonial and later republican America. Only in the 1960s did the government "discover" the health hazards related to it. But by then it was just so profitable in terms of **excise tax** yields to both federal and state governments that forbidding the sale on health grounds would mean higher taxes elsewhere. Besides, an illegal market for tobacco would immediately arise in its place that would yield "tax" revenues only to the smugglers.

This all goes to show how governments as well as people get addicted to addictive substances. We as citizens are all addicted in the sense that we depend upon smokers to disproportionately pay taxes for their vice and then graciously die prematurely without collecting their fair share of Social Security retirement benefits. What self-sacrificing patriots they are! The same can be said of alcoholics. Here we have **public choice economics** in action. The citizen smoker (or drinker) as the sovereign consumer makes intelligent (or stupid) choices in the marketplace of products and ideas. But wait you say! This is irrational. And you are right. But it is political. To understand why administration is so often irrational, we have to look at some of the underlying premises of American government.

Pluralism

The "problem" begins with the fact that American government is inherently pluralistic—composed of multiple elements. First, its constitutional arrangement requires a separation of powers, the allocation of powers among the three branches of government so that they are a check upon each other. This separation, in theory, makes a tyrannical concentration of power impossible. The U.S. Constitution contains provisions in separate articles for three branches of government—legislative, executive, and judicial. There is a significant difference in the grants of power to these branches: the first article, dealing with legislative power, vests in the Congress "all legislative powers herein granted"; the second article vests "the executive power" in the president; and the third article states that "the judicial power of the United States shall be vested in one Supreme Court, and in such inferior courts as the Congress may from time to time ordain and establish." Justice Louis D. Brandeis offered the opinion of the U.S. Supreme Court in the 1926 case of *Myers v. United States*: "The doctrine of the separation of powers was adopted by the Convention of 1787, not to promote efficiency but to preclude the exercise of arbitrary power.

---

excise tax A tax on the manufacture, sale, or consumption of a product such as gasoline or tobacco.
public choice economics An approach to public administration and politics based on microeconomic theory that views the citizen as a consumer of government goods and services. It would attempt to maximize administrative responsiveness to citizen demand by creating a market system for government activities in which public agencies would compete to provide citizens with goods and services. This might replace a portion of the current system, under which most administrative agencies in effect act as monopolies under the influence of organized pressure groups, which, the public choice economists argue, are institutionally incapable of representing the demands of individual citizens.

Box 2.3

James Madison on Angels and the Separation of Powers

Ambition must be made to counteract ambition. The interest of the man must be connected with the constitutional rights of the place. It may be a reflection on human nature that such devices should be necessary to control the abuses of government. But what is government itself but the greatest of all reflections on human nature? If men were angels, no government would be necessary. If angels were to govern men, neither external nor internal controls on government would be necessary. In framing a government which is to be administered by men over men, the great difficulty lies in this: you must first enable the government to control the governed; and in the next place oblige it to control itself. A dependence on the people is, no doubt, the primary control on the government; but experience has taught mankind the necessity of auxiliary precautions.

SOURCE: James Madison, *The Federalist*, No. 51.

The purpose was not to avoid friction, but, by means of the inevitable friction incident to the distribution of the governmental powers among three departments, to save the people from autocracy." The "friction" that Brandeis refers to is not the friction inherent in implementation that Clausewitz analyzed, but the friction of conflict caused by independent power.

Second, American political processes, being inherently pluralistic, emphasize the role of competitive groups in society. Pluralism assumes that power will shift from group to group as elements in the mass public transfer their allegiance in response to their perceptions of their individual interests. However, according to **power-elite theory**, if democracy is defined as popular participation in public affairs, then pluralist theory is inadequate as an explanation of modern U.S. government. Pluralism, according to this view, offers little direct participation, since the elite structure is closed, pyramidal, consensual, and unresponsive. Society is thus divided into two classes: the few who govern and the many who are governed; that is, pluralism is covert elitism, instead of a practical solution to preserve democracy in a mass society.

Those who subscribe to elite theory often have a paranoid political orientation, the belief that there is a nationwide conspiracy against them. Examples include

---

power-elite theory The belief that the United States is basically ruled by a political, military, and business elite whose decisional powers essentially preempt the democratic process. C. Wright Mills (1916–1962) wrote in *The Power Elite* that "the leading men in each of the three domains of power—the warlords, the corporation chieftains, the political directorate—tend to come together to form the power elite of America." Most contemporary analyses of elitism in American governance have their intellectual foundations in Mills's work, even if Mills himself is not acknowledged.

those homosexuals who believe that AIDS was "invented" by the government to destroy them, those African Americans who believe that the drug epidemic is encouraged by the government to hurt them, those right-wing militia members who believe that the federal government is conspiring to confiscate all firearms in the hands of the citizens, and politicians who—especially during the Cold War—believed that a Communist conspiracy was on the verge of taking over the country. The concept was first identified in 1965 by historian Richard Hofstadter in *The Paranoid Style in American Politics*:

> There is a vital difference between the paranoid spokesman in politics and the clinical paranoiac: although they both tend to be overheated, over suspicious, overaggressive, grandiose, and apocalyptic in expression, the clinical paranoid sees the hostile and conspiratorial world in which he feels himself to be living as directed specifically against him; whereas the spokesman of the paranoid style finds it directed against a nation, a culture, a way of life whose fate affects not himself alone but millions of others.

Third and finally, pluralism has a cultural dimension. Those who espouse this believe that a nation's overall welfare is best served by preserving ethnic cultures rather than by encouraging the integration and blending of cultures. This is in contrast to the assimilationist belief that all immigrants should take their turn in a national **melting pot** and come out homogenized. But studies have consistently shown that this "ain't necessarily so." Historian Carl N. Degler wrote: "The metaphor of the melting pot is unfortunate and misleading. A more accurate analogy would be a salad bowl, for, though the salad is an entity, the lettuce can still be distinguished from the chicory, the tomatoes from the cabbage." In recent years the term has become less fashionable and has been replaced in political rhetoric by the image of a mosaic. Without using the term, Speaker of the House Newt Gingrich resurrected the melting pot concept in 1995 when he asserted that America is a distinct civilization—and that the way for immigrants to become "civilized" is to accept the mainstream "melting pot" values.

Group Theory

The importance of pluralism and the significance of groups in the democratic political process has been recognized for over two thousand years: Aristotle noted that political associations were both significant and commonplace because of the "general advantages" that members obtained. One of the first specific references to groups in the American political process was James Madison's famous discussion of factions in *The Federalist*, No. 10. In Madison's view, the group was inherent in the nature of people, and its causes were unremovable. The only choice then was to

---

melting pot A sociological term that implies (1) that each succeeding wave of immigrants to the United States blends into the general society and (2) that this melting is ideally what should happen. The term originated in Israel Zangwill's (1864–1926) play, *The Melting Pot* (1908), in which he wrote: "America is God's Crucible, the great Melting-Pot where all races of Europe are melting and re-forming!" The phrase depicted the symbol of assimilation for several generations of American immigrants.

control the effects of group pressure and power. A more elaborate discussion of group theory can be traced to John C. Calhoun's 1853 treatise, *A Disquisition on Government*. While essentially an argument for the protection of minority interests, the treatise suggested that ideal governance must deal with all interest groups, since they represent the legitimate interests of the citizens. If all groups participated on some level of parity within the policymaking process, then all individual interests would be recognized by the policymakers.

Modern group theory has taken greater impetus from the work of **Arthur F. Bentley, David B. Truman**, and **Earl Latham**. Latham viewed the legislature as the referee of the group struggle, responsible for "ratifying the victories of the successful coalitions and recording the terms of the surrenders, compromises, and conquests in the form of statutes." The function of bureaucrats is quite different, however. They are like "armies of occupation left in the field to police the rule won by the victorious coalition." Although Latham's description was aimed primarily at regulatory agencies, he saw the bureaucrat being deluged by the losing coalitions of groups for more favorable actions despite the general rules established. The result is that "agencies are constantly besought and importuned to interpret their authorities in favor of the very groups for the regulation of which they were originally granted."

Latham distinguished three types of groups, based on phases of development: incipient, conscious, and organized. An incipient group is one "where the interest exists but is not recognized" by the potential members; a conscious group is one "in which the community sense exists but which has not become organized"; and finally an organized group is "a conscious group which has established an objective and formal apparatus to promote the common interest." Latham's incipient and conscious groups are essentially the same as Truman's potential groups,

---

Arthur F. Bentley (1870–1957) The political scientist who was one of the pioneering voices in the behavioral analysis of politics and the intellectual creator of modern interest group theory. In *The Process of Government* (1908), Bentley argued that political analysis has had to shift its focus from forms of government to actions of individuals in the context of groups, because groups are the critical action mechanisms that enable numbers of individuals to achieve their political, economic, and social desires. Bentley's work was effectively "lost" until it was rediscovered and publicized by David B. Truman.

David B. Truman (1913–) A political scientist and one of the most influential interest group theorists. Truman's principal work, *The Governmental Process* (1951), views group interaction as the real determinant of public policy and as the proper focal point of study. Truman defines the interest group as "a shared attitude group that makes certain claims upon other groups in the society. If and when it makes its claims through or upon any of the institutions of government, it becomes a public interest group." Group pressure is assured through the establishment of lines of access and influence. Truman notes that the administrative process provides a multitude of points of access comparable to the legislature. What Truman provides for group theory is a complete description and analysis of how groups interact, function, and influence in the overall political system.

Earl Latham (1907–1977) The group theorist whose *The Group Basis of Politics* (1952) was particularly significant because of his conceptualization that government itself is a group just like the various private groups attempting to access the policy process. Latham ascribed to government the same characteristics and concern for power associated with all other organized groups. Thus the state becomes more than a referee between groups in conflict, because it is also developing its own goals.

Figure 2.2   Typical Outside Forces on a Public Agency Manager

which always exist but do not come together until there is a felt need for action on an issue.

The concept of potential groups keeps the bureaucratic policymaking process honest (or perhaps balanced), given the possibility that new groups might surface or some issues may influence decision making. The potential groups concept also serves as a counterargument to the claim that group theory is undemocratic. Once the concept of potential group is married to the active role of organized groups, the claim can be made, in Truman's words, that "all interests of society by definition are taken into account in one form or another by the institutions of government" (see Figure 2.2).

So much for the theory. The problem is, according to political scientist Theodore J. Lowi, too much public authority is parceled out to private interest groups and results in a weak, decentralized government incapable of long-range planning. Powerful interest groups operate to promote private goals but do not compete to promote the public interest. Government becomes not an institution that makes hard choices among conflicting values but a holding company for interests. These interests are promoted by alliances of interest groups, relevant government agencies, and the appropriate legislative **committees** in each issue area. This is furthered by cozy triangles, the mutually supportive relations among government agencies, interest groups, and the legislative committee or subcommittee with jurisdiction over their areas of common concern. Such coalitions constantly exchange information, services, and money (in the form of campaign contributions from the interest groups to the members of the legislative committee and budget approval

committee A subdivision of a legislature that prepares legislation for action by the respective house or that makes investigations as directed by the respective house. Most standing (full) committees are divided into subcommittees, which study legislation, hold hearings, and report their recommendations to the full committee. Only the full committee can report legislation for action by the entire legislature.

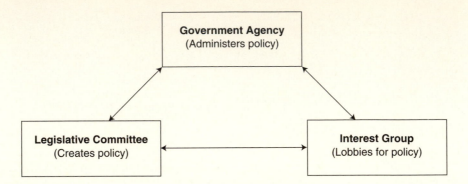

Figure 2.3   The Cozy or Iron Triangle

from the committee to the agency). As a whole, they tend to dominate policymaking in their areas of concern. The triangles are considered to be as strong as iron, because the supportive relations are so strong that others elected or appointed to control administrative policy as representatives of the public's interest are effectively prohibited from interfering on behalf of the public (see Figure 2.3).

All government agencies rise and fall, are created or dissolved, in response to an ever-changing external environment made up both of broad historical trends and everyday political maneuvering. NASA is a perfect example of this. It rose in 1958 as the American response to the space race of the Cold War—certainly a broad historical trend. Political maneuvering by cold warriors in the Truman administration allowed Nazi war criminals such as Wernher von Braun, the German rocket scientist, to give American rocketry a decided boost during the early days of the space program. Morality and ethics aside, von Braun and his team of refugees truly were the best rocket scientists available to the United States at the time. Sometimes administrative necessity is as strong a force as **military necessity**. Now that this necessity has lessened in the wake of the Cold War, it is not surprising to find NASA significantly declining in budget and numbers of employees.

Power—The Internal Perspective

George Orwell, as astute a political observer as the twentieth century has produced, was very wrong about one thing. In his book *1984* he wrote that "power is not a means, it is an end." And that "the object of power is power." This highly influential attitude was taken by a man whose only large organizational experience was as a policeman in colonial Burma for a few years in the 1920s and as the most minor of bureaucrats for little more than a year in the World War II British Broadcasting Corporation (BBC). He loathed the inherent and subtle politics of large bureaucracies—mostly because he saw such wicked ones in the fascist Europe of the World

---

military necessity A justification for actions that violate the laws of war.

Box 2.4

Power and Administration

There is no more forlorn spectacle in the administrative world than an agency and a program possessed of statutory life, armed with executive orders, sustained in the courts, yet stricken with paralysis and deprived of power. An object of contempt to its enemies and of despair to its friends.

　　The lifeblood of administration is power. Its attainment, maintenance, increase, dissipation, and loss are subjects the practitioner and student can ill afford to neglect. . . . Power is only one of the considerations that must be weighed in administration, but of all it is the most overlooked in theory and the most dangerous to overlook in practice.

SOURCE: Norton E. Long, "Power and Administration," *Public Administration Review*, Autumn 1949.

War II era. Indeed, his creation of **Big Brother** in *1984* is the ultimate expression of that loathing. Orwell is a wonderful model for a political writer because he was such a great stylist, but his analysis and disdain of power is hardly useful for would-be and practicing public administrators—because public administration in essence is the exercise of power.

　　One sure thing about power is that we all understand it. We learn about power in organizations as soon as we go to school. Most of us have a pretty good intuitive grasp of the basic concepts of organizational power by the time we reach the third grade. So, the newest thing about power in organizations is not our understanding of it but rather our intellectualizing about it.

　　Discussions of power and politics go back to Aristotle and other writers from antiquity. All of political theory is concerned with the exercise of power. The ancient field of political theory is now frequently applied to the comparatively young concepts of organization theory. Those who would limit themselves to the wisdom of modern writers are putting on intellectual blinders. Remember, it is frequently said of those who rise to rule the nation's largest organizations that they are "natural politicians." Niccolo Machiavelli is the most famous management and political analyst of the Italian Renaissance. His 1513 book of advice to would-be leaders, *The Prince*, is the progenitor of all "how to succeed" books that advocate practical rather than moral actions. In 1967, British Broadcasting Corporation executive Antony Jay reintroduced Machiavelli's concepts to a modern audience with his best-selling book, *Management and Machiavelli*, which applied Machiavelli's insights for managing a state to the problem of power and politics in organizations. Jay

---

Big Brother George Orwell's (1903–1950) symbolization, from his novel *1984* (1949), of government so big and intrusive that it literally oversaw and regulated every aspect of life. The term has evolved to mean any potentially menacing power constantly looking over one's shoulder in judgment.

concluded that Machiavelli's principles are as valid now as they were 450 years ago, because they are "rooted in human nature." According to Jay: "The new science of management is in fact only a continuation of the old art of government, and when you study management theory side by side with political theory, and management case histories side by side with political history, you realize that you are only studying two very similar branches of the same subject."

Ordinary people—as well as scholars—have hesitated to talk about power. For many, power is not a subject for polite conversation. Many of us—including Orwell—have often equated power with force, brutality, unethical behavior, manipulation, connivance, and subjugation. Harvard sociologist Rosabeth Moss Kanter contends that "power is America's last dirty word. It is easier to talk about money—and much easier to talk about sex—than it is to talk about power." Yet we must.

Organizational Goals

The traditional thinking is that organizations are institutions whose primary purpose is to accomplish established goals. Those goals are set by people in positions of formal authority. Thus the primary question for organization managers is how best to design and manage organizations to achieve their declared purposes effectively and efficiently. The personal preferences of organizational members are restrained by systems of formal rules and authority, and by norms of rational behavior. But these assumptions about organizations may be naive and unrealistic when organizations are viewed as being complex systems of individuals and **coalitions**, each having its own interests, beliefs, values, preferences, perspectives, and perceptions. These coalitions—just like the larger group theory of politics—compete with each other continuously for scarce organizational resources. Conflict is inevitable. Influence—and the power and political activities through which influence is acquired and maintained—is the primary "weapon" for use in competition and conflicts. Thus, power, politics, and influence are critically important and permanent facts of organizational life.

Only rarely are organizational goals established by those in positions of formal authority. Goals result from ongoing maneuvering and bargaining among individuals and transitory coalitions. Just as it is with outside politics in general, coalitions tend to shift with issues. Thus, organizational goals change with shifts in the balance of power among coalitions. Organizational goals are important in the same way that organizational power and politics are because they provide the "official" rationale and the legitimacy for resource allocation decisions—for who gets what money to do this or that.

Internal Power Relationships

Power relationships are permanent features of organizations primarily because specialization results in the creation of many interdependent units with varying sizes and degrees of importance that compete with each other for scarce resources. Orga-

---

coalition A temporary joining of political actors to advance legislation or to elect candidates. It is often the case that the actors in a coalition are poles apart on many issues but are able to put their continuing differences aside in the interest of joining to advance (or defeat) the issue at hand.

nization theorist Jeffrey Pfeffer emphasizes this point in his *Power in Organizations*: "Those persons and those units that have the responsibility for performing the more critical tasks in the organization have a natural advantage in developing and exercising power in the organization. . . . power is first and foremost a structural phenomenon, and should be understood as such."

Power is related to dependence. Lower-level organizational members have an arsenal of weapons—such as expertise and personal attractiveness—with which to make others dependent upon them. Servants who use their cleverness to take advantage of social betters are a stock-in-trade of classic drama. This is an intellectualization of something we all know instinctively—that some people are treated like *prima donnas* or "get away with murder" in organizations because they possess some special skill that gives them power in a specific context. The most ready example is "Hawkeye" and "Trapper" from the *M*A*S*H* movie and television series. If they had not been surgeons badly needed at the battlefront, they would have been court martialed for their college boy antics.

Traditional organization theory places high importance on "legitimate authority" (authority that flows down through the formal organizational hierarchy) and formal rules (promulgated and enforced by those in authority) to ensure that organizational behavior is directed toward the attainment of established organizational goals. Such "structuralists" tend to define power synonymously with authority. In contrast, others argue that in today's organizational world, the gap is increasing between the power one needs to get the job done and the power that comes with the job (authority). For example, Rosabeth Moss Kanter in her article "Power Failure in Management Circuits," identifies three groups of positions within organizations that are particularly susceptible to powerlessness: first-line supervisors, staff professionals, and top executives. However, she carefully distinguishes between "power" and "dominance, control, and oppression." She identifies her primary concern: at higher organizational levels, the power to "punish, to prevent, to sell off, to reduce, to fire, all without appropriate concern for consequences" grows, but the power needed for positive accomplishments does not. Managers who perceive themselves as being powerless and who think their subordinates are discounting them tend to use more dominating or punishing forms of influence. Thus, in large organizations, powerlessness (or perceived powerlessness) can be a more substantive problem than possession of power. Authority is only one of many available sources of organizational power. Power, no respecter of position, exists in *all* directions—not just down through the hierarchy.

Other forms of power and influence often prevail over authority-based power: control over scarce resources (for example, office space, discretionary funds, current and accurate information, and time and skill to work on projects), easy access to others who are perceived as having power (for example, important customers or clients, members of the board of directors, or someone else with formal authority or who controls scarce resources), a central place in a potent coalition, ability to "work the organizational rules" (knowing how to get things done or to prevent others from getting things done), and credibility (for example, that one's word can be trusted). Historian Richard E. Neustadt's landmark analysis of the presidency, *Presidential Power*, asserted that a president's real powers are informal, that presidential power

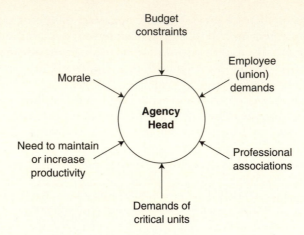

Figure 2.4   Typical Inside Forces on a Public Agency Manager

is essentially the power to persuade. Neustadt quotes President Harry S. Truman contemplating General of the Army Dwight D. Eisenhower becoming president: "He'll sit here, and he'll say, 'Do this! Do that!' *And nothing will happen.* Poor Ike—it won't be a bit like the Army. He'll find it very frustrating."

Jeffrey Pfeffer defines power as "the ability to get things done the way one wants them done; it is the latent ability to influence people." This definition offers several advantages for understanding organizations. First, it emphasizes the relativity of power. As Pfeffer points out, "power is context or relationship specific. A person is not 'powerful' or 'powerless' in general, but only with respect to other social actors in a specific social relationship." Pfeffer's phrase "the way one wants them done" is a potent reminder that conflict and the use of power often are over the choice of methods, means, approaches and/or "turf." They are not limited to battles about outcomes. This point is important because power is often a structural phenomenon—a consequence of organizational specialization. For example, competing organizational coalitions often form around professions: hospital nurses versus paramedics, sociologists versus mathematicians in a university, or business school-educated staff specialists versus generalists from the "school of hard knocks." Organizational conflicts among people representing different professions, educational backgrounds, sexes, and ages frequently do not involve goals: They center on questions about the "right" of a profession, academic discipline, sex, or age group to exercise its perception of its "professional rights," to control the way things will be done, or to protect its "turf" and status. This point is important because it reemphasizes that organizational behavior and decisions frequently are not "rational"—not necessarily directed toward accomplishing the formally stated goals of the organization (see Figure 2.4).

All would-be administrators should be aware of the personal danger in possessing significant power. Say the word power and half the people hearing it will immediately think of **Lord Acton**'s 1887 statement that "power tends to corrupt and absolute power corrupts absolutely." Certainly men like Hitler, Napoleon, Stalin, and Mao all grew more grossly corrupt the longer they held power. But petty tyrants grow proportionately corrupt. Perhaps the best advice on handling power came from Harry Truman in *Plain Speaking*: "If a man can accept a situation in a place of power with the thought that it's only temporary, he comes out all right. But when he thinks that he is the cause of the power, that can be his ruination."

The Cultures of Public Organizations

Administrative institutions are part of the greater culture of their society at the same time that they develop and nurture their own organizational cultures. We learn how to cope in these differing worlds almost instinctively from childhood. How we act in school or at home (each a relatively closed organization) is different from how we act on the street—in the outside world. This is a recognition that each culture demands different behaviors. Thus we talk differently to our friends on the street than we do to our parents or teachers. This literally acculturates us to the fact that each time we join another organization—whether for work, worship, or weight lifting—we expect to, indeed are usually eager to, learn the new jargon and accepted ways of the new group's culture. To talk of the "two cultures" of public organizations is a gross oversimplification. There are an almost infinite variety of public organization cultures. However, they all have this in common: They interact with the outside environment of the overall culture. In this sense alone it can be said that all public organizations must deal with two cultures: their unique internal culture and the common outside culture.

The Outside Cultural Environment

Public management is constantly being judged in the wrong context. It is erroneously viewed as a public sector counterpart to industrial management systems. The private sector analogy holds true only for a portion of the total public management function, and the size of that portion depends on the degree to which the administrative operations of the jurisdiction are politicized. Thus public sector operations cannot be properly understood or evaluated outside the political context—the political culture—of the host jurisdiction.

The determinant of any community's attitudes toward the quality and vigor of its governing institutions is the political culture of the geographic area concerned. Political culture is that part of the overall societal culture that determines a community's attitudes toward the quality, style, and vigor of its political processes and government operations. The only way to explain the extreme variations in public bureaucracies is by examining the cultural context of the host jurisdictions. The quality of bureaucratic operations measured by levels of citizen satisfaction, efficiency, or corruption varies for a variety of reasons—not the least of which is the

---

Lord Acton (1834–1904) English historian; original name was John Dahlberg.

substantial disagreement on just what constitutes a quality operation. But the quality or style of operations is determined only in the lesser part by critics and public officials; the crucial determinant is the political will of the community. It determines the values and resources to be applied to any given public problem; it helps establish the obligations of **citizenship**; and it establishes the parameters of activities in which an official may participate.

Even when corruption is rife, it is the political culture that sets the limits and direction of such dishonesty. For example, James Q. Wilson, in *Varieties of Police Behavior*, demonstrated that the style of **police** operations in eight communities reflected not some abstract standard of quality or professionalism but the expressed and/or implied desires of the community. Thus the police were either exceedingly lenient or exceedingly strict with minor legal violations, depending upon the perceived degree of community concern one way or the other. Wilson considers a police department to have a "watchman" style of performance if it is one in which order maintenance is perceived to be the prime function of the department. Such a police operation will tend to ignore law infringements that do not involve "serious" crimes, such as minor traffic violations, bookmaking, and illegal church bingo. Of course, all these activities or nonactivities are subject to occasional crackdowns. The police periodically shut down illegal gambling operations in response to the political needs of the police chief or mayor. The thrust of the "watchman" style is to maintain order, to ensure a smooth, nondisruptive running of the community or bureaucracy. Legal considerations and official operating mandates are paramount only when the "heat" is on. Of course, the standard operating procedures of police will tend to be more legalistic in communities that are so disposed.

Cultural Values and Administration   While a community's political culture is seldom articulated, it nevertheless serves as a source of definition. By determining the values to be applied to any given problem, the political culture ensures that the decisional process is filtered through its value system before administrative action is taken. How values influence administrative actions is illustrated by George Orwell's 1936 essay "Shooting an Elephant." In 1920s Burma, where Orwell was a police officer representing the British colonial administration, trained elephants were used for moving heavy logs. When an elephant suddenly disdained his domesticated labors in the timber industry and went on a rampage, it was the job of the local cop

---

citizenship The dynamic relation between a citizen and his or her nation. The concept of citizenship involves rules of what a citizen might do (such as vote), must do (pay taxes), and can refuse to do (pledge allegiance). Increasingly, the concept involves benefits or entitlements that a citizen has a right to demand from government. In some jurisdictions, citizenship is a requirement for public employment. Citizenship also requires loyalty to and primary residency in one's state.

police Paramilitary state and local government organizations whose most basic responsibilities include maintaining public order and safety (through the use of force if necessary), investigating and arresting persons accused of crimes, and securing the cooperation of the citizenry. The term police, while referring to all law enforcement officers in general, is usually a reference to municipal law enforcement officers. County officers are sheriffs; state officers are usually called the state police, state troopers, or highway patrol.

Willie Williams, the former police commissioner of Philadelphia, was recruited to be chief of the Los Angeles Police Department in the wake of the 1991 Rodney King beating by Los Angeles police officers. Williams was given the mandate of changing the organizational culture that led to such incidents. Seven years after the Rodney King beating, John Mack, the president of the Los Angeles Urban League was able to say: "I hear a commitment to change. There will no longer be an attitude on the part of officers on the streets, especially on the streets of South Central Los Angeles, that will presume every young black face is a gangbanger or that they are up to no good, but will indeed treat each person with respect and will be there to support and not occupy" (Associated Press, August 19, 1998). The cultures of large organizations seldom change quickly.

on the beat, in this case Orwell, to shoot him. The problem was that by the time Orwell and the local onlookers caught up with the elephant chronicled in the essay, it was peacefully eating grass and no danger to anyone. But an ever-increasing crowd expected this lone officer, this symbol of imperial presence, to act decisively. "A sahib (a master) has got to act like a sahib; he has got to appear resolute, to know his own mind and do definite things." Orwell was expected by the prevailing culture to shoot the elephant. Orwell says he felt like "an absurd puppet" who was being "pushed to and fro by the will of those" villagers. Despite that fact that there was no public safety reason to do so, he shoots and kills the elephant "solely to avoid looking a fool." The culture made him do it. Of course, today's attitudes are radically different and it is almost unthinkable that a police officer anywhere in the world would feel pressured to kill any endangered species—let alone a nonthreatening elephant.

The United States is so vast and geographically diverse that while there is an overall American political culture, it is often less influential than the local political subcultures of the individual states and regions. Differing sources of political culture, such as race, ethnicity, and religion combine with historical patterns of political behavior to yield the distinct political cultures of, for example, the Rocky Mountain West or the Deep South. All political cultures change—some more quickly than others. Germany and Japan have vastly different political cultures today than they did when they were the exemplars of **fascism** prior to and during World War II. In the wake of the Cold War the once Communist states of Eastern Europe almost overnight found themselves with new political cultures. The American political culture, with the notable exception of the Civil War of 1861 to 1865 has, in historical terms, been very stable. However, one profound change has significant implications for public administrative institutions—the growth of cynicism about government.

Toward a Culture of Cynicism   The modern beginning of an almost paranoid distrust about the intentions and capabilities of government began in 1960 with the U-2 incident. The pivotal events unfolded after an American high altitude "U-2" surveillance plane was shot down by an antiaircraft missile over the Soviet Union on May 1. Having been assured by the Central Intelligence Agency, which directed the operation, that the pilot could not have survived, President Dwight D. Eisenhower told the world a lie about how this was an off-course weather research plane. But the Soviets had both the plane wreckage and a live pilot—Francis Gary Powers. Powers was tried in Moscow and sentenced to ten years in prison. In 1962 he was exchanged for a captured Russian spy. The whole incident made the Cold War colder and undermined Eisenhower's and thus the presidency's credibility with the American public—because the president had been forced to admit that he had openly and willfully lied to the American people. This has become so commonplace today that we easily forget how shocking this admission was in 1960.

This might have remained an isolated incident had not the assassination of President John F. Kennedy in 1963, and the assassinations of presidential candidate Robert F. Kennedy and civil rights leader Dr. Martin Luther King Jr. in 1968, spawned a cottage industry of conspiracy theories. Add to this the Vietnam War, when the Johnson and Nixon administrations were discovered in one lie after another. Then there was Watergate (see Chapter 14) when Nixon told the ultimate lie—"I am not a crook"—and was forced from office in 1974 because he was. Then came the Iran-Contra affair of 1986, which embroiled both the Reagan and Bush administrations in several more years of denials that few Americans found credible. Before the U-2 incident, a president was taken at his word. Now because of all the intervening misconduct at the highest levels of American government, too many members of the press as well as ordinary citizens simply do not believe what their

---

fascism A political philosophy that advocates governance by a dictator, assisted by a hierarchically organized, strongly ideological party, in maintaining a totalitarian and regimented society through violence, intimidation, and the arbitrary use of power.

leaders say about major public policy issues. This turn toward a paranoid culture inhibits rational debate and makes it far more difficult for leaders—the overwhelming majority of whom are honest and ethical—to lead.

The Inside Cultural Environment

An organizational culture—the culture which exists within an organization—is a parallel but smaller version of a societal culture. It is made up of intangible things such as values, beliefs, assumptions, and perceptions. It is the pattern of these beliefs and attitudes that determines members' behaviors in and around the organization, persists over extended periods of time, and pervades all elements of the organization (albeit to different extents and with varying intensity).

An organizational culture is transmitted to new members through socialization (or enculturation) processes; it is maintained and transmitted through a network of rituals and interaction patterns; it is enforced and reinforced by group **norms** and the organization's system of rewards and controls. It is the unseen and unobservable force that is always behind those organizational activities that can be observed. According to Kilmann and others, "culture is to the organization what personality is to the individual—a hidden, yet unifying theme that provides meaning, direction, and mobilization."

Organizational culture is created by the attitudes and behaviors of the dominant or early organizational "shapers" and "heroes"; by the nature of the organization's work; and by the attitudes, values, and "willingness to act" of new members. It is transmitted by often-told stories and legends and by the formal and informal processes of socialization. An organization's culture provides a framework for shared understanding of events, defines behavioral expectations, and serves as a source of and focus for members' commitment and as an organizational "control system" (i.e., through group norms). But while a strong organizational culture can control organizational behavior, it can also block an organization from making those changes needed to adapt to a changing environment.

Organizational culture is particularly useful as an intellectual construct because it helps us to understand or predict how an organization will behave under different circumstances. A cultural pattern is similar to a genetic inheritance; once you know the patterns of basic assumptions, you can anticipate how the organization will act in differing circumstances. Like snowflakes, every organizational culture is different. What has worked repeatedly for one organization may not work for another—so the basic assumptions differ. And all organizational cultures are shaped by myriad factors—from the societal culture in which it resides to its technologies and competing organizations. Some organizations have strong, unified, pervasive cultures, whereas others have weaker cultures; often "subcultures" evolve in different functional or geographical areas. The most common example of this last phenomenon is the more formal culture of a headquarters office versus the informality of a field office.

---

norms The socially enforced requirements and expectations about basic responsibilities, behavior, and thought patterns of members in their organizational roles.

Although phrases like "organizational culture" and "culture of a factory" can be found in a few books on management written as early as the 1950s (for example, *The Changing Culture of a Factory* by Elliott Jaques and William H. Whyte Jr.'s book about corporate conformity, *The Organization Man*), few students of management or organizations paid much attention to the nature and content of organizational culture until the late 1970s.

Professional Socialization

During the 1960s and early 1970s, several books on organizational and professional socialization processes received wide attention. As useful as these earlier works were, they *assumed* the presence of organizational or professional cultures, and proceeded to examine issues involving the match between individuals and cultures. Two of the more widely read of these were *Boys in White* by Becker, et al., which chronicled the processes used to socialize medical students into the medical profession, and Herbert Kaufman's study of how the United States Forest Service developed the "will and capacity to conform" among its remotely stationed rangers, in *The Forest Ranger*. Once again, however, these earlier writings did not address important questions such as how cultures are formed or changed, how cultures affect leadership, or the relationship between culture and strategic planning (establishing organizational directions); rather, they focused on the process of socializing employees into existing organizational cultures, and the impacts of existing cultures on organizational members.

An entirely different orientation to organizational culture that focused on symbols started to appear in the late 1970s. Symbols are things like flags and logos which carry a wider (or different) meaning than their intrinsic content. For example, the Stars and Stripes is a symbol because it embodies values, traditions, and emotions. Symbols also can be things such as words (IBM's famous sign "Think"), phrases (*Semper fidelis*, the motto meaning "Always faithful" of the U.S. Marine Corps), and organizational structures. Because the top or seventh floor is the location of the highest officials of the U.S. Department of State, policy is frequently said to come from the seventh floor—not any particular official. Similarly, the White House is a building that can, as a symbol, speak. Reporters and political commentators frequently state that the "White House said . . ." this or that. The building speaks because it is the architectural embodiment of the bureaucratic institution that is the modern presidency. Thus the building speaks through press releases, news conferences, deep as well as shallow background briefings, and **leaks**. While the president is the main and most desired speaker, there are a few hundred other people who work there and also give it voice.

Romanticized stories about organizational heroes and ritualistic ceremonies can also be symbols—if they carry meanings that go beyond their intrinsic content. Military medals and other types of organizational awards for unusual achievement are a

---

leaks The deliberate disclosure of confidential or classified information by someone in government who wants to advance the public interest, embarrass a bureaucratic rival, or help a reporter disclose incompetence or skulduggery to the public.

major example. When a member of Napoleon's government described military decorations as "baubles," Napoleon replied, "You are pleased to call them 'baubles': well, it is with 'baubles' that mankind is governed." Wise managers will create multiple opportunities to use symbols to motivate, inspire, and thank their employees.

Symbolic Management

The manipulation of symbols and the **dramaturgy** of symbolic acts are essential elements of managing people in organizations. While such manipulations may be conscious or unconscious on the part of management, they are invariably there. Frequently, symbolic acts are easily identifiable because of their obvious **beau geste** quality. They form an integral part of everyday manners and courtesies. When an organization's chief executive accidentally meets a lower-echelon employee in a crowded elevator and says, "How's your job coming along?" the executive is not expecting an answer to this question; the words are used simply to communicate sociability—a symbolic ritual. It would be quite out of place and both annoying and surprising to the executive if the employee really answered the question instead of replying with a simple, "Fine, thank you." In cases like these, language ceases being an instrument of communication and becomes a symbol—a thing that carries a different meaning than its intrinsic content.

Symbolic management attracted only limited attention during the 1970s. The turning point for the organizational culture (and symbolism) perspective did not arrive until the early 1980s. Then, almost overnight, organizational culture became a very hot topic in books, journals, and periodicals aimed at both management practitioners and academicians. Because of the youthfulness of organizational culture as a perspective, minimal consensus exists about much of anything concerned with it. There are only a few organizational culture issues upon which there is widespread agreement. These include the following:

1. Organizational cultures exist.
2. Each organizational culture is relatively unique.
3. Organizational culture is a socially constructed concept.
4. Organizational culture provides its members with a way of understanding and making sense of events and symbols.
5. Organizational culture, because of its ability to informally approve or disapprove of behavior, can be a powerful tool for guiding organizations.

Each organization has its own unique culture that determines how it will respond to the same stimuli. At the Pentagon, the story is often told about how the

---

dramaturgy The manner in which a person acts out or theatrically stages his or her organizational or political role. Political candidates who make an effort to look or sound senatorial or presidential are engaging in dramaturgy. Of course, if they have to make an effort to look it or sound it, they may not have it. One is reminded of the traditional advice to actors: "Always be sincere. If you can fake that, you've got it made."

beau geste A noble and/or gracious gesture.

same words can have vastly different meanings in differing organizations. A good example is the use of the word "secure" in the U.S. Department of Defense. If the Army is told to secure a particular building, it will post guards at all the entrances and exits. The Marine Corps, given the same instructions, will assault the building until everyone inside surrenders. And the Air Force will achieve its mission to secure the building by negotiating a three-year lease with the owners.

Because the same words used in different organizational cultures can mean radically different outcomes, all would-be managers must be aware that organizational culture is not just something we live in. J. Steven Ott, a professor at the University of Utah, elaborates on this idea in *The Organizational Culture Perspective*. Managers must use organizational culture "as a frame of reference for the way one looks at, attempts to understand, and works with organizations." Thus even though the vocabulary may be the same, the meaning of words in their organizational context may require a manager to effectively learn a new language. Any manager who doesn't learn to "walk the walk" and "talk the talk" is walking and talking alone—not managing.

Summary

Public administration is an instrument of policy. But public policymaking in republican government is constrained by the very nature of republican institutions. Executive leadership is inherently limited both by the leader's philosophic views on how to exercise power and the legal constraints of constitutional checks and balances.

Public policymaking is cyclical. As policy decisions are made and implemented, criticism in the form of feedback puts new decisions on the policy agenda. This starts the policymaking cycle all over again. While decisions can be radical departures for the current situation, they are most likely to be incremental.

Public processes, whether public policymaking or public administration, take place within a polity, an overarching political jurisdiction. All public managers have two polities with which to contend—internal (their agency) and external (the outside political world).

Just as public policy and administration exists in two polities, it has similar double life as a culture. It is part of the greater culture of its society at the same time that it develops and nurtures its own organizational cultures.

Key Concepts

agenda setting The process by which ideas or issues bubble up through the various political channels to wind up for consideration by a political institution such as a legislature or court.

implementation Putting a government program into effect; the total process of translating a legal mandate, whether an executive order or an enacted statute, into appropriate program directives and structures that provide services or create goods.

incremental decision making model A view of the public policymaking process that assumes that small decisions made at the margins of problems are the usual reality of change.

organizational culture The culture that exists within an organization; a parallel but smaller version of a societal culture.

pluralism A theory of government that attempts to reaffirm the democratic character of society by asserting that open, multiple, competing, and responsive groups preserve traditional democratic values in a mass industrial state. Pluralism assumes that power will shift from group to group as elements in the mass public transfer their allegiance in response to their perceptions of their individual interests.

political culture   That part of the overall societal culture that determines a community's attitudes toward the quality, style, and vigor of its political processes and government operations.

program evaluation   The systematic examination of any activity undertaken by government to make a determination about its effects, both short-term and long-range.

public program   All those activities designed to implement a public policy; often this calls for

the creation of organizations, public agencies, and bureaus.

rational decision making model   A view of the public policymaking process that assumes complete information and a systematic, logical, and comprehensive approach to change.

republic   A form of government in which sovereignty resides in the people who elect agents to represent them in political decision making.

separation of powers   The allocation of powers among the three branches of government so that they are a check upon each other. This separation, in theory, makes a tyrannical concentration of power impossible.

Bibliography

Becker, H. S., et al. (1961). *Boys in White: Student Culture in Medical School.* Chicago: University of Chicago Press.

Bell, Daniel. (1960). *End of Ideology: On the Exhaustion of Political Ideas in the Fifties.* Glencoe, IL: Free Press.

Boorstin, Daniel J. (1961). *The Image: A Guide to Pseudo-Events in America.* New York: Atheneum.

Dahl, Robert A., and Charles E. Lindblom. (1953). *Politics, Economics, and Welfare.* Chicago: University of Chicago Press.

Degler, Carl. (1970). *Out of Our Past.* New York: Harper and Row.

Downs, Anthony. (1972). "Up And Down With Ecology—The Issue-Attention Cycle." *Public Interest* 28 (summer).

Easton, David. (1963). *A Systems Analysis of Political Life.* New York: Atherton.

Galbraith, John Kenneth. (1956). *American Capitalism.* Boston: Houghton Mifflin.

Gingrich, Newt. (1995). *To Renew America.* New York: HarperCollins.

Hofstadter, Richard. (1965). *The Paranoid Style in American Politics.* New York: Knopf.

Jaques, Elliott. (1951). *The Changing Culture of a Factory.* London: Tavistock Institute.

Jones, Charles O. (1977). *An Introduction to the Study of Public Policy*, 2nd ed. North Scituate, MA: Duxbury Press.

Joseph, Peter. (1947). *Good Times: An Oral History of America in the Nineteen Sixties.* New York: William Morrow.

Kanter, Rosabeth Moss. (1979). "Power Failure in Management Circuits." *Harvard Business Review* (July-August).

Kaufman, Herbert. (1960). *The Forest Ranger.* Baltimore: Johns Hopkins University Press.

Kilmann, R. H., et al., eds. (1985). *Gaining Control of the Corporate Culture.* San Francisco: Jossey-Bass.

Lasswell, Harold. (1963). *The Future of Political Science.* New York: Atherton.

———. (1936). *Politics: Who Gets What, When, How.* New York: Smith.

Latham, Earl. (1952). *The Group Basis of Politics.* Ithaca, NY: Cornell University Press.

Lindblom, Charles E. (1959). "The Science of Muddling Through." *Public Administration Review* (spring).

Lipsky, Michael. (1980). *Street-Level Bureaucracy.* New York: Russell Sage Foundation.

Lowi, Theodore, J. (1979). *The End of Liberalism*, 2nd ed. New York: Norton.

Markham, Felix. (1964). *Napoleon.* New York: New American Library.

Miller, Merle. (1974). *Plain Speaking: An Oral Biography of Harry S. Truman.* New York: Berkley.

Mills, C. Wright. (1956). *The Power Elite.* New York: Oxford University Press.

Orwell, George. (1946). *Shooting an Elephant and Other Essays.* New York: Harcourt, Brace.

Ott, J. Steven. (1989). *Organizational Cultural Perspective.* Pacific Grove, CA: Brooks/Cole.

Peters, Charles. (1993). "Tilting at Windmills." *The Washington Monthly* 25 (November).

Pfeffer, Jeffrey. (1981). *Power in Organizations.* Marshfield, MA: Pitman.

Pressman, Jeffrey, and Aaron Wildavsky. (1973). *Implementation.* Berkeley: University of California Press.

Romzek, Barbara S., and Melvin J. Dubnick. (1987). "Accountability in the Public Sector: Lessons from the *Challenger* Tragedy," *Public Administration Review* 47 (May-June).

Sheldon, Michael. (1991). *Orwell*. New York: HarperCollins.

Taft, William Howard. (1916). *Our Chief Magistrate and His Powers*. New York: Columbia University Press.

Whyte, William H., Jr. (1956). *The Organization Man*. New York: Simon and Schuster.

Wilson, James Q. (1968). *Varieties of Police Behavior*. Cambridge: Harvard University Press.

Woodward, Bob, and Carl Bernstein. (1974). *All the President's Men*. New York: Simon and Schuster.

Recommended Books

Bratton, William, with Peter Knobler. (1998). *Turnaround: How America's Top Cop Reversed the Crime Epidemic*. New York: Random House. A biographical account of how the author used modern management techniques to change the organizational culture of four major local police agencies (including the police departments of the cities of Boston and New York); this resulted in greater morale, increased productivity, and less crime.

Heady, Ferrel. (1996). *Public Administration: A Comparative Perspective*, 5th ed. New York: Marcel Dekker. The standard survey of worldwide public administration, providing both historic and contemporary contexts.

Neustadt, Richard E. (1991). *Presidential Power and Modern Presidents*. New York: Free Press. An analysis of how the essence of the power of the president—indeed, of any executive—is not to order but to persuade.

Pipes, Daniel. (1997). *Conspiracy: How the Paranoid Style Flourishes and Where It Comes From*. New York: Free Press. An updating of Richard Hofstadter's 1965 *The Paranoid Style in American Politics*. This volume deals with the latest batch of wacky theories as well as the golden oldies.

Simon, Herbert A. (1997). *Administrative Behavior: A Study of Decision-making in Administrative Organizations*, 4th ed. New York: Macmillan. The fifth anniversary edition of the groundbreaking analysis of how organizations make decisions within the context of their social values.

Related Web Sites

Abraham Lincoln online
http://www.netins.net/showcase/creative/lincoln.html
Center on Budget and Policy Priorities
http://www.cbpp.org/
Government-related servers
http://www.eff.org/govt.html
John Locke
http://www.geocities.com/Athens/Forum/5507/locke.html
National Aeronautics and Space Administration
http://www.nasa.gov

National Center for Policy Analysis
http://www.public-policy.org/~ncpa
National League of Cities
http://www.nlc.org
Nicolo Machiavelli
http://www.sas.upenn.edu/~pgrose/mach
Theodore Roosevelt
http://www.pbs.org/wgbh/pages/amex/tr/index.html

3

The Continuous Reinventing of the Machinery of Government

Keynote: The New Feudalism

What Is the Machinery of Government?

Fine-Tuning the Machinery • The Rise and Fall of Governmental Machinery

The Administrative Architecture of the U.S. Government

Executive Branch Machinery

State and Local Government Machinery

State Government • County Government • Municipal Government • Towns and Special Districts • Local Management Machinery • Metropolitan Government • Continuous State and Local Reform

Reforming the National Machinery of Government

The Brownlow Committee • The Hoover Commissions • The Ash Council • The President's Private Sector Survey on Cost Control • Reinventing Government • The Gore Report • The Reinventors Versus the Micromanagers

The Pressure for Privatization

Strategies for Privatization • The Nonprofit Gambit • Voluntarism and Philanthropy

A Comparative Perspective: The Revolution in the British Machinery of Government 1980–1999

Keynote: The New Feudalism

In 1958, economist John Kenneth Galbraith published *The Affluent Society*. This book described American society as one in which scarcity of resources was not a major problem, but where "private affluence and public squalor" existed continuously side by side. Today, this trend is becoming even more pronounced. Journalists such as Michael Lind are observing a "new feudalism" which "reverses the trend of the past thousand years toward the government's provision of basic public goods like policing, public roads, and transport networks, and public schools." Lind concludes that "in the United States—to a degree unmatched in any other industrialized democracy—these public goods are once again becoming private luxuries."

When public services deteriorate—especially in urban areas—those with enough money, increasingly, buy their way out of the problem. They send their children to private schools and hire private police. And in the best feudal tradition, they retire each night behind walled towns where guards at a gate check the identity of all who seek to enter. And we are not just talking about an apartment building with a door-keeper. We are talking about millions of citizens living in suburban "gated communities" with their own private police, private streets, and private parks.

While most popular in California, Texas, Arizona, Florida, and Virginia, such private residential communities are springing up throughout the United States, patterned after the comprehensive minicities that have long been popular with retirees in the sunbelt. What is new is that middle- and upper-income families of all ages are opting to pay hefty private taxes (community fees) and submit to stringent environmental regulations to lead the good life away from urban ills. It is estimated that over four million Americans already live in such closed-off communities. And that number is expected to double over the next decade. Ironically, according to political analyst Timothy Egan, "the very things that Republicans in Congress are trying to do away with for the nation as a whole—environmental protection, gun control, heavy regulation—are most pronounced in these predominately Republican private enclaves."

These new-fashioned feudalists, who are decidedly libertarian concerning the outside world, are surprisingly socialistic concerning the private inside world of their gated minicities. They willingly accept a wide variety of community regulations that they would challenge as unconstitutional in other contexts—from gun control, to restrictions on exterior paint colors, lawn maintenance standards, and prohibitions on basketball hoops over garages. Homeowners must abide by common mandates, including the carrying of special identification, getting permission for more than a set number of visitors, and paying user fees for a wide variety of services such as trash collection, cable TV connections, and time on tennis courts.

The new feudalism also extends beyond the guarded gates. During the Middle Ages, many of the castles on the Rhine River in Western Europe were built to enforce the collection of tolls on that portion of the river controlled by a local warlord. Today electronic "castles" are enforcing the collection of tolls on a similarly private means of transport. For example, the California Private Transportation Corporation, with state approval, has built a ten-mile, $128 million, four-lane road in the median strip of an existing but highly congested southern California freeway. This new road is certainly a way to avoid the almost daily commuter gridlock, but it is not free. Users must have a transponder installed on their vehicle's windshield that can be read by an electronic monitor—the "castle"—as they enter the road. Periodically a computer bills the driver's credit card or mails an old-fashioned paper invoice. Anyone seeking to avoid these silent sentries will have their license plates photographed and face state sanctioned fines of up to $300.

Gerald S. Pfeffer, the managing director of the corporation that owns the new road, explains his company's philosophy: "We're another example of private enterprise filling a gap in government services—the Federal Express of roads." But critics complain that the highway is elitist in that people who can afford the $2.50 rush-hour toll speed along in their luxury cars while those who can't afford an extra $5.00 a day—more than $1,000 a year—for the round trip must creep along with the poor on the old public freeway. Pfeffer sees nothing wrong with that: "You get what you pay for, the great American way." Besides, toll roads and bridges have long been common in the United States. What is new here is someone collecting tolls for profits and not for governments.

While the California legislature authorized the new toll road in 1990, Virginia was the first state in this century to actually open a new private road. In 1995 the Dulles Greenway substantially cut the time it takes to get from Washington, DC, to Dulles International Airport for a price—$2.10. The California road, which opened three months later, at the beginning of 1996 will also be a demonstration of the effectiveness of congestion-pricing; that is, the fare will vary with the time of day. In the middle of the night it will cost only 25 cents—just 10 percent of its rush hour cost. It remains to be seen whether this bargain rate will encourage the poor to get to work early—very early!

Millions of citizens obviously feel that having the private police, roads, and parks are well worth the cost in money and possible personal restrictions. The problem is that the larger sense of community is often lost. Citizens living in their affluent private enclaves are less likely to vote for spending on public services that they do not use, such as traditional public schools, public parks, and public roads. Indeed, the California legislature specifically authorized the private road because it perceived that there was not sufficient public support to pay additional taxes for new public roads.

The result of this trend toward private services is that the needs of citizens who do not have a "going private" option may be ignored. And since these enclaved communities tend to be overwhelmingly white, this leads to a further balkanization of the body politic. The essential question here is: If certain citizens can afford to buy their way out of common public problems, what kind of public services does that leave for the rest of us? It used to be that the "leading" (meaning richer) citizens would make an effort to solve the problems of their communities because, for better or worse, they were part of it. Now they can just hide behind their walls.

Even people living in the heart of a big city can buy better public services for themselves by creating a "business improvement district"—a quasi-government paid for by taxes on property owners within the district. Almost a thousand of these districts nationwide provide extra sanitation, policing, and other services for their residents. Thus

A private security guard at a gated community. Such a sight will be increasingly common in America's future as more and more citizens who pay for the luxury will opt to live in housing developments controlled by these "extra" police.

many of the richer neighborhoods in New York City are cleaner and safer because their residents can afford to pay for private sanitation services and private police.

This new feudalism is just one side of the increasing privatization of the public sector—here citizens, as is their right, buy the amount of "public" services they can afford. The other side of privatization has government itself contracting for the private provision of public functions. Thus increasingly trash is collected, public buildings are cleaned, and streets are repaired not by public employees but by private sector employees of companies with government contracts. This is often less expensive because such workers are typically paid less than public employees—especially when fringe benefits are considered.

The traditional machinery of government—the administrative structures by which public purposes are achieved—is increasingly being called into question by an angry citizenry that does not always see the contradiction between wanting ever greater government services at ever decreasing costs. Thus, privatization, even with its feudal aspects, is seen by some as one means of lowering the overall costs of government, by others as a means of reducing services to the poor, and by still others as a means of eliminating large elements of government altogether. But however it is viewed and despite the continuing danger of social balkanization, it remains one of the most important tools in reinventing the machinery of government for the twenty-first century.

Box 3.1

Is Private Government Good Business?

Unlike traditional neighborhood associations, BIDs [business improvement districts], which are chartered by state law, have the power of mandatory taxation. Once formed by a majority vote of property owners in a given area, a BID raises the money for local improvements through a special assessment on real estate. . . . And in New York City, where municipal government has increasingly shrunk from its traditional core functions of sanitation and security, BIDs have become almost a craze. The city now has thirty-three of them, with more applying for approval, and they have made the city cleaner, safer, and more charming. . . .

BIDs have often proved more effective than government in part because they can operate without bureaucracies, entrenched interests, electorial calculations, or even ideology. They offer the virtues of the private sector without the corrupting influence of the profit motive. And yet BIDs are not simply collections of citizens. . . . They are controlled by the property owners who finance them and largely make up their boards. The public, in effect, has to depend on the BIDs' sense of enlightened self-interest. Gretchen Dykstra, the president of the Times Square BID, says, "We control money, we get things done, and we are outside of democratic oversight and accountability."

SOURCE: James Traub, "Street Fight," *The New Yorker,* September 4, 1995.

What Is the Machinery of Government?

The machinery of government consists of all of the structural arrangements adopted by national, state, or local governments to deliver their legally mandated programs and services. This of necessity includes the central management arrangements of government. In all jurisdictions, the organization and eventual reorganization of executive branch agencies is the everlasting machinery of government issue.

Fine-Tuning the Machinery

In 1733 English poet Alexander Pope wrote:

For forms of government let fools contest—
That which is best administered is best.

These two lines from his *An Essay on Man* became so well known that Alexander Hamilton in *The Federalist,* No. 68, took the trouble to quote them, denounce the sentiment as "political heresy," and then go on to acknowledge "yet we may safely pronounce that the true test of a good government is its aptitude and tendency to produce a good administration." Ever since, one test of governing efficacy has been Hamilton's ideal of "good administration." The machinery that a government creates to work its will must be judged by the quality of public administration that it yields. But many political analysts of Hamilton's generation as well as today would argue that no matter how good the quality, it is the quantity that is the crucial thing. Senator Barry Goldwater's often stated warning during his unsuccessful 1964 presidential campaign still resonates: "A government big enough to give you everything you want is a government big enough to take from you everything you have."

Hamilton's contemporary, Thomas Paine, the pamphleteering propagandist of the American Revolution, wrote in *Common Sense* that "society in every state is a blessing, but government, even in its best state, is but a necessary evil; in its worst state an intolerable one." This certainly reflects the sentiments of the modern Republican party in the United States. Indeed, this party took control of the U.S. Congress during the 1994 midterm election running on a platform that differs only in detail with Paine's contention. This can all be summed up in the proposition that "government is best which governs least." New England writer Henry David Thoreau began his famous 1849 essay "Civil Disobedience" with this motto, which has also been attributed to Thomas Jefferson, Thomas Paine, and many another doubting Thomas about government.

But if so many good and wise people believed so strongly that government should be "least," how and why did it grow so large? Has the machine grown too big for its most elemental task of producing Hamilton's "good administration"? The task of this chapter is to examine the machinery of government and its effects on administrations good and bad. Always remember, however, that most of the debate over reinventing government and the best public management practices is not about fundamentally changing the nature of governing institutions—it's about fine-tuning the machinery. To use a mobile metaphor—it's not about reinventing the automobile; it's about getting more miles per gallon of fuel using fewer and less expensive parts.

The Rise and Fall of Governmental Machinery

Whenever government seeks to address a major issue, it leaves new machinery in its wake. Thus the civil rights movement that began in the 1950s left the Commission on Civil Rights (created in 1957) and the Equal Employment Opportunity Commission (created in 1964). The environmental movement that began in the 1960s left the Environmental Protection Agency (created in 1970). Governmental entities, once established, tend to last a long time and not change easily. They develop constituencies that support their cause. Often they take on new causes that also enhance their support. For example, the Equal Employment Opportunity Commission initially dealt only with cases of workplace discrimination. Today, as federal courts reinterpret the nature of discrimination, it is the nation's prime enforcer of workplace sexual harassment prohibitions as well (see Chapter 11 for more on this).

There is gravity at work in the machinery of government. What goes up can also fall down. For example, the Civil Aeronautics Board, created by the federal government to regulate the airline industry in 1938, was abolished in 1985 as economic deregulation became fashionable. The Office of Technology Assessment, created in 1972 as a support agency of the Congress to be an objective source of information on policy alternatives for technology-related issues, was abolished in 1995 as a newly elected Republican-controlled Congress sought to cut costs. In 1996 the Bureau of Mines within the Department of the Interior gave 1,200 of its employees the shaft. This 85-year-old agency was abolished by a Congress less interested in the concerns of **big labor** than in big budget savings. There is also serious consideration being given to abolishing the Departments of Commerce, Education, and Transportation. But even when a piece of the government machine is sliced off, it is seldom completely thrown away. For example, Bureau of Mines' workers engaged in coal mine safety were transferred to the Fossil Energy Division of the Department of Energy. And even the most fervent advocates of abolishing the Department of Commerce believe it would be wise to retain the National Weather Service and the Bureau of the Census.

In the United States, the national machinery of government is far more inherently conservative and, in consequence, far more hesitant to change than many other comparable—albeit smaller—democracies, such as Britain, Australia, and New Zealand. However difficult to change, the elements of the machinery of government are not immutable. They can and should be changed as societal needs alter. There is one commonly asked machinery of government question. It was posed by Representative Newt Gingrich in a December 1994 speech accepting his party's nomination to be Speaker of the House: "When you see a large government bureaucracy, is it an inevitable relic of the past that can't be changed or is it an opportunity for an extraordinary transformation to provide better services and better opportunities at lower cost?" This is one of those questions for which there is only one possible answer. Everybody wants "better services" and "lower costs." But are you willing to tinker with your government machine to get them?

The Administrative Architecture of the U.S. Government

A constitution provides the basic political and legal structure, the architecture, which prescribes the rules by which a government operates. James Madison wrote in *The Federalist*, No. 57, that "the aim of every political constitution is, or ought to be, first to obtain for rulers men who possess most wisdom to discern, and most virtue to pursue, the common good of the society; and in the next place, to take the most effectual precautions for keeping them virtuous whilst they continue to hold their public trust." While Madison asserted that the first aim was to find appropriate "men," he would certainly reconsider that word if he were writing today. To be sure he would use a sexually neutral term such as people, individuals, or persons. But this does not go far enough—because the primary task of rulers in all modern constitutional systems is administration. So administrators should replace men in Madison's political philosophy because administrators are those who run a constitution. The echo of Woodrow Wilson's famous statement that "it is getting harder

---

big labor The major American labor unions and their federations.

to run a constitution than to frame one" is loud and clear. Madison is generally considered the primary framer of the Constitution. But if he had lived to see what his handiwork hath wrought, he would be much more concerned about running it.

The Constitution, with its famous opening words, "We the people," asserts that the source of its authority is the people as opposed to the states. It then assigns powers to the various branches of government and in doing so structures the government. It limits the powers that any branch may have through a system of **checks and balances**. Most significantly, it denies certain powers to the national government by reserving them for the states and the people.

American politics has grown up around the Constitution and has been, thereby, "constitutionalized." Many domestic political issues are eventually treated in constitutional terms—for example, civil rights, crime, pornography, abortion, and impeachment, to name but some of the more obvious cases. Only the realm of foreign affairs has substantially escaped this tendency. In addressing matters of government and politics, Americans are likely to pose as the first question, "Is it constitutional?" Only afterward are the desirabilities of policies and government arrangements considered on their own merits. In the 1819 case of *McCulloch v. Maryland*, the Supreme Court explained how to tell if something is constitutional: "Let the end be legitimate, let it be within the scope of the Constitution, and all means which are appropriate, which are plainly adapted to that end, which are not prohibited, but consist with the letter and spirit of the Constitution, are constitutional."

Unlike the British parliamentary machinery of government that evolved over hundreds of years, the American machinery was created at one moment in time for its specific purpose. The Constitutional Convention of 1787 was truly the world's first reinventing government movement. And the government it invented was designed to be inefficient. Because of their experiences under British rule, Americans have historically been suspicious of a too efficient government, feeling that an overly efficient administration of public affairs could eventually eat into political liberties. Chief Justice Warren Burger, writing for the Court in *Immigration and Naturalization Service v. Chadha* (1983), offered this opinion: "It is crystal clear from the records of the [Constitutional] Convention, contemporaneous writings and debates, that the Framers ranked other values higher than efficiency. . . . The choices we discern as having been made in the Constitutional Convention impose burdens on governmental processes that often seem clumsy, inefficient, and even unworkable, but those hard choices were consciously made by men who had lived under a form of government that permitted arbitrary governmental acts to go unchecked."

---

checks and balances The notion that constitutional devices can prevent any power within a nation from becoming absolute by being balanced against, or checked by, another source of power within that same nation. The United States Constitution is often described as a system of checks and balances. For example, it allows the president to check the Congress by vetoing a bill, the Congress to check the president by overriding a veto or refusing to ratify treaties or confirm nominees to federal office; the Supreme Court can check either by declaring law passed by Congress or actions taken by the president to be unconstitutional.

The modern U.S. Supreme Court then reaffirmed the value of inefficiency when it asserted in the *Chadha* case that "there is no support in the Constitution or decisions of this Court for the proposition that the cumbersomeness and delays often encountered in complying with explicit Constitutional standards may be avoided, either by the Congress or by the President." The Court unanimously declared its support for red tape, the treasured procedural safeguards that protect us even when we do not wish to be protected, and the law's delay. And they have done this as they stated in the *Chadha* case because "with all the obvious flaws of delay, untidiness, and potential for abuse, we have not yet found a better way to preserve freedom than by making the exercise of power subject to the carefully crafted restraints spelled out in the Constitution."

Executive Branch Machinery

One glance at an organization chart of the U.S. government and we can see immediately that the most complex part of the machinery of government lies in the executive branch; the other two branches seem small by comparison, with comparatively few subdivisions. While the inefficiency of the separation of powers is to be highly valued for its protection of basic liberties, this is no excuse for individual agencies to be inefficient as organizations. Indeed, the whole thrust of American public administration reform over the past century has been to create efficient subunits within an overall inefficient system.

Although the executive branch has the most complex structure, the other two branches are also of interest from a machinery-of-government point of view. For example, the U.S. Supreme Court has ultimate administrative responsibility for the entire federal court system. And while most citizens know that the legislative branch contains the Senate and the House of Representatives, not so many realize that other important agencies are located in this branch, ranging from the Architect of the Capitol and the U.S. Botanic Garden, to the Library of Congress and the General Accounting Office (GAO). This last agency (the GAO) is of critical importance, allowing Congress to exercise financial oversight of the executive branch. The GAO would be severely diminished if its functions were located within the executive branch, as it frequently is within democracies based on the British **parliamentary system**.

The executive branch, headed by the president, contains the machinery that serves to implement national policies established by both constitutional and

---

parliamentary system A means of governance whose power is concentrated in a legislature, which selects from among its members a prime minister and his or her cabinet officers. The government—that is, the prime minister and the cabinet—stays in power as long as it commands a majority of the Parliament. When the government loses its majority (loses a vote of confidence), elections must be held within a prescribed time period (or at least every five years in British practice). The main differences between a parliamentary system (which most of the democratic countries of the world use) and the American system are (1) the ease with which a parliamentary government can be changed if it falls out of favor with a majority in the legislature and (2) the lack of checks and balances in a parliamentary system. The legislative and the executive branch are one in a parliamentary system. The prime minister represents the legislature and, through them, the voters. The major check on his or her power is the constant possibility that his or her party will lose its working majority.

Figure 3.1 The Government of the United States

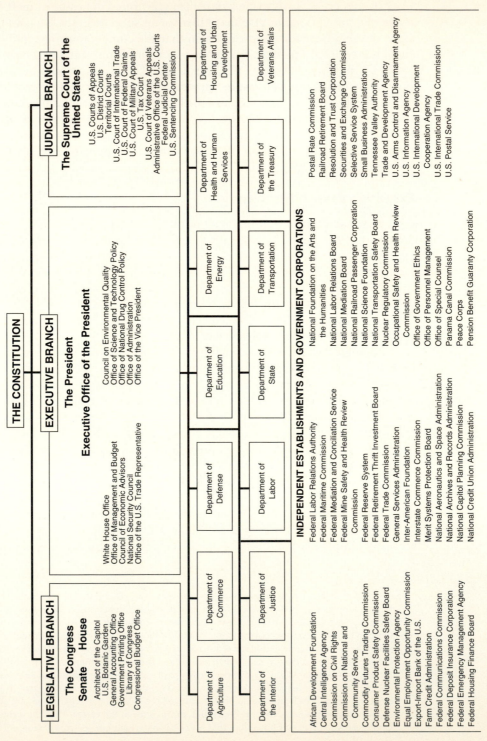

THE CONSTITUTION

LEGISLATIVE BRANCH

The Congress
Senate   House

Architect of the Capitol
U.S. Botanic Garden
General Accounting Office
Government Printing Office
Library of Congress
Congressional Budget Office

EXECUTIVE BRANCH

The President

Executive Office of the President

White House Office
Office of Management and Budget
Council of Economic Advisors
National Security Council
Office of the U.S. Trade Representative

Council on Environmental Quality
Office of Science and Technology Policy
Office of National Drug Control Policy
Office of Administration
Office of the Vice President

JUDICIAL BRANCH

**The Supreme Court of the
United States**

U.S. Courts of Appeals
U.S. District Courts
Territorial Courts
U.S. Court of International Trade
U.S. Court of Federal Claims
U.S. Court of Military Appeals
U.S. Tax Court
U.S. Court of Veterans Appeals
Administrative Office of the U.S. Courts
Federal Judicial Center
U.S. Sentencing Commission

Department of Agriculture

Department of Commerce

Department of Defense

Department of Education

Department of Energy

Department of Health and Human Services

Department of Housing and Urban Development

Department of the Interior

Department of Justice

Department of Labor

Department of State

Department of Transportation

Department of the Treasury

Department of Veterans Affairs

INDEPENDENT ESTABLISHMENTS AND GOVERNMENT CORPORATIONS

African Development Foundation
Central Intelligence Agency
Commission on Civil Rights
Commission on National and
    Community Service
Commodity Futures Trading Commission
Consumer Product Safety Commission
Defense Nuclear Facilities Safety Board
Environmental Protection Agency
Equal Employment Opportunity Commission
Export-Import Bank of the U.S.
Farm Credit Administration
Federal Communications Commission
Federal Deposit Insurance Corporation
Federal Emergency Management Agency
Federal Housing Finance Board

Federal Labor Relations Authority
Federal Maritime Commission
Federal Mediation and Conciliation Service
Federal Mine Safety and Health Review
    Commission
Federal Reserve System
Federal Retirement Thrift Investment Board
Federal Trade Commission
General Services Administration
Inter-American Foundation
Interstate Commerce Commission
Merit Systems Protection Board
National Aeronautics and Space Administration
National Archives and Records Administration
National Capitol Planning Commission
National Credit Union Administration

National Foundation on the Arts and
    the Humanities
National Labor Relations Board
National Mediation Board
National Railroad Passenger Corporation
National Science Foundation
National Transportation Safety Board
Nuclear Regulatory Commission
Occupational Safety and Health Review
    Commission
Office of Government Ethics
Office of Personnel Management
Office of Special Counsel
Panama Canal Commission
Peace Corps
Pension Benefit Guaranty Corporation

Postal Rate Commission
Railroad Retirement Board
Resolution and Trust Corporation
Securities and Exchange Commission
Selective Service System
Small Business Administration
Tennessee Valley Authority
Trade and Development Agency
U.S. Arms Control and Disarmament Agency
U.S. Information Agency
U.S. International Development
    Cooperation Agency
U.S. International Trade Commission
U.S. Postal Service

SOURCE: U.S. Government Manual 1997–1998.

legislative means. There are three main categories of organizations in the structure of the executive branch: (1) executive office agencies, (2) executive departments, and (3) independent public bodies.

Executive Office Agencies   The Executive Office of the President (EOP) is an umbrella office consisting of the top presidential staff agencies that provide the president help and advice in carrying out major responsibilities. These include, as you might expect, some agencies that are concerned with "head office" functions of policy, planning, and resource allocation, such as the Office of Management and Budget, the Council of Economic Advisers, and the National Security Council. But there are also some that are there to signify important national priorities, such as the Office of National Drug Control Policy and the Council on Environmental Quality.

Executive Departments   There are 14 executive **departments**. As a group they constitute the president's cabinet. This is an institution whose existence rests upon custom rather than constitutional provision, even though its chief members, the secretaries of the federal executive departments, must be approved by the Senate. It came into being as a single body, because President George Washington found it useful to meet with the chiefs of the several executive departments. While all subsequent presidents have considered it necessary to meet with the cabinet, their attitudes toward the institution and its members have varied greatly. Some presidents have convened their cabinet only for the most formal and routine matters, while others have relied upon it for advice and support. The president's cabinet differs from the cabinet in the British parliamentary system in that, in the United States the executive power is not shared by the cabinet as a whole but is constitutionally vested solely in the president. This is famously illustrated by a story about Abraham Lincoln. During the Civil War he called his cabinet together to discuss a pressing matter of war policy. Wanting to get a sense of their feelings, he called for a vote. They all voted "nay." Lincoln alone voted "aye." Yet as president he declared, "the ayes have it."

At the present time, cabinet membership consists of the secretaries of 14 executive departments, the newest member being the Secretary of Veterans Affairs. But a substantial part of the executive branch is not represented in the cabinet. From the earliest days, presidents have accorded to others the privilege of attending and participating in cabinet meetings. In recent years, the United States ambassador to the United Nations and the director of the Office of Management and Budget, among others, have been accorded cabinet rank to symbolize the importance of the functions they represent. However, not all cabinet members are equal. The "inner" cabinet refers to the federal departments of State, Defense, Treasury, and Justice—because they (and their secretaries) tend to be more prominent and influential in every administration than the rest of the cabinet. While all cabinet secretaries are

---

department A confusing word. While it can refer to a cabinet-level agency of the U.S. government, it can also refer to one of the three branches of government: executive, legislative, or judicial. But it is also used as a general term for any administrative subdivision. Thus the Department of the Navy is within the Department of Defense.

TABLE 3.1 U.S. Cabinet Departments

Department	Civilian Employees (in thousands)		
	1993	**1996**	**1998 (est.)**
Agriculture	114.4	100.7	99.9
Commerce	36.1	33.8	38.3
Defense	931.8	778.9	733.2
Education	4.9	4.7	4.6
Energy	20.3	19.1	17.2
Health and Human Services	66.1	57.2	57.6
Housing and Urban Development	13.3	11.4	11.0
Interior	78.1	66.7	71.4
Justice	95.4	103.8	121.8
Labor	18.0	16.0	17.1
State	25.6	22.9	23.2
Transportation	69.1	62.4	64.8
Treasury	161.1	151.1	148.1
Veterans Affairs	234.2	221.9	210.6

SOURCE: *U.S. Budget,* Fiscal Year 1998.

equal in rank and salary, the missions of those in the inner cabinet tend to give them an advantage in prestige, access, and visibility denied to those who head the rest of, or the "outer," cabinet.

But for better or worse, according to political scientists Edward Weisband and Thomas M. Frank: "Cabinet meetings in the United States, despite occasional efforts to make them into significant decision-making occasions, have, at least in this century, been characterized as vapid nonevents in which there has been a deliberate nonexchange of information as part of a process of mutual nonconsultation." The president's cabinet has never functioned as a unified team. The American machinery of government, which requires cabinet secretaries to be responsible both to the president and the Congress (with its competing interests) makes that virtually impossible.

The structure of U.S. government departments is a reasonably deft selection of topics likely to need a national focus by government. But these topics are not the only ones that could be represented at this level. They represent choices among competing priorities. There is no federal Department of the Environment, for example, which means that environmental issues must be voiced through other departments. While the Clinton administration called for such a new department, its **loyal opposition** in the Congress has not only opposed it—but has even sought to repeal much of the environmental protection legislation such a department would administer.

---

loyal opposition In a two-party system, the party out of power but loyal to the interest of the nation as a whole.

Independent Public Bodies   The third main area of the U.S. national machinery of government is formed by independent establishments and government corporations. They range in purpose from public business **corporations** (such as the U.S. Postal Service, the Export-Import Bank of the United States, and Amtrak—the National Railroad Passenger Corporation), to important regulators and watchdogs (such as the Environmental Protection Agency and the Commission on Civil Rights) to foundations committed to worthy purposes, such as the National Science Foundation and the African Development Foundation.

A regulatory **commission** is an independent agency established by the Congress to regulate some aspect of U.S. economic life. Among these are the Securities and Exchange Commission (SEC) and the Federal Communications Commission (FCC). Such agencies are, of course, not independent of the U.S. government. They are subject to the laws under which they operate as these laws are enacted and amended by the Congress. Independent agencies and regulatory commissions can be divided into two categories: (1) those units under the direct supervision and guidance of the president, and therefore responsible to him, and (2) those not under such supervision and guidance, and therefore not responsible to him.

Independent executive agencies, with rare exceptions, are headed by single administrators appointed by the president and confirmed by the Senate. These administrators serve at the pleasure of the president and can be removed by the president at any time. In addition, they must submit their budget requests to the Office of Management and Budget (OMB), which is located within the Executive Office of the President, for review and clearance. Examples of independent executive agencies include the Central Intelligence Agency, the Environmental Protection Agency, the General Services Administration, and the Small Business Administration.

Independent regulatory commissions (such as the FCC and SEC) and government-sponsored enterprises (such as the Tennessee Valley Authority) are bodies headed by several commissioners, directors, or governors who are also appointed by the president and confirmed by the Senate. But unlike administrators of independent executive agencies, they serve for fixed terms and cannot be removed at the pleasure of the president. When Franklin Roosevelt sought to dismiss commissioners of the Federal Trade Commission (FTC) for disagreements over policy, the Supreme Court ruled in *Humphrey's Executor v. United States* (1935) that the FTC "occupies no place in the executive department." Thus all such commissioners can serve to the end of their fixed terms unless impeached by the Congress.

---

corporation An organization formed under state or federal law that exists, for legal purposes, as a separate being or an artificial person. It may be public (set up by the government) or private (set up by individuals), and it may be created to carry on a business or to perform almost any function. It may be owned by the government or by a few persons, or it may be a "publicly owned corporation"—owned by members of the general public who buy its shares on an open stock market such as the New York Stock Exchange.

commission A group charged with directing a government function, whether on an ad hoc or a permanent basis. Commissions tend to be used (1) when it is desirable to have bipartisan leadership, (2) when their functions are of a quasi-judicial nature, or (3) when it is deemed important to have wide representation of ethnic groups, regions of the country, differing skills, and so on.

Note that many regulatory functions are also performed by traditional cabinet departments. For example, the Food and Drug Administration is located within the Department of Health and Human Services. And the Office of Federal Contract Compliance, which monitors behavior of corporations that do business with the government, is located within the Department of Labor.

Government corporation is the term used for a government-owned corporation or an agency of government that administers a self-supporting enterprise. Such a structure is used:

1. When an agency's business is essentially commercial,
2. When an agency can generate its own revenue, and
3. When the agency's mission requires greater flexibility than government agencies normally have.

Examples of federal government corporations include the Saint Lawrence Seaway Development Corporation, the Federal Deposit Insurance Corporation, the National Railroad Passenger Corporation (AMTRAK), and the Tennessee Valley Authority. At the state and municipal levels, corporations (often bearing different names, such as authorities) operate enterprises such as turnpikes, airports, and harbors.

State and Local Government Machinery

American subnational governments are individually smaller than the national government but collectively far larger than it. The number of public employees is a good indicator of this disparity. The federal government, excluding the armed forces, has just about 2 million civilian employees. But state and local employment exceeds 16 million. The machinery of government at the state and local levels parallels the national model with legislative, executive, and judicial branches. The Tenth Amendment, the last part of the Bill of Rights, holds that the "powers not delegated to the United States by the Constitution, nor prohibited by it to the states, are reserved to the states respectively, or to the people." This means that whatever the federal government cannot constitutionally do for the people, the states, and their subunits must or may do. Significantly, the national Constitution does not mention cities, counties, or any other type of local government. They are all creatures of their states; their powers are derived from state law; and what a state gives a state may later take away.

The primacy of state over local law is the essence of Dillon's rule—a rule famously formulated by Judge John F. Dillon in his 1911 *Commentaries on the Law of Municipal Corporations*. The rule outlines criteria developed by state courts to determine the nature and extent of powers granted to local governments. It holds that municipal corporations have only those powers (1) expressly granted in the city charter, (2) necessarily or fairly implied by or incidental to formally expressed powers, and (3) essential to the declared purposes of the corporation. "Any fair, reasonable, substantial doubt" about a power is to result in denying that power to the corporation. In some states, the rule has been relaxed, especially in dealing with

TABLE 3.2 Governments in the United States

Type	Number
National	1
State	50
County	3,043
Municipal	19,279
Townships/towns	16,656
School Districts	14,422
Special Districts	31,555
Total	85,006

SOURCE: *Statistical Abstract of the United States* (Washington: Government Printing Office, 1997).

home rule cities. The essence of Dillon's rule was upheld by the Supreme Court in *City of Trenton v. State of New Jersey* (1913).

State Government

The elected chief executive of a state government is the governor. The responsibilities of a governor usually parallel those of a U.S. president, on a smaller scale, but each governor has only the powers granted to the office by the state constitution. Some states severely limit executive powers, while others give their governors powers, such as the **item veto**, that are greater than those possessed by the president of the United States. The term of office for a governor is four years, in all states except four (Arkansas, New Hampshire, Rhode Island, and Vermont), where it is two. In one sense, it is a misnomer to call a governor the chief executive of a state. The reality is that most state constitutions provide for what amounts to a plural executive, because governors, in marked contrast to the U.S. president, typically must share powers with a variety of other independently elected executive branch officers, such as a secretary of state, an attorney general, a treasurer, and an auditor (or controller). Consequently, a governor's informal powers as a lobbyist for his or her initiatives and as head of his or her party may often be far more useful than the formal authority that comes with the office. Nevertheless, the management job of a governor compares favorably in terms of responsibility to those of the highest paid corporate executives. For example, in terms of revenues, more than half the states

home rule The ability, the power, of a municipal corporation to develop and implement its own charter. It resulted from the urban reform movement of the turn of the century, which hoped to remove urban politics from the harmful influence of state politics. Home rule can be either a statutory or a constitutional system and varies in its details from state to state.
item veto The executive power to veto separate items in a bill. This is also known as the line-item veto.

would rank among the top 100 corporations in America. Most would be among the top 200 of the **Fortune 500**.

The lieutenant governor is the elected state official who would replace the governor should he or she be unable to complete a term of office. The office parallels that of the vice president in the national government but differs in that in many states the lieutenant governor is separately elected and thus may be of a different party from the governor. This can sometimes cause considerable friction when the two officeholders are political rivals—and especially when, as in California, the lieutenant governor assumes some of the governor's powers to act whenever the governor is out of the state. Seven states (Arizona, Maine, New Hampshire, New Jersey, Oregon, West Virginia, and Wyoming) have felt no need for a lieutenant governor. In four of these states, the president of the state senate would succeed to the governorship; in the other three, the secretary of state succeeds.

The story is often told of Calvin Coolidge, then the lieutenant governor of Massachusetts, who met a woman at a dinner party. She asked, "What do you do?"

He replied, "I'm the lieutenant governor."

"How interesting, you must tell me all about it," she said.

Coolidge then replied, "I just did." While Coolidge was notoriously tight-lipped, his summation of the limited responsibilities of the office of lieutenant governor was drawn from reality.

County Government

The county is the basic unit for administrative decentralization of state government. Although it is typically governed by an elected board or commission, there is a movement at present toward a county administrator or executive (sometimes elected). In Louisiana, the comparable unit is called a parish; in Alaska, it is a borough. In 1990, the United States had 3,042 county governments. Each state determines for itself how many counties it will have. The elected officials of county government have a bewildering array of titles. According to Dade County, Florida, Commissioner Harvey Ruvin, speaking in 1989, county officials "are supervisors in California, judges in Texas, jurors in Louisiana, freeholders in New Jersey, county legislators in New York, commissioners in Dade. If I tell somebody from New York I'm a commissioner, they think I'm the dog catcher. No wonder the public and the media focus on governors and mayors."

The county seat is the capital of a county, where the courts and administrative offices are located. In much of the United States, the county seat was so located in the geographical center of the county that it would not be more than one day's ride on horseback from the farthest part of the county. This is why there are so many counties. Since few citizens ride horses to government offices today, it would seem to make a lot of sense to combine many counties and thus realize substantial savings from having fewer county clerks, county sheriffs, county courts, etc. But which clerk, sheriff, or judge is going to quietly resign? The conundrum of reforming the machinery of

---

Fortune 500 A size-ordered (based on gross revenues) directory of the 500 largest U.S. corporations published each year since 1955 by *Fortune* magazine.

Box 3.2

The Meaning of Gubernatorial

Gubernatorial is the strange word that refers to things pertaining to the office of governor. It comes from the Greek *kybernan*, meaning to direct a ship. The Romans borrowed the word from the Greeks as *guberno*. Then the French took it and sent it across the English channel as governor. When the word is used as an adjective, it goes back to its Latin roots; thus gubernatorial.

government can often be summarized by the phrase "You can't get there from here!" Of course, the multiplicity of governing entities allows for greater democratic control in that government is kept closer to the people. Nevertheless, reformers constantly ask if the benefits derived are worth the extra costs of these daily inefficiencies.

Tanis Janes Salant has classified the forms of county government as follows:

1. **Commission Form**. An elected county commission or board of supervisors, which is the most common form of county government, has legislative authority (e.g., to enact ordinances, levy certain taxes, and adopt budgets) as well as executive and administrative authority (e.g., to administer local, state, and federal policies, appoint county employees, and supervise road work). Typically, however, administrative responsibilities are also vested in independently elected constitutional officers, such as a county sheriff, treasurer, coroner, clerk, auditor, assessor, and prosecutor.
2. **Commission-Administrator**. There are three basic types of this form, some of which also have additional, independently elected constitutional officers. About 786 counties have one type of this form.
   A. **Council Manager**. The county council or board, which is the legislative body, appoints a county manager who performs executive functions, such as appointing department heads, hiring county staff, administering county programs, drafting budgets, and proposing ordinances.
   B. **Chief Administrative Officer**. The county board or commission, as the legislative and quasi-executive body, appoints a chief administrative officer to supervise and coordinate county departments, but not appoint department heads, and to prepare budgets, draft ordinances, and oversee program implementation.
   C. **County Administrative Assistant**. The county board or commission, as the legislative and executive body, appoints an administrative assistant to help carry out the commission's responsibilities.
3. **Council-Executive**. A county executive is independently elected by the people to perform specific executive functions. The county board or commission remains the legislative body, but the county executive may veto ordinances enacted by the commission, with the commission having override power by an extraordinary majority vote. The county executive's authority and responsibilities are much like those of a mayor in a strong mayor-council municipality. About 383 counties have this form.

Municipal Government

Municipal refers to something of local government concern—such as municipal bonds or municipal parks. It implies that the thing it modifies is of internal concern to a state—as opposed to international concern. It comes from the Latin word *municipium*, which meant a self-governing body within the ancient Roman Empire. A city is a municipal corporation chartered by its state. A political subdivision must meet various state requirements before it can qualify for a **city charter**; for example, it must usually have a population above a state-established minimum level.

A city council is the legislative branch, typically **unicameral**, of a municipal government. The duties of city council members vary greatly; but in almost all cases the most significant functions include passing ordinances (local laws) and controlling expenditures.

A mayor is the elected chief executive officer of a municipal corporation, the chief ceremonial officer of a city. In most modest-sized and small cities, the office of mayor is a part-time job. He or she may be directly elected. The smaller the city, the more likely that the election will be nonpartisan or that the city council will select a mayor from among its members; then the mayor simply presides as the first among equals on the council. While many big-city mayors have become national figures, no mayor has ever been able to make the leap directly from city hall to the White House—or has even been able to get a major party's nomination for president.

There has long been a bias in American government and American political thought against cities. For example, Thomas Jefferson expressed a common opinion when he wrote in a December 20, 1787 letter to James Madison: "I think our governments will remain virtuous for many centuries; as long as they are chiefly agricultural; and this will be as long as there shall be vacant lands in any part of America. When they get piled upon one another in large cities, as in Europe, they will become corrupt as in Europe." But a more tangible harm to cities was found in state and federal policies denying their residents their fair share of representatives in the Congress and in state legislatures. This bias existed until the Supreme Court, beginning in 1962 with *Baker v. Carr*, issued a series of decisions that finally ended **apportionment** in favor of rural areas. The cities were finally made political equals.

---

city charter A document that spells out the purposes and powers of a municipal corporation. To operate, a municipal corporation must have a charter like any other corporation. The municipality can perform only those functions and exercise only those powers that are in the charter. If the particular state permits home rule, a city can develop and implement its own charter. Otherwise, it is limited to statutory charters spelled out by the state legislature.

unicameral A legislature with only one chamber, as opposed to a bicameral one with two—typically a house and a senate. Nebraska is the only state with a unicameral legislature.

apportionment A determination of how many legislators should be sent to a legislative body from a given jurisdiction. The U.S. Constitution provides that each state is entitled to two senators and at least one representative. Beyond the minimum, representatives are apportioned among the states according to population. This apportionment is adjusted after every ten-year census. Under the Apportionment Act of 1929, the Congress fixed the size of the House of Representatives at 435 seats, and after each census the Congress assigns the appropriate number of seats to each state. The states themselves carry on from there: the actual redistributing process is a matter of state law with one major exception. In 1967 Congress prohibited at-large elections in all states entitled to more than one seat in the House.

TABLE 3.3   The Elected Officials Responsible for the American Machinery of Government

Type of Government	Elected Officials	Percentage of Total
Federal	542	0.1
State	18,828	3.7
Local		
Municipal	135,580	26.5
Township	127,009	24.9
School district	88,610	17.3
Special district	84,080	16.5
County	56,390	11.0
GRAND TOTAL	511,039	

SOURCE: *Governing* (April 1995).

Towns and Special Districts

A town is an urban population center—larger than a village but smaller than a city. Typically, its state statutory powers are less than those possessed by cities. The New England town combines the role of both city and county. It usually contains one or more urban areas plus surrounding rural areas. The town meeting is a method of self-government, suitable for only the smallest jurisdictions, where the entire citizenry is eligible to meet to decide local public policy. The town meeting is still the governing body for 88 percent of all New England municipalities. According to journalist Robert Preer, town meetings today are most likely to be controlled by special interests and the town's bureaucracy. Attendance is slight. Even though quorums are set at only 1 or 2 percent of registered voters, meetings are often canceled because of the lack of a quorum. "Raises and promotions pass with ease because meetings are so often packed with employees and their families and friends." Preer concludes that the modern town meeting "is a microcosm of national politics. In both cases, power has shifted from an apathetic and unorganized public to special interests, the mass media, and a bureaucratic-technocratic elite."

A special district is a unit of local government typically performing a single function and overlapping traditional political boundaries. Examples include transportation districts, fire protection districts, library districts, water districts, sewer districts, and so on. Because special districts are such useful devices, they have been multiplying rapidly. In 1942 there were only 8,299 of them in the entire United States. Today there are more than 31,000—not including school districts. They constitute one-third of all American government entities.

A school district is a special district for the provision of local public education for all children in its service area. An elected board, the typical governing body, usually hires a professional superintendent to administer the system. School districts often have their own taxing authority. Many are administratively, financially, and politically independent of other local government units. The total number of school districts has been constantly shrinking because of the increasingly common phenomenon of merging two or more districts. There were more than 108,000 school districts in 1942; today there are fewer than 15,000.

Local Management Machinery

Local government leadership in the majority of jurisdictions overwhelmingly consists of part-time elected volunteers. Tens of thousands of citizens of middle- and small-sized local governments serve as elected or appointed unpaid (or symbolically paid) council, commission, and board members. Often these amateurs appoint a full-time professional manager. The council-manager plan is a form of municipal government in which an elected city council appoints a professional city manager to administer the city government. A county-manager system offers the same essential structure at the county level.

A city manager is the chief executive of the council-manager system of local government. In contrast to the heads of other types of government, the city manager is an appointed chief executive serving at the pleasure of the council. The concept originated early in the twentieth century by progressive reformers who wanted to replace political **bossism** with municipal experts. To do this effectively, they created the concept of an administrative chief executive armed with critical administrative powers, such as appointment and removal of administrative officials, but denied any political powers, such as the veto. The city manager concept was sold to the cities as being just like a corporation with its board of directors. The dichotomy between administration and politics (remember Woodrow Wilson) upon which the system was premised was implemented by putting all of the policymaking and political functions into the city council, essentially abolishing any separation of powers in the traditional sense at the local level. The decision making ability of the council was ensured by (1) creating a small council, typically from five to nine members, elected through at-large, nonpartisan elections; and (2) permitting the council to hire and fire the city manager, their expert in the implementation of community policies.

Present council-manager systems often deviate from this traditional model. Many, particularly in bigger cities, have large councils, partisan elections, and separately elected mayors, and some if not all of the council members are elected from a **ward** or district. In fact, some recent federal court decisions have required ward elections in some cities because **at large** elections make it more difficult for minority

---

bossism An informal system of local government in which public power is concentrated in the hands of a central figure, called a political boss, who may not have a formal government position. The power is concentrated through the use of a political machine, whereby a hierarchy is created and maintained through the use of patronage and government largesse to ensure compliance with the wishes of the boss. It was a dominant system in American city government after the Civil War and was the main target of the American urban reform effort. Few authentic bosses exist today.

ward A subdivision of a city, often used as a legislative district for city council elections, as an administrative division for public services, or as a unit for the organization of political parties. A ward is often further divided into precincts.

at large An election in which one or more candidates for a legislature are chosen by all of the voters of a jurisdiction. This is in contrast to an election by legislative district, in which voters are limited to selecting one candidate to represent their district.

candidates to be elected. The council-manager system has been criticized by some political scientists as being unresponsive to some elements of the community and supported by public administration experts for its effective management in the public interest. In some larger cities, a variant of the system has evolved, utilizing a chief administrative officer often appointed by the mayor.

The mayor-council system is a form of urban government that has a separately elected executive (the mayor) and an urban legislature (the council) usually elected in partisan ward elections. It is called a strong mayor system if the office of mayor is filled by separate citywide elections and has such powers as veto, appointment, and removal. Where the office of mayor lacks such powers, it is called a weak mayor system. This designation does not take into account any informal powers possessed by the incumbent mayor, only the formal powers of the office. Hence, someone can be a strong mayor in terms of actual power in a weak mayor system.

Metropolitan Government

Most larger American cities today cover wide geographical areas. They may have an old urban center with sprawling suburbs extending for many miles, connected to the center by freeways and other forms of urban transportation. The governance of such large conurbations or metropolises presents several options and philosophical choices. There could be a single local government covering the whole area and providing for all. There could be, at the other end of the spectrum, total fragmentation, with many suburban local governments, and even fragmentation within the old center. Or there could be a variety of compromises in between—such as two-tier government in Miami-Dade County, Florida, where functions are split between an overall metropolitan government in particular localities. The Lakewood Plan, in force in California for many years, offers another option—local governments remain within the county but they contract for many of their services from the county.

The adoption of the appropriate machinery of government for a metropolis depends on values. Often, richer and predominantly white residents prefer to withdraw to the suburbs and live under a fragmented local government system, which can avoid the costs of aging urban infrastructure and the social costs of policing and welfare in poorer areas. But fragmented local government lacks the muscle to put investment into social capital that benefits everybody—such as extensive transit systems, museums, and libraries. It's no coincidence that one of the finest transit systems in North America is in Toronto, Canada, where Metro Toronto provides a strong metropolitan government approach. Of course many wealthier Americans would rather not have any local government at all, but rely on private corporations to service their (often gated) communities, distant from urban problems and exempt from both urban costs and urban politics. It's an option some like, but such a degree of civic disengagement is not for everybody. A major method for coordinating the efforts of metropolitan governments is through a council of governments (COG). These institutional forums for voluntary cooperation offer many advantages, especially in comprehensive planning and jointly seeking federal funding for regional programs. COGs are discussed further in Chapter 4.

Box 3.3

How Machinery Begins: Benjamin Franklin Invents the Fire Department in Colonial Philadelphia

I wrote a paper on the different accidents and carelessnesses by which houses were set on fire, with cautions against them, and means proposed of avoiding them. This was much spoken of as a useful piece, and gave rise to a project, which soon followed it, of forming a company for the more ready extinguishing of fires, and mutual assistance in removing and securing of goods when in danger. Associates in this scheme were presently found, amounting to thirty. Our articles of agreement oblig'd every member to keep always in good order, and fit for use, a certain number of leather buckets, with strong bags and baskets (for packing and transporting of goods), which were to be brought to every fire; and we agreed to meet once a month and spend a social evening together, in discoursing and communicating such ideas as occurred to us upon the subject of fires, as might be useful in our conduct on such occasions.

The utility of this institution soon appeared, and many more desiring to be admitted than we thought convenient for one company, they were advised to form another, which was accordingly done; and this went on, one new company being formed after another, till they became so numerous as to include most of the inhabitants who were men of property; and now, at the time of my writing this, tho' upward of fifty years since its establishment, that which I first formed, called the Union Fire Company, still subsists and flourishes, tho' the first members are all deceas'd but myself and one, who is older by a year than I am. The small fines that have been paid by members for absence at the monthly meetings have been apply'd to the purchase of fire-engines, ladders, fire-hooks, and other useful implements for each company, so that I question whether there is a city in the world better provided with the means of putting a stop to beginning conflagrations; and, in fact, since these institutions, the city has never lost by fire more than one or two houses at a time, and the flames have often been extinguished before the house in which they began has been half consumed.

SOURCE: *The Autobiography of Benjamin Franklin* (New York: Washington Square Press, 1955).

Continuous State and Local Reform

The progressive reform movement left some reform institutions in its wake that continue to encourage improvements in state and local government machinery. At the beginning of the twentieth century, municipal research bureaus—private nonprofit good government organizations—were established in most major cities. This "bureau movement" emphasized fact-finding and the application of the scientific method to urban reform; this was in marked contrast to the simplistic "throw the rascals out" tactics of earlier reform efforts. The New York Bureau of Municipal Research, founded in 1906, pioneered with investigations of wasteful municipal spending (double billing, work paid for but not performed, etc.) that when published, so shocked the community that real administrative reforms followed. The investigatory approach of the New York Bureau (now called the Institute of Public Administration) was then imitated in Philadelphia, Cincinnati, Chicago, Milwaukee, Kansas City, San Francisco, and elsewhere.

The bureau movement was the primary vehicle for developing, and then advocating the implementation of, many administrative innovations that we take for granted today—for example, executive budgeting, uniform accounting standards, merit system selection and staffing procedures, retirement systems, uniform crime statistics, and in-service training. This movement was the source of much of the early scholarly research in public administration. Indeed it is not an exaggeration to say that academic public administration was almost wholly created in its initial stages by scholars associated with the various bureaus. Today the movement continues with local good government organizations such as the Pennsylvania Economy League and institutes of government affiliated with many state universities.

Reforming the National Machinery of Government

It all started with the conquest of England in 1066. William the Conqueror appointed commissioners to make an inventory of the assets of his new kingdom. This report, known as the Doomsday Book (because its findings were as beyond appeal as a Doomsday judgment), is the predecessor of today's royal or presidential commissions and committees. Ever since, prime ministers and presidents have used these devices to investigate a matter of public concern and to issue recommendations for improvement. There is great public satisfaction to be had in the bringing together of a group of responsible, respected, supposedly objective but knowledgeable citizens to examine and report upon a national problem or major disaster.

Such commissions have proven to be handy devices for a modern president who, when faced with an intractable problem, such as crime, pornography, or urban riots, can, at slight expense, appoint a commission as a gesture to indicate his awareness of constituent distress. Whether that gesture has meaning or sincerity beyond itself is inconsequential for its immediate effect. By the time a commission makes its report, six months to a year later, attention will have been diverted to other issues, and the recommendations can be safely pigeonholed or curtailed.

Often such commissions (or committees) have been used to tinker with the machinery of government. Evolution inexorably marches on. Just as birds are now thought to be all that is left of the dinosaurs, the modern performance review can trace its lineage to the Doomsday Book. Both are efforts by the prevailing regime to assess a present situation so that it can be better repositioned. William the Conqueror used his assessment to restructure England's tax system. A later William, President William Jefferson Clinton, used his to reinvent government. We now know, after a thousand years, that the first William succeeded. It is too soon to tell how successful the second William has been.

The Brownlow Committee

The advent of the 1990s reinventing government movement has once again made reorganization a fashionable theme in the practice and literature of American public administration. However, the classic example of government reorganization, the one that to this day is still the most significant, is the structuring of the executive branch recommended by the President's Committee on Administrative Management in 1936–1937. This committee was popularly known as the Brownlow Committee, named after its chairman, Louis Brownlow, a major figure in the development of city management as a profession. The two other members of the committee were Charles Merriam of the University of Chicago and Luther Gulick of Columbia University and the Institute of Public Administration in New York City.

Government grew rapidly during the New Deal period and there was little time or inclination for planning. It was largely believed that there existed many poorly conceived and poorly implemented organizational designs that were neither economical nor effective. These poor designs were often a reflection of the considerable political conflict between the executive and legislative branches. Both the president's office and the Congress had deliberately contributed to this problem by establishing programs in new organizations or agencies only with regard to political objectives—without taking managerial considerations into account. This persistent struggle over organizational control would be addressed by the Brownlow Committee—which provided the first formal assessment of government organization from a managerial perspective.

The Brownlow Committee submitted its report to President Roosevelt in January 1937. The core proposals of the committee were simple enough. Essentially the report indicated that "the president needs help"; that he needs professional staff members around him who possessed a "passion for anonymity." This particular passion seems to have faded in recent years along with the public's belief that a modern president writes his own speeches.

Overall the committee recommended a major reorganization of the executive branch. The president agreed and appropriate legislation was submitted to Congress in 1938. But Congress, in the wake of the president's efforts to "pack"—to enlarge and thus control—the Supreme Court, and fearful of too much power in the presidency, killed the bill. The president resubmitted a considerably modified reorganization bill the following year and the Congress passed the Reorganization Act of 1939. This law created the Executive Office of the President, brought into it the Bureau of the Budget (later to be the Office of Management and Budget) from the Department of the Treasury, and authorized the president to prepare future reorganization plans subject to an after-the-fact congressional veto.

The Brownlow report, the Executive Office of the President, and many of the other recommendations of the Brownlow Committee that would eventually become law have been sanctified by time. Yet the Brownlow Committee's major proposals initially aroused considerable controversy. Modern scholars now recognize that

Box 3.4

The Brownlow Committee's Call for a Passion for Anonymity

The president needs help. His immediate staff assistance is entirely inadequate. He should be given a small number of executive assistants who would be his direct aides in dealing with the managerial agencies and administrative departments of the government. These assistants, probably not exceeding six in number, would be in addition to his present secretaries, who deal with the public, with the Congress, and with the press and radio. These aides would have no power to make decisions or issue instructions in their own right. They would not be interposed between the president and the heads of his departments. They would not be assistant presidents in any sense. Their function would be, when any matter was presented to the president for action affecting any part of the administrative work of the government, to assist him in obtaining quickly and without delay all pertinent information possessed by any of the executive departments so as to guide him in making his responsible decisions; and when the decisions have been made, to assist him in seeing to it that every administrative department and agency affected is promptly informed. Their effectiveness in assisting the president, will, we think, be directly proportional to their ability to discharge their functions with restraint. They would remain in the background, issue no orders, make no decisions, emit no public statements. Men for these positions should be carefully chosen by the president from within and without the government. They should be men in whom the president has personal confidence and whose character and attitude is such that they would not attempt to exercise power on their own account. They should be possessed of high competence, great physical vigor, and a passion for anonymity.

SOURCE: President's Committee on Administrative Management, *Administrative Management in the Government of the United States*, January 8, 1937 (Washington: U.S. Government Printing Office, 1937).

there were different schools of thought regarding the development of public administration. The executive administration school, espoused by **Frank J. Goodnow**, viewed the roles and functions of government almost exclusively as opportunities for executive actions. In contrast, the legislative administrative school, as espoused by Brookings Institution head William F. Willoughby, viewed the relationship and

---

Frank J. Goodnow (1859–1939) A leader of the progressive reform movement and one of the founders and first president (in 1903) of the American Political Science Association. Goodnow is now best known as one of the principal exponents, along with Woodrow Wilson, of public administration's politics-administration dichotomy.

especially the accountability of administration to the legislative branch as a central focus. This latter school believed that there was a considerable distinction between what was meant by "executive" and "administrative" and that the Constitution gave administrative power mainly to the Congress. The argument over who has more power over the machinery of government, the executive or the legislature, still resonates in the mid 1990s with the budgetary struggles between a Democratic president and a Republican Congress over the size and scope of the governmental machine.

While the Congress was considering the Brownlow Committee's various proposals, the forces opposed to an increase in the "administrative" powers of the president at the expense of the Congress marshaled their arguments. One of the most eloquent was Lewis Meriam's 1939 *Reorganization of the National Government*. Just as the Brownlow Committee's report argues for increased presidential power, Meriam was cautioning against it. After "noting Hitler's rise to power within constitutional forms," he warned his readers that "proposals to vest great powers in the executive" might not work "to preserve democracy as we have known it but seriously to endanger it."

Forty years later the only surviving member of the Brownlow Committee would concede a point to Meriam. In considering Richard M. Nixon's abuses of the enhanced powers of the presidency which the Brownlow Committee helped to create, Luther Gulick is quoted by Blumberg as saying that "we all assumed in the 1930s that all management, especially public management, flowed in a broad, strong stream of value-filled ethical performance. Were we blind or only naive until Nixon came along?" Nixon's 1970s subversion of constitutional government in the United States during the 1972–1974 Watergate scandal that forced his resignation differed only in degree from the subversion of republican governments that has been the hallmark of twentieth-century dictators.

Ironically, Nixon sought to enhance the power of the presidency with the creation of the Office of Management and Budget, yet he accomplished just the opposite. The Congress, upset by Nixon's budgetary double-dealing, created a parallel Congressional Budget Office so that the legislature had its own number crunchers—who presumably would crunch numbers that could be believed. So in the game of constitutional checks and balances, new machinery of government is often created to check a would-be king.

The Hoover Commissions

The first Hoover Commission (1947–1949), formally the Commission on Organization of the Executive Branch of the Government, chaired by former President Herbert Hoover, was specifically charged to reduce the number of government agencies created during World War II; but it did not do this. Instead, it found that "disorder in the administrative machinery makes the executive branch of the Government work at cross purposes within itself" and focused on strengthening the executive branch by providing for a reorganization of agencies so that there would be a coherent purpose for each department. Instead of calling for a reduction of government agencies, the commission made a vigorous call for increased managerial capacity in the Executive Office of the President (EOP) through: (1) unlimited discretion over presidential organization and staff, (2) a strengthened Bureau of the

Herbert Hoover as Secretary of Commerce in the Coolidge administration exploring the "Internet" of his day. Hoover had the great misfortune to become president (1929–1933) as the Great Depression almost destroyed the American economy. A whole generation of Americans grew up holding him personally responsible for economic events that no president of that time could have controlled. Ironically, Hoover, who made a fortune early in life as an engineer, headed allied relief operations during and after World War I, and served as Secretary of Commerce under Presidents Warren G. Harding and Calvin Coolidge, had a worldwide reputation as a preeminent administrator •

Budget, (3) an office of personnel located in the EOP, and (4) the creation of a staff secretary (what we now call a chief of staff) to provide a liaison between the president and his subordinates. The commission was considered a big success because 72 percent of its recommendations (196 out of 273) were adopted, including passage of the Reorganization Act of 1949 and the establishment of the Department of Health, Education, and Welfare in 1953.

A second Hoover Commission (1953–1955), also chaired by Hoover, is the unique example in the history of American public administration of an important commission being virtually reconvened after four years had passed, to continue its work. Many of the same commission members and staff were even retained. This second commission had three ostensible purposes:

1. the promoting of economy, efficiency, and improved service in the transaction of the public business;

2. the defining and limiting of executive functions; and

3. the curtailment and abolition of government functions and activities competitive with private enterprise.

This second commission recommended the elimination of nonessential government services and activities competitive with private enterprise, based on the assumptions that the federal government had grown beyond appropriate limits and that such growth should be reversed. In contrast to the first commission, the second commission's recommendations accomplished little. In a mere 18 volumes, the former president and his 11 fellow commissioners rigorously argued that a whole host of government activities should be turned over to the private sector. But the U.S. Congress was not so inclined and this commission's recommendations got essentially nowhere. There was no political will to undertake massive privatization in the mid 1950s. This was a banner in the dust that would not be picked up and held high again until the Reagan administration of the 1980s and, more dramatically with the Republican capture of Congress in 1994.

The Ash Council

President Richard M. Nixon's Advisory Council on Executive Organization, chaired by Roy Ash of Litton Industries, led to the transformation of the Bureau of the Budget into the Office of Management and Budget. The Ash Council's 1971 recommendations were extraordinarily ambitious in calling for a major restructuring of the cabinet agencies. President Nixon intended to implement this restructuring in his second term, beginning in 1973. But the Watergate scandal (see Chapter 14), which would force his resignation the following year, so dominated his aborted second term that no major domestic policy initiatives were possible.

The President's Private Sector Survey on Cost Control

If the second Hoover Commission is to be measured by 18 volumes of output leading nowhere, the 1982 President's Private Sector Survey on Cost Control can be measured by 47 reports from 36 major task forces with approximately similar results. The executive survey alone was 650 pages in two volumes. Like the Second Hoover Commission, President Reagan's survey was appointed from an ideological position in which it was assumed that a little private sector know-how was all that it would take to put things right in Washington—an age-old belief that has been applied time and time again with great ardor but to somewhat limited effect. The PPSSCC was chaired by businessman J. Peter Grace, and its various subcommittees were composed of business figures from many large corporations. The final report of what came to be called the Grace Commission, prepared by more than two thousand volunteer, private-sector executives, contained 2,478 recommendations on 784 different issues for improving the efficiency of the federal government. In the end, Reagan's study was a classic example of focusing on detail and missing the big picture, or being "penny wise and pound foolish." For example, the survey analyzed in a very critical manner particular actions and bodies, such as the Railroad Retirement Board, which it found to be insolvent and part of a longer pattern of institutionalized handouts to railroad workers. But on bigger issues, such as the framework of national public personnel management, the private sector executives showed limited understanding and were severely challenged in subsequent congressional hearings by Congressmen such as William D. Ford, former Chair of the House of Representatives Committee on the Post Office and Civil Service.

TABLE 3.4   Major Commissions to Reform Federal Bureaucracy

Name	Chair	Year(s)	President	Result
Brownlow Commission	Louis Brownlow	1936	Roosevelt	Enhanced presidential control of bureaucracy
First Hoover Commission	Herbert Hoover	1947–1949	Truman	Strengthened the Executive Office of the President and enhanced agency management
Second Hoover Commission	Herbert Hoover	1953–1955	Eisenhower	Nothing significant
Ash Council	Roy Ash	1971	Nixon	The Bureau of the Budget became the Office of Management and Budget
Grace Commission	J. Peter Grace	1982	Reagan	A handful of minor bureaucratic adjustments
National Performance Review	Al Gore Jr.	1993	Clinton	A somewhat more streamlined and customer friendly bureaucracy

It now seems that the Grace Commission was ill-fated from the start. The first problem was Grace himself. His true feelings notwithstanding, he came across in countless media interviews as an irascible old corporate patriarch who was condescending enough to disturb his well-earned repose by deigning to advise a misguided government on the multitudinous errors of its ways. The second problem was the commission's ignorance of one of the central precepts of modern management—employee participation. While Grace orchestrated this immense management audit by 2,000 private-sector volunteers, the committee's task force largely ignored the expertise that was freely available from within the bureaucracy and the Congress. Consequently when the report came out, it was viewed, with some justification, as an effort to "get" the bureaucracy—and to get it dishonestly at that. Thus the Grace Commission never recovered from the public relations disaster that was Grace himself and the glaring inaccuracies or misrepresentations of the analysis.

Bureaucratic reform historian Donald Savoie reports that both the General Accounting Office and the Congressional Budget Office systematically reviewed the commission's conclusions and "undermine[d] the Commission's credibility" when they demonstrated that too many of the proposed savings were nonexistent and too many of the commission's facts were not factual after all. This however "did not stop the Reagan administration from applauding the findings of the commission and from reporting that it would press ahead with their implementation." But this was largely a public relations exercise of putting a good face on a poor effort. Perhaps the most highly touted recommendation of the Commission that was actually implemented was the proposal that federal employees be issued corporate-type credit cards for official travel. While this offered legitimate savings on time previously spent on completing expense reimbursement vouchers, it was hardly worth the estimated $75 million dollar cost (all private-sector donated) for the report.

Reinventing Government

The current reinventing government movement was not started in 1992 by the David Osborne and Ted Gaebler book with that title. It represents the confluence of two long-standing influences in American public life: the progressive reform movement and management faddism. Reinventing is logically the continuation of the progressive movement's philosophy of continuous improvement. This year's or this generation's most popular management fad is the comprehensive performance audit as a logically prior step in developing a new strategic vision for a business organization or a government operation. Next year or next generation there will be a new management fad, but it will still be within the progressive tradition.

Just as every new generation writes its own history, each new managerial generation has its own way of seeing the "one best way"—even if that one way means multiple ways. What is genuinely new here is that governments at all levels are actually being forced by events to change the fundamental ways in which they operate. They must literally rethink, meaning reinvent, how they operate because they can no longer afford to simply do what they have been doing—with a reorganization here and a new public relations effort there—to assuage their critics. The simple overriding impetus to reinventing is a lack of money caused by the dual effects of the tax revolt and the Reagan revolution.

By 1980, the tax revolt movement forced 38 states to reduce or at least stabilize tax rates. Then the Reagan revolution came along and made state and local finances even more precarious. The Reagan administration, with its radical changes in the nation's fiscal and tax policies, redefined domestic priorities and curtailed federal programs—especially grants to state and local government—designed to solve social problems. As Reagan often said, "Government is not the solution to our problems. Government is the problem." In other words, the national welfare would be better served with general economic prosperity, brought about by tax cuts rather than with expanded welfare programs.

Necessity being the mother of invention, the current reinventing government movement began in the early 1980s to cope with the declining revenues caused by the tax revolt and the Reagan revolution. In 1992, Osborne and Gaebler wrote *Reinventing Government*, a book that essentially categorized many of the things the thousands of governments have been doing throughout the 1980s to cope with this crisis. Bill Clinton, as governor of Arkansas, endorsed the book. As president, he authorized the National Performance Review to seek these same kinds of innovations for the federal government—and for the same reason, money. The federal government was running record deficits. This had to be reduced by reducing (read reinventing) government.

If the federal government was off to the reinventing government races, Vice President Al Gore was the jockey riding the horse. This was unusual in itself because historically in the United States the vice president's only constitutional responsibility

President Bill Clinton and Vice President Al Gore announce their reinventing government initiative on the White House lawn in 1993 surrounded by papers representing bureaucratic regulations they promise to discard. This was a truly great photo opportunity. Before most of the cabinet, many members of Congress, and the assembled press corps, Gore then told the president (for the benefit of the press): "Mr. President, if you want to know why government doesn't work, look behind you. The answer is at least partly on those forklifts. Those forklifts hold copies of budget rules, procurement rules, and the personnel code. The personnel code alone weighs in at over 1,000 pounds. That code and those regulations stacked up there no longer help government work, they hurt it; they hurt it badly. And we recommend getting rid of it." The lesson here is that there is not much political mileage in reinventing government in a closet. Better to do it on the White House lawn and let the whole world watch •

(aside from waiting for the president to die or be removed from office) is to preside over the U.S. Senate (except when it is trying a president for impeachment) and vote in the case of a tie.

Recent presidents, however, have tended to give their vice presidents significant domestic and foreign policy assignments. Of course having the vice president play with a president's **trial balloon** has always been an effective means of insulating a president from critics if the balloon pops. So the question must be asked: how strong is the reinventing government balloon? The answer: so strong that it will not be allowed to fail. The only uncertainty is how much of a success it will be. And that question is as much a political as a managerial one—because the criteria for success, being essentially political, are moving targets.

The Gore Report

When President Bill Clinton launched the National Performance Review in 1993—a six-month study aimed at making the federal government more efficient—the language he used was familiar: "Our goal is to make the federal government both less expensive and more efficient, and to change the culture of our national bureaucracy away from complacency and entitlement toward initiative and empowerment. We intend to redesign, to reinvent, to reinvigorate the entire national government." According to the 1993 report, "Washington's failures are large and obvious"; the failures listed included:

- A fall in public trust of the national government from 76 percent in 1964 to 20 percent in 1994
- A national debt of $4 trillion, or $16,600 per capita
- Enormous waste—for example, $40 million in unnecessary Defense Department supplies
- Billions of dollars in unpaid tax bills
- Ineffective regulation, resulting in such things as the savings and loan debacle
- A $68 billion poverty bill—yet more Americans falling into poverty each year
- More than 150 different employment and training programs

Clearly these are not all issues of machinery of government. Some must be viewed as failures of political philosophy; others as the outcome of profound social and economic inequality produced by past economic policies. Some result from the structural modernization of the national and global economies; others, however, like duplication of administrative effort, the inability to combat waste, and the overall lack of trust in the system, are likely to relate in part to a structure of government that seems arthritic, resistant to change, and closed, as suggested by Gore's report no less than by its predecessors. But in pointed and emphasized contrast to the federal government's last major management reform effort (the Grace Commis-

---

trial balloon A deliberate leak of a potential policy to see what public response will be. The term comes from the meteorological practice of sending up a balloon to test weather conditions. If public response is hostile, the new policy proposal can be quietly dropped (or deflated).

sion), the Gore report would be researched and written largely by the in-house talent of the federal bureaucracy.

The National Performance Review made 258 agency-specific recommendations, affecting every national executive department, as well as the executive agencies in the Office of the President. As well, the review promised that it would spawn further reviews on more focused topics, such as the "antiquated" federal field office structure, the abandonment of obsolete programs, the elimination of unproductive subsidies, the redesign of failed programs, the redefinition of relationships between the federal government and state and local governments, and the reinvigoration of relationships between the executive and legislative branches. Whatever optimism or pessimism one might hold for the achievement of this program of change, the targets seem right, and the prospect of the U.S. national government at last being freed up, and "reinvented" does seem encouraging.

Whereas the Grace Report under the Reagan administration—which based its philosophy on the proposition that only private business executives could fix government—was an abject failure, the implementation of reinvention has been quite different. The National Partnership for Reinventing Government has relied on borrowed federal career officials to do its work. By 1998 it reported savings of $137 billion dollars, a reduction of 351,000 positions in government, and the creation of 340 reinvention laboratories in government agencies. Instead of conflict, partnership is a key theme: between labor and management (occupational health and safety has been a key focus); between regulatory agencies and regulated businesses; and between government agencies. All this has been for the common goals of best value for the taxpayer dollar, better service for customers, and better workplaces for employees.

It must also be said, however, that the Gore report is not unlike its predecessors in that it has focused on many specific programs and details, as would a conventional management consultant's report. It lacks the root and branch depth of change achieved in those bureaucracies where new fundamental principles have been adopted, rather than endeavoring to fine-tune, but not fundamentally change, the existing system. Some of the recommendations of the National Performance Review—for example, that the Railroad Retirement Board be reinvented—have a familiar ring, while others, like the recommendation that the management of the Department of Health and Human Services be reviewed, seem to be like a Russian Petrushka doll—a review that contains a recommendation for another review.

In marked contrast are the machinery of government changes that have taken place in the last decade in Britain, Australia, and New Zealand. These have involved fundamental principles and have been more radical than those of the National Performance Review. In fact, the specific machinery of government recommendations of the National Performance Review have been relatively few—considering that an organization left in place after a review lives to fight another day, and to disregard review recommendations it dislikes once the dust has settled.

The Reinventors Versus the Micromanagers

Woodrow Wilson wrote in his famous 1887 essay "The Study of Administration" that "the field of administration is a field of business"; that "it is a part of political life only as the methods of the counting-house are a part of the life of the society," and that "administrative questions are not political questions." This was institutionalized by the Brownlow Committee recommendations for greater managerial capability on the part of the executive. But as David H. Rosenbloom has observed, Congress responded to this stronger, more managerially capable, presidency "in 1946 by establishing the legal and institutional bases for its contemporary role in federal administration." Thus when Truman, a Democrat, was president while the Republicans controlled the Congress, a **divided government** brought forth this quartet of laws that sowed the seeds of **micromanagement**:

1. Administrative Procedure Act (APA) of 1946: The basic law governing the way federal agencies operate to safeguard agency clients and the general public. The APA specifies the conditions under which administrative agencies (a) publicize information about their operations; (b) make rules; (c) engage in adjudication; and (d) are subject to judicial review. Thus agencies begin with some form of legislative mandate and translate their interpretation of that mandate into policy decisions, specifications of regulations, and statements of penalties and enforcement provisions. The APA requires that rules be published 30 days before their effective date and that agencies afford any interested party the right to petition for issuance, amendment, or repeal of a rule. In effect, while the APA establishes a process of notice and time for comment, it accords administrative rulemakers the same prerogatives that legislatures have in enacting statutes, as long as the rule enacted is consistent with the enabling statute.

2. Legislative Reorganization Act of 1946: A law that dramatically reduced the number of standing committees in the Senate and House, provided for a major expansion of the Legislative Reference Service (now known as the Congressional Research Service), and promoted the creation of a professional, nonpartisan staff for committees, as well as increased staff for individual members. This was the first attempt by Congress to establish an effective staff system to decrease its dependence on executive agencies for information.

3. Tort Claims Act of 1946: The law that made federal agencies responsible for their torts—legal harms done to another person that can be the cause of a civil court suit.

4. Employment Act of 1946: The law that created the Council of Economic Advisers in the Executive Office of the President and asserted that it was the federal government's responsibility to maintain economic stability and promote full employment.

The combined effect of these laws was to unleash a mob of micromanagers. Members of Congress, once largely limited to policy oversight, now had the oppor-

divided government A government in which different political parties control the legislative and executive branches.
micromanagement A pejorative term for too-close supervision by policymakers in the implementation of programs. The Congress has been accused of micromanagement when it writes detailed rules governing programs into legislation thus denying line managers any real administrative discretion. But any manager is a micromanager if he or she refuses to allow subordinates to have any real authority or responsibility.

Box 3.5

Al Gore Assesses the Problem

Is government inherently incompetent? Absolutely not. Are federal agencies filled with incompetent people? No. The problem is much deeper. . . .

Many federal organizations are also monopolies, with few incentives to innovate or improve. Employees have virtual lifetime tenure, regardless of their performance. Success offers few rewards; failure, few penalties. And customers are captive; they can't walk away from the air traffic control system or the Internal Revenue Service and sign up with a competitor. . . .

Politics intensifies the problem. In Washington's highly politicized world, the greatest risk is not that a program will perform poorly, but that a scandal will erupt. Scandals are front-page news, while routine failure is ignored. Hence control system after control system is piled up to minimize the risk of scandal. The budget system, the personnel rules, the procurement process, the inspectors general—all are designed to prevent the tiniest misstep. We assume that we can't trust employees to make decisions, so we spell out in precise detail how they must do virtually everything, then audit them to ensure that they have obeyed every rule. The slightest deviation prompts new regulations and even more audits.

Before long, simple procedures are too complex for employees to navigate, so we hire more budget analysts, more personnel experts, and more procurement officers to make things work. By then, the process involves so much red tape that the smallest action takes far longer and costs far more than it should. . . .

This emphasis on process steals resources from the real job: serving the customer.

SOURCE: Vice President Al Gore, Report of the National Performance Review, *From Red Tape to Results: Creating a Government that Works Better and Costs Less* (Washington: Government Printing Office, 1993).

tunity to delve into the minutiae of administration on behalf of their constituents. The APA created a rulemaking process that offered unlimited possibilities for influencing rules for pork barrel motivations. The Legislative Reorganization Act gave Congress the staff it needed to constantly interfere for their specific political purposes. The Tort Claims Act meant that Congress could effectively lobby agencies to redress wrongs to constituents. And the Employment Act meant virtually unlimited justification to pump federal money into selected congressional districts. This process can be seen every time the Department of Defense has been forced into buying more of a weapon than it needs simply because the factory that makes it is in an influential member's congressional district. As Rosenbloom sarcastically noted: "Turning pork barrel politics into a virtuous national economic policy was no small achievement." But while pork by its nature is not kosher, for many Americans the very definition of a member of Congress is one who brings home the bacon. This, however, may be changing.

The import of all this is that Congress has never drawn—as the Brownlow Committee would have liked—a dichotomy between politics and administration. After all the two are not separate anyway. So what makes anybody think that the reinventing government movement—the latest effort to take politics out of administration by turning grumpy citizens into happy customers—is going to change the situation?

Now there is much tinkering that the executive branch can do on its own. It can get the Social Security Administration to answer its phones within a reasonable period. It can force Internal Revenue Service auditors to be polite. But this is minor compared to the power of Congress to determine the amount of Social Security payments and the level of taxes. Members of Congress are hardly likely to give up their ability to micromanage—with all the pork for constituents and reelection prospects that implies—for vague notions of greater efficiency. Members thrive on bureaucratic red tape and the opportunities it creates for constituent service. This is why the **ombudsman/ombudswoman** movement has never gone very far in the United States. This function is happily, even joyously, performed by the elected representatives. It is quite literally what they have their staffs spend most of their time on—because it is the key to reelection.

The conclusion of all this is in essence quite simple and obvious: To reinvent government, you must also reinvent Congress. And to reinvent state government you must reinvent the state legislature. Few things are more obvious in the study of public administration than that there is a strong relation between the organization of a legislature and that of its executive branch. According to administrative analyst Harold Seidman, "One could as well ignore the laws of aerodynamics in designing an aircraft as ignore the laws of congressional dynamics in designing executive branch structure." Thus "what may appear to be structural eccentricities and anomalies within the executive branch are often nothing but mirror images of jurisdictional conflicts within the Congress. Congressional organization and executive branch organization are interrelated and constitute two halves of a single system." The British and other parliamentary systems have been able to go much further down the reinventing road precisely because they do not have this problem. There the executive and legislature, for policy purposes, are effectively one.

The Pressure for Privatization

Nothing is more challenging, indeed threatening, to public administration than the now constant specter of privatization. Indeed, to many on the political right, reinventing is virtually synonymous with privatization. There are essentially two kinds

---

ombudsman/ombudswoman An official whose job it is to investigate the complaints of the citizenry concerning public services and to ensure that these complaints will reach the attention of those officials at levels above the original providers of service. The word is Swedish, meaning a representative of the king. Ombudsmen and ombudswomen are now found in many countries at a variety of jurisdictional levels. Many of the functions of ombudsmen in American local, state, and national governments are performed by members of their respective legislatures as casework.

of privatization. First, as discussed in the keynote, there is the private provision of services with a "public" character, such as private police and private parks. These services are public only in the sense that they are available to any who can pay for them. Second, privatization is the process of returning to the private sector property or functions previously owned or performed by government. Conservative Republicans in particular tend to be in favor of privatizing those government functions that can be performed (in their opinion) less expensively or more efficiently by the private sector. Some extreme advocates of a wholesale privatization of government functions would even return Social Security, education, and public health to the private sector.

It may be somewhat of a misnomer to even label privatization as "a movement," but clearly public administration theorists and public sector practitioners are acutely aware of the increasing frequency, and of the changes involved with, "contracting out," public-private partnerships, or whatever vehicle is being used to shift or separate the production of public sector goods and services from their provision. Privatization is a broad long-term trend, often fueled with strong and emotional conservative ideology, to reduce government expenditures, to turn (or return) government assets and operations to private enterprise and thereby to increase the effectiveness and efficiency of government.

Privatization is almost always predicated on assumptions about public sector versus private sector efficiency and productivity rates. The burden of proof is often on public sector managers to explain why they are not inferior to private enterprise managers and why they should retain their functions in the face of private sector alternatives. Perhaps no responsibility is greater for public managers today than developing the evaluation and management assessment tools needed to assure critics that public sector programs and enterprises are being managed efficiently and effectively.

Generally there are three basic forms or types of government privatization:

1. The sale of government assets (such as a railroad to a corporation or public housing units to their tenants)
2. The private financing of public facilities (such as toll highways in California or Virginia)
3. The private provision of services (such as trash collection or education)

Strategies for Privatization

Privatization is the management ideology for those fearful, suspicious, or skeptical of expanding government. It is equally ideal as a tool for those who wish to reduce the size of government. Done properly, it dovetails with the first principle of the reinventing government movement—that government should be catalytic and steer (set direction) rather than row (do the work).

However, privatization sometimes means that government will neither steer nor row. It will simply get out of an activity altogether. For example, some people strongly believe that government should have absolutely no role in birth control, sex education, or the arts. These activities, if undertaken at all, should be undertaken by private citizens at their own initiative. One counterargument was made by playwright **Arthur Miller**. He tells the story of the time he was speaking in defense of government support for theater. A man in the audience then asked him: "I manufacture shoes; if the public won't buy enough of them, why shouldn't I demand government support?" Miller couldn't think of a logical and reasoned answer to this perfectly valid question. So he responded with a question: "Can you name me one classical Greek shoemaker?" Of course, Miller was emphatically not in favor of government control of the arts; but he felt as many do that government has an obligation to further its notions of civilization—and that this is often done by subsidizing the arts.

Political analyst E. S. Savas identified four strategies of privatization that together will "halt and reverse the growth of government."

1. *Load shedding*: A term that refers to government withdrawing from the provision of goods and services, and allowing them "to be supplied by the marketplace or by voluntary arrangements."

2. *Alternative delivery systems*: Arrangements "in which government plays a relatively limited role" including services provided through voluntary or self-service arrangements, competitive markets, franchises, vouchers, grants, and contracts.

3. *Imposing user charges for goods and services*: Savas argues that government should do this whenever possible in order to expose the true costs of services and, thereby, to increase the chances that alternative delivery systems will evolve.

4. *Restoring competition and minimizing government monopolies*: Savas maintains that this "requires a conscious strategy of creating alternatives and fostering a receptive climate and mental attitude in favor of giving options to the citizen-consumers of public services."

Privatization of services usually is implemented in order to take advantage of one or more hoped-for benefits: reduced costs, improved services, short-term access to expensive specialized services, avoidance of service start-up costs, greater flexibility in service policy (through reduced inflexibility of labor and equipment), increased responsiveness to consumer demand, and improved control. In addition, privatization sometimes is pursued on the ideological grounds that government should not provide goods and services that firms in the private for-profit or non-profit sector are able and willing to provide. Government should limit itself to activities that firms in the private sector cannot or will not provide.

Privatization also has limitations and problems that may lead to misuses or abuses. Policy analyst John Donahue has found that privatization brings good news and bad news. The good news is that while privatization is not a "universal corrective," it does present some "real opportunities to make public undertakings more efficient and accountable by enlisting the private sector." The bad news is that political pressures could just as easily "tend to retain for the public sector functions

---

Arthur Miller (1915–) Pulitzer Prize-winning author of *Death of a Salesman* (1949).

where privatization would make sense, and to privatize tasks that would be better left to government."

Although the potential problems differ somewhat among the various types of privatization, there is concern and some evidence that privatization tends to lead to corruption because of its susceptibility to political influence, difficulties in monitoring contract performance and outcomes, reduced control over services, and limited numbers of competitors who are willing or able to provide services. Indeed, it was exactly these kinds of problems that led to "publicization" of many privately provided services in the first place. The progressive reformers of the municipal research bureaus early in the twentieth century forcefully advocated that the government itself provide services such as street paving and trolley lines as a way of maintaining public accountability.

One of the most vocal opponents of privatization, the American Federation of State, County, and Municipal Employees (AFSCME) has published numerous examples to demonstrate that privatization results in poor performance, fraud, bribery, and graft. AFSCME and other government employee unions are fighting to keep the jobs of their members. In New York, Philadelphia, Indianapolis, and other major jurisdictions, the unions are being forced to prove that they can compete in price and quality with the private sector. They very fact that this is a matter of discussion has had a chilling effect on public employee union militancy and has inhibited demands for wage increases and lessened the likelihood of strikes.

The Nonprofit Gambit

In chess a gambit is a play, such as the sacrifice of a pawn, by which one seeks to gain a later advantage. Governments at all levels are increasingly using nonprofit organizations for just such strategic purposes. Services previously performed by government are being turned over to them—privatized since they are private organizations—so that government can both save money and get rid of perennially troublesome social programs that seek to assuage the lot of the poor and unfortunate.

The nonprofit sector is a uniquely democratic phenomenon. In some respects it is the most capitalistic of our economic responses, reacting to **marketplace failure** by filling economic voids with **volunteers** and charitable contributions. In contrast, more socialistic economies tend to meet similar types of community needs through tax-supported government programs and services. Nonprofits provide a flexible alternative to tax-supported government action.

A nonprofit organization is in many respects a concept rather than a specific entity—and it can be defined in many different ways. The primary essence of a nonprofit organization, however, is that it is organized and operated for public or

---

marketplace failure The inability of a society's free markets to provide a needed service.

volunteer A person who provides a service without compulsion or requirement and typically without compensation. However, with the growth of the voluntary sector, the definition of a volunteer appears to be changing. For example, many volunteer ambulance services and fire departments now pay volunteers for their standby time and/or for making runs. These paid persons are still called volunteers or paid volunteers so long as their work with the ambulance service is not their primary source of income.

societal purposes (such as alleviation of poverty) rather than private benefit purposes (such as return on shareholders' investments). A second essential element of a nonprofit organization is its reliance on voluntary action for most of its financial and human resources. Despite common misconceptions to the contrary—and within well-defined limitations—nonprofit organizations can realize profits from their activities and programs, and they can engage in commercial-type enterprises. However, such profits must be returned to the operations of the agency.

Nonprofit organizations range in size and structure from large international religious denominations and seminational hospital chains to small, local, nonincorporated associations of people with common interests, goals, or concerns. From a relatively narrow, legalistic point of view, we can argue that a nonprofit organization is, in effect, an organization prescribed by the laws, rules, and codes of tax exemption. From a tax exemption viewpoint, there are two basic types of nonprofit organizations:

1. Publicly supported charitable organizations that engage directly in religious, education, and social welfare programs

2. Private foundations, which tend to support other tax-exempt organizations' programs

The Reagan administration refocused the nation on the power of voluntary, nongovernmental responses to community problems. The Reagan agenda was predicated on the assumption that issue identification and action responsibility should be returned to local communities, thus increasing community reliance on nonprofits at a time when the government was simultaneously decreasing the size of, and the sector's access to, its traditional funding sources. Never in the history of the United States had the **third sector** been called upon to do so much more with so much less.

The Bush administration did not signal the arrival of less complex times for the nonprofit sector. In fact, Bush's 1988 presidential campaign may be most remembered for its "thousand points of light," a reference to volunteerism and Bush's belief that a new, more altruistic age had begun throughout the land. Bush first used this metaphor for volunteerism and charity in American life in his acceptance speech at the 1988 Republican National Convention. In his inaugural address he further defined the "points" as "all the community organizations that are spread like stars throughout the nation doing good." Peggy Noonan, who wrote Bush's acceptance speech, said in her memoirs *What I Saw at the Revolution* (1990) that the "thousand points of light . . . became Bush's shorthand way of referring to the network of helping organizations throughout the country, and it became in some circles the object of derision, or at least of good-natured spoofing." The public as well as the press were initially confused about the exact meaning of the "thousand points."

---

third sector All those organizations that fit neither in the public sector (government) nor the private sector (business); a generic phrase for the collectivity of nonprofit organizations, or organizations that institutionalize activism to deal with issues and problems that are being ignored by the public and private sectors.

The metaphor had to be explained so often that it became a symbol of the fractured syntax of Bush's speech patterns.

The national inhibition toward more direct government funding for social programs has continued. The bottom line is that because of their charitable objectives and highly motivated, often volunteer work forces, nonprofit organizations are a cheap way to fund a legislative mandate. In these instances, the subcontracting relationship to public funders renders the nonprofit organization at least indirectly accountable to the general public. In many cases, nonprofit board decision making is quite similar to that of a public utility: the nonprofit board is free to make decisions within legislative parameters.

Voluntarism and Philanthropy

Nonprofit management, third sector organizations, and independent sector programs are only new articulations of the old concepts of charity, philanthropy, and social action. The notions of charity and philanthropy are old, but how they are influencing today's society is new. In a country where the profit motive is supreme, it is both curious and inevitable that there also exists a pervasive nonprofit sector. In most other societies voluntarism does not play as significant a role in the lives of people as it does in the United States.

This Western tradition of voluntarism has roots in two diverse ideological streams:

1. The Greco-Roman heritage of emphasis on community, citizenry, and social responsibility. The Greco-Roman ideology rests on a foundation of social reform to relieve community social problems; to improve the quality of life for all in the community.

2. The Judeo-Christian belief that relationships with a higher power affect our choices, our decision making. Thus, our purpose is not to change people's lots but rather to alleviate the (preordained) suffering of others, particularly the poor. Under Judeo-Christian tradition, one does not help others solely from concern for oneself or one's neighbors, but because a deity has given instructions to do so. We have been told to love our neighbor as we love ourself: One loves one's neighbor because one loves God first and thus seeks to obey.

These two distinct, historical, ideological themes remain clearly evident today. For example, we can distinguish between: *cause advocacy*, or leadership for social reform; and *case advocacy*, or individual service to a person or a limited group of persons in need. The influence of the two ideologies has been replayed countless times and in countless ways through the history of the American nonprofit sector. See how it is reflected in the following definitions of two types of voluntarism.

- *Philanthropy* is the giving of money or self to solve social problems; it is developmental, an investment in the future, an effort to prevent future occurrences or recurrences.

- *Charity* is relieving or alleviating specific instances of suffering; it is acts of mercy or compassion.

A contemporary cartoon of Andrew Carnegie. The popular image of Carnegie is that of an enormously wealthy robber baron giving almost all of his money away before he died. But he is an important philosopher of the movement toward nonprofit organization in twentieth-century America. He sought to create institutions whereby the working classes could better themselves. But they had to be worthy of his largesse. Thus he paid for the construction of 3,000 public libraries—but the local communities had to buy the books and maintain the buildings. He donated organs to 4,000 churches—but only to those that were financially sound and well managed. He created innumerable trusts and foundations as well as museums, institutions for art and music (Carnegie Hall but not the Carnegie Delicatessen across the street), and one of the world's great universities—Carnegie-Mellon. This man who said "He who dies rich dies disgraced" did not die disgraced. And when he did die, he gave the world the secret to his success by having this engraved on his tombstone:

Here lies a man
Who knew how to enlist
In his service
Better men than himself

We tend to view these two forms of voluntary action as complementary elements in a nonprofit system. We need philanthropy as well as charity. However, this is not always the case. For example, Andrew Carnegie, an ardent philanthropist, abhorred charity. "It were better for mankind that the millions of the rich were thrown into the sea than so spent as to encourage the slothful, the drunken, the unworthy. . . . so spent, indeed, as to produce the very evils which it hopes to mitigate or cure." Yet from the Judeo-Christian charitable tradition, almhouses, charitable hospitals, orphan homes, and charitable organizations such as the Little Sisters of the Poor, the Salvation Army, the International Red Cross, and countless others, have helped relieve untold instances of human suffering.

As this nation was founded on the democratic ideals of both individualism and pluralism, our fundamental notion of how domestic problems (such as poverty, health, child raising, housing, mental illness, homelessness, and inequitable access to employment opportunities) should be addressed is returning to its historical stable state: community-level problem solving. Our basic approach to dealing with domestic problems has progressed from individual and family-level resolution, to community problem solving (as the country urbanized), to massive state intervention, and back toward community problem solving. In part this return to the past has been a negative reaction to the perceived failure of many New Deal and Great Society social programs. Thus as we approach a new century the nexus of responsibility for charity and social action once again showed signs of shifting from a national orientation back to one of local control.

From the provision of social services to the support of metropolitan symphonies, local structures now provide for the continued survival or decide the final fate of many nonprofit organizations. The role and responsibilities of the public sector have indeed contracted, in perception if not in fact. The pioneer barn-raising spirit of neighbors helping each other in good times and bad has become the foundation for domestic public policy reform. Returning responsibility to the people, allowing and requiring communities to decide which local problems should be addressed, has become vogue.

Until recently philanthropy was largely limited to a leisure-time activity of the rich. In the last century, the great industrialists/robber barons and their families, after making their fortunes, might have donated funds for this or that public improvement. Andrew Carnegie was the most systematic example of this variety of traditional philanthropists. He gave away over $350 million while he lived. This is equivalent to $6 billion today. But this century's differing attitudes toward social responsibilities and tax laws have transformed philanthropy from the altruistic concern of a single individual or family to a huge enterprise that affects and sustains a major portion of our economy and our society.

To be sure, wealthy people as well as people of all economic means contribute money, time, energy, and property for socially desirable purposes. But the largest share of the available philanthropic dollar goes to endow foundations. There are tax advantages to the donor in doing this. Therefore, using a foundation helps to multiply the total amount of philanthropic funds available for good works.

Now that philanthropy has to a large extent been institutionalized, its role has changed from random charitable or community developmental efforts to systematic efforts to find causes for focused efforts; to alleviate poverty in certain regions, control world population growth, or preserve rare artifacts, to state only three examples. The large-scale nature of philanthropy has caused it to become bureaucratized. No longer will an emotional charitable appeal suffice. A systematic proposal must be written and maneuvered through the various levels of approval of the requesting organization to the granting organization's often equally elaborate bureaucracy. Thus the alternative to government becomes, by trying to do what government has so far failed to do, more like the government than it finds comfortable to admit.

A Comparative Perspective: The Revolution in the British Machinery of Government 1980–1999

The British machinery of government differs in important respects from that of the United States. It is a system of cabinet, rather than presidential, government. In the British system the cabinet, the collectivity of ministers, is the ultimate seat of authority, although its existence and role are not provided for in a written constitution. Each minister is an elected member of Parliament, a politician of the ruling party of the day, and is assigned his or her post by the prime minister. The clear division of powers between the executive, legislative, and judicial branches is blurred in the British system since the executive and the legislature are more closely tied. A standoff between the executive and the legislature is generally unlikely, since the cabinet and its ministers (who hold executive power) are elected from the party with the majority in the lower house of Parliament (which holds legislative power).

Just as the U.S. system puts the three dominant classes of government agencies within the Executive Office of the President, the national executive departments, and independent public bodies, we find in the British system the parallels of Crown agencies, portfolio (cabinet) departments, and public bodies. As in the United States, some of the oldest departments, like the Treasury and the Foreign Office, have long and independent traditions, and the bureaucracy of "Whitehall" has had a reputation for intransigence and self-serving behavior no less negative than that of the U.S. bureaucracy.

By 1980 the British central machinery of government had evolved into the ideal candidate for substantial reform. It had become large, unwieldy, costly, and secretive. The numbers of public bodies had grown to a point where it was difficult for any one person to understand what they did or to whom they were accountable, much less to assess whether their activities served the public interest or some narrower sectional interest. The legacy of the **nationalization** of a number of heavy industries that had not been well managed in the 1960s and 1970s represented a serious problem for the country, and their poor performance seemed to play a big

---

nationalization The taking over by government of a significant segment of a country's private sector industry, land, transportation, and so on, usually with compensation to the former owners. Socialist governments tend to favor extensive nationalization. Indeed, the level of nationalization is an accurate measure of the degree of a nation's socialism. Ironically, even conservative and nonsocialist governments have resorted to nationalization, but in an effort to save a collapsing firm or service, rather than in ideological fervor.

part in the overall decline in British economic performance. With this in view, significant reform was necessary. The British system of unitary government in which there are few of the checks and balances that exist in the U.S. Constitution and in U.S. policymaking behavior provided circumstances in which far-reaching reform could be undertaken.

The most famous of these reforms, privatization, was not part of **Margaret Thatcher**'s explicit platform when she was elected in 1979, although it was certainly part of the Conservative Party's program. Privatization was particularly focused on the nationalized industries and utilities. In Britain these included the petroleum, aerospace, and automotive industries, as well as gas, electricity, and water. Since the 1980s, these were successively sold to the private sector.

The massive reform of the national government departments, the "Next Steps" program, was launched in 1988. By 1992 more than half the British civil service—290,000 people—was included in the seventy-six new Executive Agencies. In a U.S. context, this would be comparable to a million federal government employees being reassigned to several hundred new agencies whose executives could be immediately removed if they did not achieve their performance targets. Some former departments, like Inland Revenue (equivalent to the U.S. Internal Revenue Service), were split into as many as 34 Executive Agencies, and each of these was pursuing stated quantitative performance targets. While these reforms are relatively recent, they do represent a disciplined and systematic program of reforming one of the most difficult parts of the public sector to reach and to manage—that is, the work conducted normally within civil service departments, albeit the "operational" rather than the "policy" aspects of that work. In effect, half of the traditional civil service has been placed in corporate-like structures where they will be treated more like corporate employees than public servants. This is the essence of corporatization—more flexibility for managers and less job security for all.

The results to date are encouraging, although the "arm's length relationship"—meaning no political interference—central to the Executive Agency concept can sometimes break down under sufficient political pressure. Within a decade, the British public sector was changed beyond recognition, with machinery of government changes of the most profound significance taking place. Overall, according to British professor Christopher Pollitt, "in the decade from 1979 to 1990, 800,000 employees were transferred into the private sector, and the share of the gross domestic product accounted for by state-owned industries fell from 11 percent in 1979 to 5.5 percent in 1990." In effect the Thatcher revolution cut the British public sector in half.

This revolution in the machinery of government continued even after the revolutionary party was voted out of office. In 1997 when the Labour party led by Prime Minister Tony Blair took over the British government, he declared, to the chagrin of

---

Margaret Thatcher (1925–) The conservative prime minister of Great Britain from 1979 to 1990. Elected as the first female prime minister in British history, she then held that office longer than any other twentieth-century British politician. Her championing of free-market economic policies coupled with an assertive role in world affairs, created an ideological style of leadership that came to be known as "Thatcherism."

many of the traditionally socialists members of his party, that the reforms would stay. He espoused a "third way" that went beyond the old left's preoccupation with state control but not so far as the far right's "belief that free markets are the answer to every problem." He has sought to have his "New Labour" party "rebrand Britain." And a major part of this "rebranding" was Labour's acceptance of the Conservative party's radical reforms of the machinery of government.

A key concept in the British reforms is market testing—a process that requires agencies to buy goods and services from the private sector if savings are to be had. This has led to private contractors building and managing prisons, the Passport Agency hiring outside companies to print passports, and the Inland Revenue contracting out the management of its computer databases. According to reinventing guru David Osborne, "the U.K. has gone further in reinventing government than any other country [other] than New Zealand." True, New Zealand has jumped into the deep end of the reinventing pool, but it is so small in population (less than 3.5 million) that its reinventing efforts are more comparable to those of big municipal rather than national governments.

In Britain, the late nineties saw the headlong dive into privatization slowing a little. The incoming Labour government of Tony Blair in its July 1998 White Paper on local government scrapped the compulsory local government outsourcing the Conservatives had insisted on, replacing it with a broader concept of "Best Value." In April 1999, a true watershed was reached when Conservative opposition leader William Hague, in a major public lecture, conceded that privatization should not displace predominant public funding in health, education, and welfare. This does not mean that the pendulum of privatization will swing back to the division between public and private functions which once existed, but it does indicate that, in Britain at least, a practical rather than an ideological stance on these issues is emerging on both sides of the political fence.

In the United States, the reinventing government movement renewed interest in bureaucratic innovation in general, and in aspects of commercialization in particular, but it would be fair to say that the United States has not been a leader in changes in this area. Indeed, if you read the formally stated "Principles of the National Performance Review," espoused by Vice President Al Gore, you will see that they could easily and honestly be labeled "made in Great Britain."

But the proof of all this is in the implementation. Great Britain is way ahead in this game. Of course, it started a decade earlier. Nevertheless, the U.S. machinery of government is radically different, and there is no guarantee that the United States could ever catch up. Different political cultures and different machinery require different administrative solutions.

As students and practitioners of public administration, we must thus try to be fully aware of the wealth of new management ideas and administrative experiments happening around the world—not so much to be able to imitate as to adapt. Our first responsibility is to look at the machinery of government in our own jurisdiction; to imagine ourselves having to advise on the best possible structural arrangements to serve it, and to deploy a rich knowledge of contemporary innovations to ensure that our leaders are well advised before they finalize new arrangements. All new structural arrangements have vast implications for the cohesiveness or possible balkanization of society. The installation of new machinery of government is not a light matter. In this regard we must always keep in mind the advice of that preeminent administrative analyst, Niccolo Machiavelli, who offered this advice in *The Prince* (1572): "There is nothing more difficult to take in hand, more perilous to conduct, or more uncertain in its success, than to take the lead in the introduction of a new order of things."

Summary

The machinery of government consists of all of the structural arrangements provided by a constitutional provision or a statute requiring the delivery of government services. These arrangements are not immutable. The functions of public agencies can and should be altered from time to time to reflect emerging needs and changing values.

Executive branch machinery has three main categories of organizations: (1) executive office agencies, (2) executive departments, and (3) independent public bodies. State and local arrangements parallel those of the federal level.

The advent of the 1990s reinventing government movement has made reorganization once again fashionable. But this follows a long tradition of appointed bodies given the task of recommending improvements in governing structures. The Brownlow Committee of the 1930s and the Hoover Commissions of the 1940s and 1950s have now been followed by the National Performance Review of the 1990s. But because of the micromanagers in the Congress, executive agency reforms can never get too far ahead of the legislative will.

Privatization has two faces: (1) the private provision of services for those who can afford to pay for them, and (2) the returning to the private sector functions previously performed by government. The various aspects of privatization are pivotal to reinventing government efforts throughout the world. The United States has a uniquely large nonprofit sector that it has been able to use as a vehicle for privatization.

Key Concepts

Brownlow Committee A committee appointed by President Franklin D. Roosevelt in 1936 for the purpose of diagnosing the staffing needs of the president and making appropriate recommendations for the reorganization of the executive branch.

bureau movement The efforts of progressive reformers early in the twentieth century to apply scientific methods to municipal problems. Their efforts led to the creation of research bureaus, which in turn created the academic field of public administration.

cabinet The heads of the executive departments of a jurisdiction who report to and advise its chief executive; examples would include the president's cabinet, the governor's cabinet, and the mayor's cabinet.

cabinet government The British system, whereby the cabinet as a whole, rather than only the prime minister who heads it, is considered the executive, and the cabinet is collectively responsible to the Parliament for its performance. In addition, the cabinet ministers are typically drawn from among the majority party's members in Parliament, whereas in the United States the cabinet secretaries are only from the executive branch.

constitutional architecture The administrative arrangements created by a government's constitution—from the separation of powers to the requirement that specific departments be created or services performed.

Dillon's rule   The criteria developed by state courts to determine the nature and extent of powers granted to local governments.

Executive Office of the President (EOP)   The umbrella office consisting of the top presidential staff agencies that provide the president help and advice in carrying out his major responsibilities. The EOP was created by President Franklin D. Roosevelt under the authority of the Reorganization Act of 1939. Since then, presidents have used executive orders, reorganization plans, and legislative initiatives to reorganize, expand, or contract the EOP.

Grace Commission   An attempt made by the Reagan administration to have business leaders study and reform the federal government; much was studied, little was reformed.

Hoover Commissions   The post-World War II efforts to reorganize the federal government.

nonprofit organization   An organization created and operated for public or societal purposes (such as alleviation of poverty) rather than private benefit purposes (such as return on shareholders' investments).

privatization   The process of returning to the private sector property or functions previously owned or performed by government.

regulatory commission   An independent agency created by a government to regulate some aspect of economic life.

reinventing government   The latest manifestation of the progressive tradition of continuously improving government—this time with an emphasis on privatization.

Bibliography

American Federation of State, County, and Municipal Employees. (1984). *Passing the Bucks: The Contracting out of Public Services*. Washington: AFSCME.

Blair, Tony. (1998). "Third Way, Better Way," *Washington Post National Weekly* (October 5).

Blumberg, Stephen. (1981). "Seven Decades of Public Administration: A Tribute to Luther Gulick." *Public Administration Review* 41 (March-April).

Brownlow, Louis. (1958). *A Passion for Anonymity: The Autobiography of Louis Brownlow*. Chicago: University of Chicago Press.

Carnegie, Andrew. (1900). *The Gospel of Wealth*. New York: Century.

Donahue, John M. (1989). *The Privatization Decision*. New York: Basic Books.

Egan Timothy. (1995). "Many Seek Security in Private Communities." *New York Times* (September 3).

Goodnow, Frank J. (1900). *Politics and Administration: A Study in Governments*. New York: Russell and Russell.

Gore, Al. (1993). *From Red Tape to Results: Creating a Government that Works Better and Costs Less*. Report of the National Performance Review. Washington: Government Printing Office.

Kaufman, Herbert. (1976). *Are Government Organizations Immortal?* Washington: Brookings Institution.

Kettner, P. M., and L. L. Martin. (1987). *Purchase of Service Contracting*. Beverly Hills, CA: Sage.

Lind, Michael. (1995). "To Have and Have Not: Notes on the Progress of the American Class War." *Harper's* (June).

Marlin, J. (1984). *Contracting for Municipal Services*. New York: Wiley.

McKenzie, Evan. (1994). *Privatopia: Homeowner Associations and the Rise of Residential Private Government*. New Haven: Yale University Press.

Meriam, Lewis. (1939). *Reorganization of the National Government: What Does It Involve?* Washington: Brookings Institution.

Miller, Arthur. (1995). "To Newt on Art." *The Nation* (July 31/August 7).

Morgan, D. R., and R. E. England. (1988). "The Two Faces of Privatization." *Public Administration Review* 48.

Mosher, Frederick C. (1967). *Government Reorganization: Cases and Commentary*. Indianapolis: Bobbs-Merrill.

Osborne, David, and Ted Gaebler. (1992). *Reinventing Government*. Reading, MA: Addison-Wesley.

Pollitt, Christopher. (1996). "Antistatist Reforms and New Administrative Directions: Public Administration in the United Kingdom." *Public Administration Review* 56 (January-February).

Preer, Robert. (1986). "Town Meetings Don't Work." *Washington Post* (June 13).

Rehfuss, J. A. (1989). *Contracting Out in Government*. San Francisco: Jossey-Bass.

Rosenbloom, David H. (1993). "Have an Administrative Rx? Don't Forget the Politics!" *Public Administration Review* 53 (November-December).

Ross, Bernard H. (1998). "Metropolitan Organization," *International Encyclopedia of Public Policy and Administration*, ed. Jay M. Shafritz. Boulder, CO: Westview Press.

Salant, Tanis Janes. (1998). "County," *International Encyclopedia of Public Policy and Administration*, ed. Jay M. Shafritz. Boulder, CO: Westview Press.

Savas, E. S. (1982). *Privatizing the Public Sector: How to Shrink Government*. Chatham, NJ: Chatham House.

Savoie, Donald J. (1994). *Thatcher Reagan Mulroney: In Search of a New Bureaucracy*. Pittsburgh: University of Pittsburgh Press.

Seidman, Harold. (1980). *Politics, Position, and Power: The Dynamics of Federal Organization*, 3rd ed. New York: Oxford University Press.

Szanton, Peter L., ed. (1981). *Federal Reorganization: What Have We Learned?* Chatham, NJ: Chatham House.

Weisband, Edward, and Thomas M. Frank. (1975). *Resignation in Protest*. New York: Viking Press.

Recommended Books

Downs, George W., and Patrick D. Larkey. (1986). *The Search for Government Efficiency: From Hubris to Helplessness*. Philadelphia: Temple University Press. An explanation of why efforts to reform government tend to operte in ignorance of previous reform efforts and why all such schemes have only "a miniscule chance of successful implementation."

Ingraham, Patricia W., James R. Thompson, Ronald P. Sanders, eds. (1998). *Transforming Government: Lessons from the Reinvention Laboratories*. San Francisco: Jossey-Bass. A collection of essays on the lessons for reform derived from the federal government's reinventing government effort.

Light, Paul C. (1997). *The Tides of Reform: Making Government Work, 1945–1995*. New Haven, CT: Yale University Press. The history of reforming the federal government in the fifty years after World War II.

Osborne, David, and Peter Plastrik. (1998). *Banishing Bureaucracy: The Five Strategies for Reinventing Government*. New York: Penguin Putnam. More stories of government organization turnarounds; touted as the "sequel" to the 1992 *Reinventing Government* because Osborne is the senior author of both books.

Smith, Steven R., and Michael Lipsky. (1993). *Nonprofits for Hire*. Cambridge, MA: Harvard University Press. The how and why of governmental use of nonprofit organizations.

Related Web Sites

Alliance for Redesigning Government
http://www.alliance.napawash.org/alliance/index.html

Constitutions of the World
http://www.psr.keele.ac.uk/const.htm#america

Federalist Papers
http://www.yale.edu/lawweb/avalon/federal/fed.htm

International City/County Management Association
http://www.icma.org

Library of Congress' state and local governments page
http://lcweb.loc.gov/global/state/stategov.html

National Center for Charitable Statistics
http://nccs.urban.org/

National Partnership for Reinventing Government
http://www.npr.gov/

Privatization and contracting out
http://www.afscme.org/afscme/bargtabl/cbr3973.htm

U.S. Government Manual Online
http://www.access.gpo.gov/nara/browse-gm.html

4

Intergovernmental Relations

Keynote: The Age of Devolution

The Evolution of Federal Systems

Alliances and Confederations • Defining Intergovernmental Relations

The Fundamental Settlement

The Constitution • The European Union

The American Federal System

Three Categories of Governments

The Structure of Intergovernmental Relations

The Effects of Pluralism • The Marble-Cake Metaphor • The Advisory Commission on Intergovernmental Relations

Dynamic Federalism

Dual Federalism • Cooperative Federalism • Creative Federalism • New Federalism • New New Federalism

Intergovernmental Management

Picket Fence Federalism • Councils of Government • Mandate Mania • The Cost of Compliance

Fiscal Federalism—Following the Money

The Theory of Fiscal Federalism • Grant Programs • From Contractive to Coercive Federalism

The Devolution Revolution

The Public-Choice Solution • The Race to the Bottom

Keynote: The Age of Devolution

It was a disquieting time in the United States. Many of the states in the federal system were complaining that the central government in Washington was violating the spirit if not the letter of the Constitution. There was a resurgence in the concept of states' rights, strong feelings that federal involvement within the states was both oppressive and inefficient, and that republican ideals would be best served with a smaller, less intrusive national government. These same conditions were occurring in the early 1860s, and they would emerge again in the mid-1990s. In the first instance this controversy over intergovernmental relations began its resolution with the election of Abraham Lincoln and was finally resolved by civil war. In the second instance the public sought to resolve these issues by voting for a Newt Gingrich–led Republican Congress.

Now Speaker of the House Gingrich is no Lincoln, but both men had to grapple with the core issues of the nature of the American federal system. Lincoln essentially said that devolution (returning powers to the states) can only go so far—and that secession by the eleven southern states of the confederacy was too far. More than one hundred thirty years later, Gingrich and company essentially said that centralization had gone too far—it was time to move decidedly in the other direction.

Wars, whatever else they might be (horrible, lethal, unnecessary!), are great centralizers. The world wars of the twentieth century, being total in the Clausewitzian sense (a mobilization of the entire society), have been the greatest engines of centralized governmental control of all time. Wartime governments not only told their conscripted soldiers when, where, and how they were to fight, they also regulated their home fronts to such an extent that people were told, in detail, how they were to live: how much fuel they could burn, how much food they could eat, and even where they could work.

This century's response to crises, whether military or economic, most often has been more central government. Sometimes the efforts were benign, as they were when Franklin D. Roosevelt presented the New Deal of the 1930s in the United States or when Clement Attlee led his Labour Party to socialized medicine by creating the National Health Service in the United Kingdom in the late 1940s. Often centralization has proved to be malignant, as it was with Hitler's Germany or Stalin's Soviet Union. The ending of a century that has been dominated by militarism—from the beginning of World War I in 1914 to the demise of the Soviet Union in 1991—is bringing with it renewed demands for decentralization. With the diminution of the threat from without, states throughout the world are giving more thought to demands for greater freedom within. It is a worldwide phenomenon fueled both by the end of the Cold War and the resurgence of a previously suppressed nationalism. The Soviet Union, Yugoslavia, and Czechoslovakia all disintegrated as political entities. They have been replaced by multiple smaller states that express the previously pent up tribal or nationalistic yearnings of their peoples.

On a less cataclysmic scale, similar nationalistic movements are visible even in the most stable states. Scottish and Welsh nationalists want greater autonomy from the

British central government. Quebec has been talking for decades about seceding from Canada unless it gets greater autonomy. In the United States there has been a resurgence of demands for states' rights. Once a code word for opposition to federal civil rights legislation, the phrase is now political shorthand for those who seek to decrease the powers of the federal government and increase the powers of the states. This multifaceted international movement to reduce the power of national governments, to reduce the power of presidents and prime ministers, and to concomitantly increase the power of legislatures and subnational governments is a direct result of the reduction of external threats. In wartime, whether hot or cold, political leaders get extraordinary powers and deference. Peace diminishes both them and their office. Without the need to rally around the commander-in-chief, American national politics seems to be returning to a government dominated more by its legislative than by its executive branch. This was the normal condition of American government during most of the nineteenth century (the Civil War being the major period of exception).

The key word in the new American thrust toward devolution is *mandate*. Normally this word refers to the perceived popular or electoral support for a public program, political party, or a particular politician. U.S. presidents who win elections by overwhelming majorities may rightly feel the vote was a mandate to carry out their proposed policies. But mandate has another equally important meaning; it is one level of government requiring another to offer—or pay for—a program as a matter of law or as a prerequisite to partial or full funding for either the program in question or other programs. It is the federal government ordering, by means of passing a law, state governments to reduce air pollution. Or it is a state government ordering, by means of passing a law, municipal governments to recycle trash collections. Mandates are orders pure and simple. And the movement toward devolution is spurred on by jurisdictions and constituencies that increasingly resent taking such orders. In the United States these jurisdictions cite the "fact" that they are sovereign states and shouldn't have to put up with this administrative tyranny.

Hypocrisy is what makes it possible for the states to demand federal action and funding on this or that program while complaining that federal regulations on their use of federal funds insult their sovereignty. It is like a grown child demanding his or her parents are obligated to pay for this and that while at the same time insisting that he or she be treated like an independent adult. Neither the states nor such children can have it both ways. As Shakespeare's King Lear reluctantly learned: "How sharper than a serpent's tooth it is to have a thankless child." But who is the child here? The federal government is the creature (if not the child) of the states. Yet the states, like old King Lear, gave up their sovereign pretensions to "form a more perfect union." Now they complain when things are not perfect enough. But that was not the agreement. The deal made at the 1787 Constitutional Convention was "more perfect"—not perfect. Those who might say to the states "Quit your whining and act your age" miss the point. The whining, the complaining, the hypocrisy is an inherent and beneficial part of a never-ending process of intergovernmental give and take. Besides, the complaining often leads to useful change.

Perhaps the best example of this give-and-take aspect of the federal system is that if a government function is not working at one level, it can be shifted onto another level to see if it can be done any better. A good example of a program that has bounced between the intergovernmental levels is welfare. When the Social Security Act was passed in 1935, it included a small program to help widows and orphans. This was the origin of Aid to Families with Dependent Children (AFDC), the program by which the federal government matched state spending on welfare. AFDC provided federal funds, administered by the states, for children living with a parent or a relative who met state standards of need. The program was controversial because of charges that it not only promoted illegitimacy but also encouraged fathers to abandon their families so they could become eligible for AFDC. In 1994 more than 14 million people were receiving AFDC, up from just over 2 million in 1955.

Claiming that the system had produced "welfare queens," women conceiving children out of wedlock to qualify for AFDC benefits, and a cycle of generational poverty encouraged by the welfare system, the Republican-controlled Congress in 1995 decided to act. It would change the system by giving the problem back to the states. Welfare was a local problem to begin with. The tradition of the county poor farm or workhouse can be traced back to sixteenth-century England. The money spent on AFDC would be converted to block grants with which the states in their 50 varieties of wisdom would decide who was worthy of the new style welfare and under what conditions. In essence most of the federal strings would be removed, and the states would overall get less than before, but they would have far greater discretion on how to spend it. Thus a comprehensive welfare reform bill was passed by the Congress in 1996. This repealed the entitlement aspect of AFDC and was signed into law by President Clinton. The states—with the encouragement of the federal government—are now busy simultaneously reinventing welfare programs while they seek to discourage the expansion of the welfare rolls by holding fathers more responsible for supporting their children. Simply put, the problem has proved so difficult that the Congress is giving up on it and seeking to dump it back on the states. Ah, federalism!

Two years after the 1996 enactment of the Welfare Reform Law it is being hailed as a great success. States are reporting dramatic declines in their welfare rolls—27 percent overall. Some states have had astounding drops. For example, Idaho dropped 76 percent and Wyoming 72 percent. One reason is the booming economy. Even without reform we would expect welfare rolls to decrease when jobs are plentiful. But other more lasting factors are at work as well—factors that suggest that the rolls will not "automatically" go up to with a modest economic downturn. First, devolution means that welfare isn't what it used to be; most importantly, it is no longer an entitlement. According to Vobejda and Havemann, in at least three dozen states welfare managers actively seek to prevent applicants from getting welfare once they apply.

"Welfare offices are urging applicants to ask for help from relatives instead of signing up for government assistance, writing one time emergency checks in place of monthly benefits, or requiring applicants to spend weeks searching for work before they receive their first welfare payment." This raises questions "of whether

This 1937 picture with its juxtaposition of rich and poor has long symbolized welfare in a land of plenty. But the photo, taken in Louisville, Kentucky, is triply misleading. First, it is not about traditional welfare at all; the people waiting in the bread line were the victims of flooding. Second, it implies that most welfare recipients are black, when the absolute majority of welfare recipients are white. This was as true in 1937 as it is today. According to the U.S. Census Bureau figures, twice as many whites are welfare recipients than blacks: 23 million versus 12 million. However, just about a third of all blacks receive welfare while only about ten percent of whites do. (*Charlotte Observer*, September 11, 1997). And last, the U.S. does not have a "world's highest standard of living" when judged by overall social indicators such as infant mortality. A United Nations report ranked the U.S. 4th in overall quality of life (behind Canada, France and Norway) and 17th in poverty levels behind almost all of the major industrialized states despite the fact that the U.S. has the highest per capita income. It is just that this income isn't as evenly distributed as in the 16 other countries with lower poverty rates (*Pittsburgh Post Gazette*, September 9, 1998) •

they have found jobs on their own, never truly needed them in the first place, or have been scared off or intimidated from applying for help that their children genuinely require."

Such diversion tactics are now commonplace. California, Kansas, Florida, Oregon, and New York, among other states, all seek to direct applicants into jobs or one time cash payments (they cannot then reapply for a prescribed period). This leads to the second major new factor. The traditional welfare office is evolving into a new administrative animal. According to Rachel L. Swarns, in New York City "job centers are replacing welfare offices. Financial planners are replacing caseworkers. And the entire bureaucracy is morphing into the Family Independence Administration. In truth the same workers still do business in the same buildings, but the city has been infected by a name-changing frenzy that has been sweeping the country. Massachusetts' Department of Public Welfare is now the Department of Transitional Assistance. Florida's welfare program is now the Work and Gain Economic Self-Sufficiency Program." Indicative of this major change in terminology is the 1998 decision of the American Public Welfare Association (which represents social service agencies) to change its name after 66 years to the American Public Human Services Association. Devolution may not yet have killed welfare in fact, but it has certainly killed it in name.

Welfare is just one example of how the age of devolution is bringing us back to the first principles of the age of revolution. Alexander Hamilton, the high priest of an energetic national government among the founding fathers, felt strongly that essentially local issues, as he wrote in *The Federalist*, No. 17 "can never be desirable cares of a general jurisdiction." Hamilton believed it "improbable that there should exist a disposition in the federal councils to usurp the [local] powers . . . because the attempt to exercise those powers would be as troublesome as it would be nugatory; and the possession of them, for that reason, would contribute nothing to the dignity, to the importance, or to the splendor of the national government." Will a rollback of the welfare state contribute to the "dignity" and "splendor" of the federal government? That depends if it is your welfare that is being rolled back! According to political analyst Gareth G. Cook at least one thing is certain: "Devolution is the theme that runs through nearly all of the Republican's high-profile domestic initiatives. . . . Whether it's cops on the street, environmental protection, or school lunches for poor kids, the Republican solution is to devolve it."

The Evolution of Federal Systems

History indicates clearly that the principal factor in the formation of federal systems of government has been a common external threat. Tribes, villages, cities, colonies, or states have joined together in voluntary unions to defend themselves. However, not all systems so formed have been federal. A true federal system such as that in the United States must have the following features:

1. a written constitution that divides government powers between the central government and the constituent governments, giving substantial powers to each;

2. levels of government, through their own instrumentalities, exercising power directly over citizens (unlike a confederation, in which only subnational units act directly on citizens while the central government acts only on the subnational governments); and

3. a constitutional distribution of powers that cannot be changed unilaterally by any level of government or by the ordinary process of legislation.

Alliances and Confederations

In the beginning there was the alliance, a coalition of states agreeing to help each other in the event of war or crises. Alliances do not only involve cooperation and aggregation of capabilities; they are generally directed toward an actual or potential enemy and the actual or potential use of force. The agreement on which an alliance is based is often embodied formally in a treaty, but it can also be based upon a tacit or informal understanding. Alliances can be between states that are relatively equal in power and involve mutual security guarantees, or they can be between unequal states, in which case the more powerful state generally extends a unilateral guarantee to the less powerful one. This is always a dangerous situation for the weaker state. Too often a willingness to protect and preserve has turned into a desire to take over and annex. Alliances differ in duration, number of members, and the extent to which there are common interests among the members. The greater the common interest, the stronger and more durable the alliance is likely to be.

Then came the confederation, a group of independent states that delegate powers on selected issues to a central government. In a confederation, the central government is deliberately limited, designed to be inherently weak, and has few independent powers. The United States was a confederation from 1781 to 1789. But the central government was so ineffectual in dealing with problems such as **Shays' Rebellion** and interstate commerce that the Constitutional Convention of 1787 was called to discuss the inadequacies of confederation government. To the great surprise of many who sent them to the convention, the delegates recommended not improvements in the confederation—which was expected—but a whole new form of national government.

Defining Intergovernmental Relations

Finally, when there was need for even stronger bonding among governments, along came federalism, a system of governance in which a national, overarching government shares power with subnational or state governments. Intergovernmental relations is federalism in action. It is the complex network of day-to-day interrelationships among the governments within a federal system. It is the political, fiscal, programmatic, and administrative processes by which higher units of government share revenues and other resources with lower units of government, generally accompanied by special conditions that the lower units must satisfy as prerequisites to receiving the assistance.

In essence, intergovernmental relations are the sets of policies and mechanisms by which the interplay between different levels of government serving a common geographical area is managed. Such relations reflect the basic constitutional framework that links the levels of government, as well as dynamic contemporary factors including relative power, financial strengths, ethnic divisions, geographical factors, and so on. The essence of this constitutional framework is well captured by this famous 1763 statement by **William Pitt**, the elder, in the British House of Lords: "The

---

Shays' Rebellion A futile armed revolt (1786–1787) led by Daniel Shays (1747–1825), a Revolutionary War officer, in New England to protest the discontent of small farmers over debts and taxes. The rebellion was never a serious military threat, but it raised concern over the inadequacy of the Articles of Confederation to handle internal disorders and thus helped to create support for a stronger national government.

William Pitt (1708–1778) The First Earl of Chatham, known as the Great Commoner for his leadership in the House of Commons. The City of Pittsburgh is named in his honor. Historians call him "the elder" because his son with the same name was later prime minister.

poorest man may in his cottage bid defiance to all the forces of the Crown. It may be frail—its roof may shake—the wind may blow through it—the storm may enter—the rain may enter—but the King of England cannot enter!—all his force dares not cross the threshold of the ruined tenement!"

In the United States today the "crown"—the federal government—may not interfere unless this "poorest man" commits the proverbial "federal offense" and federal officials obtain a search or arrest warrant. And only local officials can obtain warrants for local crimes. This is why the investigation of President John F. Kennedy's 1963 **assassination** was undertaken by the local police in Dallas, Texas. In the eyes of the law, Kennedy was just the victim of a local murder. In 1963 it was a federal crime to rob a bank if it was insured, as most are, by a federal agency, but it was not a federal crime to murder a president. (It is now!) After the local police so botched the investigation that they inadvertently spawned a conspiracy theory industry, Congress made it a federal offense to threaten or attack a president, vice president, or their immediate families. The point here is that within a federal system different levels of government often perform similar functions, law enforcement in this case, that are constitutionally separate. Each level has constitutional limitations.

An understanding of intergovernmental relations is essential for every public administrator, since this area defines the scope and territory of the administrative world in which he or she lives. It is not just a question of territorial boundaries, though the boundaries of all political units are established by laws, constitutions, and accords, the study of which is central to intergovernmental relations. It is equally a question of functional allocations, because most countries have found it necessary to distinguish among national, regional, and local issues and to allocate them in various ways to different levels of government. This allocation, the question of who does what and with what resources, is the essential core, the heart of intergovernmental relations.

The Fundamental Settlement

The most critical dimension of intergovernmental relations, that which forms and shapes the context of every government, is the fundamental settlement or accord by which the government was created. Such accords can never ultimately be unilateral—they must always involve a settlement between a plurality of communities. Federalism, like most institutional forms, is a solution of, or an attempt to solve, a certain kind of problem of political organization. Viable federal systems accommodate regional or subsystem diversity, thereby enhancing the strength of the greater federation. Both the United States and the European Community offer illustrations

---

assassination The deliberate murder of someone, especially of a politically prominent personage for political motives. The original assassins were thirteenth-century Muslims whose main goal was the murder of Christian Crusaders and other political rivals. Assassination is a time-honored though not honorable way of removing people from public office. Presidents Lincoln, Garfield, McKinley, and Kennedy were assassinated; Presidents Theodore Roosevelt, Franklin Roosevelt, Truman, Ford, and Reagan all narrowly escaped death in various attempted assassinations.

of settlements whose terms determine the nature, scope, and powers of the governments involved.

The Constitution

The 1789 Constitution of the United States is the oldest written constitution continuously in force and an enduring example to the rest of the world of the benefits and effectiveness of such a well-crafted document. Its famous beginning, "We the people," asserts that the source of its authority is the people as opposed to the states. It then assigns powers to the various branches of government and in doing so structures the government. It limits the powers that any branch may have and allows each branch to check and balance the others. Most significantly, it denies certain powers to the national government, reserving them for the states and the people. But aside from its legal force as law and its physical existence as a piece of fading parchment in the National Archives, the U.S. Constitution is the national icon, the premier symbol of American freedom and governance; above all, it represents the collective political will of the American people over two centuries to maintain their republican form of government. Nevertheless, because of the nature of judicial review, the Constitution is ultimately, as New York governor Charles Evans Hughes asserted in 1907, "what the judges [of the Supreme Court] say it is." It is as Thomas Jefferson angrily wrote in a September 6, 1819, letter to Spencer Roane, "a mere thing of wax in the hands of the judiciary, which they may twist and shape into any form they please."

The 85 essays in *The Federalist* published in 1787–1788, are the classic commentary on the U.S. Constitution and the theories behind it. They are considered by many political scientists to be the most important work of political theory written in the United States—the one product of the American mind counted among the classics of political philosophy. The papers were originally newspaper articles written by Alexander Hamilton, James Madison, and John Jay (all under the pseudonym **Publius**) to encourage New York to ratify the new Constitution. The papers reflect the genius of the balance achieved in the American system between the views of Madison, an exponent of limited government, and Hamilton, an admirer of an energetic national government. It has been suggested that the papers reflected the thinking of the minority of Americans who wanted a more nationalist government than that desired by most of the post-revolutionary generation.

Jay wrote only a few of the Federalist papers but he was the first chief justice of the United States—a job he considered so insignificant that he resigned to become governor of New York. His resignation had the beneficial effect of making room for a later chief justice, John Marshall, the Revolutionary War soldier who became the third chief justice of the Supreme Court and, by almost universal agreement, the one who did the most to establish the independent authority of the Court. From 1801 to 1835, he led the struggle for the Court to be the final arbiter of the Constitution

---

Publius An ancient Roman who was famous for his devotion to republican government. It was common in the late eighteenth century for political writers to use a pseudonym of ancient lineage that reflected their political leanings.

and, by sheer force of will and legal cunning, made the federal judiciary a true check on the power of the other two branches.

Marshall, in a wide-ranging series of decisions, helped to create the American style of federalism. For example, in 1819 in *McCulloch v. Maryland* the Court upheld the implied powers granted to the Congress by the **necessary and proper clause** of the Constitution, upheld the supremacy of the national government in carrying out functions assigned to it by the Constitution, and established the doctrine of intergovernmental tax immunity. In stating that "the power to tax is the power to destroy," the Court held that the Bank of the United States was not subject to taxation by the State of Maryland. And "destroy" is exactly what the Maryland State Legislature wanted to do to the bank. It viewed the "Monster Bank" so much the tool of the privileged elite and of the still hated British interests that it specifically passed a law taxing the bank's operations in Maryland in the hopes of crippling it.

The European Union

Sometimes the fundamental settlement occurs all at once, as it did with the creation of the American federal system by the U.S. Constitution. Sometimes it evolves over a series of accords, as it has with the European Union, which is still evolving. It may eventually become a "sort of United States of Europe" as Winston Churchill envisioned in 1946; or it could fracture in warring (both hot or cold) camps as it did so often in the twentieth century. Remember, the U.S. experience with federalism was not a ride in a continuous direction. The Civil War was a major setback. Of course, after the war the Union was stronger than ever. Historian James M. McPherson reminds us in his *Battle Cry of Freedom* (1988), that "Before 1861 the two words 'United States' were generally rendered as a plural noun: 'the United States *are* a republic.' The war marked a transition of the United States to a singular noun." Only after the Civil War were we "one nation under God, indivisible" as it says in the Pledge of Allegiance. The war had decided once and forever the issue of divisibility.

Political integration occurs as a result of a process, whether peaceful or forceful, of joining together to create a new political community—one that is generally regarded as larger than the traditional nation state. Foreign policy analyst Ernst Haas in *The Uniting of Europe* (1958) wrote of integration as a process "whereby political actors in several distinct national settings are persuaded to shift their loyalties, expectations, and political activities toward a new center, whose institutions possess or demand jurisdiction over the preexisting national states." This process has been at work in the European Union and is still going on as the community moves toward building a new political reality. To be viable, this new community must evoke loyalty from the populations of the individual units that have joined together. If it does not, then a process of disintegration will take place. What we do not know about the current movement toward European integration is how far it

---

necessary and proper clause That portion of Article I, Section 8, of the U.S. Constitution (sometimes called the elastic clause) that makes it possible for the Congress to enact all "necessary and proper" laws to carry out its responsibilities.

will go or if it will last. But without a formal overarching structure for European integration, there can be no framework for intergovernmental relations.

The American Federal System

The U.S. Constitution is the fundamental settlement defining federalism and also defining the permanent features of intergovernmental relations in the United States. Like the constitutions of many countries, the U.S. Constitution is capable both of amendment as to its formal terms and evolution as to its meaning as a result of such things as Supreme Court judgments. Yet in essence it represents a relatively unchanging element of the framework within which intergovernmental relations are conducted.

The most fundamental aspects include the Constitution's provisions in three areas:

1. Its creation of a federal system, that is, one in which there is both a national government and state governments
2. Its allocation of certain functions to the national government
3. Its embodiment of certain principles, particularly through the interpretation of the Constitution and the **Bill of Rights**, which provide scope for Supreme Court judgments that can profoundly alter the respective powers and functions of the national and state governments over time.

If we grow up within a federal system and are used to belonging to a state as well as a nation, it is difficult to imagine what it would be like to live in a country without states. Yet this is the case in countries such as France and New Zealand, which have unitary governments, with all significant decisions being made at the national level.

Three Categories of Governments

There are three main categories into which we can allocate nations: (1) unitary governments, (2) federal governments, and (3) confederations. Each has certain strengths and weaknesses, and it is interesting to consider what would be the effects of altering the system from one of these to another, as New Zealand did in 1879 when it abolished its federal system and moved to unitary government. In Australia today, a significant minority would like to abandon federalism, abolish state governments, and perhaps introduce a new level of less costly, more numerous regional administrations.

Sometimes the reform impetus goes in the other direction. For example, Great Britain, formally the United Kingdom, is on the verge of moving from a unitary government to a federal structure now that Scotland and Wales will have their own legislatures with broad powers.

Bill of Rights The first ten amendments to the U.S. Constitution. Only a few individual rights were specified in the Constitution that was ratified in 1788. Shortly after its adoption, however, ten amendments—called the Bill of Rights—were added to the Constitution to guarantee basic individual liberties.

TABLE 4.1 Types of Government

Type	Examples	
Unitary Governments There are no state governments: all important power lies with the national government.	Denmark France	Japan New Zealand
Federal Governments There is a national government and a number of state governments; power is shared between them.	Australia Brazil Canada Germany	India Mexico Switzerland United States
Confederations Power rests with "sovereign" state governments, and an overarching government has some defined powers	European Union Commonwealth of Independent States (former USSR)	

Unitary Government Advantages   Unitary governments do have some significant strengths. The following are four key advantages they usually have over a federal system or a confederation:

1. National direction is clear; policies can be made by a single government without the need for negotiation or conflict with subnational states.

2. There can be no confusion as to **accountability**. It is clear to voters which level of government is responsible for a particular problem or function. (Legislators who wish to spend money must raise it; it is not possible for legislators to seek to pass the **buck** for failure to another level of government.)

3. Duplication of legislatures, bureaucracies, and programs is avoided with significant savings in direct costs—and the more subtle but no less real costs of needless duplication.

4. Issues of fairness in raising and spending money between levels of government (vertical fiscal imbalance) simply do not arise.

---

accountability The extent to which one must answer to higher authority—legal or organizational—for one's actions in society at large or within one's particular organizational position. Elected public officials are theoretically accountable to the political sovereignty of the voters. In this sense, appointed officials—from file clerks to cabinet secretaries—are less accountable than elected officials. The former are accountable mainly to their organizational supervisors, while the latter must answer to their constituents.

buck Responsibility. To avoid a problem or a responsibility is to *pass the buck*. President Truman was famous for having a sign on his desk that read "The Buck Stops Here." Buck, a term from poker, refers to the marker put in front of the player who next had to deal. Bureaucrats in many jurisdictions refer to the form memos that they use to direct paper from one to another as buck slips.

Federal Government Advantages   Unitary governments also have major drawbacks, which in turn correspond to the major strengths of federal systems. These include the following:

1. A federal system has greater scope for diversity and experimentation in policy.

2. The need to debate issues rather than enact them instantly may provide a more considered and viable policy outcome. This tendency toward incrementalism is seen as integral to democracy.

3. A federal system must consider the different ethnic or cultural groupings that may predominate in a particular state and wish to pursue a distinct cultural or social policy—such as the French Canadians in Quebec. (As the cases of Quebec and Bosnia show, membership in a federation may still fail to fulfill the nationalist aspirations of many people.)

4. The danger always exists in a large country that a unitary government may be too remote for appropriate democratic participation by regional centers located away from the capital; a federal system encourages, indeed demands, regional participation in governance.

5. The danger that in a unitary government the stronger regions, the larger racial groups, or more powerful interests will provide insufficient allowance for the needs of minorities or weaker groups.

In *The Federalist*, No. 10, James Madison discusses the problem of such factions and the danger they pose to a political system. Madison feared that the interests of parties and pressure groups could destabilize a government, but he believed that an overarching representative government, with a functional as well as a territorial separation of powers, could prevent this.

Confederations   Confederal systems are inherently weak as central governments. The United States was originally a confederal system. The Articles of Confederation were the original framework for the government of the new United States; they went into effect in 1781 and were superseded by the U.S. Constitution in 1789. The Articles said that the states were entering into a "firm league of friendship" and a "perpetual union for the common defense, the security of their liberties, and their mutual and general welfare." The Articles provided for a weak central government, which could not compel states to respect treaties, could not regulate interstate and foreign commerce, could neither collect taxes directly from the people nor compel the states to pay for the costs of the national government, and could not create a sense of national unity and national purpose. It nonetheless provided the experience of state cooperation out of which the consciousness of the need for a stronger union could emerge.

All confederations such as the present European Union and the Commonwealth of Independent States (the former Soviet Union) pose the same question. Which way are they going? Will they evolve, as the United States did, into a strong federal system? Or will they follow the route of the **Confederate States of America**, or the **Confederation of the Rhine**, and simply disintegrate and be replaced by new governing structures?

The Structure of Intergovernmental Relations

There are eternal questions concerning the structure of intergovernmental relations: Which level of government will have overall responsibility for what functions? When functions are shared between levels of government, how will each function be divided among national, state, and local governments? Should the taxes needed to finance local government be raised by the government that is to spend them, or by the higher level of government most successful at tax raising? Should a national government have an objective of redistributing revenues to reduce the differential between the richest and poorest regions of a nation?

Some of these questions are answered by the very nature of a federal system; for example, only a national legislature can establish policies of redistribution. Others are answered by the structure of intergovernmental relations created over time by a multitude of laws, court precedents, and traditional political expediency. Intergovernmental relations structures are almost always designed to accommodate differing communities of interest—social, ethnic, and political—as the boundaries of governments often possess or soon acquire symbolic meanings for communities that identify with them. This applies whether we are speaking of what it means to be a European or an American, a Luxemburger or a Texan, a Londoner or a San Franciscan. For example, localities in the United States often create fire, library, and school districts that for obvious reasons of **economies of scale** serve the citizens of a variety of small general-purpose jurisdictions such as boroughs or towns. These communities may develop a strong sense of identity that is focused on volunteer fire companies or high school sports teams.

The Effects of Pluralism

Sometimes a community is so dominated by one ethnic group that this impacts their relations—their intergovernmental relations—with other levels of government. Thus the people of Quebec, because of their strong French cultural identity, have been able to get special advantages from the Canadian national government. Alternatively, ethnically dominated communities in other countries have complained that they get fewer resources from their national governments because of their minority status. Sometimes national policies even encourage political ghettoization. For

---

Confederate States of America The short-lived confederation formed by the eleven states that sought to secede from the Union. That they could not do so was decided by the Civil War of 1861 to 1865. Those states, in alphabetical order, were Alabama, Arkansas, Florida, Georgia, Louisiana, Mississippi, North Carolina, South Carolina, Tennessee, Texas, and Virginia.

Confederation of the Rhine The 1806–1813 union of the smaller German-speaking states in the Rhine River region.

economies of scale Cost savings realized by doing things in larger rather than smaller units. This decreases the overall average cost.

example, the United States has long practiced the art of gerrymandering, the reshaping of an electoral district to enhance the political fortunes of the party in power, as opposed to creating a district with geographic compactness. The term first arose in 1811, when Massachusetts Governor Elbridge Gerry reluctantly signed a redistricting bill, creating a district shaped like a salamander.

In 1986 the Supreme Court ruled in *Davis v. Bandemer* that partisan gerrymandering is unconstitutional "when the electoral system is arranged in a manner that will consistently degrade a voter's or a group of voters' influence on the political process as a whole." This encouraged a spate of affirmative gerrymandering, redistricting to consolidate minority votes so that a minority group member will most likely win the next election. This has resulted in more minorities, especially African Americans, being elected to the U.S. Congress than ever before. The effect of this is to give them representation in numbers that approximates their percentage of the population. Just like all other members, they fight the political wars to bring resources to the myriad governments within their legislative districts. However, in the 1995 case of *Louisiana v. Hays* the Supreme Court seemed to put severe inhibitions on this when it ruled that congressional district lines are unconstitutional if race is the "predominant factor" in drawing them. Nevertheless the Court did not say that race could not be a factor at all.

The Marble-Cake Metaphor

People who have not worked in or studied public administration are often unaware of the complicated nature of intergovernmental relations. It is not simply a question of dividing the work between the levels: of assigning local issues to local government, and national issues to federal government. The majority of issues have national, regional, and local implications. The popular image of the federal system as a layer cake, each layer of government neatly on top of the other, is deceptive. The reality is more like a marble cake. This metaphor holds that the cooperative relations among the varying levels of government result in an intermingling of activities; in contrast to the more traditional view of layer-cake federalism, which holds that the three levels of government are totally or almost totally separate. Marble-cake federalism is usually associated with **Morton Grodzins**, who made a famous example out of the case of rural county health officials called sanitarians: sanitarians are appointed by the state government under merit standards established by the federal government, and while their base salaries come from state and federal funds, the county provides them with offices and office amenities and pays a portion of their expenses.

> It is impossible from moment to moment to tell under which governmental that the sanitarian operates. His work of inspecting the purity of food is carried out under federal standards; but he is enforcing state laws when inspecting commodities that have not been in interstate commerce; and somewhat perversely, he also acts under state authority when inspecting milk coming into the county from producing areas across the state border. He is a federal officer when impounding impure drugs shipped from a neighboring state; a federal-state officer when distributing typhoid immunization serum; a state

---

Morton Grodzins (1917–1964) A University of Chicago political scientist.

officer when enforcing standards of industrial hygiene; a state-local officer when inspecting the city's water supply; and (to complete the circle) a local officer when insisting that the city butchers adopt more hygienic methods of handling their garbage.

The essential story of the sanitarian could be told of hundreds of other public sector jobs. Bus drivers, police officers, and teachers are all caught up in the intergovernmental maze. Consequently, mass transit, law enforcement, and education policies, for example, must be the subject of attention at all levels of government. It takes wise legislators at each level to comprehend how their legislation will fit in with that being developed at other levels—and officials working at each level may find it a major task to see that their work is compatible with that of people working on similar topics in other levels of government. It is not surprising that modern nations have immensely complex sets of rules and procedures, innumerable committees, and frequent conferences designed to gain the best results from this immensely complex machine.

The Advisory Commission on Intergovernmental Relations

To better cope with its federal maze, the U.S. Congress in 1959 created the Advisory Commission on Intergovernmental Relations (ACIR) to monitor the operation of the federal system and to recommend improvements. The ACIR was a permanent, national, bipartisan body composed of 26 members, who serve two-year terms and were representative of the federal, state, and local governments and the public. As a continuing body, the commission approached its work by addressing itself to specific issues and problems, the resolution of which would improve cooperation among the levels of government and the functioning of the federal system. One of the long-range efforts of the commission has been to seek ways to improve federal, state, and local government taxing practices and policies to achieve equitable allocation of resources, increased efficiency in collection and administration, and reduced compliance burdens upon the taxpayers. Nevertheless, the ACIR became a victim of the budget wars in Congress. It was phased out and shut down by the end of 1996. Many states have created "little ACIRs" to study state and local developments within states.

Remember that it may not be simply a task of maximizing cooperation to implement shared goals. Very often, constituencies elect different parties when they are voting for different levels of government, or a local or state government may be working within a higher framework controlled by a political machine with different and conflicting purposes from their own. In these circumstances, political gamesmanship is common. Conferences designed to facilitate cooperation may be transformed into political arenas to embarrass the party controlling the other level of government. And in implementation, allocations may be left unspent or twisted to serve local purposes quite unintended by the legislators who voted the money at higher levels.

Dynamic Federalism

The formal structure of powers, roles, and relationships underlying the intergovernmental relations of a federal system is rather like the trunk and branches of an old tree. It sways in the wind, leaves come and go, and sometimes entire branches are lost

Box 4.1

One Method of Pump Priming

If the Treasury were to fill old bottles with bank notes, bury them at suitable depths in disused coal mines which are then filled up to the surface with town rubbish, and leave it to private enterprise on well-tried principles of *laissez-faire* to dig the notes up again . . . there need be no more unemployment, and with the help of the repercussions, the real income of the community would probably become a good deal larger than it is. It would, indeed, be more sensible to build houses and the like; but if there are practical difficulties in the way of doing this, the above would be better than nothing.

SOURCE: John Maynard Keynes, *General Theory of Employment, Interest, and Money* (Cambridge: Cambridge University Press, 1936).

in a storm. The more rigid the tree, the greater the possibility that a major storm (such as a civil war) may uproot it entirely. If the tree is more supple, it will adapt and change, it will weather the storm—and may be all the stronger for the experience.

Some federations have collapsed entirely in recent political history. The Union of Soviet Socialist Republics and Yugoslavia are leading examples. Others such as Malaysia have lost a major branch (Singapore) but survived. Still others like Canada have been close several times to losing a very major branch (Quebec).

In the United States, there has been a series of major phases of intergovernmental relations.

Dual Federalism

This was the nineteenth-century concept, now no longer operational, that the functions and responsibilities of the federal and state governments were theoretically distinguished and functionally separate from each other. With this philosophy—which existed during the last century, when each level of the government could and did pretend the other level did not exist—rival lawmen rode through the old West. In the absence of cooperation between jurisdictions, an outlaw could evade capture simply by "crossing the state line."

Some analysts suggest that this kind of federalism, which went out when the New Deal of 1933 came in, is what the Reagan administration sought, at least rhetorically, to eventually get back to. The basic idea of dual federalism was expressed succinctly in 1891 in *The American Commonwealth*, by British historian James Bryce, who visited the United States in the 1880s to observe its political system:

The characteristic feature and special interest of the American Union is that it shows us two governments covering the same ground yet distinct and separate in their action. It is like a great factory wherein two sets of machinery are at work, their revolving wheels apparently intermixed, their bands crossing one another, yet each doing its own work without touching or hampering the other.

Cooperative Federalism

This is the notion that the national, state, and local governments are cooperating, interacting agents, working jointly to solve common problems, rather than conflicting, sometimes hostile competitors pursuing similar or, more likely, conflicting ends. While some cooperation has always been evident in spite of the conflict, competition, and complexity of intergovernmental relations, cooperation was most prominent between the 1930s and the 1950s. The emergency funding arrangements of the Depression years, known collectively as the New Deal, and the cooperation among federal, state, and local authorities during World War II to administer civilian defense, rationing, and other wartime programs are noteworthy examples of cooperative federalism in the United States.

The New Deal's scheme of economic reconstruction involved many new federal grants to the states aimed at providing jobs. During this time, the concept of using federal spending to create demand—**pump priming**—led to an entirely new position for federal government as the shaper of programs in the states. This was the economic prescription of the British economist **John Maynard Keynes**, which called for stimulating the economy during a time of economic decline by borrowing money to spend on public works, defense, welfare, and so on. In theory, the prosperity generated by such expenditures would increase tax revenues, which in turn would pay for the borrowing.

Cooperative federalism also has a horizontal dimension—state-to-state interactions and relations. Such interstate relations take many forms, including **interstate compacts** and commissions established for specific purposes: river basin management, transportation, **extradition** of criminals, conservation of forests and wildlife, and administration of parks and recreation. Horizontal relations between local governments also are numerous. Cities frequently contract for services from various neighboring local governments (and even from private providers). The Lakewood plan, established in southern California in 1954, is the best known example of interlocal contracting for services in the United States. Under this plan, the City of Lakewood

---

pump priming Government spending to stimulate an economy during a time of economic decline.

John Maynard Keynes (1883–1946) The English economist who wrote the most influential book on economics of this century, *The General Theory of Employment, Interest, and Money* (1936). Keynes founded a school of thought known as Keynesian economics, which called for using a government's fiscal and monetary policies to positively influence a capitalistic economy, and developed the framework of modern macroeconomic theory. All U.S. presidents since Franklin D. Roosevelt have used Keynes's theories to, admittedly or unadmittedly, justify deficit spending to stimulate the economy.

interstate compacts Formal arrangements entered into by two or more states, generally with the approval of the U.S. Congress, to operate joint programs. While Article I, Section 10, of the Constitution requires that interstate compacts be approved by the Congress, as a practical matter many agreements on minor matters ignore this requirement. The initial intent was to prevent states from forming regional alliances that might threaten national unity.

extradition The surrender by one nation or state to another of a person accused or convicted of an offense in the second nation or state.

contracted for a rather comprehensive package of services from Los Angeles County, where Lakewood is located.

Creative Federalism

This was the Lyndon B. Johnson administration's term for its approach to intergovernmental relations, which was characterized by joint planning and decision making among all levels of government (as well as the private sector) in the management of intergovernmental programs. Many new programs of this period had an urban-metropolitan focus, and much attention was given to antipoverty issues. Creative federalism sought to foster the development of a singular **Great Society** by integrating the poor into mainstream America. Its expansive efforts were marked by the rapid development of categorical grant programs to state and local governments and direct federal grants to cities, frequently bypassing state governments entirely. Great Society programs such as **Head Start** and the **War on Poverty** were all based on the concept of federal grants shaping activities and directions at the state and local levels. However, the idea that all wisdom rested in Washington was not always well received in state capitals or city halls. The Nixon administration's New Federalism sought to alter this balance.

New Federalism

This was President Richard Nixon's attempt to return autonomy to the states while maintaining significant levels of federal funding. From 1972 onward, New Federalism entailed establishing aggregate grant levels by formula, but allowing state and local governments substantial latitude in applying the funds in their own area. The term has its origins in the liberal Republican effort to find an alternative to the centralized state perceived as having been set up by the New Deal, but an alternative that nonetheless recognized the need for effective national government. During the Nixon administration, New Federalism referred to the style of decentralized management at the federal level symbolized by such programs as general revenue sharing (see following page), and the decentralization of federal regional management to ten coterminous regions, each with a common regional center.

New Federalism as developed by the Reagan administration disregarded the Nixon approach of decentralized federal regional management and turned to development of direct relations between the federal government and the state governments. The intent was to return power and responsibility to the states and to dramatically reduce the role of the federal government in domestic programs, rang-

---

Great Society The label for the 1960s domestic policies of the Johnson administration, which were premised on the belief that social and economic problems could be solved by new federal programs. This was Johnson's effort to revive the federal reform presence in social change represented in the Progressive movement, the New Deal, and the Fair Deal.

Head Start The federal program designed to provide early education opportunities for poor children prior to kindergarten. Head Start centers exist nationwide and offer not only preacademic instruction but also health, social, nutritional, and psychological services.

War on Poverty The phrase used by the Johnson administration for those 1960s Great Society programs designed to eliminate the causes and effects of poverty in the United States.

ing from community mental health to crime prevention. This was reminiscent of the dual federalism that prevailed in the United States in the nineteenth century.

New New Federalism

First proposed in its modern form in the early 1960s by Walter Heller, then chairman of President John F. Kennedy's Council of Economic Advisers, revenue sharing was designed to arrest the rising fiscal burdens of many state and local governments. Part of its original rationale was the concern of some economists about the accumulation of federal budget surpluses.

Given the subsequent record federal deficits, this sounds a bit unreal; nevertheless, excessive budget surpluses were a true concern of the early 1960s. The theory was that a budget surplus would produce a fiscal drag on the economy and that the money ought to be put back into the economy in some efficient way. Revenue sharing seemed a natural. Another justification for revenue sharing was its ability to mitigate fiscal imbalances among the states, where variances in per capita personal income are significant. Finally, the argument was made that revenue sharing is economically justified by the federal government's monopolization of the most efficient and **progressive tax** source—the federal income tax. In 1972, revenue sharing was enacted with the passage of the State and Local Fiscal Assistance Act. But the Reagan administration, opposed to general revenue sharing, allowed it to expire in 1986. The subsequent burgeoning of federal budget deficits became an enormous obstacle to renewal.

The Reagan administration imposed new policy objectives on intergovernmental arrangements. This was also called, Nixon fashion, "new federalism." Confusing? Yes. But it made sense in that it was basically an extension of the Nixon initiatives. Reagan and his advisers viewed much activity by the national government, especially many expenditures on social programs, as wasteful and unnecessary. Thus they turned their attention to cutting federal grants, attempting to transfer functions "back" to the states and away from Washington. The Reaganites destroyed general revenue sharing, the unrestricted distribution of a portion of federal tax revenues to state governments.

Because Reagan succeeded in making such large cuts in the funds available from Washington to state and local governments, the subnational jurisdictions had no choice but to curtail or close facilities and programs, or to look for energetic ways of funding those they wished to retain. In some respects, the entrepreneurship in state and local government documented by Osborne and Gaebler in *Reinventing Government* (1992) was the inventiveness mothered by the financial necessity imposed on them by Reagan administration policies. While the policy directions of the Reagan and Bush administrations, through their cuts in state and local aid, heavily impacted the poor in the U.S., they failed to address the perception of **malaise** in Washington. Thus the Clinton administration began with public confidence in government at record low levels—especially with regard to intergovernmental issues such as welfare and crime.

---

progressive tax Any tax that has people of greater wealth paying a larger percentage in tax than people of lesser means. Income taxes are often progressive.

malaise The medical term for a vague feeling of illness that is used in other contexts to express a lassitude or ineffectiveness not traceable to a specific source and not exhibiting a specific set of symptoms. Malaise was President Jimmy Carter's word for the political uneasiness he found in America.

Then history, as is its wont, repeated itself. The Republican Congress elected in 1994 declared in 1995 that it was determined to create, what else, a new federalism. But according to political journalist Alan Ehrenhalt, "it would be more accurate to describe it as the New New New Federalism—the 1995 revival of the Reagan revival of the Nixon revival of some ideas that Dwight D. Eisenhower placed before the country almost 40 years ago." Ehrenhalt views the 1995 Republican version of federalism as "the fourth modern incarnation of the simple-enough notion that Washington ought to be doing less governing and the states ought to be doing more." You may well be thinking by now "the more things change, the more they remain the same." This now trite observation was first credited to Alphonse Karr, the nineteenth-century French journalist, in a January 1849 issue of *Les Guépes*, a satirical review of intergovernmental relations in Paris.

Intergovernmental Management

We cannot usually "see" intergovernmental relations, just as we cannot see other aspects of government machinery. But there are times when intergovernmental management bubbles to the surface and becomes visible. Unfortunately these times usually involve great tragedies such as a major earthquake in California or a terrorist bomb at the World Trade Center in New York or the federal building in Oklahoma City. In each case the various levels are literally on the scene. First to arrive are local police and fire personnel. They are backed up by appropriate state agencies such as the **National Guard**. The federal government is represented by the FBI (when a crime is suspected, as in a bombing) and the Federal Emergency Management Agency (FEMA), which plans for and coordinates emergency preparedness and response for all levels of government and for all kinds of emergencies—both civilian and military. FEMA is the organization that decides what the various governments should be doing after such a catastrophe.

The political dialogue in American politics is always full of intergovernmental management issues. Politicians running for president or Congress love nothing better than telling the voters what they are going to do about crime or education once elected. But these are only marginal concerns of the federal government. State and local police are responsible for law enforcement. The FBI, while highly visible in the public's crime-fighting imagery, is minuscule in comparison. State and local governments employ more than half a million uniformed police officers. The FBI has only about ten thousand special agents. Education is the province of local school boards. The bottom line is that aside from minor funding for special programs there is practically nothing the federal government can do about these issues—nothing but talk. And federal officials, and would-be federal officials, spend so much time talking about such hot button issues that the public often thinks there is something, usually

---

National Guard The military forces of the states, which often are used for civil emergencies, such as major fires or floods. Normally, under the command of each state's governor, any or all of the states' individual guard units may be called (by the U.S. Congress) into federal service at any time. Once a guard unit is called into federal service, it is no longer subject to state control. The National Guard was organized in 1916. Until that time, each state had a volunteer militia.

something simple like mandating more homework for third graders or telling teenagers not to become sexually active before marriage, that the federal government can do that will make a real difference. But while the politicians may think the public naive, there are no simple answers to the complex questions of intergovernmental management.

In the past, discussions of intergovernmental relations were very much preoccupied with legal and structural questions on the one hand, and federal financial relations on the other. While these categories are of course fundamentally important, the structuring of various philosophies for, and types of, federal grants programs themselves set basic parameters of federal-state-local interaction. However, an additional strand of public administration studies in federalism emphasizes other dimensions of intergovernmental relations, namely, issues surrounding the management processes that are needed to make a federation work successfully.

Key issues from this perspective include: a focus on implementation and problem solving in federal systems; the nature of coordination; accountability in a multiorganizational setting; and an interest in competence and capacity building (the development of both the physical and human infrastructure for economic advancement).

Any government servant who wishes to successfully manage a program that is intergovernmental in nature must come to grips with these issues. The most common danger with intergovernmental management is the tendency for each higher level to "micromanage" those below them. The Congress has been accused of micromanagement when it writes detailed rules for program management into legislation, thus denying line managers any real administrative discretion. But any manager is a micromanager if he or she refuses to allow subordinates to have any real authority or responsibility. Even the federal courts play the micromanagement game. For example, according to *New York* magazine, they require New York City to provide inmates in municipal jails with free daily newspapers in both English and Spanish at a cost of $200,000 per year. They also require the windows of each city prison to be washed at least four times a year at an annual cost of $400,000.

Picket Fence Federalism

The human body depends on the interplay of a variety of comprehensive systems—from the cardiovascular system to the respiratory system to the nervous system—each of these as critical as the next one. It is similarly true that a federal system of government is built around several pervasive systems—systems a lot less predictable than those serving the human body, but just as pervasive and critical. *Picket fence federalism* is the metaphor most commonly used for this systemic process. This concept implies that bureaucratic specialists at the various levels of government (along with clientele groups) exercise considerable power over the nature of intergovernmental programs. Bureaucratic or program specialists at national, state, and local government levels for such fields as public housing, vocational education, health and hospitals, and higher education represent the pickets in the picket fence. They communicate with each other in daily work, belong to the same professional organizations, and have similar professional training. They are likely to be in conflict with general-purpose government officials (mayors, governors, the president), who attempt to coordinate the vertical power structures, or pickets. The general-purpose officials are the crosspieces of the fence. The metaphor is credited to Terry Sanford, when he was governor of the state of North Carolina. It was initially presented in his *Storm Over the States* (1967).

Councils of Government

Any multijurisdictional cooperative arrangement to permit a regional approach to planning, development, transportation, environment, and other problems that affect a region as a whole tends to be known as a Council of Government (COG), even if the word "council" is not part of its formal title. COGs are typically substate regional planning agencies established by states. They are usually responsible for areawide review of projects applying for federal funds and for development of regional plans and other areawide special purpose arrangements. They are composed of designated policymaking representatives from each participating government within the region. Some COGs have assumed a more enterprising role beginning in the 1980s by acting as contractors for, and service providers to, their local governments. For example, the COG for Lee and Russell counties in Alabama helped form a waste management authority to negotiate a single landfill contract with the private company that owns the landfills they use. According to journalist Eileen Shanahan, there is a tendency for COGs to be "transformed into regional entities that amount to multipurpose special districts, with real powers."

But that tendency has not been pronounced, because all councils of government suffer from being only advisory in nature. They have few, if any, independent sources of revenue. Bernard H. Ross has compared them to the General Assembly of the United Nations in that both institutions "can debate, discuss, and suggest, but they cannot enforce action" on any of their members.

Mandate Mania

Nothing sours intergovernmental relations faster than mandates. (The nature and scope of mandates were discussed in this chapter's keynote.) It is difficult to even determine how many mandates impact any given jurisdiction. For example, according to journalist Eric Pooley, the New York State Governor's Office of Mandate Relief counted 1,700 state and federal mandates in 1992. But in 1994 the *New York Times* discovered that there were 3,200 from the state alone that affected local government. There is obviously a major problem of definition here. Different things were being counted.

The only way to comprehend the full scope of the mandate problem is to look at their different categories. First, are they direct orders (which imply civil or criminal penalties for disobeying) or merely conditions for receiving aid? If they are the latter, they may not be considered mandates at all for they do not have any effect unless you want the aid. Then you must also take the strings, the mandates, that come with it. Second, are they programmatic or procedural? Programmatic mandates state the type and quality of program to be implemented—a school lunch program must meet specified national standards for nutrition. A procedural mandate requires jurisdictions to do what they were going to do anyway, but according to

Box 4.2

Mandating from Above

Nearly 3,300 years ago, on the banks of the Nile, Ramses II issued an order that has an all-too-familiar ring to it.

"Ye shall no more give the people straw to make brick, as heretofore," the Pharaoh commanded his overseers. "Let them go and gather straw for themselves." And yet the workers were supposed to produce as much brick as ever.

Ramses had invented the unfunded mandate. In the short run, it was not much of a public policy success. The Hebrew people, against whom the order was directed, thought it so unfair that they eventually seceded from the Egyptian government altogether.

Over the ensuing centuries, however, countless government officials at all levels have played it Pharaoh's way. They have seized upon the idea that, if you have power, you can tell people at the next level down to do anything you want . . .

"It all rolls downhill," one cynical small-town Michigan mayor said not long ago.

He is right. If financially strapped localities across the country could find any lower level of government to ship their problems to, they no doubt would. The only thing that keeps them righteous on this score is that no such destination exists.

Of course, the localities do have some options. A delegation of mayors could copy the tactics of the Hebrews against Ramses and descend on Lansing (the capital of Michigan) or Springfield (the capital of Illinois) with a plague of frogs or locusts. But that didn't work particularly well in ancient Egypt and it would be extremely risky from a public relations point of view.

SOURCE: Alan Ehrenhalt, "Mandating from Above," *Governing* (September 1995).

new requirements—personnel have to be hired according to equal opportunity provisions; formal meetings and records have to be open to the public. While programmatic mandates may cost a great deal, many procedural mandates may cost little or nothing, or have a one time only cost.

Some mandates merely constrain. But the constraints can hurt, as they do when state laws specify the kinds of government, religious, and nonprofit organization property that is exempt from local property taxes. Or when states put limits on property taxes or tax increases for veterans or retired citizens.

Some mandates involve not one but large numbers of programs at once. These so-called crosscutting mandates are often found in virtually all state and federal aid programs. For example, if you accept federal funds, you are subject to the Anti-Kickback Act of 1934 (the Copeland Act) which should inhibit you from extorting money from employees or contractors.

While it is possible to classify mandates, they are so integral to all of public administration that it is virtually impossible to accurately count them without first creating a classification scheme that defines what you mean by a mandate. There is no **czar** of mandates statistics. There are only countless studies by countless groups such as the U.S. Conference of Mayors and the Advisory Commission on Intergovernmental Relations that all conclude, essentially, that there are more mandates than you can shake a stick at!

The Cost of Compliance

The real crux of the mandates controversy is the cost of compliance. Just consider, for example, the Americans with Disabilities Act (ADA) of 1990, the federal law that bans discrimination against physically and mentally handicapped individuals in employment, transportation, telecommunications, and public accommodations. (See Chapter 11 for more details on the ADA.) Businesses with more than 25 workers are required to accommodate disabled employees. New buses and trains will have to be accessible to people in wheelchairs. Telephone companies will have to provide hearing- or voice-impaired people with equipment to place and receive calls from ordinary telephones. Renovated or new hotels, stores, and restaurants will have to be wheelchair accessible. Existing barriers must be removed, if the work is "readily achievable." Businesses that can demonstrate that these changes would be too costly or disruptive could be exempt from the law. But asserting that something is "too costly" may cost more in legal fees for court challenges than it is worth.

This laudable law certainly sounds reasonable on the surface. But what about Aurora, the largest suburb of Denver. It has 28,000 street corner curbs that need to be cut to meet ADA standards. At $1,500 each, the complete cost of compliance would be $30 million. According to André Henderson, the city was only able to budget $200,000 in 1994 for this. The big money needed for total compliance simply isn't there—not in Aurora and not in many other jurisdictions, too. And this is just one aspect of one mandate. There are many other parts to ADA and other mandates that are all competing for increasingly scarce budgeting resources. This one law, Henderson reports, noble in intent as it is, will cost the nation's cities and counties $5 billion from 1994 to 1998—more than $1 billion a year. Not a penny of this comes from the federal government. This is the raw meaning of an unfunded mandate.

In order to address this problem, at least symbolically, Congress passed the Unfunded Mandate Reform Act of 1995. This law holds that any future **bill** might be out of order if it imposes a financial mandate of more than $50 million on any one state, local, or Native American tribal government. But this requirement could always be rescinded by a majority vote. The law did nothing to end current unfunded mandates. It was basically designed to force Congress to be more aware of the im-

---

czar A former Russian absolute monarch; a nickname for any high-ranking administrator who is given great authority over something—for example, an energy czar, a housing czar.

bill A legislative proposal formally introduced for consideration; unfinished legislation. After a bill is passed and signed into law, it becomes an act.

plications of possible future mandates. Thus the **Congressional Budget Office** has been assigned the task of developing estimates of the costs of all future mandates. The new CBO assignment amounted to an unfunded mandate in itself. So the then head of the CBO, Robert Reischauer, told a congressional appropriation subcommittee in February 1995 that the CBO would need $7.1 million in additional funds to carry out its new duties. No unfunded mandates for his agency!

Intergovernmental management, then, is the multiplicity of hourly relationships between governments, as well as the dynamic relationships with higher and lower levels of government and with peer governments on the same level. The currency of these relationships is broad; included are political negotiations and old fashioned "horse trading," legal wrangling, and fiscal maneuvering. Over time, political acumen and economic power will alter the status of governments one to the other, and this dynamism will give rise to anguish—sometimes even to nostalgic attempts to restore past relationships. However, the student of public administration is well advised to begin with a detached assessment as to where his or her government stands in this regard, to acknowledge that the standing and independence of all governments wax and wane, and to demand managers who can administratively "sniff the wind" to ascertain the appropriate response.

Fiscal Federalism—Following the Money

In the infancy of federalism in the eighteenth century, it may have been grandiose to think of the policy arrangements in national and state government as a system. Geographic separation, painfully slow systems of communication, and a relatively clear differentiation of functions gave each level of government a role that could be carried out with only limited interaction with other levels of government.

Several factors permanently changed this picture during the twentieth century. First, the galvanizing effect of the world wars and the Cold War saw national direction and planning emerge more thoroughly than had ever been necessary before. Second, a revolution occurred in transport and communications that has permanently ended the possibility for states to behave with the completely unilateral autonomy they once had. Third, there emerged with the 1930s New Deal, and with the 1960s civil rights and antipoverty programs, legislation embodying national values that needed to be uniformly implemented across the entire country. The cumulative effect of these fundamental changes gave rise to a concept of national policymaking and state policy implementation overlaid on the traditional and continuing functions of national and state government.

How could a national government bring about actions at the state level that state governments, left to themselves, might find neither palatable nor affordable? Certainly, at times, the federal courts have ordered state governments to adopt

---

Congressional Budget Office (CBO) A support agency of the U.S. Congress created in 1974 by the Congressional Budget and Impoundment Act to provide the Congress with basic budget data and with analyses of alternative fiscal, budgetary, and programmatic policy issues, independent of the executive branch and of the Office of Management and Budget.

TABLE 4.2 Federal Aid to State and Local Governments

Year	Total (in millions of dollars)	As a percentage of federal outlays
1970	24,065	12.3%
1975	49,791	15.0
1980	91,385	15.5
1985	105,852	11.2
1989	121,928	10.7
1990	135,325	10.8
1991	154,519	11.7
1992	178,065	12.9
1993	193,612	13.7
1994	210,596	14.4
1995	224,991	14.8
1996	227,811	14.6
1997 (est.)	244,794	15.0

SOURCE: *Statistical Abstract of the U.S.,* (1997)

policies and actions based on judicial interpretations of the meaning of federal legislation or the Constitution. For example, the courts have ordered states to integrate schools (by **busing** if necessary) and to relieve prison overcrowding if it amounts to **cruel and unusual punishment**. However, the federal government, under the Tenth Amendment to the Constitution, does not have a general power to give directions to the states in their primary areas of power. Consequently, more often than not, financial inducement, through grants of money tied to a particular policy objective, has been the preferred instrument for achieving federal purposes. Financial arrangements have been the predominant vehicle within intergovernmental relations by which national policies have been implemented by and through the states.

The Theory of Fiscal Federalism

Fiscal federalism refers to the fiscal (financial) relationships that exist between and among units of government in a federal system. The theory of fiscal federalism, or

---

busing The transporting of children by bus to schools at a greater distance than those the children would otherwise attend to achieve racial desegregation. Busing has often been mandated by the federal courts as a remedy for past practices of discrimination. It has been heartily objected to by parents who want their children to attend neighborhood schools and has, in consequence, been a major factor in "white flight" from central cities. Busing is often used as an example of government by the judiciary, because busing, one of the most controversial domestic policies in the history of the United States, has never been specifically sanctioned by the Congress.

cruel and unusual punishment The criminal penalty prohibited by the Eighth Amendment, which not only bars government from imposing punishment that is barbarous but, as the U.S. Supreme Court has announced, forbids punishment that society's "evolving standards of decency" would mark as excessive.

multiunit governmental finance, addresses the question of the optimal design of governments in a multilevel (or federal) governmental system.

The public sector has three principal economic problems to solve:

1. The attainment of the most equitable distribution of income
2. The maintenance of high employment with stable prices
3. The establishment of an efficient pattern of resource allocation

The theory of fiscal federalism postulates that a federal form of government can be especially effective in solving these problems because of the flexibility it has in dealing with some problems at the national or central level and some at the local or regional levels. It argues that, for a variety of reasons, the first two problems, equitable distribution of income and maintenance of high employment with stable prices, are problems that the national level of government is best equipped to handle. However, according to the theory, the decentralized regional or local units of government can more efficiently deal with the third problem, allocation of resources, because such units of government are more familiar than the central or national government with local needs and the desires of citizens for public services. Even so, grants-in-aid from the national level of government to local levels may be needed to stimulate local government spending for national purposes, to provide for uniform or minimum service levels (as in education), or to compensate citizens of one area for benefits from services they finance that spill over to residents of another area. Spillover benefits are especially frequent in such programs as clean water and air pollution control, health, and education.

In theory, an accountable government should involve representatives only voting for programs for which they have voted the taxes. The representatives would be accountable to the voters, who could directly assess whether the "purchase" of services and programs they had made at election time was what they wanted, and whether they got good value for their tax money. But in a large nation, need for services can vary greatly between communities, and the capacity to pay taxes also varies greatly among the categories of those who are taxed. This issue focuses attention on several of the central problems of the federal concept—the difficult notion of two or more governments overlaid on the same geographical territory; the difficulty of persuading voters that they need to pay their taxes twice (or more) to different levels of taxing authority; and the difficulty of persuading taxpayers that it is fair that some of their taxes should produce no direct benefit to them but be used to assist some other community or some ill-defined goal dear to an official in a remote office in another city.

Attitudes toward these issues illustrate the level of confidence citizens have in a democratic federation. If confidence is high, and a sense of common national purpose is high—as it was during a "popular" war such as World War II or during the early days of the Great Society programs, citizens are more prepared to entrust politicians and bureaucrats to redistribute taxes to promote national goals elsewhere. If, however, confidence in politicians and the bureaucracy is low—as it has been in the United States in the mid 1990s—citizens may well take some convincing that spending programs are fair and necessary. A confident, successful federal democracy that has confidence in its political leaders and has honest and efficient bureaucrats and well-articulated national aspirations will be one in which there is more room for redistributive programs—an admirable goal to strive for, or perhaps not!

All too often the same central question of fiscal federalism is asked in countless congressional and presidential elections: Why can't the citizens of the states just keep their money (meaning, have their federal taxes reduced) rather than paying it to the federal government so they can return it in grants and services? The answer is deceptively simple: not all states are fiscally equal. If there are more poor people in one state, federal welfare funds from other states will in effect subsidize them. Would Delaware and Connecticut, for example, otherwise transfer tax dollars from their citizens to the overall poorer citizens of Mississippi and Alabama? Federal spending for military bases, while concentrated in more southern states for reasons of climate, benefit the entire nation—even if they benefit the local economy of Georgia more. While bases and ports may be concentrated in the South, defense contractors are widely distributed. Indeed, to gain support for many defense systems, the **Pentagon** quite consciously procures goods and services from companies in as many congressional districts as possible. Even NASA once boasted, in order to drum up congressional support, that the parts for the space shuttle were built in most of the 50 states.

Lobbying by defense contractors aside, the federal government justifies taking its measure of taxes from the states and distributing them in an uneven fashion because this furthers national policies for welfare, for defense, for conservation, for environmental protection and so on. In this process, some states are winners and some losers. And while no one would deny that any given program could not be better managed or more economically operated, these redistribution programs all exist because lawmakers representing all the citizens thought them to be in the public interest. The members of Congress cannot have it both ways—they cannot argue that the federal government is too full of pork barrel programs for the congressional districts while at the same time they kick and claw to bring home the bacon for their constituents. Fortunately this is becoming, though only gradually, a truth more universally acknowledged than before.

Grant Programs

Grants by formula or category are the most significant means by which federal moneys are transmitted to the states. A grant is simply an intergovernmental transfer of funds (or other assets). Since the New Deal, state and local governments have become increasingly dependent upon federal grants for an almost infinite variety of programs. Grant money had grown to more than 21 percent of all state and local expenditures by 1993. By comparison, it was only 10 percent in 1955. From almost the beginning of the republic to the present, a grant by the federal government has been a continuing means of providing states, localities, public (and private) educational or research institutions, and individuals with funds to support projects the national government considered useful for a wide range of purposes. In recent years, grants have been

---

Pentagon The building that has become the symbol of the U.S. Department of Defense.

TABLE 4.3   Winners and Losers in the Game of Fiscal Federalism

Top Ten States

(whose citizens on average get back more in federal spending than they pay in federal taxes)

New Mexico	$3,531*
Mississippi	2,184
Virginia	2,051
North Dakota	1,804
West Virginia	1,676
Alaska	1,536
Montana	1,524
Alabama	1,472
Maine	1,397
Maryland	1,301

Bottom Ten States

(whose citizens on average pay more in federal taxes than they get back in federal spending)

Indiana	−407
Wisconsin	−793
New York	−815
Nevada	−825
Michigan	−963
Minnesota	−993
Illinois	−1,371
New Hampshire	−1,473
Delaware	−1,771
Connecticut	−1,805

SOURCE: Statistics from *Time*, May 29, 1995

*Per capita data for 1993.

made to support the arts as well as the sciences. All such grants are capable of generating debate over what the public as a whole, acting through the grant-making agencies of the federal government, considers useful and in the national interest.

A "grant-in-aid" is the term used for federal or state payments to local governments for specified purposes and usually subject to supervision and review by the granting government or agency in accordance with prescribed standards and requirements. One function of a federal grant-in-aid is to direct state or local funding to a purpose considered nationally useful by providing federal money, on condition that the jurisdiction receiving it match a certain percentage of it. The federal government actively monitors the grantee's spending of the funds to ensure compliance with the spirit and letter of federal intent. Grants-in-aid have other public policy implications as well, because a jurisdiction that accepts federal money must also accept the federal "strings," or guidelines, that come with it. All federal grantees must comply with federal standards on equal employment opportunity in the selection of personnel and contractors, for example.

Historically, the most common grants have been "categorical"—those that can be used only for specified purposes. But there has been a trend, ever since the Nixon administration, to move toward block grants that give the states more discretion over the funds. This trend decidedly accelerated in the mid-1990s as the Republican-controlled Congress sought to reduce the size and role of the federal bureaucracy by reducing congressional oversight of grant programs—and at the same time permanently removing the federal employees who performed many of the oversight functions. For the public administrator, fiscal federalism refers, first and foremost, to the politics and administration of complex intergovernmental grant-in-aid systems.

The federal government distributes money to the states through hundreds of grant programs, of which about half are related to **Medicaid**; some 20 percent are for infrastructure such as transportation, water, or sewage treatment, and the remainder relate to various social and labor market programs. During the 1970s, the Nixon administration introduced less-specific block grants to counter the criticism that too greatly specifying the way in which federal moneys were to be spent tended to reduce state governments to an extremely mechanical role not consistent with their status as governments in their own right. A block grant is distributed in accordance with a statutory formula for use in a variety of activities within a broad functional area, largely at the recipient's discretion. For example, the community development block grant program, administered by the Department of Housing and Urban Development, funds community and economic development programs in cities, counties, Indian reservations, and U.S. territories. The nature of the block grant allows these jurisdictions to allocate the funds to supplement other resources in ways they choose. The problem with block grants is that Washington loses control and the money may be spent even less wisely than it would if more federal strings were attached.

From Contractive to Coercive Federalism

Political scientist Deil S. Wright has developed a series of federalism metaphors—short descriptions for the intergovernmental administrative realities of each era in

---

Medicaid The federally aided, state-operated, and state-administered program that provides medical benefits for certain low-income people in need of health and medical care. Authorized by 1965 amendments to the Social Security Act, it covers only members of one of the categories of people who can be covered under the welfare cash payment programs—the aged, the blind, the disabled, and members of families with dependent children where one parent is absent, incapacitated, or unemployed. Under limited circumstances, states may also provide Medicaid coverage for children under twenty-one years of age who are not categorically related. Subject to broad federal guidelines, states determine coverage, eligibility, payment to health care providers, and the methods of administering the program.

Figure 4.1   The Changing Nature of Federal Grants to State and Local Governments

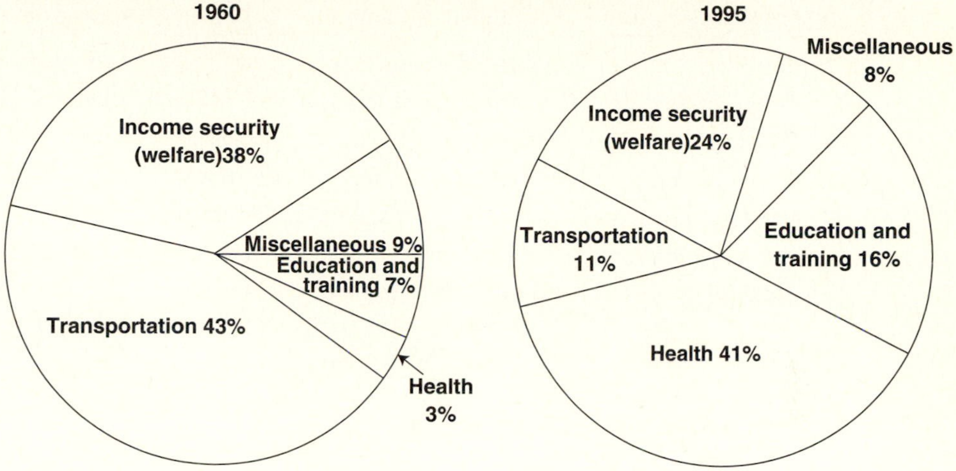

1960

- Income security (welfare) 38%
- Miscellaneous 9%
- Education and training 7%
- Transportation 43%
- Health 3%

1995

- Miscellaneous 8%
- Income security (welfare) 24%
- Transportation 11%
- Education and training 16%
- Health 41%

SOURCE: Office of Management and Budget. *Budget of the United States Government, Fiscal Year 1996: Analytical Perspectives* (1995).

American federalism. He sees the United States leaving a period of Reagan administration-inspired "contractive federalism" known for its cuts in federal aid. Today he sees the United States as entering a period of "coercive-collage" federalism. The "coercive" refers to the continuing problems of unfunded mandates (discussed above); the "collage" refers to the fact that modern-day federalism is so much like a Salvador Dali painting (with melting clocks in surreal landscapes) in that both lack "thematic coherence." There are so many factors (so many reinventors) at work, so many conflicting political actors playing with the intergovernmental system, that "kaleidoscopic" may be the only way to describe the current situation.

This is made all the more complicated by the fact that some internal American federal issues have been internationalized. For example, the North American Free Trade Agreement has allowed Canada to mount a successful legal challenge to state preferences (lower taxes) for in-state beer and wine. Now American six-packs and Canadian six-packs are equal in this regard. But the moral of this story is that state laws can be nullified by international agreement. This was a major surprise to American brewers, vintners, and state legislators.

The Devolution Revolution

The dilemmas of intergovernmental relations illustrated so clearly by the problem of federal-state financial relationships have always been critical issues in democratic federations. The only certainty here is that the states have become addicted to intergovernmental funding. The question remains whether their political leaders will gradually wean them from it or feed their habit. On this front there is good news and bad news. The good news is that many state governments seem genuinely caught up in the devolution revolution. In late 1994, all of the Republican governors and governors-elect

TABLE 4.4 Phases of Intergovernmental Relations

Phase Description	Federalism Metaphor	Appropriate Time Period
Conflict	Layer-cake federalism	19th century to 1930s
Cooperative	Marble-cake federalism	1930s–1950s
Concentrated	Water taps (focused or channeled)	1940s–1960s
Creative	Flowering (proliferated and fused)	1950s–1960s
Competitive	Picket fence (fragmented federalism)	1960s–1970s
Calculative	Facade (confrontational federalism)	1970s–1980s
Contractive	De facto, telescope, and whiplash federalism	1980s–1990s
Coercive-collage	Kaleidoscopic federalism	1990s–?

SOURCE: Adapted from Deil S. Wright, *Understanding Intergovernmental Relations*, 3rd ed., (Pacific Grove, CA: Brooks/Cole, 1988), updated by Deil S. Wright in 1995.

met in Williamsburg, Virginia—the colonial capital of that state. Representing a clear majority (30) of the states with an overwhelming (70 percent) majority of the population, they issued the "Williamsburg Resolve," which called for reversing the power that had been going to Washington since the New Deal. They said grandiose things appropriate to the place where Patrick Henry said in 1775 "Give me liberty or give me death!" California Governor Pete Wilson said that the "states are not colonies of the federal government." Governor Tommy Thompson of Wisconsin said they should no longer have to go to Washington "on bended knee to kiss the ring."

The bad news is that this is somewhat hypocritical. After all, what their "resolve" essentially calls for is the federal money without the federal strings. But these "strings" have important public policy implications—like ensuring the relatively equal treatment of all citizens no matter in which state they may reside. The current movement toward devolution is similar to the Sagebrush Rebellion. This term, first heard in the 1980s, covers any number of dissatisfactions—hardly a rebellion—that some people in the states of the American West have with the federal government's management and use of the federal lands within their borders. In general, they feel that the states should have more control over the lands and how they are used. The counterargument is that such lands are national trusts and can only legitimately be dealt with by representatives of the national government. According to historian Robert Hughes in *The Culture of Complaint*, the American West "is archetypally the place where Big Government is distrusted, the land of the independent man going it alone. Yet much of it—states like Arizona, for instance—has depended, not marginally or occasionally but always and totally, on federal money from Washington for its economic existence." Consequently, "the Southwestern states could never have been settled at their present human density without immense expenditure of government funds on water-engineering. They are less the John Wayne than the Welfare Queen of American development."

Yet these western states, mostly Republican at that, do not like to be reminded of the role that Washington played in creating and economically developing them.

The federal lands within them belong just as much to the rest of the nation. While the political leaders of these western states are quick to assert their "rights" over federal lands, other citizens of other states are just as quick to note that these lands were paid for, indeed fought for, by the entire country.

The latest wrinkle in this Sagebrush Rebellion is to resurrect **Gifford Pinchot**'s definition of conservation as the "wise use" of resources. But this modern wise-use movement is not traditional conservation, but a cover for those who advocate greater economic development of public lands. By asserting the legitimacy of multiple uses of public lands, they seek to roll back environmental protections now extant. One legal technique to achieve this rollback is to assert county supremacy by means of local land-use ordinances. This has engendered considerable conflict between local officials and federal land managers. The only certainty here is that as one contemplates the vast expanses of federal land in the West, much litigation can be seen on the horizon.

The web of intergovernmental relations is such a tangled one that there are no easy solutions to the understandable desire for devolution. Even a national administration completely sympathetic to the devolutionist will find it difficult to return powers and lands back to the states. It will take far more than a Williamsburg Resolve and a Sagebrush Rebellion to simply locate, let alone repeal, two centuries' worth of centralizing legislation.

The Public Choice Solution

The Reagan Revolution of the 1980s, which was continued by the 1990s Republican Congress, coincided with public administration's increasing embrace of public-choice theory. This theory rejected the concept of welfare economics that emerged out of the New Deal: that when private markets failed, the government had to step in to effectively carry out the public interest, and the governmental level best suited to do this was the federal one.

Public-choice theory seriously questioned whether such governmental decisions really represented the wishes of the majority of citizens. More emphatically, public choice denounced governments as being basically inefficient and completely lacking in incentives to perform well unless the expansion of their own programs and the increase of their budgets was involved. The better solution, public-choice advocates argued, was to place as much governmental action (and expenditures) at the lowest possible levels—i.e., at the local government level. The feeling here was that local governments would provide more experimentation, true competition, and innovation. At the local level, citizens could "vote with their feet"—that is, if the citizens had access to appropriate information, they would be able to readily compare the levels of taxation to the quality of services they received. They could then reject inefficient or unresponsive governments by voting down budgets, by voting out big spenders or even by moving elsewhere—or not moving in at all. Thus the solution to devolution offered by the public-choice advocates is to increase the discretion in

---

Gifford Pinchot (1865–1946) America's first professional forester, who is credited with coining the term *conservation*. Twice governor of Pennsylvania (1923–1927; 1931–1935), he became internationally famous as President Theodore Roosevelt's partner in making conservation a national issue.

TABLE 4.5 Average Monthly Welfare Payments for a Family of Three

High Benefits		Low Benefits	
California	$607	Arkansas	$204
New York	577	Indiana	288
Vermont	638	Mississippi	120
Washington	546	Tennessee	185
Wisconsin	518	Texas	188

SOURCE: *Newsweek*, August 14, 1995.

the hands of the individual voter by maximizing "user-pay systems" (whether for trash collection or through fees at state park camping grounds), and by placing vouchers (for schools or housing) for spending in the hands of recipients rather than compelling them to use particular government services or institutions.

The Race to the Bottom

The ultimate devolution, of course, is to get government out of a particular activity altogether. Certainly privatization, as discussed in Chapter 3, has a major role to play here. But those who would privatize many aspects of the welfare system are relying on private charitable giving to make up the difference between reduced government spending and the actual life-sustaining needs of the poor. But the very welfare programs that are being criticized were created in the first place because private charity proved insufficient.

Charity notwithstanding, the real issue in the devolution of welfare programs is that of a "race to the bottom." In this race states and their counties increasingly lower their welfare benefits to discourage the out-of-state poor from moving in to collect more generous aid than was possible where they were. "Generous" states increasingly resent the fact that "stingy" states are effectively exporting their poor. But as Minnesota Governor Arne Carlson said, "We do not want to be in the importing business. We will devise a range of policies to make sure we take care of Minnesotans, but we're not in the business of subsidizing Gary, Indiana." This is the crux of the intergovernmental welfare dilemma. A state designs a responsible welfare system to take care of its own only to become a welfare magnet to outsiders. But by "racing to the bottom" in terms of benefits, states discourage the out-of-state poor from moving in. Senator Daniel Patrick Moynihan offers this explanation: "The hidden agenda of the Devolution Revolution is a large-scale withdrawal of support for social welfare, no matter how well conceived. The result would be a race to the bottom, as states, deprived of federal matching funds, compete with one another to reduce spending by depriving their own dependent population of help."

There is already a major differential among the states. The block granting of federal welfare funding that withdraws the federal matching requirement (which was, in effect, an entitlement to the states) may make that differential far worse. Now that welfare eligibility is state- (as opposed to nationally) determined, the differential in benefits can vastly increase. Many states now offer a low level of benefits. The block grant reforms now allow them to offer no benefits. As this problem shows, the core issues of intergovernmental relations can be reduced to stark realities. It comes down to this: intergovernmental fiscal arrangements ultimately determine—for a large class of citizens—who eats and who goes hungry.

Summary

Intergovernmental relations is federalism in action. It is the complex network of day-to-day interrelationships among the governments within a federal system. It is the political, fiscal, programmatic, and administrative processes by which higher units of government share revenues and other resources with lower units of government, generally accompanied by special conditions that the lower units must satisfy as prerequisites to receiving the assistance.

The U.S. Constitution created the permanent features of intergovernmental relations in the United States. The popular image of the federal system as a layer cake, with each layer of government neatly on top of the other, is deceptive. The reality is more like a marble cake in which the cooperative relations among the varying levels of government result in an intermingling—not a layering of activities.

The key word in the new American thrust toward decentralization or devolution is mandate: one level of government requires another to offer—or pay for—a program as a matter of law or as a prerequisite to partial or full funding for either the program in question or other programs. Mandates are orders. The movement toward devolution is spurred on by jurisdictions and constituencies that increasingly resent taking such orders.

Fiscal federalism refers to the financial relationships that exist between units of government in a federal system. A central question is frequently asked about fiscal federalism: Why can't the citizens of the states just keep their money (meaning have their federal taxes reduced) rather than paying it to the federal government so that it can be returned in grants and services? The only certainty here is that the states have become addicted to intergovernmental funding. The question remains whether their political leaders will gradually wean them from it or feed their habit.

Key Concepts

block grant   A grant distributed in accordance with a statutory formula for use in a variety of activities within a broad functional area, largely at the recipient's discretion.

categorical grant   A grant that can be used only for specific, narrowly defined activities—for example, to construct an interstate highway.

council of government (COG)   An organization of cooperating local governments seeking a regional approach to planning, development, transportation, environment, and other issues.

devolution   The transfer of power from a central to a local authority.

federalism   A system of governance in which a national, overarching government shares power with subnational or state governments.

federalism, cooperative   The notion that the national, state, and local governments are cooperating, interacting agents jointly working to solve common problems, rather than conflicting, sometimes hostile competitors, pursuing similar or possibly conflicting ends.

federalism, dual The nineteenth-century concept, now no longer operational, that the functions and responsibilities of the federal and state governments were theoretically distinguished and functionally separate from each other.

federalism, marble-cake The concept that the cooperative relations among the varying levels of government result in an intermingling of activities; in contrast to the more traditional view of layer-cake federalism, which holds that the three levels of government are totally or almost totally separate.

Federalism, New The Republican efforts begun during the Nixon administration to decentralize governmental functions by returning power and responsibility to the states. This trend was continued in the 1980s by the Reagan administration and culminated in the 1990s movement toward devolution.

federalism, picket fence The concept that bureaucratic specialists at the various levels of government (along with clientele groups) exercise considerable power over the nature of intergovernmental programs.

fiscal federalism The financial relations between and among units of government in a federal system. The theory of fiscal federalism, or multiunit government finance, is one part of the branch of applied economics known as public finance.

grant An intergovernmental transfer of funds (or other assets). Since the New Deal, state and local governments have become increasingly dependent upon federal grants for an almost infinite variety of programs.

intergovernmental relations The complex network of interrelationships among governments; the political, fiscal, programmatic, and administrative processes by which higher units of government share revenues and other resources with lower units of government, generally accompanied by special conditions that the lower units must satisfy as prerequisites to receiving the assistance.

mandating One level of government requiring another to offer—and/or pay for—a program as a matter of law or as a prerequisite to partial or full funding for either the program in question or other programs.

Bibliography

Arrandale, Tom. (1994). "The Sagebrush Gang Rides Again," *Governing* (March).

Cohen, Richard. (1995). "States Aren't Saints, Either," *Washington Post National Weekly* (April 9).

Cook, Gareth G. (1995). "Devolution Chic: Why Sending Power to the States Could Make a Monkey Out of Uncle Sam," *Washington Monthly* (April).

Ehrenhalt, Alan. (1995). "The Locust in the Garden of Government," *Governing* (March).

Elazar, Daniel J. (1962). *The American Partnership: Intergovernmental Cooperation in the 19th Century United States*. Chicago: University of Chicago Press.

Furtwangler, Albert. (1984). *The Authority of Publius: A Reading of the Federalist Papers*. Ithaca, NY: Cornell University Press.

Grodzins, Morton. (1966). *The American System*, ed. Daniel J. Elazar. Chicago: Rand McNally.

Helvarg, David. (1994). *The War Against the Greens: The Wise Use Movement, the New Right, and Anti-Environmental Violence*. San Francisco: Sierra Club Books.

Henderson, André. (1994). "The Looming Disabilities Deadline," *Governing* (December).

Hughes, Robert. (1993). *The Culture of Complaint*. New York: Oxford University Press.

Larkin, John. (1995). "Mandate Protesters to Gain Limited Relief," *Public Administration Times* (March 1).

Lloyd, Alan. (1974). *The Scorching of Washington: The War of 1812*. Washington: Robert B. Luce.

Marando, Vincent, and Patricia S. Florestano. (1990). "Intergovernmental Management: The State of the Discipline." In *Public Administration: The State of the Discipline*, eds. Naomi B. Lynn and Aaron Wildavsky. Chatham, NJ: Chatham House.

McCurdy, Howard E. (1984). "Public Ownership of Land and the 'Sagebrush Rebellion,'" *Policy Studies Journal* 12 (March).

McDonald, Forrest. (1985). *Novus Ordo Seclorum: The Intellectual Origins of the Constitution*. Lawrence: University Press of Kansas.

Moynihan, Daniel Patrick. (1995). "The Devolution Revolution," *New York Times*, August 6.

Pooley, Eric. (1995). "Things That Make Rudy Nuts: The Mayor's Real Top Ten List: Unfunded Federal, State, and Judicial Mandates That Push the City into the Red," *New York* (January 30).

Popper, Frank J. (1984). "The Timely End of the Sagebrush Rebellion," *Public Interest* 76 (summer).

Rainwater, Lee, and William Yancey. (1967). *The Moynihan Report and the Politics of Controversy.* Cambridge: MIT Press.

Ross, Bernard H. (1998). "Metropolitan Organization." *International Encyclopedia of Public Policy and Administration,* ed. Jay M. Shafritz. Boulder, CO: Westview Press.

Sanford, Terry. (1967). *Storm Over the States.* New York: McGraw-Hill.

Shanahan, Eileen. (1991). "Going It Jointly: Regional Solutions for Local Problems," *Governing* (August).

Swarns, Rachel L. (1998). "A New Broom Needs a New Handle: Welfare as We Know It Goes Incognito," *New York Times* (July 5)

Swartz, Thomas R., and John E. Peck, eds. (1990). *The Changing Face of Fiscal Federalism.* Armonk, NY: M. E. Sharpe.

Vobejda, Barbara, and Judith Havemann. (1998). "States' Welfare Shift: Stop It Before It Starts," *Washington Post* (August 12).

Vobejda, Barbara. (1995). "Will There Be a Race to the Bottom on Welfare?" *Washington Post National Weekly* (September 18–24).

White, Leonard D. (1948). *The Federalists.* New York: Macmillan.

Wikstrom, Nelson. (1985). *Councils of Governments: A Study of Political Incrementalism.* Chicago: Nelson-Hall.

Wills, Garry. (1981). *Explaining America: The Federalist.* Garden City, NY: Doubleday.

Wright, Deil S. (1988). *Understanding Intergovernmental Relations,* 3rd ed. Pacific Grove, CA: Brooks/Cole.

Recommended Books

Conlan, Timothy. (1998). *From New Federalism to Devolution: Twenty-five Years of Intergovernmental Reform.* Washington, DC: Brookings Institution. The history of American federalism from the 1970s through the 1990s.

Dilulio, John, and Donald F. Kettl. (1995). *Fine Print: The Contract with America, Devolution, and the Administrative Realities of American Federalism.* Washington, DC: Brookings Institution. The story of what happens when Republican party ideology seeks to cope with and reform the immutable facts of intergovernmental relations.

Peterson, Paul E. (1995). *The Price of Federalism.* Washington, DC: Brookings Institution. A historical account and optimistic contemporary assessment of the intergovernmental fiscal relationships among the differing levels of government.

Posner, Paul L. *The Politics of Unfunded Mandates: Whither Federalism?* (1998). Washington, DC: Georgetown University Press. The origins and politics of congressional requirements for state and local governments to implement federal policies.

Related Web Sites

Council of State Governments
http://www.csg.org
Intergovernmental Enterprise Panel
http://www.iep.fedworld.gov
Local Government Network
http://civic.net/lgnet/
Metropolitan Councils of Government
http://www.cais.net/mwcog
National Association of Counties
http://www.naco.org

National Association of Towns and Townships
http://www.natat.org
National Association of Regional Councils
http://narc.org/narc/index.html
National Governors' Association
http://www.nga.org
National League of Cities
http://www.nic.org

5

The Evolution of Management and Organization Theory

Keynote: Moses Meets the First Management Consultant

The scene is set as in the Bible: Moses (in Exodus, Chapter 18) has led the Israelites out of the land of Egypt. Now . . .

> Moses sat to judge the people: and the people stood by Moses from the morning unto the evening.
>
> And when Moses' father-in-law saw all that he did to the people, he said, "What is this thing that thou doest to the people? Why sittest thou thyself alone, and all the people stand by thee from morning unto even?"
>
> And Moses said unto his father-in-law, "Because the people . . . when they have a matter, they come unto me; and I judge between one and another. . . ."

Moses, while certainly an effective and charismatic leader, could not delegate. "The system" he created would not let him let go. He literally had thousands of people reporting to him. The managerial workload became overwhelming, The ancient Israelites by the hundreds were unhappily standing in line "from the morning unto the evening" to confer with him. Finally, Jethro, Moses' father-in-law, became the first known management consultant when he gave Moses the reengineering advice he needed to create a more competent organization. First he assessed the problem:

> And Moses' father-in-law said, "The thing that thou doest is not good. Thou wilt surely wear away, both thou, and this people that is with thee: for this thing is too heavy for thee: thou art not able to perform it thyself alone.
>
> Hearken now unto my voice, I will give thee counsel . . . thou shalt teach them ordinances and laws, and shalt show them the way wherein they must walk.

Here is the beginning of modern bureaucratic structures. A body of laws, a book of regulations, that apply to everyone means that all similar problems are treated alike; the organization does not have to "reinvent the wheel" each time a common problem reoccurs. Jethro next lays out the most basic principles of all hierarchical organizations, the very same principles that are today used in literally all large organizations whether they be military or civilian, private or public.

> Moreover thou shalt provide out of all the people able men . . . to be rulers of thousands, and rulers of hundreds, rulers of fifties, and rulers of tens:
>
> And let them judge the people at all seasons: and it shall be, that every great matter they shall bring unto thee, but every small matter they shall judge: so shall it be easier for thyself, and they shall bear the burden with thee.
>
> If thou shalt do this thing . . . then thou shalt be able to endure . . ."

In those three verses we have the origins of all large-scale enterprises. Jethro's advice of putting able people to be "rulers of thousands, and rulers of hundreds, rulers of fifties, and rulers of tens" was followed by the ancient Roman army, the early Catholic Church, and every major organization since. Early in the twentieth century, Frederick Taylor, the so-called "father of scientific management," called bringing "every great matter" to the top "management by exception"—meaning that if all was going well there was no reason to bother the next higher layer of management. This is exactly what Jethro advised. He then stated the main advantage of abiding by this advice: "If thou shalt do this thing, . . . then thou shalt be able to endure." The essential problem of the nondelegating manager is not that he or she is not able and wise, but that in large organizations no one person "is able to endure" without delegating. Thus an otherwise extremely competent manager becomes incompetent by seeking to be super-competent—by trying to do it all.

But what did Moses do with all this good advice?

> So Moses hearkened to the voice of his father-in-law, and did all that he had said.
>
> And Moses chose able men out of all Israel, and made them heads over the people, rulers of thousands, and rulers of hundreds, rulers of fifties, and rulers of tens.
>
> And they judged the people at all seasons: the hard causes they brought unto Moses, but every small matter they judged themselves.

Moses took his consultant's advice and became a more competent leader. He had to deal only with "the hard causes" because he adopted a system by which "every small matter" would be dealt with by others. Not only did Moses make himself more competent, but his structural reforms made all of his lieutenants better managers as well. Moses had, to use a modern term, reinvented tribal management.

Now, what happened to Jethro, the consultant who turned Moses from an over-controlling to an empowering manager? All we know is that Moses "let his father-in-law depart; and he went his way into his own land." He then disappeared from the Bible and from history. It just goes to show that even in biblical times it was true that all management consultants eventually wear out their welcome. But it gets worse as far as Jethro's reputation is concerned. Later on in the Bible (Deut. 1:9–18), Moses is giving a kind of annual report to the Israelites. He recounts the reorganization plan he adopted with Jethro's advice and, like many a modern executive, does not give any credit at all to the person who had the ideas that he successfully implemented. And this is not unjust. After all, the job of the consultant— the reason he or she is hired in the first place—is to make the person who hires them look good. A consultant's final task is to take the money he or she has earned—and run.

The Origins of Public Management

Civilization and administration have always gone hand in hand. Since ancient times, a city was defined by the walls created for its defense. Even today many **municipalities** will award someone a key to the city in symbolic remembrance of when the only way into a city was through a locked gate in the wall. This meant that once primitive tribes gathered in cities—when they literally became civilized (meaning to

---

municipalities Local governments. The word and concept comes from the Latin in which *municipium* referred to any self-governing body within the Roman Empire.

Charlton Heston as Moses in the 1956 film *The Ten Commandments*. Here he demands that Pharaoh (played by Yul Brynner) stop reading his book about Egyptian public administration and "let my people go!" Ever since playing Moses in one of the most successful films of all time, Heston's voice has been the patriarchal voice of authority. This was reinforced by many subsequent films in which he played strong historical characters such as El Cid, Cardinal Richelieu, and Andrew Jackson. Thus, when in 1998 he was elected president of the National Rifle Association, the preeminent gun lobby, his denunciation of President Clinton in his inaugural speech as head of the NRA, had a resonance far beyond these damning words: "Mr. Clinton, America didn't trust you with our health care sytem . . . America doesn't trust you with our 21-year-old daughters, and we sure, Lord, don't trust you with our guns!" Heston was particularly annoyed that during the course of the Lewinsky affair the president seemed to have violated at least three of the Ten Commandments (See Chapter 14 for more on this) •

live in cities)—they had to be sufficiently organized for war to build their strong-hold and defend it from attackers. This necessitated a sophisticated system of administration. Cities without walls only became possible in relatively recent times, when an overarching state authority was able to impose peace over a large area.

Thus the profession of **management** began and developed as the **profession of arms**. To the extent that the history of the world is the history of warfare, then it is also the history of public administration—because war at the state level is quite

---

management A term that can refer to both (1) the people responsible for running an organization and (2) the running process itself—the utilizing of numerous resources to accomplish an organizational goal.

profession of arms The practice of the art and science of war; the occupation of a career military officer.

literally not possible without an effective system of public administration behind it. Military officers were the first public administrators. Societies beyond the extended family only became possible with the rise of an officer class. Thus the first armies were mobs with managers.

Only gradually did these mob managers develop the organizational skills to command large armies and rule large areas. These early martial skills constitute the most basic elements of all administrative processes. **Hierarchy**, line and staff personnel, **logistics**, and communications were all highly developed by ancient armies. Even *reform* is of military origin. After all, it means to once again (the "re") organize the ranks (the "form") for an additional assault—whether on another army or on a difficult management problem. And there is hardly any core concept in modern strategic thought that has not been anticipated by **Sun-Tzu** in ancient China. The word *strategy* itself comes from the ancient Greek meaning "the art of the general."

The vocabulary of public administration is so heavily indebted to its military origins that the field would be literally tongue-tied without it. Next time you see an organization's slogan (such as New Hampshire's "Live Free or Die") printed on a sheet of its letterhead, remember that "quality first" or some other inane would-be motivator had its beginnings as a war cry of the Highland clans of Scotland. If you don't get what you initially want and go for your fall-back position, remember that fall-backs were prepared fortified sites that soldiers ran to once the enemy broke through their first line of defense. If you are in an organization's rear echelon, console yourself with the fact that the French are to blame because they used their word for the rung of a ladder—*échelon*—to describe parallel military formations. And if you cherish a particular tax loophole, remember that a loophole was a small opening in a fort from which soldiers could shoot out of, or use as a means of escape from, depending upon the circumstances. They are still a means of escape—from taxes.

The Continuing Influence of Ancient Rome

In his landmark 1941 book, *The Managerial Revolution*, James Burnham contended that as the control of large corporations passes from the hands of the owners into the hands of professional administrators, the society's new governing class would be the possessors not of wealth but of technical expertise. But Burnham was two millennia off in his analysis because this managerial changeover from those of wealth and power to those of professional expertise first occurred in the ancient Roman army. According to military historian John Keegan, "The Roman centurions, long-service unit leaders drawn from the best of the enlisted ranks, formed the first

---

hierarchy Any ordering of persons, things, or ideas by rank or level. Administrative structures are typically hierarchical in that each level has authority over levels below and must take orders from levels above.

logistics Traditionally the art and science of moving military forces and keeping them supplied; those inventory, production, and traffic-management activities that seek the timely placement of materiel and personnel at the proper time and in the appropriate quantities.

Sun-Tzu (fourth century B.C.E.) The ancient Chinese writer whose essays, traditionally published as *The Art of War*, have influenced all Western military analysts since they were first available in European editions in the late eighteenth century.

Box 5.1

Listen Up!

The ancient Egyptians were highly skilled administrators—how else could they have built the pyramids? Here is an example of their wisdom—4,000-year-old advice for supervisors that could be found in any industrial psychology text today:

> Be calm as thou listenest to what the petitioner has to say. Do not rebuff him before he has swept out his body or before he has said that for which he came. . . . It is not [necessary] that everything about which he was petitioned should come to pass, [for] a good hearing is soothing to the heart.

Some things haven't changed much in the last four millennia!

SOURCE OF QUOTE: John A. Wilson, *The Culture of Ancient Egypt* (Chicago: University of Chicago Press, 1951).

body of professional fighting officers known to history." This middle-management class transmitted from generation to generation the technical skills and discipline by which Rome dominated the world for five centuries. They were the managers who allowed the **patrician** governing class to exercise actual command. They were motivated by loyalty to their legion, pride in their profession, regular pay, and retirement payments that were an additional inducement to good behavior. Here is the beginning of the modern **merit system**. The West would not see its like again until **Napoléon**, espousing the best in French revolutionary idealism, announced "careers open to talent" in both the civilian and military spheres.

The regulating of pay and pensions in ancient Rome was the key to maintaining the army—and to this end the first civil service was created (by the Emperor **Augustus Caesar**) to raise the taxes necessary to support the legions. Thus out of military necessity was born civilian public administration. The same Augustus would boast that "I found Rome a city of bricks and left it a city of marble." While spoken by an emperor, these are also the words of a proud municipal **public works** administrator.

patrician A member of the upper class in ancient Rome; by analogy, a member of any high-ranking group or governing class. The opposite was a plebeian, a member of the lower class.

merit system A public sector concept of staffing that implies that no test of party membership is involved in the selection, promotion, or retention of government employees and that a constant effort is made to select the best qualified individuals available for appointment and advancement.

Napoléon Bonaparte (1769–1821) The Corsican-born French general and dictator who dominated the political and military affairs of Europe from the time he seized control of France in a coup d'état in 1799 until his final defeat at the Battle of Waterloo in 1815.

Augustus Caesar (63 B.C.E.–14 C.E.) The nephew of Julius Caesar who became the first Roman emperor after defeating his rivals Mark Anthony and Marcus Brutus in the civil war that followed his uncle's assassination in 44 B.C.E.

public works A general term for government-sponsored construction projects.

While many ancient kingdoms, such as Egypt and China, had sophisticated administrative institutions, the core features of modern public administration in the Western world were first found in the Roman Empire. The Roman state was depersonalized. It had existed independent of any political leader or king; it was not "owned" by anyone. Significantly, the state's public finances were separate from the private funds of its leadership. Second, it made use of a centralized hierarchical structure. At the top was the central government, then the province, and finally the diocese. These structures are still familiar, still in use. Finally, the Romans introduced several units of functional specialization that form the heart of most modern public administrative systems. They had organizational units for military affairs, finance, justice, and **police**. This last function was so broadly conceived that it included transportation, health, education, agriculture, and commerce.

Ever since the time of ancient Rome, young men have viewed a stint of service as a military officer as a logical prelude to larger public service or to greater political office. Indeed, during the days of the Roman Republic it was a condition of elective office that a candidate have a decade of military service. Not only was this a seasoning period for youths, it was the only social institution that offered systematic training in administration. It was thought reasonable that those who could demonstrate the ability to command and administer should be considered legitimate candidates. This is still true today. Most U.S. presidents and countless lesser politicians have used their military experience as a springboard for their political careers. Has your member of Congress served in the armed forces?

When Governor Bill Clinton of Arkansas announced he would be running in the 1992 presidential race, the very legitimacy of his candidacy was called into question because he not only lacked military experience but conspicuously sought to avoid it during the Vietnam War. While many who opposed the war thought that Clinton's legal avoidance of the draft was a more honorable course of action than serving in this unpopular war, the depth of reaction to his lack of prior military service continued to make it difficult for him to function as **commander in chief** well into his presidency. Thus the ancient Roman attitude toward the desirability of youthful military service as preparation for later public office still strongly affects modern American politics and administration.

The Military Heritage of Public Administration

The history of the world can be viewed as the rise and fall of public administrative institutions. Those ancient empires that rose and prevailed for a while were those with better administrative institutions than their competitors. Brave soldiers have been plentiful in every society, but they are ultimately wasted if not backed up by

---

police Paramilitary state and local government organizations whose most basic responsibilities include maintaining public order and safety (through the use of force if necessary), investigating and arresting persons accused of crimes, and securing the cooperation of the citizenry. But a state's police power goes far beyond the criminal justice system; it is the legal basis by which governments regulate such areas as public health, safety, and morals.

commander in chief The authority granted under Article III, Section 2, of the U.S. Constitution that "the president shall be commander in chief of the army and the navy of the United States and of the militia of the several states when called into the actual service of the United States."

TABLE 5.1   Military Service of U.S. Presidents Since World War II

President	Service
Harry S. Truman	Army
Dwight D. Eisenhower	Army
John F. Kennedy	Navy
Lyndon B. Johnson	Navy
Richard M. Nixon	Navy
Gerald R. Ford	Navy
Jimmy Carter	Navy
Ronald Reagan	Army
George Bush	Navy
Bill Clinton	None

Note: While only Eisenhower—as head of Allied Forces in Western Europe during World War II—used his military career as a direct stepping stone to the presidency, all of the others found their military service to be a decided boost in their early political efforts.

administrators who can feed and pay them. **Marcus Tullius Cicero,** the ancient Roman orator, is usually credited with first saying that "the sinews of war are infinite money." And this was a trite sentiment way back when he said it!

Rome, like Egypt, Persia, and other empires before it, conquered the ancient world because it had an organizational doctrine that made its soldiers far more effective than competing forces—and because its legions were backed up by a sophisticated administrative system of supply based on regular if not equitable taxes. The Roman Empire only fell when its legions degenerated into corps of mercenaries and when its supply and tax bases were corrupted. Napoléon was wrong. Armies do not "march on their stomachs," as he said; they march on the proverbial backs of the tax collectors and on the roads built by administrators. Regular pay allows for discipline. Strict discipline is what makes a mob an army. And a disciplined military, obedient to the leaders of the state, is a precondition for civilization. This is the classic chicken-and-egg problem. Which comes first—effective public administration or an effective military? The rise and fall of ancient Rome proved that you could not have one without the other.

Early bureaucrats in ancient Rome and modern Europe literally wore uniforms that paralleled military dress. After all, the household servants of rulers traditionally wore **livery.** It indicated that the wearer was not free but the servant of another. Government administrators are still considered servants in this sense; they

---

Marcus Tullius Cicero (106–43 B.C.E.) The Roman senator who was killed by henchmen of Augustus Caesar because Cicero was a republican and Augustus was a murderous dictator. This in no way diminishes Augustus' reputation as a fine administrator. Public administrators throughout the ages have used murder as an administrative tool. Only relatively recently has this become less fashionable.

livery The uniform of a servant; any identical and identifying item of dress—such as a necktie, scarf, or blazer—worn by members of the same organization.

General Dwight D. Eisenhower preparing for high political office by leading the Allied invasion of Nazi-occupied France on D Day, June 6, 1944. Here he is giving a pep talk to the soldiers who are about to parachute into France the night before the dawn invasion. Eisenhower's chief air staff advisor has urged him to cancel this aspect of the invasion, as it was considered a suicide mission for the more than 30,000 paratroopers; the estimate was that 80 percent would be killed or wounded within hours. This photo exists because Eisenhower felt it only honorable to look these men in the eye before sending so many off to their deaths. But Eisenhower also believed that the soldiers invading from the sea on D Day needed every possible break, even if the paratroopers were practically wiped out while trying to disrupt the enemy's rear. In the end the paratroopers performed better than expected, had "only" 30 percent casualties, and Eisenhower got the credit for winning the war in western Europe. He was acutely aware that he eventually became president because of the spilt blood and unstinting valor of these men •

are public servants because they, too, have accepted obligations, which means they are not completely free. Indeed, until early in this century many otherwise civilian public officials in Europe—most notably diplomats—had prescribed uniforms.

Both victorious soldiers and successful managers tend to be inordinately admired and disproportionately rewarded as risk takers. True, the specific risks and rewards are different; but the phenomenon is the same. They both may have to put their careers, and sometimes significant parts of their anatomy as well, "on the line" to obtain a goal for their state or organization. Notice again the military language, for "the line" originally referred to the line of battle where you faced the enemy. This is why line officers today are still those who perform the services for which the organization exists. This is the direct link between the Roman centurion and the modern fire captain, chief of detectives, or elementary school principal. Life on the line is still a daily struggle.

The Significance of Administrative Doctrine

All organizations are guided by a doctrine of management that reflects basic values. Doctrines and values may be stated or unstated, conscious or unconscious, advertent or inadvertent; but they are always there. No management program can be viable without a guiding doctrine and compatible behavioral techniques for implementing it. The first administrative doctrine was that contained in the brutality of military discipline: "Do this or die." Indeed, one of the main reasons officers traditionally carried pistols was to shoot their own men if they were not sufficiently enthusiastic about obeying an order—especially one involving great danger. As Edward Gibbon wrote in *The Decline and Fall of the Roman Empire* (1776), "It was an inflexible maxim of Roman discipline that a good soldier should dread his own officers far more than the enemy."

A more modern example of a doctrine is **Henry Ford**'s famous simplistic dictum: "All that we ask of the men is that they do the work which is set before them." With Ford there was an underlying assumption that employees who do not respond adequately to the "work which is set before them" should be dismissed. (A much better alternative than being shot!) The behavioral technique used here is the same as that applied to those small experimental animals who have spent generations running through mazes for psychologists. The more work, the more cheese.

More sophisticated doctrines are needed when meaningful and fulfilling work for its employees is a central goal of the organization. Here the underlying assumptions are radically different. Wages are not the only reason for working! Strategies that emerge from this management value and philosophy are more conducive to long-term organizational **effectiveness** and **productivity**. Just as religious doctrine often defines an individual's attitude toward life, a managerial doctrine defines management's values and attitude toward work and people at work. By the exercise of its doctrinal philosophy, management earns a reciprocal attitude from others toward their responsibilities. This is why doctrines, values, and attitudes on the part of management so often become self-fulfilling prophecies. Employees and managers, like students and teachers, tend to live up (or down) to expectations.

Henry Ford (1863–1947) The founder of Ford Motor Company, which was first to mass-produce automobiles on a moving assembly line.

effectiveness Traditionally, the extent to which an organization accomplishes some predetermined goal or objective; more recently, the overall performance of an organization from the viewpoint of some strategic constituency. Effectiveness is not entirely dependent upon the efficiency of a program, because program outputs may increase without necessarily increasing effectiveness.

productivity The measured relationship between the quantity (and quality) of results produced and the quantity of resources required for production. Productivity is, in essence, a measure of the work efficiency of an individual, a work unit, or a whole organization.

But doctrine and attitudes do far more than affect the **morale** and performance of individual employees; they are part of the culture of the organization, and the organizational culture affects the overall competence or incompetence of an organization. When managers are heavily constrained by official doctrine, by standard operating procedures, and by "the book," they cannot use discretion to respond to changing circumstances. Faced with an obviously right decision that is contrary to formal policy, they all too often dutifully make the wrong decision, feeling that they have no choice. This is a faulty conception of managerial responsibility. Any organization that does not allow its managers to appropriately respond to changing conditions is headed for a fall. It is this conception, this philosophy, this doctrine of leadership as expressed by the organization's culture and as manifest in the organization's policies that ultimately determines success or failure, victory or defeat, competence or incompetence.

Administrative doctrines resemble the paradigms of Thomas S. Kuhn. In his landmark 1962 book, *The Structure of Scientific Revolutions*, Kuhn explained that as the natural sciences progressed, they amassed a body of ever-changing theory. Scientific advances were based not on the accumulation of knowledge and facts, but rather on a dominant paradigm (or model) used in any specific period to explain the phenomena under study. Rather than refuting previous theories, each paradigm would build upon the body of relevant knowledge and theories. Once a paradigm was accepted by consensus among current scholars, it would last as long as it was useful. Ultimately, it would be replaced by a more relevant and useful paradigm; this process of replacement was Kuhn's "scientific revolution."

While paradigms have their own time frames and contents, they overlap both in time and content because they are constantly evolving. In a parallel sense, doctrinal development in administration has been inherently cyclical. A successful innovation by reformers is followed by a period of increased effectiveness, at least until competing organizations adopt similar reforms. But over time advancing technologies and changing environments allow the innovation to deteriorate relative to other arrangements, first to become less competent, then to become incompetent. After an innovative change remedies the problem, the cycle of competence and incompetence repeats. This "time lag" phenomena is similar to the traditional boom-and-bust business cycle, with incompetence occurring when the cycle is in recession. Thus, maintaining organizational competence is a never-ending struggle.

This is why competing organizations tend to look like each other over time. Whenever an innovation earns a reputation for being successful, it is copied by others wishing to be equally successful. But equality in structure and equipment is not always enough to ensure being a successful competitor. A famous example will illustrate. During the spring of 1940, Nazi Germany conquered France using tanks and troops in a **blitzkrieg** formation. Germany won despite the fact that France not

---

morale The collective attitude of the workforce toward their work environment; a crude measure of the organizational climate.

blitzkrieg German for "lightning war," the tactical method used by the German army in the invasion of Poland, France, and the Soviet Union during World War II. The classic blitzkrieg campaign involves swift strikes with tanks and planes and a series of army columns exploiting weak spots in the enemy line. Advance units pass behind the enemy, destroying its lines of communication and disrupting unit cohesion.

only had more troops but significantly more tanks that were of better quality. What made the difference was the fact that the Germans had a better tactical doctrine for the use of their tanks—in massed assaults as opposed to piecemeal support for infantry.

Remember that the military, the seminal administrative institution of all societies, only has to be led in battle a relatively few days of any year. But it has to be administered every day. Societies may be protected by their standing armies or navies; but armed forces cannot stand or float without administrative institutions to support them. It is often true, as Mao Tse-tung famously said, that "political power grows out of the barrel of a gun." But political power is empty and meaningless without concomitant economic and administrative power. Historian Paul Kennedy in his *The Rise and Fall of the Great Powers* demonstrated how in modern times ultimate victory went to the state that was economically strong. Those that were merely militarily strong—Austria, France, Great Britain, Germany, Spain and the Soviet Union—all suffered from "imperial overstretch" and declined as great powers.

Revolutionaries with their guns can start a revolution, but only the administrators that follow in their wake can solidify and complete it. Thus all conquering armies have necessarily been followed by hordes of bureaucrats. Napoléon solidified the French Revolution of 1789 with the administrative reforms embodied in the Code Napoléon and the creation of a merit-based civil service. The U.S. Constitution of 1787, which followed the Revolution of 1776, still provides the administrative framework of American government. The Russian Revolution of 1917 led to the administrative apparatus of a socialist state that with its **command economy** was so cumbersome and inefficient that a subsequent revolution in 1991 replaced it with a regime that had greater hopes for efficiency. All the political revolutions in Eastern Europe during the late 1980s, while initially politically motivated, increasingly became administrative revolutions to secure for their people the blessings of a new administrative doctrine, one that allows a state's economy to function with the greater efficiency offered by a free market.

Every major political revolution—from the American to the French to the Russian—can be said to have been caused by the same thing—poor public administration. Remember that the large middle section of the American Declaration of Independence is a list consisting largely of administrative complaints against George III, the British king. For example, the Declaration asserted that the king "has obstructed the administration of justice," has imposed "taxes on us without our consent," and "has erected a multitude of new offices and sent hither swarms of officers to harass our people, and eat out their substance." Simply put: Happy and prosperous people do not revolt. Revolutions are caused by incompetent public administration, and they are made by disgruntled consumers of government services. This is why an effective public administration doctrine is so important—because no society can live in peace and prosperity, or prevail in war, without it. It is a matter of national security!

---

command economy The traditional economic model offered by communism wherein all industry is controlled by a central government that makes all decisions and appoints all managers.

The Evolution of Management Principles

Authoritarian or traditional management is the classic model of military governance applied to civilian purposes. Managers under an authoritarian doctrine value order, precision, consistency, and obedience. To them, the power that flows from structure is supreme. Relationships are hierarchical, based on dominance and dependence. This authoritarian style has gradually given way to less centralized, more participative management styles—not because management developed an altruistic desire to be nice to the workers, but because participation has proved to be more competent than authoritarianism when dealing with sophisticated workers. This change takes nothing away from the fact that at an earlier time authoritarianism was the most competent management posture. Thus, in judging the competence of an organization at any given time, you must, as with a stock market, learn whether the level of competence (as with the price of a stock) is high or low relative to others in the market.

Since antiquity, the military has evolved principles about how their authoritarian organizations were best managed. While there are many versions of the principles of war that reflect local conditions, they all contain the same basic elements. Those elements having civilian applications have been incorporated into principles of management. Thus concepts once military—such as **span of control** and **unity of command**—are now thoroughly civilian as well.

Comparing Military and Civilian Principles

There is no **royal road** to administrative wisdom. There are no generally accepted principles of management, no one list upon which there is general agreement. However, there is a principles approach that has its origins in the principles of war. While these precepts can be traced back to ancient times, for comparison's sake it is convenient to use the nine principles of war currently used by the U.S. Army:

1. Objective: Direct every military operation toward a clearly defined, decisive, and attainable objective.
2. Offensive: Seize, retain, and exploit the initiative.
3. Mass: Concentrate combat power at the decisive place and time.
4. Economy of force: Allocate minimum essential combat power to secondary efforts.
5. Maneuver: Place the enemy in a position of disadvantage through the flexible application of combat power.
6. Unity of command: For every objective, ensure unity of effort under one responsible commander.

---

span of control The extent of an administrator's or agency's responsibility. The span of control has usually been expressed as the number of subordinates that a manager should supervise.

unity of command The concept that each individual in an organization should be accountable to a single superior.

royal road An easy way. The Greek mathematician Euclid in about 300 B.C.E. supposedly told the mathematically challenged Ptolemy I of Egypt that there was no royal road to geometry. There still isn't!

7. Security: Never permit the enemy to acquire an advantage.

8. Surprise: Strike the enemy at a time and/or place and in a manner for which he is unprepared.

9. Simplicity: Prepare clear, uncomplicated plans and clear, concise orders to ensure thorough understanding.

All nine principles are not always important. But in any large-scale operation they are always all there. Which ones dominate at any given time is a function of context, of the evolving situation. These principles are inherently interrelating and reinforcing. They represent the distilled science of war as it has evolved over thousands of years. But they are merely the colors with which the commander paints. If he or she is artful in execution, then victory, promotion, and acclaim will follow. If clumsy, then removal by death or disgrace will. Note that the principles of war (and management) are not really designed for experienced officers. These are instructions for the inexperienced. Military historian John Keegan even called them "words to the unwise."

There are a large number of formulations of the principles of management from which to choose. Those below are from **Catheryn Seckler-Hudson**, who wrote them in 1955 when she was dean of the School of Government and Public Administration at the American University. Her 12 principles, distilled from the literature of business and public administration and presented in her book, *Organization and Management*, came with a warning label: "It should never be assumed that principles of organization are immutable laws to be applied automatically."

1. Policy should be defined and imparted to those who are responsible for its achievement.

2. Work should be subdivided, systematically planned, and programmed.

3. Tasks and responsibilities should be specifically assigned and understood.

4. Appropriate methods and procedures should be developed and utilized by those responsible for policy achievement.

5. Appropriate resources (men, money, material) in terms of availability and priority should be equitably allocated.

6. Authority commensurate with responsibility should be delegated and located as close as possible to the point where operations occur and decisions need to be made.

7. Adequate structural relationships through which to operate should be established.

8. Effective and qualified leadership should head each organization and each subdivision of the organization.

9. Unity of command and purpose should permeate the organization.

Catheryn Seckler-Hudson (1902–1963) A pioneer in developing the "nuts and bolts" of public management technology, she was the author of many groundbreaking works on public sector planning, budgeting, and organization.

10. Continuous accountability for utilization of resources and for the production of results should be required.

11. Effective coordination of all individual and group efforts within the organization should be achieved.

12. Continuous reconsideration of all matters pertaining to the organization should be a part of regular operations.

These principles represent the received wisdom of public administration at mid-century by one of its most acknowledged scholars. Yet when they are compared with the principles of war, they seem mushy and vacillating—hardly any guidance for leadership at all. (True, in the book from which these are taken the author includes many pages of additional explanation.) Part of the reason for this is that these are guidelines for administrators, not for leaders. Her guidelines and principles try to be so all-encompassing that they defeat themselves by their complexity. **Herbert Simon** gained much of his early reputation by attacking the principles approach in his 1946 article condescendingly titled "The Proverbs of Administration." He denounced the whole principles approach to public administration that then dominated administrative thinking. He found the management principles of his era inconsistent, conflicting, and inapplicable to too many of the administrative situations facing managers. He concluded that they were little more than proverbs. Simon would later write in his memoirs that this article, which "secured my instant and permanent visibility in public administration," came "almost purely from the logical structure and internal inconsistency of the principles themselves. No experience of organization was required to detect it."

Simon's criticism of these "proverbs" was valid only to a point. Principles of either kind—military or management—were never meant to be dogma. Even Napoléon warned that "no rule of war is so absolute as to allow no exceptions." But rules can be, nevertheless, very useful. As **Bernard Brodie** wrote, "It may be well that the consideration of a catalog of numbered principles (usually fewer than a dozen) with the barest definition of the meaning of each may be necessary to communicate to second-order minds (or minds too busy with the execution of plans to worry much about the specific validity of the ideas behind them) some conception of what the business is all about."

What is striking about the two lists is how the military list is more policy oriented, more leadership directed, than the civilian list. The latter seems obsessed with the routines of administration—as opposed to breaking new ground with innovation. The military principles are far more proactive and appropriately aggressive. But strangely enough, aggression is back in fashion in contemporary management thinking. The thrust of the military approach with its emphasis on strategy can be found, for example, in the philosophic underpinnings of the reinventing government and to-

---

Herbert Simon (1916–) The winner of the 1978 Nobel Prize in economics for his pioneering work in management decision making.

Bernard Brodie (1910–1978) The American who was the first major academic theorist of nuclear warfare.

tal quality management movements of the 1990s. Far from being of mere historical interest, they seem almost fresh when compared with the staid principles of management—and certainly relevant. When used with common sense and attention to experience, the principles of war can be extremely useful to those public managers who would join the never-ending battle against the evil trinity of waste, fraud, and abuse. This is all the more true for those public sector organizations forced to compete with private sector competitors. Competition by creating "enemies" clarifies objectives. The difference between a lean mean fighting machine, as the U.S. Marine Corps aspires to be, and a lean mean management machine is, in essence, one of objectives.

The Principles Approach

The principles approach to management, whether of the civilian or military variety, was a pivotal development in the advancement of management as a profession. Why? Because it seeks to make a science out of what was once considered only art. Antoine-Henri Jomini was the Swiss bank clerk turned Napoléonic era general who wrote dozens of books explaining why some generals (mainly Napoléon) and some armies (mainly the French) were consistently more successful than their rivals. The answer was to be found in scientific principles of strategy. Jomini proved in literally dozens of major books that victory went to those who instinctively followed the principles that he had distilled from historical accounts and years of experience campaigning with Napoléon—simply put, victory went to the general who used massive forces in an offensive action against a decisive point. Yet Jomini was keenly aware that art had a major role to play in this science. As he wrote in *The Art of War*, "It is almost always easy to determine the decisive point of a field of battle, but not so with the decisive moment; and it is precisely here that genius and experience are everything, and mere theory of little value."

While simple enough and mostly common sense, Jomini's principles were enormously influential. Because Jomini was *the* military theorist of the nineteenth century, his ideas were widely disseminated. His basic teaching, his doctrine, was that the management of war could be taught—just study the principles and how they are applied in specific situations. (Today this technique is known as the **case study** method.) Since so many of the activities of war—planning, training, logistics, and so on—are more management than fighting, it was not much of a leap of the imagination to apply similar principles to management. The timing was certainly right, because the mid-nineteenth century saw the beginning of large-scale industrial enterprise, especially railroads, the scope of which was similar to managing a large army.

By the time business administration emerged as an academic field toward the end of the nineteenth century, it seemed only natural to take a principles approach to teaching management. But these early efforts at developing and teaching principles were authoritarian in that they were premised on the notion that all direction and innovation came from the top—that the people in power, while not necessarily

---

case study A research design that focuses upon the in-depth analysis of a single subject. It is particularly useful for the understanding of dynamic processes over time.

Box 5.2

Napoléon First Learns of Jomini's Principles

[Napoleon says, after an aide read to him a few pages of Jomini's book,] "Why here is a young major, a Swiss at that, who teaches us what my professors never taught me, and what very few generals understand!"

After hearing a little more he said, much excited: "Why did Fouché [the Minister of War] allow such a work to be published? It teaches my whole system of war to my enemies! The book must be seized and its circulation prevented!"

After a few moments' reflection, he again said: "But I attach too much importance to this publication. The old generals who command against me will never read it, and the young men who will read it do not command. Nevertheless, such works must not be published hereafter without my permission."

He then directed that young Jomini's name be placed on the list of promotions [to colonel].

SOURCE: George B. McClellan, "General Jomini," *The Galaxy*, vol. 7 (January–June 1869). Napoleon was concerned with Jomini's first book, *Treatise on Great Military Operations*, published in 1805.

---

having a monopoly on brains in the organization, had the only brains that mattered. Thus success or failure was a function of how smart the boss was. Bosses would certainly be more effective if they adopted principles, but they were inherently limited by their own abilities.

The explosion of textbooks and self-improvement and "how to succeed" books on management that take a principles approach began early in this century and has never abated. Next time you see a best-seller offering a new management system, remember that while the author may never acknowledge it, he or she is an intellectual disciple of Jomini—because the authors of these best- and would-be best-sellers all premise their works on the belief that management is a skill that can be taught.

The Cross-Fertilization of Military and Civilian Management

Even today, military and civilian management constantly influence one another. There has been a constant cross-fertilization of management thinking in the American **military-industrial complex**. For example, during World War II, the U.S. Army

---

military-industrial complex A nation's armed forces and their industrial suppliers. During his farewell address in 1961, President Dwight D. Eisenhower warned that "in the councils of government we must guard against the acquisition of unwarranted influence, whether sought or unsought, by the military-industrial complex. The potential for the disastrous rise of misplaced power exists and will persist." Malcolm C. Moos (1916–1982), Eisenhower's chief speechwriter during the second term, is usually credited with coining what has become Eisenhower's single most memorable warning: to "guard against . . . the military-industrial complex."

Air Corps (the U.S. Air Force was not created until after the war in 1947) used statistical control with great effectiveness. By developing techniques to count almost everything, they were able to offer the kind of policy advice that saved millions of dollars and thousands of lives. For example, the B-17 bomber was to be gradually replaced by the newer B-24, which would carry 50 percent more bombs. But statistics proved that the B-24 had so many defects that the overall performance of the B-17 was greater. Result: production of the B-24s was scaled down and more air crews survived the war because the B-17 could take far more combat damage and return to base. Once a B-24 was hit, the crew's chances of survival were far less. Number crunching pays off—sometimes in lives!

After the war, the head of the Air Corps statistical control unit, Colonel Charles "Tex" Thornton and nine of his best analysts "sold" themselves to the Ford Motor Company as a team. Using the techniques they had pioneered during the war, now renamed management control, they turned around Ford, which was on the verge of being run out of the auto business by competition from General Motors. They were known as the "whiz kids" because of their high-powered intellects and obvious youth. According to management historian John A. Byrne, they "built a mystique for the methods of rational management they invented during the war—a system of tight financial controls that made quantitative analysis of every business problem essential." Because of their enormous influence, "a postwar generation of managers became slaves to numbers, taught to squeeze out costs in every part and every product while building looming hierarchies of white-collar staffs that centralized authority and decision making."

And just who was the number one "whiz kid," the so-called "human computer" who was the first of the group to rise to be president of Ford in 1960? None other than Robert S. McNamara, who as Secretary of Defense under Presidents Kennedy and Johnson used this same kind of quantitatively based decision making to fight and lose the Vietnam War. So the military, which helped to create modern management control of far-flung operations, was being influenced by a corporate version of it that put control over the more traditional values of morale and culture. By seeking to solve problems just by using numbers, it lost sight of too many other factors. By viewing the war as an exchange of firepower, McNamara ignored the morale and motivation of the enemy.

McNamara's whole Vietnam strategy of piecemeal escalation at indecisive points was in gross violation of the principles of war. His managerial approach to problem solving undermined the effectiveness of the military down to the smallest units. For example, officers—in order to give more of them combat experience—were allowed six-month tours of duty with front-line troops. But the troops had a one-year tour. It has been known since ancient times that **unit cohesion** is the glue that holds armies together. This necessitates a belief among soldiers that their officers will fight and, if necessary, die with them. According to military historians Richard Gabriel and Paul Savage, "In Vietnam the record is absolutely clear on this point: the officer corps simply did not die in sufficient numbers or in the presence of their men often enough. . . . The troops began to perceive that their officers simply

---

unit cohesion Solidarity within a work group as demonstrated by commitment to common goals, to the organization as a whole, and by the members to each other.

were not prepared to share the risk of the ultimate sacrifice—and they came to despise them for it."

Overall, McNamara's number-crunching approach to military leaderships was a disaster at all levels, strategic and tactical. Numbers alone are never the whole story. This is why the notorious **body count** statistics were so misleading—leaving aside the fact that they were also notoriously inaccurate. Such policies destroyed the effectiveness of the U.S. Army for a generation. Fortunately, organizations can renew themselves. But it was not until the Persian Gulf War in 1991 that the army was able to demonstrate its full recovery from the trauma of Vietnam and McNamara. Now the pendulum is swinging the other way and the military, because of its superb equal employment opportunity record, is showing the rest of the nation how racial integration can be achieved without compromising efficiency. This process of military-civilian cross-fertilization is never-ending.

What Is Organization Theory?

An "organization" is a group of people who jointly work to achieve at least one common goal. A "theory" is a proposition or set of propositions that seeks to explain or predict something. The something in the case of organization theory is how groups and individuals behave in differing organizational arrangements. This is critically important information for any manager or leader. It is not an exaggeration to say that the world is ruled by the underlying premises of organization theory. This has been true ever since humankind first organized itself for hunting, war, and even family life. Indeed, the newest thing about organization theory is the study of it.

Only in the twentieth century has intellectual substance and tradition been given to a field that was the instinctual artistic domain of adventuresome entrepreneurs and cunning politicos. It was artistic in the sense that it was done naturally without formal learning. Leaders in every field during every age used organization theory as naturally as they used their oratorical powers. In neither case did they need to intellectualize about it. Thus the pirate captain in the seventeenth-century Caribbean, the revolutionary leader in eighteenth-century colonial America, and the suffragist leader in late nineteenth-century America were all organization theorists—because none of them could have made it as leaders without understanding, if only subliminally, how to structure and motivate a group.

Organization theory was always there in the authoritarian model offered by the military. While many of its premises were understood by the ancients, it did not co-

---

body count The quantitative manner in which the American forces measured success during the Vietnam War. As soldiers naturally want to please their superiors, these counts became greatly exaggerated. Thus the progress of the war was grossly distorted and misled both military planners and the public. According to David H. Hackworth in *About Face* (1989), "Sometimes a body count was completely made up to mask a screwed-up mission. In just one instance, a battalion commander asked one of his company COs over the radio to tell him his college football jersey number to have something to report for a botched operation. ("Eighty-six," said the company commander. "Eighty-six!" exclaimed the battalion commander. "Great body count!") Because body count mathematics were so discredited by the Vietnam War, the U.S. military made it a policy of never estimating the number of enemy dead during the Persian Gulf War.

alesce as a self-conscious field of knowledge until society found a practical use for it—to help manage the ever-burgeoning national (as opposed to local) industries and institutions brought about by the **industrial revolution**. When the problems of managing an organization grew to be more than one head could cope with, the search for guidance on how to manage and arrange large-scale organizations became as noble a quest as the secular world of business could offer. If a commercial society ever had prophets, it was those pioneers of industrial engineering who claimed that the path to ever greater prosperity was to be found in the relentless search for the "one best way." They were offering society a theory—abstract guidance for those who knew where they wanted to go but did not quite know how to get there. They already knew what social psychologist Kurt Lewin would assert years later: "There is nothing so practical as a good theory."

What was once said of the first atomic bomb has also been said of the first U.S. voyage to the moon: It was as much an achievement of organization as it was of engineering and science. Have our more recent theories of organization kept pace with our industrial and technical achievements? Maybe. But certainly yes when they are compared with the "primitive" authoritarian management. Yet many of the basics remain the same—remain as givens. The laws of physics and gravity do not change with intellectual fashions or technological advances; nor do the basic social and physical characteristics of people. Just as those who would build spaceships have to start by studying the physics of Isaac Newton, those who would design and manage organizations must start with Adam Smith, Frederick Taylor, and Henri Fayol. The future will always build upon what is enduring from the past.

It was T. E. Lawrence (of Arabia) who wrote: "With 2,000 years of examples behind us, we have no excuse when fighting, for not fighting well." The same, even double, can be said of organization theory: With 4,000 years of examples behind us, we have no excuse when organizing, for not organizing well.

While it is always great fun to delve into the wisdom of the ancients, most analysts of the origins of organization theory view the beginnings of the **factory system** in Great Britain in the eighteenth century as the birth point of complex economic organizations and, consequently, of the field of organization theory.

Classical Organization Theory

Classical organization theory, as its name implies, was the first theory of its kind, is considered traditional, and continues to be the base upon which other schools of organization theory have been built. Its basic tenets and assumptions, however, which were rooted in the industrial revolution of the 1700s and the professions of mechanical engineering, industrial engineering, and economics, have never changed. They were only expanded upon, refined, and made more sophisticated. Thus, an understanding of classical organization theory is essential not only because of its

---

industrial revolution A very general term that refers to a society's change from an agrarian to an industrial economy. The Industrial Revolution of the Western world is considered to have begun in England in the eighteenth century.

factory system Any production process that has individual workers specializing in the varying aspects of a larger task.

historical interest but also, more importantly, because subsequent analyses and theories presume a knowledge of it.

The fundamental tenets of organization theory can be summarized as follows:

1. Organizations exist to accomplish production-related and economic goals.
2. There is one best way to organize for production, and that way can be found through systematic, scientific inquiry.
3. Production is maximized through specialization and division of labor.
4. People and organizations act in accordance with rational economic principles.

The evolution of any theory must be viewed in context. The beliefs of early management theorists about how organizations worked or should work were a direct reflection of the societal values of their times. And the times were harsh. It was well into the twentieth century before the industrial workers of the United States and Europe began to enjoy even limited "rights" as organizational citizens. Workers were not viewed as individuals but as the interchangeable parts in an industrial machine whose parts were made of flesh only when it was impractical to make them of steel.

The advent of power-driven machinery and hence the modern factory system spawned our current concepts of economic organizations and organization for production. Power-driven equipment was expensive. Production workers could not purchase and use their own equipment as they once had their own tools. The memorable phrase for being fired—"get the sack"—comes from the earliest days of the industrial revolution, when a dismissed worker literally was given a sack in which to gather up his tools. Increasingly, workers without their own tools and often without any special skills had to gather for work where the equipment was—in factories. Expensive equipment had to produce enough output to justify its acquisition and maintenance costs.

Under the factory system, organizational success resulted from well-organized production systems that kept machines busy and costs under control. Industrial and mechanical engineers—and their machines—were the keys to production. Organizational structures and production systems were needed to take best advantage of the machines. Organizations, it was thought, should work like machines, using people, capital, and machines as their parts. Just as industrial engineers sought to design "the best" machines to keep factories productive, industrial and mechanical engineering-type thinking dominated theories about "the best way" to organize for production. Thus, the first theories of organizations were concerned primarily with the anatomy or structure—of formal organizations. This was the milieu, or the environment, the mode of thinking, which shaped and influenced the tenets of classical organization theory.

Adam Smith and the Pin Factory

Centralization of equipment and labor in factories, division of specialized labor, management of specialization, and economic paybacks on factory equipment all were concerns identified by the Scottish economist Adam Smith (1723–1790) in his work, *An Inquiry into the Nature and Causes of the Wealth of Nations*. Smith and James Watt (1736–1819), the inventor of the steam engine, are the two peo-

Box 5.3

The Invisible Hand

Every individual endeavors to employ his capital so that its produce may be of greatest value. He generally neither intends to promote the public interest, nor knows how much he is promoting it. He intends only his own gain. And he is in this led by an invisible hand to promote an end which was no part of his intention. By pursuing his own interest he frequently promotes that of society more effectually than when he really intends it.

SOURCE: Adam Smith, *The Wealth of Nations* (1776).

ple who are most often named as being responsible for pushing the world into industrialization.

Smith, considered the "father" of the academic discipline of **economics**, provided the intellectual foundation for **laissez-faire** capitalism. But Smith's *The Wealth of Nations* devotes its first chapter, "Of the Division of Labour," to a discussion of the optimum organization of a pin factory. Why? Because specialization of labor was one of the pillars of Smith's "invisible hand" market mechanism in which the greatest rewards would go to those who were the most efficient in the competitive marketplace.

Traditional pin makers could produce only a few dozen pins a day. When organized in a factory with each worker performing a limited operation, they could produce tens of thousands a day. Smith's chapter, coming as it did at the dawn of the Industrial Revolution, is the most famous and influential statement on the economic rationale of the factory system, even though factory systems had been known since ancient times. For example, in 370 B.C.E., Xenophon described the division of labor in a shoe factory. But it was not until centuries later that the popularity of Smith's 1776 book revolutionized thinking about economics and organizations. Hence, 1776 is the year that is traditionally considered the starting point of organization theory as an applied science and academic discipline. Besides, 1776 is easy to remember as it was a good year for other events as well.

All formal organizations, whether Smith's eighteenth-century factory or the most sophisticated modern corporation, are *force multipliers* in the sense that they allow the combined individual efforts to be far greater than the sum of their parts. Smith's pin makers acting individually could make a few dozen pins a day at best; as a team, they could make thousands. Proper organization thus means that 2 plus 2 does not equal 4; it probably equals 100.

---

economics The study of how people or states use their limited resources to satisfy their unlimited wants; how scarce resources are allocated among competing needs.

laissez-faire A hands-off style of governance that emphasizes economic freedom so the capitalist invisible hand can work its will.

Box 5.4

Adam Smith on the Division of Labour

The way in which this business [pin making] is now carried on, not only the whole work is a peculiar trade, but it is divided into a number of branches. . . . One man draws out the wire, another straights it, a third cuts it, a fourth points it, a fifth grinds it at the top for receiving the head; to make the head requires two or three distinct operations; to put it on, is a peculiar business, to whiten the pins is another; it is even a trade by itself to put them into the paper; and the important business of making a pin is, in this manner, divided into about 18 distinct operations. . . . I have seen a small manufactory of this kind where ten men only were employed, and where some of them consequently performed two or three distinct operations. But though they were very poor, and therefore but indifferently accommodated with the necessary machine, they could, when they exerted themselves, make among them about 12 pounds of pins in a day. There are in a pound upwards of 4,000 pins of a middling size. Those ten persons, therefore, could make among them upwards of 48,000 pins in a day. Each person, therefore, making a tenth part of 48,000 pins, might be considered as making 4,800 pins in a day. But if they had all wrought separately and independently, and without any of them having been educated to this peculiar business, they certainly could not each of them have made 20, perhaps not one pin in a day. . . . In every other art and manufacture, the effects of the division of labour are similar to what they are in this very trifling one.

SOURCE: Adam Smith, *The Wealth of Nations* (1776).

This phenomenon is also illustrated by a story playwright George Bernard Shaw tells in *Everybody's Political What's What*: "More than 50 years ago I was marching in a procession which numbered at least a thousand men. It was broken up and scattered in hopeless confusion and terror by 20 pale nervous policemen armed with nothing more deadly than their clubs. Not one of the thousand knew what to do or what any of the others would do; so they all ran away, except those who were overtaken and knocked on the head." The policemen, because they were effectively organized, had their force multiplied. "Each of the 20 policemen knew what the other 19 were going to do, and had the law on his side. He had a uniform, a helmet, and a weapon, and could depend on the cooperation of 19 uniformed, helmeted, weaponed comrades. It was a triumph of expected behavior over mistrust and anarchy." It was a triumph of good organization over bad organization. The leaders of the demonstration organized their men to march but did not provide any guidance on what to do when the police arrived. In the absence of leadership, in the absence of organization, they ran away.

The military uses the term force multiplier to refer to any new technology that makes a soldier more effective on the battlefield. Thus the machine gun is a force multiplier because it means that one soldier with it is as effective as, say, a hundred soldiers with traditional rifles. Modern computers and word processors are force multipliers in a civilian context because one word processor operator can be as effective as dozens of traditional typists. But as both Smith and Shaw have shown, it is not just technology that can be a force multiplier. Good organization is a technology in its own right, is as powerful a force multiplier as any machine—and far cheaper, too!

The Origins of Scientific Management

The basic problem with the traditional hierarchical organization was that it was dependent upon the proper enculturation of individual supervisors at every level for its success. Under stable conditions, properly trained military officers and factory supervisors performed well. But as military affairs and factory production became increasingly unstable during the **French Revolution**, the Age of Napoléon, and the industrial revolution, mechanisms had to evolve to compensate for the inherent rigidity of the traditional hierarchy. Individual officers and supervisors, competent enough under stable conditions, became less competent under revolutionary conditions. Whether on the "field of honor" or the factory floor, they could not cope with the competition—organizations that adopted the major structural innovation of that era, the staff concept.

While traditional hierarchical organizations allowed leaders to extend their reach, the organization was still dependent upon the necessarily limited intellectual energy at the top. But even the greatest mind with the best advisors has limits. The staff concept evolved to overcome the inherent limitations of a single mind and ever-fleeting time.

Staff refers to two mutually supporting ideas that gradually evolved in both military and civilian contexts. As the management function becomes increasingly complex and differentiated, managers started using assistants—secretaries and clerks at first, later personnel and purchasing specialists. This traditional use of staff was followed by the staff principle (or staff concept), which created a specific unit in the larger organization whose primary responsibility was to think and plan, to ponder over innovations and plan for their implementation. Under the factory system that emerged from the industrial revolution, business success resulted from well-organized production systems that kept machines busy and costs under control. Industrial and mechanical engineers—and their machines—were the keys to production. Organizational structures and production systems needed constant tinkering and refining to take best advantage of ever-evolving technology. Organizations, it was thought, should work like machines, using people as their parts. Just as industrial engineers sought to design "the best" machines to keep factories productive, industrial and mechanical engineering-type thinking dominated theories about "the best way" to organize people for their role as part of the overall industrial machine.

French Revolution The political convulsions that began in Paris when the citizens stormed the Bastille (a prison) on July 14, 1789. These convulsions have continued ever since.

Beginning with the industrial revolution (and Napoleonic era military organizations) the staff concept has made ever-increasing inroads into the public and private sector. The concept was first formally instituted in the military, and it can be traced back to the ancient Greek armies of Alexander the Great. While generals have always had **aides-de-camp**, the modern military general staff principally originates from the Prussian military reforms that transformed an inefficient army into the foremost military machine in Europe by the middle of the nineteenth century. The Prussian, later German, General Staff has been admired for its efficiency (if not its ethics), though seldom fully imitated, by military analysts ever since. It consisted of a small group of the most intellectually able officers, drawn from the main officer corps relatively early in their careers, who then spent their professional lives in the central planning unit known as the general staff. The general staff then developed the strategies and tactics that Germany would use in future wars. By the end of the nineteenth century, all of the major military powers, including the United States and Japan, had adopted a variant of the German general staff for their militaries.

The general staff concept, modified to reflect local conditions, was increasingly adopted by burgeoning industrial and governmental organizations. In the latter part of the nineteenth century, American industrial engineers began asserting that factory workers could be much more productive if their work was designed scientifically. And who would these designers be? They would be the civilian counterparts of the military general staff. Their job was to conduct the research and do the planning that would make the organization more competitive relative to other organizations. Thus scientific management grew out of engineering—which brings up another connection to our old friend Jomini. The greatest single source of the nineteenth-century American engineers who built the railroads, canals, harbors, and bridges came from one school, West Point—where the principles espoused by Jomini were and are still taught. The professional paper that management historians considered to be the first call for scientific management was entitled "The Engineer as an Economist." And it was presented by **Henry R. Towne** at the 1886 meeting of the American Society of Mechanical Engineers. Those nineteenth-century engineers, whether educated at West Point or not, tended to know good principles when they saw them.

The Influence of Frederick W. Taylor

Frederick Winslow Taylor became the acknowledged father of the scientific management movement. He pioneered the development of **time-and-motion studies**, originally under the name "Taylorism" or the "Taylor system." Taylorism, or its successor, scientific management, was not a single invention but rather a series of methods and organizational arrangements designed by Taylor and his associates to increase the efficiency and speed of machine shop production. Premised upon the notion that there was "one best way" of accomplishing any given task, Taylor's sci-

---

aide-de-camp A young officer serving as a personal assistant to a general.

Henry R. Towne (1844–1924) An early scientific management advocate whose efforts predated and influenced Frederick W. Taylor.

time-and-motion studies Various techniques for establishing time standards for the performance of manual work.

entific management sought to increase output by using special staff to discover the fastest, most efficient, and least fatiguing production methods.

Scientific management emerged as a national movement in the United States during a series of events in 1910. Some eastern railroads filed for increased freight rates with the **Interstate Commerce Commission**. Louis D. Brandeis, the populist lawyer who would later be a Supreme Court justice, took the case against the railroads. He called in **Harrington Emerson**, a consultant who had "systematized" the Santa Fe Railroad, to testify that the railroads did not need increased rates: They could "save a million dollars a day" by using what Brandeis initially called "scientific management" methods. According to historians Harold Smiddy and Lionel Naum, this "sudden realization among business leaders everywhere that the then proudest industrial achievement, the system of railroads, was actually something less than the flawless gem of American enterprise, brought at last the needed widespread attention and support the management movement had lacked." It was a managerial epiphany similar to, but less nationwide in effect than, the shock of *Sputnik* in 1957. It was, as the saying went, "a hell of a way to run a railroad!"

At first Taylor was reluctant to use the phrase "scientific management" because it sounded too academic. But, the ICC hearings meant that the national scientific management boom was underway, and Taylor was its leader. Taylor had a profound—indeed revolutionary—effect on the fields of business and public administration. His work and fame gave ever-increasing credence to the notion that organizational operations could be planned and controlled systematically by staff experts using scientific principles.

Taylor echoed Jomini when he asserted that "the remedy for . . . inefficiency lies in systematic management, rather than in searching for some unusual or extraordinary man." Jomini's goal was to make any would-be Napoléon as skillful as the legendary general if they adopted Jomini's principles. Taylor sought "to prove that the best management is a true science, resting upon clearly defined laws, rules, and principles, as a foundation." Taylor—indeed all the scientific managers of his generation—took Jomini's approach to teaching war and applied it to management.

Many people unfamiliar with Jomini think that Clausewitz was *the* greatest nineteenth-century theoretician of war. After all, his classic *On War* was published in 1832. Yes, but being published is not the same as being read. Clausewitz had to wait for the beginning of the twentieth century and good translators to become influential. Fortunately, Taylor had better luck. His classic book, *The Principles of Scientific Management*, was an instant success when it was published in 1911 and has been in print ever since. Unfortunately, Taylor, because he died in 1915, had only a few years to enjoy his success. Still, he fared better than Clausewitz, whose great book was published a year after he died. Posthumous publication is a much overrated joy!

Taylor's greatest public sector popularity came in 1912, after he presented his ideas to a Special Committee of the House of Representatives to Investigate the

---

Interstate Commerce Commission (ICC) The federal agency that regulated interstate surface transportation. Established in 1887, it was abolished in 1996.

Harrington Emerson (1853–1931) One of the first management consultants in the United States; known as the "high priest of efficiency" because of his advocacy of eliminating "wanton, wicked waste."

Frederick W. Taylor, a strange man. Born to wealth, he graduated from Phillips Exeter Academy and passed the entrance exam to Harvard with honors, but declined to go. Instead he had family friends arrange a job for him as an apprentice pattern maker and machinist at the Enterprise Hydraulic Works of Philadelphia. In the following years he led a double life: a genuine member of the working class by day who on any night he wished could be found in Philadelphia's most exclusive clubs. Indeed, in 1881 he won (with his brother-in-law) the first U.S. Lawn Tennis Association doubles championship—this when tennis was the most upper-class of sports. Meanwhile he earned an engineering degree through correspondence at the Stevens Institute of Technology of Hoboken, New Jersey. As he advanced into management jobs, he never lost his understanding of workers, his hostility of poor supervision, and his profound belief that labor should be paid for performance, not mere attendance. Thus was formed his religious zeal to measure output as a means towards greater productivity and more equitable pay •

Taylor and Other Systems of Shop Management. Taylor's comprehensive statement of scientific management principles was focused on what he called the "duties of management":

1. Replacing traditional, rule-of-thumb methods of work accomplishment with systematic, more scientific methods of measuring and managing individual work elements

2. The scientific study of the selection and sequential development of workers to ensure optimal placement of workers into work roles

3. Obtaining the cooperation of workers to ensure full application of scientific principles

4. Establishing logical divisions within work roles and responsibilities between workers and management

Taylor's duties seem so obvious today, but they were revolutionary in 1912. Taylor himself even insisted in his *Principles of Scientific Management* that "scientific management does not necessarily involve any great invention, nor the discovery of new or startling facts." Nevertheless, it did "involve a certain combination of elements which have not existed in the past, namely, old knowledge so collected, analyzed, grouped and classified into laws and rules that it constitutes a science."

Box 5.5

Taylor Compares Scientific Management to Baseball

There is one illustration of the application of the principles of scientific management with which all of us are familiar and with which most of us have been familiar since we were small boys, and I think this instance represents one of the best illustrations of the application of the principles of scientific management. I refer to the management of a first-class American baseball team. In such a team you will find almost all of the elements of scientific management.

You will see that the science of doing every little act that is done by every player on the baseball field has been developed. Every single element of the game of baseball has been the subject of the most intimate, the closest study of many men, and, finally, the best way of doing each act that takes place on the baseball field has been fairly well agreed upon and established as a standard throughout the country. The players have not only been told the best way of making each important motion or play, but they have been taught, coached, and trained to it through months of drilling. And I think that every man who has watched first-class play, or who knows anything of the management of the modern baseball team, realizes fully the utter impossibility of winning with the best team of individual players that was ever gotten together unless every man on the team obeys the signals or orders of the coach and obeys them at once when the coach gives those orders; that is, without the intimate cooperation between all members of the team and the management, which is characteristic of scientific management.

SOURCE: Frederick W. Taylor, testimony before the U.S. House of Representatives, January 25, 1912.

Fayol's General Theory of Management

While the ideas of Adam Smith, Frederick Winslow Taylor, and others are still dominant influences on the design and management of organizations, it was Henri Fayol (1841–1925), a French executive engineer, who developed the first comprehensive theory of management. While Taylor was tinkering with the technology employed by the individual worker, Fayol was theorizing about all of the elements necessary to organize and manage a major corporation. Fayol's major work, *Administration Industrielle et Generale* (published in France in 1916), was almost ignored in the United States until Constance Storr's English translation, *General and Industrial Management* appeared in 1949. Since that time, Fayol's theoretical contributions have been widely recognized and his work is considered fully as significant as that of Taylor.

Fayol believed that his concept of management was universally applicable to every type of organization. While he had six principles—(1) technical (production of goods), (2) commercial (buying, selling, and exchange activities), (3) financial (raising and using capital), (4) security (protection of property and people),

(5) accounting, and (6) managerial (coordination, control, organization, planning and command of people)—Fayol's primary interest and emphasis was on his final principle—managerial. His managerial principle addressed such variables as division of work, authority and responsibility, discipline, unity of command, unity of direction, subordination of individual interest to general interest, remuneration of personnel, centralization, **scalar chains**, order, equity, stability of personnel tenure, initiative, and **esprit de corps**.

Fayol was the first to explain why principles beyond the golden rule and other moral precepts were needed. "Surprise might be expressed at the outset that the eternal moral principles . . . are not sufficient guide for the manager. . . . The explanation is this: the higher laws of religious or moral order envisage the individual only, or else interests which are not of this world, whereas management principles aim at the success of associations of individuals and at the satisfying of economic interests. Given that the aim is different, it is not surprising that the means are not the same."

The Period of Orthodoxy

It is hardly possible to exaggerate the influence that scientific management has had and continues to have on the intellectual development of public administration. Those who have traced the historical evolution of public administration, such as Dwight Waldo, Vincent Ostrom, Nicholas Henry, and Howard McCurdy, would describe the pattern of development within public administration between the world wars as a "period of orthodoxy." The tenets of this orthodox ideology held that the work of government could be neatly divided into decision making and execution (the politics-administration dichotomy of Woodrow Wilson), and that administration was a science with discoverable principles (scientific management). This dichotomy, which played such an important part in the historical development of public administration, would hardly have been possible if scientific management had not evolved when it did.

The notion that politics could, let alone should, be separated from administration, was quickly disposed of by the New Deal and World War II. While those wars against depression and oppression were primarily economic and military operations, they were also immense managerial undertakings. The experience of those years called into question much of what was then the **conventional wisdom** of public administration. The politics-administration dichotomy of the progressive reform movement lost its viability amid the New Deal and the war effort because it was increasingly seen that it simply was not possible to take value-free processes of business and apply them to government. Government, in spite of the best efforts of many reformers, was not a business and was not value-free.

---

scalar chain The chain of supervisors from the top of an organization to the bottom.
esprit de corps The spirit or morale of a group; traditionally, the pride that soldiers take in their military units.
conventional wisdom That which is generally believed to be true. However, any writer who uses the phrase is setting something up to be knocked down; so conventional wisdom really means that which most people believe to be true, but really is not. The phrase first gained currency after John Kenneth Galbraith used it in *The Affluent Society* (1958): "Only posterity is unkind to the man of conventional wisdom, and all posterity does is bury him in a blanket of neglect."

The attack on the politics-administration dichotomy came from many quarters at once. David E. Lilienthal, writing of his experiences as chairman of the Tennessee Valley Authority—the federal government's flood control and electric power corporation for the Tennessee River Valley—found the planning process of government to be a blatantly political enterprise. One that was, not incidentally, both healthy and beneficial for a democratic society.

Paul Appleby's Polemic

But it remained for Paul Appleby, a prominent New Deal administrator and dean of the Maxwell School at Syracuse University, to write the most skillful polemic of the era, which asserted that this theoretical insistence on apolitical governmental processes went against the grain of the American experience. In his book *Big Democracy* Appleby emphatically shattered public administration's self-imposed demarcation between politics and administration. He held that it was a myth that politics was separate and could somehow be taken out of administration. This was good, not evil as many of the progressive reformers had asserted, because this political involvement in administration acted as a check on the arbitrary exercise of bureaucratic power. In the future those who would describe the political ramifications and issues of administration would not begin by contesting the politics-administration dichotomy as incorrect or irrelevant—they would begin from the premise, as Appleby put it so succinctly, that "government is different because government is politics."

Luther Gulick's POSDCORB

The second tenet of the interwar "orthodoxy," that administration was a science with discoverable principles, has never left us. The influence of scientific management continues to be pervasive. Taylor's scientific management sought to increase output by discovering the fastest, most efficient, and least fatiguing production methods. The job of the scientific manager, once the "one best way" was found, was to impose this procedure upon his or her organization. Classical organization theory derives from a corollary of this proposition. If there was one best way to accomplish any given production task, then correspondingly, there must also be one best way to accomplish any task of social organization—including organizing firms. Such principles of social organization were assumed to exist and to be waiting to be discovered by diligent scientific observation and analysis. Thus the methodology used to divine the "one best way" to accomplish physical tasks was increasingly applied to the problem of social organization.

Luther Gulick's "Notes on the Theory of Organization" is without doubt the best-known statement of this "principles" approach to managing organizations. In 1937, he and Lyndall Urwick edited a collection entitled *Papers on the Science of*

Luther Gulick (1892–1993) Perhaps the most highly honored reformer, researcher, and practitioner of public administration in the United States. Often called the dean of American public administration, Gulick was intimately involved with the pioneering development and installation of new budget, personnel, and management systems at all levels of government. He was a founder of the Institute of Public Administration, the American Society for Public Administration, and the National Academy of Public Administration.

Administration. Originally this was intended to be a staff report for the Brownlow Committee (see Chapter 3). Overall, these *Papers* were a statement of the "state of the art" of organization theory. It was here that Gulick introduced his famous mnemonic, POSDCORB, which stands for the seven major functions of management:

Planning, that is working out in broad outline the things that need to be done and the methods for doing them to accomplish the purpose set for the enterprise

Organizing, that is the establishment of the formal structure of authority through which work subdivisions are arranged, defined, and coordinated for the defined objective

Staffing, that is the whole personnel function of bringing in and training the staff and maintaining favorable conditions of work

Directing, that is the continuous task of making decisions and embodying them in specific and general orders and instructions and serving as the leader of the enterprise

Coordinating, that is the all important duty of interrelating the various parts of the work

Reporting, that is keeping those to whom the executive is responsible informed as to what is going on, which thus includes keeping himself and his subordinates informed through records, research, and inspection

Budgeting, with all that goes with budgeting in the form of fiscal planning, accounting, and control

Gulick helped shape a critical distinction in orthodox public administration; that the study of management and administration was to be focused on the role of upper-level management. Its organizational outlook, as demonstrated by POSDCORB, took the point of view of the top. But this narrow focus was to be increasingly challenged. Even as Gulick wrote, his "scientific" approach to management was being confronted by the more humanistic focus that would increasingly challenge it. Although this was not immediately apparent, the theoreticians of the human relations and **behavioral science** approaches to management were very much contemporaries of Gulick; they were simply prophets before their time.

The Many Meanings of Bureaucracy

The bureaucratic institutions of the modern state with their hierarchies of officials have their origins in ancient times, as the keynote story about Moses illustrated. Ever since, most large organizations, both in the public and private sectors, have been hierarchical structures. Thus bureaucracy has always been one of the central

---

behavioral science A general term for all of the academic disciplines that study human and animal behavior by means of experimental research. The phrase was first put into wide use in the early 1950s by the Ford Foundation to describe its funding for interdisciplinary research in the social sciences; and by faculty at the University of Chicago seeking federal funding for research—and concerned in an era of McCarthyism that their social science research might be confused with socialism.

concerns of organization theory. But before we can deal with this concern, we must explore the many meanings of the word itself.

All Government Offices

First, "the bureaucracy" is the totality of government offices or bureaus (a French word meaning "office") that constitute the permanent government of a state; that is, those public functions that continue irrespective of changes in political leadership. Modern Western-style bureaucracies originated in Europe when the governing affairs of centralized autocratic regimes became so complicated that it became necessary to delegate the king's authority to his representatives. American bureaucracy has never fully recovered from its nondemocratic European origins. This has allowed politicians to continually rejoice in attacking the "unresponsive" bureaucracy. At the same time, "good government" groups often contend that, once in office, politicians make the bureaucracy all too responsive to special **interests** instead of leaving it alone to impartially administer the programs for which it was originally established.

All Public Officials

Second, "the bureaucracy" refers to all of the public officials of a government—both high and low, elected and appointed. Thus the secretary of the treasury is a bureaucrat, but so is a lowly secretary in the Treasury Department. We typically think of a bureaucrat sitting at a desk shuffling papers on behalf of the citizenry. But most bureaucrats lead far more active lives. They are police officers, teachers, firefighters, scientists, and astronauts. While many fit the image and do sit behind a desk all day—somebody has to shuffle the papers—they are no more representative of bureaucrats as a whole than are other major categories such as trash collectors and street maintenance workers. However, the paper shufflers often finish the day cleaner.

A General Invective

Third, bureaucracy is often used as a general invective to refer to any inefficient organization encumbered by **red tape**. We've all heard the jokes. There was the malfunctioning rocket that was named "the civil servant" because it would not work and you could not fire it. When a voter registration card arrived in the mail for her recently deceased husband, the bereaved widow dutifully informed the Bureau of

---

interests A group of persons who share a common cause, which puts them into political competition with other groups or interests. Thus the oil interests want better tax breaks for the oil industry, and the consumer interests want new laws protecting consumer rights vis-à-vis the business interests, who want fewer laws protecting consumer rights.

red tape A symbol of excessive formality and attention to routine. It has its origins in the red ribbon with which clerks bound official documents in the nineteenth century. The ribbon has disappeared, but the practices it represents linger on. Herbert Kaufman, in *Red Tape: Its Origins, Uses and Abuses* (1977), found that the term "is applied to a bewildering variety of organizational practices and features." After all, "one person's 'red tape' may be another's treasured procedural safeguard." Kaufman concluded that "red tape turns out to be at the core of our institutions rather than an excrescence on them."

Elections of his passing and promptly received an absentee ballot for him. Then there is the story of the spy sent to discover which Washington agencies could be sabotaged. He reports back: "Suggested plan hopeless. Americans brilliantly prepared. For each agency we destroy two more are already fully staffed and doing exactly the same work." There is a germ of truth in all these stories and their ilk. Some rockets do not work. Some agencies send letters (and even checks) to the dead. And duplication of efforts is not uncommon. This does not mean that the government organization involved is always inefficient. Many government agencies have longstanding reputations for efficient operations. We do not hear much about them because normal everyday efficiency does not generate much publicity—and bad publicity is a long-lasting stain. For example, NASA (as the keynote in Chapter 2 showed) has an an extraordinary reputation for efficient operations. But the *Challenger* disaster of 1986 has been a long-lasting stain. Nevertheless, efficient operations, whether in NASA, the Postal Service or your municipality, are the norm in government. But widespread perceptions of inefficiency have given an additional meaning to the word bureaucracy.

Max Weber's Structural Arrangements

Fourth, bureaucracy refers to a specific set of structural arrangements. The dominant structural definition of bureaucracy, indeed the point of departure for all further analyses on the subject, is that of the German sociologist **Max Weber**, who used an "ideal type" approach to extrapolate from the real world the central core of features that would characterize the most fully developed bureaucratic form of organization. This ideal type is neither a description of reality nor a statement of normative preference; it is merely an identification of the major variables or features that characterize bureaucracy. The fact that such features might not be fully present in a given organization does not necessarily imply that the organization is not bureaucratic. It may be an immature rather than a fully developed bureaucracy. At some point, however, it may be necessary to conclude that the characteristics of bureaucracy are so lacking in an organization that it could neither reasonably be termed bureaucratic nor be expected to produce patterns of bureaucratic behavior.

Weber's ideal type of bureaucracy possesses the following characteristics:

1. The bureaucrats must be free as individuals; they can only be bossed around with respect to the impersonal duties of their offices.

2. The bureaucrats are arranged in a clearly defined hierarchy of offices, the traditional scalar chain wherein every bureaucrat has an unambiguous place—and knows his or her place!

3. The functions of each office are clearly specified in writing.

4. The bureaucrats accept and maintain their appointments freely—without duress. Slave bureaucrats, while once fashionable in the Ottoman Empire and

---

Max Weber (1864–1920) The German sociologist who produced an analysis of an ideal type bureaucracy that is still the most influential statement—the point of departure for all further analyses—on the subject. Weber also pioneered the concepts of the Protestant ethic, charismatic authority, and a value-free approach to social research.

Imperial China, are an inherent contradiction except within military or prison organizations.

5. Appointments to office are made on the basis of technical qualifications, which ideally are substantiated by examinations administered by the appointing authority, a university, or both.

6. The bureaucrats receive money salaries and pension rights, which reflect the varying levels of the hierarchy. While the bureaucrats are free to leave the organization, they can be removed from their offices only under previously stated, specific circumstances.

7. The office must be the bureaucrat's sole or at least major occupation.

8. A career system is essential; while promotion may be the result of either seniority or merit, it must be premised on the judgment of hierarchical superiors.

9. The bureaucrats do not have property rights to their office nor any personal claim to the resources that go with it.

10. The bureaucrat's conduct must be subject to systematic control and strict discipline.

While Weber's structural identification of bureaucratic organization (first published in 1922) is perhaps the most comprehensive statement on the subject in the literature of the social sciences, it is not always considered satisfactory as an intellectual construct. For example, Anthony Downs, in *Inside Bureaucracy* (1967), argued that at least two elements should be added to Weber's definition. First, the organization must be large. According to Downs, "any organization in which the highest ranking members know less than half of the other members can be considered large." Second, most of the organization's output cannot be "directly or indirectly evaluated in any markets external to the organization by means of voluntary **quid pro quo** transactions." This latter element is what economist Ludwig von Mises meant when he said that the work of a government bureaucracy had "no cash value." It is not that the "successful handling of public affairs has no value, but that it has no price on the market, that its value cannot be realized in a market transaction and consequently cannot be expressed in terms of money."

Definitions of bureaucracy apply equally to organizations in the public as well as the private sector. However, public sector bureaucracies tend to operate in a somewhat different climate from those in the private sector. What has come to be known as the "third sector"—not-for-profit organizations such as hospitals, universities, and foundations—would analytically be classed with public organizations because of the lack of free-market forces upon them. In short, bureaucracy is best conceptualized as a specific form of organization, and public bureaucracy should be considered a special variant of bureaucratic organization. Yet, in the popular imagination a bureaucracy is any organization in which people arranged in hierarchical ranks have to obey lots of rules.

---

quid pro quo A Latin phrase meaning something for something; initially meaning the exchange of one thing for another. In politics it suggests actions taken because of some promised action in return.

Neoclassical Organization Theory

There is no precise definition for "neoclassical" in the context of organization theory. The general connotation is that of a theoretical perspective that revises and/or is critical of classical organization theory—particularly for minimizing issues related to the humanness of organizational members, coordination needs among administrative units, internal-external organizational relations, and organizational decision processes. The major writers of the classical school did their most significant work before World War II. The Neoclassical writers gained their reputations as organization theorists by attacking the classical writers after the end of the war. They sought to "save" classical theory by introducing modifications based upon research findings in the behavioral sciences.

The neoclassical school was important first because it initiated the theoretical movement away from the over-simplistic mechanistic views of the classical school. The neoclassicists challenged some of the basic tenets of the classical school head on—and they did so when the classical school was the only school. Organization theory and classical organization theory were effectively synonymous.

Second, in the process of challenging the classical school, the neoclassicalists raised issues and initiated theories that became central to the foundations of most of the schools or approaches to organization theory that have followed. Thus the neoclassical school was a critically important forerunner to the "power and politics" and the "organizational culture" perspective discussed in Chapter 2 and the "systems theory" school discussed below.

Herbert A. Simon's Influence

Herbert A. Simon was the most influential of the neoclassical organization theorists. He was the first to seriously challenge the principles approach proposed by Fayol, Gulick, and others. (His assertion that those principles were more like proverbs was discussed earlier in this chapter.) Simon was also a firm believer that decision making should be the focus of a new "administrative science." He wrote that organization theory is, in fact, the theory of the **bounded rationality** of human beings who **satisfice** because they do not have the intellectual capacity to maximize. He was also the first analyst to draw a distinction between "programmed" and "unprogrammed" organizational decisions; he highlighted the importance of the distinction for management information systems. His work on administrative science and decision making went in two major directions: first, he was a pioneer in developing the "science" of improved organizational decision making through quantitative methods such as operations research and computer technology. Second, and perhaps even more important, he was a leader in studying the processes by which administrative organizations make decisions.

---

bounded rationality The "bounds" that people put on their decisions. Because truly rational research on any problem can never be complete, humans make decisions on satisfactory as opposed to optimal information.

satisfice Accept a satisfactory and sufficient amount of information upon which to base a decision. Herbert Simon invented this word to help explain his theory of bounded rationality.

TABLE 5.2   *Classical Organization Theory: A Chronology*

1776   Adam Smith's *The Wealth of Nations* discusses the optimal organization of a pin factory: this becomes the most famous and inlfuential statement on the economic rationale of the factory sytem and the division of labor.

1832   Charles Babbage's *On the Economy of Machinery and Manufactures* anticipates many of the notions of the scientific management movement, including "basic principles of management" such as the division of labor.

1855   Daniel C. McCallum, in his annual report as superintendent of the New York and Erie Railroad Company, states his six basic principles of administration; the first was to use internally generated data for managerial purposes.

1885   Captain Henry Metcalfe, the manager of an army arsenal, published *The Cost of Manufactures and the Administration of Workshops, Public and Private*, which asserts that there is a "science of administration" that is based upon principles discoverable by diligent observation.

1886   Henry R. Towne's paper "The Engineer as an Economist," read to the American Society of Mechanical Engineers, encourages the scientific management movement.

1903   Frederick W. Taylor publishes *Shop Management*.

1904   Frank B. and Lillian M. Gilbreth marry; they then proceed to produce many of the pioneering works on time and motion study, scientific management, and applied psychology, as well as 12 children.

1910   Louis D. Brandeis, an associate of Frederick W. Taylor (and later a U.S. Supreme Court justice) coins and popularizes the term "scientific management" in his Eastern Rate Case testimony before the Interstate Commerce Commission by arguing that railroad rate increases should be denied because the railroads could save "a million dollars a day" by applying scientific management methods.

1911   Frederick W. Taylor publishes *The Principles of Scientific Management*.

1912   Harrington Emerson publishes *The Twelve Principles of Efficiency*, which put forth an interdependent but coordinated management system.

1916   In France, Henri Fayol publishes his *General and Industrial Management*, the first complete theory of management.

1922   Max Weber's structural definition of bureaucracy is published posthumously; it uses an "ideal type" approach to extrapolate from the real world the central core of features that characterizes the most fully developed form of bureaucratic organization.

1931   Mooney and Reiley in *Onward Industry* (republished in 1939 as *The Principles of Organization*) show how the newly discovered "principles of organization" have really been known since ancient times.

1937   Luther Gulick's "Notes on the Theory of Organization" uses a mnemonic device (POSDCORB) to draw attention to the functional elements of the work of an executive.

SOURCE: Adapted from Jay F. Shafritz and J. Steven Ott, *Classics of Organization Theory*, 4th edition (Fort Worth, TX: Harcourt Brace, 1996).

Box 5.6

What Herbert Simon Really Thought of Public Administration

My actual research career started in an academic backwater: public administration. However important that field was and is to public affairs, it is attracted few scholars with a real understanding of what research is all about, or of how to construct theoretical foundations for an applied field. Viewed by the norms of science, many of the books published in public administration (and management generally) are positively embarrassing. For these and other reasons, this field was nearly invisible to mainstream social scientists. Even if a researcher made a contribution with potential beyond administration, it was unlikely that it would be noticed by anyone outside the field.

My case was even worse. I spent my first three working years (1936–1939) largely on very practical tasks at the International City Managers' Association. Mary, my first college sweetheart who once visited me in Chicago long after our affair had ended, expressed amazement that I should be devoting my life to such trivia. I replied that it was a job . . . . and that sooner or later I would probably finish.

SOURCE: Herbert A. Simon, *Models of My Life* (New York: Basic Books, 1991).

Simon writes in his 1991 memoir that his "Proverbs" article "got plenty of attention, not all of it favorable. Urwick never quite forgave me this attack on his life work, but Gulick was quite friendly in later years. Presumably he made allowance for the hubris of a young man. Hubris, arrogance, or whatever, that article secured my instant and permanent visibility in public administration."

The Impact of Sociology

One of the major themes of the neoclassical organization theorists was that organizations did not, indeed could not, exist as self-contained islands isolated from their environments. As might be expected, the first significant efforts to "open up" organizations (theoretically speaking) came from analysts whose professional identity required them to take a broad view of things—from sociologists. One such analyst was Philip Selznick, who in his 1948 *American Sociological Review* article, "Foundations of the Theory of Organization," asserted that while it is possible to describe and design organizations in a purely rational manner, such efforts can never hope to cope with the nonrational aspects of organizational behavior. In contrast with the classical theorists, Selznick maintained that organizations were made up of individuals whose goals and aspirations might not necessarily coincide with the formal goals of the organization—as opposed to consisting of just a number of positions for management to control. Neoclassical writers such as Simon and Selznick opened up the field of organization theory. Thereafter, it would be inherently interdisciplinary and open to the perspectives of sociology, cultural anthropology, political science, business administration, economics and, of course, public administration.

"Modern" Structural Organization Theory

Usually when someone refers to the structure of an organization, that person is talking about the relatively stable relationships among the positions and groups of positions (units) that comprise the organization. Structural organization theory is concerned with vertical differentiations—hierarchical levels of organizational authority and coordination, and horizontal differentiations between organizational units—for example, between product or service lines, geographical areas, or skills. The organization chart is the ever-present "tool" of a structural organization theorist.

Basic Assumptions

The label "modern" is used to distinguish the more recent writers of structural organization theory from the pre-World War II classical theorists such as Taylor and Weber. Management analysts Lee Bolman and Terrence Deal identified the basic assumptions of the "modern" structural school:

1. Organizations are rational institutions whose primary purpose is to accomplish established objectives; rational organizational behavior is achieved best through systems of defined rules and formal authority. Organizational control and coordination are key for maintaining organizational rationality.

2. There is a "best" structure for any organization—or at least a most appropriate structure—in light of its given objectives, the environmental conditions surrounding it (for example, its markets, the competition, and the extent of government regulation), the nature of its products and/or services (the "best" structure for a management consulting firm probably is substantially different than for a certified public accounting firm), and the technology of the production processes (a coal mining company has a different "best structure" than the manufacturer of computer microcomponents).

3. Specialization and the division of labor increase the quality and quantity of production—particularly in highly skilled operations and professions.

4. Most problems in an organization result from structural flaws and can be solved by changing the structure.

Mechanistic and Organic Systems

The most immediate issue in the design of any organization is the question of structure. What should it look like? How should it work? How will it deal with the most common structural questions of specialization, departmentalization, span of control, and the coordination and control of specialized units? A famous example of structural organization theory in action was provided by two British researchers, Tom Burns and G. M. Stalker of the Tavistock Institute in London. They developed a widely cited theory of "mechanistic" and "organic systems" of organization while examining rapid technological change in the British and Scottish electronics industry.

Burns and Stalker found that stable conditions may suggest the use of a mechanistic form of organization, where a traditional pattern of hierarchy, reliance on formal rules and regulations, vertical communications, and structured decision making is possible. However, more dynamic conditions—situations in which the environment changes rapidly—require the use of an organic form of organization where there is less rigidity, more participation, and more reliance on workers to define and redefine their positions and relationships. For example, technological creativity, an essential ingredient in an organic system, requires an organizational climate and management systems that are supportive of innovation. The impacts of these two organizational forms on individuals are substantially different. Supervisors and managers find that the mechanistic form provides them with a greater sense of security in dealing with their environment than the organic form, which introduces much greater uncertainty. Thus either form may be appropriate in particular situations.

Systems Theory

Since World War II, the social sciences have increasingly used **systems analysis** to examine their assertions about human behavior. The field of management, which to the extent that it deals with human resources can be said to be a social science, has been no exception.

Systems theory views an organization as a complex set of dynamically intertwined and interconnected elements, including its inputs, processes, outputs, feedback loops, and the environment in which it operates and with which it continuously interacts. Any change in any element of the system causes changes in other elements. The interconnections tend to be complex, dynamic (constantly changing), and often unknown. Thus when management makes decisions involving one organizational element, unanticipated impacts usually occur throughout the organizational system. Systems theorists study these interconnections, frequently using organizational decision processes and information and control systems as their focal points for analysis.

Whereas classical organization theory tends to be one-dimensional and somewhat simplistic, systems theories tend to be multidimensional and complex in their assumptions about organizational cause-and-effect relationships. The classicalists viewed organizations as static (unchanging) structures; systems theorists see organizations as continually changing processes of interactions among organizational and environmental elements. Organizations, not being static, are in constantly shifting states of dynamic equilibrium. The maintenance of this dynamic equilibrium was the task referred to in the title of the 1938 classic, *The Functions of the Executive*, by **Chester I. Barnard**. Barnard viewed organizations as cooperative systems where "the function of the executive" was to maintain the dynamic equilibrium between the needs of the organization and the needs of its employees. In order to do this, management had to be aware of the interdependent nature of the formal and informal organization. Barnard's analysis of the significance and role of informal organizations provided the theoretical foundations for a whole generation of empirical research.

---

systems analysis The methodologically rigorous collection, manipulation, and evaluation of data on social units (as small as an organization or as large as a polity) to determine the best way to improve their functioning and to aid a decision maker in selecting a preferred choice among alternatives.

Chester I. Barnard (1886–1961) The Bell System executive closely associated with the Harvard Business School, best known for his sociological analyses of organizations that encouraged and foreshadowed the post-World War II behavioral revolution.

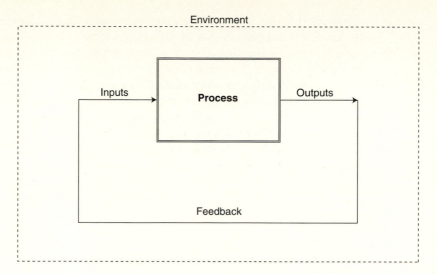

Environment

Inputs

Process

Outputs

Feedback

Figure 5.1   Norbert Wiener's Model of an Organization as an Adaptive System.

Cybernetics

Because organizations are adaptive systems that are integral parts of their environments, they must adjust to changes in their environment if they are to survive; in turn, virtually all of their decisions and actions affect their environment. Norbert Wiener's model of an organization as an adaptive system, from his 1948 book *Cybernetics*, epitomizes the basic theoretical perspectives of the systems perspective. Cybernetics, from a Greek word meaning "steersman," was used by Wiener to mean the multidisciplinary study of the structures and functions of control and information processing systems in animals and machines. The basic concept behind cybernetics is self-regulation—biological, social, or technological systems that can identify problems, do something about them, and then receive feedback to adjust themselves automatically. Wiener, a mathematician, developed the concept of cybernetics while working on anti-aircraft systems during World War II. Variations on this simple model of a system have been used extensively by systems theorists for many years—particularly around the development and use of management information systems.

The search for order among complex variables has led to an extensive reliance on quantitative analytical methods and models. The systems approach is strongly cause-and-effect oriented (logical-positivist) in its philosophy and methods. In these respects, systems theories have close ties to Taylor's scientific management approach. Whereas Taylor used quantitative scientific methods to find "the one best way," the systems theorist uses quantitative scientific methods to identify cause-effect relationships and to find optimal solutions. In this sense, the conceptual approaches and purposes between the two perspectives are strikingly similar. Thus, systems approaches are often called management sciences or administrative sciences. But be careful never to make the unpardonable error of calling them scientific management!

Systems thinking is critically important because the whole world, in essence, is a collection of interrelated systems. Nothing happens in isolation. Your reading this page is made possible by your visual system. Your turning to the next page is a function of your nervous system and muscular system—which is also related to your visual system. How else would you know when to turn the page? The systems of the world seem so infinite that another theory—chaos theory—has evolved to explain why they are often unexplainable. This theory postulates that the tiniest change in the smallest part of a system can eventually produce enormous effects. In weather forecasting this has become known as the Butterfly Effect. According to James Gleick, this is "the notion that a butterfly stirring the air today in Peking can transform storm systems next month in New York." All of chaos theory seeks to explain how the smallest elements of a system, whether weather or organizational, can have the biggest consequences. Yet all this was summed up by Benjamin Franklin in a 1758 issue of *Poor Richard's Almanac*:

> For the want of a nail the shoe was lost,
> For the want of a shoe the horse was lost,
> For the want of a horse the rider was lost,
> For the want of a rider the battle was lost,
> For the want of a battle the kingdom was lost—
> And all for want of a horseshoe-nail.

The Learning Organization

MIT Professor Peter Senge's *The Fifth Discipline* has become one of the most influential "systems" books of the 1990s. Senge seeks to destroy the "illusion that the world is created of separate, unrelated forces. When we give up this illusion—we can then build 'learning organizations.'" This phrase is Senge's term for "organizations where people continually expand their capacity to create the results they truly desire, where new and expansive patterns of thinking are nurtured, where collective aspiration is set free, and where people are continually learning how to learn together." Thus Senge's particular variant of the systems approach builds upon the doctrines of participation. He, too, builds upon the work of Abraham Maslow (discussed in Chapter 6). Indeed Senge's **yellow brick road** to the "learning organization" is in essence the route to Maslow's concept of **self-actualization**.

Senge argues that five new "component technologies" are gradually converging that will collectively permit the emergence of learning organizations. He labels these component technologies the "five disciplines": (1) personal mastery—how people approach life and work; (2) mental models—our deeply ingrained assumptions or mental images "that influence how we understand the world and how we take action"; (3) building shared vision—because "when there is a genuine vision . . . people excel

---

yellow brick road A clearly marked path such as the one provided for Dorothy in the 1939 film, *The Wizard of Oz*.

self-actualization The apex of Abraham Maslow's needs hierarchy, where an individual theoretically reaches self-fulfillment and becomes all that he or she is capable of becoming. The importance of the concept of self-actualization was established long before Maslow gave it voice. The nineteenth-century poet Robert Browning described its essence when he said, "A man's reach should exceed his grasp, or what's a heaven for?"

and learn, not because they are told to, but because they want to"; (4) team learning—where team members engage in true dialogue with their assumptions suspended; (5) systems thinking—the integrative discipline that fuses the others into a coherent body of theory and practice. Thus, without an understanding of systems, we can neither grow nor thrive as an organization or as an individual.

Summary

Modern management has its origins in the military institutions of the ancient world. While many ancient kingdoms, such as Egypt and China, had sophisticated administrative institutions, the core features of modern public administration in the Western world were first found in the Roman Empire.

All organizations are guided by a doctrine of management that reflects the basic values of the cultural environment. No management program can be viable without such guiding doctrines and compatible behavioral techniques for implementing them. The first doctrines were authoritarian and paralleled the brutality of military discipline. Since antiquity the military has evolved principles about how their authoritarian organizations were best managed. Those elements having civilian applications have been incorporated into principles of management. Thus concepts once military—such as span of control and unity of command—are now thoroughly civilian as well.

Advances in organization theory are not based on the accumulation of knowledge and facts, but rather on a dominant paradigm (or model) used in any specific period. Rather than refuting previous theories, each paradigm builds upon the body of relevant knowledge and theories. Once a paradigm is accepted by consensus, it lasts as long as it is useful. Ultimately, it is replaced by a more relevant and useful paradigm.

Classical organization theory (which includes bureaucracy), as its name implies, was the first theory of its kind, is considered traditional, and continues to be the base upon which other schools of organization theory have been built.

In the latter part of the nineteenth century, American industrial engineers began asserting that factory workers could be much more productive if their work was designed scientifically; their job was to conduct the research and do the planning that would make the organization more competitive relative to other organizations. Thus scientific management grew out of engineering. The progressive reformers were able to use scientific management as the core rationale for their call to separate politics from administration.

The pattern of development within public administration between World Wars I and II became known as a "period of orthodoxy." This ideology held that the work of government could be neatly divided into decision making and execution (the politics-administration dichotomy), and that administration was a science with discoverable principles (scientific management). This dichotomy would hardly have been possible if scientific management had not evolved when it did.

All the subsequent perspectives on organization theory—for example, the neoclassical, the "modern" structuralists, and systems theory—are essentially revisions and expansions of the classical writers. There is no consensus on what constitutes knowledge in organization theory. Anyone who studies this subject is free to join the school of organization theory of his or her choice and is free to accept the philosophic boundaries of one group of serious thinkers over another. No single perspective may deserve your loyalty because each contains important information and insights that are useful in differing circumstances.

Key Concepts

administrative doctrine   The rules, procedures, and ways of doing things that reflect the basic values of an organization.

bureaucracy   The totality of government officers; all of a government's employees; a general invective to refer to any inefficient organization encumbered by red tape or a specific set of structural arrangements.

classical theory   The original theory about organizations that closely resembles military structures.

learning organization   Peter Senge's term for organizations in which new patterns of thinking are nurtured and people are continually learning together to improve both the organization and their personal lives.

neoclassical theory   Theoretical perspectives that revise, expand, or are critical of classical organization theory.

organization   A group of people who jointly work to achieve at least one common goal.

organization theory   A set of propositions that seeks to explain or predict how groups and individuals behave in differing organizational arrangements.

paradigm   An intellectual model for a situation or condition.

POSDCORB   The mnemonic device invented by Luther Gulick in 1937 to call attention to the various functional elements of the work of a chief executive.

principles of management   Fundamental truths or working hypotheses that serve as guidelines to management thinking and action.

scientific management   A systematic approach to managing that seeks the "one best way" of accomplishing any given task by discovering the fastest, most efficient, and least fatiguing production methods.

systems theory   A view of an organization as a complex set of dynamically intertwined and interconnected elements, including its inputs, processes, outputs, feedback loops, and the environment in which it operates and with which it continuously interacts.

Bibliography

Appleby, Paul. (1945). *Big Democracy*. New York: Knopf.

Barker, Ernest. (1944). *The Development of Public Services in Western Europe, 1660–1930*. London: Oxford University Press.

Bolman, L. G., and T. E. Deal. (1984). *Modern Approaches to Understanding and Managing Organizations*. San Francisco: Jossey-Bass.

Brodie, Bernard. (1973). *War and Politics*. New York: Oxford University Press.

Burnham, James. (1941). *The Managerial Revolution*. New York: John Day.

Burns, T., and G. M. Stalker. (1961). *The Management of Innovation*. London: Tavistock Publications.

Byrne, John A. (1993). *The Whiz Kids: The Founding Fathers of American Business—and the Legacy They Left Us*. New York: Doubleday.

Downs, Anthony. (1967). *Inside Bureaucracy*. Boston: Little, Brown.

Drucker, Peter F. (1950). *The New Society: The Anatomy of the Industrial Order*. New York: Harper.

Gabriel, Richard A., and Paul L. Savage. (1978). *Crisis in Command: Mismanagement in the Army*. New York: Hill and Wang.

Gerth, H. H., and C. Wright Mills, eds. (1946). *From Max Weber: Essays in Sociology*. New York: Oxford University Press.

Gladden, E. N. (1972). *A History of Public Administration*, 2 vols. London: Frank Cass.

Gleick, James. (1987). *Chaos: Making a New Science*. New York: Viking.

Grant, Michael. (1991). *The Founders of the Western World: A History of Greece and Rome*. New York: Charles Scribner's.

Gulick, Luther, and Lyndall Urwick. (1937). *Papers on the Science of Administration*. New York: Institute of Public Administration.

Handel, Michael I. (1992). *Masters of War: Sun-Tzu, Clausewitz, and Jomini*. London: Frank Cass.

Henry, Nicholas. (1975). *Public Administration and Public Affairs*. Englewood Cliffs, NJ: Prentice Hall.

Jomini, Antoine-Henri. (1862). *The Art of War*. Philadelphia: Lippincott.

———. (1805). *Treatise on Great Military Operations*. New York: Van Nostrand.

Keegan, John. (1993). *A History of Warfare*. New York: Knopf.

Kennedy, Paul. (1987). *The Rise and Fall of the Great Powers*. New York: Random House.

Kuhn, T. S. (1970). *The Structure of Scientific Revolutions*, 2nd ed., enlarged. Chicago: University of Chicago Press.

Lilienthal, David E. (1944). *TVA: Democracy on the March*. New York: Harper & Bros.

Livingston, J. Sterling. "Pygmalion in Management." *Harvard Business Review* (July-August 1969).

Marini, Frank E. (1971). *Toward a New Public Administration*. San Francisco: Chandler.

Marrow, Alfred J. (1969). *The Practical Theorist: The Life and Works of Kurt Lewin*. New York: Basic Books.

McCurdy, Howard E. (1986). *Public Administration: A Bibliographic Guide to the Literature*. New York: Marcel Dekker.

Mises, Ludwig von. (1944). *Bureaucracy*. New Haven: Yale University Press.

Osborne, David, and Ted Gaebler. (1992). *Reinventing Government*. Reading, MA: Addison-Wesley.

Ostrom, Vincent. (1974). *The Intellectual Crisis in American Public Administration*, rev. ed. University: University of Alabama Press.

Ott, J. Steven. (1989). *The Organizational Culture Perspective*. Pacific Grove, CA: Brooks/Cole.

Seckler-Hudson, Catheryn. (1955). *Organization and Management: Theory and Practice*. Washington, DC: The American University Press.

Senge, Peter M. (1994). *The Fifth Discipline: The Art and Practice of the Learning Organization*. New York: Doubleday.

Shapley, Deborah. (1993). *Promise and Power: The Life and Times of Robert McNamara*. Boston: Little, Brown.

Shaw, George Bernard. (1944). *Everybody's Political What's What*. New York: Dodd, Mead.

Simon, Herbert A. (1991). *Models of My Life*. New York: Basic Books.

———. (1946). "The Proverbs of Administration." *Public Administration Review* (winter).

Smiddy, Harold F., and Lionel Naum. (1954). "Evolution of a Science of Managing in America," *Management Science* 1 (October).

Taylor, Frederick W. (1911). *The Principles of Scientific Management*. New York: Harper.

Waldo, Dwight. (1948). *The Administrative State: A Study of the Political Theory of American Public Administration*. New York: Ronald Press.

Wiener, Norbert. (1948). *Cybernetics*. Cambridge, MA: MIT Press.

Wilson, John A. (1951). *The Culture of Ancient Egypt*. Chicago: University of Chicago Press.

Wren, Daniel A. (1987). *The Evolution of Management Thought*, 3rd ed. New York: Wiley.

Recommended Books

Kanigel, Robert. (1997) *The One Best Way: Frederick Winslow Taylor and the Enigma of Efficiency*. New York: Viking. More than you ever wanted to know about the man, his times, his movement and his continuing influence.

Merkle, Judith A. (1980) *Management and Ideology: The Legacy of the International Scientific Management Movement*. Berkeley, CA: University of California Press. A highly readable historical analysis of the continuing influence of Frederick Taylor and scientific management in business and public administration.

Shafritz, Jay M., and J. Steven Ott, eds. (1996). *Classics of Organization Theory*, 4th ed. Forth Worth: TX: Harcourt Brace. A comprehensive collection of the most important writings on organization from ancient times to the present, from Socrates to postmodernism.

Wren, Daniel A., and Ronald G. Greenwood. (1998). *Management Innovators: The People and Ideas That Have Shaped Modern Business*. New York: Oxford University Press. A collection of mini-biographies of all the major thinkers on and experimenters with management techniques, from Eli Whitney to Peter Drucker.

Related Web Sites

Adam Smith's *Wealth of Nations*
   http://www.bibliomania.com/NonFiction/Smith/
   Wealth/index.html
Frederick W. Taylor archive
   http://www.lib.stevens-tech.edu/collections/
   taylor/
Herbert A. Simon
   http://www.psy.cmu.edu/psy/faculty/hsimon/
   hsimon.html
International Society for Performance Improvement
   http://www.ispi.org/

Management history
   http://www.fitapg.org/mhd/mhd.html
Max Weber's home page
   http://msumusik.mursuky.edu/~felwell/http/
   weber/whome.html
Napoleon Bonaparte Internet guide
   http://www.iselinge.nl/napoleon/
Organization and management theory
   http://www.nbs.ntu.ac.uk/staff/lyerji/list/hromt.htm

6

Organizational Behavior

Keynote: Organization Development in Hollywood: From *The Sands of Iwo Jima* to *G.I. Jane*

Demi Moore is the new John Wayne. In the 1997 film *G.I. Jane* she takes a disparate group of would-be Navy SEALs (sea-air-land teams) and forges them into a competent combat team—just in time to see "real" action on a fictional mission off the coast of Libya. What she did was not much different from what John Wayne did in the World War II films *The Sands of Iwo Jima* (1949) and *Flying Leathernecks* (1951). In the former Wayne is the sergeant of a Marine infantry squad; in the latter he is the commanding officer of a Marine fighter squadron. In both cases he forges his unruly and high spirited young charges into an effective, highly disciplined fighting force. He, as an older, more mature character, teaches them by example and instruction. And when someone inevitably dies because one of his men failed the group, Wayne is ready (in *The Sands*) with the kind of after-action fatherly consolation that makes his charges determined not to screw up again. "A lot of guys make mistakes, I guess, but every one we make, a whole stack of chips goes with it. We make a mistake, and some guy don't walk away—forevermore, he don't walk away." He says this with his eyes welling up with moisture and his voice choking to give it greater poignancy. Wayne was always most effective as here, when he gets almost to the point of crying but manfully holds it in.

Taking a cue from the John Wayne school of acting, Demi Moore also "manfully" holds in her tears throughout much of *G.I. Jane*. Never more so than when she demonstrates extraordinary bravery during a brutal mock prisoner-of-war interrogation. She is finally accepted by the SEALs as one of the guys when she, hands tied behind her back, attacks her sadistic interrogator with a brutal kick to the groin (thus denying him—at least temporarily—his masculine advantage) and lets forth with a blue streak of verbal abuse that shows once and for all that she can use the foul language of the barracks like the toughest of the guys. After this the men she commands are ready to follow her anywhere. The point is that her actions, her example, just like Wayne's, forges them into an effective team, whereas before they lacked group cohesion. *G.I. Jane* and many other war movies such as those of John Wayne demonstrate how organization development is, and always has been, an inherent part of military training.

Of course Moore, even with her hair in a crew-cut, is not really the new John Wayne. After all, it is highly unlikely that she will make a career of war movies and become the symbol of an aggressive American military. Wayne first became that symbol in a major way in 1949 when he played Sergeant Stryker in *The Sands*. Wayne earned his first Academy Award nomination with his portrayal of a tough disciplinarian whose men hated him for his rigorous training methods until toward the end of the film, when they realize that his toughness saved many of their lives by making them an effective combat team. According to Lawrence Suid, Wayne himself described the plot of *The Sands* as "the story of Mr. Chips [a benevolent English boarding school teacher] put in the military. A man takes eight boys and has to make men out of them." But Roberts and Olson add: "If one can imagine Mr. Chips cracking the jaw of one of his students with the butt of a rifle, the comparison is an apt one."

This film, made with the complete cooperation of the U.S. Marine Corps (the "cast of thousands" are mostly real Marines), has often been derided by "serious" critics, but has nevertheless become one of the more influential films of the twentieth century. It taught a whole generation of Americans what it meant to be a leader—especially of small groups. Stryker's hallmark shouts of impending action—"saddle up" and "lock and load"—are still commonly heard in both military and civil-

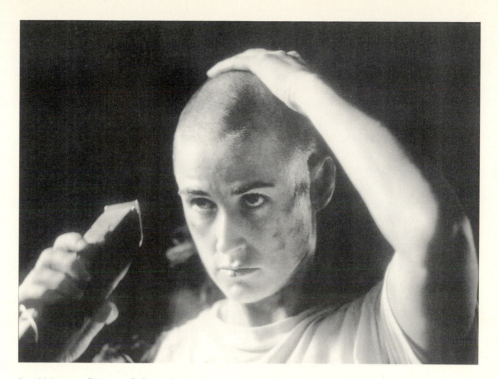

Demi Moore as "G.I. Jane" shaves her head to prove by looking more like one of the guys her total commitment to becoming a Navy SEAL •

ian contexts. For example, journalist Pat Buchanan, who never served in the military, often used those phrases during his ill-fated political campaign for the 1996 Republican presidential nomination. The Speaker of the House of Representatives, Newt Gingrich of Georgia, told Elizabeth Drew that *The Sands* was "the formative movie of my life." Stryker's style of leadership—make them tough and effective even if they hate you for it—is Gingrich's self-confessed tactic for shaping up his Republican insurgents for their successful 1994 assault on the House of Representatives.

Wayne played similar roles, outwardly tough but inwardly caring older leaders of younger men, in *Flying Leathernecks* (1951) and director John Ford's U.S. Cavalry trilogy: *Fort Apache* (1948), *She Wore a Yellow Ribbon* (1949), and *Rio Grande* (1950). But only his *The Cowboys* (1971) was a reprise of his role as Sergeant Stryker in a different guise. Here he is a Texas rancher who must use untrained boys to drive his cattle herd to the railhead many hundreds of miles away. But the plot, the organization development effort, is essentially the same: make these boys men enough for the job at hand. In both cases the boys dislike him at first but then learn to love him because they realize his way will see them through. In both cases Wayne is killed—by a Japanese sniper as the U.S. flag is raised on Iwo Jima in *The Sands* and by a despicable cattle rustler played by Bruce Dern in *The Cowboys*. In both cases the team can now carry on without him because he has trained, nurtured, and developed them so well. In

The Sands the squad goes on to secure the island as the Marine Corps hymn reminds us that this same kind of thing has been going on "from the halls of Montezuma to the shores of Tripoli." In *The Cowboys* the group realizes that they—because of *him*—are now strong enough to go it alone, to take back the herd from the rustlers and kill the villains for good measure. In both cases Wayne, much like the Old Testament Moses, gets his people almost to the "promised land," but dies before they can achieve it. They must go on without him. They *can* go on because of him. It is just this patriarchal aspect of Wayne that makes him, his characters, and his movies so sublimely moving and ultimately lasting.

But alas, the real John Wayne was no "John Wayne." The archetypal hero of so many movies and of America's popular imagination, far form being a hero, was quite the opposite. As a warrior he was a complete phony. Unlike many of his contemporary film stars, such as Clark Gable, Robert Taylor, James Stewart, Tyrone Power, Henry Fonda, Glenn Ford, and Sterling Hayden, to name a few, who gave up established Hollywood careers to serve in World War II with distinction—Wayne made every effort to avoid military service during the war. He was, more than any other major public figure, an active, artful, and successful draft dodger many times over. He simply arranged for the movie studios to say he was in a job essential to the war effort. However, by 1943 Wayne decided he would serve his country if he could get the assignment he wanted—working for director (but now naval officer) John Ford's naval photography unit. But Ford couldn't get him in because all such billets were frozen at that time. According to Ford's grandson Dan Ford, "Wayne tried other avenues but couldn't get a commission. The only way he could get in the service was to enlist in the army as a private." Wayne explained: "I felt that it would be a waste of time to spend two years picking up cigarette buts. I thought I could do more for the war effort if I stayed in Hollywood."

Wayne's career thrived during the war when so many other leading men were in uniform facing the enemy while he faced the cameras. Many in the film industry never forgave Wayne for refusing to serve. Political analyst Garry Wills wrote: "A few even claim that Wayne did not forgive himself—that the compensatory super patriotism of later years, when he urged the country on to wars in Korea and Vietnam, was a form of expiation. If so, it was not enough. This is a man who called on other generations to sacrifice their lives, and called them 'soft' if they refused."

Wayne's personal honor and patriotism notwithstanding, in the postwar era he became—and remains—the national icon of organization development. Wayne's performance in *The Sands*, while excellent in its own right, was a movie cliché even then. The stern fatherly taskmaster who takes error-prone "boys" under his wing and makes men out of them is a dramatic device that can be found as far back as the works of Homer in ancient Greece. It became the standard plot device for so many war movies because it lent itself so well to a story line needing a neat beginning, middle, and end. *The Sands* is simply the leading example of this genre. Other films with almost identical plot structures include *Gung Ho!* (1943) starring Randolph Scott, *Battle Cry* (1954) starring Van Heflin, *Cockleshell Heroes* (1956) starring José Ferrer, *Darby's Rangers* (1958) starring James Garner, *The Dirty Dozen* (1967) starring Lee Marvin, *The Devil's Brigade* (1968) starring William Holden, *Gallipoli* (1981) starring Mel Gibson, and *Heartbreak Ridge* (1986) starring Clint Eastwood.

Box 6.1

Forging a Band of Brothers

Unlike the Civil War, when army units were recruited from a single state, in World War II men, in most cases, were thrown together willy-nilly—so much so that a war-spawned cliché of film and fiction is the squad made up of the hillbilly from Arkansas, the Jew from Brooklyn, the coal miner from Pennsylvania, the farmer from Ohio, the lumberman from Oregon, the Italian from Chicago, the Pole from Milwaukee, and the Cajun from Louisiana. At first they hate each other; training draws them together; combat welds them into a band of brothers; they emerge by the final scene as just plain Americans with a strong sense of nationalism. And the truth is that this happened in life before it happened in art.

SOURCE: Stephen E. Ambrose, *Americans at War* (Jackson, MI: University Press of Mississippi, 1997).

The formula used by these films has three acts. In the first, the disparate group is assembled and seen as a bunch of individualists not capable of functioning as a team. Almost always, the group is ethnically diverse to represent the tensions and composition of the larger society. Thus there is often the college boy, the lumberjack, the "dead-end" kid, the farmer, and the urban ethnics (characters that are obviously meant to be Polish, Italian, or Jewish). Later, as U.S. society became more inclusive, Hispanic, Asian, and African Americans would appear. The first "act" always has the various types gradually lose their "street" identities and, under the harsh but benevolent guidance of the father-figure drill instructor, mold themselves into a team whose motto might well be that of Alexander Dumas' *Three Musketeers* (1844): "All for one, one for all."

The second act has the group performing as a team in training exercises and, often equally important, while on leave. For the purposes of the plot, it is equally valid for the group to realize they are a team in a barroom brawl as on field maneuvers. It's the group adventure, the sharing of mutual stress and danger, that finally cements the individuals into a team. (For the same reason, retreats and outdoor adventures are still popular means of developing civilian groups. The team that drinks together and climbs mountains together will perform the mundane duties of their everyday work in a more cooperative manner.) Once team status is achieved and the young soldiers realize how good the tough training they initially hated has been for them, they are ready for the third act—combat.

The third act validates the first two. It "proves" that the training works. While lives are inevitably lost, discipline and teamwork are shown to save lives and save the day. The father figure—whether John Wayne or Randolph Scott—is never more fatherly than when he leads them into danger and helps them fulfill their destiny as soldiers or cannon fodder.

One of the reasons films that follow this three-act formula have been so popular is that they ring true. While they have been decidedly sanitized for the mass public, they are true in that this *is* how the military—of all countries for seemingly all times—has indoctrinated and readied new soldiers for service. Thus the genre represents a time-tested method of organization development. The problem, of course, is that this particularly brutal method cannot be universally applied. First-line supervisors (the industrial equivalent of sergeants) cannot demand an instant fifty push-ups from an errant worker. In the industrial world the punishments must be more psychological than physical.

So far we have discussed the low end of war movie organization development. While such small unit plots offer the greatest opportunity for character development and audience identification, there is also a high end—organization development at the command level. This is best illustrated by films such as *Patton* (1970), starring George C. Scott, and *Twelve O'Clock High* (1949), starring Gregory Peck. In both instances new generals take charge of large units whose performance has been deficient. Yet even though they are generals, not sergeants, they use the same techniques as John Wayne's Sergeant Stryker to change the dysfunctional organizational culture that has led to failed operations and the sacking of the previous commanders. When Scott and Peck use their general's stars to impose a harsh disciplinary regime on their errant outfits, they are following Stryker's example and techniques but on a higher organizational level. And they get the same results—an effective team that yields high morale and successful operations.

The essence of this little essay has been to demonstrate that the military throughout the ages—and American war movies in particular—have evidenced a sophisticated understanding of organization development long before this became a formal element of modern management education. Wayne's Sergeant Stryker may not have been anyone's ideal of your friendly organization development facilitator or consultant, but he—quite literally—knew the drill. Even without an advanced degree in applied behavioral science or public administration, he and his brothers-in-arms going back to the legions of ancient Rome and beyond, knew how to instill planned organizational change. Higher education is a wonderful thing. But sometimes you can learn just as much by staying home and watching a bunch of old war movies.

Organizational Behavior

The study of organizational behavior comprises those aspects of the behavioral sciences that focus on the understanding of human behavior in organizations. Students of public administration have always been interested in the behavior of people in government organizations. But fundamental assumptions about the behavior of such people at their work did not change dramatically from ancient efforts at organization until only a few decades ago. Using the traditional authoritarian, militaristic, and "papa knows best" set of attitudes toward work organizations, **Hugo Münsterberg** pioneered the application of psychological findings from laboratory experiments to practical matters. He sought to match the abilities of new hires with a company's work demands, to positively influence employee attitudes toward their work and their company, and to understand the impact of psychological conditions on employee productivity. Münsterberg's pre-World War I approach was typical of how the behavioral sciences tended to be applied in organizations well into the 1950s.

In contrast to Münsterberg's traditional perspective on organizational behavior, a new style of applied behavioral science emerged in the 1960s. It focused attention on seeking to answer questions such as how organizations could encourage their workers to grow and develop. The belief was that organizational creativity, flexibility, and prosperity would flow naturally from employee growth and development. The essence of the relationship between organization and people was redefined from dependence to codependence. In contrast, managers in Münsterberg's day did not believe (assume) that codependence was the "right" relationship between an organization and its employees.

There has long been considerable interest in the behavior of people inside bureaucracies. After all, the whole purpose of organization theory, as discussed in the previous chapter, is to create mechanisms for regulating the behavior of people in organizations. However, it was not until about 1960, with the publication of Douglas MacGregor's *Human Side of Enterprise*, that our basic assumptions about the relationship between organizations and people truly began to change. This new approach to analyzing organizations focused on people, groups, and the relationships among them and the organizational environment. It was built around the following assumptions:

1. Organizations are created to serve human ends.

2. Organizations and people need each other (organizations need ideas, energy, and talent; people need careers, salaries, and work opportunities).

3. When the fit between the needs of the individual and the organization is poor, one or both will suffer: individuals may be exploited, or may seek to exploit the organizations or both.

4. A good fit between individuals and organizations benefits both because people gain meaningful and satisfying work—and organizations receive the talent and energy they need to thrive.

It is instructive to contrast these assumptions with the paternalistic authoritarian attitudes that preceded them. Previously, when new technology was to be introduced, new orders were given for its installation and operation. There was no concern about what the workers would think about such changes. They simply had

---

Hugo Münsterberg (1863–1916) The German-born psychologist whose later work at Harvard would earn him the title of "father" of industrial or applied psychology.

no say. Once in awhile some **Luddites** might surface but they were quickly suppressed. Compare this "orders is orders" approach to how modern organizational behaviorists contemplate the introduction of a new technology. They immediately start thinking about and planning a specific approach:

1. Minimize fear of change by involving people at all levels in designing the introduction of the changes.
2. Minimize the negative impacts of the change on groups of workers at risk (such as older, less-skilled, or younger workers).
3. **Co-opt** informal and formal (usually union) leaders, especially those who might become antagonistic.
4. Find alternatives for employees who do not see the changes as consistent with their personal goals.

Because the modern perspective places a high value on the individual, employees are provided with maximum amounts of accurate information, so they can make informed decisions about their future.

The assumptions of the Münsterberg traditional perspective continue to be alive and well in many less sophisticated organizations—where it is still assumed that people should be fitted to the organization. With the classical organization theory of Frederick Taylor and others, the organizational role of the applied behavioral sciences largely consisted of helping organizations find and shape people to serve as human replacement parts for the organizational machine.

Yet, under the right circumstances, people and organizations will grow and prosper together. Individuals and organizations are not necessarily antagonists. Managers can learn to unleash previously stifled energies and creativities. Two of the most important "tools" for doing this are group dynamics and organization development.

Group Dynamics

Since the earliest days of the Industrial Revolution, workplace organizations have been constructed on the foundation principles of specialization and division of labor (remember Adam Smith's pin factory). In our complex organizations of today, few jobs can be done from start to finish by one person. Specialization allows an organization to use people's skills and efforts more systematically and to focus their knowledge and energy on a limited number of tasks. Employee **learning curves** are minimized.

Luddites Originally English workers in the early nineteenth century who destroyed new textile machinery that was displacing them in factories; now the term, after the legendary Ned Ludd, refers to anyone who sabotages high-tech equipment to protect jobs.

co-opt To include potentially dissident group members in an organization's policymaking process to prevent such elements from being a threat to the organization or its mission. The classic analysis of co-optation is found in Philip Selznick's *TVA and the Grass Roots* (1949).

learning curve The time it takes to achieve optimal efficiency in performing a task. When workers repeatedly do a new task, the amount of labor per unit of output initially decreases according to a pattern that can be plotted as a curve on a graph.

Most employees who perform sets of specialized functions are organizationally clustered in work groups, which are organized into units or branches, which are organized into divisions or departments, which are organized into agencies, and so forth. Work groups attract people with like backgrounds; for example, professional training, socialization, and experience as accountants, teachers, engineers, or computer programmers. All such shared backgrounds involve the socialization of people into common value/belief/behavior systems. We learn how to think and act like lawyers, teachers, or accountants—and like Virginians or Southern Californians.

Practically all groups, and particularly purposeful, specialized, organizational groups, develop their own sets of norms of behavioral assumptions about things like the nature of their organizational environment and appropriate relations with other groups. All groups expect their members to conform to their norms. By rewarding activities the organization wants done and punishing counterproductive behavior, managers engineer the accomplishment of organizational goals. Virtually all organizations attempt to motivate employees through combinations of rewards and punishments. **Reinforcement** theories of motivation assume that people at work seek rewards and try to avoid punishments.

Acceptance of and adherence to group norms permits people to know what to expect from each other and to predict what other members will do in different circumstances. Norms cause people to behave in patterned and predictable ways. Thus by institutionalizing common expectations, they stabilize the organization. Always remember, though, that too much adherence to norms causes overconformity. This can hurt or destroy individualism—and even lead to groupthink (see the section on groupthink in this chapter). The potential damage here is not limited to individuals who work in organizations. Excessive conformity may result in so much organizational rigidity that the organization's overall ability to achieve its mission is degraded.

When a group becomes institutionalized in an organization, such as a production unit or a branch office, these shared beliefs, values, and assumptions—these norms—become the essence of a cohesive group and of an organizational subculture. Most group subcultures have a resemblance to the overall organizational culture, but also contain unique elements that form through the impacts of events, circumstances, and personalities. Considering the normal loyalties that groups demand and the affiliational needs they meet, it becomes easy to understand why ingroups and outgroups and feelings of we-and-they and we-versus-they are so characteristic of life in organizations.

Group dynamics is the subfield of organization behavior concerned with the nature of groups, how they develop, and how they interrelate with individuals and other groups. Usually the term "group" refers to what is more technically known as a primary group—a group small enough to permit face-to-face interaction among its

---

reinforcement An inducement to perform in a particular manner. Positive reinforcement occurs when an individual receives a desired reward that is contingent upon some prescribed behavior. Negative reinforcement occurs when an individual works to avoid an undesirable outcome.

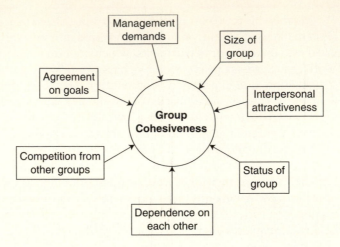

Figure 6.1   Factors Contributing to Group Cohesiveness

members that remains in existence long enough for some personal relations, sentiments, and feelings of identification or belonging to develop. There are two basic kinds of primary groups: formal and informal.

Formal groups are officially created by a larger organization, usually for the purpose of accomplishing tasks. Employees are assigned to formal groups based upon their position in the organization. There are two basic types of formal groups. First, there are command groups that are specified in a formal organization chart. These include both supervisors and the people who report directly to them. Groups of this type are the essential building blocks of organizational structure. They vary from a mail room staff, to the employees of a small branch office, to an entire headquarters staff. Second, there are task groups, formally sanctioned job-oriented units with short lives. Here you will find employees who work together to complete a particular project or task and then are disbanded. Any ad hoc ("for this") **task force** or temporary ("for this") committee is an example.

Informal groups are spontaneously developed relationships and patterns of interactions in work situations. Included here are employees who associate voluntarily, primarily to satisfy social needs. Although informal groups at work may have goals and tasks (for example, ethnic support groups, bowling clubs, and luncheon speaker groups), their primary reasons for existence are friendship, affiliation, and shared interests. Although informal groups seldom are formally sanctioned, they are extremely important to the working of organizations. Their norms, values, beliefs, and expectations have significant impacts on work-related behavior and attitudes.

---

task force A temporary interdisciplinary team within a larger organization charged with accomplishing a specific goal. Task forces are typically used in government when a problem crosses departmental lines.

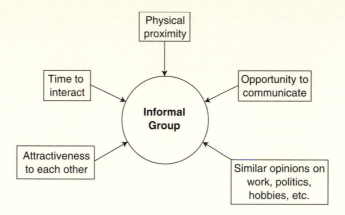

Figure 6.2 Factors Leading to the Creation of Informal Groups

Chester I. Barnard in *The Functions of the Executive* has provided the classic statement on the vital significance of informal groups:

> Informal organization, although comprising the processes of society which are unconscious as contrasted with those of formal organization which are conscious, has two important classes of effects: (a) it establishes certain attitudes, understandings, customs, habits, institutions; and (b) it creates the condition under which formal organization may arise.

Groups in organizations of all types are of high importance and interest to students and practitioners of organizational behavior, both for what happens in them (and why) and what happens between them.

Organization Development

The French Foreign Legion, when it occupied most of the North African desert early in the twentieth century, had the slogan "march or die"—which meant that a legionnaire could not survive unless he kept his place in the moving column. A similar slogan should be on the walls of all organizations: "change or die." The message here is that without constant change, renovation—indeed reinventing—this social organism will die just as surely as the solitary legionnaire of old.

Organization Development (O.D.) is planned organizational change. Organizations exist in a dynamic environment both internally and externally to which they must respond or become ineffectual. The responsibility of O.D. advisors, specialists on applied behavioral science, is to facilitate change—to use their knowledge of the behavioral sciences for organizational improvement. These advisors can be internal in that they already work for the organization or external independent consultants. A frequently desired change is the installation of a beneficent managerial philosophy. More modest goals might be the creation of an atmosphere of trust in order to facilitate communications or the development of participatory mechanisms that would stimulate productivity. Any organization that wishes to survive or simply to remain healthy must periodically divest itself of those parts or characteristics that contribute to its malaise.

O.D. itself is not a philosophy. It is an approach or strategy for increasing organizational effectiveness. As a process, it has no value biases, but it is usually associated with the idea that effectiveness is found by integrating the individual's desire for growth with organizational goals. There is no universal O.D. model that can easily be plugged into a troubled organization. The basic task of the O.D. advisor is to adapt appropriate portions of the generally available O.D. technology to the immediate demands of his or her organizational problem. This is why the O.D. advisor must be thoroughly conversant with the findings of the behavioral technology of modern management. Since no textbook will have a case study of the exact organizational problem to be remedied, these advisors must be prepared to draw upon their backgrounds to improvise. O.D. advising, like much of the rest of public administration, contains a large element of art.

The O.D. process is made all the more difficult to implement in the public sector because top management, which must first be sold on the O.D. process, is fractured, consisting of political and career executives, legislative committees, client groups, etc. Hostility can also be expected from line management. As an O.D. role for the personnel department implies a greater involvement with management's traditional line prerogatives, it may take some time before personnel's agitation in this regard is viewed as supportive instead of threatening.

A decision on the part of top management to suddenly replace a highly structured authoritarian organizational climate with an atmosphere of greater employee participation and collaboration probably would create a great sense of shock and suspicion among employees. All changes in organizational climate or culture must be well planned in advance and implemented gradually. O.D. is not something that can be accomplished in an afternoon. It is a slow process that extends, at the very least, over many months and requires the commitment and cooperation of all of the principal actors in the organizational drama. The first phase of almost all O.D. models is the education of top management in basic O.D. objectives and strategies. O.D. as a process is one that must flow from the top down. As leadership sets the tone of organizational life, it is futile to seek to change the pace and quality of that life without uninhibited cooperation from the top down.

O.D. is concerned with deep, long-lasting organization-wide change or improvement—not in superficial changes in isolated organizational pockets. This concern for broad-based and long-term change led O.D. practitioners to an interest in the concept of organizational culture long before it became a fashionable management topic in the 1980s. O.D. advisors have developed numerous strategies and techniques for improving organizations: Most of them utilize **interventions** facilitated by outsiders (often called change agents). Some of the most common strategies include organizational diagnosis, **process consultation**, team building (in many

---

intervention The entering of an outsider into an ongoing system of relationships, such as an organization, to help make it perform better.

process consultation The interventionist activities of an organization development advisor.

forms), action research, data feedback, **job enlargement, job enrichment,** and conflict management. But each advisor has his or her own preferred tactics.

The origins of the organization development movement can be generally traced to the Hawthorne studies (discussed later in this chapter). But the specific understandings of organizational behavior-oriented change processes came out of the sensitivity training (or **T-group**) movement that started in 1946 when Kurt Lewin and associates collaboratively conducted a training workshop to help improve racial relations and community leadership in New Britain, Connecticut. During their evening staff meetings, they discussed the behavior of workshop participants and the dynamics of events. Several workshop participants asked to join the night discussions, and the results of the process eventually led to the initiation and institutionalization of T-group technology. Although the early T-groups focused primarily on individual growth and development, they quickly were adapted for organizational application. T-groups became the method by which organizational members learned how to communicate honestly and directly about facts and feelings. (From the human relations perspective, feelings are facts.) Thus T-groups became a keystone strategy for increasing organizational effectiveness by improving interpersonal communications (e.g., feedback), reducing defensiveness (and thus rigidity), and otherwise helping organizations achieve greater effectiveness through the development of coping processes. The meaning of coping here is twofold—coping with the job as well as with fellow workers.

But the T-group needed to be part of a larger overarching methodology. Survey research methodology, when combined with feedback/communication (T-group) techniques, and applied to planned organizational change, resulted in the development of the action research model of organizational change—the mainstay of O.D. practitioners and theorists. The action research model is a process for identifying needs for organizational improvement through the use of external consultation but also through **psychological ownership** of problems and solutions by organizational members. Briefly, action research involves the following:

1. Collecting organizational diagnostic data (ascertaining the problem) usually either through written questionnaires or interviews

2. Systematically feeding back information to the organization members who provided input

3. Discussing what the information means to members and its implications for the organization, in order to be certain if the "diagnosis" is accurate and to generate psychological ownership of the need for actions to improve the situation

---

job enlargement Adding additional but similar duties to a job.

job enrichment Adding differing kinds of duties so that the work is both at a higher level and more personally satisfying.

T-group A training group. According to Chris Argyris, a leading authority on O.D. techniques, the T-Group experience is "designed to provide maximum possible opportunity for the individuals to expose their behavior, give and receive feedbacks, experiment with new behavior, and develop everlasting awareness and acceptance of self and others."

psychological ownership Emotional involvement with, and commitment to, an intangible something such as an organizational reform effort.

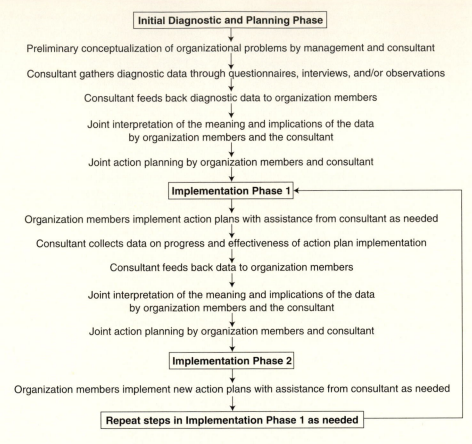

Figure 6.3 The Organization Development Action Research Model   SOURCE: Adapted from J. Steven Ott, ed., *Classic Readings in Organizational Behavior*, 2nd ed. (Belmont, CA: Wadsworth, 1996).

4. Jointly developing an improvement plan, using both the knowledge and skills of the consultant and the insider perspective of members

5. Repeating all of the above as needed

The key to long-term O.D. success is this very last step—repeat as needed. Lewin is well known for his assertion that social change must be viewed as a three-step process of unfreezing, change, and refreezing. If one focuses only on the change process per se, change will be short-lived at best. The organization must put the change in place to see if it takes. The process is called action research because the thing being experimented on, the organization, is constantly in action. When Lewin says "unfreezing," he means opening up the organization to change. The "refreezing" process is installing the new change, then watching it to see if the "refreezing" is an improvement. This O.D. effort toward continuous improvement is a precursor to the total quality management (TQM) movement discussed in Chapter 7.

The ultimate question here is not whether organizations should change. They are constantly changing in response to the dynamic environments in which they all exist. Of course, some environments are more dynamic than others. But change, fast or slow, is inexorable. The best line Thomas Wolfe ever wrote was the title of his 1940 novel *You Can't Go Home Again*. The home you left, because of the simple passage of time, is no longer the home to which you return. The home in which you once lived, just like the office in which you once worked, changes every day. People get older, attitudes evolve, and new skills are learned no matter what we do. So the question for would-be managers of organizations is not change: yes or no, but unplanned change or planned change. O.D. as planned change is just a tool for managers to gain control of and give direction to the inevitable changes within their organizations.

The Impact of Personality

Chris Argyris, a preeminent analyst of organizational phenomena for over four decades, first became noteworthy with the publication of his 1957 book *Personality and Organization*. In it he claimed that there was an inherent conflict between the mature adult personality and the needs of modern organizations. The problem, simply put, was that most organizations were treating adults like children. As the truth of this finding was made increasingly evident, treatments changed. A new dogma evolved that organizations should give their citizens all the responsibilities they could handle—and then some.

While this nicely dovetailed with concerns for greater productivity and effectiveness, the inherent problem of personality was not so much superseded as ignored. After all, in the era of equal employment opportunity and workforce diversity, efforts to address the impact of individual personalities on organizations could be dangerous. Who needs lawsuits claiming that an employee's cultural heritage is being "attacked" by an inherently oppressive organization and a supervisor insensitive to the subtleties of managing in a multicultural environment?

Nevertheless, organizational analysts have once again begun, despite the diversity issue minefield, to look anew at the impact of personality. And they are beginning to say things that will make some people uncomfortable. They are not rejecting what Argyris said about adults and organizations. But they are saying that different kinds of adults fit organizations differently; that individuals who might have been heroes in an earlier age because of their inherent aggressiveness and disdain for established authority are too often misfits in a contemporary bureaucratic culture.

The issue here is inherent temperament. According to Winifred Gallagher, there is still much to be said for the validity of four basic human temperaments first described in ancient Greece by Hippocrates 2,500 years ago. His four "humors" are still commonly used today to informally describe personality types. We have all seen people who are sanguine (optimistic and energetic), melancholic (moody and withdrawn), choleric (irritable and impulsive), and phlegmatic (calm and slow). Indeed, many people have displayed all of these "humors" or moods at one time or another.

Even if we discard Hippocrates' "humors" as a classification system, it is just common sense that a "dirty Harry" (the archetypal aggressive police officer portrayed by Clint Eastwood in a series of films) should not be placed in charge of the police department's computer system. Similarly, an extremely shy, soft-spoken person would not usually be the best individual to represent your organization on radio and TV. And someone prone to constant anxiety and worry will probably not do well in a high-stress position. Yet such mismatches are so commonplace that they are a leading cause of organizational incompetence.

The Dangers of Groupthink

In a classic 1951 article, "Effects of Group Pressure upon the Modification and Distortion of Judgments," Solomon Asch described his investigations into the ways individuals cope when a group's majority opinion is contrary to the facts of a situation. Asch put lone experimental subjects in rooms with people who had been instructed to give blatantly wrong answers to factual questions. For example, saying a chair was green when it was obviously blue. Only the experimental subjects did not know what was going on. Although a slim majority of subjects retained their independence and reported the facts accurately, a sizable minority of them altered their judgment to match that of the majority. When faced with a group opinion that was obviously wrong, they were not willing to report what they saw. They changed their minds.

Asch's experiments provided dramatic evidence of group impacts on people in organizations. From a managerial perspective, they showed why it is extremely important to focus attention on a work group's beliefs, values, and composition. But for the most part, informal groups are outside of the formal organization's direct sphere of influence.

Twenty years after Asch's experiments, Irving Janis published his now even better-known study on "groupthink." Like Asch, Janis explored pressures for conformance—the reason why social conformity is encountered frequently in groups. But unlike Asch's experimental use of college students, Janis looked at high-level decision makers at the time of the following major fiascoes:

- The 1941 failure to prepare for the Japanese attach on Pearl Harbor. This brought the United States into World War II.
- The 1950 decision during the Korean War to send General Douglas MacArthur to the Yalu River, the boundary between North Korea and China. This provoked Chinese intervention and expanded the war.
- The 1961 decisions to allow an American-sponsored invasion of Cuba by expatriate Cubans trained by the CIA to overthrow the government of Fidel Castro. The landing at the Bay of Pigs was a total failure and a major embarrassment to the Kennedy administration.

Groupthink is "the mode of thinking that persons engage in when concurrence seeking becomes so dominant in a cohesive in-group that it tends to override realistic appraisal of alternative courses of action." Thus a "desperate drive for consensus at any cost . . . suppresses dissent"—and information that might encourage or support dissent as well. The organizational culture that allows groupthink also stifles information. Janis identified eight easily observable symptoms of groupthink that lead to incompent—and sometimes disastrous—decisions:

1. An illusion of invulnerability
2. Collective construction of rationalizations that permit group members to ignore warnings or other forms of negative feedback
3. Unquestioning belief in the morality of the in-group
4. Strong, negative, stereotyped views about the leaders of enemy groups
5. Rapid application of pressure against group members who express even momentary doubts about virtually any illusions the group shares
6. Careful, conscious, personal avoidance of deviation from what appears to be a group consensus
7. Shared illusions of unanimity of opinion
8. Establishment of mind guards—people who "protect" the leader and fellow members from adverse information that might break the complacency they shared about the effectiveness and morality of past decisions

The groupthink phenomenon is hardly limited to high-level decision makers in the government. Groupthink tends to occur when individuals value membership in a group and identify strongly with their colleagues. It may also occur because the group leader does not encourage dissent or because of stressful situations that make the group more cohesive. In essence, group members suppress doubts and criticisms about proposed courses of action, with the result that the group chooses riskier and more ill-advised policies than would otherwise have been the case. Groupthink, because it refers to a deterioration of mental efficiency and moral judgment due to in-group pressures, has now developed an invidious connotation.

Janis concluded that groupthink has a negative influence on executive decision making because it leads to an overestimation of the group's capabilities and a self-imposed isolation from new or opposing information and points of view. Note that there is nothing new about groupthink. For example, what happened at the Bay of Pigs in 1961 is in groupthink essence no different than what happened to the Spanish Armada's attempted invasion of England in 1588. In both cases leaders (John F. Kennedy and Philip II of Spain) expected small landings of hostile forces to lead to a general uprising against the established regime. False intelligence led to false premises which, in turn, led to failed invasions. In the cases concerning the Pearl Harbor attack and the Korean War, false intelligence was not the issue. Here there was plenty of intelligence. The failure was to accurately interpret and act upon it.

What's really new about groupthink is that we can now label it with an official social science word. Kennedy speechwriter Theodore C. Sorensen, in his biography of his old boss, quotes the president assessing his judgment on the Bay of Pigs: "All my life I've known better than to depend on the experts. How could I have been so stupid, to let them go ahead?"

The Impact of Bureaucratic Structure on Behavior

The impact of bureaucratic structure on the behavior of its denizens results from their unique personalities interacting with the organizational structures in which they must function. Each organization has structures that define the unique ways labor is divided, how specialized roles and functions are coordinated (related to each other and to other organizational levels and functions), how information flows among people and groups, and how the system of controls (how tasks are measured, evaluated, and altered) is to work. These structures, often visualized in the form of an **organization chart**, establish how roles, expectations, and resource allocations are determined for people and groups in any given organization. Structure is a primary reason why organizational behavior differs from behavior in everyday life, and thus why organizational behavior developed as a separate field of study within the applied behavioral sciences. Structure, however, is only one of a variety of forces that affect the behavior of people in organizations. Attitudes and behaviors are also shaped by **peer group** pressure, shared group norms of behavior, social and technical aspects of work tasks, and the organization's internal and external cultures (discussed in Chapter 2).

The structures of a large bureaucracy are inherently conservative in that they are slow to change. Thus one of the perennial complaints about bureaucracy is its lack of responsiveness to changing conditions. But this notorious slowness to change is very often a function of its legal mandate. No public bureaucracy in a democratic government does anything that is not provided for by its enabling legislature. This alleged slowness, from another point of view, is simply its obedience to the law. What a chief executive would streamline and make more efficient, the power brokers of the legislature would just as often keep bloated and inefficient. And if government jobs for their constituents are at stake, efficiency and economy in government suffer even more. This is exactly what members of the U.S. Congress must confront every time the Department of Defense seeks to close military bases. Congressional **doves** suddenly turn into defense **hawks** when it is the jobs of the voters in their district at stake.

As organizations grew from small offices and shops into large corporations and government agencies, the disciplined hierarchies and unambiguous functional assignments of bureaucracy evolved as the ideal structural form. This structure allowed for pervasive control from the top of an organizational pyramid. But tight control is a good news/bad news story. The good news is that it is possible to centrally monitor and regulate the behavior of the employees. The bad news is that there are high costs involved with excessive control and the line between tight control and excessive control is a thin one. Employees in organizational straitjackets are unlikely to exercise

---

organization chart The visual representation of the structure of an organization, usually in the form of a diagram.

peer group People at the same organizational level in terms of rank, title, or salary.

dove A peaceful bird in metaphor; a symbol of peace since ancient times.

hawk Person inclined toward military action. Its antithetical term is dove.

initiative. Like automatons—human robots—they perform their prescribed duties until appropriate bureaucratic authority tells them otherwise. A properly designed bureaucratic organization can be impressively efficient even though none of its individual bureaucrats are in any way exceptional individuals. This is why Herman Wouk in his 1951 novel *The Caine Mutiny* called the U.S. Navy "a machine invented by geniuses, to be run by idiots." These machines, whether governmental or industrial, can be extraordinarily impressive in performance even when run by mediocre people. Thus the French novelist Honoré de Balzac called bureaucracy "the giant power wielded by pygmies." In this sense bureaucracy, far from being incompetent, is a bastion of super-competence—its overall performance far exceeding the quality that could otherwise be expected from its miscellaneous human parts.

Bureaucratic Dysfunctions

Unfortunately, bureaucracies often have within them the seeds of their own incompetence, like a bad genetic inheritance. Contemporary writers such as Robert K. Merton and Victor A. Thompson have argued that bureaucracies have inherent dysfunctional and pathological elements that make them inefficient in operations. Merton found that bureaucracies have a "trained incapacity." This refers to a "state of affairs in which one's abilities function as inadequacies or blind spots. Actions based upon training and skills which have been successfully applied in the past may result in inappropriate responses under changed conditions." According to Merton, bureaucracy exerts constant pressures on people to be methodical and disciplined, to conform to patterns of obligations. These pressures eventually cause people to adhere to rules as an end rather than a means—as a matter of blind conformance.

It is this blind conformance that gives bureaucracy its catch-22 quality, its trained incapability to respond to contradictory requirements. This "catch" from Joseph Heller's 1961 novel of the same name about American bomber crews in World War II meant that you could get out of flying combat missions if you were insane. All you had to do was ask. But if you asked, you were not insane because seeking to avoid combat was a rational, not an insane, act. In Heller's words a pilot "would be crazy to fly more missions and sane if he didn't, but if he was sane, he had to fly them. If he flew them he was crazy and didn't have to, but if he didn't, he was sane and had to." The "catch" is beautifully circular in its perversity. Because the book was such an enormous bestseller, catch-22 entered the language as the code word for the essence of bureaucratic dysfunctionalism, for being trapped between contradictory bureaucratic regulations. A common example of catch-22 is this double bind: a person can't get a job without experience but can't get experience without first having a job.

Bureaucratic structure also stresses depersonalized relations, and power and authority gained by virtue of organizational position rather than by thought or action. Thus, ideas and opinions are valued not according to their intrinsic merit but according to one's rank. This would be perfectly fine if the bosses truly were always smarter than the workers. Without question, Merton sees bureaucratic structure as more than affecting organizational behavior and thinking: it also determines and controls. It determines that not all of the organization's brain power will be used

Box 6.2

The Most Famous Song of Bureaucratic Upward Mobility

I cleaned the windows and I swept the floor,
And I polished up the handle of the big front door.
Then I was promoted to the post of junior clerk.
I served the writs with a smile so bland,
And I copied all the letters in a big round hand.
Finally I became a lawyer and was given a partnership,
Which was the only *ship* I'd ever seen!
I grew so rich I was sent to Parliament.
I always voted at my party's call,
And I never thought of thinking for myself at all.
As a matter of fact—
I thought so little, they rewarded me
By making me the Ruler of the Queen's Navy!
Now landsmen all, whoever you may be,
If you want to rise to the top of the tree,
Stick close to your desks and never go to sea,
And you *all* may be Rulers of the Queen's Navy!

SOURCE: William S. Gilbert, *H. M. S. Pinafore* (1878).

and that the objectively less deserving may remain in control. Of course, there is always the bright aspiring bureaucratic leader who holds his tongue or her brains in check while they climb the bureaucratic career ladder. But the danger here is that they suffer from "evaporation." Historian B. H. Liddell Hart observed in his *Why Don't We Learn from History?* that "ambitious officers when they came in sight of promotion" to high rank, "would decide that they would bottle up their thoughts and ideas, as a safety precaution, until they reached the top and could put these ideas into practice. Unfortunately the usual result, after years of such self-repression for the sake of their ambition, was that when the bottle was eventually uncorked the contents had evaporated."

As a form of organization, bureaucracy has many advantages: order, predictability, stability, professionalism, and consistency. Nevertheless, the behavioral consequences of bureaucratic structure are often negative. To illustrate this, Thompson combined "bureaucracy" with "pathological" to describe the all-too-familiar "bureaupathic official." Such a person "usually exaggerates the official, nontechnical aspects of relationships and suppresses the technical and the informal." Being insecure he or she "may be expected to insist on petty rights and prerogatives, on protocol, on procedure—in short, on those things least likely to affect directly the goal accomplishment of the organization." This is the classic stereotype of "the bureaucrat." Thus an otherwise "functionless reviewing officer will often insist most violently on his right to review and scream like an injured animal if he is bypassed." Moreover, "if he has a counterpart at a higher organizational level, he will probably insist on exclusive contact with that higher clearance point. By controlling this particular communication channel, he protects his authority and influence." This stereotype has been around, quite literally, for ages. In *Measure for Measure* (Act II, Scene 2) Shakespeare writes of the "petty officer," the "proud man, dress'd in a little brief authority, most ignorant of what he's most assur'd." This "petty officer" with his or her "little brief authority" is also probably performing at a bureaucracy near you—right now!

Bureaucratic Impersonality

Max Weber referred to bureaucracy's "special virtue" as "dehumanization." Hardly anyone would argue that bureaucracy does not have dehumanizing consequences for its employees and, to a lesser extent, for its clients as well. By dehumanization, Weber meant the elimination "from official business [of] love, hatred and all purely personal, irrational, and emotional elements." In Weber's view, formalization, hierarchy, and the other central features of bureaucracy render the individual bureaucrat "only a single cog in an ever-moving mechanism which prescribes to him an essentially fixed route of march." Consequently, "the individual bureaucrat is forged to the community of all functionaries who are integrated into the mechanism." He cannot "squirm out of the apparatus in which he is harnessed." Today the term "impersonality" is generally used in referring to this aspect of bureaucratic behavior. Viewed against a historical background of administrative organizations characterized by such "irrational" elements as **nepotism,** personal subjugation, and capricious and uninformed judgment, impersonality can be seen as a step in the direction of greater rationality; a step further in the direction of Aristotle's ideal of "a **government of laws**; not of men."

Bureaucratic impersonality has three major advantages. First, it increases organizational effectiveness by enabling administrators to do things that are otherwise difficult for people to do. In the course of their normal functioning, organizations may create considerable hardships for individuals. This is especially true of public organizations, which are often engaged in punishment, taxation, and the withholding of benefits such as food stamps, unemployment compensation, or welfare funds.

---

nepotism Any practice by which officeholders award positions to members of their immediate family. It is derived from the Latin *nepos*, meaning nephew or grandson. The rulers of the medieval church were often thought to give special preference to their nephews in distributing churchly offices, at that time, "nephew" being a euphemism for an illegitimate son.

government of laws A governing system in which the highest authority is a body of law that applies equally to all (as opposed to the rule of men, in which the personal whim of those in power can decide any issue). The idea of the desirability of a "government of laws, and not of men" can be traced back to Aristotle. The earliest American reference is in the 1779 Massachusetts Constitution. John Marshall also used this succinct legal description in *Marbury v. Madison* (1803): "The government of the United States has been emphatically termed a government of laws, and not of men. It will certainly cease to deserve this high appellation, if the laws furnish no remedy for the violation of a vested legal right."

Impersonality creates a desirable moral insensitivity. For example, it is much easier—emotionally speaking—for military planners on a general staff to select targets for bombardment than it is for a rifleman to shoot an enemy soldier who is a few yards ahead of him and whose face is clearly visible. Similarly, it is far easier for welfare agency budget analysts to cut school lunch funding for poor students than for a food service worker at a school cafeteria to see children go hungry when they cannot pay for lunch.

A second advantage of impersonality flows from the fact that as Blau and Meyer observed in *Bureaucracy in Modern Society*, "efficiency also suffers when emotions or personal considerations influence administrative decisions." If, for example, recruitment and promotions within an organization are based on personal preference, or ascriptive criteria (such as race or class), rather than competence, that organization's administrative processes will over time become less efficient.

Finally, impersonality tends to produce relatively evenhanded rule application. Thus procedural, if not necessarily actual, justice is ensured. "Go by the book" behavior requires equal treatment of those in the same categories, regardless of their social status. While this attitude may cause hardship for some, there has long been great philosophic support for it. For example, eighteenth-century philosopher Jean Jacques Rousseau denied that it was an abridgment of anyone's freedom to do the **general will**. Rousseau defined freedom in this context as simply being treated the same as everyone else. He would have loudly applauded modern bureaucracy's institutionalized lack of respect for a person's station in life.

Although impersonality may further procedural justice, it may at the same time fail to provide substantive or actual justice. The decisions bureaucrats reach may fail to fit the individual cases in terms of providing a just resolution. Many people fail to accept that their case is no different from those of others. They resent being treated on the basis of categories to which they do not feel they rightly belong. This tendency of bureaucracy has often aroused considerable hostility—sometimes even violence—on the part of clients. But the nature of impersonal organization is such that bureaucrats must apply established rules and procedures, even when they realize that these will not provide a reasonable or just resolution of a specific problem. Consequently, it has frequently been argued that a characteristic pathology of bureaucracy is an inversion of ends and means whereby the rules become more important than the objectives underlying their creation.

While impersonality is acknowledged as a central feature of bureaucratic behavior, there is disagreement over its desirability. Given that it has both advantages and dysfunctions, it would appear that the most sensible approach is to try to maximize the former while minimizing the latter. At the very least, this requires that students and practitioners of public administration avoid sweeping generalizations about bureaucratic behavior. The focus of concern ought to be the operations of individual bureaucratic units. By the same token it is imperative that the serious student recognize that some popular analyses of bureaucratic behavior—for example,

---

general will Jean Jacques Rousseau's ideal from *The Social Contract* (1761) that there is a collective will or consensus among the people, which is the ultimate locus of all political power.

Parkinson's Law that "work expands so as to fill the time available for its completion" and the **Peter Principle** that "in a hierarchy every employee tends to rise to his level of incompetence" are generally more amusing than descriptive of reality.

Bureaucrat Bashing

Bashing is extreme and public criticism (often unwarranted and irrational) of a person, policy, or nation. Domestically, bashing has often followed the word "bureaucrat." During the 1980s, the constant complaints and jokes about the competence of government employees—led by President Ronald "Government Is the Problem" Reagan—helped to create an acceptance of bureaucrat-bashing. Following his 1964 campaign for governor of California, Reagan was constantly complaining that "government is like a big baby—an alimentary canal with a big appetite at one end and no sense of responsibility at the other."

The term *bureaucrat bashing* has been used so frequently in so many contexts that it has taken on two meanings that are the opposite of each other. Those on the ideological right who tend to oppose big government use it to refer to justified criticism of "lazy and incompetent" government employees. At the same time, those on the ideological left, who tend to be more supportive of big government, use it to refer to the political right's "unnecessary and inappropriate" condemnation of public employees. But the meaning goes beyond rhetoric. The term now also refers to widespread support for specific policies that adversely impact or demean public employees. For example, monitoring phone calls to prevent personal use, reducing office sizes, and curtailing free parking privileges all reduce the quality of bureaucratic life on the job. And being asked to take a urine test to detect drug use or to sign an antileak (of information) pledge may be personally demeaning.

The problem with bureaucracy from the point of view of the cultural conservatives is that the values they most cherish seem to be under attack by bureaucratic institutions. They see a **red** flag in both the literal (meaning danger) and political sense when a government agency such as the National Endowment for the Arts subsidizes works of art they consider to be obscene; or when a government welfare agency takes the social stigma out of illegitimacy by making no distinction between widowed (or divorced) women with dependent children in financial need and never-married mothers. The bureaucratic grouping of them together as simply "single mothers" is morally offensive to many cultural conservatives who view it as a policy

---

Parkinson's Law The title of a 1957 bestseller by C. Northcote Parkinson (1909–1993), an otherwise serious British naval and economic historian. Parkinson also "discovered" that any public administrative department will invariably increase its staff an average of 5.75 percent per year. In anticipation of suggestions that he advise what might be done about this problem, he asserted that "it is not the business of the botanist to eradicate the weeds. Enough for him if he can tell us just how fast they grow."

Peter Principle The 1969 bestseller of the same name by Laurence J. Peter (1919–1990), then an obscure professor of education, offered the corollary that "in time, every post tends to be occupied by an employee who is incompetent to carry out its duties."

red A Communist; the red flag is the international symbol of communism. This is why someone thought to be leaning toward communism might be called *pink* or a *pinko*.

Ronald Reagan cheerfully bashing the bureaucracy at the National Press Club in 1966. Three of his favorite bashes were: (1) Government is like a big baby—an alimentary canal with a big appetite at one end and no sense of responsibility at the other; (2) Government does not solve problems; it subsidizes them; and (3) The nine most terrifying words in the English language are, "I'm from the government and I'm here to help." Ironically, the most expensive federal building ever constructed is now named after this critic of the bureaucracy. The huge Ronald Reagan Building and International Trade Center cost $818 million. Only the Pentagon houses more federal workers. According to Gloria Borger, the behemoth is "an embarrassment to Republicans who believe that it represents everything Reagan fought against—big-spending government, inefficient bureaucracy, waste, fraud, and abuse. Reagan himself authorized the building, which makes it awkward for his flock to openly abandon it. And guess who will work there? Employees of the Environmental Protection Agency, one of Reagan's favorite targets" (*U.S. News*, December 15, 1997) •

that only encourages a continual rise in the number of children born outside of marriage (30 percent of all U.S. births in 1995). Thus the bureaucracy with its subsidizing of single motherhood is castigated by conservatives as seeking to destroy the traditional family, the indispensable weaver of the social fabric.

There is really nothing new in American politics about attacking the bureaucracy. Indeed the middle of the Declaration of Independence of 1776 contains a major assault on the bureaucracy of King George's colonial government. But what is new is that the people running the bureaucracies, not just their political opposition, are also on the attack. Ronald Reagan won election in 1980 by running against the federal bureaucracy. After four years of being responsible for it, he successfully ran against it again in 1984. Bill Clinton pledged in his successful 1992 presidential campaign to reinvent federal bureaucracy. His reinventing cost 200,000 federal bureaucrats their

Box 6.3

Bureaucratic Impersonality in Action

Historians have often written of the Nazi Germany bureaucrats who murdered millions of innocent victims in gas chambers. However, you probably haven't heard of the few American bureaucrats who nearly gassed to death hundreds of equally innocent people in Philadelphia on the night of July 4, 1977. It happened in Independence Mall, the site where the Declaration of Independence was signed in 1776. Under this mall, a three-level, 650-car garage was built to accommodate all the visitors to the historic sites. Normally people come and go at odd times and the cashiers at the underground garage exits are not overburdened.

On this Independence Day, there was a big celebration, as might be expected. After it was over, hundreds of motorists returned to their cars in the underground garage, started their engines, and headed for the garage exits. But, because of stalled and illegally parked cars, there were not sufficient exit lanes open. The ventilation system of any underground garage cannot cope with the exhaust fumes of hundreds of automobile engines running at once. But the cashiers' duty was clear—collect payment from every car before it leaves. Because this was a slow process, the fumes built up. Some people began to get sick. But the cashiers, in best bureaucratic fashion, kept methodically collecting their tolls. The backup was made worse by the refusal of the cashiers to allow vehicles to leave the garage until their drivers had stopped to pay the parking fee—even though many people were obviously passing out from the exhaust fumes.

For only a few dollars, you could exit this impromptu municipal gas chamber. The problem was that you had to still be alive when it came your turn to pay. These minimum-wage cashiers were about to inadvertently kill hundreds of innocent civilians because they were not about to disobey orders and ignore policies. They felt that they had no choices. A lot of lives may have been at stake, but so were their jobs! Tragedy was only averted when firefighters wearing gas masks ordered the motorists to turn off their engines and walk out—if they could. Over 60 people were taken to area hospitals. No one died. But it was close.

Any bureaucracy has within itself the seeds of "bureaupathologies"—sicknesses that make it morally incompetent or inefficient. Gas chambers in Germany or Philadelphia aside, who has not seen plans frustrated because of silly organizational rules? But no organization has a Vice President for Silly Rules whose job it is to frustrate the plans of clients or others in the organization. Bureaucracies, to be efficient, must deal in wholesale policies—the same rules for everyone. But that is precisely the problem because these same rules often seem silly and become inefficient when applied to a specific retail or individual situation.

jobs by 1996. The bureaucracy is an easy political target to bash because, being largely politically neutral, it does not bash back.

The Case for Bureaucracy

Despite widespread berating of "the bureaucracy" and a constant stream of jokes about the efficiency of government employees, Americans often like their bureaucrats and think highly of the quality of the services they recieve. Charles T. Goodsell, a professor of public administration at Virginia Polytechnic Institute and State University, got so enraged about the popular "vision of a failed bureaucracy" that he wrote a book, *The Case for Bureaucracy*, exploring what he called "the great falsehood about American government." After reviewing a wealth of research reports, he found "satisfactory citizen treatment as the *norm* rather than the *exception*."

Moreover, Goodsell argued, "the commonly accepted view of political conservatives that government never performs as well as business is also shown to be a patent falsehood." In addition, "a comparison of American bureaucracy to that of other countries reveals that we experience one of the best levels of service in the world, light years ahead of that endured by most national populations." Goodsell's book is a perennial rebuttal to all those misguided or malicious bureaucrat bashers.

Motivation

Theatrical lore has it that as a famous actor struggled to find just the right characterization for a scene, he turned to his director and asked: "What's my motivation?" The director sarcastically replied: "To keep your job!" And so it is with most work done off the stage as well. "Keeping the job" has been the primary goal of industrial workers ever since they abandoned their farms to find work in the factories of the city. The perennial problem for managers is to motivate the workers to do more than is minimally necessary to keep that job.

While there always has been consensus about the need for motivated employees, the same cannot be said for beliefs about how to induce higher levels of motivation—and concomitant productivity. Not only have prevailing views (or theories) of motivation changed radically over time, but incompatible theories usually have competed with each other at the same points in time. Some theories assume that employees act rationally: managers simply need to manipulate rewards and punishments logically, fairly, and consistently. Other theories start from the position that managerial assumptions about employees—which undergird such systems of rewards and punishments—actually stifle employee motivation. This section summarizes some of the more important theories.

The Hawthorne Experiments

It was during the late 1920s and early 1930s that the Hawthorne experiments were undertaken at the Hawthorne Works of the Western Electric Company near Chicago. This study consisting of the most famous management experiments ever reported, was conducted by Elton Mayo and his associates from the Harvard Business School. The decade-long series of experiments started out as traditional scientific

Box 6.4

How Bureaucracy Is "Set Up"

A major cause for chronic underestimation of American bureaucratic performance is our tendency to hold unrealistic expectations for it. Belonging to a culture accustomed to optimism and habituated to progress, we Americans tend to assume that if bureaucracies do not succeed in changing the world in the ways we wish, they have somehow failed. But in reality we often "set up" bureaucracy in such a way as to make complete success impossible. We give administrative organizations inconsistent or contradictory goals, creating disappointments no matter what happens. We make effective implementation of laws unduly difficult in many policy areas by holding several different organizations responsible for the job. . . . Bureaucracy is further handicapped by the tendency of Americans to expect it to solve any and all problems, no matter how solvable or unsolvable they may be, even when the bureaucrats have no control whatever over the causes of the problems.

SOURCE: Charles T. Goodsell, *The Case for Bureaucracy*, 3rd ed. (Chatham, NJ: Chatham House, 1994).

management examinations of the relationship between work environment and productivity. But the experimenters, because they were initially unable to explain the results of their findings, literally stumbled upon a finding that today seems so obvious—that factories and other work situations are first of all social situations. The workers, as **Mary Parker Follett** had suggested a decade earlier, were more responsive to peer pressure than to management controls. The Hawthorne studies are generally considered to be the genesis of the human relations school of management thought, providing the first major empirical challenge to the scientific management notion that the worker was primarily an economic animal who would work solely for money.

It is important to note that the Mayo team began its work trying to fit into the mold of classical organization theory thinking. The team phrased its questions in the language and concepts industry was accustomed to using in order to see and explain certain problems, among them productivity in relationship to such factors as the amount of light, the rate of flow of materials, and alternative wage payment plans. The Mayo team succeeded in making significant breakthroughs in understanding only after it redefined the Hawthorne problems as social psychological problems—problems conceptualized in such terms as interpersonal relations in groups, group norms, control over one's own environment, and personal recognition. It was only

---

Mary Parker Follett (1868–1933) An early social psychologist who anticipated, in the 1920s, many of the conclusions of the Hawthorne experiments of the 1930s and of the post-World War II behavioral movement.

after the Mayo team achieved this breakthrough that it became the "grandfather"— the direct precursor—of the field of organizational behavior and human resource theory. The Hawthorne experiments were the emotional and intellectual wellspring of modern theories of motivation. They showed that complex, interactional variables make the difference in motivating people—things like attention paid to workers as individuals, workers' control over their own work, differences between individuals' needs, management's willingness to listen, group norms, and direct feedback.

A particularly notable discovery that came out of the Hawthorne experiments was the Hawthorne effect—the discovery that production increases were due to the known presence of benign observers. The researchers' concern for and attention to the workers led the workers, who naturally wanted to be reciprocally nice, to increase production. This "effect" caused great confusion at first because the changing physical conditions (lighting, rest breaks, etc.) seemed to make no difference. Output just kept going up. Once they realized that the workers' perception of participation was the true "variable," the effects of the "effect" were understood.

The Needs Hierarchy

Abraham H. Maslow, a psychologist, took the basic Hawthorne finding that workers are as much social as economic creatures a step further when he first proposed his famous "needs hierarchy" in his 1943 *Psychological Review* article, "A Theory of Human Motivation." Maslow asserted that humans had five sets of goals or basic needs arranged in a hierarchy of prepotency: (1) physiological needs (food, water, shelter, etc.), (2) safety needs, (3) love or affiliation needs, (4) esteem needs, and (5) self-actualization needs—when an individual theoretically reaches self-fulfillment and becomes all that he or she is capable of becoming. Once the lower needs are satisfied, they cease to be motivators of behavior. Conversely, higher needs cannot motivate until lower needs are satisfied. Simply put—a person will risk being eaten by a hungry lion if that risk is the only way to get food and water. Only after the body is sustained can thoughts turn to safety and the other higher needs.

According to Maslow, "It is quite true that man lives by bread alone—when there is no bread. But what happens to man's desires when there is plenty of bread and when his belly is chronically filled? At once other (and higher) needs emerge and these, rather than physiological hungers, dominate the organism." When these in turn are satisfied, new even higher needs will emerge. Maslow's psychological analysis of motivation proved to be the foundation for much subsequent research. While other researchers, such as Herzberg, McGregor, and Bennis (all discussed on the following pages), would take Maslow's concepts and develop them into more comprehensive theories of motivation and organizational behavior, Maslow's work remains the point of departure.

The Motivation-Hygiene Theory

One of the first extensive empirical demonstrations of the primacy of internal worker motivation was the motivation-hygiene theory put forth by Frederick Herzberg, Bernard Mausner, and Barbara Snyderman, in a landmark 1959 study

Figure 6.4   Maslow's Needs Hierarchy

entitled *The Motivation to Work*. Five factors were isolated as determiners of job satisfaction: (1) achievement, (2) recognition, (3) work itself, (4) responsibility, and (5) advancement. Five factors associated with job dissatisfaction were similarly realized: (1) company policy and administration, (2) supervision, (3) salary, (4) interpersonal relations, and (5) working conditions. The satisfying factors were all related to job content, the dissatisfying factors to the environmental context of the job. The factors that were associated with job satisfaction were quite separate from those factors associated with job dissatisfaction. Herzberg later made this observation in *Personnel Administration*:

> Since separate factors need to be considered depending on whether job satisfaction or job dissatisfaction was involved, it followed that these two feelings were not the obverse of each other. The opposite of job satisfaction would not be job dissatisfaction, but rather NO job satisfaction; and similarly the opposite of job dissatisfaction is NO job dissatisfaction—not job satisfaction.

Because the environmental context of jobs, such as working conditions, interpersonal relations, and salary, served primarily as preventatives, they were termed hygiene factors, as an analogy to the medical use of hygiene meaning preventative and environmental. The job-content factors such as achievement, advancement, and responsibility were termed motivators because these are the things that motivate people to superior performance. Herzberg wrote this in *Work and the Nature of Man*:

> The principal result of the analysis of this data was to suggest that the hygiene or maintenance events led to job dissatisfaction because of a need to avoid unpleasantness; the motivator events led to job satisfaction because of a need for growth or self-actualization. At the psychological level, the two dimensions of job attitudes reflected a two-dimensional need structure: one need system for the avoidance of unpleasantness and a parallel need system for personal growth.

Since its original presentation, a considerable number of empirical investigations by a wide variety of researchers has tended to confirm the motivation-hygiene theory. Its chief fault seems to be its rejection of the view that pay is a unique incentive capable, in differing circumstances, of being a hygiene factor as well as a motivator. But the theory's main holding—that worker motivation is essentially internal—remains largely unchallenged.

Toward a Democratic Environment

According to Warren Bennis, a preeminent sage of organizational futures, democracy in an organization context "is inevitable." Its inevitability has been determined by its empirically proven effectiveness when compared to the more traditional, autocratic methods of organizational management. While the evidence is not complete, the whole thrust of behavioral research concerning employee motivation and productivity supports the notion of extending democracy to the lowest levels of the organizational hierarchy. That extension includes sharing power and policy decisions.

Three basic stratagems have evolved to meet the demands for a more democratic environment in the workplace. First—and historically the most common in the public as well as the private sector—top management tries to meet an expressed need for greater participatory management with a symbolic sop rather than with a meaningful program. When an employee "crisis" erupts because of the general **alienation** of the workforce or because of some specific reason such as perceived racism or the dehumanizing nature of the work, management seeks to mollify the situation. If it is unable to make any substantial changes, it can often defuse a present crisis by providing a limited upward mobility program or employee representation on the decisional councils of the organization. However, this tactic can only mitigate or alleviate the current problem; there is no real change. There is only an increase in what Frederick Herzberg has called the "hygiene" factors of work—salary, working conditions, interpersonal relations, etc. These in turn lead to an insatiable appetite for still more "hygiene." Like heroin, it soon takes more and more to produce less and less effect. In such a context, a manager is called upon to play the morally corrupt role of a narcotics pusher, rather than the more beneficial role of an organizational physician.

Yet, this is not all dysfunctional. It is a gross misunderstanding to view symbolic rewards as mere deception. In redressing a real or imagined grievance with a symbolic gesture, management, perhaps unwittingly, is taking its first step toward actually resolving the grievance. Responding to an employee demand with a symbolic reward simultaneously acknowledges the appropriateness of the demand and establishes its legitimacy. Once the legitimacy of a demand is established, its eventual achievement is practically preordained, though it may be many years in coming.

To attempt to deal with the question of employee participation in decision making on the plane of symbolic action, however, is not to deal with the question at all. It is merely a delaying tactic, and delay becomes less and less of an option as public sector unions take ever-increasing interest in participatory management. Therefore, the manager sincerely interested in increasing productivity and de-

---

alienation A term adopted by Marxism to describe the inevitable feeling of dissociation of industrial workers because of their lack of control over their work (thus making them ripe for revolution). The word has largely lost its Marxist meaning and now refers to any feelings of estrangement from one's work, family, government, society, and the like. In the context of politics and voting behavior, alienation refers to a voluntary dropping out of the political process, to nonvoting, to feelings of contempt or indifference toward government.

creasing **turnover** will adopt one of the remaining two stratagems: participation implemented by management from above or participation implemented in cooperation with an employee organization such as a union.

Theory X and Theory Y

Psychologists have long been noted for their studies of human and animal motivation. Why else have so many rats gotten so lost in so many mazes? But the operative discipline in organizational motivation is philosophy. The sincerity and rigor of the motivation of employees toward their duties is a direct reflection of management's philosophy toward them. That an operative philosophy is neither written down nor formally stated is irrelevant to its existence. Many organizations have commendable formal managerial philosophies. Reams upon reams of paper have been dedicated to espousing an official view of what an idyllic place the jurisdiction is in which to work. The only problem with these fine-sounding philosophies is that they are seldom operational, tending to exist only on paper. Subordinates soon perceive the reality of the situation.

All managerial philosophies are premised upon a set of assumptions about human behavior. Douglas McGregor, through his 1960 book *The Human Side of Enterprise*, popularized the contending concepts of managerial philosophy with his now famous Theory X and Theory Y sets of assumptions. McGregor hypothesized that a manager's assumptions about human behavior predetermined his administrative style. Because of the dominance of traditional theory in managerial thought, many managers had long accepted and acted upon a set of assumptions that are at best true of only a minority of the population. McGregor labeled as Theory X the following assumptions:

1. The average human being has an inherent dislike of work.
2. Most people must be coerced or threatened with punishment to get them to put forth adequate effort.
3. People prefer to be directed and wish to avoid responsibility.

Theory X sounds very much like a traditional military organization which, indeed, is where it comes from. While McGregor's portrait of the modern industrial citizen can be criticized for implying greater pessimism concerning human nature on the part of managers than is perhaps warranted, Theory X is all the more valuable as a memorable theoretical construct because it serves as such a polar opposite of Theory Y, which assumes the following:

1. The expenditure of physical and mental effort in work is as natural as play or rest.
2. A person will exercise self-direction and self-control in the service of objectives to which he is committed.
3. Avoidance of responsibility, lack of ambition, and emphasis on security are generally consequences of experience, not inherent human characteristics.

---

turnover The rate at which employees leave an organization—usually expressed as a percentage of all workers who resign or are fired each year.

In this scene from *Ben-Hur*, the Roman officers discuss using a kind of Theory X management style to motivate the galley slaves. Later in this scene the Roman general played by Jack Hawkins (standing left) walks over to slave number 41, Charlton Heston, in the title role and offers this eternal bit of motivational advice: "There is hatred in your eyes number 41. That's good. Hatred keeps a man alive." Unfortunately, getting your subordinates to hate you is a much-used, if inadvertent and too often ineffectual, management technique •

4. The capacity to exercise a relatively high degree of imagination, ingenuity, and creativity in the solution of organizational problems is widely, not narrowly, distributed in the population.

Of course, these differing philosophic orientations are extremes for purposes of example. Most work situations would require a mix rather than a simplistic acceptance of either construct. Nevertheless, assumptions shape destiny; they tend to create self-fulfilling prophecies. Just as it has been shown in experiments with schoolchildren that a teacher's attitude toward any given child helps to determine that child's classroom performance, so it has been shown in similar studies that management's attitude toward workers has the same effect. Simply put, if management assumes that employees are "no damn good" and acts upon these assumptions, their employees are going to live down to management expectations.

Different philosophies are appropriate to differing organizational environments and work situations. The philosophy appropriate to a military combat unit would hardly be suitable for a research program in computer science. Unfortunately, the environment in which a public sector personnel program tends to operate frequently mitigates against the development of a coherent managerial philosophy. The most basic reason for this is external to the nature of the individuals comprising the organization. While private organizations typically exist in response to a specific goal, the objectives of public organizations are seldom as definite. It has frequently been shown that the professed objectives of a public organization are only vaguely related to its actual mission. For example, the goal of a correctional institution may be reform, but the organization's specific mission is more likely to be simply that of detention. The goal of a police department may be to enforce all of the laws of the community, but its specific mission is more likely to be the maintenance of public order. One goal of a public personnel unit may be to find the best qualified managers for its agency, but its specific mission in some cases may be limited to processing the papers of those candidates with prior **political clearance**. When the public policy process is so schizophrenic, it is little wonder that coherent managerial philosophies find it difficult or impossible to emerge.

How can organizational policies premised on one set of rhetorical conditions be implemented in a real world operating on contradictory premises? It is a gross understatement to assert that this aspect of public management tends to severely hinder the development of comprehensive managerial strategies and objectives. This is one of the reasons that management by objectives (see Chapter 8) has not been able to provide a comprehensive answer to the need to set direction in the public sector. Objectives in public administration tend to fall victim to expediencies. Many organizational objectives in government tend to be inherently unstable in reaction to the dynamics of the political process.

By the end of the 1960s, the basic relationship between people and the organizations they work in was being redefined from the old world of dependence to the new world of codependence. The whole focus of organization management began to shift from executive control to executive nurturing of the people, groups, and relationships in the organizational environment. The new goal of management was less leadership than the unleashing of the previously stifled energies and creativities of the organization. This trend was fine as far as it went. But a happy organization is not necessarily the most productive one.

The Future of Organizations

Be assured—organizations have a future. What that future will be is far more difficult to predict. But change is inevitable. Here are the major trends that will have impact on government organizations in the years ahead.

Postbureaucratic Organizations

In 1952 administrative historian Dwight Waldo prophesied a future society in which "bureaucracy in the Weberian sense would have been replaced by more democratic,

---

political clearance The process by which qualified applicants for both patronage and merit system appointments are hired only after there is an appropriate indication of partisan political sponsorship. While it is illegal to require political clearance for merit system appointments, it remains a common practice.

more flexible, though more complex, forms of large-scale organization." Waldo called such a society "postbureaucratic." However, it remained for Warren G. Bennis, in the 1960s, to make the term particularly his own with a series of articles and books predicting the "end of bureaucracy." In its place, Bennis wrote in *The Temporary Society*, "there will be adaptive, rapidly changing temporary systems. These will be task forces composed of groups of relative strangers with diverse professional backgrounds and skills organized around problems to be solved." The various task forces would "be arranged in an organic, rather than mechanical, model, meaning that they will evolve in response to a problem rather than to present, programmed expectations." Thus employees would "be evaluated not vertically according to rank and status, but flexibly according to competence. Organizational charts will consist of project groups rather than stratified functional groups."

Bennis wasn't a voice in the wilderness. Many other organization analysts of the time (such as Leonard Sayles, George Berkley, and Victor Thompson) were making similar noises. But it remained for **future shock** theorist Alvin Toffler, in his 1970 worldwide bestseller *Future Shock*, to give the popular name to the post bureaucratic lack of structure: "ad hocracy"—a contraction of **ad hoc** and bureaucracy—for "the fast-moving, information-rich, kinetic organization of the future, filled with transient cells and extremely mobile individuals."

Is the bureaucratic form of organization on an inevitable road to extinction? Is it being replaced by systems of temporary democratic networks or structures without hierarchical layers of authority, responsibility, and accountability? If so, the trend is not apparent yet. The announcement of bureaucracy's death seems, once again, to be premature—or at the very least, as in Mark Twain's case, "greatly exaggerated." Actually, bureaucracy appears to be holding its own quite well in practice—even if not in the mainstream literature of organization theory. Within the discipline of public administration, defenders (such as Kaufman, Krislov, and Goodsell) have emerged who justify the bureaucratic form of organization both for its efficiency as well as for its promotion of equity and representativeness.

Elliot Jaques has emerged as the foremost defender of the hierarchical-bureaucratic form of organization in the 1990s. Jaques contends that those who argue against hierarchy are "simply wrong, and all their proposals are based on an inadequate understanding of not only hierarchy but also human nature." Hierarchical layers add value to organizations by separating tasks into manageable series of steps: "What we need is not some new kind of organization. What we need is managerial hierarchy that understands its own nature and purpose." According to Jaques, hierarchy is *the* best alternative for large organizations: "We need to stop casting about fruitlessly for organizational Holy Grails and settle down to the hard work of putting our managerial hierarchies in order." Well said!

---

future shock Alvin Toffler's term, from his book *Future Shock*, for the "distress, both physical and psychological, that arises from an overload of the human organism's physical adaptive systems and its decision making processes. Put more simply, future shock is the human response to over-stimulation."

ad hoc A Latin term meaning temporarily, for this one time. It is sometimes used to criticize methods that substitute for standard procedures.

TABLE 6.1 Alternatives to the Bureaucratic Paradigm

The Bureaucratic Agency	The Customer-Driven Agency
Focuses on own needs	Focuses on customer needs
Defined by the resources it controls	Defined by results it achieves for customers
Controls costs	Creates value
Sticks to routine	Responds to changing customer demands
Fights for turf	Competes for business
Follows standard procedures	Builds choice into operating systems
Separates thinking from doing	Empowers all front-line employees

SOURCE: Adapted from Michael Barzelay, *Breaking Through Bureaucracy* (Berkeley: University of California Press, 1992).

The enduring strength of the hierarchical structure is elegantly illustrated by Leon E. Panetta, a U.S. representative from California who became President Clinton's first director of the Office of Management and Budget. After the president realized that there was much validity in the widespread criticism about how the White House was managed, he promoted Panetta to chief of staff in 1994. Panetta thereupon set about creating the most ancient of organizational structures for the White House. According to *New York Times* reporter Alison Mitchell: "Panetta set about creating a hierarchy, with himself and his two deputies . . . at the top. He instituted a 7:30 A.M. meeting for a handful of senior staff members—the restrictiveness of the meeting sending a message about the chain of command." There's nothing like a chain of command for creating organizational order out of chaos—even at the White House.

So if the traditional hierarchy (which is all that most people think of when they hear the word bureaucracy) continues to hold its own, what will happen to all these highly structured government agencies aching for reinvigoration? After the polemical bashing of bureaucracies by angry politicos and "end of bureaucracy" futurists subsides, what will remain is a kernel of reform that calls for traditional bureaucracies to be transformed into customer-driven service organizations. In *Breaking Through Bureaucracy*, Michael Barzelay outlines the new style government organization that offers "responsive, user-friendly, dynamic, and competitive providers of valuable services" as the alternative to traditional Weberian bureaucracy. In essence, modern government bureaucracies are fighting a two-front war. They are being denounced from without at the same time they are being reformed from within.

Postmodernism

Nothing is changing bureaucracies—both public and private—faster than postmodernism, an "ism" that embraces constant change and accepts as a new fact of life that large organizations today are living on the edge, on the boundary between order and chaos. In this context, however, "chaos" is not synonymous with "anarchy." Instead, it refers to a pervasive condition of unpredictability and complexity. The chaos and uncertainty of this approaching postmodern era has been accompanied by—and accelerated by—rapidly advancing information technology, particularly information networks. In the space of only a few years, information technology has evolved from mainframes to personal computers, local area networks, remote bulletin boards, information networks, and the Internet—the "information superhighway."

We have been experiencing technological advancement, however, almost since time began. Is something different happening now? The answer is a resounding yes. Information—and information technology—can extend human mental capability. We are not certain, though, what effects information technology will have on interpersonal relations, working teams, and thus organizations as we know them. Emerging forms of communication technology already are spanning time and space. The differences between information technology in premodern, modern, and postmodern organizations can be illustrated by examining the changing nature of the passport. This ubiquitous document is of ancient origins. It is essentially an instruction from the ruler (the state) to allow the bearer to "pass" through the "port"— the gateway to a city whether on a waterway or a highway. In the modern period it became a small printed book with pages for visa stamps and personal information about the bearer (address, next of kin, etc.). A suspicious-looking traveler might have his or her passport closely inspected to see if the seals upon it were truly official or forgeries. The traveler's name might be checked against a list of undesirables. But today's postmodern passports may contain encrypted information on an attached plastic strip allowing immigration officials access to much of the bearer's life and medical history. Or the document can be fed into a mainframe computer at headquarters that reveals even more about the bearer. What do officials do with all this information? What implications are here for the abuse of civil liberties? The postmodern passport illustrates both the potentialities as well as the dangers of a total information age.

Information networks that tap into (and simultaneously update) real-time databases are providing empowered, self-managing work teams with the information they need to schedule and coordinate their own tasks as well as discipline their own members. Layer upon layer of supervisors and middle-managers that are no longer needed are being eliminated. The traditional hierarchy (remember Moses in Chapter 5) was created in the first place so that information could be efficiently communicated up and down the line (often, the line of battle). If all of the organization members now (because they are each online in the computer sense) instantly have the same information, the traditional communicators—the hoards of middle managers—are, at the very least, less necessary if not totally superfluous.

Information networks in the postmodern era are raising vexing questions that tax existing theories of organization. Those postmodernists who consider themselves deconstructionists (because they intellectually take things apart to analyze their parts) like to think of organizations not as entities in their own right but just simply as a web of relationships. To them an organization can have no goals; it is simply the vehicle by which individuals pursue their personal goals.

Technology and postmodernism also raise questions about the experience of people who work in—or around—organizations. Will Warren Bennis's prediction finally come true? Will bureaucratic organizations as we know them disappear because they are unable to adapt to rapidly changing environments? Will working at home and "telecommuting" become the norm for some public service occupations? If so, how will government employees be held accountable for their time? Can trusting relations be established through interpersonal communications along the information highway in cyberspace?

Old familiar machine analogies of organization simply do not apply in the postmodern era. The texture of the relationships between individuals, their work, and their organization is changed irreversibly by information technology. Shoshana Zuboff, in her book *In the Age of the Smart Machine*, describes this irreversible change in the texture of work relationships when she visited a large bank's offices; "I witnessed a sight that would eventually become so familiar as to defy notice—an entire floor of people seated at their partitioned workstations, staring into the screens of desktop terminals. . . . Many [of these] people voiced distress, describing their work as 'floating in space' or 'lost behind the screen.' They complained that they were no longer able to see or touch their work." Zuboff "saw that a world of sensibilities and expectations was being irretrievably displaced by a new world."

The Problem of Technocracy

Organizations today must wrestle with complex dilemmas about participating in this "new world" where the workers who once interacted face to face with other people now "float in space" and stare at computer screens instead of faces. In 1965 Don K. Price formulated a new hypothesis on the impact of decisional authority. In his book, *The Scientific Estate*, he posited that decisional authority inexorably flowed from executive to technical offices. Consequently, a major distinction had to be made between the legal authority to make a policy decision and the technical ability to make the same decisions. Price's work predated John Kenneth Galbraith's *The New Industrial State* (1967), in which Galbraith made a similar claim for the decisional processes of the large corporations. This theme is destined to be a continuing one in the study of public administration, involving the dilemmas of control of power, information, and technical expertise—what many writers have called the problem of technocracy.

Zuboff, in newly expanding upon this old problem of technocracy, coined the term "informate" to highlight a duality that is central to the issues and dilemmas of this postmodern world. Technology can be used to automate operations using the same logic that was in place before the automating was initiated. This use of technology, to "automate," enables a task to be performed with more control and predictability than when it was performed by humans. Automation, then, is a logical, evolutionary extension of the work begun by Frederick Taylor and the scientific management movement early in the twentieth century.

Although "automating" represented an information technology revolution in the 1960s, it does not now. In contrast, "informating" is concerned with "radical changes as it alters the intrinsic character of work" and requires the adoption of new concepts of authority. Zuboff contends that the coming of the "information age" will require us to critically revisit our notions of systems, power, authority, accountability, and the role of people in organizations. An organization that merely automates is locked into the predictability and control system logic of the modern era. An organization that informates has the potential to adapt to the changes and uncertainties of the postmodern era.

The Core Themes of Postmodernism

Organization theorist William Bergquist has analyzed postmodernism extensively: "In many ways, postmodernism is a fad—and is at the same time about fads. Even though postmodernism is characterized by superficial, facile, and often internally contradictory analyses, it must not be dismissed, for these analyses offer insightful and valuable (even essential) perspectives on and criticisms of an emerging era." Bergquist identifies the four core themes of postmodernism:

1. *Objectivism versus constructivism*: "Objectivism"—which predominated in the modern era—is "rational." It assumes that there is an objective reality that can be discovered. "Constructivism," which is a postmodern phenomenon, "believe[s] that we construct our own social realities. . . . There are no universal truths or principles, nor are there any global models of justice or order. . . . Ways of knowing may themselves change over time and in differing situations."

2. *Language as reality*: Language, and the use of verbal symbols and signs, is more than a means for communicating information about reality. It is (at least a part of) reality. "The language being used to describe . . . elusive and changing reality is itself a major source of this social construction."

3. *Globalization and segmentalism*: "According to the postmodernists, our world is becoming progressively more global, while at the same time becoming progressively more segmented and differentiated." At the same time that information technology is allowing us to know more about our commonalties with people around the world, we seem to have lost our sense of community and organization. Thus perhaps we live in an era of "contradiction between globalism and localism in many aspects of our daily lives."

4. *Fragmented and inconsistent images*: "Postmodernists are enthralled with the superficial and the trendy." Virtual reality machines "convey the sense of depth, yet like holographic devices, they actually replicate only the surface, never the depth of the experience. We are tricked into believing that we have experienced depth or virtual reality when in fact we have seen only the surface."

These four themes represent the central realities of a fragmented and inconsistent postmodern world. "The modern manager sees systems as the ultimate tool for making sense out of chaos." In contrast, "the postmodern manager sees chaos as what is to be managed and systems, though very useful, as merely one aspect of the chaotic environment. To the postmodern manager chaos is not bad. It is what is."

The postmodern world can be extremely frightening to people of traditional bureaucratic sensibilities. There is something comforting about knowing, quite literally, where you stand in your organizations and what your duties are. The premodern, modern, and postmodern organizational worlds will continue to live side by side for the foreseeable future—sometimes even in the same overall organization. The post office, for example, has premodern door-to-door mail delivery, it has modern automated mail-sorting operations, and somewhere in the depths of its research and development operations it has postmodern units trying to discover a role for the Postal Service on the Internet. In the premodern world land was the dominant form of capital. In modern times money and buildings became more important. In the postmodern world information is the new capital. This is why Bill Gates of Microsoft, the world's leading computer software company, is now the richest person in America.

A Feminist Perspective

Viewing organizational behavior from a feminist perspective is important for two reasons. First, there is an ever-increasing body of literature on the differing ways that the genders operate in organizations. Any managers, whether male or female or from the private or public sector, who are ignorant of this perspective are figuratively walking into an unmarked minefield. No matter how careful they seek to be, they will eventually step on something that will do them great damage. Reinforcing the importance of this first reason is the simple fact that women in the United States are an ever-increasing majority of public sector workers. Women constituted 24 percent of all public officials and administrators in 1970. By 1990 they constituted 59 percent. According to U.S. Department of Education data published in the *Chronicle of Higher Education* (June 9, 1995), women are earning bachelor's degrees in public administration and related service areas at more than three times the rate of men, master's degrees at twice the rate of men, and doctorates at about even the rate of men. However, if you would take out the numbers of foreign students in these degree fields, who are almost all men, then the percentage of female predominance in America is even greater. So we may conclude that a feminist perspective on public administration is important because this profession is being feminized in the most literal possible sense.

Feminist organizational analysts such as Joan Acker have argued that longstanding male control of organizations has been accompanied and maintained by male perspectives of organization theory. Thus it has been mainly through male lenses that we see and analyze organizations. At least four sets of gendered processes perpetuate this male reality of organizations:

1. Gender divisions that produce gender patterning of jobs
2. Creation of masculine organizational symbols and images
3. Interactions characterized by dominance and subordination
4. "The internal mental work of individuals as they consciously construct their understandings of the organization's gendered structure of work and opportunity and the demands for gender-appropriate behaviors and attitudes"

Anti- and pro-Equal Rights Amendment (ERA) demonstrators at the Illinois State Capital in 1980. This proposed amendment to the U.S. Constitution was passed by Congress in 1972. It said in part: "Equality of rights under the law shall not be denied or abridged by the United States or any state on account of sex." At first, the ERA seemed headed for quick passage. By the end of 1972, over 22 states had ratified it. But when it became apparent that ERA would eventually become law, a conservative opposition organized. It argued that the ERA would not only subject women to a potential military draft, but also to combat duty, and that women would lose the legal advantages they hold under many state domestic relations law and labor codes. As the ERA became more controversial, fewer states moved to ratify it. On March 27, 1982, the final deadline, three states were still needed for ratification, and the ERA was dead. The women's movement thought that the ERA was essential for legal equity at work. But so many barriers have been broken down by the sex discrimination prohibition of the Civil Rights Act of 1964 as amended, that in retrospect, the ERA seems far less essential than it did at first ●

Ordinary activities in organizations are not gender-neutral. They perpetuate the "gendered substructure within the organization itself and within the wider society"—as well as in organization theory. So what do we do about this? One option is nothing. Just wait—and think about lung cancer. It used to be that lung cancer was pretty much a male problem. Then women started smoking as much as men. Since lung cancer takes a few decades to develop, it takes awhile to catch up. But "progress" is slowly being made. Complete equality, thanks to continued cigarette advertising and government subsidies of tobacco farmers, is approaching ever nearer.

What happened with women and lung cancer is also happening today in organizations. As women increasingly climb the organizational ladders, they leave their mark—they gradually change the culture. Substantial research has already shown that women tend to have different management styles from men. For example, Judy B. Rosener has shown women to be more cooperative and to share leadership; they are less apt to use the traditional authoritarian "command and control" militaristic style so favored by men. The greatest beneficiaries of the last three decades of affirmative action hiring policies have been women. The seed has been planted. Organizations, as they are increasingly impacted by feminine management styles, will gradually change their operating styles to reflect ever-increasing female influences. The alternative hypothesis is that in-

Box 6.5

The Assertions of Feminist Theory

Feminist theory asserts that women's influence in the workforce will result in significant changes in the workplace:

- Organizational hierarchies will become less rigid.
- Organizational climates will become more cooperative, less competitive, and less aggressive.
- Values of trust, openness, and acceptance will replace the quest for individual power.

SOURCE: Mary E. Guy, "The Feminization of Public Administration," in *Public Management in an Interconnected World*, eds. Mary Timney Bailey and Richard T. Mayer (New York: Greenwood Press, 1992).

stead of making their organizations more hospitable to feminine management culture, the women managers—subject to the same stimuli for increased production as men have traditionally been—will become more like the men, will adapt more masculine attitudes because that is the way to thrive in the competitive environment of organizational life.

According to Camilla Stivers, "as long as we go on viewing the enterprise of administration as genderless, women will continue to face their present **Hobson's choice**, which is either to adopt a masculine administrative identity or accept marginalization in the bureaucratic hierarchy." So the leaders of today's organizations have three options: (1) do nothing and wait for the problem to resolve itself over time, (2) intervene to consciously create organizations more hospitable to women, or (3) hope that managerial women will be content to become more like men. These options are not mutually exclusive. Time inexorably moves on. Considerable progress is constantly being made. In the end the best hope is that women will not necessarily become the organizational infighters that men traditionally have been, but that a mutual accommodation will evolve.

Summary

Organizational behavior examines individuals, groups, and the relationships among them within their organizational environments. Typically, people are clustered in work groups; when a group, such as a branch office, becomes institutionalized in an organization, it evolves shared beliefs, values, and assumptions—norms that become the essence of a cohesive group and of an organizational subculture. Formal groups are officially created by a larger organization. Informal groups are formed through spontaneously developed relationships.

Hobson's choice A dilemma; a difficult decision; a choice of only the lesser of two evils. No choice at all is the original meaning. Thomas Hobson (1544–1631) ran a stable in England. When someone came to rent a horse, Hobson made him take the next horse in line.

Organization development is planned organizational change necessitated by the fact that organizations exist in a dynamic environment, both internally and externally, to which they must respond or become ineffectual. This process is especially difficult to implement in the public sector because top management, which must first be committed to the process, is so fractured.

As a form of organization, bureaucracy has many advantages; nevertheless, the behavioral consequences of bureaucratic structure are often negative. Because structure stresses depersonalized relations and authority gained by virtue of position, individual ideas and opinions are often valued not according to their intrinsic merit but according to rank.

While there always has been consensus about the need for motivated employees, the same cannot be said for beliefs about how to induce higher levels of motivation. The Hawthorne experiments provided the first major empirical challenge to the scientific management notion that the worker was primarily an economic animal who worked solely for money. Abraham H. Maslow took these findings a step further with his "needs hierarchy." Based on this, Douglas McGregor developed his Theory X and Theory Y sets of managerial assumptions.

Postbureaucratic organizational theorists predict a future society in which traditional bureaucracy is replaced by more flexible forms of large-scale organization. Nevertheless, the hierarchical-bureaucratic form of organization is still highly defended because of its ability to add value to organizations by separating tasks into manageable series of steps.

Two new forces are rapidly changing the organizational world. Postmodernism, with its acceptance of unpredictability and complexity, is being accelerated by rapidly advancing information technology. And as women increasingly climb organizational ladders, they are changing organizational cultures, causing them to be more cooperative and less militaristic.

Key Concepts

bureaucrat bashing   Either justified criticism or inappropriate condemnation of public employees.

bureaucratic dysfunctions   The pathological elements of bureaucratic structures that often make them inefficient in operation; the pressures on workers to conform that cause them to adhere to rules as an end rather than a means.

bureaucratic impersonality   The dehumanizing consequences of formal organizational structures eliminating personal and emotional consideration from organizational life so that the individual bureaucrat functions only as a cog in an ever-moving machine.

group cohesion   The shared beliefs, values, and assumptions of a group that allow it to function as a team.

group dynamics   The subfield of organization behavior concerned about the nature of groups, how they develop, and how they interrelate with individuals and other groups.

Hawthorne experiments   The late 1920s and early 1930s management studies undertaken at the Hawthorne Works of the Western Electric Company near Chicago. Conducted by Elton Mayo and his associates from the Harvard Business School, they became the most famous management experiments ever reported.

motivation   An amalgam of all of the factors in one's working environment that foster (positively or negatively) productive efforts.

needs hierarchy   Five sets of goals or basic needs arranged in a hierarchy of prepotency: physiological needs (food, water, shelter, etc.), safety needs, love or affiliation needs, esteem needs, and the need for self-actualization.

organization development   An approach or strategy for increasing organizational effectiveness. As a process it has no value biases, but it is usually associated with the idea that effectiveness is found by integrating the individual's desire for growth with organizational goals.

postbureaucratic organization   Constantly changing temporary organizational systems; task forces composed of groups of relative strangers with diverse skills created in response to a special problem rather than to a continuing need.

postmodernism   The belief that constant change is a new fact of life for large organizations that are living on the edge, on the boundary, between order and chaos.

technocracy   A contraction of "technical" and "bureaucracy," which refers to the high-tech organizational environments of the postmodern world.

Theory X   The assumptions that the average human being has an inherent dislike of work, that most people must be threatened to get them to put forth adequate effort, and that people prefer to be directed and to avoid responsibility.

Theory Y   The assumptions that work is as natural as play, that workers can exercise self-direction and self-control, and that imagination, ingenuity, and creativity are widespread.

Bibliography

Acker, Joan. (1992). "Gendering Organizational Theory." In *Gendering Organizational Analysis*, eds. A. J. Mills and P. Tancred. Newbury Park, CA: Sage.

Argyris, Chris. (1964). "T-Groups for Organizational Effectiveness." *Harvard Business Review* (March-April).

———. (1957). *Personality and Organization*. New York: Harper and Row.

Asch, S. E. (1951). "Effects of group pressure upon the Modification and Distortion of Judgments." In H. S. Guetzkow (ed.), *Groups, Leadership, and Men*. Pittsburgh, PA: Carnegie Press.

Barnard, Chester I. (1938). *The Functions of the Executive*. Cambridge: Harvard University Press.

Barzelay, Michael. (1992). *Breaking Through Bureaucracy*. Berkeley: University of California Press.

Bennis, Warren G. (1966). *Changing Organizations*. New York: McGraw-Hill.

Bennis, Warren G., and Philip E. Slater. (1969). *The Temporary Society*. New York: Harper Colophon Books.

Bergquist, William. (1993). *The Postmodern Organization: Mastering the Art of Irreversible Change*. San Francisco: Jossey-Bass.

Berkley, George E. (1971). *The Administrative Revolution*. Englewood Cliffs, NJ: Prentice Hall.

Bernstein, R. J. (1992). *The New Constellation: The Ethical-Political Horizons of Modernity/Postmodernity*. Cambridge: MIT Press.

Blau, Peter, and Marshall Meyer. (1971). *Bureaucracy in Modern Society*. New York: Random House.

Clegg, S. (1990). *Modern Organizations: Organizational Studies in the Postmodern World*. Newbury Park, CA: Sage.

Cooper, Dick, and Edgar William. (1977). "Unfortunate Chain of Events Led to Fumes." *Philadelphia Inquirer*, July 6.

Drew, Elizabeth. (1996). *Showdown*. New York: Simon and Schuster.

Drucker, Peter F. (1988). "The Coming of the New Organization." *Harvard Business Review* (January-February).

Ford, Dan. (1979). *Pappy: The Life of John Ford*. Englewood Cliffs, NJ: Prentice Hall.

Fox, Charles J., and Hugh T. Miller. (1995). *Postmodern Public Administration: Toward Discourse*. Thousand Oaks, CA: Sage.

Gallagher, Winifred. (1994). "How We Became What We Are." *Atlantic Monthly* (September).

Goodman, P. S., and L. S. Sproull, eds. (1990). *Technology and Organizations*. San Francisco: Jossey-Bass.

Goodsell, Charles T. (1994). *The Case for Bureaucracy*, 3rd ed. Chatham, NJ: Chatham House.

Guy, Mary. (1992). "The Feminization of Public Administration," in *Public Management in an Interconnected World*, eds. Mary Timney Bailey and Richard T. Mayer. New York: Greenwood Press.

Hayles, N. I., ed. (1991). *Chaos and Order: Complex Dynamics in Literature and Science*. Chicago: University of Chicago Press.

Herzberg, Frederick. (1964). "The Motivation-Hygiene Concept," *Personnel Administration* (January-February).

———. (1966). *Work and the Nature of Man*. Cleveland: World.

Hoesterey, I., ed. (1991). *Zeitgeist in Babel: The Post-Modernist Controversy*. Bloomington: Indiana

University Press.

Janis, Irving L. (1972). *Victims of Groupthink*. Boston: Houghton Mifflin.

Jaques, Elliot. (1990). "In Praise of Hierarchy." *Harvard Business Review* (January-February).

Kaufman, H. (1977). *Red Tape*. Washington: Brookings Institution.

Keil, L. Douglas. (1995). *Managing Chaos and Complexity in Government*. San Francisco: Jossey-Bass.

Kellert, Steven H. (1993). *In the Wake of Chaos: Unpredictable Order in Dynamical Systems*. Chicago: University of Chicago Press.

Krislov, S., and D. H. Rosenbloom. (1981). *Representative Bureaucracy and the American Political System*. New York: Praeger.

Liddell Hart, B. H. (1972). *Why Don't We Learn from History?* NY: Hawthorn Books.

Mayo, Elton. (1933). *The Human Problems of an Industrial Civilization*. New York: Viking.

McGregor, Douglas M. (1960). *The Human Side of Enterprise*. New York: McGraw-Hill.

Merton, Robert K. (1957). *Social Theory and Social Structure*. New York: Free Press.

Mitchell, Alison. (1995). "Panetta's Sure Step in High-wire Job." *New York Times*, August 17.

Osborn, Alex F. (1953). *Applied Imagination*. New York: Scribner's.

Price, Don K. (1965). *The Scientific Estate*. Cambridge: The Belknap Press of Harvard University Press.

Rheingold, H. (1993). *The Virtual Community*. Reading, MA: Addison-Wesley.

Roberts, Rand, and James S. Olson. (1995). *John Wayne American*. New York: The Free Press.

Rosener, Judy B. (1995). *America's Competitive Secret: Utilizing Women as a Management Strategy*. New York: Oxford University Press.

Sayles, Leonard R., and Margaret Chandler. (1971). *Managing Large Systems*. New York: Harper and Row.

Schein, Edgar H. (1969). *Process Consultation: Its Role in Organization Development*. Reading, MA: Addison-Wesley.

Sorensen, Theodore C. (1965). *Kennedy*. New York: Harper and Row.

Sproull, L. S., and P. S. Goodman. (1990). "Technology and Organizations: Integration and Opportunities." In P. S. Goodman and L. S. Sproull, eds., *Technology and Organizations*. San Francisco: Jossey-Bass.

Stivers, Camilla. (1993). *Gender Images in Public Administration: Legitimacy and the Administrative State*. Newbury Park, CA: Sage.

Suid, Lawrence. (1978). *Guts and Glory: Great American War Movies*. Reading, MA: Addison-Wesley.

Thompson, Victor A. (1961). *Modern Organization*. New York: Knopf.

Toffler, Alvin. (1970). *Future Shock*. New York: Random House.

Truman, David B. (1951). *The Governmental Process*. New York: Knopf.

Villa, D. R. (1992). "Postmodernism and the Public Sphere." *American Political Science Review* 86.

Waldo, Dwight. (1952). "Development of Theory of Democratic Administration." *American Political Science Review* 44 (March).

Weick, Karl E. (1990). "Technology as Equivoque: Sensemaking in New Technologies." In P. S. Goodman and L. S. Sproull, eds., *Technology and Organizations*. San Francisco: Jossey-Bass.

Wills, Garry. (1977). *John Wayne's America*. New York: Simon and Schuster.

Wilson, James Q. (1989). *Bureaucracy*. New York: Basic Books.

Zuboff, Shoshana. (1988). *In the Age of the Smart Machine: The Future of Work and Power*. New York: Basic Books.

Recommended Books

French, Wendell L., and Cecil H. Bell. (1995). *Organizational Development: Behavioral Science Intervention for Organization Improvement*, 5th ed. Englewood Cliffs, NJ: Prentice Hall. Everything you always wanted to know about how to do organizational development.

Kaufman, Herbert. (1977). *Red Tape: Its Origins, Uses and Abuses*. Washington, DC: Brookings Institution. A very engaging account of the bureaucratic origins of red tape; after defining this elusive term, Kaufman assesses its pros and cons.

Lipsky, Michael. (1980). *Street-Level Bureaucracy: Dilemmas of the Individual in Public Services*. New York: Russell Sage Foundation. Many were genuinely surprised when the author first asserted that public employees who interacted directly with the public—police, social workers, etc.—were also, by default, the makers of bureaucratic policy, albeit on a small scale but with vast implications for accountability.

Stivers, Camila. (1993). *Gender Images in Public Administration: Legitimacy and the Administrative State*. Newbury Park, CA: Sage. An analysis of how the core ideas of modern administration, having to do with expertise, leadership, and virtue, have masculine attributes that give the advantage to masculinity over femininity; this leaves women with the choice of adopting masculine roles or becoming marginalized—unless the rules of perception are changed.

Wilson, James Q. (1989). *Bureaucracy: What Government Agencies Do and Why They Do It*. New York: Basic Books. A now classic analysis of bureaucratic behavior in a wide variety of institutional settings; might have been retitled "everything Max Weber would have said about modern bureaucracy if he were still alive and working as an American professor of public administration."

Related Web Sites

Abraham Maslow
   http://www.nidus.org/
Association for Quality and Participation
   http://www.aqp.org.
Center for the Study of Work Teams
   http://www.workteams.unt.edu/
Journal of Managerial Psychology
   http://www.mcb.co.uk/cgi-bin/journal1/jmp
Mary Parker Follett
   http://www.plgrm.com/history/women/F/Mary_
   Parker_Follett.HTM

Organizational Development Network
   http://www.tmn.com/odn/index.html
People management
   http://www.peoplemanagement.co.uk/index.html
Performance Management Network
   http://www.pmn.net/
Postmodernism
   http://www.alphalink.com.au/~pashton/essays/
   postmodernism.htm
Society for Industrial and Organizational Psychology
   http://www.siop.org/

7

Managerialism and Performance Management

Keynote: Socrates Discovers Universal Management

In ancient Greece, Socrates was busy establishing the intellectual foundations of modern educational testing when he discovered that "the unexamined life is not worth living." Still he found time to argue for the universality of management, that a successful business leader could be an equally effective general. Universal or generic management refers to management practices that are equally applicable in the public, private, and nonprofit sectors. The underlying doctrine holds that a properly trained manager will be effective in any type of organization, whether public or private, whether in service or manufacturing.

In a dialog recorded by Xenophon, an experienced soldier named Nicomachides complains to Socrates about being passed over for promotion to general despite "having received so many wounds from the enemy" [as he says this he opens his cloak to reveal his scars] in favor of a businessman "who has never served in the heavy-armed infantry and who indeed knows nothing but how to get money."

Socrates tells the brave soldier that a leader who "knows what he needs, and is able to provide it, [can] be a good president, whether he have the direction of a chorus, a family, a city, or an army."

"By Jupiter, Socrates," cried Nicomachides, "I should never have expected to hear from you that good managers of a family [business] would also be good generals."

"Come then," proceeded Socrates, "let us consider what are the duties of each of them, that we may understand whether they are the same, or are in any respect different."

"By all means."

"Is it not, then, the duty of both," asked Socrates, "to render those under their command obedient and submissive to them?"

"Unquestionably."

"Is it not also the duty of both to intrust various employments to such as are fitted to execute them?"

"That is also unquestionable."

"To punish the bad, and to honor the good, too, belongs, I think to each of them."

"Undoubtedly."

"And do you think it for the interest of both to gain for themselves allies and auxiliaries or not?"

"It assuredly is for their interest."

"Is it not proper for both also to be careful of their resources?"

"Assuredly."

"And is it not proper for both, therefore, to be attentive and industrious in their respective duties?"

"All these particulars," said Nicomachides, "are common alike to both; but it is not common to both to fight."

"Yet both have doubtless enemies," rejoined Socrates.

"That is probably the case," said the other.

Why is this man (Ross Perot) smiling? Because he knows that Socrates taught that a successful private sector manager could also be a successful public sector manager. So without any experience in elective office, he ran for president of the United States in 1992 and received 19 percent of the vote. Conclusion: Millions of Americans who may never have heard of Socrates nevertheless believe in his assertion of the universality of management •

"Is it not for the interest of both to gain the superiority over those enemies?"

"Certainly; but to say something on that point, what, I ask, will skill in managing a household avail, if it be necessary to fight?"

"It will doubtless in that case, be of the greatest avail," said Socrates, "for a good manager of a house, knowing that nothing is so advantageous or profitable as to get the better of your enemies when you contend with them, nothing so unprofitable and prejudicial as to be defeated, will zealously seek and provide everything that may conduce to victory, will carefully watch and guard against whatever tends to defeat, will vigorously engage if he sees that his force is likely to conquer, and, what is not the least important point, will cautiously avoid engaging if he finds himself insufficiently prepared."

Socrates in listing and discussing the duties of all good leaders—of public as well as private institutions—emphasized their similarities. He then states that "the conduct of private affairs differs from that of public concerns only in magnitude; in other respects they are similar." Socrates concludes that "those who conduct public business make use of men not at all differing in nature from those whom the managers of private affairs employ; and those who know how to employ them conduct either public or private affairs judiciously, while those who do not know will err in the management of both." His is the first known statement that managerial competence was transferable. Thus a manager who could cope well with one type of organization would be equally adept at coping with others, even though their purposes and functions might be widely disparate. Ever since, the generalist manager has been an ideal.

Socrates was not the only ancient Greek to provide significant insights into modern management. Plato, a student of Socrates, is often considered to be the first political scientist. His *Republic* is the Western world's first systematic analysis of the political process. There he provided an intellectual rationale for the "divine right of kings" even before Christianity sanctioned the notion. To Plato, only an elite of philosopher kings or "guardians" had the political wisdom necessary to govern; he would not have been an equal opportunity employer. His just society was one where each person had a predetermined place—with the guardians on top. Yet, in essence, Plato's elitism is a call for professionalism—a challenge to his contemporaries who thought that no training or aptitude was necessary to manage public affairs.

In his *Politics*, Aristotle, a student of Plato, wrote of the division of labor, departmentalization, centralization, decentralization, and delegation of authority. But most importantly he presented the first comprehensive analysis of the nature of a state and any political community. To Aristotle, the state was a natural development because "man is by nature a political animal." The state was even more important than family because, while a family exists for comfort, the state can be a vehicle for glory and the good life.

Perhaps Aristotle's most famous analytical construct is his classification of the three basic forms of government. He found that every political community had to be governed by either the one, the few, or the many. This corresponds to his three governing types: kingship, aristocracy, and polity (majority rule). Unfortunately, each of these had its perversions, the conditions to which it degenerated when the rulers ceased ruling in the interests of the whole community. Kingship often degenerated into tyranny; aristocracy (rule by a talented and virtuous elite) into an oligarchy (rule by a small group in its own interest); and a polity or constitutional system (where a large middle class rules for the common interest) into democracy (mob rule in the interests of the lower classes). Overall, Aristotle favored a mixed constitution—one in which all citizens "rule and are ruled by turn," where no class monopolizes power and a large middle class provides stability.

It is only in this last situation that administrative institutions evolve to be responsive to the needs of the mass of the citizenry. Still the Greeks limited citizen participation. Manual workers, merchants, and other "disreputable" types (including large numbers of slaves) were excluded from citizenship. Because work itself was disdained, no professional corps of administrators emerged. The relatively few citizens, competent or not, took turns managing the public's business. As Pericles said in his funeral oration over the Athenians who died in the Peloponnesian War: "We are called a democracy, for the administration is in the hands of the many and not of the few." The Athenians assumed that all citizens would participate in government. Pericles proudly asserted that "we are the only people to regard the man who takes no interest in politics not as careless, but as useless." Thus it made sense to them that most offices were filled by lot for short terms. Effectively, the gods decided who did what. However, some offices such as treasurer or military commander were elected—they were simply too important to give the gods free rein. As any student of Greek mythology knows, the gods often proved to be perverse.

Aristotle's most famous student was Alexander the Great. He did not write any books; he just used what Aristotle taught him and conquered the world. But because he never created an institutional foundation for his empire, it dissipated shortly after his death. The Greeks simply lacked the knack—lacked the doctrine—for large-scale administrative structures. They never got beyond the city-state. So it was relatively easy for the better organized Romans to take them over in the middle of the second century B.C.E. It just goes to show that in the game of chutes and ladders that is the rise and fall of civilizations, the better organized—those who have the best public administration doctrine—win. And it has been that way since the beginning of recorded history. Aristotle might just as well have said that "man is an administrative animal" because states do not get very far politically or militarily unless they also develop administratively.

Managerialism

In the 1960s and 1970s there was a vast expansion in the intellectual development and technical capabilities of public administration. The new tools of program evaluation and policy analysis, with quantitative precision, called into question the efficacy and utility of long-standing public programs—especially those having to do with social services and education. New budgeting techniques—from **PPBS** to **zero-based budgeting**—meant that political executives and legislators could better see, if not better control, where money was spent. The traditional management focus was expanded to include greater emphasis on strategic planning (see Chapter 8), **internal control** and ethical responsibility (see Chapter 14). Nevertheless, in spite of all these advances in the art and science of public administration, the 1980s became a period of decline in the public service—declining budgets, declining productivity, declining quality of services, and the declining reputation of the public service itself. In response a new doctrine—managerialism—would emerge and ride, if not to the rescue, then at least, into the fray.

Managerialism as a term has long been used by sociologists with reference to the economic and bureaucratic elites that run an industrial society. **James Burnham** in his 1941 *The Managerial Revolution* announced that the world was in transition "*from* the type of society which we have called capitalist or bourgeois *to* a type of

---

PPBS Planning, programming, budgeting systems; a budgeting process that requires agency directors to identify program objectives, to develop methods of measuring program output, to calculate total program costs over the long run, to prepare detailed multiyear program and financial plans, and to analyze the costs and benefits of alternative program designs.

zero-based budgeting A budgeting process that is, first and foremost, a rejection of the incremental decision making model of budgeting. It demands a rejustification of the entire budget submission (from ground zero), whereas incremental budgeting essentially respects the outcomes of previous budgetary decisions (collectively referred to as the budget base) and focuses examination on the margin of change from year to year.

internal control The sum of the many diverse procedures that management uses to administer an agency, from accounting systems to training programs.

James Burnham (1905–1987) The professor of philosophy at New York University who, after an early career as a Communist of the anti-Stalinist, Trotsky type, became a leading conservative writer who advocated defeating and rolling back the Soviet Empire.

society which we shall call *managerial*." Burnham asserted that as control of large businesses moved from the original owners to professional managers, society's new governing class would be not the traditional possessors of wealth—but those who have the professional expertise to manage, to lead, those large organizations. The same phenomenon was occurring at roughly the same time in the Communist world. **Milovan Djilas** wrote in his 1957 *The New Class* that instead of producing a classless society, the Communists had instead developed a new class system consisting of party officials, managers of the nationalized industries, and bureaucrats. These people, especially those near the top, were the only ones in the Communist states to have any power. They used the repressive forces of the state, especially the secret police, to ensure total obedience. This enabled them to enjoy a standard of living vastly higher than ordinary members of society. And they were able to pass on this privilege to their children. Even though they could not legally own much more than ordinary citizens, access to high quality education and easy entrance to prestige jobs guaranteed their children the same status that they possessed themselves. Thus they constituted an upper social class, albeit a nontraditional one.

In the 1980s managerialism, now a well-established sociological "ism," took on new connotations. When Margaret Thatcher began her eleven-year stint as British prime minister in 1979, she immediately sought to refocus the civil service from policy toward management. Thus she tried to force the bureaucracy to be more responsive to the needs of its customers (into which citizens were to be transformed). Managerialism, entrepreneurial management that goes beyond participative management to unleash the creative abilities of public managers at all levels, became the prevailing public sector doctrine. As a philosophy of continuous reform, it seeks to prevent an organization from ever degenerating into incompetence. Paradoxically, managerialism is also a retreat from participative management in that it romantically assumes that a managerial elite can radically change and control the direction, culture, and purpose of organizations. The romance of managerialism would not be possible if there were not heroes to romanticize. Who are these new-style heroes? Why, the managers themselves, who have come to revitalize the public service by slaying the dragons of self-serving unions and inefficient bureaucrats. Plato would have felt right at home with these modern philosopher-kings.

A New Managerial Revolution

The core theme of managerialism is management rights—giving managers enough room to maneuver so that they can accomplish their goals. This additional managerial room is necessarily taken from the **rank and file**. Thus managerialism is quite comfortable with authoritarian management styles and a new version of scientific management—except the search for the "one best way" has been updated to the

---

Milovan Djilas (1911–) The Yugoslavian vice president whose writings attacking European communism cost him his job and earned him a lengthy stay in jail.

rank and file A colloquial expression for the masses. When used in an organizational context, it refers to those members of the organization who are not part of management; those who are the workers and have no status as officers. Rank and file was originally a military term, referring to the enlisted men who had to line up in ranks, side by side, and files, one behind the other. Officers, being gentlemen, were spared such indignities.

British Prime Minister Margaret Thatcher discussing managerialism with then–Vice President George Bush. They are standing in front of Number 10 Downing Street, the home and office (much like the White House) of British prime ministers. In 1990 Thatcher staunchly encouraged President Bush as he assembled the worldwide coalition that would rebuff the Iraqi invasion of Kuwait during the Persian Gulf War. Perhaps she repeated to him her words on her conduct during the Falklands War of 1982: "It is exciting to have a real crisis on your hands, when you have spent half your political life dealing with humdrum issues like the environment" •

constant installation of the latest in behavioral and mechanistic technologies. In an effort to gain maximum control of personnel costs, and minimal problems with introducing labor-saving technologies, managerialism seeks to contract out to the private sector as much of the public's business as it can. The techniques of administrative improvement advocated by managerialism, such as management audits and program evaluations, are comparatively old. What's new is that these same old techniques, like the same old tanks (remember the 1940 blitzkrieg discussed in Chapter 5), are being reinvigorated by a new doctrine or guiding philosophy.

It is no longer sufficient for a public manager to be the traditional "neutral gun for hire" passively performing the tasks set by political masters. In 1923 Charles G. Dawes, the first modern budget director of the U.S. government (and later vice president from 1925 to 1929), explained the traditional concept of neutral competence thusly: "If Congress . . . passed a law that garbage should be put on the White House steps, it would be our regrettable duty, as a bureau, in an impartial, nonpolitical and nonpartisan way to advise the Executive and Congress as to how the largest amount of garbage could be spread in the most expeditious and economical manner."

Policy Entrepreneurs

Today such an attitude by a senior administrator would find him or her in bad odor—and not just because of the garbage. Modern public managers are expected to be policy entrepreneurs who forcefully develop, argue for, and yes, sell, creative solutions to vexing problems. Current thinking calls for the most aggressive actions on the part of administrators to fight the never-ending threats of waste, fraud, and **abuse**. These modern crusaders go into the administrative battles shouting their slogans in the same manner that the French revolutionaries of 1789 chanted "Liberty, Equality, Fraternity." But today's administrative chant, also of French etymological origin, is "reengineering, empowerment, and entrepreneurialism."

The current horde of administrative revolutionaries preach as if they are the first to ever see the light of divine bureaucratic guidance. But none of this is new. Franz Kafka, the preeminent novelist of bureaucratic oppression, warned us that "every revolution evaporates leaving behind only the slime of a new bureaucracy." In a parallel sense, every revolution in management thinking and dogma leaves in its wake only the slime of a new vocabulary.

Reengineering

Reengineering is an old-fashioned reorganization with a college education. Traditional reorganization calls for changes in the administrative structure or formal procedures of government that do not require fundamental constitutional change or the creation of new bodies not previously established by the legislature. Many reorganizations are undertaken for the purposes of departmental consolidation, executive office expansion, budgetary reform, and personnel administration—primarily to promote bureaucratic responsiveness to central executive control and, secondly, to simplify or professionalize administrative affairs. Of course all those contemplating a major reorganization should first heed John Kenneth Galbraith's timeless advice: "When things are not good, it is usually imagined that a review, or possibly a reorganization, will make things better. No one ever asks whether the best is being made of a lousy situation."

Radical as Opposed to Incremental Change

The "message" of reengineering is that all large organizations must undertake a radical reinvention of what they do, how they do it, and how they are structured. There is no room for incremental improvement—for small and cautious steps. Organizations

---

abuse The furnishing of excessive services to beneficiaries of government programs, violating program regulations, or performing improper practices—none of which involves prosecutable fraud. Fraud, a more serious offense, is the obtaining of something of value by unlawful means through willful misrepresentation.

need to quit asking, "How can we do things faster?" or "How can we do our current work at the lowest cost?" The question needs to be, "Why do we do what we do—at all?" In *Reengineering the Corporation*, reengineering proselytizers Michael Hammer and James Champy claim that reengineering "is to the next revolution of business what the specialization of labor was to the last." It is the process of asking: "If I were re-creating this company today, given what I know and given current technology, what would it look like?" More formally, reengineering is the "fundamental rethinking and radical redesign of business processes to achieve dramatic improvements in critical, contemporary measures of performance, such as cost, quality, service, and speed." Thus, reengineering is the search for new models for organizing work.

Reengineering takes reorganization beyond its traditional focus by seeking to totally rethink and refocus how programs are managed and to take maximum advantage of new technology—especially computers. Laudable intentions indeed! But neither reorganization nor reengineering happens in a political vacuum. Harold Seidman warns that all potential reengineers should be aware of the strong relationship between the organization of a legislature and its executive branch. "One could as well ignore the laws of aerodynamics in designing an aircraft as ignore the laws of congressional dynamics in designing executive branch structure. What may appear to be structural eccentricities and anomalies within the executive branch are often nothing but mirror images of jurisdictional conflicts within the Congress." Legislative and executive branch organizations are "interrelated and constitute two halves of a single system."

The most famous warning on reorganization applies equally to reengineering. It is usually attributed to Petronius Arbiter, a Roman writer of the first century: "I was to learn later in life that we tend to meet any new situation by reorganizing; and a wonderful method it can be for creating the illusion of progress while producing confusion, inefficiency, and demoralization."

Note that Hammer and Champy's best seller contains a reformulation of what has been known since ancient times. Remember the story of the Trojan horse, about how the besieging Greeks finally defeated the defenders of Troy in Asia Minor? For years the Greeks used conventional siege tactics to no avail. Then Ulysses said that the besieging Greeks had to completely rethink what they were doing. With the help of Minerva, the goddess of wisdom no less, Ulysses reengineered the siege. The new approach was to feign abandoning the siege while leaving behind a wooden horse large enough to contain a squad of Greek soldiers inside. The Trojans, thinking the horse a tribute from the fleeing Greeks, took it within their city's walls and had a party. Later that night the Greeks hiding in the horse came out to open the gates for their returning comrades. Then they sacked and looted Troy in the classic manner. Hammer and Champy could not offer a better example of a "fundamental rethinking and radical redesign" of a business effort. Ever since, Ulysses the reengineer has retained his reputation for cunning.

Becoming a Reengineer

Reengineering is as much a mental discipline and a philosophy as it is a process. The reengineer's primary skill is an ability to look at things such as work processes and organizational structures with new eyes. Reengineering is a radical change strategy, not an incremental "grass-roots" employee involvement approach. Reengineering literally means what its name implies. According to Hammer and Champy, "When someone asks us for a quick definition of business reengineering, we say that it means 'starting over.' It *doesn't* mean tinkering with what already exists or making incremental changes that leave basic structures intact. . . . It involves going back to the beginning and inventing a better way of doing work."

While there are various paths to reengineering, they all usually include the following three steps:

1. *Process mapping*: The flow-charting of how an organization presently delivers its services and products as a process. This emphasis on process is why reengineering is often called "process reengineering."

2. *Customer assessments*: The evaluation of the organization's customers' needs, both presently and in the future, by means of **focus groups**, surveys, and meetings with consumers of the organization's products and services.

3. *Process visioning*: A total rethinking of how the work processes ought to function, keeping in mind the latest available technology.

The key to successful reengineering efforts is the ability to challenge the assumptions underlying the current system. Just as there are **barriers to entry** that face all new business ventures, there are a parallel set of barriers to reengineering. They include bureaucratic turf concerns, employee resistance to change, lack of incentives, and general skepticism about just another in a long line of reform efforts. But with a strategic commitment from top management these barriers can be overcome. For example, a 1994 International City/County Management Association report illustrates how Charlottesville, Virginia, reengineered their process for issuing new business licenses to take less than a half hour instead of two days; how Merced County, California, reengineered their social service eligibility process to take less than three days instead of the previous 40 days; and how Phoenix, Arizona, reengineered the time it took to get city property maps from five days to five minutes.

Robert M. Melia, as first deputy commissioner of the Massachusetts Department of Revenue, became a famous reengineer to many "deadbeat dads" in the early 1990s when he reengineered how past-due child support payments are collected. According to John Martin, because "there was no money for throwing more caseworkers at the problem . . . [Melia] forced the department to rethink child-support enforcement from the ground up—the essence of reengineering." Consequently, "these days, it's a computer, rather than expensive caseworkers, that

---

focus group A relatively small number (6 to 20) of people with a common characteristic brought to a neutral setting to participate in a discussion on products or politics led by a trained researcher. Focus groups are a major tool of marketing research. They allow analysts to delve deeply into the motivations for buying a product or voting for a politician.

barriers to entry Impediments to further competition in an industry, whether they be legal (critical patents owned by others), economic (start-up costs too high), political (unstable government), or social (the market has established brand preference).

handles the bulk of the commonwealth's child-support cases. The computer issues a single warning before proceeding to collect overdue child support anywhere it can: garnishing wages, raiding bank accounts and intercepting tax refunds, unemployment benefit checks, and lottery winnings." Collections have gone up 30 percent. But more important, the average number of families leaving the welfare rolls, because of improved child support, is now double its previous monthly rate.

Reengineering, thinking from the ground up, is hardly new. In the nineteenth-century operetta *The Mikado* by Gilbert and Sullivan, the Mikado's (the emperor of Japan's) efforts at reengineering the Japanese judicial system are explained in Act 1: "Our logical Mikado, seeing no moral difference between the dignified judge who condemns a criminal to die, and the industrious mechanic who carries out the sentence, has rolled the two offices into one, and every judge is now his own executioner." Then as now, reengineering is merely a combination of applied logical and strategic will.

Empowerment

Power is the fuel of organizational life. It is what makes things go. It is relatively easy for managers to get the traditional authoritarian powers of domination that allow them to control and punish subordinates; what is far more difficult is obtaining the power needed for positive accomplishment. This kind of power is less formally given than informally earned—often by empowering others. Thus the paradox that managers can often make themselves more powerful by giving power away. By empowering others, leaders actually acquire more "productive power"—the power truly needed to accomplish organizational goals.

Managers who cannot delegate, who will not trust or empower subordinates, become less and less powerful, and correspondingly more and more incompetent, as they increasingly seek to hoard power. Remember power, much as with money—a variant of power—is like manure: you have to spread it around for it to do any good. Perhaps the most common example of the dysfunctional withholding of power concerns the way managers are punished for not spending all of their budgeted funds. The typical punishment is to take the money away by reallocating the funds and then, to add insult to injury, budget less money during the next budget cycle. No wonder managers have become adept at spending their allocations down to virtually the last penny. Not only is this wasteful, but it discourages cost-cutting to achieve real savings and greater productivity. Empowering managers to control their budget savings is one of the main thrusts of the entrepreneurial management movement in the United States.

Nor are universities immune from this problem. University administrators seem constantly surprised when academic departments vote tenure for mediocre or marginally competent professors. This tends to happen when the administration maintains a policy of automatically taking budget authority for professional positions away from departments whenever a position becomes vacant. Thus, from the point of view of the department, a faculty slot filled by a mediocrity is better than being understaffed. So the department's tenure decision all too often is based not on merit or competence but on whether the individual in question is better than nothing.

Empowering Teams

Virtually all of the "new" approaches to management that are being advocated, the attempts to find solutions to the "productivity problem"—have blended traditional management methods with new forms of employee involvement and participative management. For the past two decades, we have witnessed a never-ending series of "new" management approaches, particularly approaches that emphasize organizational flexibility through the development and **empowerment** of individuals and work groups.

All of these team-based approaches assume that groups provide individuals with opportunities for personal and professional growth and self-expression and **job satisfaction**. They also assume that these opportunities cannot become available to workers in traditional hierarchical organizations. Groups provide structure and discipline for individuals at work. Therefore, organizations that permit empowerment do not need multiple levels of supervisors to coordinate, control, and monitor production.

While empowerment is a proven means of enhancing productivity, Marc Holzer warns: "One danger in employee involvement, especially within the TQM envelope, is the extent to which it will parallel or bypass the union. In those cases the gains to be made through participation may run up against the losses resulting from political alienation of the union hierarchy." It is reasonable to conclude that the "most effective systems might involve both union and workplace committees. In both sectors the most effective organizations are those which treat unions as real partners, not imagined enemies. Excellent union relationships are especially important in the more heavily unionized public sector."

The Self-Directed Work Team

Work groups can and will accept responsibility for their processes and products—as well as the behavior of other group members. This has been illustrated by the research on the "self-directed work team" undertaken by management consultant J. D. Orsburn and others. They define a self-directed work team as a "highly trained group of employees, from 6 to 18, on average, fully responsible for turning out a well-defined segment of finished work." Therefore, self-directed work teams differ in several "revolutionary" ways from conventional work groups:

1. *Fewer job categories*: Each member of a self-directed work team performs multiple tasks. "When a conventional machine shop converts to self-direction, for example, 10 or so job categories may collapse into 1 or 2."

2. *Authority*: Because self-directed work teams handle tasks that historically have been the purview of management, the teams need adequate authority. First-level supervisors usually work at a distance, or their role is changed to facilitator.

---

empowerment Giving a person or organization the formal authority to do something.
job satisfaction The totality of an employee's feelings about the various aspects of his or her work; an emotional appraisal of whether a job lives up to an employee's values.

3. *Reward system*: If self-directed teams are to produce their potential benefits, the organization needs to reward individual behaviors that promote team flexibility. This usually means compensating team members for mastering a range of skills. Gain-sharing and profit-sharing programs are often introduced.

Orsburn and his colleagues found that teams that are successful use self-directing teams for "downloading" duties to the lower levels. "Work teams release their managers to perform duties now exercised by managers at the level above." Executives have more time for strategic planning, and mid-managers have time to engage in activities such as **coaching**, championing innovative ideas, and working with vendors or customers. Ongoing training is the "engine that drives the transition." Training provides team members with operational know-how and also helps them to cope with the transition. All in all, self-directing work teams lead to organizational productivity, streamlining, flexibility, quality, commitment, and customer satisfaction.

Most of the experience with employee involvement, empowerment, and self-directed teams to date has been in manufacturing industries. Service industry and government applications have largely been overlooked in practice and in the literature. Management professors David E. Bowen and Edward E. Lawler III examined the benefits and costs of empowering employees in service industries, the range of management practices available for empowering employees to varying degrees, and the key business characteristics that affect the desirability of using empowerment approaches. Bowen and Lawler concluded that "empowerment" is the sharing of four organizational "ingredients" with front-line service employees: (1) information about the organization's performance, (2) rewards based on organizational performance, (3) information and knowledge, and (4) power to make decisions.

Entrepreneurialism

The last and potentially the most powerful element of the revolutionary credo is entrepreneurialism. This calls for managers to be transformational leaders who strive to change organizational culture. Each must develop a new vision for the organization—then convert that vision into reality.

President George Bush was not a man to inadvertently create many new phrases. But "the vision thing" inadvertently became uniquely his own after he first complained about it in 1988 because he seemed to lack it, knew he seemed to lack it, and couldn't get it. This lack of vision created an image of domestic policy incompetence that greatly contributed to his failure to win reelection in 1992. Perhaps President Bush should have paid more attention to the biblical Moses. There was a man with vision. He took a people who were slaves in Egypt and transformed them into an independent nation. Now we cannot all be a Moses and get our vision from a burning bush; but we can all avoid being a Bush with no vision.

Entrepreneurial vision cannot and should not be limited to the top; at every organizational level managers need vision and dreams, need the ability to assess the situation and plan for a better future. Those who cannot do this, who cannot visualize

---

coaching Face-to-face discussions with a subordinate in order to effect a change in his or her behavior.

and plan for change, are by definition incompetent. After all, organizations that do not change must eventually die—even in the public sector. Besides, if you don't have a dream—if you don't have a vision—how will you ever know if it comes true?

But be aware that the true believers of any philosophic system or ideology are often headed for a fall. This is nowhere more true than with theories of management. We constantly fool ourselves into thinking we're onto something really new until we discover that, for example, Socrates in ancient Greece espoused the merits of generic management, that Aristotle anticipated the underlying premises of organizational culture, and that during the Italian Renaissance Niccolo Machiavelli wrote *The Prince*, the first of an endless series of "how to succeed" books of management advice.

Too many organizations become infatuated with each new management fad and slick-talking consultant that comes along. They buy books for their managers, send them to training programs—and then expect them to manage by **MBO, OD, ZBB, QC, TQM**, and a host of other acronyms submerged in a bowl of alphabet soup.

But be careful of swallowing any of this soup whole. Both you and your organization could get a bad case of indigestion because management philosophy taken to extremes is one of the leading causes of incompetence. For example, the scientific management of Frederick Taylor was premised upon the notion that there was "one best way" of accomplishing any given task. The job of the line manager then, once the "one best way" was found by the staff, was to impose this procedure upon the organization. The problem with traditional scientific management is its paternalistic "papa knows best" attitude. It presupposes that the managers have a monopoly on brains, that input from the workers is a distraction to be avoided. But every worker comes with a brain. Only an incompetent organization wastes or ignores this resource. Thus scientific management, a good idea in principle, becomes scientific incompetence when taken to extremes.

Public administration and management in general, is newly concerned, indeed newly obsessed, with an issue variously described as quality, competence, more bang for the buck, or meeting the needs of your customers. The whole thrust of this trend toward managerialism is with instilling a new-found sense of competence in organizations—to ward off the evils of incompetence. Unfortunately, competence and incompetence are two sides of the same trick coin. It is a trick coin because there is no common agreement on which side wins—no universal agreement on

---

MBO Management by objectives; an approach to managing, the hallmark of which is a mutual setting—by both organizational subordinate and superior—of measurable goals to be accomplished by an individual or team over a set period of time.

OD Organization development; a process for increasing an organization's effectiveness. As a process it has no value bias, yet it is usually associated with the idea that maximum effectiveness is to be found by integrating an individual's desire for personal growth with organizational goals.

ZBB Zero base budgeting.

QC Quality circles; small groups of employees working in the same organizational unit who, with the approval of management, voluntarily meet on a regular basis to identify and solve problems that directly affect their work.

TQM Total quality management; processes to ensure that all aspects of an organization are performing at an optimal level.

what constitutes either competence or incompetence. This problem is much like Supreme Court Justice Potter Stewart's famous dilemma over defining pornography. He asserted that while he could not define it, he nevertheless knew it when he saw it. Competence suffers from a similar problem of perception. After all, while one person may see obstructing red tape, another, looking at the same thing, may see a treasured procedural safeguard.

Toward a Competitive Public Administration

The great flaw in managerialism is the logic by which it approaches reform. The problem is not so much the fine people who populate the public service but the systems under which they must work. Just bring in hardheaded managers, presumably with considerable private sector experience, and they will whip things into shape in no time. While it is always true that public service operations can be improved, it does not necessarily follow that the wholesale adoption of private sector tactics will do the job. What the would-be reformers so often forget is that government operations are not inefficient because stupid people work there; they are inefficient because they have been designed by the legislature to reflect the competing interests of patronage, representativeness, and due process. Efficiency has to take its turn with these other factors. And no upstart executive most recently from some hotshot corporation is going to push these other factors out of line—because they are just as much part of the agency's legal mandate as efficiency.

This is why the managerialist impulse initially rode into town on the back of conservative or right-of-center governments such as the Reagan (U.S.) and Thatcher (U.K.) administrations of the 1980s. They both talked a better managerial game than they played; but nevertheless their influence has been both lasting and ultimately bipartisan in that politically center and left-of-center governments in the early 1990s in the United States, Australia, and New Zealand, for example, have also adopted the essence of managerialism. As the guru of managerialism Christopher Pollitt has argued, "managerialism is the 'acceptable face' of new-right theory concerning the state. . . . [It] provides a label under which private-sector disciplines can be introduced to the public services, political control can be strengthened, budgets trimmed, professional autonomy reduced, public service unions weakened, and a quasi-competitive framework erected to flush out the 'natural' inefficiencies of bureaucracy."

The myriad managerialist intiatives have been favorably received by the public because of the general antipathy toward "the bureaucracy," the increasing reluctance of citizens to pay more taxes, the widespread belief (which is often erroneous) that privatization will cost the public less, and the fact that reform of whatever ilk is often good politics.

Practically all the managerialists' goals can be achieved by what has come to be known as **competitive public administration**. At all levels of government under

---

competitive public administration Public sector policies that force differing organizations to compete with each other for the opportunity to do the public's work. Thus private contractors compete with a government agency, government agencies compete with each other, etc.

regimes of vastly differing political philosophies, self-standing bureaucratic components such as building-maintenance staffs or trash collection operations are being forced to compete in price with private sector contractors that are ready and willing to put the jobs in question into the private sector. Various **voucher systems** allow this same strategy to be applied to public education and housing—even free meals for the homeless. This Darwinian atmosphere of the "survival of the cheapest" is indeed introducing private-sector discipline, is strengthening political control, is trimming budgets, and is curtailing unionism and professionalism. What was once right wing is now mainstream. In the United States this is often referred to as the "reinventing government" movement after the book of that same title by David Osborne and Ted Gaebler.

A perennial theme in American politics is that government's administrative problems will be solved just as soon as some successful business leaders show those bureaucrats what's what. Yet managerialism's doctrine of transferability, this genericism that goes back to Socrates, when tried, has usually been far less successful than initially anticipated. Within private corporations, a parallel genericism has been equally destructive. As managers skilled in finance increasingly gained control of manufacturing corporations, products and eventually sales suffered. This problem of a top management cadre skilled in juggling numbers but ignorant of how their products are made has become so great as to call into question the core beliefs of genericism. Indeed, there is now talk of what economist Robert Samuelson calls the "death of management," the death of the notion that a manager with an MBA (master of business administration) degree "should be able to manage any enterprise, anywhere, any time."

The New Public Management

As a doctrine, managerialism continues to evolve, its essence having been distilled under the label "the new public management," which according to Christopher Pollitt has four main aspects:

1. A much bolder and larger scale use of marketlike mechanisms for those parts of the public sector that could not be transferred directly into private ownership (quasi-markets)

2. Intensified organizational and spatial decentralization of the management and production of services

3. A constant rhetorical emphasis on the need to improve service 'quality'

4. An equally relentless insistence that greater attention had to be given to the wishes of the individual service user/'consumer'

---

voucher systems A government program that issues redeemable vouchers to eligible citizens to purchase services on the open market. For example, housing vouchers have been suggested as an alternative to public housing and education vouchers have been suggested as an alternative to public education. The idea of using vouchers was popularized by economist Milton Friedman in *Capitalism and Freedom* (1962).

The new public management is ambitious. It is far more than the traditional management aspects of public administration (which can be called the "old" public management), and according to Owen Hughes it is a "new Paradigm" that heralds a major change in the role of government in society. Like any good paradigm, it seeks to replace the earlier model of public administration because that model "has been discredited theoretically and practically." While one can admire Hughes's intensity of feeling, it is difficult not to figuratively shout "Mind you don't throw out the baby with the bathwater!"

All reform movements seek vehicles for proselytizing, for educating new converts. The most prominent vehicle for this has been Osborne and Gaebler's *Reinventing Government*. This 1992 surprise best-seller has become the bible of the new public management movement. And just as the original Bible warns us that "there is no new thing under the sun," (Ecclesiastes), the Osborne and Gaebler bible preaches its gospels using ten principles. The ghost of Jomini reasserts itself! (See Chapter 5.)

Will these new principles "solve the major problems we experience with bureaucratic government" as their authors intend? To find out, stay tuned to another exciting chapter in the history of public administration! There is no official "new public management." No government has formally sanctioned a group of practices with that title. There only exists a disparate group of structural reforms and informal management initiatives that reflect the doctrine of managerialism and can usefully be grouped under the rubric of the "new public management."

Subsequent chapters will constantly return to these themes not because they are supplanting a "discredited" public administration, but because they are an almost expected revitalization of public administration in the tradition of the progressive movement that started more than one hundred years ago. The progressives got their name from the fact that they believed in the doctrine of progress—that governing institutions could be improved by bringing science to bear on public problems. It was a disparate movement, with each reform group targeting a level of government, a particular policy, and so on. Common beliefs were that good government was possible and that "the cure for democracy is *more* democracy." To achieve this, they only had to "throw the rascals out." And it was the progressive influence that initially forged the fledgling discipline of public administration.

Doctrines come and doctrines go; but public administration is always and inherently progressive. Managerialism, the new public management, and the reinventing government movements are just the latest landmarks on the yellow brick road of progressivism. All these reforms are like Macbeth's "poor player that struts and frets his hour upon the stage and then is heard no more." In 1933 Leonard D. White, the preeminent historian of American public administration, published *Trends in Public Administration*, in which he devoted several chapters to "the new management" that had evolved since 1900. In 1971 Frank E. Marini published his highly influential edited volume *Toward a New Public Administration*. New! New! New! But all this new stuff is just the reaffirmation of the progressive doctrine. There can be no end to the doctrine of public administration; there is only continuous doctrinal reform.

Box 7.1

The Ten Principles for Reinventing Government

1. Catalytic government: steering rather than rowing
2. Community-owned government: empowering rather than serving
3. Competitive government: injecting competition into service delivery
4. Mission-driven government: transforming rule-driven organizations
5. Results-oriented government: funding outcomes, not inputs
6. Customer-driven government: meeting the needs of the customer, not the bureaucracy
7. Enterprising government: earning rather than spending
8. Anticipatory government: prevention rather than cure
9. Decentralized government: from hierarchy to participation and teamwork
10. Market-oriented government: leveraging change through the market

Source: David Osborne and Ted Gaebler, *Reinventing Government* (Reading, MA: Addison-Wesley, 1992).

What Is Performance Management?

Performance management is what leaders do; it is the primary responsibility of an organizational leader. It is the systematic integration of an organization's efforts to achieve its objectives. What makes performance management different from mere management is this emphasis on systematic integration. Thus it includes the comprehensive control, audit, and evaluation of all aspects of organizational performance. The components of performance management are long-established management tools that encompass most of the other senses in which the term performance is used in the language of public sector management. These components include:

1. The specification of clear and measurable organizational objectives (i.e., management by objectives), which is the essence of strategic management (discussed in Chapter 8)

2. The systematic use of performance indicators, measures of organizational performance, to assess organizational output (this is closely linked to concepts of performance standards to allow the performance measured in one organization to be compared with industry averages, **best practice**, and benchmarking—the systematic comparison of performance between or among organizations)

---

best practice The generally recognized optimal way of performing a task.

3. The application of the performance appraisal of individual employees to assist in harmonizing their efforts and focusing them toward organizational objectives

4. The use of performance incentives, such as **performance pay** to reward exceptional personal efforts toward organizational goals

5. The linking of human and financial resource allocation to an annual management or budget cycle

6. Regular review at the end of each planning cycle of the extent to which goals have been achieved and the reasons for performance that is better or worse than planned. This creates the feedback that helps start the cycle anew.

Most organizations operate within a calendar or management cycle. This, in its simplest terms, plots against a calendar the main management actions that must be taken in the coming year. As a minimum, such calendars normally record the meeting dates of the governing board of the body, if there is one, and dates surrounding the preparation, consideration, and finalization of the budget. This reflects the de facto role of the budget in many organizations as the central focus of decision making concerning resource allocation for the coming year. A management cycle not only forces decisions to be made with a calendar in mind, it also serves as a conceptual diagram, which implies a logical interaction, sequencing, and above all linking of related categories of management activity. Moreover, a logical performance management cycle will indicate which classes of decisions must be made by which management actors—and when they must be made.

A performance management system of this type may be adopted at the level of an entire national, regional, or local government, or by a particular public enterprise or government agency. At the present time, such systems are rapidly being adopted by governments, not because the components are new but because the need to closely focus and target activities toward desired results is felt to be pressing. By the mid-1990s, governments in Australia, New Zealand, the United Kingdom, and the United States had all adopted explicit performance management programs to a greater or lesser extent. In the United States, the new interest in performance management took the form of a national review of performance management, led by Vice President Al Gore, and significantly influenced by David Osborne, coauthor of *Reinventing Government*. The U.S. federal government process employs a slightly less focused version of performance management, termed performance review. The American review does emphasize heightened accountability and improved focus on overall objectives, both features of the performance management concept. But it does not embrace some of the other key features of contemporary performance management models, particularly the comprehensive aligning and linking of individual and unit performance targets to a cyclical plan for organizational achievement.

It is not uncommon for governments to adopt mandatory performance management frameworks extending to many agencies and enterprises. Such across-the-board implementation involves serious risks. In the United States, the failed

---

performance pay Extra compensation for extraordinary efforts on the job.

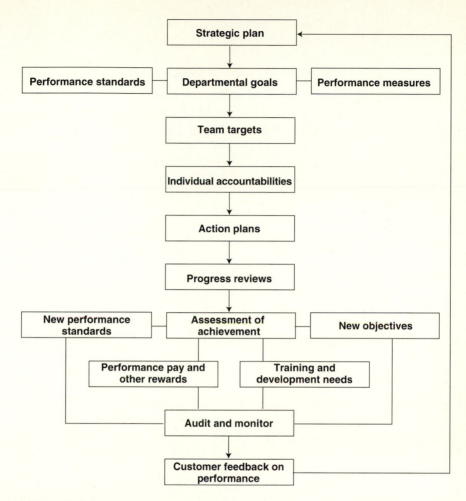

Figure 7.1 The Performance Management Cycle

implementation of PPBS (Planning-Programming-Budgeting Systems) by the Johnson administration (1963–1969) and zero-based budgeting in the Carter administration (1977–1981) has left a profound skepticism as to the feasibility of national implementation of complex public sector management systems. The risks include the likelihood of major differences in agency preparedness, shortages, and competition for the limited number of highly skilled staff familiar with the new approach and its requirements, and, in the past, a lack of reliable and comparable basic data concerning agency performance. Nevertheless, governments may attempt to shoot for across-the-board implementation of performance management because of its promise to address some of the most important standing challenges facing any government—the need for enhanced accountability, the need to know what is happening on a systematic and comparable basis, the need to link agency effort to government objectives, and the need to harmonize budgeting, planning, and staffing actions. These are such fundamental issues that the offer of performance management to systematically address them is hard to turn down.

The Politics of Performance Management

Performance management begins with a plan. It is tempting to think of planning as a rational, linear, straightforward process of collecting and analyzing data, establishing and assigning priorities to strategic targets, assessing alternative methods for achieving ends, designing implementation programs, and evaluating programs so as to use the information to improve program and agency impact and performance. However, this is an illusion. Planning is neither straightforward nor linear. Planning never occurs in a vacuum; it is an inherently political process. Consequently, the success of a plan of any kind is often a function of the political astuteness of the planner. Things are still the same as they were in 1788, when Alexander Hamilton advised in *The Federalist*, No. 70, "Men often oppose a thing merely because they have had no agency in planning it, or because it may have been planned by those whom they dislike."

In the public sector, plans often begin out of political necessity. The citizens literally vote for the plans espoused by elected political executives in their campaign promises. For example, Jimmy Carter promised, if elected president, to implement zero-based budgeting. He was and did—but his successor, Ronald Reagan, used an executive order to abolish zero-based budgeting for the federal government on his first day in office. Rudolph W. Giuliani ran for mayor of New York in 1993 promising to reduce crime. During his first year in office, crime—especially the murder rate—went down. Whether this was caused by changing demographics or better police management, nobody really knows. What is certain is that the mayor—as any mayor would—took credit for the decline. In 1994 the Republican party offered a "contract with America" which would radically affect federal budgeting practices. Because of their electoral victory, many federal agencies had to begin planning for downsizing. And opposition party President Bill Clinton has been no less ambitious with his reinventing government plans to significantly reduce federal employment.

Performance management plans do not have to wait upon elected officials. In the early 1990s the postmaster general did not have to run for office to hear the political winds blowing. All he had to do was read the newspaper accounts of increasing criticisms of mail services, of members of Congress calling for the dismemberment of the Postal Service, and of business leaders calling for an end to the government's first-class mail monopoly. He got the message. Performance, meaning on-time mail delivery, started going up; complaints and calls for dismemberment started going down.

The most comprehensive adoption of performance management by the U.S. government to date has been the Government Performance and Results Act of 1993—sometimes known just as the "Results Act." This legislation is a typical performance management system in that it seeks to link resource allocations and results, to improve program performance, to provide better information for congressional policymaking, to force agencies to specify their missions, objectives and strategies, and to require them to advise the Congress on just how they've gone about the consultation process. The General Accounting office has been given a special role in monitoring the implementation of the Results Act. This is the most comprehensive performance management effort ever undertaken by the federal government. The GAO, in a 1997 report, explains why the Results Act should work when similar initiatives have failed:

- Where past efforts failed to link executive branch performance planning with measurement with congressional resource allocation, GPRA requires explicit consultation between the executive and legislative branches on agency strategic plans. Past initiative experiences suggest that efforts to link resources with results must begin in the planning phase with some fundamental understanding about program goals.
- Where past initiatives devised unique performance information formats often unconnected to the structures used in congressional budget presentations, GPRA requires agencies to plan and measure performance using the program activities listed in their budget submissions.
- Where past initiatives were generally unprepared for the difficulties associated with measuring the outcomes of federal programs and often resorted to simple output or workload measures, GPRA states a preference for outcome measures. Focusing on outcomes shifts the definition of accountability from the traditional focus on inputs processes and projects to a perspective centered on results.
- Past initiatives often foundered because there was no mechanism to reconcile legislative staff's concentration on oversighting, and near term performance with agency staff's emphasis on long-term goals, adaptability and flexibility in execution.

Management Control

Management information and **control** systems are instituted in public agencies for two primary reasons: (1) to allow administrators to find out what is going on in an organization (and in the environment as the result of an agency's activities) and thereby to manage the activities of others, and (2) to respond to the need to report (to be accountable) to external groups. Control systems are employed to see whether plans are being executed as intended, to monitor goal-oriented behavior, and to make corrections when behavior or results veer from planned goals. This monitoring is essential because organizational goals, quite simply, often get lost. This happens in part because organizations, as artificial entities, cannot have true goals; only people can. And people, despite the fact that they create or join organizations with professed goals, all too often have goals of their own that do not coincide with the ostensible goals of the organization.

The more an organization's stakeholders, the people affected directly or indirectly by the organization's activities, work toward their own separate goals, as opposed to the "official" goals of the organization, the more incompetent the organization must necessarily become. For example, while British incompetence during the American Revolution was caused only in part by structural rigidity, it was also aided by unclear and conflicting goals. The first priority for the British was

---

control That aspect of management concerned with the comparison of actual versus planned performance as well as the development and implementation of procedures to correct substandard performance. Control, which is inherent to all levels of management, is a feedback process that ideally should report only unexpected situations.

to keep its North American colonies as a vital source of raw materials for its factories and customers for its merchants. If the Brits had kept this mission clearly in mind—had followed strategies to accomplish this one purpose—the course of world history would have been very different. But the administrators in London allowed a second goal to affect their decisions: forcing subservient compliance on the upstarts. These two goals began to conflict, to cause the British government to take actions that steadily diminished its ability to accomplish either purpose.

Organizational goals get displaced when employees become more concerned with what they can get out of, as opposed to what they must contribute to, the organization. The most essential task of a manager, indeed the "function of the executive," as Chester I. Barnard asserted, is to maintain the "dynamic equilibrium" between the needs of the organization and the needs of its employees. The performance management movement toward "quality" and instilling a customer service orientation is essentially an effort to forestall or prevent incompetence by aligning stakeholders' goals and bringing them to the forefront. The power of performance management is that it is a linking or integrative framework by which vital components of the management process are identified and connected in a meaningful pattern. For example, it links the separate management systems within an agency such as the budgeting, staffing, performance measurement, and individual performance appraisal systems. It links the wishes of the top with service delivery at the bottom; those at the center of decision making are linked with those responsible away from the center for delivering programs and dealing with customers. It can be made to link effort to reward through performance pay at the individual level and through the shifting of priorities at the organizational unit level. It is the absence of this linking process that is one of the chief causes of wasted, duplicated, or ineffective activity. The extent to which the performance management approach can provide focus and links within the organization is undoubtedly a key reason for its power, an explanation for its increasing acceptance, and a basis for the enthusiasm with which it is now being adopted.

Contracting for Performance

Intimately associated with performance management is the concept of contracting. Individual or organizational goals set in the framework of performance management are frequently embodied in a structure of quasi-commercial **contracts**. Such contracts, whether formal, informal, or only psychological, exist between supervisors and subordinates and are often used for performance appraisals. However, the analogy can be, and in some public sector settings is, also extended to the organizational level. In this extension, the organizational service contracts may be external—between a cen-

---

contract An agreement that affects the legal relationships between two or more persons. To be a contract, an agreement must involve at least one promise, consideration (something of value promised or given), persons legally capable of making binding agreements, and a reasonable amount of agreement between the persons as to what the contract means. A contract is called bilateral if both sides expressly make promises (such as the promise to deliver a book on one side and a promise to pay for it on the other) or unilateral if the promises are on one side only (usually because the other side has already done its part).

tral government department that funds a program and the dispersed agencies that receive funds and must deliver agreed levels of performance. Or they may be intraorganizational between the chief executive of an agency and a particular division; for example, the mayor of Philadelphia allows department heads to keep (for their departments) a portion of cost savings for favored new projects. Such arrangements provide a setting where the **contracting out** of any particular role and function is simplified, since expectations, roles, and rewards can be made very clear. The contracts involved may be binding—supported by the full force of the law—or they may be less formal quasi-contracts in which respective roles and responsibilities are defined, but neither the law nor real sanctions for nonperformance apply.

Performance management provides a series of conceptual links within an organization, designed to align and direct effort toward agreed ends. People need to know how the work they have agreed with their supervisor to do "fits into the picture." A unit head needs to see how the work of the unit contributes. An agency executive needs to see how the agency's work fits against the goals of the elected officials. But a conceptual link is all too often not enough. A system of rewards and sanctions may be needed to make the conceptual links into the formal contracts that define roles and responsibilities. Any comprehensive performance management system will operate through both individual and organizational unit contracts.

Individual Contracts

The phrase "individual employment contract" does not strike the ear kindly if one has any sympathy with the history of the **labor movement**. This was the traditional justification that employers used against collective bargaining (see Chapter 10); that since every worker had an individual contract with the employer, collective efforts at negotiating a contract were superfluous. Indeed, until the nineteenth century, employee efforts at collective bargaining were considered criminal conspiracies by both employers and the law. How times change! Now individual employment contracts and performance contracts are becoming commonplace in the public sector. And it is no accident that this is occurring during a period of labor union decline.

An individual employment contract may simply state the role, responsibilities, and terms of conditions under which a person is employed, without providing much detail on performance objectives sought and how performance is to be matched with rewards and sanctions. A performance contract, however, is an employment

contracting out Having work performed outside an organization's own workforce. Contracting out is often an area of union-management disagreement, especially in the public sector. While many unions recognize management's right to occasionally subcontract a job requiring specialized skills and equipment not possessed by the organization or its employees, they oppose the letting of work that could be done by the organization's own workforce. In particular, unions are concerned if work normally performed by its members is contracted out to firms having inferior wages or working conditions or if such action may result in reduced earnings or layoffs of regular employees. Contracting out is one of the major means of privatizing and thus reducing the size of the public sector.

labor movement An inclusive phrase for the progressive history of unionism in the United States. Sometimes it is used in a broader sense to encompass the fate of the workers. The political influence of American unions has been declining precipitously in recent decades. In 1955, close to 40 percent of all nonfarm workers belonged to unions. By the late 1990s, that number had dropped to about 13 percent.

contract in which specific goals are required of the employee within the term of the contract, and significant rewards and sanctions are included—especially financial rewards that will be paid if certain key targets are met. Such contracts are rarely applied to all jobs within an agency. Two areas in which they are frequently found however are (1) at the level of the chief executive and his or her most senior executives, and (2) in those other areas where measurable output improvement can conveniently be made the subject of rewards.

Executive-level performance contracts, especially those outside of the United States, are often secret. The details of the performance objectives to be rewarded may be secret, too. One chief executive of a public enterprise in New Zealand is reputed to have had over 400 particular targets written into his contract; another in Australia was to be rewarded according to the alteration in the credit rating status accorded to the government by the Standard and Poors ratings agency during the term of the contract. There is often a degree of skepticism and suspicion associated with secret contracts of this nature, where there is likely to be no independent public audit of the validity of the goals, of their measurement, of the contribution of the individual to their attainment, or as to their relative weightings. Yet on the other hand, it is surely not unreasonable for a senior manager to seek a contract that is quite explicit as to what he or she will be judged on, and in which there are good rewards for the attainment of difficult goals.

Senior executive performance contracts are also a matter for debate, but perhaps they are less contentious than secret top-level contracts suspected to contain "hidden agendas." Senior executive **performance pay** was contained in the **senior executive service** package adopted by the federal government in 1979. Today at least 20 states also have senior executive management systems that allow for flexibility in the assignments of individual executives. A senior executive below the chief executive is likely to have more focused goals—perhaps responsibility for a particular organizational unit or outcome. In this regard, senior executive performance contracts may be more concrete and clearly task-focused than those of chief executives. However, controversy remains. How much of the effort being rewarded is due to the executive and how much to subordinates? How difficult were the constraints on goal achievement? What unforeseen diversions in responsibility were placed on the person? How adequately were ongoing, time-consuming, but unglamorous functions of the job recognized? How finely tuned was the system of performance assessment and how fair were its results? The questions raised are significant, and the outcome to date in many jurisdictions is equivocal.

Contracts for Organizational Performance

The performance management model is distinguished by its twin concerns for individual and organizational performance and for linking these. Thus it is not surpris-

---

performance pay Any formal system of one-time bonuses or permanent salary increases for above average on-the-job efforts.

senior executive service (SES) The federal government's top management corps, established by the Civil Service Reform Act of 1978.

ing that emphasis on individual performance contracting is matched by the development of contracting approaches to organizational performance.

Capture theory is the proposition advanced by public choice theorists that government agencies will tend to become captured by employees or clients at the expense of the governments that seek to direct them. Organizational performance contracts seek to prevent such "captures" by closely connecting an agency's work to the will of its masters—presumably representative of the people. Notwithstanding public choice theories, however, it is clearly reasonable for an organizational unit to seek express relationships with its masters as to the performance expected, and the rewards and sanctions that will apply. There are a variety of versions of such contracts; in general, their adoption provides a setting in which privatization—whether in the form of competitive tendering, contracting-out, franchising or divestiture—is somewhat facilitated through the process of making goals, rewards, and sanctions explicit. This is an added attraction for their adoption in some jurisdictions.

The Purchaser-Provider Model

The purchaser-provider model is one of the most common and important variants of organizational performance contracting. The model is applicable to circumstances in which a government wishes to obtain certain program objectives to be delivered through a variety of agencies. The government, which votes funds, is the purchaser—its role is to specify the desired outcomes and to enter into contracts with others who will deliver the services. Those who deliver the services—the providers—may be other agencies of the same government. But they could also be agencies of another level of government, state or local. They could be nonprofit organizations or business firms. The purchaser-provider distinction views the purchaser role as a core role of government; the service delivery role, because it is to be judged strictly on performance efficiency criteria, could be played by a variety of institutions—public, private, or in between. Thus the contracts that link the purchaser, say a health department, to its providers—hospitals or medical practitioners—are performance contracts.

Sometimes the structure of arrangements within an organization is analogous to a purchaser-provider arrangement. Here a set of service agreements may be entered into between a central organization and its delivery units—for example, between a board of education and its local schools, between a police department and its local precincts, or between a federal agency and its field offices. Such service agreements may in most respects replicate a purchaser-provider contract but be less formal in structure.

The most comprehensive adoption of internal contracting within government departments occurs in New Zealand, where a hierarchy of contractual relationships has been established within departments. The minister, instead of being viewed as the person in whose name the work of the department is done (the traditional position of a minister within the **Westminster model** of government), is defined as purchaser.

Westminster model The parliamentary system used in the United Kingdom (the Houses of Parliament are located in the Palace at Westminster). It forms the basis of parliamentary government in most countries of the former British Commonwealth of Nations.

He or she enters into a purchase contract with the departmental head, to purchase for the coming year certain services on behalf of the government. This purchase agreement is quite lengthy and specific, and it defines exactly what it is that the government is buying. In parallel, the minister enters into a chief executive performance agreement with the chief executive specifying individual goals and rewards. Within the department, individual staff and their units are bound by a range of additional contracts. This overall process is also at the heart of the Next Steps reforms (see Chapter 3) adopted in Britain.

In the United States, local governments have long used **service contracts**. According to the International City Management Association, most U.S. cities and towns contract for some services, most typically for such professional, one-time services as engineering or architectural consulting, auditing, and legal counsel. Contracting for short-term professional services rarely is controversial. However, some municipalities contract for a much wider variety of services, including vehicle towing, refuse collection, street lighting, tree trimming, operation of public hospitals, municipal data processing services, animal control, planning/zoning, library management, and (in rare instances) such public safety functions as police and fire protection. Municipal privatization through franchising is also common—and usually noncontroversial—for such services as cable television, taxicab operations, and ambulance services.

The various forms of privatization and contracting out continue to add new terminology to the language of public administration. A major example is the public-private partnership, a term representing arrangements in which a public agency and a private corporation work together. It may be that the partnership is simply one of contracting out or "outsourcing"; it may be a franchise arrangement in which government sets quite strict performance requirements for a service; or it may be a fully integrated long-term joint venture in which government and business combine their skills and organizations to deliver a product or service. Such partnerships include those under contracting out, or franchising, where government is clearly the principal and the private sector the contractor; but they differ from privatization, in which the initiative is passed wholly to the private sector. Under a public-private partnership, government may just be one member of a team of organizations with a shared vision or purpose.

Productivity Improvement

Productivity in private and public sector organizations has become the overriding issue in top management suites as well as in the legislative corridors of power. The ultimate aim of all performance management efforts is greater productivity. Productivity is a measured relationship between the quantity (and quality) of results produced and the quantity of resources required for the production of goods or services. Productivity is, in essence, a measure of the work efficiency of an individual, a work unit, or a whole organization.

---

service contract An agreement between local units of government for one unit (usually larger) to provide a service for another (usually smaller). It is often called the Lakewood plan, because it was first extensively used between the County of Los Angeles and the City of Lakewood, California.

Productivity Measurement

Measuring the productivity of any jurisdiction, organization, program, or individual is particularly problematic in the public sector because of the problem of defining outputs and of quantifying measures of efficiency, effectiveness, and impact.

Organizations that provide public services often have multiple and sometimes intangible outputs. In evaluating efficiency, selecting from among the many possible input/output ratios is troublesome. A considerable danger exists in selecting only certain input and output variables because a single efficiency measure may be, in truth, a meaningless or oversimplified measure of performance.

The productivity measurement issue is further complicated by the fact that different efficiency and effectiveness measures must be selected depending upon certain organizational variables: highly routine work versus nonroutine work; high or low degrees of employee discretion; outputs that are standard or novel; or simple as opposed to complex work processes. Another way of stating this problem is that from the variety of available productivity measures, those selected must differentiate between intermediate outputs (outputs used by other members of the organization) and final outputs (those absorbed by the outside environment) and between staff and line functions (some individuals/units perform support functions whose impact can be assessed only in terms of increased performance of line departments). Productivity measurement is beset by many obstacles, not the least of which is the insecurity felt by managers attempting to undertake productivity assessments.

And none of this is new. In 1776 Adam Smith in his *Wealth of Nations* wrote: "The labor of some of the most respectable orders in the society is, like that of menial servants, unproductive of any value, and does not fix or realize itself in any permanent subject or vendible commodity, which endures after that labor is past." The eternal problem is that in some areas, when government produces a service, the labor that goes into it cannot be measured as to impact and evaluated as to quality as if it were a manufactured product. Thus it is easy to measure and even improve government productivity when factory-like operations lend themselves to engineered **work measurement standard**s. But service workers such as police officers, social workers, and grade school guidance counselors do not always create a product that is directly measurable except by broad **social indicators**.

Barriers to Productivity Improvement

The barriers to increased public employee productivity are legion. They can often appear insurmountable: cumbersome and rigid civil service procedural rules that prevent management from reallocating and reorganizing work; a public personnel management approach that has created endless, cumbersome, inflexible systems of position descriptions, job classifications, testing and Equal Employment Opportunity and Affirmative Action requirements, which in combination have resulted in

---

work measurement standard A numerical value applied to the units of work an employee or group can be expected to produce in a given period of time.

social indicators Statistical measures that aid in the description of conditions in the social environment (e.g., measures of income distribution, poverty, crime, health, physical environment).

what Wallace Sayre called a "triumph of techniques over purpose"; union intransigence; and combinations of procedural and structural rules that inhibit management's ability to reward and punish workers for performance or lack thereof.

The public sector productivity problem also ties directly into the privatization debate. Again, there are assumptions about inferior public sector versus private sector productivity rates. Although researchers such as Downs and Larkey have gone to great lengths to explain why these comparisons cannot be made, are not made correctly, and should not be made in the first place, the simple truth remains that the burden is on public sector organizations to demonstrate that they are not inferior in terms of their productivity. This is doubly difficult because productivity in the public sector frequently involves multiple client groups and conflicting objectives and priorities. In comparison, private sector counterparts like to make single horizontal comparisons and to stack one set of products or services against another.

Public sector organizations can certainly be faulted for not being willing to do productivity measurements, but one should be clear about both the context and reasons for that unwillingness. There are far too many system "disincentives" built into productivity measurement, from fears of having budgets cut, personnel levels trimmed, or other penalties for producing above budgeted levels, to the serious measurement problems that are inherently biased against public sector goods and products.

There is yet another major difference to be considered. There is a common assumption that private sector organizations use productivity measurement and improvement in the same way public sector organizations do. They do not. Most private sector organizations use productivity measurement systems to assign more work, more responsibility, more financial reward, more capital resources, and more power to the units that demonstrate the highest levels of productivity. They do not cut the most productive units. Instead they tend to give them more resources or more rewards. This also affects the investment strategy that goes into productivity improvement efforts. Most public sector organizations commission productivity efforts by assignment without up-front investment. In other words, staff members are reassigned or reprogrammed to take on productivity responsibilities. In short, productivity improvement endeavors must be financed internally. In contrast, private sector organizations expect to pay up-front costs to start a productivity measurement or participative management effort and then evaluate the results against total costs.

Because it traditionally has been so difficult for government organizations, already fiscally strapped, to find the funds to invest in productivity improvement efforts (especially new technology), many jurisdictions have created "innovation funds" to finance such ventures. For example, both the Internal Revenue Service and the state of Florida use this approach. The city of Philadelphia uses savings from cost-cutting for productivity improvement. Mayor Ed Rendell told the National Performance Review Staff, "We tell a department, 'You go out there and do good work. You produce more revenue. You cut waste. And we'll let you keep some of the savings of the increased revenue.'"

Traditionally, the mayor said, "every nickel that they would have saved would have gone right back to the general fund . . . They would have gotten a pat on the back, but nothing else." Now municipal departments can keep some of the money they save to finance productivity improvement projects. For example, when Philadelphia's Department of Licenses and Inspection generated $2.8 million more than expected in 1992, the city let the department keep $1 million of the savings to hire more inspectors, which in turn led to increased collections in subsequent years.

The National Performance Review *Report* states that Philadelphia "also opened a Productivity Bank, from which departments can borrow for investment-type projects—that is, capital equipment—to produce either savings or enough revenues to repay the loan in five years. To ensure that departments don't apply frivolously, the city subtracts loan payments from annual departmental budgets."

A major thrust of the performance management movement is to refocus thinking about how to increase productivity. If so much of government work does not lend itself effectively to productivity measurement, the solution may be to change the nature of the work to either make it amenable to measurement or subject it to the competition of the marketplace.

Total Quality Management

Although comprehensive productivity improvement movements have taken different shapes, developed much jargon, and took off in many directions in the 1980s and 1990s, the origins of all of them can be traced back to **W. Edwards Deming** and his 1950 trip to Japan. Deming, a New York University professor, was invited by Japanese executives to teach them his approach to **statistical quality control**. Joseph Juran, who emphasizes the "management" part of "quality," followed Deming to Japan in 1954. In turn, Armand V. Feigenbaum followed Juran with "total quality control" (TQC), a management approach that required all employees to participate in quality improvement activities—from the chair of the board to hourly workers, from suppliers to customers, and the community.

By 1975, Japan had developed into the world leader in quality and productivity. In contrast, "quality teachings" were mostly ignored in the United States. According to Keki Bhote, "Deming's popularity in Japan was in contrast to an almost total ignorance about him in the United States. . . . Deming remained in the quality wilderness of America for a whole generation."

W. Edwards Deming (1900–1993) The professor of management who developed his philosophy of customer service and statistical quality control while working at AT&T's Hawthorne plant (see Chapter 6) in the 1920s and 1930s.

statistical quality control A statistical technique for maintaining product quality at the desired level without 100-percent inspection. Statistical quality control uses acceptance sampling to determine whether a large lot of finished products meets preset quality levels. Using statistical techniques, a random sample is taken from a lot of goods and the sample is inspected. From this analysis, an inference as to the quality level of the entire lot is made. This technique is often used in conjunction with periodic inspection along the production line that permits corrective action to be taken before finally assembly of the product.

Box 7.2

The Emperor Caligula Finds a "Double Economy" in Government

[In ancient Rome] the money went faster and faster and at last Caligula decided to make economies. He said one day, for instance, "What is the use of putting men in prison for forgery and theft and breaches of the peace? They don't enjoy themselves there and they are a great expense for me to feed and guard; yet if I were to let them go they would only start their career of crime again. I'll visit the prisons today and look into the matter." He did. He weeded out the men whom he considered the most hardened criminals, and had them executed. Their bodies were cut up and used as meat for the wild beasts waiting to be killed in the amphitheatre: which made it a double economy.

Source: Robert Graves, *I, Claudius* (New York: Modern Library, 1934).

If any one event can be said to have triggered the total quality movement in the United States, it was a June 24, 1980, NBC television documentary, "If Japan Can . . . Why Can't We?" The program documented Deming's experiences and successes in Japan. The response was overwhelming. Within months, hundreds of major U.S. corporations and government agencies had scrambled aboard the quality bandwagon. Quality circles—voluntary work groups that cut across organizational layers and boundaries to analyze and recommend solutions to organizational problems—appeared everywhere as if by magic.

In 1991 the U.S. Government Accounting Office defined "quality management":

> A leadership philosophy that demands a relentless pursuit of quality and the stamina for continuous improvement in all aspects of operations: product, service, processes, and communications. The major components of quality management are leadership, a customer focus, continuous improvement, employee empowerment. . . .

"How to Do It" TQM materials are now abundant, but Deming's 14 points of management is its most famous formulation. Note how Deming's "theory of TQM" is the intellectual descendent of Jomini's (see Chapter 5) principles of war—a road map for organizational, as opposed to military, victory. In *Out of the Crisis* Deming provides this 14-point guide, which we have paraphrased, for would-be quality managers:

1. Create constancy of purpose for improvement of product and service. (A long-term focus is thus essential.)
2. Adopt the new philosophy. (Be prepared for a total transformation.)
3. Cease dependence on mass inspections. (Quality must be built in; defects must be prevented rather than detected.)

4. End the practice of awarding business on the basis of price tag alone. (Low bids lead to low quality. Long-term relationships must be established with single suppliers.)

5. Improve constantly and forever the system of production and service. (Continuous improvement becomes a philosophy, not just a goal.)

6. Institute training. (Training at all organizational levels is a necessity, not an option.)

7. Adopt and institute leadership. (Managers must lead, not supervise.)

8. Drive out fear. (All employees must feel secure enough to express ideas and ask questions.)

9. Break down barriers between staff areas. (Work in organizations is inherently teamwork.)

10. Eliminate slogans, exhortations, and targets for the workforce. (Problems are caused by the system; not by individuals. Posters and slogans tend to create resentment.)

11. Eliminate numerical quotas for the workforce and numerical goals for people in management. (Production quotas yield defective products; replace work standards with intelligent leadership.)

12. Remove barriers that rob people of pride of workmanship. (The individual performance appraisal is a barrier, not an aid, to productivity.)

13. Encourage education and self-improvement for everyone. (Education never ends, for anybody at any level of the organization.)

14. Take action to accomplish the transformation. (Both top management and employee commitment is essential.)

Even though Deming was a Ph.D. in physics (Yale, 1928) and the world's leading authority on statistical quality control, he believed—and he wrote and he preached—that the key to quality was organizational culture and management philosophy, that "85 percent" of quality problems were caused by management, not employee, errors. The biggest problem here is a lack of a sustaining vision from the top, a "lack of constancy of purpose." This problem is identical in both the private and public sectors. In the private sector the pressures of the quarterly dividend and the **annual report** force managers to think short term. If they do not look good soon, they will soon be out of a job. The pressure is the same in the public sector but for a different reason; there a short-term perspective is created by the short-term nature of elected public offices. TQM is necessarily long-term. There is no quick fix.

Deming, being a quantitative type, loved to make lists. So while he offered 14 points to transform an organization, he also warned of 7 deadly diseases and 16

---

annual report The report most corporations are legally required to provide each year to stockholders and to the government. Most companies also make it freely available to the public. The report usually contains a balance sheet, statements of income, spending, retained earnings, and other financial data, plus a breakdown of the company's stocks and bonds, an explanation of accounting principles used, an auditor's report, comments about the year's business and future prospects, etc.

W. Edwards Deming proselytizing on TQM. Deming first went to Japan in 1947. His job, as a civilian employee of the U.S. occupation authorities, was to help arrange for a national census. Becoming interested in Japanese culture and society, he frequently socialized with the Japanese. In 1950 he was invited by the Union of Japanese Scientists and Engineers to give a series of lectures on statistical quality control—first in Tokyo, then in other major cities. As he was being paid by the U.S. government, Deming refused all payment—and even allowed his hosts to freely translate and publish his lectures. The lectures sold so well that in 1951 the royalties were used to endow the now highly-coveted Deming Prize, which is still given •

obstacles that tended to inhibit or altogether prevent such transformation. As Steve Wall, the director of Ohio's Office of Quality Services told Jonathan Walters in *Governing* "This [TQM] isn't about hitting home runs. This is about hitting single after single after single. You score a lot more runs that way." The problem is too many managers want to use TQM just to hit a few home runs so that they can look good and go on to higher positions.

TQM is further hampered by an emphasis on short-term profits (in the private sector) or short-term "looking good" results (in the public sector). The whole thrust of TQM is to change the organizational culture to one that values long-term, long-lasting effectiveness. This is why Deming finds short-term numerical ratings of productivity or individuals to be ineffective. Deming believes the effects of annual performance appraisals or management by numbers to be devastating. "Management by fear would be a better name." Such systems force managers to manage defects rather than lead toward constant quality.

Still the question must be asked, as Albert C. Hyde of the Brookings Institution puts it: "Is it a fad, or is it for real?" Hyde laments the fact that "for over two decades the public management experience seems to replicate one management fad after another, each promising more and delivering less. Little wonder that there is so much cynicism about quality management." Yet quality seems to be a major movement now.

Most public sector organizations are now concerned with installing if not the reality, at least the veneer of quality in their programs. One example of helping with the veneer of quality is the removal of clocks from post office lobbies. The Postal Service asserts that this is designed to give post offices a more "retail" look and is most emphatically not designed to inhibit "customers from watching their lives tick away while buying stamps." According to Postal Service spokesperson Sandra Harding, "Clocks look bureaucratic. They are not an imperative part of the post office experience." Nevertheless, the Postal Service is jumping on the quality bandwagon. The October 1, 1995 *New York Times* ran this advertisement:

QUALITY MANAGEMENT PROFESSIONALS . . . THIS IS YOUR OPPORTUNITY! . . . The United States Postal Service is seeking Quality Professionals with a successful track record in implementing TQM. . . . In addition to excellent communication, consulting and interpersonal skills, successful candidates will possess:
- strong process management and policy management skills
- problem-solving skills, proven history of delivering concrete, quantifiable results
- ability to work with senior management in a team environment
- staff management skills (management positions)
- experience in designing and evaluating TQM training materials
- ability to effectively integrate new quality tools/techniques such as benchmarking. . . .

And the Postal Service was not looking for just one person; it was recruiting a whole team.

Quality Is Free shouts the title of a book by Philip Crosby, urging organizations to constantly do their best and focus on the needs of the customers. It's "free" because it doesn't really cost any more to do your best as an individual or as an organization. But what does cost is superficial hypocritical quality—the quality that is touted but not delivered. This reduces the perception of the organization's competence in the eyes of both its employees and its customers. The slogan of the Ford Motor Company is "Quality is Job 1." But you only have to have owned one Ford car with a few minor defects to see the slogan as cynical.

Quality must be consistent. A case can even be made that consistent mediocrity is better than high quality goals that are not consistently met. For example, consider this actual scene in a large Brooklyn post office, as reported by the *New York Times*. A long line of impatient customers stood before the one open service window. "All at once, five postal workers appeared carrying a ladder, balloons, and a banner that read, CUSTOMER APPRECIATION WEEK. Slowly, the workers proceeded to hang the banner. The customer line, meanwhile, barely moved." When one of the customers who had been waiting more than half an hour in line pointed out to the leader of this "banner group" that it was inconsistent to have only one postal worker serving customers at the window while her group was hanging the "customer appreciation" banner, the response he got was: "Oh that! That doesn't start until next week." All those quality experts that the Postal Service is hiring certainly have a big job ahead of them!

It's the Customer, Stupid!

Bill Clinton's 1992 presidential campaign headquarters had what became a famous sign on its wall: "It's the economy, stupid!" This was designed to keep the campaign focused. Similarly, all public managers might well keep a sign on their walls that reads: "It's the customer, stupid!" The customer is government's new focus. And governments at all levels would be "stupid" to forget it.

A customer service orientation is inherently part of the workplace quality movement. And, in line with TQM theory, it means not just good service in the present but a constant striving for continuously better service. The 1993 National Performance Review listed the following eight principles to govern the provision of customer service:

1. Survey customers frequently to find out what kind and quality of services they want.
2. Post standards and results measured against them.
3. Benchmark performance against "the best in business."
4. Provide choices in both source of service and delivery means.
5. Make information, services, and complaint systems easily accessible.
6. Handle inquiries and deliver services with courtesy.
7. Provide pleasant surroundings for customers.
8. Provide redress for poor services.

All federal agencies dealing directly with the public, in line with principle 2 above, must now issue standards of performance that the public can expect of them. For example, the Postal Service standards include the following:

1. Your first class mail will be delivered anywhere in the United States within 3 days.
2. Your local first class mail will be delivered overnight.
3. You will receive service at post office counters within 5 minutes.
4. You can get postal information 24 hours a day by calling a local number.

You may well snicker at standard number 3—especially if you have gone to any big city post office at lunch time. But at least now there is a standard about which you can complain. A standard violated is better than no standard at all. Besides most people are happy with their mail service. According to a U.S. News/CNN poll reported in *U.S. News & World Report* on March 13, 1995, eight out of nine Americans are basically satisfied with their mail services. About 10 percent of all citizens give their individual mail carriers cash presents at Christmas. Can you think

Box 7.3

The Management Fad Cycle

The average management fad, like the average love affair, goes through a fairly predictable cycle from infatuation to disillusionment. First, a management guru comes up with an idea, coins a buzzword, and sweet-talks the press. Next, one or two big companies, threatened with bankruptcy or desperate to seem with it, give the idea a go. Stories are published about sensational results, the corporate world clamors for advice, and the guru forms a million-dollar consultancy. Finally, some business-school professor produces an authoritative report arguing that the fad is a fraud; the press discovers a raft of sensational failures; and the guru, muttering that he was misunderstood, comes up with another idea.

Source: The *Economist*, July 2, 1994.

of any other group of public employees who are so regularly given such cash "tips"? Actually it is quite dangerous to offer cash to other public employees—especially police officers who stop you for a traffic violation or an Internal Revenue Service auditor examining your tax returns. They and the local district attorney may think you are offering them a bribe instead of showing them the kind of affection so many Americans reserve for their mail carriers at Christmas.

In the 1950s when Ronald Reagan, then an actor, was hosting the TV program *General Electric Theater*, he would close each episode by reminding the audience, on behalf of the sponsor, that "progress is our most important product." Many governments today are picking up on this product orientation by asserting, in effect, that "service is our most important product." Service for whom? The citizens. That is why the purveyors of these services are historically and rightly called public servants. The only thing really new here is that the public sector has picked up a word more traditionally used in private business—customer. So the public is now the customer. And a customer service orientation simply means that all activities are focused on pleasing the customer. That has always been known by the best businesses, and governments are increasingly becoming aware of it.

Summary

Managerialism as a term has long been used by sociologists as a reference to the economic and bureaucratic elites that run an industrial society. In the 1980s this well-established sociological "ism" took on new connotations when the British government sought to refocus the civil service from policy toward management. Now managerialism is used worldwide to refer to efforts to force the bureaucracy to be more responsive to the needs of its customers. Thus it is no longer sufficient for public managers to be the traditional "neutral guns for hire." They are now expected to be policy entrepreneurs who forcefully develop creative solutions to vexing problems.

There are three major aspects to managerialism: (1) reengineering, which takes reorganization beyond its traditional focus by seeking to totally rethink and refocus how programs are managed and to take maximum advantage of new technology—especially computers; (2) empowering others, which reflects the paradox that managers can often make themselves more powerful by giving power away; and (3) entrepreneurialism, which calls for managers to be transformational leaders who strive to change organizational culture—to develop a new vision for the organization and then convert that vision into reality.

Performance management, the primary responsibility of an organizational leader, is the systematic integration of an organization's efforts to achieve its objectives. It includes the comprehensive control, audit, and evaluation of all aspects of organizational performance. Closely associated with this is the concept of contracting, because individual or organizational goals are often embodied in quasi-commercial contracts.

Measuring the productivity of any jurisdiction, organization, program, or individual is particularly problematic in the public sector because of the problem of defining outputs and of quantifying measures of efficiency, effectiveness, and impact. Total quality management programs require all employees to participate in quality improvement activities; the thrust is to change the organizational culture to one that values long-term, lasting effectiveness. A customer service orientation is inherently part of the workplace quality movement. This means not just good service in the present but a constant striving for better service.

Key Concepts

empowerment   Giving a person or organization the formal authority to do something.

management control   That aspect of management concerned with the comparison of actual versus planned performance, as well as the development and implementation of procedures to correct substandard performance.

managerial revolution   James Burham's concept that as control of large businesses moved from the original owners to professional managers, society's new governing class became not the traditional possessors of wealth but those having the professional expertise to manage, to lead, large organizations.

managerialism   An entrepreneurial approach to public management that emphasizes management rights and a reinvigorated scientific management.

new public management   A disparate group of structural reforms and informal management initiatives that reflects the doctrine of managerialism in the public sector.

performance management   The systematic integration of an organization's efforts to achieve its objectives.

productivity   A measured relationship between the quantity (and quality) of results produced and the quantity of resources required for production. Productivity is, in essence, a measure of the work efficiency of an individual, a work unit, or a whole organization.

reengineering   The fundamental rethinking and redesign of organizational processes to achieve significant improvements in critical measures of performance, such as costs or quality of services.

self-directed work team   A work group that will accept responsibility for their processes and products—as well as the behavior of other group members.

total quality management (TQM)   A new phrase for quality control in its most expanded sense of a total and continuing concern for quality in the production of goods and services.

Bibliography

Aristotle. (1952). *Politics*, trans. B. Jowett. Chicago: Great Books, Encyclopedia Britannica.

Barnard, Chester I. (1938). *The Functions of the Executive*. Cambridge: Harvard University Press.

Barzelay, M. (1992). *Breaking Through Bureaucracy: A New Vision for Managing in Government*. Berkeley: University of California Press.

Bhote, Keki R. (1991). *World Class Quality*. New York: Amacom.

Bowen, D. E., and E. E. Lawler III. (1992). "The Empowerment of Service Workers: What, Why, How, and When." *Sloan Management Review* (spring).

Burnham, James. *The Managerial Revolution*. New York: John Day, 1941.

Crosby, P. B. (1979). *Quality is Free*. New York: McGraw-Hill.

———. (1984). *Quality Without Tears*. New York: McGraw-Hill.

Deming, W. E. (1986). *Out of the Crisis*. Cambridge: MIT Press.

———. (1993). *The New Economics*. Cambridge: MIT Press.

Djilas, Milovan. (1957). *The New Class*. New York: Praeger.

Downs, G., and P. D. Larkey. (1986). *The Search for Government Efficiency*. New York: Random House.

Dynes, Michael, and David Walker. (1995). *The New British State*. London: Times Books.

Fiegenbaum, Armand V. (1983). *Total Quality Control*. New York: McGraw-Hill.

Galbraith, John Kenneth. (1998). *Letters to Kennedy*, ed. James Goodman. Cambridge: Harvard University Press.

Halachmi, Arie, and Geert Bouckaert, eds. (1995). *Public Productivity Through Quality and Strategic Management*. Amsterdam: IOS Press.

Hammer, Michael, and James Champy. (1993). *Reengineering the Corporation*. New York: HarperCollins.

Holzer, Marc. (1955). "Productivity and Quality Management." In *Handbook of Public Personnel Administration*, ed. Jack Rabin, et al. New York: Marcel Dekker.

Hughes, Owen. (1994). *Public Management and Administration*. London: Macmillan.

Hyde, Albert C. (1991). "Productivity Management for Public Sector Organizations." In *Public Management: The Essential Readings*, J. S. Ott, A. C. Hyde, and J. M. Shafritz., eds. Chicago: Lyceum Books/Nelson-Hall.

———. (1992). "Implications of Total Quality Management for the Public Sector." *Public Productivity and Management Review* 16 (fall).

International City Management Association. (1986). 1985 *Municipal Year Book*. Washington: ICMA.

Juran, J. M. (1992). J*uran On Quality By Design*. New York: Free Press.

Juran, J. M., and F. M. Gryna, eds. (1988). *Juran's Quality Control Handbook*, 4th ed. New York: McGraw-Hill.

Katzenbach, J. R., and D. K. Smith. (1993). *The Wisdom of Teams: Creating the High-Performance Organization*. Boston: Harvard Business School Press.

Lawler, E. E. III, S. A. Mohrman, and G. E. Ledford Jr. (1992). *Employee Involvement and Total Quality Management*. San Francisco: Jossey-Bass.

Linden, Russ. (1994). *MIS Report: Re-Engineering Local Government*. Washington: International City/County Management Association.

Marini, Frank E. (1971). *Toward a New Public Administration*. San Francisco: Chandler.

Martin, John. (1994). "Robert M. Melia: The Soul of a Child Support Machine." *Governing* (December).

M.I.T. Commission on Industrial Productivity. (1989). *Made in America: Regaining the Productive Edge*. Cambridge: MIT Press.

Mitroff, I. I. (1987). *Business Not as Usual*. San Francisco: Jossey-Bass.

Orsburn, J. D., L. Moran, E. Musselwhite, J. H. Zenger, with C. Perrin. (1990). *Self-directed Work Teams: The New American Challenge*. Homewood, IL: Business One Irwin.

Osborne, D., and T. Gaebler. (1992). *Reinventing Government: How the Entrepreneurial Spirit Is Transforming the Public Sector*. Reading, MA: Addison-Wesley.

Pascale, R. T., and A. G. Athos. (1981). *The Art of Japanese Management*. New York: Simon and Schuster.

Peters, T. J., and R. H. Waterman Jr. (1982). *In Search of Excellence*. New York: Harper and Row.

Plato. *The Republic*. (1925). Oxford: Clarendon Press.

Pollitt, Christopher. (1993). *Managerialism and the Public Services*, 2nd ed. Oxford, England: Blackwell.

Pollitt, Christopher, and Geert Bouckaert, eds. (1995). *Quality Improvement in European Public Services*. London: Sage.

Samuelson, Robert J. "The Death of Management." *Newsweek* (May 10, 1993).

Sayre, Wallace S. (1948). "The Triumph of Techniques Over Purpose." In *Public Administration Review*, Vol. 8 (spring).

Seidman, Harold. (1980). *Politics, Position, and Power*, 3rd ed. New York: Oxford University Press.

Tichy, N. M., and D. O. Ulrich. (1984). "The Leadership Challenge—A Call for the Transformational Leader." *Sloan Management Review* 26.

U.S. General Accounting Office. (1997). "Performance Budgeting: Past Initiatives Offer Insights for GPRA Implementation." Washington, DC: GAO (March).

Walters, Jonathan. (1994). "TQM: Surviving the Cynics." *Governing* (September).

Weisbord, M. R. (1991). *Productive Workplaces: Organizing and Managing for Dignity, Meaning, and Community*. San Francisco: Jossey-Bass.

White, Leonard D. (1933). *Trends in Public Administration*. New York: McGraw-Hill.

Xenophon. (1859). *The Anabasis or Expedition of Cyrus and the Memorabilia of Socrates*, trans. J. S. Watson. New York: Harper and Row.

Recommended Books

Hammer, Michael. (1996). *Beyond Reengineering: How the Process-Centered Organization Is Changing Our Work and Our Lives*. New York: HarperCollins. What to do after you reengineer, by the author who first popularized the concept.

Hilmer, Frederick G., and Lex Donaldson. (1996). *Management Redeemed: Debunking the Fads That Undermine Our Corporations*. New York: Free Press. An exposé on how the latest management trends all-too-often lead managers down "false trails."

Holzer, Marc, and Kathe Calahan. (1998). *Government at Work: Best Practices and Model Programs*. Thousand Oaks, CA: Sage. After presenting a model for comprehensive productivity improvement, the authors give an outstanding number of good examples in which such "best practices and model programs" are succeeding every day.

Pollitt, Christopher. (1993). *Managerialism and the Public Services*, 2nd ed. London: Blackwell. The first major work applying managerialism to public administration; unfortunately, it has decidedly difficult diction—a book more to be aware of than to read.

Related Web Sites

American Productivity and Quality Center
http://www.apqc.org

American Society for Quality Control
http://www.asqc.org

Best practices
http://web.bham.ac.uk/l.montiel/government/good.htm

Management tips
http://www.inc.com/301/management.html

Managerialism
http://labor.org.au/evatt/Efficiency.html

National Center for Public Productivity
http://andromeda.rutgers.edu/~ncpp/

National Institute of Standards and Technology Quality Program
http://www.quality.nist.gov

Performance measurement resources
http://www.npr.gov/library/resource/measure.html

Quality Network
http://www.quality.co.uk/quality/hometext.htm

Reengineering
http://www.utsi.com/wbp/reengineering/

W. Edwards Deming Institute
http://deming.org

8

Strategic Management in the Public Sector

Keynote: When Short-Term People Do Long-Term Planning

What Is Stragetic Management?

Objectives • The Planning Horizon • Capabilities • Environment

Four Strategic Factors

The Public-Private Paradox • The Importance of Being Close to the Center • Organizational Language and Culture • Organizational Place

Contemporary Strategic Challenges

The Challenge of Mandate • The Challenge of Efficiency • The Challenge of Competitiveness • The Challenge of Boundaries • The Challenge of Service • The Challenge of the Public Interest

Keynote: When Short-Term People Do Long-Term Planning

Strategic management—the achievement of long-term organizational goals—is not a tidy business. It is not that managers do not want to be neat; it is just that the managerial environment, especially in the public sector, is inherently and notoriously lacking in neatness. It is not exactly what the Scottish poet Robert Burns had in mind when he said that the "best laid schemes of mice and men" often go awry; it is instead that these plans are seldom comprehensive documents—if they exist at all. Often the overall strategy exists only as a vague document or unwritten philosophy. The full implementation of a strategic plan usually takes many years—sometimes decades or even more. The usefulness of a strategic plan is that it provides the long-term doctrine, the overall guidance, so essential for short-term, or tactical, management decisions.

Ancient Rome was into strategic management in a big way. Of course, there was no one single document entitled "The Strategic Plan for the Roman Empire" but all of its elements lay scattered about in various laws, policies, and proclamations. It was much like the British Constitution of today, unwritten but nevertheless thoroughly understood by all those with the responsibility for its implementation. Indeed, the process of strategic planning has always been done—especially in a military context where it began. However, the Romans of old were among the first to apply strategic concepts to the large-scale nonmilitary aspects of government as well.

Julius Caesar espoused a strategic doctrine that so enraged the Roman aristocracy they assassinated him in 44 B.C.E. Nevertheless, his successors implemented the plan that became known as the Pax Romana. This established relatively stable borders and co-opted possible opposition to Roman governance by expanding Roman citizenship. The several centuries of mostly peace that followed were made possible by a relatively small military establishment that was so well trained and managed that disturbances within the empire could be suppressed with the utmost efficiency and ruthlessness. An unremitting management discipline was the critical element in the tactical doctrine that provided for the peace and prosperity envisioned by the strategic plan.

In the twentieth century arguably the most significant single strategic plan has been the Truman Doctrine, the policy of President Harry S. Truman's administration of extending military and economic aid to those countries (originally Greece and Turkey) seeking to resist "totalitarian aggression." The Truman Doctrine became the corner-stone of the U.S. policy of containing (restricting the influence of) the Soviet Union, the underlying basis of U.S. foreign, military, and much of domestic policy after World War II. The demise of the Soviet Union in 1991 can be seen as the ultimate vindication of the containment strategy.

While there was broad agreement on the objective of containment, at least until the reaction against American involvement in Vietnam in the late 1960s, different strategies have been used to implement this objective. From 1947 until 1950, the emphasis was upon rebuilding allies in Western Europe; this massive infusion of economic aid became known as the Marshall Plan—so named by Truman to honor Secretary of State George C. Marshall Jr., who headed the U.S. Army during World War II. During the Korean War, the emphasis moved to actual fighting on the borders of the free world to prevent the spread of communism. The Eisenhower administration emphasized the possibility of nuclear retaliation. Then the Kennedy and Johnson administrations used containment as the rationale for massively escalating the limited war in Vietnam. The Nixon administration did not abandon containment but tried instead to uphold it through greater reliance on allies and on détente (a lessening of military and diplomatic tensions) with the Soviet Union. The Carter administration initially tried to ignore containment, but embraced it after the Soviet invasion of Afghanistan. The Reagan administration not only pursued a highly military containment policy but tried to go beyond it and roll back some of the Soviet gains of the 1970s in the Third World through support for anti-Communist revolutionary movements. The Bush administration saw containment come to an end with the demise of the Soviet Union— a development that vindicated the logic of the initial architects of containment.

The Truman Doctrine provided the vision, the overall philosophy for all of these efforts. Its strategic vision guided all of the details of the Cold War that followed—

Then-Vice President Harry Truman playing the piano for actress Lauren Bacall. This February 1945 photo illustrates how good intentions can easily turn into political embarrassment. Truman, an accomplished amateur piano player, agreed to perform at a variety show for 800 servicemen at the Washington Press Club. Sensing an ideal photo op, young Bacall's press agent perched her atop the piano. The crowd of soldiers loved it, roared their approval, and Truman just kept playing. The many photos became a minor scandal. Truman's wife, Bess, was said to be furious and forbade any more public performances. Two months after this picture, President Franklin Roosevelt died, and President Truman had less time to play the piano •

from the Marshall Plan to the Korean and Vietnam Wars. President Truman made this statement to a joint session of Congress, on March 12, 1947:

> At the present moment in world history nearly every nation must choose between alternative ways of life. The choice is too often not a free one.
>
> One way of life is based upon the will of the majority, and is distinguished by free institutions, representative government, free elections, guaranties of individual liberty, freedom of speech and religion, and freedom from political oppression.
>
> The second way of life is based upon the will of a minority forcibly imposed upon the majority. It relies upon terror and oppression, a controlled press and radio, fixed elections, and the suppression of personal freedoms.
>
> I believe that it must be the policy of the United States to support free peoples who are resisting attempted subjugation by armed minorities or by outside pressures.
>
> I believe that we must assist free peoples to work out their own destinies in their own way.
>
> I believe that our help should be primarily through economic and financial aid which is essential to economic stability and orderly political processes.

The domestic implications of the Truman Doctrine were equally important. For example, the Communist threat justified the Federal Aid Highway Act of 1956 (which built the U.S. interstate road network—the National Defense Highway System), the National Defense Education Act of 1958 (which provides loans and fellowships for students and grants to schools and colleges), and the National Aeronautics and Space Administration Act of 1958 (for the peaceful exploration of space).

Of course, Truman never envisioned his doctrine supporting local public works or graduate student education. But the Cold War goal of defeating communism meant that anything that could be presented as part of this international struggle would get a more sympathetic legislative reception. Thus graduate student fellowships and academic research in almost every field were justified as aiding the national defense effort. As more and more people got with the plan, it turned out that there was hardly any worthwhile government project that could not be designed, however far-fetched, to defeat communism. It turned out that every single member of Congress was willing, indeed eager, to fight the worldwide Communist menace by bringing pork barrel projects home to his or her district.

This combination of limited wars on the perimeter, interstate highways, and fellowships for graduate students was more than the Soviet Union could bear. When the great Communist experiment finally failed, credit was given to the containment policies of the Truman administration and its successors and more recently to the Reagan administration's massive arms build-up that the Soviets could not match. But no direct credit was given to the overall strategic plan. That's because there was no plan as such. There was the Truman strategic vision and all that followed. Thousands of programs and millions of people each played their part in an effort to achieve a goal that often seemed impossible. It was messy. Only retrospectively can we behold all the oars in the water rowing to the same philosophy. All the warriors, diplomats, highway builders, and scholars rowed out of faith, out of self-interest, or out of the simple desire to have a job. But in the end and because of the overall philosophy, they rowed in the same direction. What more could you ask of a plan?

What Is Strategic Management?

Strategy, the ancient art of generalship, is the employment of, the management of, overall resources (classically soldiers) to gain an objective. Tactics are the use of a subset of these resources to gain a part of the overall objective. Strategic management is the modern application of this ancient art to contemporary business and public administration. It is the conscious selection of policies, development of capability, and interpretation of the environment by managers in order to focus organizational efforts toward the achievement of preset objectives. These objectives necessarily vary. In the private sector it could be the doubling of annual dividends to stockholders within so many years. In the nonprofit sector it could be the creation of a repertory theater or a significant increase in attendance at symphony orchestra concerts. In the public sector it could be a reduction in the crime rate, an increase in the high school graduation rate or, as we have seen in the keynote, the defeat of worldwide communism.

All strategic management efforts take an essentially similar approach to planning where an organization wants to be by a future target date. These are the six features that identify a strategic, as opposed to a nonstrategic, management approach:

1. The identification of objectives to be achieved in the future (these are often announced in a vision statement)

2. The adoption of a time frame (or "planning horizon") in which these objectives are to be achieved

3. A systematic analysis of the current circumstances of an organization, especially its capabilities

4. An assessment of the environment surrounding the organization—both now and within the planning horizon

5. The selection of a strategy for the achievement of desired objectives by a future date, often comparing various alternatives

6. The integration of organizational efforts around this strategy

The overall strategy chosen is in essence the package of actions selected after analyzing alternatives, assessing the outside environment, and determining the internal capabilities of an organization to achieve specified future objectives through the integration of organizational effort. The strategic management process is often conducted by a strategic planning unit within the organization. Eventually its findings are presented in a detailed document known as the strategic plan. Many of the core elements of strategic management listed above have unique considerations when they are applied to public sector organizations.

Objectives

Objectives-based thinking in management has become so pervasive that it is as hard to think of management without objectives as living rooms without television sets. Originally, objectives were part of military thinking. The Swiss-born Napoleonic era general, Henri Jomini, in his 1838 book *The Art of War*, taught how battles should be conducted, with soldiers' moves being planned either for strategic benefit (a qualitative improvement in the long-term position, particularly vis-à-vis the enemy) or tactical benefit (that is, a shorter-term move designed to win the problems—the fighting—of the day and create a better position for the next day's battle).

In this context, we can think of a tactical objective such as "Hill 45"—a specific location that must be taken from the enemy to further the purpose of the overall plan of battle. A strategic objective might be victory on the whole of a battlefront or theater of war. This military vocabulary is now commonly applied to business. For example, when Honda, the Japanese company, started selling motorcycles in the United States in the early 1960s, it secured a tactical objective; but when it forced British motorcycles out of the American market, it secured a strategic victory.

The public sector was slower than the private sector in embracing strategic management notions. This is because, traditionally, public administrators were expected to focus not on their objectives—what they were trying to achieve—but on their functions and responsibilities—that is, the duties assigned to them by law. Indeed,

Figure 8.1 The Strategic Management Process

public administration was traditionally defined as the enforcement or implementation of public policy—that is, the law. This emphasis on the responsibility to discharge ongoing functions set down by law has been the focus of traditional public administration. The seniority principle in promotions often accompanied this attitude. After all, if a detailed knowledge of how to administer the laws in a certain functional area were critical, it logically followed that it must be better to have a more senior—and therefore more knowledgeable—employee than to hire someone fresh, who might take years to acquire a parallel level of knowledge. Job descriptions even emphasized knowledge of laws and regulations as a key selection criterion.

In contrast, today's most sophisticated selection officers tend to instead look for a record of achievement, as opposed to highly specific knowledge of this kind. A world in which public administrators take responsibility for unchanging functions still exists in some corners of the public sector in most countries, but it is increas-

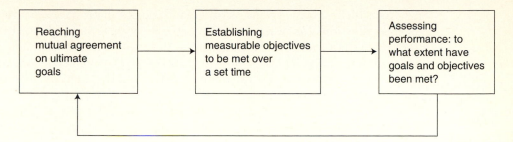

Figure 8.2 The Management by Objectives Process

ingly being replaced by a focus on objectives. No longer do we begin by asking a public administrator "What do you do?" (i.e., *What is your function?*). Today the question more likely to be asked is "What are you trying to achieve?" (i.e., *What are your objectives?*). While there are many reasons for this change in perspective, three are paramount.

The first is the popularization of the concept of management by objectives (MBO) by Peter Drucker through his pioneering 1954 work, *The Practice of Management*. MBO as espoused by Drucker and, by now, countless others is an approach to managing whose hallmark is the mutual—by both organizational subordinate and superior—establishment of measurable goals to be accomplished by an individual or team over a set period of time. The widespread adoption of the MBO concept across the world has aided in the distinction between a function and an objective. It is now widely understood that an emphasis on the latter can stimulate a focus on performance and effort as opposed to the more traditional custodial focus toward one's organizational obligations.

Second, the ever more rapid pace of change in the communities served by the public sector is such that there are now few functions that can go on unchanged from year to year and decade to decade. The public organizations of today must generally fight and compete in a less sheltered environment—where the luxury of just "administering" timeless functions rarely exists. The objectives of public sector organizations have become moving targets—and public sector managers must move with them.

Third, the ideas of strategic management and the use of objectives are pervasive in the private sector. Since there is no **Berlin Wall** dividing the sectors, and staff move increasingly in and out of each sector, there is an ever-increasing unification of language, concepts, and standards between the sectors.

Peter Drucker (1909–) The preeminent philosopher of management during the post-World War II era.
Berlin Wall The concrete and barbed wire wall built by East Germany in 1961 to divide East and West Berlin. The wall became the symbol of the division of Eastern and Western Europe. It was dismantled in 1989.

Nonetheless, many public sector organizations still produce separate statements of their functions (or responsibilities) and objectives. You can broadly distinguish the language of each. Since a statement of functions is about what an organization is responsible for under law, it broadly answers the question "What do we do?" The answer is normally a static description, timeless and without directionality. A statement of objectives (often called a mission statement) however, answers the question, "What are we trying to achieve?" Instead of a static description, this normally implies a direction being pursued, along with specific measures so that we will know when we get there. A statement of functions might say "we are in charge of childcare"; a statement of objectives might say "we intend to provide a preschool place for every child in the county by 1998." A statement of objectives should be:

1. Succinct, and limited to the organization's sphere of influence
2. Directional, with specific future states to be achieved
3. Time limited, with indications when each objective is to be achieved
4. Measurable, so that achievement or progress can be evaluated

The Planning Horizon

Sometimes when you apply for a job, the recruitment officer or selection committee may say to you, "Where do you see yourself in ten years' time?" This is often perceived to be a silly question to put to an individual, and with respect to the structure of women's careers, possibly a discriminatory one. But in asking this question, a selection committee is trying to see whether the applicant for the job has a personal career strategy, or is drifting in an opportunistic way without a strategy, without personal objectives, and without a career plan.

The same question is most decidedly not silly when addressed to public sector organizations. It is of the utmost importance to assess whether or not they have strategic intent—that is, the will to shape their future, rather than merely reacting to changes driven by others. Any organization's planning horizon, the time limit of organizational planning beyond which the future is considered too uncertain or unimportant to waste time on, is an important factor in assessing its short- as well as long-term viability. While private corporations have the luxury of determining their own planning horizons, severe obstacles are put in the path of those who advocate the most rational possible planning in the public sector. The inherently political nature of public administration can place a premium on short-term thinking. It was the late British Prime Minister Harold Wilson who said, "A week is a long time in politics." By this he was drawing attention to the fickle nature of the public's attention, to the fact that an issue of premier significance one week may be forgotten the next. Political leaders may lose power—and even office—in a very short time, often unexpectedly. "Today a rooster, tomorrow a feather duster" sums up the uncertain job prospects of those who would lead the political barnyard. Thus the reigning administrations in developed democracies feel they must be very sensitive to the results of very short-term opinion polling. These factors and all others that bring a short-term focus to bear on public policymaking work—and work very hard—against strategic management efforts.

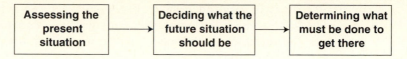

Figure 8.3 The Essence of Planning

Public budgeting procedures, because of their annual nature, reinforce this tendency toward short-term thinking. National, state, and local legislators are accustomed to exercising oversight authority during the annual rituals of the budget formulation and review process. To them, biennial and multiyear budgeting represent immediate threats to their political powers and patronage prerogatives. Aaron Wildavsky discussed this problem in a famous article, "A Budget for All Seasons: Why the Traditional Budget Lasts." It lasts because it is the basis of the political power of so many legislators. Otherwise rational reforms leading to multiyear budgets are simply not in their personal political interests. Despite the many efforts that have been made over the years to introduce longer budget cycles, success has been limited. Thus short-term budgeting continues to reinforce short-term policymaking and inhibit the inherently long-term nature of strategic planning.

Despite the constraints mentioned above, long-term planning is inescapable in some areas of public sector activity. Some endeavors clearly require long-term planning horizons because they need both gradual development and enormous capital investment. Publicly owned power, water, and transit utilities must operate in this way. They must have long forward plans, and multiyear lead times to complete a new transit system, power station, or water purification plant. Here the constraints of traditional short-term government planning cannot apply. Often, such utilities, if they are not already in the private sector, are placed in semiautonomous public corporations or commissions. There they have more freedom to think, plan, and operate within a longer-term time horizon than if they were to operate as traditional government departments. Government-owned utilities, with their heavy investment and long lead times, illustrate areas of the public sector where long-term strategy and concomitant long-term planning are inescapable.

Longer-term strategic planning can occur close to the heart of power. If a government wishes to bring about a fundamental change in community attitudes or lifestyle, a national strategy of some kind may be needed. A national energy strategy may be desirable to persuade citizens, over time, to be more responsible in the way they use finite energy resources. But ever since the **oil embargo** of 1973–1974, successive national administrations in the United States have tried but failed to develop a politically acceptable comprehensive energy policy. As happened with the Clinton administration's comprehensive health care reform efforts, much planning was done but little was actually implemented. Sometimes such planning efforts are an end in themselves. Many a planning effort is undertaken

---

oil embargo The 1973–1974 effort by the Arab members of OPEC to change Western policies toward
the Middle East by refusing to export oil to those countries that supported Israel during the October 1973 Yom Kippur War.

by an agency or by a presidential or royal commission to assuage a political constituency. It is just because long-term national strategies are notoriously difficult to achieve in developed economies that strategies are often developed for the crassest political motives.

In developing and less-democratic countries, longer-term strategy may come naturally. In Indonesia, for example, the country has proceeded since independence in 1945 through a series of five-year plans that have helped it to modernize and industrialize despite many difficulties. Attitudes to national strategy may differ significantly between developed and developing countries in large measure because so many developing countries offer their citizens only the minimum of political freedoms. Consequently, there is less need to consult obstreperous interest groups seeking to influence the policy process. The problem with democratic government is that planning is inherently messy when so many interests must be accommodated. The "neatness" of planning in authoritarian regimes may be admirable in technique, but at what cost?

Policy analyst Charles E. Lindblom, in his classic 1959 article "The Science of Muddling Through," argued that in pluralistic democracies, step-by-step decision making—muddling through toward an acceptable decision—was a more appropriate model for public decision making than leaping forward toward a desired strategic objective chosen as part of a rational planning process. Lindblom views a rational model as unrealistic. The policymaking process is above all, he asserts, complex and disorderly. Interestingly, policy analyst Yehezkel Dror made the point that incremental, step-by-step muddling through might be all right for a wealthy and confident democracy such as the United States, but developing nations with massive problems needed the certainty of rational planning and confident movement toward a known set of goals. Incremental decision making is in many respects highly compatible with the pluralistic compromise typical of the American political system. But it is important to note in these times of international economic competition how countries more attuned to rational planning, such as the economies of Southeast Asia, have used rational planning successfully.

When strategic management is adopted in a corporation, municipality, or bureau, or in a presidential initiative, a choice is made for rational decision making. In this sense, there is now a greater commitment to rational planning in American institutions than ever before. For example, the Government Performance and Results Act of 1993 requires that "federal agencies must prepare and submit strategic plans to the Office of Management and Budget and Congress." The states are increasingly passing similar legislation. For example, according to House Bill 2009, passed by the Texas State Legislature in 1991, all state agencies must use strategic plans as the basis for developing their "requests for legislative appropriations, and measure agency effectiveness by the outcomes and outputs they achieve."

Capabilities

Strategic management has been described, most notably by H. Igor Ansoff, as "a matching process" in which the variables of strategy, capability, and environment are matched as the organization seeks to manage change through strategy. As the environment moves from stable to turbulent, Ansoff argues, the required capa-

---

Box 8.1

Strategic Planning Is Now Compulsory For Federal Agencies

The strategic approach to management is no longer just an option, it's compulsory if you work in a U.S. federal agency. The Government Performance and Results Act (GPRA) of 1993 requires every federal agency to ask itself, "What is our mission?" "What are our goals?" and "How will we achieve them?"

The GPRA requires each agency's strategic plan to have six components:
- A comprehensive mission statement
- Agency-wide, long-term goals and objectives for all major functions and operations
- Approaches (or strategies) to achieve the goals and objectives
- A relationship between the long-term goals/objectives and the annual performance goals
- An identification of key factors, external to the agency and beyond its control, that could significantly affect achievement
- A description of how program evaluations were used to establish or revise strategic goals

An important feature of the approach to strategic planning required by GPRA is that agencies cannot "go it alone"—they must consult with Congress and other stakeholders. They are required by an Office of Management and Budget Circular (A-11 of September 1995) to send their proposed plans to Congress with a letter explaining how they've consulted with stakeholders, including consultants, customers, contractors, and state governments.

---

bility moves from "custodial" toward "entrepreneurial." In a stable environment, a custodial, unchanging capability may suffice. But as the environment becomes surprising and turbulent, a more entrepreneurial and risk-taking capability is needed.

When mismatch exists between environment and capability, management must take action to better match its human resources capability with the emerging environment. The actions required may include hiring new employees who are better oriented by disposition or training to a new entrepreneurial environment. Existing employees could be given additional training. Unfortunately, it is often the case that some employees may no longer be suited to what the present environment requires. For example, a juvenile correctional institution moving toward a counseling and support model may find difficulties if its staff capability exclusively consisted of tough custodial officers. Similarly, many organizations in the public sector whose strengths have traditionally been in technical or professional excellence may find that new requirements for customer orientation require, at the very least, extra training programs, but more likely the hiring of some new staff with new attitudes and skills.

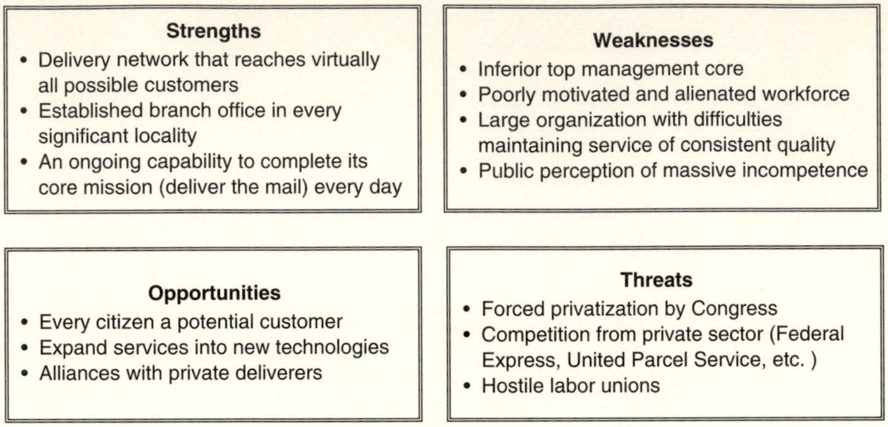

```
┌─────────────────────────────────────┐   ┌─────────────────────────────────────┐
│              Strengths               │   │             Weaknesses              │
│ • Delivery network that reaches      │   │ • Inferior top management core       │
│   virtually all possible customers   │   │ • Poorly motivated and alienated     │
│ • Established branch office in every  │   │   workforce                          │
│   significant locality               │   │ • Large organization with            │
│ • An ongoing capability to complete   │   │   difficulties maintaining service   │
│   its core mission (deliver the mail) │   │   of consistent quality              │
│   every day                          │   │ • Public perception of massive       │
│                                      │   │   incompetence                       │
└─────────────────────────────────────┘   └─────────────────────────────────────┘

┌─────────────────────────────────────┐   ┌─────────────────────────────────────┐
│            Opportunities             │   │               Threats               │
│ • Every citizen a potential customer  │   │ • Forced privatization by Congress   │
│ • Expand services into new            │   │ • Competition from private sector    │
│   technologies                       │   │   (Federal Express, United Parcel    │
│ • Alliances with private deliverers   │   │   Service, etc. )                    │
│                                      │   │ • Hostile labor unions               │
└─────────────────────────────────────┘   └─────────────────────────────────────┘
```

Figure 8.4 SWOT Analysis for the U.S. Postal Service

What is true of human resources capability is also likely to be the case with systems capability, or financial capability—indeed capability in whatever dimension is critical to the organization's ability to adapt to an emerging environment. For example, years ago, the task of servicing lighthouses—traditionally a public sector function—was viewed as requiring a capability to maintain a fleet of tough little ships that could reach remote areas. This capability later gave way to a capability to service remote locations by helicopter. Eventually, as global positioning systems developed, that capability in turn became obsolete.

The SWOT analysis—a review of an organization's Strengths, Weaknesses, Opportunities, and Threats—is a technique widely used to provide another test of strategic viability. SWOT analysis is often conducted by consultants or senior management groups in an interactive, brainstorming mode, in which the group turns its attention sequentially to each aspect of the organization's position. Analysis of strengths and weaknesses highlights capability issues, while attention to opportunities and threats turns attention to the opportunistic as well as the predatory aspects of organizational survival. A SWOT analysis is often undertaken as part of a situation audit, an assessment of an organization's performance in absolute terms or in comparison to a competing or parallel organization.

In considering future strategic directions, managers must contemplate whether they have or can obtain the personnel, systems, finance, structure, and other requirements that might be essential to realize their vision. If these cannot be obtained, a less ambitious strategy may be the only alternative. Strategic vision cannot be developed without ultimate regard for the feasibility of assembling the necessary organizational capability.

Environment

An assessment of an organization's present, currently emerging, and likely future environments is a critical aspect of strategic management. Of course, it has always been the case that forward planners assessing the need for a new highway, transit system, water supply reservoir, or public health facility have had to pay considerable attention to demand forecasting—the estimating of how much of something will be needed in the future.

Whenever a new program requiring major investment is being advocated—often in the context of **infrastructure** development—it is necessary to critically examine the approach to demand forecasting that has been adopted. A sound demand forecast should employ independent statistics concerning likely population and economic growth in the area concerned. It must examine whether contemporary patterns of consumer behavior can be extrapolated or are likely to be modified. Those proposing major new programs or investments can sometimes be overoptimistic about growth, and in many countries, including the United States, significant overinvestment in areas such as power generation capacity has resulted from unrealistic demand forecasts. Where power utilities are privately owned, as they are in most of the United States, the resultant costs have been borne by private stockholders. Nevertheless, whenever an inappropriate level of investment takes place, there will be a marked **opportunity cost**. If too much is spent on water supply reservoirs and too little on sewage treatment, there may be clean water and polluted rivers. If too much is spent on highways and too little on mass transit, there may be clogged roads and a struggling transit system. In developing countries, mistakes in these areas can prove disastrous in economic and human terms—as billions can be poured into power stations and highways while infant mortality remains very high due to polluted drinking water. But demand forecasting is just one method by which managers seek to cope with their environment. More comprehensive methods of assessing the future environment are also necessary.

Futures analysis is another important mode in which formal attention can be given to assessing the environmental circumstances an organization may be facing in the future. Since the pioneering work of Alvin Toffler in his book *Future Shock*, futures studies have become much more familiar and commonplace. For example, civil services of the United States, Canada, and Australia, among others, have all engaged in formal studies directed at identifying the service's most likely characteristics around the year 2000. Organizations in all sectors now routinely obtain advice from futures consultants. In Australia there is even a federal government body called the Commission for the Future, which seeks to study and popularize understanding of futures issues.

Four Strategic Factors

Strategic management, in its focus on measurable objectives to be achieved, contrasts with the older form of functional management, which emphasizes responsibilities to be discharged and things to be done, without a primary focus on what is to be achieved. Strategic management may embrace strategic leadership, strategic direction, and strategic planning; but it is broader than any of these. Strategic

---

infrastructure A general term for a jurisdiction's fixed assets, such as bridges, highways, tunnels, and water treatment plants.

opportunity cost The value that resources, used in a particular way, would have if used in the best possible or another specified alternative way. When opportunity costs exceed the value the resources have in the way they are being used, they represent lost opportunities to get value from the resources. Opportunity cost is sometimes more narrowly defined as the rate of profit earned by investing your money rather than putting it into a particular project.

management requires the deployment of all the organization's managerial functions toward getting results. Strategic planning, for example, while it is an important and logical precondition, should not be equated with strategic management. After all, strategic management often occurs without formal strategic planning; but strategic planning is impotent and meaningless without strategic management.

Are policy and strategy different? We know that strategic management is a central concern of virtually all large organizations. Since the 1970s, the study of strategic management has assumed a central role in both the teaching and practice of management. Every major management school—both public and private sector—now has its experts in strategic management. The word "policy" does not seem as natural coming from the lips of private business executives. Policy has always been a looser word than strategy. As used in the context of government it usually refers to a statement of goals that can be translated into a plan or program by specifying the objectives to be obtained. Goals are a far more general statement of aims than are objectives. Goal-objective ambiguity may exist for a variety of reasons. The original sponsors of the policy or program may not have had a precise idea of the end results desired. Formal statements of objectives may be intentionally ambiguous, if such vagueness makes it easier to obtain a consensus on action. After all, value judgments underlying the objectives may not be shared by influential groups. Consequently, the result intended may be perceived by some as implying ill effects for them. So explicit statements of objectives, which tend to imply a specific assignment of priorities and commitment of resources, may be purposely avoided.

Consequently, it is hardly a surprise that in many MBA programs, the course unit that used to be called "business policy" is now called "strategic management." The public sector has been as uncomfortable with the word "strategy" as the private sector has been with "policy." While all administrative and political analysts are obsessed with policy—its formulation, its direction, and its implementation—many elected political executives and appointed agency administrators feel reluctant to use the word strategy for fear of its Machiavellian and militaristic connotations.

But clearly it is not the case that strategic management concepts are inapplicable or even foreign in many parts of the public sector. From the national administration through to the smallest local governments, the concepts and language of strategic management are in ever-growing use. To understand this, we need to appreciate four important factors that affect the use of strategic management concepts in the public sector:

1. The public-private paradox
2. The importance of being close to the center
3. Organizational language and culture
4. Organizational place

A review of these factors will establish bearings on the road map of strategic management, which will help to explain how organizations use strategic management concepts and how these concepts are constantly encountered in the daily lives of virtually all public administrators.

The Public-Private Paradox

Over the years, scholars and managers have come to appreciate two interconnected propositions about the relationship between business and government—and thus about the relationships between business management and public administration. The first is that business and government are ultimately different; the second is that business administration and public administration have very much in common. This paradox lies at the heart of public administration as a discipline. There is much that is unique about government and about the work of the public administrators within it that distinguishes public sector from private sector management. In modern democracies, the work of government has the mandate of political **legitimacy**—no private company, however important, can claim this. The work of government can be embodied in law and, if necessary, implemented by force. Government is owned by all, is responsible to all, and must be equitable to all. So the work of its officials must be fair and defensible, based on the principle of fear and favor to no one. Modern administrative states contain many groups and interests; so the work of government necessarily involves accommodation, compromise, and incremental decision making. Political leaders and public administrators work in a complex web of interconnections, and make unilateral decisions at their peril. Finally, bottom-line profit in itself is almost never the test of success.

In contrast, managers in private corporations live in a world ruled by different fundamental principles. They are there to pursue the interests of their shareholders, not those of the public as a whole. They must pursue a designated private interest and may at times ignore or even act against the public interest in doing so. The most famous statement on this was made by William Henry Vanderbilt, the executive of the New York Central Railroad, who in 1882 answered a reporter's question about whether the railroad would maintain a particularly unprofitable train service "for the benefit of the public." Vanderbilt's response was "the public be damned"— which seemed to epitomize the **robber baron** attitude toward social responsibility and helped create the climate for greater public regulation of the railroad industry. Yet most of those who have complained about Vanderbilt's callous remark have also ignored the inherent sensibleness of what he went on to say—that "railroads are not run on sentiment but on business principles." And those principles may force a business sometimes to act against the public interest. This is essentially the attitude of **Milton Friedman**, who has long argued that the resolution of social problems is the task of governments, not businesses, and managers who so spend money on them act irresponsibly.

---

legitimacy A characteristic of a social institution, such as a government or a family, whereby it has both a legal and a perceived right to make binding decisions for its members.

robber barons The label first applied to the big business titans of the United States toward the end of the nineteenth century. Now it is an invidious term for corporate leadership in general.

Milton Friedman (1912–) A conservative economist of the Chicago school, generally considered the leading proponent of a return to laissez-faire economics. A 1976 Nobel Prize winner, Friedman has been a major influence on thinking about monetary policy, consumption, and government regulation. He is generally considered to be the intellectual godfather to the movement toward government deregulation.

Rather than focusing on equity and fairness to all, private corporation executives often focus on differentiating products and markets to "position" themselves selectively and advantageously for their bottom lines. The leadership, the boards of directors of private corporations, though they may have strategic alliances and a conglomerate structure, have far greater autonomy and capability to make strategy unilaterally than is generally the case for their public sector counterparts. The bottom line, the stock exchanges, the possibility of mergers and acquisitions, sales and profit margins—in short, the signals of the competitive market—rule the priorities of business executives. Their public sector counterparts are more focused on political promises, election and issue polling, budget making, inter- and intragovernmental power plays, media attention, and citizen perceptions.

Thus at the extremes, public management leadership and business management leadership seem to be marching to different tunes. So the question must be asked: Can we expect a common language and approach in the way they approach setting directions for their organizations? To begin to answer this, we must return to the other side of the public-private paradox—that there is very much in common at the heart of both business and public administration.

Both the public and private sectors possess large bureaucracies and comparatively small leadership structures. Both possess professional elements (such as hospitals and research units), as well as mass production and transportation organizations. Many features of organizational culture and decision making are more a product of the type of organization and its place in "the system" than whether it exists in a public or private context. While it is true that there are special languages and cultures peculiar to organizations in each sector, it is also true that the same people and overall culture are shared by both. After all, both sectors recruit from the same pool of college and university graduates. Individuals move in their careers from private to public and back again, even more so than in the past—and, significantly, they bring their ideas with them. So while there is no impenetrable cultural wall dividing the two sectors, there are some significant differentiations.

Today the public sectors in all modern nations are focusing on bringing in the best of private sector management ideas, including **competitiveness**, customer orientation, contracting out, strategic management, and so on. There is an increasing recognition that because of the profit incentive, the private sector is more efficient at generating, experimenting with, and rapidly installing new management techniques. The public sector is inherently and necessarily more conservative in this sense. Corporate executives rightly and regularly, with the support of their boards of directors, risk the firm if they believe a new product or process will offer ap-

---

competitiveness The ability of the United States to compete economically with other developed nations—especially Japan. In the late 1980s, the term became an abbreviated way of referring to the concern for a comprehensive national industrial policy, to the persistent problem of lagging productivity of American workers, and to an increasingly unfavorable U.S. balance of trade. Competitiveness goes beyond the concerns of international trade to a concern for, indeed a reevaluation of, the entire American business structure. This is because the countries with which the United States mainly competes, ironically its closest military allies in most cases, play the competitiveness game by radically different rules using business-government partnership (corporatism) in ways that are for all practical purposes unknown in the United States.

propriate gains. But it would be irresponsible for public sector managers to take similar risks. Thus the public sector constantly benefits from the inherently more experimental nature of private sector management. Additionally, an increasing proportion of public programs are delivered via private corporations or not-for-profits. So while there are barriers, there is also daily cooperation and interaction between the sectors.

Technology presents a common basic language for many of the daily tasks in each sector. The software a clerk in a public organization is using today will almost certainly be the same essential product that his or her private sector counterpart is using. And standard medical procedures are no different in public as opposed to private hospitals even though the food and quality of hotel-type services may vary considerably. And all sectors now ride the information superhighway via the Internet.

Thus it is fair to conclude that both the public and private sectors have very much in common—and that the public-private paradox remains very true today. Strategic management concepts, largely developed in the private sector, are now applied daily in public sector organizations. But how they are applied is heavily influenced by organizational role, size, and structure—and by the political environment.

The Importance of Being Close to the Center

Many of the key phrases in Osborne and Gaebler's book *Reinventing Government* have become familiar arguments in public debate, none more so than the subtitle of the first chapter, "Steering Rather Than Rowing." This proposes that governments should direct their attention more to shaping and ensuring the outcomes of programs (the steering) rather than being preoccupied with their delivery (the rowing). This in effect is a call for governments to center themselves, to focus, on setting overall strategy rather than on the tactical details of delivery. Trash collection, schooling, or water supply may, perhaps should, be privatized, this argument goes, as long as government ensures that the outcomes are those that meet the public's needs.

However, there is an equally strong proposition that, with respect to many services that they have traditionally provided, governments should be neither steering nor rowing—that strategy itself can be set by those who deliver programs, and that there may be no role for government in the steering process. Many jurisdictions in privatizing particular assets (such as railroads), services (such as telephones), or functions (such as trash collection) are implicitly accepting that they should neither steer nor row. Strategy making, if it happens at all, will occur in the boardrooms of corporations, presumably on commercial criteria. In such a context the "will of the people" is made evident by customer demand.

Sweden has long made the most emphatic distinction between steering and rowing in designing its machinery of government. There a separation exists between "policy ministries," which decide what is to be done, and "executive agencies," which do not make policy but deliver set programs for which they are responsible. In Britain, a major reform of the machinery of government in the 1990s has involved the emulation of aspects of the Swedish model through the creation of what are termed the "Next Steps" agencies, which like executive agencies in Sweden are there to deliver set programs in an autonomous way, but not to deliberate on policy. In federal systems, such as that in the United States, another variant on this problem occurs: Policies are determined nationally—in Washington—but are designed to be delivered through state or local government agencies. Here again a conceptual distinction is made between steering or strategy making as the center's role, and delivery, as the role of the periphery. Pressman and Wildavsky, in their classic study *Implementation,* documented how easy it is for the best centrally made plans to be subverted, misunderstood, or bungled by service deliverers with limited ownership of the plans they are given to implement. More recently, not-for-profit organizations have often been substituted for state or local governments in the role of program deliverers for the central government, usually with the aim of cost savings in program delivery.

Yet in assigning the role of strategy making to the center, we face another significant issue. At the center, the predominant form taken by the machinery of government is the bureau or department. Such organizations lie deep at the heart of decision making. But according to management analyst Nancy Roberts, there are at least four key reasons why it may be difficult to adopt strategic management in such organizations:

1. Bureau managers must share power with other important actors as they seek to make decisions. These actors can be nearby, within the organization or far-flung, in another branch of government (the legislature or judiciary) or an outside interest group.

2. Because bureaus function in a political as opposed to a rational environment, they often do not concur as to measures of adequate performance. After all, what one group of taxpayers perceives to be an overly generous bureaucratic effort to ameliorate a social program, another group of service recipients may see as too meager to do any lasting good.

3. Government managers have far less overall autonomy and control than their private sector counterparts. This makes it far more difficult for government to implement and coordinate any plan of action.

4. Strategic decision making in government, because of the above factors, is far more complex and difficult than in the private sector environment.

In the industrialized states of the Western world, strategy making generally has been the role of the national or state capital, while delivery has been the role of the **grass roots**. But there is an equally strong tradition that values the role of local decision making. National programs are often designed to provide for or even maximize local or individual discretion. The American tradition of local choice goes back to the **town meetings** of colonial New England, and to the tradition of electing many officials (like judges and **sheriffs**) who would be appointed public servants in

---

grass roots The rank and file of a political party or of a large bureaucracy.

town meeting A method of self-government, suitable for only the smallest jurisdictions, where the entire citizenry meets to decide local public policy. The town meeting is still the governing body for 88 percent of all New England municipalities.

sheriff In all states but Rhode Island, the elected chief officer of a county law enforcement agency, usually responsible for law enforcement in unincorporated areas of the county and for the operation of the county jail.

other administrative traditions. School boards, university councils, and many other locally elected public boards have a capacity to plan their own operations, and to make strategy themselves, limited only by the constraints that may be attached to grant funding received from governments. More recently, the teachings of public choice economics have promoted the values of local choice, and advocated voucher systems for financing various types of public projects. Such voucher systems maximize the opportunity for individuals to influence what is funded by government, and provide scope for strategy making to be pushed down into smaller and smaller autonomous providers of services.

Organizational Language and Culture

The application of the behavioral sciences to management studies has heightened our awareness that issues of language and style, of culture, are central to how an organization approaches its task (see Chapter 2). Quite simply, the special language of strategic management—however widespread in many public organizations—does not fit with the culture of all of them. Some years ago, one of the authors of this book visited Whitehall in London to ask a senior British civil servant about strategic management and how the concepts of objectives, strategies, and performance measurement were used. "Objectives, my dear chap," was the reply, "we don't bother about objectives. Good chaps know what good chaps ought to do!" It is highly likely that this "good chap" is now gone from the Whitehall scene (and not just because of advancing age). Beginning with the conservative Thatcher administration in 1979, the British public sector has radically changed its organizational culture. One manifestation of this is its embrace of strategic management. This has been more difficult to achieve in the United States because as both a federal system with independent levels of government and a presidential system with a separation of powers, it is far more difficult for any one actor to mandate the implementation of systematic strategic management. Nevertheless, strategic management is well on its way to becoming the norm rather than the exception in American governments.

Strategic management entails a special culture and language. It is easier to adopt this language and develop this culture in environments where staff members are likely to have undergone postgraduate training in management. Also, the more open government organizations are to new talent, the more likely strategic management is to be adopted. Executives who move to and from the various organizational sectors are worker bees who bring about the pollination of new ideas. Finally, strategic management is more likely to be adopted in an organization where there has been a successful culture of change rather than one where new approaches to management are viewed with skepticism and reserve.

Organizational Place

The old saying in real estate is that three factors determine the price of a property: location, location, and location. The same can be said of strategic management. The most important single factor in the effectiveness of public sector strategic management efforts is location. The closer an organization is to the center of national decision making, the more difficult it is to sustain a successful strategic management effort. President Bill Clinton's attempt to reform the American health care system during his first two years in office, 1993 and 1994, was a massive strategic effort—and a massive failure. Nothing was accomplished despite the fact that impressive resources were devoted to the problem by the executive, the legislature, and a host of health care industry lobbies. The problem was so large and aroused such competing interests that the national ability to cope, even to reach a compromise, was paralyzed. This is why strategic management is so difficult with the really big issues.

While strategic management can succeed at the presidential level, it is often displaced by the hurly-burly of politics and horse-trading that properly occupies much time at all levels in Washington. On the other hand, local school districts, public hospitals, or state departments of highways are more likely to be consistently successful in using strategic management.

As rules of thumb, we can say that strategic management approaches in the public sector can more readily be adopted under these conditions:

1. The further a public organization is from the heart of political leadership in its nation, state, or local government

2. The more the organization undertaking strategic management is self-contained and autonomous as to its funding, personnel decisions, and overall destiny

3. The smaller it is (providing that it has the minimum critical mass needed to manage, plan, and operate independently)

4. The more its results are consistently measurable

5. The greater the proportion of its income is raised directly from its customers (from **user charges/user fees** for example)

In short, strategic management approaches fit better if an organization has a reasonable amount of autonomy in its decision making—a prerequisite if strategic management is to be adopted and successfully implemented. If the organization is highly dependent, and inseparably tied into the workings of a political administration, it may not in truth be able to make independent strategic decisions at all, or if it can make them, not do so well. For some organizations, this problem can be overcome by "commercializing" them—that is, changing structural arrangements to give them substantial autonomy and freedom over key decisions, such as pricing, staffing, and budgets. Others may be so bound up in the central work of government that such commercialization is neither feasible nor proper. Yet even these public-policy dominated organizations can benefit from and employ strategic management techniques albeit in a more limited context.

Contemporary Strategic Challenges

While all managers will have some unique strategic challenges to contend with, there are a number of similar challenges faced by most if not all contemporary public sector managers. There are six key challenges specifically faced by public sector

---

user charges/user fees Specific sums that users or consumers of a government service pay to receive that service. For example, a homeowner's water bill, if based upon usage, would be a user charge. Other examples include toll roads and bridges and charges to use public swimming pools.

managers: (1) mandate, (2) efficiency, (3) competitiveness, (4) boundaries, (5) service, and (6) public interest.

The Challenge of Mandate

Should the public sector continue to operate in this area? Since the widespread implementation of privatization around the world, it has become customary for the mandate of many traditional functions of government to be challenged. The question of "Why should government carry out this function" is often a call to action—and a call to privatization. The posing of this question represents as fundamental a strategic challenge as many managers would wish to have, since it questions not the positioning, marketing, or efficiency of a governmental entity, but rather its right to exist at all. Yet public sector managers must respond constructively when the question is raised. There are few cases today in which the entry of government into manufacturing, or retailing, would be widely advocated—though there are many instances around the world where the public sector continues its historic involvements in these fields. For example, the United States still mints its own coins and prints its own paper currency, but many small nations have this done by private contractors.

On the other hand, there is a wide range of good reasons why governments continue their involvements in any number of activities. Thus the manager challenged by the question, "Why is your organization in the public sector?" would be wise to review the following questions before formulating an answer.

1. Is the organization a natural **monopoly**? In some circumstances, the provision of high voltage electricity transmission lines, railroad track and facilities, or roads may be in the nature of a natural monopoly, where it would be inefficient to provide duplicate facilities, and where it is impracticable to bring about competition through division of the facilities or the provision of wider access to them.

2. Are defense or strategic interests critical? There may be a need to maintain an activity so that know-how in some sensitive or specialized area is retained for strategic (in the military sense) purposes. Weapons design and manufacture is a common example.

3. Does the organization serve special community or **development** purposes? Some government bodies exist to pursue social or developmental goals that will be neglected or ignored if left to the market to provide.

---

monopoly A situation in which one or only a few companies control the manufacture, sale, distribution, or price of something. Under antitrust laws, a monopoly may be prohibited if a company deliberately built its power to fix prices or exclude competition. While the term monopoly suggests gigantic national or international business firms, smaller firms can illegally monopolize a local or regional market. Monopoly power has often been assumed to exist by courts when a single firm is responsible for the sales of 70 percent or more of a specific product within a specific geographic area.

development The gradual process of increasing economic growth so that the benefits of increased production and a more equitable distribution of income improve social and political conditions. The word is usually used in the context of the Third World, but the differences are only a matter of degree. After all, the comparatively rich industrialized states are still developing, too. The ultimate goals of development are higher standards of living, better health and nutrition, more widespread educational opportunity, and increased personal freedoms.

4. Is the organization part of the rule-making apparatus? Some government bodies exist to be the umpires, and to research, draft, and administer the laws and regulations under which private corporations operate. It would involve a **conflict of interest** if corporations could acquire interests in or control of such regulators—infringing upon the old adage that you "can't be judge and advocate in your own cause." So, although senior officials of national regulators sometimes after retirement accept positions as consultants or advisors to corporations they have spent their working lives regulating, the bodies that form part of the regulatory apparatus are generally viewed as inappropriate candidates for privatization—though even this is occasionally proposed, often under the designation of "industry self-regulation."

5. Does the organization principally produce "public goods"—goods shared by all members of society, from the enjoyment of which nobody can be excluded? Examples would include national defense, safe streets, or cleaner air. These are basically inappropriate targets for privatization, albeit many of their supply and support services may be suitable for contracting out.

6. Is the body part of the central administrative machinery of the state? Some bureaus—for example, those involved in budgeting or central government administration—are unsuitable candidates for privatization, although again there may be many aspects of the work that can be outsourced. These range from certain aspects of policy advice, which can be contracted to consultants, to payroll and personnel services, which can be delivered by private agencies.

The boundaries of the mandate of government are not fixed, although the above categories may be helpful in thinking about the problem. The broad position during the last quarter of the twentieth century has been that the scope of governmental activities in most countries has contracted to some extent, but there are big differences from country to country. A public sector manager faced with the challenge of potential privatization faces a profound strategic issue: Should that manager seek to develop the rationale for continued public provision of the function concerned, or work on a strategy of accommodating or facilitating commercialization, contracting out, or privatization? There is no set answer to this question, but managers finding themselves in this position should consider carefully why their organization received its existing mandate, and the extent to which that mandate will remain valid in future years. And of course, in the end it will be the community and its elected representatives who most often will be the final arbiters of this—and rightly so!

The Challenge of Efficiency

Is this organization efficient by industry standards? For public sector managers, the challenge to maximize operational efficiency is critical because public organizations may lose their credibility or even their right to exist if their managers cannot oper-

---

conflict of interest Any situation in which the personal interest of an officeholder may influence or appear to influence that officeholder's decision on a matter of public interest.

TABLE 8.1 The Move to Privitalization

Service	Percentage of Cities Contracting Out
Food services at public facilities	100
Major construction projects	100
Janitorial services	70
Solid waste management	50
Building maintenance	42
Security services	40
Automobile towing	40
Parking garages	35
Park maintenance	30
Tree trimming	30
Data processing	30
Street maintenance and repair	35
Golf courses	25
Health and medical services	28
Animal control services	22
Ambulance services	20
Bill collection	20
Street sweeping	18
Municipal cafeterias	12
Jail food services	14

SOURCE: Based on a 1995 survey of 82 cities in 34 states reported in the *New York Times*, March 2, 1995.

ate them in such a way as to demonstrate acceptable standards of competence. In past years, managers could sometimes obfuscate discussion of the efficiency of public sector organizations by references to unique characteristics, measurement difficulties, and the complexity of public sector life. While there is a measure of truth in all these as reasons making the assessment of the efficiency of public sector organizations difficult to deal with, it is also true that we now have, through benchmarking and studies of comparative performance, a good deal more data to consider—especially in those parts of the public sector where measurements and comparisons are easiest, that is, where there are "hard," measurable outputs.

Despite the problems and subtleties of measuring performance and productivity in the public sector, an objective baseline is indispensable if any manager or government wishes to bring about better performance. Almost as indispensable is a systematic way of comparing how you are doing with the efforts of others working in the same sphere. This latter problem is not unique to public sector management; it is a problem all managers face. This technique of comparison, known as benchmarking, was developed by the Xerox corporation just for this purpose. It has now spread around the world and is widely used in the public sector.

Benchmarking systematically compares work processes with those of competitors or with best practices in an industry. It involves choosing and studying key performance areas in an organization and often involves entering into cooperative arrangements with partner organizations. The process may be carried out internally (perhaps comparing how the organization's regional offices perform); it may be carried out externally (for example, a study of local tax collection efficiency comparing two municipalities); or it may involve like functions (such as customer service) in unlike organizations. Whatever the scope or focus, benchmarking should not be carried out in isolation. It must be linked to the strategic plans of the organization (to ensure that the most relevant areas are chosen for study) and to formal quality improvement efforts, since any shortfall in performance, once pinpointed, must be attacked and improved.

One of the most creative applications of benchmarking in the public sector has been in the state of Oregon, where the Oregon Benchmarks Project is run by the governor's office. Each agency is required to define long-term goals, benchmarks, mission statements, and performance measures. In aggregate, the process achieves integrated strategic planning for the state. [You can see these benchmarks on the Internet at www.econ.state.or.us\opb] Oregon has used this concept very creatively; it even has detailed (and quantified) benchmarks for "civic engagement."

In Australia, benchmarking was first promoted heavily within industry in the 1980s by the federal government, as a means of encouraging private enterprise to become more internationally competitive. Then it was used in the struggle to make public enterprises more efficient. In the 1990s, a number of benchmarking studies compared the performance of Australian public enterprises (like railroads, ports, and electricity undertakings) with each other and with those overseas. Then benchmarking was extensively applied in local government. Benchmarking can be a valuable aid to judging the efficiency of a public organization. However, the technique is susceptible to misuse and poor application if inappropriate comparisons are made and if sufficient explanation of variances is not provided in published results.

Where public and private sector organizations are able to compete with one another on a "level playing field"—that is, under circumstances where regulatory controls, policy latitude, and other key determinants are impartial—public sector organizations often compare well with private sector counterparts. This has been demonstrated in Australia, where public/private competition in the airline and banking industries existed for many years, and where the large public operators often defeated large private operators under comparable operating conditions. Such examples reinforce the proposition that competition is a more important precondition of organizational efficiency than ownership as such.

Such ideal laboratory conditions rarely exist in practice. Public sector organizations often have to compete while handicapped by special government policy directions, community service obligations, or restrictions on access to capital. It is interesting to observe how often public organizations are able to markedly improve their measured efficiency in the run-up to privatization, a period often

Focus

How public, private, and nonprofit organizations
compare with each other. Strategic benchmarking
is seldom industry-focused. It moves across
industries and cities to determine the best-in-class
strategic outcomes.

How public, private, and nonprofit organizations
compare with each other in terms of product and
service. Performance benchmarking usually
focuses on elements of price, technical quality,
ancillary product or service features, speed,
reliability, and other performance features.

How public, private, and nonprofit organizations
compare, through the identification of the
most effective operating practices of many
organizations that perform similar work
processes.

Figure 8.5 Three Types of Benchmarks   SOURCE: Adapted from Anthony H. Rainey, "Benchmarking to Become Best in Class," *Government Finance Review* (February 1997).

marked by the removal of government restrictions. British Airways, for example, experienced a legendary improvement in performance during this phase, prior to its privatization in 1987. On-time service went dramatically up while complaints went significantly down.

International benchmarking studies tend to focus on public enterprises rather than government agencies, and to some extent highlight the measurable. Such studies are of great interest, and often indicate that for whatever reasons, public organizations often have scope for considerable improvement in their efficiency on those criteria that are easily measured.

Many areas in the public sector do not have similar comparative data available, but nonetheless also face a significant strategic challenge in meeting the new expectation that they can achieve, measure, and demonstrate standards of efficiency comparable with **best practices**. Managers who neglect these issues leave their organizations extremely vulnerable to externally imposed change, as legislators and the community seek to be assured that the area in question is not a sinkhole of waste and incompetence.

The Challenge of Competitiveness

Can this organization compete well in its markets? If you consult most public administration texts written only a decade ago, you will find no mention in the index of "competition." Like other concepts now taken into public sector thinking from the private sector, the concept of competitiveness is increasingly a feature of the thinking of public sector managers, as many of them come to realize that the notion

---

best practices Ideal management standards; the state of the art in any given area of management.

that "competition is the driver of strategy" has relevance in many unexpected parts of the public sector.

The post office provides a simple example. For years, post offices around the world were largely free of competition. They typically had a legislated monopoly for the delivery of first class mail. They had a practical monopoly as well, since they possessed a unique national distribution network, and via the **Universal Postal Union**, an international distribution network of substantial reliability. These practical monopolies have now been substantially offset. Private courier companies now offer excellent national and international distribution facilities for the delivery of packages, and much material that in the past would have been mailed is now delivered by companies such as Federal Express and United Parcel Service. These companies have used their market position to establish extended "value-added" roles, so that Federal Express is now involved in warehousing and logistics, and actually stocks and distributes spare parts for IBM in some areas, relieving IBM of some of its inventory requirements. Then again, facsimile machines and electronic mail networks also pose direct competition if the traffic is information, not just objects.

To deal with these threats, public sector postal enterprises have had to develop competitive strategies as clever and complex as those of any large corporation. They have had to introduce special express delivery services at premium rates. They have had to expand their traditional niche market in collector stamps. (Thus the U.S. Postal Service created major media events when it introduced the Elvis Presley and Marilyn Monroe stamps—products that held great appeal for people who did not ordinarily collect stamps.) They have introduced attractive storefronts, with many related packaging and gift products on display. They have extended their hours to accommodate the changing work patterns of dual career couples. And they have had to give quality management principles their careful attention. These innovations are strategic; they are about survival, **market share**, and continuing relevance; but they are driven by competition from the private sector. The post office is only the most obvious case. How many public sector managers can say confidently that competition offers no threat to their function?

The Challenge of Boundaries

What is the territorial and organizational scope? Public sector enterprises, agencies, and bureaus are created by governments—national, state, or local. All government agencies are in part defined by their boundaries. Indeed, the names of many public agencies often include some statement about the boundaries of the jurisdiction of the government that created them. So we think of the *United States* Department of Agriculture, the *California* Highway Patrol, or the Port Authority

---

Universal Postal Union The specialized agency of the United Nations that facilitates the flow of mail across international borders.

market share The percentage of sales of a particular item that one company controls in a particular geographic area.

of *New York* and *New Jersey*. Once, this jurisdictional signal was the end of the story, but today, public sector agencies as never before are challenging their boundaries. National bodies are operating overseas, state bodies are operating interstate, and local government bodies are operating in neighborhoods away from their bases.

There are three main reasons for this. First, technological expertise is no respecter of jurisdictional boundaries. If a public agency in one territory has know-how, its expertise will be sought elsewhere. For example, the FBI crime laboratory and fingerprinting identification services have long been used by local government. Second, the ease and low cost of modern transportation and communications mean that service can be readily provided to extended areas. A private sector example of this is a major software company, whose worldwide telephone help line is operated from just two bases, one in the United States and one in Australia; calls are routed according to time of day. Third, an aspect of competition has emerged. As many public enterprises are now required to compete for work over which they once held a monopoly, so now they demand a right to compete for work elsewhere.

The Challenge of Service

Is the organization effectively consumer-oriented? In the past, the concept of **consumer sovereignty** has hardly been of central concern to public sector managers. Government agencies have traditionally been concerned with discharging their legal obligations, delivering on political promises, or doing efficiently what they have always done. But simple customer service has not always been a strong point. Government agencies, involved in delivering services to the public, would often be open from 10 to 12 in the morning and 2 to 4 in the afternoon—hours which suited the staff well and ensured the orderly progress of business within the office. But this did not necessarily coincide with what the public wanted. Indeed, the simple extension of operating hours to suit customers has been a feature of service improvements in many service industries in recent years—not only those in the public sector.

The move toward customer orientation, toward viewing members of the public as "customers" deserving "service" is a revolutionary change in public sector thinking in recent years. The country in which this move has been most entrenched has been Britain, where the "Citizen's Charter" was introduced to spell out the standards of service citizens could expect from every government agency. The Citizen's Charter involves imposing a set of customer service principles on all public services—schools, hospitals, town halls, police forces, and railroads. Interestingly, it has even been extended to privatized public utility services such as gas, electricity, and water. The charter concept involves both industry specific requirements and general customer service principles. These include requirements for all

---

consumer sovereignty The power of individual customers in a free market economy to, as an unorganized group, determine what products get produced. They literally use their money to "vote" on goods and services.

public servants who are in contact with the public to wear name badges and for performance standards to be published. Each year, a lengthy report is published detailing how well these principles have been applied, and brochures explaining the concept are on the counter in most public agencies. You will even see the British Customs Service version of the Citizen's Charter as you arrive at London's Heathrow Airport on vacation.

A comprehensive charter of this kind, imposed from above, is a major innovation in public administration. Yet in the end the success of public sector managers in dealing with the strategic challenges of effective service provision lie at the point of service delivery. The public manager who cannot, in the end, adopt strategies that result in higher levels of customer satisfaction runs a real chance today of being replaced by some other person or organization that does put the customer first.

The Challenge of the Public Interest

Does the organization clearly serve the public interest? Commitment to serving the public weal or the **commonwealth** has always been an important motivator for people to join government service. Government service has never put cash rewards as high as alternative rewards in the satisfaction of serving the public in some useful role—whether in policing or nursing, teaching, or some aspect of administration. On the other hand, the question of ensuring that public services are designed to meet the public interest rather than sectional interests or even the interests of the staff who provide them, is an important strategic challenge. The reality is that most public organizations produce mixed outputs and have mixed objectives. Some of these are close to commercial in nature; others are produced because an expectation has developed in the community that they will be available, while still others are public goods or statutory requirements for which the public agency operates within parameters tightly defined by the legislature.

Theorists of the public choice school argue that, in general, public services become "captured" by special constituencies, and result in a suboptimal allocation of resources in the interests of those constituencies. We all know instances where this seems to be true—where regulators come to identify with the industry being regulated, or where the staff seem to be the major beneficiaries of the activity. More commonly, we are faced with genuine dilemmas in identifying the precise nature of the public interest served by public agency outputs.

A useful technique in assessing the public's interest in a program is often to develop a clear list of "community service obligations"—that is, public services produced by an agency on a noncommercial basis because they are thought to serve some public interest. This listing process requires the identification of the

---

commonwealth The notion of Thomas Hobbes (1588–1679) and other philosophers of his era that the members of a social order have a common weal, which is in their collective interest to preserve and protect. Common weal evolved into commonwealth, which came to mean the state. Thus the republic established in Britain under Oliver Cromwell from 1649 to 1660 was called the Commonwealth. Four American states (Pennsylvania, Virginia, Massachusetts, and Kentucky) are formally commonwealths rather than states.

costs and beneficiaries of each product or service, and serves several important purposes. First, the searchlight is thrown on outdated activities whose constituency has disappeared and that may have been continued out of respect for the staff involved and on the basis of a now expired public interest. For example, in 1993 the Clinton administration curtailed federal government subsidies to mohair (goat wool) producers first established during the Korean War in the early 1950s to maintain a reliable supply of specially warm wool for military use. (This subsidy was kept in place by members of Congress who got campaign contributions from the wool producers; today synthetic fabrics have long replaced mohair for military purposes.) Second, the process of specification provides a firm basis to seek specific directions and funding for those community service obligations the legislature wishes continued. Third, this process allows constituencies and interest groups to be linked to products and services ostensibly produced for them, allowing them to be polled as to the relevance of existing arrangements to service them.

The astute use of a review of community service obligations to revise and update how an agency services the public interest is but one illustration of how a public manager may think strategically about public interest obligations. Such a manager will persistently seek ways to engage with legislators and with the constituencies the agency services in order to ensure that the public interest in question is a source of strategic support, rather than a vulnerability.

Summary

Strategy is the employment of resources to gain an objective. Tactics are the use of a subset of these resources to gain a part of the overall objective. Strategic management is the application of this ancient art to contemporary business and public administration. Strategic planning should not be equated with strategic management because strategic management often occurs without formal strategic planning; but strategic planning is meaningless without strategic management.

All strategic management efforts entail all of the following:

1. The identification of objectives to be achieved
2. The adoption of a time frame
3. An assessment of organization capabilities
4. An assessment of the organization's environment
5. The selection of a strategy from among alternatives

Overall, strategic management approaches in the public sector can more readily be adopted (1) the further a public organization is from the heart of its political leadership, (2) the more the organization undertaking strategic management is self-contained and autonomous, (3) the smaller it is (providing that it has the minimum critical mass), and (4) the more its results are consistently measurable.

Strategic management has become an indispensable perspective for many public sector managers. Such perspectives do not displace traditional management concerns, but rather add a new dimension.

Key Concepts

objective A short-term goal; something that must be achieved on the way to a larger overall achievement.

planning horizon The time frame during which the objectives of a strategic plan are to be achieved.

strategic management A philosophy of management that links strategic planning with day-to-day decision making. Strategic management seeks a fit between an organization's external and internal environments.

strategic plan The formal document that presents the ways and means by which a strategic goal will be achieved.

strategic planning The set of processes used by an organization to assess the strategic situation and develop strategy for the future.

strategy The overall conduct of a major enterprise to achieve long-term goals; the pattern to be found in a series of organizational decisions.

SWOT analysis A review of an organization's Strengths, Weaknesses, Opportunities, and Threats. This technique is widely used to examine the viability of strategic plans.

tactics The short-term immediate decisions that in their totality lead to the achievement of strategic goals.

vision A view of an organization's future. The purpose of strategic management is to make such a vision a reality.

vision statement The identification of objectives to be achieved in the future.

Bibliography

Ansoff, H. Igor. (1965). *Corporate Strategy*. New York: McGraw-Hill.

Bryson, John M. (1995). *Strategic Planning for Public and Nonprofit Organizations*, 2nd ed. San Francisco: Jossey-Bass.

Dror, Yehezkel. (1964). "Muddling Through—'Science' or Inertia," *Public Administration Review* 24 (September).

Drucker, Peter F. (1954). *The Practice of Management*. New York: Harper

Gordon, Gerald C. (1993). *Strategic Planning for Local Government*. Washington: International City Management Association.

Kennan, George F. [x] (1947). "The Sources of Soviet Conduct," *Foreign Affairs* (July).

Lindblom, Charles E. (1959). "The Science of Muddling Through." *Public Administration Review* 19.

Luttwak, Edward N. (1976). *The Grand Strategy of the Roman Empire*. Baltimore: Johns Hopkins University Press.

Mintzberg, Henry. (1994). *The Rise and Fall of Strategic Planning*. New York: Free Press.

Osborne, David, and Ted Gaebler. (1992). *Reinventing Government*. Reading, MA: Addison-Wesley.

Pascale, Richard T. (1993). "The Honda Effect." In *The Strategy Process*, James Brian Quinn, Henry Mintzberg, and Robert M. James, eds. Englewood Cliffs, NJ: Prentice Hall.

Porter, Michael E. (1980). *Competitive Strategy*. New York: Free Press.

Pressman, Jeffrey L., and Aaron Wildavsky. (1973). *Implementation: How Great Expectations in Washington Are Dashed in Oakland; Or, Why It's Amazing that Federal Programs Work at All. . . .* Berkeley: University of California Press.

Roberts, Nancy C. (1993). "Limitations of Strategic Action in Bureaus." In *Public Management: The State of the Art*. Barry W. Bozeman, ed. San Francisco: Jossey-Bass.

Rumelt, Richard. (1992). "The Evaluation of Business Strategy." In *The Strategy Process*, James Brian Quinn, Henry Mintzberg, and Robert M. James, eds. Englewood Cliffs, NJ: Prentice Hall.

Toffler, Alvin. (1970). *Future Shock*. New York: Random House.

Wettenhall, Roger, and Colm O. Nuallain, eds. (1990). *Public Enterprise Performance: Seven Country Studies*. Brussels: International Institute of Administrative Studies.

Wildavsky, Aaron. (1978). "A Budget for All Seasons: Why the Traditional Budget Lasts," *Public Administration Review* 38, No. 6 (November-December).

Recommended Books

Bryson, John M. (1995). *Strategic Planning for Public and Nonprofit Organizations*, rev. ed. San Francisco, CA: Jossey-Bass. A comprehensive guide to all aspects of strategic leadership, with an emphasis on planning, implementation, and strategy evaluation.

Koteen, Jack. (1997). *Strategic Management in Public and Nonprofit Organizations in Managing Public Concerns in an Era of Limits*, 2nd ed. Westport, CT: Praeger. A comprehensive how-to-do-it manual on creating, installing, and evaluating strategic management systems.

Mitchell, Jerry. (1998). *The American Experiment with Government Corporations*. Armonk, New York: M. E. Sharpe. A survey of the organizational form that incorporates the best features of public and private management to accomplish tasks that are deemed unsuited for commercialization or traditional bureaucracy.

Moore, Mark, H. (1995). *Creating Public Value: Strategic Management in Government*. Cambridge, MA: Harvard University Press. A call for public managers to go beyond being competent bureaucratic technicians; they must retool as strategic managers who "search for public value"—that is, more bang for the buck, better quality or quantities for each dollar spent.

Related Web Sites

Center for Strategic Management
   http://www.csmweb.com
Contingency analysis
   http://www.contingencyanalysis.com/
Government Performance and Results Act
   http://server.conginst.org/conginst/results/
Milton Friedman
   http://adam.hhss.se/utskott/Friedmans/
   MILTON.HTM
National Strategy Forum
   http://www.natstratfm.org/nsf/htm

Peter Drucker
   http://www.dgsys.com/~tristan/technodrucker.html
Strategic planning in Canada
   http://www.city.grande-prairie.ab.ca
Strategic Planning Institute Council on Benchmarking
   http://www.spinet.org/
Strategic plans of federal agencies
   http://www.financenet.gov/financenet/fed/docs/
   strat.htm

9

Leadership and Accountability

Keynote: Transforming the Post Office

Leading for Performance

Defining Leadership • Leadership and Management • Trait Theories • Transactional Approaches • Contingency Approaches • Transformational Leadership

Too Much Leadership

Micromanagement • Overmanagement

Moral Leadership

The Bully Pulpit • Rhetorical Leadership

The Challenge of Accountability

Constitutional and Legal Constraints • Obsessive Accountability • Avoiding Accountability

Legislative Oversight

Hearings • Casework

Keynote: Transforming the Post Office

Ever since the nineteenth century, when stamps were first used on letters, people have been collecting them for both their artistic merit and investment value. The United States first issued adhesive postage stamps in 1847. They had portraits of Benjamin Franklin and George Washington. Governments have conscientiously produced a multitude of commemorative stamps for the collectors' market. After all, a stamp purchased and saved is almost pure profit to the post office.

When the U.S. Postal Service decided to issue a stamp commemorating rock and roll star Elvis Presley, it created publicity by asking Americans to "vote" on stamp designs featuring either the young or old Elvis. When the "polling" was complete, the young Elvis design won by 4 to 1. More importantly, this created a ready audience, a ready market, for the stamp when it was released in 1992. Nevertheless, the Postal Service was surprised at the depth of the public's enthusiasm. People who had never saved stamps before suddenly become collectors—at least of this stamp. The Postal Service could barely keep up with the initial demand for the Elvis stamp. Since hardly anyone bought the first Elvis stamps to use on letters, the Postal Service, from its point of view, was almost literally printing money.

Taken by surprise by the public's tremendous response to the Elvis stamp, the Postal Service was determined that the next time they would be ready—ready with more stamps to sell. But stamps of what? Most commemorative stamps are issued, bought by collectors or by people who prefer stamps with some distinction, then forgotten. The Postal Service searched for another dead national icon with a following comparable to Elvis's. "Dead" was an important consideration here. Contrary to the philatelic policies in monarchies and dictatorships, only likenesses of the deceased are allowed on American stamps. Marilyn Monroe, dead since 1962, had never faded from the public's mind. As with Elvis, her face and persona were instantly recognizable. Both had died prematurely of drug overdoses when they were still enormously popular.

Realizing the market potential, the Postal Service gave the Marilyn stamp a lavish publicity sendoff. Postmaster General Marvin Runyon made the rounds of the TV and radio talk shows as if he were hawking a book. He scheduled visits to shopping malls where he would judge Marilyn Monroe look-alike contests. They even advertised her on TV. Over old news clips of Marilyn, an announcer asks: "When is a stamp not just a stamp? The Marilyn stamp [picture of stamp replaces news film]—now at your Post Office." Many people give great patriotic service to their government when they are alive; to do so after death, as Marilyn has done—is still doing—is patriotism indeed.

Today's Postal Service was created by the Postal Reorganization Act of 1970. This federal statute converted the Post Office Department into an independent establishment—within the executive branch of the government—to own and operate the nation's postal system, thereafter known as the U.S. Postal Service. The old Post Office Department was "reinvented" (before this term was in common usage in government) as a public enterprise because the Nixon administration was unhappy with its poor management and constant need for public subsidies.

Amidst a dramatic postal strike in the spring of 1970, the government for the first time in history agreed to allow wages, which hitherto had always been set through the legislative process, to be negotiated between union and government representatives. That ended the strike. Subsequently, the Postal Reorganization Act was passed, establishing the corporate framework sought by Nixon and providing for collective bargaining with postal employees in the future. The Postal Service remains the only federal agency whose employees are governed by a collective bargaining process that permits negotiations over wages.

The chief executive officer of the Postal Service, the postmaster general, is appointed by the nine governors of the Postal Service, who are appointed by the president, with the advice and consent of the Senate, for overlapping nine-year terms. The ambiguous legal status of the Postal Service has been the source of political controversy since it was established in 1970. It does not report to the president and is only indirectly responsible to the Congress. Even though it is an "independent" government corporation, it cannot even set its own prices for services. A Postal Rate Commission, created by the 1970 Reorganization Act, must approve all postage rates, fees, and mail classifications. The commission also has appellate jurisdiction to review Postal Service determinations to close or consolidate small post offices. There have been a number of bills introduced in recent congresses to return the Postal Service to the status of a regular executive department—and to greater political control. Such proposals tend to increase dramatically whenever local post offices are forced to merge or close.

Despite perennial criticism, what the Postal Service does is impressive: More than 180 billion pieces of mail are delivered annually to 125 million residences and businesses by more than 800,000 employees in 40,000 post offices. With annual revenues of more than $58 billion, it delivers more than 40 percent of the world's mail each day. And while most Americans do not realize it, their daily mail is cheap, comparatively speaking. The United States has the lowest first-class postage of any of the larger industrialized nations. For the price of a first-class stamp, even one with Marilyn or Elvis on it, the Postal Service will take your letter—if properly addressed—to the bottom of the Grand Canyon by mule, to the Arctic Circle in Alaska by bush pilot, or to ships on America's remote rivers by mailboat. The current motto of the postal service is "We Deliver for You." They know that if they do not, that if there are too many complaints, the Congress may change their mandate.

The Postal Service's worst nightmare is that Congress will jeopardize the service's solvency by allowing others—maybe Federal Express or United Parcel Service—the right to deliver first-class mail. Such totally private corporations could then easily skim off the easy and profitable urban delivery routes and leave the Postal Service with all the unprofitable and difficult ones. Fearful of losing its monopoly and viability, the Postal Service is hustling to improve its core services, to create new products such as Marilyn and Elvis and self-adhesive stamps, and to match the competition. Thus "express mail" overnight delivery was created in 1977 specifically to compete with Federal Express, and the Postal Service has conducted quarterly performance evaluations since 1990 to monitor the timeliness of its first-class mail delivery.

The Marilyn and Elvis stamps are indicators of a major new trend in public administration in general and the Postal Service in particular—the concern for marketing. Marketing, entrepreneurship, and promotional management are relatively new areas of interest in the public and nonprofit sector. The first published argument (that we have been able to locate) that nonprofit organizations should engage in marketing even though they face somewhat unique circumstances is in Philip Kotler and Sidney Levy's 1969 article, "Broadening the Concept of Marketing." The first textbook on the subject, also by Kotler, was not published until 1975. Although some nonprofit organizations have engaged in business enterprise-type activities at least since the beginning of the twentieth century—for example, the Metropolitan Museum of Art in New York City opened its first official

AIR MAIL
is Socially Correct

5¢ for the First Ounce 10¢ for each additional Ounce

This 1929 poster illustrates more than airmail. It shows that the post office has been continuously reinventing itself as technology progresses. Because airmail letters had to be written on flimsy, lightweight paper, the poster uses an obvious "society type" (only they still wrote with feather quills) to encourage customers to use the new service •

retail store in 1908—only scattered attention was paid to such income-generating activities prior to 1980.

Entreprenurial-type business ventures by agencies of the public sector are not limited to the Postal Service. Creating and capitalizing on chances to make money—the core of entrepreneurship—is becoming increasingly fashionable. Thus organizations as diverse as the Chicago Public Library and the Los Angeles County Coroner's Office sell a wide range of memorabilia. The Coroner's Office, which had a better reputation prior to the 1994–1995 O. J. Simpson trial, sells literally thousands of chalked-body-outline beach towels, caps, mugs, tote bags, and skeletons. In the first two years after it started selling logo imprinted souvenirs in 1993, the Coroner's Office grossed more than half a million dollars. Its line of boxer shorts, called "undertakers," is very popular. And in Crown Point, Indiana, a funeral home pays the city to advertise on the back of police cars. The City of Atlanta sold its name to Visa for the "official credit card" of the 1996 Summer Olympics. New York City plans to create its own nationally distributed line of products, from shirts to paperweights. According to William J. Diamond, the city's Commissioner of General Services, "We'll spread the name and fame of New York City into every major mall in America, while making money at the same time." But *New York Times* journalist Steven Lee Myers offers this warning:

> Not everyone is thrilled. For some, the flurry of entrepreneurship raises troubling questions about the very nature of municipal government. Does the drive for profits clash with the primary goal of public service? Are the entrepreneurial novices of the public sector up to the Darwinian challenges of the market-place and the wiles of the shrewd operators they could be dealing with in many cases?

Up to it or not, they are going to try. The pressure for additional revenue sources is just too great.

The result of entrepreneurial forays by the Postal Service and other public sector entities is to raise revenue through nontraditional methods rather than increasing taxes or user fees (or stamp prices). Entrepreneurship is a frame of mind, a willingness to create and to be receptive to opportunities, an orientation toward risk-taking ventures. But nonprofit organizations cannot allow the current interest in entrepreneurship to allow them to forget their traditional purposes. Business ventures can be dangerous when they compromise the organization's original mission. Marilyn and Elvis stamps, pins, and other souvenir items are like best-selling books. They generate tremendous income when first offered for sale and even have comfortable backlist sales; but they are no substitute for the organization's core function—selling a service.

So what's the lesson here? The public sector can benefit from some entrepreneurial techniques. If stamps with Washington, Franklin, and other dignitaries do not sell well enough as collectibles, then sell what sells. Sell Marilyn and Elvis. Marilyn sold 46.3 million stamps in 1995. But the "King" is still the king; Elvis sold 124 million in 1993. The Postal Service, by being made a public enterprise, has simply used its discretion to branch out into the entertainment industry. In so doing, it has found a way to improve its financial health so as to better fulfill its primary purpose: delivering the mail.

Leading for Performance

There are many characteristics of public sector management that call for knowledge and skills somewhat distinct from those required in private sector management. We have seen how the political context and governance arrangements that exist in the public sector present constraints and frameworks of decision making that must be understood and in many respects "managed" by public officials. We have discussed the special problems, in public sector strategic management, of converting political programs and managerial imperatives into a well-sequenced path to be followed. We have examined how the external and internal structures through which government is managed—intergovernmental relations and the machinery of government—give a framework that public sector managers must acknowledge and accommodate if they are to work effectively.

All of these areas, however fundamental, really amount to parts of the context in which the public sector manager is to operate. It is as though we have examined a theater—its lighting, its marketing arrangements, its ownership, the way the supporting cast of actors and dancers are hired and fired. But we have now to turn to the heart of the question—how good is the performance going to be? What do the producer and director, the managers, have to do to exact from the cast the best performances of which they are capable?

The word performance is shared here by the world of management and the theatrical world—it also permeates the sporting world. There, too, the task is to exact a personal best from an athlete or a supreme performance from a team. There, too, issues like training, team functioning, leadership, comparison with the best, total quality in the sense of trying never to miss a trick, and of course strategy are central ideas. *Performance*, above all, means the demonstration of a skill, the display of competence. In public sector management there are now many senses in which the term performance is applied. There are so many because knowing what kind of performance we are getting, and setting up means for individuals and teams to do better, are central concerns of public sector leaders. Thus performance management really begins with leadership.

Defining Leadership

As a callow youth, one of the authors of this book took an undergraduate course in medieval history. Having seen dozens of films in which castles were stormed by a cast of thousands, this youth asked the professor: "How do they get large numbers of men in real life to storm castles and the like when it appears to be, and indeed often is, certain death?" The professor's answer was memorable: "That's leadership for you!"

And so it is. The job of the leader of any organization is to get people to do things they have never done before, to do things that are not routine, and to take risks—and sometimes even to die—for the common good. Once the organization accepts the credo of Alexander Dumas's three musketeers—"one for all and all for one"—then they have been led, and only then have they been molded into an organization. In essence, that is the most basic task of a leader—to create organization out of disorder, to make people more capable as a cohesive group than they are as unorganized individuals.

Leadership is the exercise of authority, whether formal or informal, in directing and coordinating the work of others. The best leaders are those who can simultaneously exercise both kinds of leadership: the formal, based on the authority of rank or office, and the informal, based on the willingness of others to give service to a person whose special qualities of authority they admire. It has long been known that leaders who must rely only upon formal authority are at a disadvantage when compared to those who can also mobilize the informal strength of an organization or nation. Shakespeare observed this when in *Macbeth* (Act V, Scene 2) he has Angus describe Macbeth's waning ability to command the loyalty of his troops:

> Those he commands move only in command,
> Nothing in love: now does he feel his title
> Hang loose about him, like a giant's robe
> Upon a dwarfish thief.

Macbeth had become the very definition of an incompetent leader. Once he lost the respect and admiration of his followers, his organization was as doomed as he was.

The power that a leader possesses implies a hierarchy of control of stronger over weaker. French and Raven, in "The Bases of Social Power," suggest that there are five major bases of power: (1) expert power, which is based on the perception that the leader possesses some special knowledge or expertise; (2) referent power, which is based on the follower's liking, admiring, or identifying with the leader; (3) reward power, which is based on the leader's ability to mediate rewards for the follower; (4) legitimate power, which is based on the follower's perception that the leader has the legitimate right or authority to exercise influence over him or her; and (5) coercive power, which is based on the follower's fear that noncompliance with the leader's wishes will lead to punishment. Subsequent research on these power bases has indicated that the first two (expert and referent power) are more positively related to subordinate performance and satisfaction than the last three (reward, legitimate, and coercive power).

Leadership and Management

We need to distinguish between leadership and management. The two functions and roles overlap substantially. Management involves power (usually formal authority) bestowed on the occupant of a position by a higher organizational authority. With the power of management comes responsibility and accountability for the use of organizational resources. In contrast, leadership cannot be bestowed upon a person by a higher authority. Effective managers must also be leaders, and many leaders become managers, but the two sets of roles and functions differ.

The subject of leadership raises many complex issues that have plagued the behavioral sciences for generations. For example, what gives a manager or a leader legitimacy? Simply put, legitimacy is a characteristic of a social institution, such as a government, a family, or an organization, whereby it has both a legal and a perceived right to make binding decisions. Thus managers presumably have legitimacy because of the legal and perceived rights that accompany their organizational positions. In contrast, the legitimacy of a leader—separate and distinct from the legitimacy of a manager—cannot be addressed without introducing the concept of charisma, leadership based on the compelling personality of the leader rather than on formal position.

This last concept was first articulated by our old friend Max Weber—he wasn't called a universal genius for nothing—who distinguished charismatic authority from the traditional authority of a monarch and the legal authority one receives by virtue of law, such as the authority that legitimizes organizational executives. The word charisma is derived from the Greek word for divine grace. Charismatic leadership, if it is to survive, must eventually be institutionalized or routinized. Thus the founder of a movement or organization may be a charismatic spellbinder, but his or her successors are often, of necessity, comparatively dull bureaucrats.

Despite the differences and the unresolved questions, two things are evident: First, leadership involves a relationship between people in which influence and power are unevenly distributed on a legitimate basis; and second, a leader cannot function in isolation. In order for there to be a leader, someone must follow.

Perhaps the most accepted pure definition of the organizational leadership function comes from Chester I. Barnard. In his 1938 study, *The Functions of the Executive*, he defines three essential functions of leaders or executives:

1. To provide a system of communication
2. To promote the securing of essential efforts
3. To formulate and define the purposes and goals of an organization

Note how he was decades ahead of his time in arguing that the most critical function of a chief executive is to establish and communicate a system of organizational values among organizational members. "The formulation and definition of purpose is then a widely distributed function only the more general part of which is executive. In this fact lies the most important inherent difficulty in the operation of cooperative systems—the necessity for indoctrinating those at the lower levels with general purposes." Here Barnard is referring to the necessity for top management to develop and instill a strategic vision for the organization. "Without that up-and-down-the-line coordination of purposeful decisions, general decisions and general purposes are mere intellectual processes in an organization vacuum, insulated from realities by layers of misunderstanding. The function of formulating grand purposes and providing for their redefinition is one that needs sensitive systems of communication, experience in interpretation, imagination, and delegation of responsibility." Barnard knew, in part because he was a real executive, that if the value system of the organization was clear and strong, the day-to-day concerns would take care of themselves.

Trait Theories

The trait approach to leadership assumes that leaders possess traits that make them fundamentally different from followers. Advocates of trait theory believe that some people have unique leadership characteristics and qualities that enable them to assume responsibilities not everyone can execute. Therefore they are "born" leaders.

It is no longer fashionable to contend that people will be effective leaders because they possess certain traits—without also considering other variables that influence leadership effectiveness. The arguments against trait theory are persuasive and come from a number of points of view. First, trait theory has largely fallen out of favor because reality never matched the theory. Instead, starting in the late 1950s, it has become standard practice to view leadership as a relationship, an interaction between individuals. The interaction was called a transaction, so that the term transactional leadership has become the umbrella label encompassing many theories of leadership. Second, the situation strongly influences leadership. The situation is now viewed as an enormous influence in determining the qualities, characteristics, and skills needed in a leader. There is even a **law of the situation** that deals with this.

Probably the most damaging criticism of trait theory, however, has been its lack of ability to identify which traits make an effective leader. Even among the traits that have been most commonly cited—intelligence, energy, achievement, dependability, and socioeconomic status—there is a lack of consensus across studies. The most obvious proof that leadership involves more than possessing certain

---

law of the situation A notion developed by social psychologist Mary Parker Follett (1868–1933) that one person should not give orders to another person, but both should agree to take their orders from the situation. If orders are simply part of the situation, the question of someone giving and someone receiving does not come up.

traits is the simple fact that a leader may be effective in one setting and ineffective in another. It all depends on the situation.

Transactional Approaches

While the central question for the trait approach was who was a leader, transactional approaches sought to determine how leadership was established and exerted. Leadership style-oriented **transactional approaches** all follow in the tradition of the famous Lewin, Lippitt, and White (1939) studies of the effectiveness of leadership styles on the group efforts of ten-year-old children engaged in hobby activities. The leader in each group was classified as authoritarian, democratic, or laissez-faire oriented.

Authoritarian leaders determined all policies, set all work assignments, were personal in their criticisms, and were product (or task) oriented. Democratic leaders shared decision making powers with subordinates, left decisions about assignments up to the group, and participated in group activities but tried not to monopolize. They exhibited high levels of consideration for others. Laissez-faire leaders allowed freedom for individual and group decision making, provided information (or supplies) only when requested, and did not participate in the group except when called upon. They functioned more as facilitators.

Groups with democratic leaders were the most satisfied and productive. The authoritarian-led groups showed the most aggressive behavior and were the least satisfied, but they were highly productive (possibly because of fear of the leader). The groups with laissez-faire leaders showed low satisfaction and low production, and they were behaviorally aggressive toward group members and other groups. Thousands of subsequent studies have essentially presented the same findings. Democracy, meaning participative management, works.

Managers with authoritarian personalities and styles value order, precision, consistency, obedience, rules, law, and organization. To them, the power that flows from structure is supreme. Relationships are hierarchical, based on dominance and dependence. Authoritarianism, control through structure, is rigidly unbending. Yet, authoritarians, while often initially successful, cannot survive over the long term. Whether large scale (such as Hitler or Stalin) or pint size (such as an oppressive supervisor), authoritarians will ultimately fail because "democracy is inevitable." It is inevitable not just because it is good but because it is more effective—especially in the modern world, with its high-tech workforce. In the meanwhile, however, authoritarians cause considerable psychic damage in individuals and generate lost productivity in the internal organizational polity while often sustaining **authoritarianism** in the outside polity.

---

transactional approaches Any means of analyzing leadership style that focuses on how leaders interact, how they treat, those they seek to lead.

authoritarianism Rule by an individual whose claim to sole power is supported by subordinates who sustain control of the system by carrying out the ruler's orders and by a public that is unwilling or unable to rebel against that control. The ruler's personality may be a significant element in maintaining the necessary balance of loyalty and fear. Authoritarianism differs from totalitarianism only in that the latter may have a specific ideology that rationalizes it, although it may require a leader who embodies that ideology to sustain public support. An authoritarian state may be further distinguished from a totalitarian one by the fact that under some circumstances, an authoritarian state could allow limited freedom of expression and political opposition, as long as the regime does not feel threatened.

Because it is so easy and tempting for authoritarian personalities to rise to power, they must be all the more resisted because of their inherent tendencies toward destruction. People, groups, and organizations must evolve and adapt to their environment. Authoritarians do not adapt willingly to changing circumstances and new ideas. They are conservative in the worst sense of the word. Thus their need to protect and preserve the past and to inhibit constructive change leads to organizational rigidity and incompetence. Authoritarians dominate; their disciples obey. Organizational authoritarians and democrats cannot coincide; they are mutually exclusive.

Democracy, whether it takes the form of representative government or participative management, is in marked contrast. It allows for a peaceful evolution and change. Dissent is not suppressed; it is instead used as a creative force leading to greater effectiveness and less incompetence. The Soviet Union and its Communist party disintegrated in 1991 because its authoritarian command economy was increasingly unable to provide its citizens an adequate standard of living. Democratic institutions are more competent because they allow for inevitable mistakes to be corrected in an evolutionary manner—before they lead to revolution.

Authoritarian rigidity is an important structural cause of organizational incompetence. It inhibits an organization's ability to learn and adapt to its environment. It concentrates decision making and responsibility in too few places and individuals. It denies others the right and opportunity to influence or to grow as employees and as people. Rigidity is illustrated by the British contingent of soldiers continuing to march in formation between Lexington and Concord, Massachusetts Colony, in 1775 despite colonial sharpshooters diminishing their ranks. Why did the dedicated targets keep on marching in file? Because the structure (the rules, lines of authority, the policies and procedures) said that was how wars were to be fought and soldiers were to behave. British structural rigidity—in all aspects of its eighteenth-century relationships with its American colonies—not only caused the American Revolution but led to the British defeat as they tried to suppress it.

Transactional leadership approaches assumed that leaders could be trained to act in the appropriate way as called for by their organization. This has proved to be wishful thinking. When leaders return to their organization after leadership training sessions, they seldom exhibit behavior changes. Despite training, department heads will not necessarily act considerately toward subordinates if their own supervisors do not act supportively toward them. One obvious implication is that changes must be introduced into an organization as a whole—not just to certain employees. In practice, leaders apply different styles in different situations. Thus the "pure" leadership style emphasis has given way to contingency approaches.

Contingency Approaches

We have all seen examples of the heroic leader: the general who leads troops from the front lines is the managerial cousin to the supervisor who leads from the assembly line. Each finds it almost impossible to delegate responsibility and, by trying to do it all alone, ultimately fails. This inherently theatrical style of leadership was appropriate for ancient armies when an Alexander the Great, sword in hand, would be the first to engage the enemy. This lead worker (or lead killer) approach had by the middle of the twentieth century become discredited. True, there will always be

---

Box 9.1

Oligarchic Leadership

"Who says organization says oligarchy." This is Robert Michels's "iron law of oligarchy," stated in his *Political Parties* (1915), which holds that organizations are by their nature oligarchic because majorities within an organization are not capable of ruling themselves:

> Organization implies the tendency to oligarchy. In every organization, whether it be a political party, a professional union, or any other association of the kind, the aristocratic tendency manifests itself very clearly. The mechanism of the organization, while conferring a solidity of structure, induces serious changes in the organized mass, completely inverting the respective position of the leaders and the led. As a result of organization, every party or professional union becomes divided into a minority of directors and a majority of the directed.

SOURCE: Robert Michels, *Political Parties* (Glencoe, IL: The Free Press, 1915, 1949)

---

organizational heroes. But their heroism will be more situational, a response to an urgent need or crisis—not a way of organizational life.

Heroic style managers are stress carriers. They create high levels of stress for themselves and transmit it to others around them. Such managers typically will give a secretary a handwritten letter to type and then *watch*, with ever-increasing nervousness for everyone concerned, as it is typed; or will give an assignment to subordinates and then tell them exactly how to do it; or will insist on being the center and controller of all organizational communications—thereby causing information bottlenecks and corresponding organizational incompetence. When heroic leadership is allowed by the organization's top managers, it is reinforced and imitated by lower level managers. While no organization would advocate self-destructive leadership styles, tolerating them amounts to the same thing. Modern organizational leadership is inherently more situational or contingent than heroic.

Unlike the trait theory and transactional leadership approaches, contingency approaches take into consideration the many factors that may influence a leader's style. There is a recognition that a successful leader in one type of organization may not be successful in another simply because it differs from the previous one. Its situation (or context) is different, and the choice of a style needs to be contingent upon the situation. As leadership historian Ralph Stogdill notes, the contingency theories stress:

1. The type, structure, size and purpose of the organization
2. The external environment in which the organization functions
3. The orientation, values, goals, and expectations of the leader, his superiors, and subordinates
4. The expert or professional knowledge required of the position

The contingency approaches assert that different leadership styles will differ in their effects in different situations. The situation (not traits or styles themselves) determines whether a leadership style or a particular leader will be effective. Thus, contingency theorists maintain that there is no "one best way"—as in the scientific management of Frederick Taylor—of effective leadership. Just think of Ulysses S. Grant, the victorious general of the American Civil War. On the basis of his war record, he was elected president in 1868. But he was as good a general as he was bad as president. He is rated among the best generals in American history; at the same time historians almost universally concede that he was one of the very worst presidents. Other American generals were able to make the leap from military to civilian leadership—George Washington, Andrew Jackson, and Dwight D. Eisenhower being the most famous examples. But poor President Grant just did not have it in him. He wasn't able to spontaneously retool his mind as a civilian leader. While Grant himself was honest, he consistently showed blind loyalty to corrupt friends.

Robert Tannenbaum and Warren Schmidt conducted one of the first studies that actually indicated a need for leaders to evaluate the situational factors prior to the implementation of a particular leadership style. They concluded that "the successful manager . . . can be primarily characterized neither as a strong leader nor as a permissive one." Indeed, he or she "is one who maintains a high batting average in accurately assessing the forces that determine what his most appropriate behavior at any given time should be and in actually being able to behave accordingly."

While Tannenbaum and Schmidt assert that leaders should adjust their styles to accommodate followers, University of Washington professor Fred Fiedler found that the opposite was often true. It is sometimes easier to change the work environment, the situation, to fit a leader's style. The underlying leadership style depends upon personality. According to Fiedler, a leader's personality is not likely to change because of a few lectures or a few weeks of intensive training. Therefore, an organization should not choose a leader who fits a situation, but should change the situation to mesh with the style of its leader. But this is easier said than done. The choices are clearly expressed by the new boss who tells the staff: "We can do things my way, your way, or the company's way. If you do things my way, we'll get along just fine."

Transformational Leadership

A transformational leader is one with the ability to change an imbedded organizational culture by creating a new vision for the organization and marshalling the appropriate support to make that vision the new reality. The best-known transformational leader is General George S. Patton Jr., who during World War II took charge of a defeated and demoralized American Army in North Africa and transformed it into a winning team. The task was different but no less difficult for Lee Iacocca when he took charge of a Chrysler Corporation on the verge of bankruptcy and disintegration in the late 1970s and brought it back into profit. Similar challenges faced the leadership of AT&T when it went from a monopoly public utility to a company that had to change its corporate culture to compete in the open market.

Edward G. Rendell faced a similar problem (but different in its content) when he became mayor of Philadelphia in 1992. Philadelphia was a "loser"—in just

Box 9.2

Machiavelli on Leadership Style

From this arises the question whether it is better to be loved more than feared, or feared more than loved. The reply is, that one ought to be both feared and loved, but as it is difficult for the two to go together, it is much safer to be feared than loved, if one of the two has to be wanting. . . . And men have less scruple in offending one who makes himself loved than one who makes himself feared; for love is held by a chain of obligation which, men being selfish, is broken whenever it serves their purpose; but fear is maintained by a dread of punishment which never fails.

SOURCE: Niccolo Machiavelli, *The Prince* (1513).

about every way—in the eyes of employees, potential employers, bond holders, suppliers, and citizens. It was simply *assumed* that the city could not compete head-on with comparable cities. Rendell had to change not only an organizational culture, but also just about *everybody's perception* of that culture. He effectively told the municipal unions to get with the plan or "kiss off." After a brief strike that was notable for its lack of public support, they got with the plan. Philadelphia needed and got in Rendell a transformational leader, a person who could totally transform an imbedded organizational culture by creating a new vision of and for the organization, and successfully selling that vision—by rallying commitment and loyalty to make the vision become a reality.

Noel Tichy and David Ulrich describe transformational leaders as those rare individuals who can lead employees through their fears and uncertainties to the realization of the new vision. This requires strategic leadership that successfully changes people's perceptions of the organization. Transformational change is more than a rational, technical, incremental approach to change. The leader's primary function is to lead and support through carefully conceived change stages, acting as a cheerleader and as a belief model—verbally and nonverbally communicating belief in the benefits to all that will accrue from the changes.

Historian Stephen E. Ambrose wrote that during World War II General Dwight D. Eisenhower felt that it was critical that he, no matter what his personal feelings at the time, maintain an air of absolute confidence. He knew that confidence, or "cheerleading," at the top would permeate down through every level of his immense organization. Eisenhower instinctively knew, as social science now proves, that a confident organization is far more likely to succeed than a doubtful one—even if its leader in reality has doubts.

Whereas the transactional theories of leadership apply primarily to leadership roles, functions, and behavior within an existing organizational culture, transformative leadership is about leadership to change a culture. Transactional leadership focuses on incremental change. Transformative leadership is about radical change.

Sometimes the radical changes call for co-optation, the inclusion of new, potentially dissident group members into an organization's policymaking process to prevent such elements from being a threat to the organization or its mission. More often it is the implementation of a new strategic vision.

It is interesting to observe that transformational leadership theories have many similarities with the trait theories of leadership. Transformational leadership borders on "great man" theory—the belief that leaders are born, not made. In many ways, leadership theory is once again involved in seeking to find the basis of leadership in traits—rather than in relational and cultural factors. We have come full circle!

Too Much Leadership

Structural rigidity often causes managers to overmanage—to lead too much. "Micromanage" is the pejorative term for supervising too closely. Any manager may be guilty of micromanagement for refusing to allow subordinates to have any real authority or responsibility, thereby ensuring that subordinates can neither function as, or grow into, effective managers. Further, the managers are kept so busy micromanaging that they never have time to do what managers are supposed to do—like develop long-term strategy and overall vision. Legislators at all levels of government are frequently practitioners of micromanagement. By writing detailed rules for programs into legislation, by demanding that particular items be procured from suppliers in their districts, or mandating that certain employees be hired or promoted for patronage purposes, they deny public managers a large measure of the real administrative discretion that all effective managers need.

Micromanagement

An apt example of legislative micromanagement is provided by Philip Howard. In *The Death of Common Sense*, his denouncement of governmental micromanagement, he recounts the story of Mother Teresa's Missionaries of Charity trying to build a homeless shelter in New York City. A group of nuns from the organization proposed refurbishing an abandoned four-story building that would house 64 residents. But all four-story buildings in New York had to have an elevator—which would have added $100,000 to the cost. This lack of amenities did not deter the nuns, who shun modern conveniences and did not want an elevator anyway—or a dishwasher. It was to be a no-frills basic shelter. But regulations are regulations. When the Mother Teresa group could not find anyone who had the authority to waive the elevator requirement after 18 months of navigating the hallways of the municipal bureaucracy, they gave up and went on to other good works.

While there is some legitimate justification for micromanagement by legislators and directors (after all they are the legitimate representatives of the owners of the government or corporation), there is no justification for micromanagement along the traditional chain of hierarchical authority. While close supervision is appropriate for a trainee, it is insulting and disabling for any employee who is presumably able. And it can be dangerous. Micromanagement can drive employees over the edge into violence. For example, in recent years the U.S. Postal Service has had a spate of enraged workers going berserk and murdering their supervisors. These tensions are common in many industries. But according to Peter Kilborn, in post offices they "fester[ed] within an archaic, Army-like culture in which many top managers communicate by directive, and front-line supervisors often hover over their charges, waiting for a mistake and timing workers' trips to the bathroom." Shootings have killed three dozen people in U.S. Post Offices from the mid-1980s to the mid-1990s. In 1994 the "Federal Centers for Disease Control and Prevention found that murder was the second leading cause of death on the job for postal workers."

Micromanagement will not make a competent employee more competent; it only makes things worse by wasting time, by damaging interpersonal relationships, by demonstrating that the micromanagers themselves are not competent supervisors, and by distracting managers from the kinds of activities that can prevent organizational incompetence. Instead, micromanagement—and overmanagement—lead to overcommitment and bureaucratic overcontrol, two of the classic symptoms of organizational incompetence.

Overmanagement

Having too many managers for the nature of the organization or task—overmanagement—is related to and inevitably leads to micromanagement and organizational rigidity. Overmanagement has become a particularly important problem in recent years as computer-driven information systems render once-useful layers of middle management obsolete. These threatened managers struggle to find new roles for themselves and ways to retain their long-standing sources of authority, which have depended on their exclusive control of organizations' knowledge bases. They get in the way of more productive organizational units until periodic downsizing efforts permanently remove them. But until they are sought out and expelled, they are among the major structural causes of organizational incompetence.

Moral Leadership

Garry Wills warns that "if the leader is just an expediter of what other people want, a resource for their use, the people are not being *led* but *serviced*." Thus it is moving people in new directions—taking them to places where they did not know they wanted or needed to go—that is the essence of leadership, and has been since ancient times. Thucydides, in his *History of the Peloponnesian War*, describes Pericles, the leader of ancient Athens, as someone who, because he was so "clearly above corruption, was enabled, by the respect others had for him and his own wise policy, to hold the multitude in a voluntary restraint." Thus "he led them, not they him; and since he did not win his power on compromising terms, he could say not only what pleased others but what displeased them, relying on their respect."

The Bully Pulpit

Pericles exercised moral leadership. He was able to send people in new directions of action and thought because it was the right and decent thing to do. During the presidential campaign of 1932, then-New York Governor Franklin D. Roosevelt spoke for all political executives when he said "The presidency is not merely an adminis-

The "inventor" of the bully pulpit, President Theodore Roosevelt. He was such an energetic speaker—really a civil preacher—that once in 1912, when a would-be assassin shot him in the chest, he refused medical treatment until he had finished his speech. He told his Milwaukee audience: "I have just been shot; but it takes more than that to kill a Bull Moose!" They looked on in shocked admiration as he continued to bleed and talk. What saved Roosevelt's life was the fact that the bullet went into his breast pocket and through a folded speech and metal eyeglass case before hitting him. While the event was dramatic and bloody, Roosevelt, with his extensive experience during the Spanish-American War, knew that he had suffered only a flesh wound. And why let that ruin a good speech on an otherwise fine day! •

trative office. That's the least of it. It is more than an engineering job, efficient or in-efficient. It is pre-eminently a place of moral leadership. All our great presidents were leaders of thought at times when certain historic ideas in the life of the nation had to be clarified." Presidents have traditionally used what President Theodore Roosevelt called their bully (meaning "first-rate") pulpit to provide this clarification.

Rhetorical Leadership

Political scientists James Caeser, Glen Thurow, Jeffrey Tulis, and Joseph Bessette in "The Rise of the Rhetorical Presidency," argue that, historically, leadership through rhetoric was suspect, that presidents rarely spoke directly to the people, and that, in any event, presidents relied much more heavily on party and political leadership in the Congress for their electoral and programmatic support. But today's presidents attempt to move mass opinion by speeches that exhort the public to support their policies and programs. Presidents are obliged to do this for three reasons: (1) the modern doctrine of the presidency, which avers that the presidency is a place of moral leadership and should employ rhetoric to lead public opinion; (2) the advent of the modern mass media, especially television, which facilitates the use of rhetoric; and (3) the modern presidential campaign, which blurs campaigning and governing.

According to Caeser, et al., "Popular or mass rhetoric, which presidents once employed only rarely, now serves as one of their principal tools in attempting to govern the nation. Whatever doubts Americans may now entertain about the limitations of presidential leadership, they do not consider it unfitting or inappropriate for presidents to attempt to 'move' the public by programmatic speeches that exhort and set forth grand and ennobling views." But just as it was with ancient Pericles, their views are only accepted as "grand and ennobling" if they themselves are perceived as noble, worthy, and above corruption.

The "two presidencies" phenomena is telling here. This is Aaron Wildavsky's division of the presidency into two differing spheres of influence: foreign policy and domestic policy. Wildavsky contended that presidential leadership in foreign policy will, generally speaking, find greater support among the public than leadership in domestic policy. To test his hypothesis, Wildavsky examined congressional action on presidential proposals from 1948 to 1964. For this period, the Congress approved 58.5 percent of the foreign policy bills; 73.3 percent of the defense policy bills; and 70.8 percent of general foreign relations, State Department, foreign aid bills, and treaties. During this same period, the Congress approved only 40.2 percent of the president's domestic policy proposals. Thus the two-presidencies thesis was confirmed. Wildavsky's work has spawned a bevy of research articles. While Wildavsky himself in "Reconsidering the Two Presidencies," would in 1989 concede that his thesis was decidedly "time and culture bound," nothing has materially diminished the essence of his original thesis put forth in 1966. The reason the president is so much more successful in foreign policy is that he comes to the table with cleaner hands—he is less the conniving politician and more the noble statesman.

But more people than presidents can offer moral leadership. For example, Secretary of Health and Human Services Louis W. Sullivan was considered one of the most ineffectual members of the Bush administration until 1990, when he started attacking cigarette companies for targeting the marketing of cigarettes to minorities and women. His popularity and stature immediately soared. More important, he was effective. R.J. Reynolds, one of the largest U.S. tobacco companies, was test marketing a new brand called "Uptown," which was specifically aimed at African Americans. Sullivan said: "This brand is cynically and deliberately targeted toward black Americans. . . . At a time when we must cultivate greater responsibility among our citizens, Uptown's slick and sinister advertising proposes instead a great degree of personal irresponsibility." After Sullivan's attack, the brand was withdrawn. While moral leadership may not move mountains, it can sometimes move cigarette companies.

The Challenge of Accountability

Accountability is the obverse of leadership in all democratic societies. Without accountability leadership is an undemocratic dictatorship. Therefore, to fully understand democratic leadership, we must explore the means by which leaders are held accountable and their dictatorial tendencies are inhibited.

Accountability is the extent to which one must answer to higher authority—legal or organizational—for one's actions in society at large or within one's particular organizational position. Elected public officials are theoretically accountable to the political sovereignty of the voters. In this sense, appointed officials—from file clerks to cabinet secretaries—are less accountable than elected officials. The former are accountable mainly to their organizational supervisors, while the latter must answer to the people of their jurisdiction.

Administrative accountability is that aspect of administrative responsibility by which officials are held answerable for general notions of democracy and morality as well as for specific legal mandates. The two basic approaches to administrative accountability were first delineated by political scientists Carl J. Friedrich (1901–1984) and Herman Finer (1898–1969). Friedrich argued that administrative responsibility can be ensured only internally, through professionalism or professional standards or codes, because the increasing complexities of modern policies require extensive policy expertise and specialized abilities on the part of bureaucrats. Finer, on the other hand, argued that administrative responsibility could be maintained only externally, through legislative or popular controls, because internal power or control would ultimately lead to corruption. The tension between these two approaches continues today. Thus the challenge of accountability is to find a balance between completely trusting government officials to use their best professional judgment in the public's interest, and watching them so closely through legislative committees or executive review agencies that it inhibits their ability to function.

Because we aspire to a democratic form of government, we need to consider how the links between democratic government and public administration work. What are the things we do, must do, and indeed must avoid if we are to be public administrators in a democracy rather than cogs in a despotic mechanism? Under the totalitarian communism of the former Soviet Union, the Russians had a word for people who served the apparatus of state without question. They were called **apparatchiks**—a term implying that the individual mindlessly follows orders. What stops us from being apparatchiks in all but name?

The answer to this question is that public administrators in a democracy work within the rule of law—a governing system in which the highest authority is a body of law that applies equally to all (as opposed to the rule of men, in which the personal whim of those in power can decide any issue). The idea of the desirability of a "government of laws, and not of men" can be traced back to Aristotle. The earliest American reference is in the 1779 Massachusetts Constitution. John Marshall also used this succinct legal description in *Marbury v. Madison* (1803): "The government of the United States has been emphatically termed a government of laws, and not of men. It will certainly cease to deserve this high appellation, if the laws furnish no remedy for the violation of a vested legal right." The rule of law and the concomitant notion that no one is above the law have been continuously critical concepts. When Ford succeeded Nixon (who was forced to resign because

---

apparatchik This Russian word for a bureaucrat is now used colloquially to refer to any administrative functionary.

of his illegal activities during the Watergate scandal), he told the nation right after taking the oath of office (August 9, 1974): "My fellow Americans, our long national nightmare is over. Our Constitution works; our great Republic is a government of laws and not of men." This was difficult for many citizens to reconcile with his **pardon** of Nixon one month later; so they voted Ford out of office the first chance they got. Now that's accountability!

In democratic societies, we require our administrators to work within a system of democratic accountability, to respond to a complex system of checks and balances, and be subject to scrutiny by official auditors, by the media and by community watchdogs and whistleblowers (as Finer advocated). But in the end, they are individually responsible for their own ethical and honorable behavior (as Friedrich believed). We often (but not always) remove from office those public administrators who seek to ignore their responsibilities to democracy. Occasionally, as in the case of J. Edgar Hoover of the FBI, there will be public administrators in democratic societies who seem to be above the law. But they, too, will fall from power in the end—if only because they eventually die.

Sometimes we purposely create public institutions that seem to have an "above the law" status. Security organizations sometimes seem to have this characteristic, best exemplified by the fictional British secret agent James Bond's "license to kill." Intelligence agencies have always had a certain mystical quality—perhaps because they are so associated with fictional exploits. This even affects presidents. Arthur M. Schlesinger Jr., in *A Thousand Days* (1965), quoted President John F. Kennedy: "If someone comes in to tell me this or that about the minimum wage bill, I have no hesitation in overruling them. But you always assume that the military and intelligence people have some secret skill not available to ordinary mortals." The review of the policies and activities of U.S. intelligence agencies by appropriate legislative review committees was not formally done by the Congress until the 1970s, when reports of FBI and CIA abuses of their operating mandates encouraged both houses of the Congress to create committees that would systematically and formally watch over the intelligence operations of the executive branch. Parliamentary systems, which are used in most of the world, have far less opportunity for comparable oversight because prime ministers, who ultimately direct intelligence agencies, lead both the executive and the legislative branches of government.

More generally, however, abuse of authority in public administration is a central target for condemnation in democratic societies, and a likely route to disgrace and dismissal. Yet in many societies around the world to hold official office, to be a public administrator, is to be able to take **arbitrary** decisions, to confer benefits on

---

pardon An executive's granting of a release from the legal consequences of a criminal act. This may occur before or after indictment or conviction. The U.S. president's power to pardon people for federal offenses is absolute except for convictions in impeachment cases. A pardon prior to indictment stops all criminal proceedings. This is what happened when President Gerald Ford pardoned Richard M. Nixon in 1974 for all offenses that he "has committed or may have committed or taken part in while president."

arbitrary Decided on the basis of individual judgments that do not meet commonly understood rules of procedure and hence may not appear justifiable to those seeking to explain them to others or to replicate them in similar circumstances.

family and friends, and to be open to corrupt, unethical—even inhuman—behavior. So we must ask: what legal and institutional arrangements, conventions, and ethical values essentially distinguish democratic from despotic public administration? In truly democratic societies—as opposed to those that are democratic in name only—there is a framework of constitutional, legal, and procedural requirements that subject public administrators to rigorous monitoring and oversight by a democratic legislature, independent courts, and other institutions at arm's length from the government. This leads to the expectation on the part of public administrators that, for the most part, they must work in the open, not only expecting but welcoming the scrutiny of elected representatives and the others whose task it is to make public accountability work.

Constitutional and Legal Constraints

Like it or not, public administrators always work within some kind of legal framework. In Europe, particularly in Germany, the legal setting of public administration is so all-encompassing that a senior official normally cannot be appointed without a formal law degree. In other parts of the world, a law degree is usually not required, but some understanding of constitutional and administrative law is. For American public administrators, the Constitution serves as an invisible fence surrounding their field of operation. Specific laws deriving from it delineate and regulate in finer and finer detail what public administrators can do to whom, when, and how.

David H. Rosenbloom states that there are three reasons why public administrators should understand the Constitution:

1. Public administration must have democratic policy very much at heart, so that managerial and political approaches are taken that are compatible with constitutional principles and values.

2. Many public administrators in America take an oath to support the Constitution, and this may be more important than routine administrative functions.

3. Public administrators may be personally liable for civil damages if they act in contravention to the Constitution.

As Rosenbloom emphasizes, it is no easy task to achieve the necessary understanding of the Constitution, since its contemporary meaning extends not only to the letter of the document, but to **case law** and extensive interpretation, derived from legal, philosophical, moral, and political considerations as to how the law should be applied.

Public administrators in each policy domain—health, civil defense, education, or whatever it may be—need to maintain an awareness that the Constitution impacts on what they can do by virtue of specific judgments and case law in the past, or alternatively because in a general sense what they propose to do may be seen to conflict with the Bill of Rights or some other fundamental Constitutional precept. For example, in *Wood v. Strickland* (1975) the U.S. Supreme Court held that a

---

case law All recorded judicial and administrative agency decisions.

school board member (and by implication other public employees) is not immune from liability for damages "if he knew or reasonably should have known that the action he took within his sphere of official responsibility would violate the constitutional rights of the students affected, or if he took the action with the malicious intention to cause a deprivation of constitutional rights or other injury to the student."

Apart from the general constraints and freedoms conferred on administrators by the Constitution, the laws creating governing institutions and regulating their particular policy domain must also remain foremost in administrators' minds. Sometimes this component of the framework of democratic oversight can involve the president and a committee of the Congress working with officials to design the legislation that will guide future administration. They all know that the **legislative history** may be used in writing rules, or by courts in interpreting the law, to ascertain the intent of the Congress if the act is ambiguous or lacking in detail. The history, particularly the committee reports, often contains the only complete explanation of the meaning and intent of the law. Thus members of the Congress, their staffs, and other interested parties often try to influence a legislative history to help shape the way the law is eventually administered by agencies and interpreted by the courts. Sometimes, during the legislative debate on a bill, a member of the legislature will specifically talk about what is intended or not intended by the bill so that the ensuing legislative history will be a better guide to future interpretations of the **legislative intent**.

Arthur E. Morgan, the first chairman of the Tennessee Valley Authority, described how, after he had been chosen for the role, President Franklin D. Roosevelt gave him permission to meet and work with the **conference committee** of the House and Senate, which was designing the enabling legislation. The scope of the discussions extended to the composition of the board of the proposed agency and its powers and policies. In the course of the discussions, Morgan was able to make scores of suggestions for changes to the legislation within which he would have to work for many years. Few public administrators enjoy this rare privilege. For the most part, they must work within a framework laid down by others and hope that it provides scope for the needs that emerge—sometimes years later in very different contexts than originally anticipated.

Obsessive Accountability

It was Napoléon's foreign minister Charles-Maurice de Talleyrand who is usually credited with first saying of administrative affairs, "Above all, not too much zeal." Yet it is an excess of zeal in the form of obsessive attention to minor details that so

---

legislative history The written record of the writing of an act of the U.S. Congress.
legislative intent The supposed real meaning of a statute as interpreted from its legislative history.
conference committee A meeting between the representatives of the two houses of a legislature to reconcile the differences over the provisions of a bill. Unless all differences between the houses are finally adjusted, the bill fails. The conference committee process can sometimes have a dramatic effect on a bill. As President Ronald Reagan once said, "You know, if an orange and an apple went into conference consultations, it might come out a pear" (*New York Times*, December 18, 1982).

often leads to incompetence in modern organizations. Some of this dysfunctional zeal is caused by aberrant personalities, but the real culprit is the formally mandated zeal of governing rules and regulations. Much required zeal is good. No one can argue with requirements for punctuality. But once organization-wide standard procedures are established for major functions, there is an inevitable tendency for minutiae to be covered as well. These minutiae then, quite literally, take more time than they are worth.

For example, in 1993 the U.S. General Accounting Office reported that "each year the military spends some $20 million moving and storing a half-million items worth less than the cost of processing." Thus a U.S. base in Europe returns a few dollars, worth of metal bolts or nylon cord to a Defense Department warehouse in Ohio. But since it costs $40 to process these small items, it would have been far less expensive to give or throw away the stuff. However, there is no provision in the rules for disposing of unneeded items in this way. Such practices would give too much discretion to individual employees. The formal organization, in its zeal to prevent theft, mandates many such wasteful practices.

Peter Drucker maintains that organizations, most typically governments, that are obsessed with accountability are inherently less competent than they might be. New procedures are created in response to possible or previous abuses. Since individuals once showed themselves incapable of being responsible for specified organizational assets, discretion over them was taken out of their hands and given to unemotional, unbending, and, in some circumstances, irrational procedures. Accountability was placed in procedures rather than in individuals, the rationale being that the honest administration was too important a matter to leave to an individual's discretion. It is precisely because of governments' attempts to assign accountability for everything they control that public management operations grow to be outrageously expensive when compared to similar functions in private industry. According to Drucker, government must always tolerate this extra expense—not out of some unwarranted affection for red tape but because a "little dishonesty" in government is a corrosive disease that rapidly spreads to infect the entire polity. To fear such corruption is quite rational. Consequently, government "bureaucracy" and its attendant high costs cannot and should not be eliminated.

While the high costs of accountability can never be totally eliminated, some of the dysfunction of its associated procedures can be mitigated. Such mitigation frequently has organizations bending, ignoring, and subverting regulations in the interests of good management. The discretion that the regulations deny to the executive may be restored by the machinations of administrative operatives. When the flexibility deemed essential for mission accomplishment is formally denied to line managers, it is almost invariably obtained informally through administrative finesse. This is an idea that has not only been demonstrated in countless empirical studies, but also sanctioned and revered in American popular culture. The nation has a tremendous appetite for movies and television programs about war and other violent escapades. As any aficionado with sufficient exposure to this genre of entertainment can explain, you cannot have a successful military operation without a scrounger in your unit—at least not according to Hollywood's version of World War II. A scrounger was that member of the team assigned to obtain all the essential requirements of the mission that could not be obtained through official channels. It hardly mattered what methods the scroungers used to secure the needed supplies as long as they succeeded—and there were no official complaints. The war seems to have been won in large measure because our scroungers were better at overcoming organizational constraints than their scroungers.

The obvious danger of managers using excessive zeal in seeking to achieve an organization's mission, and thereby going beyond the proper range of discretion, is well recognized. This is an inherent and necessary risk in all managerial delegation. Unreasonable constraints only exacerbate the danger and increase the frustration. When mandates from on high reflect neither administrative wisdom nor experience, they are viewed as barriers to managerial effectiveness—which must be overcome. There is even significant evidence that organizational superiors discourage subordinates from reporting fully just how they have accomplished their missions because of concerns for formal or legal culpability. According to Herbert Kaufman, executives "may resort to the strategy of discouraging feedback about administrative behavior because they privately *approve* of the behavior they know they should, according to law and morality, prevent." Thus rookie police officers are told by their more experienced associates that they will have to forget what they learned at the police academy before they can operate effectively—and survive—in a real-world situation. Any new public manager must suffer through an on-the-job acquisition of administrative **realpolitik**. They learn by the unfortunate consequences of violating norms that are discovered only when they are breached. While this may seem at first to be an unnecessary and gratuitous bit of trauma to impose upon innocent individuals, it is a critical rite of passage in the loss of administrative innocence and the learning of organizational norms and the inculcation of an organization's culture.

Avoiding Accountability

The public rightly expects an executive to be accountable for the actions of the subordinates he or she has selected, whether or not the executive had actual knowledge of the actions. It is based on the belief that the selection of subordinates and the monitoring of their behavior is an executive responsibility. Nowhere is primitive ritual or **Machiavellian** feigning more apparent than in the periodic

---

realpolitik A German word, now absorbed into English, meaning the politics of realism; an injunction not to allow wishful thinking or sentimentality to cloud one's judgment. At its most moderate, the word is used to describe an overcynical approach, one that allows little room for human altruism, that always seeks an ulterior motive behind another actor's statements or justifications. At its strongest, it suggests that no moral values should be allowed to affect the single-minded pursuit of one's own self-interest or patriotism. It also makes an absolute assumption that any opponent will certainly behave in this way.

Machiavellian Referring to Niccolo Machiavelli (1469–1527), the Italian Renaissance political philosopher whose book of advice to would-be leaders, *The Prince* (1532), is the progenitor of all how-to-succeed books. Its exploration of how political power is grasped, used, and kept is the benchmark against which all subsequent analyses are judged. Machiavelli's amoral tone and detached analysis have caused him to be both soundly denounced as well as greatly imitated. While his name has become synonymous with political deception, no other writer has given the world such a brilliant lesson in how to think in terms of cold political power.

assumption of full responsibility by an organization's chief executive. Although one of the advantages of delegating a problem is the ease with which the cunning leader can shift the blame for the situation if it sours, modern executives are seldom so crude as to lay blame. The appropriate tactic is to assume full responsibility for the situation. Paradoxically, in assuming full responsibility, the executive is seemingly relieved of it. Political scientist Murray Edelman observed that whenever this ritual is enacted, all of the participants tend to experience "a warm glow of satisfaction and relief that responsibility has been assumed and can be pinpointed. It once again conveys the message that the incumbent is the leader, that he knows he is able to cope, and that he should be followed." In reality, however, this ritual proves to have no substance. It "emphatically does not mean that the chief executive will be penalized for the mistakes of subordinates or that the latter will not be penalized."

This is the tactic that President Richard M. Nixon employed when he first addressed the nation concerning the Watergate scandals in the spring of 1973. He boldly proclaimed that all of the possibly illegal actions of the White House officials were his responsibility and that he fully accepted that responsibility. Certainly Nixon did not mean to imply—at that point in time—that he should be punished for the transgressions of his underlings. Nor did Ronald Reagan in 1987 when he took full responsibility for the Iran-Contra affair. Bill Clinton, during an August 17, 1998, television address to the nation, took full responsibility for lying to his wife, his cabinet, his staff, and his nation about his affair with White House intern Monica Lewinsky. But his hopes that this would be enough to stop an impeachment inquiry were short-lived. Government officials of lesser rank are no less sophisticated with their manipulations of the ritualistic and symbolic aspects of their offices. Of course, the risk they take is that the legislature will investigate the situation thoroughly enough to expose any wrongdoing.

Legislative Oversight

While constitutional and legal frameworks themselves amount to a passive exercise of democratic control over the discretion of public administrators, there is no substitute for active control through energetic elected representatives. The main reason the U.S. Congress (or a state legislature or a city council) monitors the activities of executive branch agencies is to determine if the laws are being faithfully executed. After all, the president has the constitutional obligation (given in Article 2, Section 3) to "take care that the laws be faithfully executed." Congressional oversight is designed in our system of "checks and balances" to check that he does.

Hearings

Oversight takes many forms. The most obvious are the annual congressional hearings on agency budget requests, in which agency activities have to be justified to the satisfaction of the Congress. Both the House and the Senate hold budget hearings. But only the Senate holds hearings on the confirmation of major appointees such as cabinet secretaries and Supreme Court nominees.

Any member of the Congress can instigate an investigation. Many of these investigations are small matters concerning the interests of a single constituent (see the section on casework below). But if something significant turns up worthy of a larger inquiry, an appropriate committee or subcommittee always has the right to initiate a further examination. The oversight function is primarily implemented through the process of hearings that often call for sworn testimony from officials, through consultancy reports and through the publication of findings. Committees that have investigated scandals such as Watergate and the Iran-Contra affair and issues such as whether gays should be permitted to serve in the military, illustrate how important and central a role this aspect of democratic government can be. In consequence, those who become chair of an influential committee of Congress occupy powerful positions indeed.

The entire Congress is in effect a permanently sitting **grand jury** always waiting to hear of improper acts by executive branch agencies so that **hearings** can be launched and witnesses called. Some members of the Congress are so zealous in their oversight concerns that they will go to the trouble of traveling all over the world (at government expense) to see how federal programs and policies are operating. These visits are derisively called junkets, but they are an important part of the oversight process. Some members of the Congress simply cannot understand why it is necessary to vote for money for American forces in NATO unless they first visit Europe and make a thorough investigation of the situation.

Of course, the oversight function may be abused, especially when it is done for partisan advantage. Such political oversight often happens when the executive and legislative branches of a government are controlled by opposing parties; then its purpose may be to embarrass the administration. Two famous examples of this are the Democratic party-sponsored Watergate hearings of 1973–1974 which helped force Republican President Richard Nixon to resign in 1974, and the Republican party-sponsored Whitewater hearings of 1995–1996, which were designed to embarrass the Democratic President Bill Clinton. Of course, whether an oversight action is simply in the interest of good government or whether it is a play in a game of partisan one-upmanship is in the eye of the beholder.

Casework

Casework is the term used for the services performed by legislators and their staffs at the request of and on behalf of constituents. For example, a U.S. representative may be asked to discover why a Social Security check has been delayed or why a

---

grand jury A group of citizens selected to review evidence against accused persons to determine whether there is sufficient evidence to bring the accused to trial—to indict or not to indict. A grand jury usually has from 12 to 23 members and operates in secrecy to protect the reputation of those not indicted. Grand juries have been both criticized for being easily manipulated tools in the hands of prosecutors and praised for protecting the rights of those falsely accused.

hearings A legislative committee session for hearing witnesses. At hearings on legislation, witnesses usually include specialists, government officials, and representatives of those affected by the bills under study. Subpoena power may be used to summon reluctant witnesses. The public and press may attend open hearings but are barred from closed (executive) hearings.

Box 9.3

Casework in Action

I would relate to the crowds how I called on a certain rural constituent and was shocked to hear him say he was thinking of voting for my opponent. I reminded him of the many things I had done for him as prosecuting attorney, as county judge, as congressman, and senator. I recalled how I had helped get an access road built to his farm, how I had visited him in a military hospital in France when he was wounded in World War I, how I had assisted him in securing his veteran's benefits, how I had arranged his loan from the Farm Credit Administration, how I had got him a disaster loan when the flood destroyed his home, etc., etc.

"How can you think of voting for my opponent?" I exhorted at the end of this long recital. "Surely you remember all these things I have done for you!"

"Yeah," he said, "I remember. But what in hell have you done for me lately?"

SOURCE: Alben W. Barkley, *That Reminds Me* (Garden City, NY: Doubleday, 1954). Barkley was vice president under Truman.

veteran's claim for benefits has been denied. Casework is an important means by which legislators maintain oversight of the bureaucracy and solidify their political base with constituents.

Casework offers many advantages for legislators. First, it's cheap and noncontroversial. For the price of some minor staff time, a politician can make a voter happy. After dealing with thousands of cases over several years, this can pay back big on election day. Of course, there is always the danger that the legislator will not be able to solve the constituent's problem. But if the situation is handled with promptness and tactfulness, the case can still be a net gain from a public relations viewpoint. Even if the "customer" did not get what was wanted from the bureaucracy, a perception of fair treatment will still go a long way.

Agency administrators can also benefit from good casework service. The responsive handling of constituent problems will tend to make legislators more receptive to next year's budget requests. And a pattern of similar casework complaints could indicate administrative problems that need to be fixed before the numbers explode. Naturally, there is a thin line between administrative troubleshooting and special treatment. This is a line that astute administrators must walk straight—well, almost straight!

Summary

Leadership is the exercise of authority, whether formal or informal, in directing and coordinating the work of others. The best leaders are those who can simultaneously exercise both kinds of leadership: the formal, based on the authority of rank or office, and the informal, based on the willingness of others to give service to a person with special qualities of authority.

There is a difference between leadership and management: management involves power (formal authority) bestowed on the occupant of a position by a higher organizational authority; leadership, in contrast, cannot be bestowed by a higher authority—it must be earned.

Administrative accountability is that aspect of administrative responsibility by which officials are held answerable for general notions of democracy and morality as well as for specific legal mandates. In democratic societies administrators are required to respond to a complex system of checks and balances and to be subject to scrutiny by official auditors, by the media, and by community watchdogs and potential whistleblowers.

While a government's constitutional and legal frameworks are a passive exercise of democratic control over the discretion of public administrators, there is no substitute for the active control of energetic elected representatives. This control, known as legislative oversight, takes many forms. The most obvious form is the annual congressional hearings on agency budget requests, in which agency activities have to be justified to the satisfaction of the Congress.

Key Concepts

accountability   The extent to which one must answer to higher authority—legal or organizational—for one's actions in society at large or within one's particular organizational position.

casework   The services performed by legislators and their staffs at the request of and on behalf of constituents.

charisma   Leadership based on the compelling personality of the leader rather than upon formal position. The word charisma is derived from the Greek word for divine grace. The concept was first developed by Max Weber, who distinguished charismatic authority from both the traditional authority of a monarch and the legal authority given to someone by law.

congressional oversight   The total means by which the U.S. Congress monitors the activities of executive branch agencies to determine if the laws are being faithfully executed.

contingency theory   An approach to leadership asserting that leadership styles will vary in their effects in different situations. The situation (not traits or styles themselves) determines whether a leadership style or a particular leader will be effective.

leadership   The exercise of authority, whether formal or informal, in directing and coordinating the work of others.

moral leadership   Leading people in specific directions of action and thought based on morals and decency.

rule of law   A governing system in which the highest authority is a body of law that applies equally to all (as opposed to the traditional "rule of men," in which the personal whim of those in power can decide any issue).

trait theory   An approach to leadership that assumes leaders possess traits that make them fundamentally different from followers. Advocates of trait theory believe that some people have unique leadership characteristics and qualities that enable them to assume responsibilities not everyone can execute. Therefore they are "born" leaders.

transformational leadership   Leadership that strives to change organizational culture and directions. It reflects the ability of a leader to develop a values-based vision for the organization, to convert the vision into reality, and to maintain it over time.

Bibliography

Ambrose, Stephen E. (1994). *D-Day*. New York: Simon and Schuster.

Barnard, Chester I. (1938). *The Functions of the Executive*. Cambridge: Harvard University Press.

Caeser, James, Glen Thurow, Jeffrey Tulis, and Joseph Bessette. (1981). "The Rise of the Rhetorical Presidency," *Presidential Studies Quarterly* (Spring 1981).

Cohen, Jeffrey E. (1982). "A Historical Reassessment of Wildavsky's 'Two Presidencies,'" *Social Science Quarterly* (September).

Downs, G., and P. D. Larkey. (1986). *The Search for Government Efficiency*. New York: Random House.

Drucker, Peter F. (1969). "The Sickness of Government," *Public Interest* 14 (Winter).

Dynes, Michael, and David Walker. (1995). *The New British State*. London: Times Books.

Edelman, Murray. (1967). *The Symbolic Uses of Politics*. Urbana: University of Illinois Press.

Edwards, George C., III. (1986). "The Two Presidencies: A Reevaluation," *American Politics Quarterly* (July).

Fiedler, Fred. E. (1967). *A Theory of Leadership Effectiveness*. New York: McGraw-Hill.

Fielder, F. E., and M. M. Chemers. (1974). *Leadership Style and Effective Management*. Glenview, IL: Scott, Foresman.

Fielder, F. E., M. M. Chemers, and L. Mahar. (1976). *Improving Leadership Effectiveness: The Leader Match Concept*. New York: Wiley.

Finer, Herman. (1941). "Administrative Responsibility in Democratic Government," *Public Administration Review* 1.

Fink, S. L. (1992). *High Commitment Workplaces*. New York: Quorum Books.

French, J. R. P., and B. Raven. (1959). "The Bases of Social Power." In D. Cartwright and A. Zander, eds., *Studies in Social Power*. Ann Arbor: University of Michigan, Institute of Social Research.

Friedrich, Carl J. (1940). "The Nature of Administrative Responsibility." In Carl J. Friedrich, ed., *Public Policy*. Cambridge: Harvard University Press.

Howard, Philip K. (1995). *The Death of Common Sense*. New York: Random House.

Kilborn, Peter T. (1993). "Inside Post Offices, the Mail Is Only Part of the Pressure," *New York Times* (May 17).

Kotler, Philip. (1982). "The Responsive Organization: Meeting Consumer Needs." *Marketing for Non-profit Organizations*, 2nd ed. Englewood Cliffs, NJ: Prentice Hall.

Kotler, Philip, and Sidney J. Levy. (1969). "Broadening the Concept of Marketing," *Journal of Marketing* (January).

Lewin, K., R. Lippitt, and R. K. White. (1939). "Patterns of Aggressive Behavior in Experimentally Created Social Climates," *Journal of Social Psychology* 10.

Metcalf, Henry C., and Lyndall Urwick, eds. (1940). *Dynamic Administration: The Collected Papers of Mary Parker Follett*. New York: Harper.

Morgan, Arthur E. (1974). *The Making of the TVA*. New York: Prometheus Books.

Mustafa, Husain, and Anthony A. Salomone. (1971). "Administrative Circumvention of Public Policy," *Midwest Review of Public Administration* 5, No. 1.

Myers, Steven Lee. (1995). "City Hall's Going Retail in *Wholesale Fashion*," New York Times (July 9).

Oldfield, Duane M., and Aaron Wildavsky. (1989). "Reconsidering the Two Presidencies," *Society* 26 (July-August).

Popkin, James. (1993). "Wasteline: By the Book," *U.S. News & World Report* (May 24).

Riccucci, Norma M. (1995). *Unsung Heroes: Federal Execucrats Making a Difference*. Washington: Georgetown University Press.

Romzek, Barbara, and Melvin J. Dubnick. (1987). "Accountability in the Public Sector," *Public Administration Review* (May-June).

Rosenbloom, David H. (1993a). "Have an Administrative Rx? Don't Forget the Politics!" *Public Administration Review* 53 (November-December).

———. (1993b). *Public Administration*, 3rd ed. New York: McGraw-Hill.

Sayre, W. (1948). "The Triumph of Techniques Over Purpose," *Public Administration Review* 8 (Spring).

Slater, Philip E., and Warren Bennis. (1964). "Democracy Is Inevitable," *Harvard Business Review* 42 (March-April).

Stogdill, Ralph M. (1974). *Handbook of Leadership: A Study of Theory and Research*. New York: Free Press.

Tannenbaum, Robert J., and Warren H. Schmidt. (1973). "How to Choose a Leadership Pattern," *Harvard Business Review* 51 (May-June).

Tichy, N. M., and D. O. Ulrich. (1984). "The Leadership Challenge—A Call for the Transformational Leader," *Sloan Management Review* 26.

Wildavsky, Aaron. (1966). "The Two Presidencies," *Trans-Action* (December).

Wills, Garry. (1994). "What Makes a Good Leader?" *Atlantic Monthly* (April).

Recommended Books

Barnard, Chester I. (1968). *The Functions of the Executive*, 30th anniversary ed. Cambridge, MA: Harvard University Press. The classic analysis of organizations as cooperative systems wherein the function of the executive was to maintain the "dynamic equilibrium" between the needs of the organization and the needs of its employees.

Kearns, Kevin P. (1996). *Managing for Accountability: Preserving the Public Trust in Public and Nonprofit Organizations*. San Francisco, CA: Jossey-Bass. A strategic management approach to organizational accountability; accountability should not be undertaken as an afterthought—it must be integrated with all aspects of management.

Light, Paul C. (1995). *Thickening Government: Federal Hierarchy and the Diffusion of Accountability*. Washington, DC: Brookings Institution. A study of how the federal government has constantly expanded the number of its high-level positions (during the period 1935–1992) to increase efficiency and accountability.

Rosen, Bernard. (1998). *Holding Government Bureaucracies Accountable*, 3rd ed. Westport: CT: Praeger. A survey of the mechanisms of accountability in the federal government, with excellent coverage of 1990s accountability legislation such as the Government Performance and Results Act of 1993.

Wren, J. Thomas. (1995) *The Leader's Companion: Insights on Leadership Through the Ages*. New York: Free Press. Sixty-four selections of the best writing on leadership, from ancient classicists to modern social scientists.

Related Web Sites

Center for Creative Leadership
http://www.ccl.org/
Citizens' Circle For Accountability
http://www.magi.com/~hemccand.cca.html
Congressional Accountability Project
http://www.essential.org/orgs/CAP/CAP.html
Council for Excellence in Government
http://www.excelgov.org/Default.htm

Government Accountability Project
http://www.whistleblower.org
Leadership development
http://leadership/mindgarden.com/demo/index.html?133,21
U.S. Postal Service
http://www.usps.gov

10

Personnel Management and Labor Relations

Keynote: The Adventures of a Young Man as a Personnel Technician

I didn't mean to discover the netherworld of personnel administration in 1965. I was just looking for a job. This was complicated by the fact that I had no skills. A bachelor's degree in English from Temple University and a decidedly undistinguished academic record did not suggest any immediate directions. I thought it might be fun to be a librarian, so off I went to the Free Library of Philadelphia. I asked a bored circulation clerk, "Could you please tell me who to see about becoming a librarian?" She sent me to Mr. Greenberg in the personnel office.

I bounded into his office and politely inquired if he could advise me on how to get a job as a librarian. Never in 30 subsequent years of going in and out of other people's offices have I been greeted with such genuine warmth and solicitude. And I didn't even have an appointment! But I had something going for me that Mr. Greenberg needed very badly—my gender; that is, I was a male college graduate and thus met all of his needs in a new librarian trainee. Even today, careers as professional librarians attract a disproportionate number of females. It was much more so in the mid-1960s. This caused a very particular staffing problem for the library because it had recently purchased a new bookmobile. But the female librarians were exceedingly reluctant to work on a bookmobile that traveled through Philadelphia's poorer neighborhoods. They felt, and with good reason, that it was too dangerous. This accounts for Mr. Greenberg's immediate warm regard for me. He was very much in need of a brave young man to take literacy into the neighborhoods of the inner city.

There was just one minor technicality to attend to before I could gain the command of a municipal bookmobile. I had to pass a civil service examination. Mr. Greenberg was almost apologetic about the inconvenience as he told me where in City Hall I would find the continuous testing room of the Civil Service Commission. There I would take a general entrance examination for new college graduates desiring a variety of entry-level professional positions. The test, he assured me, would be scored immediately after I completed it; and he would be able to formally put me on the payroll and in the bookmobile within a few days. He was very pleased to have solved a personnel problem using the much unappreciated but classic technique of sitting at his desk waiting for someone to walk in the door.

But I was fated never to be a librarian, never to ride the bookmobile, and never to see Mr. Greenberg again. Yet this was my start in the world of personnel. The examination I took was used by the city for a dozen different professional trainee positions. On the first page I was asked to check off the names of all the jobs for which I wished to be considered. I checked every one. After being told by the examinations proctor that I had easily passed the hour-long multiple-choice examination, I went home to await my call to the bookmobile. Instead it was Mrs. Margolis, a certification clerk for the Civil Service Commission, who called. It was her job to take the names of job applicants who passed various civil service examinations and officially certify them as eligible for appointment. Whenever a municipal department had a vacancy in a given job category, she would contact the highest scorers on the list of eligibles to see if they were still interested in employment with the city. If so, she would arrange a job interview. I told her of my meeting with Mr. Greenberg and how anxious I was to get started on my new career on the bookmobile. She immediately and emphatically responded with these immortal words of career advice: "Don't be an idiot! That's not for you."

She went on to explain that I ought to take the highest paying of all the entry positions for which my test score now qualified me. The job for me, she insisted, was management trainee. This paid a whopping 20 percent more than librarian trainee, $6,000 a year as opposed to $5,000. I told her that I didn't know anything about management but knew lots about books. She assured me that it didn't matter. They would train me; that's why the job was called management *trainee*. A 20-percent raise even before I started working for the city and not being an idiot were pretty powerful inducements. So I agreed.

"Good," she said. "I'll schedule you for an oral exam at three o'clock tomorrow afternoon."

"What oral exam?" I asked in amazement.

"All management trainee applicants must take an oral exam. You put on your suit and come to the sixth floor of the Municipal Services Building at three," she demanded of me as if she were my mother. To this day I still wonder how she knew that I had only one suit.

The next day I put on that suit, as ordered, and having never taken an oral exam before, and not knowing what to expect, I also brushed my teeth very carefully. Upon my arrival at the designated place at the designated time, a receptionist ushered me into a small room in which three men were seated behind a table. I would later learn they were all personnel officers for the city. They each wore a dark suit with a thin tie atop a white shirt. They could easily have been mistaken for the FBI agents or IBM salesmen of those days who were all required to wear white shirts, thin ties, and short hair. After a round of handshakes, they offered me a chair and proceeded to ask me a series of questions that I could not possibly answer. I had never given any thought to the problems of perpetually tardy employees and clogged typing pools. I didn't even know that typists were allowed to swim! So I responded to their questions by just making up stuff off the top of my head all the while thinking: "Bookmobile, here I come."

To make matters worse, one of my examiners took an immediate dislike to me. He was unusually rude and kept badgering me with hostilely phrased questions. He would constantly interrupt my sentences and often call my answers stupid. I soon realized that the situation was hopeless; so I relaxed and took what Californians would call a mellow approach to the examination. I calmly answered all questions as best I could and didn't let the badgerer upset me no matter what his antics. Consequently, I exhibited a degree of self-confidence that was as convincing as it was artificial.

A few weeks later I would learn that the oral exam had no purpose except to size up the physical deportment and extemporaneous speaking ability of the applicant. One member of the examining board was always hostile to see if the examinee could be emotionally shaken by a disagreeable exchange. My badgerer didn't dislike me after all; it was simply his turn to be the bad guy. Nevertheless, I left the Municipal Services Building confident that the bookmobile was my destiny. Shortly after nine the next morning Mrs. Margolis called again. Before I could tell her how sorry I was that I did so poorly on the oral exam, she said, "Congratulations, you've passed the oral."

"You've got to be kidding," I said in contradiction. "I was terrible."

"No. You got a very high score. They even want you for personnel. You have to come to an interview this afternoon at two."

"But I did the interview yesterday," I complained.

"No, that was the oral exam. The job interview is today. Put your suit back on."

The subsequent job interview was my first introduction to position classification. Two nice but seemingly elderly senior supervisors in the Department of Personnel (which is administratively under the Civil Service Commission) spent an hour asking me about my whole life. At twenty-one there was not much to tell. When they seemed on the verge of ending the discussion and offering me a position, I bluntly asked what the duties would be. They said I would start in the Division of Position Classification and Pay doing reports that would ultimately determine how much city employees would be paid.

"But I thought the mayor did that," I explained in honest ignorance.

"No," I was corrected, "the city has over 30,000 employees. He couldn't possibly do it all. That's why we have position classification."

"Oh," I responded still not really sure what they meant by classification.

They seemed to understand my discomfort about the strange nature of the work they were describing. To conclude, they said they had only one final question, "if we forced you to state the one area that you really know well, what would it be?"

I quickly thought about all that I had studied in college and replied with great seriousness and complete honesty, "The only thing I really know well is modern American fiction."

They thereupon hired me to write job descriptions for the employees of the City of Philadelphia. I would report to work on the following Monday and be a management trainee in the personnel technician series, meaning that I would later be eligible for promotion to Personnel Technician I, Personnel Technician II, and so on. By going to the library to seek a job that would allow me the leisure to write fiction, I stumbled upon a job for which I would be paid to write fiction—although I wouldn't be allowed to call it that.

I started my new job with every intention of doing well and pleasing my superiors. It was my first real job after college and I was determined to be a success. Unfortunately, within eight weeks I had become such a problem for my employers that I was about to be dismissed.

The Division of Classification and Pay occupied one quarter of the sixth floor of the Municipal Services Building. There were two private offices for the division chief and his deputy. Everyone else, a dozen professionals and four clerk-typists, had desks in one large open area whose walls were lined with file cabinets. Promptly at 8:30 Monday morning I reported to Mrs. L. the deputy chief, who introduced me to everyone and assigned me a desk directly in front of her door. She then told me that my first week would be spent in training. She handed me a very thick book with small print that she described as "the bible" of position classification—Ismar Baruch's *Position Classification in the Public Service*, written in 1940. This was my training—to sit at my desk under the helpful eye of Mrs. L. and read. It was just like the library except that I could read only one book.

The theory underlying position classification is quite rational and logical. In the bad old days the salaries of public employees were determined by whatever entity had authority over the budget, usually the legislature. Any individual salary was a function of that individual's influence with the legislature. Vast disparities in pay grew up over the years as public servants worked the political system; one clerk would often be paid twice as much as another in the same job, all because an uncle or sugar daddy was on an appropriate legislative committee. Position classification was put forth by reformers early in this century as a way of curbing the corruption inherent in the old system. Jobs would be grouped according to their duties and responsibilities so that all similar positions would be paid the same.

After a week reading "the bible" of classification, I spent another week following an experienced classifier around as he did desk audits—that is, as he traveled to the "desk" or workstation of an employee to interview him or her about his or her job to ascertain if it was properly classified. After talking to the incumbent and the incumbent's supervisor, the classifier would write an elaborate report, which was technically a memorandum to the Civil Service Commission. Only one of three recommendations was possible: that the job be reclassified to a higher level or a lower level, or that it remain the same. Since the whole point of classification was ultimately to determine salary levels, everybody wanted to be reclassified upward. Consequently, much of the work of the Division of Classification and Pay consisted of dealing with reclassification requests by means of desk audit reports.

Finally, my several weeks' training complete, I was let loose to play in the fields of municipal administration. Assigned to do a desk audit on a variety of relatively uncomplicated junior clerk-typists who wanted to be senior clerk-typists, I became the boy investigative reporter I was fated to be.

A few days later, Mrs. L. was quite annoyed. She held up my report and asked in a tone of controlled fury, "Just what do you think you are doing?"

"What do you mean by 'just what do you think you are doing?'" I asked back in all innocence. But this only agitated her further.

"You know very well what I mean," she insisted in a loud voice.

"No, I don't," I replied suddenly realizing I must be in a lot of trouble for something.

"Where did you get the information that went into your desk audit report?"

"I did just what you told me to do. I spoke to the incumbent and to the incumbent's supervisor."

"But they didn't tell you all this?"

"No. Much of the information came from coworkers and other people around the office such as the security guards, the mail room guy, and the other secretaries."

"But you weren't supposed to speak to them," she lamented.

"Who was I supposed to speak to?"

"Just to the incumbent and to the supervisor."

"But they lied," I said in explanation.

"That's none of your business," she responded in exasperation.

"You mean I'm just supposed to take down their lies and write them up as if they were the truth. You've got to be kidding!"

"I never joke about classification."

"And I don't write lies, with all due respect, for you or anyone."

"No one's asking you to lie," she explained. "We just don't want you talking to the wrong people and getting the wrong idea about things."

"But it's a good thing that I did speak to those additional people. Otherwise I would never have been able to write up the whole story."

"You just don't understand. Your job is to interview just the people we tell you to. Then write up what they say."

"But what if they lie?" I asked.

"That's not for you to determine."

"Then who does?"

"This is getting us nowhere. Please wait outside."

"Should I continue with my work?"

"No. Just sit at your desk."

I sat and tried to figure out what went wrong. As an idealistic youth I genuinely wanted to do well by my city but had only managed to get myself fired. A short while later the ax fell. The deputy director of personnel came by and told me that it had been decided that I wasn't quite ready for the arduous life of a position classifier. I assumed that his next words would herald the end of my life in municipal administration. I wondered if the bookmobile was still available. But to my astonishment he offered to transfer me to the Division of Recruitment and Examinations. So I was only half fired. What a break! My budding career in public administration had been salvaged by the kindness of strangers. For my sins, such as they were, I would spend the next year writing civil service examinations for such exciting jobs as morgue attendant and sewer crawler.

It would be several years before I fully realized what had happened to me in classification. I had stumbled upon the netherworld, but hadn't seen it. Of course nobody calls it that. The netherworld is just my term for the underground or black market in personnel decision making that exists in all large governmental organizations. It was just an accident that I first discovered it in Philadelphia. It exists almost everywhere. It exists whenever a government manager wants to reward an unusually productive employee but cannot because the system denies managers any real discretion over salaries. So they play the position classification game to informally win the discretion that they are formally denied.

Suppose you have a secretary who is the best ever. You are going to lose her if you cannot get her salary raised. What's worse, she would then be replaced by someone not half as good. That was the quality of secretary—"not half as good"—that you could typically expect to come from civil service lists. Consequently you'll do anything to keep your current secretary happy—even lie, cheat, and steal. Fortunately, that is exactly what you must do to win the position classification game.

But all this I would discover later. At the time, all I knew was that I had bumped into some strange ethics. And I felt extremely fortunate to be exiled into the world of civil service examinations, where I would spend the next year writing multiple-choice tests and avoiding the moral mazes of position classification. But it was a dull life for an adventurous soul. The library would have been more exciting. I yearned for something more and found it in the *New York Times*. I came upon an advertisement that graduate assistantships were available at the Baruch School of Business and Public Administration of the City University of New York. I applied in October of 1966. Before Christmas I received a letter congratulating me on the scholarly attainments that had earned me a research assistantship beginning in January. I felt like a fraud. But I was equally determined to take full advantage of my ill-deserved appointment. So off I went to the Big Apple to earn a master's degree in public administration.

Years later, after I had earned my Ph.D. and was a new assistant professor attending a professional conference, I chanced to come upon the late Professor Samuel Thomas, then still dean of the Baruch School. It was he who awarded me the graduate research assistantship that started my academic career. We exchanged a few pleasantries and when the moment seemed right, I popped the question: why had I been awarded the assistantship when my record was so undistinguished and comparatively undeserving? "Oh, that's easy to recall," he said with an impish grin. "You, Dr. Shafritz, were the only one to apply." It seems that Woody Allen was right: "Eighty percent of success is showing up."

The Personnel Function

The function of a personnel staff, or even an entire personnel agency, is service to line management. Typical services include recruiting, selection, training, evaluation, compensation, discipline, and termination. *Personnel* is a collective term for all of the employees of an organization. The word is of military origin—the two basic components of a traditional army being materiel and personnel. Personnel is also commonly used to refer to the personnel management function or the organizational unit responsible for administering personnel programs. While the terms *personnel administration* and *personnel management* tend to be used

Two views of Philadelphia Government. City Hall in Philadelphia: The netherworld lurks below.
Philadelphia Mayor Ed Rendell cleans up City Hall. Why is the mayor doing this? He is demonstrating that all city employees should be more flexible about their job duties, that it shouldn't take, for example, three workers to change a lightbulb, as he found was the policy at the Philadelphia International Airport—a mechanic to remove the cover, an electrician to replace the bulb, and a custodian to sweep up the inevitable debris. This issue of work rules would cause a major confrontation between the mayor and the municipal unions during his first year in office. But on the so called "non-economic issues" having to do with new work rules, the major held firm. We may assume that worn-out lightbulbs all over the city are being replaced by a newly-lonely worker.

interchangeably, there is a distinction. The former is mainly concerned with the technical aspects of maintaining a full complement of employees within an organization, while the latter concerns itself as well with the larger problems of the viability of an organization's human resources—how motivated and productive they are.

Not very long ago, it would have been absurd to refer to the occupation of the public personnel administrator as a professional practice. The traditional professions all presupposed a large measure of formal training in preparation for the ensuing professional practice—a practice that was highlighted by the personal autonomy and independent judgments of the practitioner. Just as the repugnant caterpillar evolves into the graceful butterfly, personnel management is undergoing a similar metamorphosis. From its origins as a clerical function, it has gradually been evolving into an in-house consultant to management on labor relations, job redesign, EEO provisions, organization development, productivity measurement, and other pressing concerns. Top management values and seeks out the professional opinion of the personnel practitioner because that opinion is backed up by expertise that is essential if the organization is to thrive. Unfortunately, in the majority of U.S. jurisdictions this metamorphosis is only just beginning. The in-house expertise either does not yet exist or is ignored by political executives. Butterfly status is many years away. All the more reason to now begin raising the consciousness of the occupation.

As with many questions in public administration, the issue of how the overall public personnel function should be organized has been plagued by an attempt to realize several incompatible values at once. Foremost among these values have been those of "merit" or neutral competence, executive leadership, political accountability, and managerial flexibility; and representativeness. The main problem of the structure and policy thrusts of central personnel agencies has been that maximizing some of these values requires arrangements ill-suited for the achievement of others. Thus, achieving neutral competence requires the creation of a relatively independent agency to help insulate public employees from the partisan demands of political executives. Yet the same structural arrangement will tend to frustrate executive leadership and the ability of political executives to manage their agencies. To facilitate executive leadership, on the other hand, the central personnel agency should be an adjunct of the president, governor, or other chief executive. Similarly, maximizing the value of representativeness may require less emphasis on traditional merit concepts and examinations, and the placement of personnel functions having an impact on equal employment opportunity in an equal employment or human rights agency. So doing, however, will also complicate the possibilities of achieving a high degree of executive leadership and neutral competence, as traditionally conceived.

Matters are further confused by the rise of public-sector collective bargaining, which emphasizes employee-employer **codetermination** of personnel policy and the creation of independent public-sector labor relations authorities. The desire to maxi-

---

codetermination Union participation in all aspects of management, even to the extent of having union representatives share equal membership on an organization's board of directors.

mize simultaneously these incompatible values accounts for many of the problematic aspects of the organization of the central personnel function. Arrangements satisfying some values inevitably raise complaints that others are being inadequately achieved.

Recruitment

Recruitment is the process of advertising job openings and encouraging candidates to apply. It is designed to provide an organization with an adequate number of viable candidates from which to make its selection decision. One indicator of the economic health of a community is the number of applicants for public employment. In poor economic times, government agencies are flooded with applications from the qualified and unqualified alike.

The main objective of recruitment is the generating of an adequate number of qualified applicants. An applicant is any individual who submits a completed application form for consideration. Indeed, it is often said that the first phase of the examining process consists of filling out the application form. If applicants do not provide the necessary information documenting their minimum qualifications, they are not given any further consideration—they are not permitted to take the formal examination. However, it is not uncommon for applicants who qualify in every respect for a position to be refused consideration. Many positions above the entry level are open only to individuals already employed within the jurisdiction. Outsiders, no matter how qualified, may not be admitted to such promotional examinations. For example, only currently-employed police officers may be permitted to take the police sergeant's examination; only police sergeants may take the police lieutenant's examination.

Merit Selection

Selection is the oldest function of public personnel administration. The 1883 Pendleton Act, which put the federal government on the road to widespread, merit-system coverage, foreshadowed the character of the examinations process when it mandated that "examinations shall be practical in their character." As the British civil service was the greatest single example and influence upon the U.S. reform movement, there was considerable concern that a merit system based upon the British system of competitive academic examinations would be automatically biased in favor of college graduates. Because higher education in the United States was essentially an upper-class prerogative in the last century, this was reminiscent of the aristocratic civil service that the Jacksonian movement found so objectionable only 50 years earlier. Mandating that all examinations be "practical in their character" presumably neutralized any advantage that a college graduate might have, for in those days there was little that was "practical" taught in most U.S. colleges. Indeed, it would not be until 1934 that the U.S. Civil Service Commission offered its first entrance examination designed especially for liberal arts graduates.

Over the years, the primacy of examination practicality was often breached. However, that primacy was loudly reaffirmed by the U.S. Supreme Court in the *Griggs v. Duke Power Company* decision of 1971—the most significant single decision concerning the validity of employment examinations. The Court unanimously ruled that Title VII of the Civil Rights Act of 1964 "proscribes not only overt discrimination but also practices that are discriminatory in operation." Thus, if employment practices operating to exclude minorities "cannot be shown to be related to job performance, the practice is prohibited." The ruling dealt a blow to **restrictive credentialism**, stating that, while diplomas and tests are useful, the "Congress has mandated the commonsense proposition that they are not to become masters of reality." In essence, the court held that the law requires that tests used for employment purposes "must measure the person for the job and not the person in the abstract." The *Griggs* decision applied only to the private sector until the **Equal Employment Opportunity Act of 1972** extended the provisions of Title VII to cover public employees.

Job relatedness is now the paramount consideration in developing a selection device. The legality of any test hinges on its capability in predicting job success, and validation is the process of demonstrating how well the testing device actually can predict success on the job. While examinations were once simply technical and administrative problems of the personnel department, they are now of equal concern to a jurisdiction's legal office. The thrust of the Equal Employment Opportunity Act of 1972 is to stop, by providing legal remedies for, acts of discrimination in hiring, assignments, promotional opportunities, or any other benefits or conditions of employment. Theoretically, there is no inherent conflict between a merit selection program and equal employment opportunity laws. Each requires selection without regard to race, color, religion, sex, quotas, or compensatory hiring (although the courts retain discretion to impose remedies for proved past patterns of discrimination). While there are no legal limits on an organization's use of tests, all examining tools may now be challenged as discriminatory in effect. Job success is a complex matter and not generally attributable to any single factor. To ensure job relatedness, organizations must identify the appropriate criteria that "contribute" to job success and must ensure that the testing devices used accurately measure those criteria. Those responsible for the preparation of examinations have no choice but to develop their testing techniques on the assumption they will have to be defended in a court challenge.

In the United States every important public issue becomes a legal problem. Such an issue is the central question of civil service examinations—test validity. While the validity of such exams could be theoretically determined by psychologists and other social scientists who could offer their professional opinions, the opinion of a federal judge provides binding social legitimacy. When the historians of personnel operations look back at the last few decades, they no doubt will write that the courts markedly accelerated the sophistication of aptitude examinations, which became so sophisticated and valid they were able to withstand considerable litigation.

---

restrictive credentialism A general term for any selection policy adversely affecting disadvantaged groups because they lack the formal qualifications for positions that, in the opinion of those adversely affected, do not truly need such formal qualifications.

Equal Employment Opportunity Act of 1972 An amendment to Title VII of the 1964 Civil Rights Act strengthening the authority of the Equal Employment Opportunity Commission and extending antidiscrimination provisions to state and local governments and labor organizations with 15 or more employees, and to public and private employment agencies.

Position Classification and Pay

A fable is sometimes told about position classification. Once upon a time a new tiger was brought to a municipal zoo. He was put into a habitat, cages being passé, next to another tiger. At mealtime, 10 pounds of raw red meat was thrown into the habitat of the tiger next to him. "Yummy," thought the new tiger as he eagerly awaited the first meal in his new home. You can imagine his surprise, however, when the zookeeper tossed him not the decaying portions of a bloody carcass, but 20 pounds of bananas. After a few days of enforced vegetarianism, the tiger finally asked the zookeeper why his neighbor got meat and he only got yellow finger food. "Well," said the zookeeper, "this is a government zoo and we didn't have money in our budget that was authorized for another tiger. But we did have approval to buy more monkeys. Because we bought you instead, you get the food for six monkeys."

While this is but a fable, it does contain a large germ of truth. For example, it is true that a large municipal hospital on the East Coast of the United States once employed a janitor to perform brain surgery. Just as with the tiger/monkey story, the hospital was authorized to hire an additional full-time janitor, but really needed a part-time brain surgeon. So they hired the brain surgeon to work one day a week, but paid him the full-time salary of the janitor—and kept him on the official books as a janitor. While the personnel staff thought it was a very funny way of solving a very real management problem, it also illustrates—and reinforces our keynote adventure about—how position classification systems create much dysfunctional and sometimes silly activity.

Position classifications are formal job descriptions that organize all jobs in a civil service merit system into classes on the basis of duties and responsibilities, for the purposes of delineating authority, establishing chains of command, and providing equitable salary scales. The principles and practices of position classification that are generally used in the public service are throwbacks to the heyday of the scientific management movement. They were conceived at a time—before 1920—when this school of management thought held sway, and they have never really adapted to modern currents of management thought. Reduced to its essentials, a classification plan is nothing more than a time-and-motion study for the governmental function. The duties of the larger organization are divided into positions in order to prevent duplication and promote efficiency. In this schema, a position merely represents a set of duties and responsibilities, not a person. While position classifications tend to be universally recognized as essential for the administration of a public personnel program, their allegiance to notions of the past cause them to be frequently denounced as unreasonable constraints on top management and sappers of employee morale, or for being little more than polite fictions in substance.

Because the most basic doctrines of position classification were established prior to World War II, current practices ignore many of the advances in management science and theory that have occurred since then. In addition, the kind of workforce that classification plans were originally designed to accommodate no longer exists. Classification principles assume, in the best scientific management tradition, that work can most efficiently be organized by imitating industrial machinery and creating a system of human interchangeable parts. Thus one person in any given class was considered absolutely equal to any other person in that class.

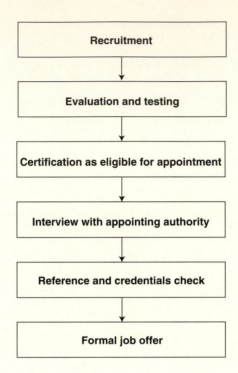

Figure 10.1 The Selection Process

However, because of advances in the social sciences and radical changes in the nature of the workforce, conventional classification systems are obsolete for many categories of employees, in terms of simply not being as efficient as other modes of organization. They have also proved themselves to be frequently counterproductive in achieving the organizational mission.

Because of the ever-increasing rise in U.S. educational levels, the bulk of the labor force now consists of highly skilled technical and professional employees. Such workers should not be treated as if they were semi-skilled laborers, menials, or clerical functionaries. Yet classification systems, designed to meet the needs of these latter employees, are being imposed upon administrative, professional, and technical employees for reasons that are hardly defensible in light of what is known today about organizing and motivating a workforce. The old dichotomy between managers and workers is no longer valid. Workers in the traditional sense are an ever-decreasing minority. They are being replaced by technical and professional employees. This group is more likely to consider itself part of management than of the oppressed proletariat.

Even employees at the bottom of the organizational hierarchy are at such a level of education and consciousness that they cannot be casually treated as so many human, interchangeable spare parts. Relying on a management tool—position classification—that has not changed in two generations is akin to relying on a pre-World War I Model T Ford for transportation in the supersonic age. Is there another field of endeavor in the United States that is so backward? An engineer or architect could not design very much for today's world if limited to the technology of the 1930s.

Box 10.1

Position Classification Principles

Here are basic principles of position classification that constitute the foundation of most position classification systems in government. They were promulgated by the 1919 Congressional Joint Commission on Reclassification of Salaries:

1. Positions and not individuals should be classified.
2. The duties and responsibilities pertaining to a position constitute the outstanding characteristics that distinguish it from, or mark its similarity to, other positions.
3. Qualifications in respect to education, experience, knowledge, and skill necessary for the performance of certain duties are determined by the nature of those duties. (Therefore, the qualifications for a position are an important factor in the determination of the classification of a position.)
4. The individual characteristics of an employee occupying a position should have no bearing on the classification of the position.
5. Persons holding positions in the same class should be considered equally qualified for any other position in that class.

SOURCE: *Report of the Congressional Joint Commission on Reclassification of Salaries*, 66th Cong., 2nd sess., 1920, H.Doc.686.

This is exactly what public personnel administrators are doing to the employees of their jurisdictions—engaging in a presumably professional practice using a technology that predates World War II.

Performance Appraisal

Performance appraisal is the title usually given to the formal method by which an organization documents the work performance of its employees. An employee evaluation process is essential for managerial decisions on retention, advancement, and separation. Lamentably, most performance evaluation systems have not been very successful. The main reason may be that supervisors have a great deal of difficulty writing useful and objective performance reports. They submit appraisals that tend to be very subjective, impressionistic, and noncomparable with the reports of other raters.

Performance appraisals are designed to serve a variety of functions, among them: (1) changing or modifying dysfunctional work behavior; (2) communicating to employees managerial perceptions of the quality and quantity of their work; (3) assessing the future potential of an employee in order to recommend appropriate training or developmental assignments; (4) assessing whether the present duties of an employee's position have an appropriate compensation level; and (5) providing a documented record for disciplinary and separation actions.

There are five basic types of appraisals.

1. *Supervisory ratings:* The most common type of appraisal, whereby the supervisor evaluates the performance of subordinates
2. *Self-ratings:* Individuals rate themselves by completing a standard form, writing a narrative report on their work, or submitting a work product as documentation of performance.
3. *Peer ratings:* Each individual rates every employee in his or her division or office at a parallel level in the organization.
4. *Subordinated ratings:* Subordinates rate the performance of a supervisor.
5. *Group ratings:* An independent rater, usually a qualified expert, rates the performance of an entire work unit based on selected interviews or on-the-job visitations.

When significant numbers of employees must be evaluated, rating forms often offer multiple choices to the evaluator. Then all the evaluator must do is check the appropriate boxes. Typically, these forms are behaviorally anchored; that is, they are premised upon varying levels of performance. Here is an example of a behaviorally anchored numerical rating scale for tennis players:

Rating	Behavioral Anchor
1	Knows rules of tennis, can bounce ball and hit it over the net
2	Hits forehand strokes with consistency, backhand weak
3	Hits both forehand and backhand strokes with consistency
4	Can place ball accurately, including serves, volleys, and half volleys
5	All strokes are accurate, firm, and consistent; topspin and underspin strokes can be employed as required

Strong-minded supervisors with very high standards will do their better employees an injustice when their reports are compared with those of supervisors who have low standards or are less professional. The result is a vast quantity of inflated reports filled with superlatives so that any review of performance appraisals will boil down to a consideration of who wrote the report, what other reports they have prepared, and what was left unsaid. More often than not, reports submitted on employees will primarily reflect the strengths and weaknesses of the rater. The impact of this factor substantially limits the validity and use of an individual performance appraisal. To complicate matters even further, supervisors are often not sure of "what" is really being rated—their subordinates' work performance, or their own ability to use the **critical-incident method** of evaluative narration. Nevertheless, appraisal systems will

---

critical-incident method   Identifying, classifying, and recording significant examples—critical incidents—of an employee's behavior for purposes of performance evaluation. The theory behind the critical-incident approach holds that there are certain key acts of behavior that make the difference between success and failure. After the incidents are collected, they can be ranked in order of frequency and importance and assigned numerical weights. Once scored, they can be as useful for employee development and counseling as for formal appraisals.

always be with us if only because so many civil service laws and regulations require them as a precondition to annual salary increases. Employees without at least a satisfactory rating may be denied even "automatic" wage increases based on longevity.

The question remains: Why do so few employees receive poor evaluations—the first step toward dismissing them? The answer is that there is seldom adequate incentive for a line supervisor to be held accountable for his or her lack of punitive action toward deserving employees. Why should a supervisor risk creating a difficult interpersonal situation with all other subordinates for some vague notion of the public interest? Unless there is some extraordinary pressure for productivity, there is simply no incentive to take the hard action that is occasionally the duty of all managers. The public manager is not, after all, the proprietor of his or her own small business; the actions or inactions of employees, unless they exhibit some gross misconduct, do not directly affect his or her own interests. Why should he or she be the one manager in the jurisdiction to take the waste of public funds seriously enough to take concrete action? Does it not take an individual of intense ideological conviction to act upon his beliefs when all others indicate contrary attitudes? Before interfering with a system that tolerates marginally performing employees, a reasonable person would have to be sure of the legitimacy of his or her actions. Precedence creates legitimacy. To upset what has evolved as the natural order of things may be socially and morally illegitimate, and simultaneously legally appropriate.

Training

Training has frequently been a victim of organizational neglect. In a budget squeeze, training funds have tended to be cut in favor of the examination and the classification functions frequently mandated by legislation or charter. Training was considered to be an option, a luxury, or worse—illegal. Prior to the 1950s, many jurisdictions operated on the premise that employees hired via the merit system were fully qualified for their duties. Training almost by definition was superfluous. Why should a jurisdiction suffer the expense of training individuals to do a job that they had to have a proven capability of performing before they were employed? Attitudes changed as merit systems grew stronger, as more and more occupations became limited to the public service, and as public jobs came to be thought of as career positions requiring continuous upgrading rather than as sets of static duties.

It was not until 1958 that Congress passed the Government Employees Training Act that required federal agencies to provide for employee training. It would be yet another decade before the U.S. Civil Service Commission would be authorized to create the federal government's first in-residence management training facility—the Federal Executive Institute in Charlottesville, Virginia. And it was not until the Intergovernmental Personnel Act of 1970 that the federal government was able to provide any funds for state and local government training programs. But this was only temporary. The Reagan administration discontinued such grants in the mid-1980s. With such a recent history as a serious concern for personnel, it is no wonder that the state of the training art is, at the very least, immature.

A training program is not complete without an evaluation of its effectiveness and usefulness. Yet most government training efforts that do not simply stop at the training itself are given only the most cursory of evaluations. While evaluation is the last phase of a training program, preparations for it must be made prior to the commencement of the program. If base points of performance are not established prior to training, subsequent attempts to measure progress are likely to yield spurious results.

The essential question is whether or not a training effort has met its objective. While this is relatively easy when you are dealing with word processors, the matter becomes vastly more complicated when your training population consists of police officers, research scientists, or administrators. The measurement and evaluation of training programs for these latter classes require a great deal of subtlety, technical skill, and time. A word processor training program can be evaluated immediately thereafter, but it could easily take months and in some cases years to objectively measure the effectiveness of training for police officers, administrators, and scientists.

Although there is a great variety of training formats, almost all will fall into one of the following categories:

1. *Skills training:* Teaching specific skills such as word processing, welding, or computer operation

2. *Coaching:* Personal instruction in which an expert oversees the efforts of a learner and provides continual advice

3. *Formal or informal classroom instruction:* Traditional classroom instruction, including courses at nearby academic institutions, whereby groups of employees are instructed (with jurisdictions often providing subsidies for job-related college courses)

4. *Sensitivity or "T-group" training:* Assembling small groups of employees to deal with the problems of interpersonal relationships (usually requiring a professional "facilitator" and relying heavily on the willingness of individuals to confront the emotional aspects of their behavior)

5. *Job rotation:* Providing employees with differing work activities in order to increase their experience (a variant of this being cross-training, where each job, and thus the entire work of an office, is learned by each employee)

6. *Special conferences and seminars:* Meetings of employees or professional groups to discuss and exchange ideas about common processes, problems, and techniques

7. *Modeling, games, and simulation training:* Simulated real-life situations providing employees with various experiences

8. *Exchange and sabbatical programs:* Getting the individual out of the organizational environment and into a totally different one for a substantial period of time—several months to a year

All the training options listed above are limited by the availability of funding. While all large organizations have training budgets, these are among the most tempting targets to cut during times of financial strain. Nevertheless, annual reports frequently boast of the number of employees who have been trained during the past

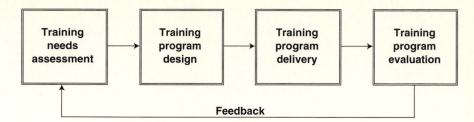

Figure 10.2   The Training System

year. But such statistics must be looked upon with great suspicion. It is a common mistake to assume that the number of people who have been subjected to training is equal to the number that have actually been trained. No statement of training accomplishment can honestly be made unless it is supported by sophisticated measures of evaluation.

Management Development

Management development is a hybrid of training and selection. Any conscious effort on the part of an organization to provide a manager with the skills needed for future duties such as rotational assignments or formal educational experiences constitutes management development. The semantic difference between *training workers* and *developing managers* is significant. Workers are trained so that they can better perform their present duties; managers are developed so that they can be of greater organizational value in both present and future assignments. In such a context, the development investment made by the organization in a junior manager may pay off only if and when that individual grows into a bureau chief. One common method of developing managers is to provide them with the kinds of assignments and experiences that will allow them to grow professionally. Unfortunately, rank-in-position personnel systems—the norm in the U.S. public service—very much inhibit such efforts.

The secondary focus of management development is selection. The range of experiences, both on and off the job, that managers are exposed to over the years leaves records in terms of specific scores or subjective evaluations upon which future advancements may be based. While it is not overly difficult to make promotional decisions based upon this array of information, what criteria should an organization use in selecting relatively inexperienced managers in whom to invest its development resources? **Assessment centers** have proved to be an increasingly popular way of establishing the criteria upon which to base management-development program selection. The assessment-center process typically consists of the intense observation of a subject undergoing a variety of management simulations and stress situations over a period of several days. The resulting evaluations have proved to be remarkably accurate in indicating capability and potential.

---

assessment center Not a particular place but a process consisting of the intense observation of a person undergoing a variety of simulations and stress situations over a period of several days.

TABLE 10.1   Training and Development Compared

	Training	Development
Time Frame	Short term	Long term
Goals	To learn specific techniques, behaviors, and processes	To understand the context of management, to develop judgment, and to enlarge personal abilities
Measures of Effectiveness	Performance appraisals, testing, and/or certification	Promotion of those developed; an overall organization with a competent managerial corps

The assessment-center concept is far from new. Assessment-center techniques were used by the German Army for selecting officers in World War I, and the Office of Strategic Services used them for selecting secret agents in World War II. However, the assessment-center concept did not reach U.S. industry until the mid-1950s, when AT&T pioneered a program. The practice spread during the 1960s, but it was not until 1969 that a U.S. government agency, the Internal Revenue Service, used assessment-center methodology on a large scale. Today such techniques are being rapidly adopted by government agencies at all jurisdictional levels.

The Bittersweet Heritage of Civil Service Reform

The perversion of most civil service merit systems for private, administrative, and especially partisan ends is one of the worst kept, yet least written about, secrets in government. It is one of the dirty little secrets of life. ("Dirty" because it is less than honorable; and "little" because it is not really a secret at all—just a much neglected topic of conversation.) Books on government management tend to deal with this subject as if it were an abnormal malignancy instead of an inherent and frequently beneficial part of civil service systems. But this is a faulty perspective. The perversion of merit systems is a normal, even healthy, condition. Indeed, such perversions are essential if actual merit is often to be rewarded within the merit system.

"Civil service" and "merit system" are concepts that are frequently confused. A civil service consists of all those civilians who work for a government. Any government employee who is not in the military is part of the civil service. A jurisdiction's merit system, if it has one, consists of all those members of the civil service who are selected by a formally established merit process. Of course, to be intellectually honest, "merit system" should always be proceeded by the phrase "so-called" because merit may or may not be an integral part of any given "so-called merit system." Because of the netherworld of personnel administration, determining the true level of merit in any given merit system is almost impossible. It is much like counting the virgins at a high school graduation—a process that is both methodologically very difficult and likely to be embarrassing to the individuals under scrutiny.

The Netherworld of Public Personnel Administration

Throughout the United States, public personnel merit systems tend to operate on three different planes within the same jurisdiction. In effect, parallel administrative universes, invisible to the untrained eye, occupy the same physical space. This notion of parallel universes was a plot device used on the "Star Trek" television series during the late 1960s. It seemed that the "good" starship Enterprise had a parallel but "evil" twin operating in a hidden dimension. The personnel netherworld is much the same in that both good and bad occupy the same space, but on different planes. The vast majority of civil service employees within the merit system enter, perform, and advance on the basis of their own talents and the design of the system. However, at the same time and within the same system there are two groups of employees who enter the system and advance according to criteria other than those provided for by merit system regulations.

The first group consists of all those employees who were appointed for considerations other than personal fitness. Here are hidden the political appointees in excess of those policymaking and confidential positions that are legally the chief executive's prerogative. These positions are obtained only after months of diligent effort performing political good works such as aiding the mayor's, the governor's, or the president's election campaign or playing up to some other influential political actor. *Washington Post* columnist Mike Causey wrote that both the White House and the Congress "all too often defend the career civil service system up to the point where a friend or brother-in-law needs a job badly." The same can be said of governors and state legislators; of mayors and city councils.

It is a time-honored practice for a limited number of such politicos to be fudged into presumably merit system positions. Fudge, meaning to cheat or grossly exaggerate, is one of the most important words in personnel management. Indeed, it can be said that the whole public personnel netherworld only exists because of the ability of personnel administrators to produce a seemingly endless supply of fudge. The extent of such placements depends upon such factors as the strength and longevity of the merit system, the political culture of the community, and the personal integrity of a chief executive who, having taken an oath to uphold all of the laws of the jurisdiction, can only make such appointments in violation of the spirit, if not the letter, of that oath.

While the merit system is frequently perverted for traditional political purposes, it is similarly abused for more scrupulous purposes. The excessively rigid procedures for entering and advancing in most merit systems have long been recognized as being hindrances to effective management practices. In order to compensate for the lack of management discretion caused by these rigidities, career civil servants as well as other highly qualified individuals from outside the system have been advanced or initially installed through a fudging of the civil service regulations similar to the processes by which politicos are foisted on the merit system. The formal system with its attendant procedural morass simply does not allow for the timely promotion or placement of such meritorious individuals.

Consequently, what frequently exists in fact, although nowhere is it officially recognized, is a first-class and a second-class civil service. This is not an indicator of

TABLE 10.2 A Few Examples of How Civil Service Systems Are "Fudged"

Model	Process
"Tailoring"	"Preferred" candidate is identified. Qualifications for position in vacancy announcement tailored to skills of preferred candidate. Preferred candidate hired or promoted. This practice is technically legal, but goes beyond the spirit of civil service law.
"Bridging" a permanent appointment	Agency targets highly qualified (i.e., "preferred") candidate. To avoid a hiring delay, candidate is hired on a temporary line, which is later converted, or bridged to a permanent line. This practice is technically legal, but goes beyond the spirit of civil service law.
Provisional appointment	This practice is technically legal, but goes beyond the spirit of civil service law.
"Soliciting" a declination	Convince persons ranked high on civil service list to turn job offer down. To do so, candidate must be convinced that the work is undesirable and unpleasant. Or, a bargain will be made whereby the candidate is promised a "helping hand" for some other current or future job vacancy. This practice is clearly illegal.

NOTE: This represents just a sample of techniques, all of which have been employed at least at the federal level of government.

SOURCE: Adapted from Carolyn Ban, "The Realities of the Merit System," In *Public Personnel Management: Current Concerns, Future Challenges*, eds. Carolyn Ban and Norma M. Riccucci (White Plains, NY: Longman Press, 1991).

the quality of any individual or of the productive value of each class; it is merely a reference as to how people are treated by the merit system. While the politically uninfluential who comprise the civil service proletariat must be content with careers bounded by the full force of the frequently unreasonable and always constraining regulations, others—fortunate enough to be recognized for their talents or in spite of their talents—benefit markedly by having these same regulations waived, fraudulently complied with, or simply ignored.

From Spoils to Merit

Of course, all this—the formal merit system and the informal netherworld—was brought about by the civil service reform movement. While federal civil service reform is generally dated from the post–Civil War period, the political roots of the reform effort go back much earlier—to the beginning of the republic. Thomas Jefferson was the first president to face the problem of a philosophically hostile bureaucracy. While sorely pressed by his supporters to remove Federalist officeholders and replace them with Republican partisans, Jefferson was determined not to remove officials for political reasons alone. He maintained that only "malconduct is a just ground of removal: mere difference of political opinion is not." With occasional defections from this principle, even by Jefferson himself, this policy was the norm rather than the exception down through the administration of Andrew Jackson. President Jackson's rhetoric on the nature of public service was far more influential than his administrative example. In claiming that all men, especially the newly enfranchised who did so much to elect him, should have an equal opportunity for public office, Jackson played to his plebeian constituency and put the patrician civil service on notice that they had no natural monopoly on public office. The spoils system, used only modestly by Jackson, flourished under his successors. The doctrine of rotation of office progressively prevailed over the earlier notion of stability in office.

Depending upon your point of view, the advent of modern merit systems is either an economic, a political, or a moral development. Economic historians would maintain that the demands of industrial expansion—a dependable postal service, a viable transportation network, and so on—necessitated a government service based upon merit. Political analysts could argue rather persuasively that it was the demands of an expanded **suffrage** and democratic rhetoric that sought to replace favoritism with merit. Economic and political considerations are so intertwined that it is impossible to say which factor is the true midwife of the merit system. The moral impetus behind reform is even more difficult to define. As moral impulses tend to hide economic and political motives, the weight of moral concern undiluted by other considerations is impossible to measure. Nevertheless, the cosmetic effect of moral overtones was of significant aid to the civil service reform movement, because it accentuated the social legitimacy of the reform proposals.

With the ever-present impetus of achieving maximum public services for minimum tax dollars, business interests were quite comfortable in supporting civil service reform, one of a variety of strategies they used to have power pass from the politicos to themselves. The political parties of the time were almost totally dependent for financing upon **assessments** made on the wages of their members in public office; with the decline of patronage, the parties had to seek new funding sources, and American business was more than willing to assume this new financial burden—and its concomitant influence.

The Pendleton Act

There is no doubt that civil service reform would have come about without the 1881 assassination of President James A. Garfield; there is also no doubt that the assassination by a disappointed office seeker helped. Garfield was shot by Charles Guiteau, an insane, self-styled attorney who had worked for Garfield's election and

---

suffrage The right to vote. Property ownership was commonly required for voters in the early years of the United States, but, by the time Andrew Jackson became president in 1829, universal white male suffrage had been effectively achieved. Since then, various constitutional amendments have been devoted to expanding the suffrage. In 1870, the Fifteenth Amendment held that suffrage shall not be denied "on account of race, color, or previous condition of servitude." In 1920, the Nineteenth Amendment held that citizens of either sex had the right to vote.

assessment The contributions to political parties determined according to a schedule of rates and made in order to retain a civil service patronage appointment.

Box 10.2

An Assassin's Letter to a Future Victim

March 26, 1881

Gen. Garfield:

I understand from Col. Hooker of the Nat'l committee that I am to have a consulship. I hope it is the consulship at Paris, as that is the only one I care to take. Wish you would send in my name for the consulship at Paris. Mr. Walker, the present consul, has no claim on you for the office, I think as the men that did the business last fall are the ones to be remembered.

Very respectfully,

Charles Guiteau

SOURCE: U.S. Office of Personnel Management. Reprinted in Jay M. Shafritz, Albert C. Hyde, Norma Riccucci, and David H. Rosenbloom, *Personal Management in Government: Politics and Process*, 4th ed. (New York: Marcel Dekker, 1992).

was angry about not receiving a patronage appointment. While the twentieth president's death was certainly instrumental in creating the appropriate climate for the passage of the Pendleton Act, historians maintain that the Republican reversals during the midterm elections of 1882 had the more immediate effect on enactment. Civil service reform had been the deciding issue in a number of congressional contests. Thus, when President Chester A. Arthur signed the Pendleton Act into law on January 16, 1883, and created the U.S. Civil Service Commission, it was essentially a gesture by reluctant politicians to assuage public opinion and the reform elements.

The Pendleton Act or "An Act to Regulate and Improve the Civil Service of the United States" has been a remarkably durable piece of legislation. Within it is the framework for personnel management that is still the heart of the federal civil service system. The act created the U.S. Civil Service Commission as the personnel management arm of the president. While it was termed a **commission**, it was by no means independent. It was an executive agency that for all practical purposes was subject to the administrative discretion of the president. Written into the act were requirements for open competitive examinations, probationary periods, and protection from political pressures. While the personnel program was to remain decentralized and in the control of the departments, the commission was authorized to supervise the conduct of examinations and make investigations to determine the degree of departmental enforcement of its rules.

---

commission A group charged with directing a government function, whether on an ad hoc or a permanent basis. Commissions tend to be used (1) when it is desirable to have bipartisan leadership, (2) when their functions are of a quasi-judicial nature, or (3) when it is deemed important to have wide representation of ethnic groups, regions of the country, differing skills, and so on.

The Pendleton Act was hardly a total victory for the reformers. It only covered just over 10 percent of the federal service. Actually the reformers were not at all anxious for near universal merit system coverage. They recognized the problems of creating the appropriate administrative machinery and were concerned that the reform program would be overburdened and subject to failure if complete reform were attempted all at once. Over the years, federal employees were brought more and more under the jurisdiction of the Civil Service Commission or of other federal merit systems, such as those of the Foreign Service, Tennessee Valley Authority, and so forth.

American presidents during the reform period typically entered office taking full advantage of their patronage prerogatives and left office with extensions of the merit system to their credit. This was the case with every president from Arthur to Wilson. Merit system coverage went from 10 percent in 1884 to over 70 percent by the end of World War I. Generally, lame duck presidents being succeeded by someone of a different party would **blanket in** large numbers of employees in order to reduce the amount of patronage available to the opposition party. One of the ironies of civil service reform brought about by such blanketing in is that such initial reforms had a tendency to benefit employees who were the least meritorious.

State and Local Reform

Influenced by the example of the 1883 Pendleton Act, state and local jurisdictions began to institute civil service commissions. But this was a very slow process. While New York adopted a merit system that same year and Massachusetts did so during the following year, it was more than 20 years before another state did so in 1905. By 1935, only 12 states had formally instituted merit systems. These early efforts were not all successes. Connecticut had its first civil service law repealed, while Kansas kept the statute as law but "made it innocuous by refusing to vote appropriations." Nor were these laws necessarily effective even when kept on the books. For example, New York State, which since 1883 had the most stringent prohibitions against political assessments on the salaries of public employees, had widespread "voluntary" contributions to the party at least through the 1930s. It wouldn't be until well after World War II that most states would install merit systems—initially, in many cases, only to qualify for federal grants. Today almost all states have general merit system coverage for their employees.

Only 65 cities had created civil service commissions by 1900. By 1930, that number had risen to 250. Today less than 12 percent of cities with populations exceeding 50,000 do not have merit systems. The percentage lacking merit system coverage is almost double that for all cities in the 25,000 to 50,000 population range. Only six of the more than 3,000 counties had adopted merit systems by 1933. Today less than 10 percent have instituted general merit systems.

It is important to note that all statistics concerning merit system coverage are inherently deceptive. While such figures may be numerically accurate, they merely

---

blanket in A term for the large-scale importation of previously noncareer jobs into the regular civil service merit system. In the short run, blanketing-in can be (and has been) used to protect political favorites from the next administration. In the long run, blanketing-in is one of the major means through which the civil service merit system has been enlarged.

Box 10.3

George Washington Plunkitt on "The Curse of Civil Service Reform"

This civil service law is the biggest fraud of the age. It is the curse of the nation. There can't be no real patriotism while it lasts. How are you goin' to interest our young men in their country if you have no offices to give them when they work for their party? Just look at things in this city to-day. There are ten thousand good offices, but we can't get at more than a few hundred of them. How are we goin' to provide for the thousands of men who worked for the Tammany ticket? It can't be done. These men were full of patriotism a short time ago. They expected to be servin' their city, but when we tell them that we can't place them, do you think their patriotism is goin' to last? Not much. They say: 'What's the use of workin' for your country anyhow? There's nothin in the game.' And what can they do? I don't know, but I'll tell you what I do know. I know more than one young man in past years who worked for the ticket and was just overflowin' with patriotism, but when he was knocked out by the civil service humbug he got to hate his country and became an Anarchist.

This ain't no exaggeration. I have good reason for sayin' that most of the Anarchists in this city to-day are men who ran up against civil service examinations. Isn't it enough to make a man sour on his country when he wants to serve it and won't be allowed unless he answers a lot of fool questions about the number of cubic inches of water in the Atlantic and the quality of sand in the Sahara desert? There was once a bright young man in my district who tackled one of these examinations. The next I heard of him he had settled down in Herr Most's saloon smokin' and drinkin' beer and talkin' socialism all day. Before that time he had never drank anything but whisky. I knew what was comin' when a young Irishman drops whisky and takes to beer and long pipes in a German saloon. That young man is to-day one of the wildest Anarchists in town. And just to think! He might be a patriot but for that cussed civil service.

SOURCE: William C. Riordon, *Plunkitt of Tammany Hall* (New York: McClure Phillips, 1905).

---

indicate that merit systems are "on the books," not that they exist in practice. The surveys of merit system coverage that are annually undertaken by a variety of good-government groups are typically administered by mailed questionnaire. These statistics are by no means ascertained by empirical investigation. Consequently, while the arithmetic of these surveys may be impeccable, the resulting summaries frequently belie the true extent of merit system coverage. Remember, the city of Chicago has an excellent merit system on the books, yet it manages to retain its well-earned reputation as the largest American city with the most notorious patronage abuses.

The Rise and Fall of the Civil Service Commission

Subnational jurisdictions followed the federal merit system example in many respects: Bipartisan civil service commissions became common, examining methods and related administrative detail were frequently similar, and prohibitions concerning assessments and other varieties of political interference were legally binding many years before a general pattern of compliance appeared. In some areas, such as position classifications programs and retirement provisions, a variety of local jurisdictions were many years ahead of the federal service. However, at the local level the pattern of reform that evolved contained a crucial difference—the civil service commission was made administratively and presumably politically independent of the jurisdiction's chief executive officer.

The commission format was mandated by political, not administrative, considerations. Then, as now, the illogic of divorcing the control of personnel from programmatic authority was recognized. Nevertheless, the more immediate goal of defeating the influences of spoils was paramount. With this in mind, the rationale for the commission device was quite reasonable. Not only would it be independent from the party-controlled government, but its three- or five-part membership would be in a better position to resist political pressures than could any single administrator. **Appellate** functions, especially, are better undertaken by a tribunal than by a solitary judge. Not insignificantly, a commission provides a political safety valve by making room for representatives of special interests such as racial or employee groups.

It was not very long before the rationale for the independent commission was seriously challenged. As the city manager movement developed early in this century, managers—nonpartisan reform-type managers at that—found themselves burdened with the same kinds of restrictions upon their authority over personnel that had been designed to thwart the spoilsmen. They felt, quite reasonably, that the personnel function should be integrated with the other administrative functions under the executive.

While this line of reasoning made considerable headway where the city manager concept was firmly entrenched, it had little applicability for most of the larger cities where merit system provisions implemented only a few years earlier had degenerated into a sham. This was achieved by the dual process of appointing persons unsympathetic to merit system ideals as civil service commissioners and by restricting the work of the commission by denying adequate appropriations. In response to such "starve 'em out" tactics, many jurisdictions later enacted **ordinances** providing that a fixed percentage of each year's budget would be for the administration of the merit system.

Despite these rather inauspicious beginnings, the merit system has now taken a firm hold on most sizable public jurisdictions. Two basic factors have accounted for the continued growth of merit systems at the state and local level. First, as the scope and nature of state and local employment changed, it was almost inevitable that patronage appointees would have to give way to those with greater technical training

---

appellate Any court that considers appeals concerning a lower court's actions.

ordinances Regulations enacted by a local government that have the force of law but must be in compliance with state and national laws. They are issued under the authority derived from a grant of power (such as a city charter) from a sovereign entity (such as a state).

and an interest in public service careers. It should be remembered in this context that even in the federal government at its worst, the spoils system never substantially abused positions requiring technical skills. For the most part, then, the complex functions of government, rather than the ideals of civil service reformers, have led to the relative demise of spoils practices.

Second, the federal government threw its weight in favor of the development of forceful merit systems at the state and local levels. Beginning in the 1930s, it has adopted a variety of measures to coerce or induce states to use merit procedures where federal funding is involved. Federal standards for this purpose were first issued in 1939 and have been periodically revised ever since.

Ironically, at the same time that the federal government has been pressuring state and local governments to adopt and strengthen merit systems, the commission form of administering them has been on the wane for reasons similar to the abolition of the commission format at the federal level. Put simply: independent, structurally and politically isolated personnel agencies of a regulatory nature have great difficulty in serving the needs of elected executives and public managers.

The advent of the civil service commission as a political device was not synonymous with the development of personnel administration as such. The commission impetus was decidedly negative and heavily moralistic. Its goals were to smite out "evil" as personified by the spoils system. Viewed historically and dispassionately, one could argue that considerable good in the guise of executive discretion also got washed away with the evil. Administrative historian Frederick C. Mosher saw two lasting efforts from the widespread implementation of civil service commissions. They not only "perpetuated the association of public personnel and its administration with morality," but they also "divorced personnel administration from general management—from the executives responsible for carrying out the programs and activities of governments." Unlike its private sector counterpart, the personnel function in government has two frequently conflicting roles. Of necessity, it must attend both to service and to control. Is it possible to be both an integral member of the management team and the organization's policeman at the same time? In its various manifestations, this is the central dilemma of public personnel administration today.

The Civil Service Reform Act of 1978

On March 2, 1978, President Jimmy Carter, with the enthusiastic support of his Civil Service Commission leadership, submitted his civil service reform proposals to Congress. On that same day, before the National Press Club, he further called his proposals to the attention of the Congress by charging that the present federal personnel system had become a "bureaucratic maze which neglects merit, tolerates poor performance, and permits abuse of legitimate employee rights, and mires every personnel action in red tape, delay, and confusion."

The reform bill faced considerable opposition from federal employee unions (which thought the bill was too management oriented) and from veterans' groups (which were aghast at the bill's curtailment of veterans' preferences). The unions lost. The veterans won. The bill passed almost intact, thanks in great measure to the efforts of Alan K. "Scotty" Campbell, the last chairman of the U.S. Civil Service Commission, who was both the architect of the reform act and its most fervent advocate before Congress. (Campbell would then serve as the first director of the new Office of Personnel Management during 1979–1980.)

The Civil Service Reform Act of 1978 mandated that the U.S. Civil Service Commission would be divided into two agencies—an Office of Personnel Management (OPM) to serve as the personnel arm of the chief executive and an independent Merit Systems Protection Board (MSPB) to provide recourse for aggrieved employees. In addition, the act created the Federal Labor Relations Authority (FLRA) to oversee federal labor-management policies.

Was the OPM nothing more than the old commission with a face lift? A case can be made that the whole Civil Service Reform Act was not much more than reorganization for cosmetic effect—that is, much-changed on the surface but essentially the same underneath. While some criticize the act as too little too late, others concede their misgivings and say "better a symbolic act than no act." The show must go on! For if the act fails in substance, it is an overwhelming success as a symbol. Because of the scandals that arose during the Nixon-Ford years, the U.S. Civil Service Commission grew to symbolize corruption and incompetence. Of course only a minority of individuals engaged in corrupt behavior or exhibited incompetent tendencies. But that was enough to ruin a reputation.

The commission's "good name" could not be salvaged. Only a new name could remove the stigma of past indiscretions. The stigma was so great that the reformers went so far as to formally assert that it was not the giant Office of Personnel Management that would be the successor agency to the commission, but the little Merit Systems Protection Board. OPM would be a totally new entity—an organization without a history starting with a clean slate. It's a nice thought. But quite untrue except as a symbolic purging of the evils of the past. Yet on this plane of symbolic

A woman exiled to a turkey farm. Turkeys may be good eating but they are among the dumbest of farm animals. Thus a "turkey farm" has come to mean a government office with little work and slight, if any, responsibility. Government managers frequently find it easier to place troublesome or incompetent employees on turkey farms, rather than go through the hassle of adverse action proceedings to have them removed.

action it has been a considerable success. Alan K. Campbell and company deserve a lot of credit. You cannot help but admire a federal manager who, upon inheriting a troubled and demoralized agency, destroys it only to find himself and practically all of his previously troubled agency born again on the White House organization chart.

Reinventing Public Personnel Administration

Personnel management in government has been heavily impacted by the reinventing government movement. Indeed, civil service reform is a major theme of the 1993 *National Performance Review* (the Gore Report), which states that "to create an effective federal government, we must reform virtually the entire personnel system: recruitment, hiring, classification, promotion, pay and reward systems." If one word sums up the overall focus of the reform agenda, that word is decentralization. Accordingly, the federal government has done the following:

1. Deregulated personnel policy by phasing out the 10,000-page Federal Personnel Manual and all agency implementing directives

2. Gave all departments and agencies authority to conduct their own recruiting and examinations for all positions, and abolished all central registers and standard application forms

3. Dramatically simplified the current classification system to give agencies greater flexibility in how they classify and pay their employees

4. Allowed agencies to design their own performance management and reward systems, with the objective of improving the performance of individuals and organizations

5. Sought to reduce by half the time required to terminate federal managers and employees for **cause**.

For over 100 years, the concept of merit employment progressively spread across U.S. governments. However, in 1996, Georgia introduced Senate Bill 635 to "eliminate" the merit system the state had introduced in 1943. In practice, the legislation drew on common themes of increasing decentralization, employment flexibility and ease of hiring and firing. But it went further and abolished the state's merit system as well, including employment protections and grievance appeal processes.

Is this an aberration or a turning point? Advocates of the change note greater simplicity and ease of personnel action by management, especially simplicity of firing. But the way has been opened for the return of a political spoils system, and it is doubtful whether a regime with no due process rights for employees and a capacity to diminish minority rights will withstand constitutional scrutiny.

Nevertheless, it is difficult to usher in the brave new world of reinvented government in an era of downsizing and privatization. Downsizing is reducing the total number of an agency's employees by **attrition**, buy-outs (financial incentives to retire or resign), and layoffs—often called "reductions-in-force." Privatization entails sending

---

cause The reason given for removing someone from an office or job (short for just cause). The cause cited may or may not be the real reason for the removal.

attrition The reduction in the size of a workforce that naturally occurs through voluntary resignations, retirements, and deaths.

Box 10.4

Merit System Principles

The Civil Service Reform Act of 1978 put into law the nine basic merit principles that should govern all personnel practices in the federal government:

1. Recruitment from all segments of society, and selection and advancement on the basis of ability, knowledge and skills, under fair and open competition
2. Fair and equitable treatment in all personnel management matters, without regard to politics, race, color, religion, national origin, sex, marital status, age, or handicapping condition, and with proper regard for individual privacy and constitutional rights
3. Equal pay for work of equal value, considering both national and local rates paid by private employers, with incentives and recognition for excellent performance
4. High standards of integrity, conduct, and concern for the public interest
5. Efficient and effective use of the federal workforce
6. Retention of employees who perform well, correcting the performance of those whose work is inadequate, and separation of those who cannot or will not meet required standards
7. Improved performance through effective education and training
8. Protection of employees from arbitrary action, personal favoritism, or political coercion
9. Protection of employees against reprisal for lawful disclosures of information

both a function and the employees who performed it to a private company. With this, the U.S. Office of Personnel Management has led the way. The Clinton administration's first major privatization of a federal program took place in 1995, when about 125 former employees of the Office of Personnel Management's Workforce Training Service started work for the U.S. Department of Agriculture's Graduate School. While affiliated with the Department of Agriculture, this "graduate school" is a nonprofit organization that receives no federal funds; it supports itself through tuition fees.

The ultimate goal of the reinventors of public personnel administration is to force government personnel offices to always remember the customer, as stated in the Gore Report: "Personnel officers must shift from reactive processors of paperwork to responsive consultants and advisors." This new focus requires personnel officers to look at the federal manager "as a customer" with needs that must be anticipated and met with responsive service.

Note the significant change here. The manager is the customer, the manager is the priority. The traditional public personnel agency concerns of protecting the rights of employees and maintaining the integrity of the merit system have been relegated to the appeals agencies such as the Merit Systems Protection Board and to the public employees' unions.

Patronage Appointments

Patronage is the power of elected and appointed officials to make partisan appointments to office or to confer contracts, honors, or other benefits on their political supporters. While subject to frequent attack from reformers, patronage has traditionally been the method by which political leaders assure themselves a loyal support system of people who will carry out their policies and organize voters for their continued political control. The patronage appointments process is more commonly known as the spoils system. The spoils system got its name in 1832 when Senator William L. Marcy (1786–1854) asserted in a Senate debate that "that the politicians of the United States . . . see nothing wrong in the rule, that to the victor belong the spoils of the enemy."

The Plum Book

Whenever there is a change of administration—whether in Washington, a state capital, or a city hall—there is a concomitant patronage feeding frenzy. When the national government changes administrations this frenzy is encouraged by "the Plum Book," formally, *United States Government: Policy and Supporting Positions*. This publication comes out every four years, right after the presidential election. It lists all the jobs that a new president can fill at his or her discretion.

In response to the fact that jobs such as "Confidential Assistant to the Executive Assistant to the Secretary of Agriculture" and "Commissioner, Inter-American Tropical Tuna Commission" are now open, thousands of patriotic citizens send their résumés to the White House. For most it will be a totally futile effort. In 1993, according to *Washington Monthly* editor Charles Peters, "the Clinton Administration has dumped 25,000 unread, unprocessed résumés out of the 40,000 it received from citizens hoping to serve as a part of the new administration." And the earlier Bush and Reagan administrations did the same. Despite the fact that every new administration states it is seeking to hire the best people the nation can offer, don't think that just submitting a résumé—however impressive it might be—will land you a plum job from the Plum Book. The brutal political fact is that no one will even look at unsolicited credentials for high-level patronage jobs unless they are politically sponsored. Only phone calls and letters from influential people will get you seriously considered. The reason they call it patronage is that you need a patron.

The Constitutionality of Patronage

Patronage has always been one of the major tools by which executives at all levels in all sectors consolidate their power and attempt to control a bureaucracy. In the 1990 case of *Rutan v. Republican Party*, the U.S. Supreme Court ruled that traditional patronage in public employment is unconstitutional. Writing the majority opinion, Justice William J. Brennan Jr. said: "To the victor belong only those spoils that may be constitutionally obtained." In earlier cases, *Elrod v. Burns* (1976) and *Branti v. Finkel* (1980), the Court held that the First Amendment forbids government officials to discharge or threaten to discharge public employees solely for not being supporters of the political party in power, unless party affiliation is an appropriate requirement for the position involved.

In the *Rutan* case the Court was asked to decide the constitutionality of several related political patronage practices—"whether promotion, transfer, recall and hiring decisions involving low-level public employees may be constitutionally based on party affiliation and support. We hold that they may not." In a stinging dissent, Justice Antonin Scalia said, "The new principle that the Court today announces will be enforced by a corps of judges (the members of this Court included) who overwhelmingly owe their office to its violation. Something must be wrong here, and I suggest it is the Court." The Supreme Court notwithstanding, patronage will turn out to be like prostitution: It can be outlawed but it cannot be stopped. Laws barring either will merely drive the practice underground—into the netherworld.

Veterans' Preference

Patronage appointments are essentially a means of implementing a society's values. The United States has always sought to advance the interests of its military veterans. Thus veterans' preference—special influence earned by honorable military service—has become a special variant of patronage. While veterans have always been given special benefits by their governments, the formal concept dates from 1865, when the Congress, toward the end of the Civil War, affirmed that "persons honorably discharged from the military or naval service by reason of disability resulting from wounds or sickness incurred in the line of duty, shall be preferred for appointments to civil offices, provided they are found to possess the business capacity necessary for the proper discharge of the duties of such offices." The 1865 law was superseded in 1919, when preference was extended to all "honorably discharged" veterans, their widows, and wives of disabled veterans. The Veterans' Preference Act of 1944 expanded the scope of veterans' preference by providing for a five-point bonus on federal examination scores for all honorably separated veterans (except for those with a service-connected disability, who are entitled to a ten-point bonus). Veterans also received other advantages in federal employment (such as protections against arbitrary dismissal and preference in the event of a reduction in force).

All states and many other jurisdictions have veterans' preference laws of varying intensity. New Jersey, an extreme example, offers veterans absolute preference; if a veteran passes an entrance examination, he or she must be hired (no matter what the score) before nonveterans can be hired. Veterans competing with each other are rank-ordered, and all disabled veterans receive preference over other veterans. Veterans' preference laws have been criticized because they have allegedly made it difficult for government agencies to hire and promote more women and minorities. Although the original version of the Civil Service Reform Act of 1978 sought to limit veterans' preference in the federal service, the final version contained a variety of new provisions strengthening veterans' preference.

In *Personnel Administrator of Massachusetts v. Feeney* (1979) the Supreme Court held that a state law operating to the advantage of males by giving veterans lifetime preference for state employment was not in violation of the equal protection clause of the Fourteenth Amendment. The Court found that a veterans' preference law's disproportionate impact on women did not prove intentional bias.

Public Sector Labor Relations

Unions are groups of employees who create a formal organization (the union) to represent their interests before management. Labor relations is the term for all of the interactions between the union leaders (representing the employees) and management (representing the corporation or jurisdiction). The importance of labor relations in the public sector is painfully evident to anyone who has ever sniffed through a garbage strike, walked through a transit strike, or suffered through the **blue flu**. A reasonable person would seem to have adequate cause to be alternately optimistic or pessimistic concerning the emergence of militant, public employee unions. Job actions notwithstanding, the extraordinary ability of such unions to gain fiscally crippling pay raises from their jurisdictions without exchanging corresponding increases in productivity is certainly adequate cause for pessimism. On the other hand, the future of unions as vehicles to replace part of the merit system's worn-out regalia and as a source of leadership in the fight for greater productivity is exceedingly hopeful.

Why have the unions been so successful in so many instances? Simply put, union leaders have been better politicians than the elected political executives. Their acceptance of a militant posture directly followed their recognition that nontraditional forms of political behavior had been exceedingly productive for other interest groups—especially the civil rights advocates of the early 1960s whose use of civil disobedience was exceedingly effective.

Public personnel departments have traditionally had the dual function of simultaneously representing management while enforcing and interpreting civil service regulations. This institutionalized degree of conflict over what role personnel should play on what occasion has often been noted, but the problem is reaching its resolution. Unions, opting for the pluralistic conflictive model of ascertaining the public interest, reject the proposition that personnel in the public sector has an equal responsibility to employees as it does to management. No less an authority than the longtime public employees union chief Jerry Wurf has flatly stated that the "civil service is nothing more—and not much less—than management's personnel system." The unions see their prime role as representing the public employee. Any remaining pretensions on the part of personnel that this is not the case will eventually be negotiated away. Even the sacrosanct, independent, civil service commission will gradually see its duties considerably narrowed by the more vigilant and better staffed unions. This situation begs a significant question. If the civil service commissions are not to play a role in the collective bargaining process, how are they to remain relevant? The National Civil Service League—the organization that drafted the original 1883 Pendleton Act, which established the U.S. Civil Service Commission—has concluded that other forces have so lessened the significance of the independent civil service commission that the league's current Model Public Personnel Administration Law now recommends the abolition of such commissions.

---

blue flu An informal strike by police officers, who call in sick; the blue refers to their uniforms.

The AFL-CIO

The American Federation of Labor–Congress of Industrial Organizations is a voluntary federation of over a hundred national and international labor unions operating in the United States and representing in total over 13 million workers. The AFL–CIO is not itself a union; it does no bargaining. It is perhaps best thought of as a union of unions. The affiliated unions created the AFL–CIO to represent them in the creation and execution of broad national and international policies and to coordinate a wide range of joint activities. The American Federation of Labor (organized in 1881 as a federation of craft unions, the Federation of Organized Trade and Labor Unions), changed its name in 1886 after merging with those craft unions that had become disenchanted with the more idealistic national labor organization, the Knights of Labor. In 1955, the AFL merged with the Congress of Industrial Organizations to become the AFL–CIO. Each member union of the AFL–CIO remains autonomous, conducting its own affairs in the manner determined by its own members. Each has its own headquarters, officers, and staff. Each decides its own economic policies, carries on its own contract negotiations, sets its own dues, and provides its own membership services. Each is free to withdraw at any time. But through such voluntary participation, the AFL–CIO, based in Washington, plays a role in establishing overall policies for the U.S. labor movement, which in turn advances the interests of every union.

All of the major public sector unions are members of the AFL–CIO. The National Education Association, representing teachers, is the largest, with 1.7 million members. While the International Association of Firefighters, with 150,000 members, may seem small in comparison, a greater percentage of firefighters are union members than workers in any other public sector occupation.

Box 10.5

Solidarity Forever

The union movement encouraged the singing of stirring "message" songs as a way of building morale and gaining membership. Some unions even issued official songbooks designed to fit into a hip pocket. Perhaps the most famous of all union songs (many of which were parodies of well-known hymns) is *Solidarity Forever*, which should be sung to the tune of *The Battle Hymn of the Republic*.

> It is we who plowed the prairies, built the cities where they trade,
> Dug the mines and built the workshops, endless miles of railroad laid;
> Now we stand outcast and starving mid the wonders we have made
> But the union makes us strong!
> Solidarity forever!
> Solidarity forever!
> Solidarity forever!
> For the union makes us strong!

Administrative Agencies

In the context of labor relations, an administrative agency is any impartial private or government organization that oversees or facilitates the labor relations process. The contemporary pattern of labor relations in both the public and private sectors relies on administrative agencies to provide ongoing supervision of the collective bargaining process. While generally headed by a board of three to five members, these agencies make rulings on unfair labor practices, on the appropriateness of bargaining units, and sometimes on the proper interpretation of a contract or the legitimacy of a scope of bargaining. They also oversee **authorization elections** and certify the winners as the exclusive bargaining agents for all of the employees in a bargaining unit. The National Labor Relations Board (NLRB), created in 1935 by an act of Congress, is the prototype of administrative agencies dealing with labor relations. The NLRB seeks to protect the rights of employees and employers, to encourage collective bargaining, and to eliminate practices on the part of labor and management that are harmful to the general welfare. The NLRB establishes procedures by which workers can exercise their choice at a secret ballot election and determines whether certain practices of employers or unions are unfair labor practices. The NLRB model has been adapted to the public sector by the federal government and several states.

The equivalent agency for federal employees is the Federal Labor Relations Authority, created by the Civil Service Reform Act of 1978 to oversee the creation of bargaining units, to supervise elections, and to otherwise deal with labor-management issues in federal agencies. The FLRA is headed by a three-member panel—a chair and two members—who are appointed on a bipartisan basis to staggered five-year terms. The FLRA replaced the Federal Labor Relations Council (FLRC). A general counsel, also appointed to a five-year term, investigates alleged unfair labor practices and prosecutes them before the FLRA. Also within the FLRA and acting as a separate body, the Federal Service Impasses Panel (FSIP) acts to resolve negotiation impasses.

In the states, such agencies are generally called Public Employment Relations Boards (or PERBs). Typically, their functions parallel those of the NLRB, as do the methods by which they are appointed, their terms of office, and their administrative procedures. One important difference in the public sector is that binding arbitration over questions of contract interpretation may be used instead of strikes as the final means of resolving disputes. When this is the case, the PERB may have a role in overseeing the use of arbitration and even the substance of the arbitrators' rulings when they raise serious issues about the scope of bargaining or public policy.

Collective Bargaining

Collective bargaining is bargaining on behalf of a group of employees, as opposed to individual bargaining, in which each worker represents only himself or herself. Collective bargaining is a comprehensive term that encompasses the negotiating

---

authorization election Polls conducted by the National Labor Relations Board (or other administrative agency) to determine if a particular group of employees will be represented by a particular union or not. Authorization election is used interchangeably with certification election (because, if the union wins, it is certified as the representative of the workers by the administrative agency) and representative election (because a winning union becomes just that, the representative of the workers).

TABLE 10.3 The Labor Relations Legal System

Sector	Legal Base	Administrative Agency
Private industry	National Labor Relations Act, as amended	National Labor Relations Board
Railroads and airlines	Railway Labor Act, as amended	National Mediation Board
Postal Service	Postal Reorganization Act of 1970	National Labor Relations Board
Federal government	Civil Service Reform Act of 1978	Federal Labor Relations Authority
State and local government	Public employees relations acts	Public employment relations boards

SOURCE: Jay M. Shafritz, *Facts on File Dictionary of Public Administration* (New York: Facts on File, 1985).

process that leads to a contract between labor and management on wages, hours, and other conditions of employment as well as to the subsequent administration and interpretation of the signed contract. Collective bargaining is, in effect, the continuous relation between union representatives and employers. There are four basic stages of collective bargaining:

1. The establishment of organizations for bargaining
2. The formulation of demands
3. The negotiation of demands
4. The administration of the labor agreement

Collective bargaining is one of the keystones of the **National Labor Relations Act** (the Wagner Act) of 1935, which declares that the policy of the United States is to be carried out

> by encouraging the practice and procedure of collective bargaining and by protecting the exercise by workers of full freedom of association, self organization, and designation of representatives of their own choosing, for the purpose of negotiating the terms and conditions of their employment or other mutual aid or protection.

The predominant public sector labor relations model comes from the private sector. But this fit has been long recognized as far from perfect. This is one reason why public sector labor relations were at first opposed and then organized as **meet-and-confer discussions** rather than as a collective bargaining process. The term "collective negotiations" was often used to further avoid the suggestion of actual bargaining. But today those jurisdictions with well-developed labor relations programs rely upon the private sector model. The ramifications are considerable.

National Labor Relations Act In common usage, the National Labor Relations Act refers not just to the act of 1935 but to the act as amended by the Labor-Management Relations (Taft-Hartley) Act of 1947 and the Labor-Management Reporting and Disclosure (Landrum-Griffin) Act of 1959.

meet-and-confer discussions A technique used mostly in the public sector for determining conditions of employment whereby the representatives of the employer and the employee organization hold periodic discussions to seek agreement on matters within the scope of representation. Any written agreement is in the form of a nonbinding memorandum of understanding. This technique is often used where formal collective bargaining is not authorized.

Instead of accepting the "public interest" or some equally saccharine goal as the watchword of the negotiating process, they have tended to adopt the adversary model of negotiations so common in the private sector. This model assumes that for one side to win the other must lose. Essentially, each party is haggling over its share of the organization's profits. There being no legal profits as such in government, has the private sector model based on conflict and individual acquisitiveness been appropriately applied to the public sector?

This private sector model of labor relations was consolidated by the National Labor Relations Act. It provides for negotiations between workers and management on the assumption that the outcome will reflect the inherent **bargaining strength** of each. Rules for fair labor relations practices were established and the **National Labor Relations Board** was created to adjudicate disputes over their application. Workers retain the right to strike and to bargain as equals with management over virtually all employment-related issues not constrained by law. Although relations are assumed to be adversarial, the model is based on the belief that the free market imposes an ultimate harmony of interest between employer and employee: Neither party favors the economic demise of the employer.

Employing this basic model in the public sector is problematic because some of its crucial assumptions do not fit. It is difficult to assume equality between the parties in public sector collective bargaining. What does it mean to say that a union is equal to the government, or to the people as a whole? Elected legislative bodies and elected executives are generally considered the appropriate policymaking bodies in American government. Public managers bargaining with organized employees are not. The basic adjustment to the inequality of the parties in labor disputes has been to recognize the government's greater authority by restricting the **scope of bargaining**.

Since it is not assumed that the parties in public sector collective bargaining are equal in principle, it follows that the outcome of disputes should not depend upon their relative strengths; consequently, there should be no need to strike. But public sector strikes are not necessarily intended to harm the employer economically. They tend to do more political than economic damage, at least in the short run. This is because the governmental employer is likely to derive its revenues from taxation, rather than exclusively from user fees. Yet, when a strike interrupts a government service, tax dollars are not refunded; nor are they paid out in compensation to striking employees. So a strike may temporarily enhance a government's economic position. In short, the function of a strike in the public sector is substantially different from that in the private sector.

---

bargaining strength The relative power each party holds during negotiation. Management has greater bargaining strength than labor if it believes that a short strike would be desirable. Final settlements often reflect the bargaining power of each side.

National Labor Relations Board The federal agency created by the National Labor Relations Act of 1935 that administers the nation's laws relating to labor relations in the private and nonprofit sectors. (Also under its jurisdiction is the U.S. Postal Service.) The NLRB is vested with the power to safeguard employees' rights to organize, to determine through elections whether workers want unions as their bargaining representatives, and to prevent and remedy unfair labor practices.

scope of bargaining Those issues over which management and labor negotiate during the collective bargaining process.

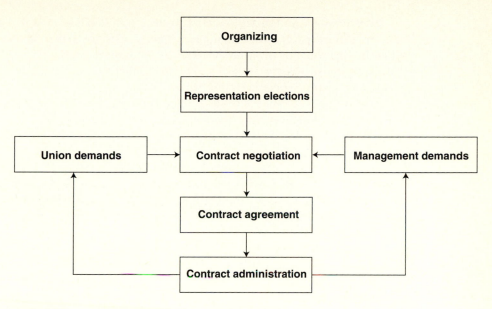

Figure 10.3 An Overview of the Collective Bargaining Cycle

Overall, the public sector is incredibly fragmented in terms of collective bargaining. There is no national law on the subject. States and cities vary widely in their practices. The law differs from one to another, placing substantial burdens on national labor unions and dispute resolution personnel who work in different jurisdictions. While the opportunity to experiment and to adapt to local conditions is valuable, such fragmentation makes it hard to speak of "public sector collective bargaining" without engaging in overgeneralization.

Impasse Resolution

An impasse is a condition that exists during labor-management negotiations when either party feels that no further progress can be made toward a settlement—unless the process of negotiating changes. The most common techniques used to break the impasse are mediation, fact-finding, and arbitration.

Mediation or conciliation is any attempt by an impartial third party to help settle disputes. A mediator has no power but that of persuasion; the mediator's suggestions are advisory and may be rejected by both parties. Mediation and conciliation tend to be used interchangeably to denote the entrance of an impartial third party into a labor dispute. However, there is a distinction. Conciliation is the less active term. It technically refers just to efforts to bring the parties together so that they may resolve their problems themselves. Mediation, in contrast, is a more active term. It implies that an active effort will be made to help the parties reach agreement by clarifying issues, asking questions, and making specific proposals. However, the usage of the two terms has been so blurred that the only place where it is absolutely necessary to distinguish between them is in a dictionary.

Fact-finding is an impartial review of the issues in a labor dispute by a specially appointed third party, whether it be a single individual, panel, or board. The fact finder holds formal or informal hearings and submits a report to the administrative agency and/or the parties involved. The fact finder's report, usually considered advisory, may contain specific recommendations.

Arbitration is the means of settling a dispute by having an impartial third party (the arbitrator) hold a formal hearing and render a decision that may or may not be binding on both sides. The arbitrator may be a single individual or a board of three, five, or more (usually an uneven number). When boards are used, they may include, in addition to impartial members, representatives from both of the disputants. In the context of labor relations, arbitrators are selected jointly by labor and management, or recommended by the Federal Mediation and Conciliation Service, by a state or local agency offering similar referrals, or by the private American Arbitration Association.

Compulsory arbitration is a negotiating process whereby the parties are required by law to arbitrate their dispute. Some state statutes concerning collective bargaining impasses in the public sector mandate that parties who have exhausted all other means of achieving a settlement must submit their dispute to an arbitrator. The intent of such requirements for compulsory arbitration is to induce the parties to reach agreement by presenting them with an alternative that is certain, even though it may be unpleasant in some respects to everyone involved.

Final or last-offer arbitration is a negotiating stratagem that has an arbitrator choose from among the disputing parties' final or last offer.

The most common effort to adjust public sector collective bargaining in the absence of the legalized strike has been to introduce some form of binding arbitration. But this raises a host of different problems. Arbitration inherently undercuts the bargaining process itself. If both sides are convinced a dispute will go to arbitration, they will tend to spend most of their time posturing rather than negotiating or compromising. Moreover, arbitration cannot resolve the concern that the sovereign—the state and not its employees—makes public policy. And arbitrators' decisions are not automatically sensible or in the public interest. Sometimes, they may even disregard a jurisdiction's ability to pay for the awards they authorize.

The nature of the arbitration of public sector labor disputes is also related to the remoteness of the "market" as a constraint on the total compensation of employees. In fact, the economic aspects of public sector labor relations tend to work best when cities are on the threshold of bankruptcy and therefore the "market" is not so remote. Since the market does not serve as a constraint as directly in the public sector as in the private sector, some substitute for it must be devised to resolve labor disputes. Unfortunately, arbitration has not always fared well in this context. Often, arbitrators will look to comparable jurisdictions to determine what is equitable. But there is a built-in redundancy in this approach and the selection of "comparable" jurisdictions is always somewhat arbitrary. In the private sector, an arbitration award is sometimes based on the relative strength of the parties, but this approach is not very meaningful in the public sector since the parties are fundamentally so unequal. In other words, the remoteness of the market has required arbitrators to develop other standards for reaching their awards—standards that are fraught with difficulty.

TABLE 10.4   Types of Impasse Resolution

	Mediation	Fact-Finding	Arbitration
Process	Intervention by Federal Mediation and Concilliation Service or other appropriate third party at request of negotiating parties or on own proffering of services.	A Procedure for compelling settlement, frequently a final alternative to arbitration	A terminal procedure alternative to or following fact-finding
Subject Matter	Terms of new agreement being negotiated	Terms of agreement being negotiated	Terms of agreement being negotiated (also final step in grievance procedure)
Setting	Mediator tries to determine basis for agreement and persuade parties to reach agreement	Parties try to persuade fact finder by arguments	Parties try to persuade arbitrators by arguments (same as fact-finding)
Third Party	Mediator—a Federal Commissioner of Mediation and Conciliation or other third party	Fact finder—a public employee or a private citizen selected by parties or by an administrative agency.	Arbitrator—a public employee or a private citizen selected by parties or by an administrative agency
Power Factor	Mediator limited to persuasion and ability to find compromise	Fact finder may make recommendations for impasse resolution	Arbitrator makes binding decision
Publicity	Confidential process— no public record kept	Quasi-public process with recommendations recorded and reported	Quasi-public process with decisions recorded and reported

SOURCE: Jay M. Shafritz, *Facts on File Dictionary of Public Administration* (New York: Facts on File, 1985).

Strikes

A strike is a mutual agreement among workers (whether members of a union or not) to a temporary work stoppage to obtain—or to resist—a change in their working conditions. The term is thought to have nautical origins because sailors would stop work by striking or taking down their sails. A strike or potential strike is considered an essential element of the collective bargaining process. Many labor leaders claim that collective bargaining can never be more than a charade without the right to strike. Major strikes have been declining in frequency in recent years, as unions in both the public and private sectors have lost a large measure of economic clout and political support. Public employee strikes also have been declining for another reason as well. A great percentage of public sector strikes in the 1960s and early 1970s were over one issue: recognition of the union for purposes of collective bargaining. Because recognition strikes tend to be one-time issues and because many states have in the last three decades passed comprehensive public employee relations laws, public-sector labor strife has been less than it once was.

The use of strikes is becoming somewhat outmoded. The use of economic force can be too damaging and unpredictable in today's economy and, consequently, the strike is viewed as a last-resort means of producing an agreement. Moreover, it is sometimes argued that the fundamental character of the strike is changing due to the maturing of collective bargaining relationships. Violence is sometimes incidental to strikes nowadays, but physical force no longer plays a central role. Rather, the parties tend to view the strike as a continuation of the bargaining process. Indeed, negotiations may avidly continue during the entire length of a strike. Again, it is important to remember that both sides have an overriding interest in common—the economic vitality of the employer and the concomitant maintenance of the employees' jobs. Another general factor affecting strike behavior is what folk singer Bob Dylan refers to as "Union Sundown." Because the public's image of unions has changed, they are no longer considered weak underdogs struggling for justice in the workplace. In contrast, many segments of the population see them as too powerful and too greedy. Since organized labor now seeks to achieve many of its goals through political means such as lobbying and electioneering, it cannot be oblivious to its public standing.

Why Strikes Occur

Strikes do occur and it is possible to identify at least five sets of concerns that promote them. First, it is often the case that workers will not work after a contract has expired. "No contract, no work" remains fundamental to the system of collective bargaining, since the purpose of negotiations is to arrive at agreements to govern the workplace. Sometimes, as negotiations reach the hour for the termination of the existing contract, the "clock is stopped" and marathon, all night/all day, bargaining sessions take place. There is no doubt that "no contract, no work" places a great deal of pressure on both sides to arrive at an agreement.

Second, the union leader is often in a complicated political position. A strike and the solidarity it promotes may be necessary for the leader to maintain his or her position. Union leaders tend to oversell their ability to dictate conditions to management. In order to justify their leadership and the exclusive representative position of the union, they tend to generate very high expectations. Eventually, the gap between these expectations and reality leads the membership to think it has been "sold out" by the union leader. (Many readers will notice a parallel with the election and subsequent performance of U.S. presidents in this regard.) Subsequent contract rejection by the membership can be viewed as a technique to compel management to further concessions. In the public sector, this ploy raises an interesting problem because management's concessions to labor may also be subject to outside ratification by a legislative body. In some cases, the legislature has used the city's negotiators as "surface bargainers," intending later on to reject the contract and force further concessions from the union. This practice is a breach of **good faith** and illegal in many jurisdictions, but if used with sophistication, it is hard to identify and challenge.

---

good faith Honesty; in the context of equal employment opportunity, good faith is the absence of discriminating intent. Good-faith bargaining is a requirement of the National Labor Relations Act, which makes it illegal for an employer to refuse to bargain in good faith about wages, hours, and other conditions of employment with the representative selected by a majority of the employees in a unit appropriate for collective bargaining.

Third, a strike may be used as a political weapon against public officials. It may be intended to embarrass an official, such as a mayor, who is running for reelection. It may also be intended to show public officials "who's boss." Municipal strikes have resembled urban guerrilla warfare: tons of garbage have been left in the streets, buildings allowed to burn, drawbridges left in uncrossable positions, and sewage spewed into waterways and upon public beaches. One of the acute problems in public-sector labor relations is the tendency for unions to play a major role in a candidate's election, only to find later on that all their economic demands will not be met. This too leads to frustrations caused by a gap between expectations and reality.

A fourth general factor contributing to strikes has been management's efforts to provoke them at a time when unions are relatively weak. It may be too evocative and emotive to call this a "union busting" technique. Perhaps "union taming" would be a better term. However, today a failed strike can lead to a decertification election, and unions are now losing such elections (and the right to represent workers) with greater frequency than ever before. A tame union will be an aid to the employer in selling management's view of what conditions in the workplace should be left to the employees. It will also be more willing to engage in givebacks, demands that a union accept lower salaries or benefits, ostensibly to preserve jobs. The most common giveback of recent years is union agreement that its members will pay a larger portion of the cost of health insurance than before.

Finally, strikes are related to the economic positions of the two sides. An economic weapon can backfire if it cannot be afforded. Unions with limited membership may have difficulty developing large and sufficient strike funds to aid the workers during the length of a strike. The timing of strikes can also be of great importance. Strikes during periods of economic recession and high unemployment are very risky because they make it easier for the employer to find **scabs** and replacement workers; and because the public's sympathy is hardly likely to be extended to those people fortunate enough to have jobs but unwilling to work them.

Two Famous Strikes

The Boston police strike of 1919 was the nation's first taste of large-scale municipal labor problems. While the patrolmen struck mainly for higher wages, they also wanted the right to form a union and affiliate with the American Federation of Labor. The strike brought chaos to the city. Samuel Gompers, the longtime leader of the American Federation of Labor, protested the police commissioner's refusal to allow the union to affiliate with the national federation. Calvin Coolidge, then governor of Massachusetts, responded with his famous assertion in a September 14, 1919 telegram to Gompers: "There is no right to strike against the public safety by anybody, anywhere, anytime." These words so expressed the public's outlook that a tidal wave of support gained him the Republican vice presidential nomination in 1920 (and when President Warren G. Harding died in 1923, Coolidge became

---

scab Generally, an employee who continues to work for an organization while it is being struck by coworkers. Since the 1500s, scab has been used as a term for a rascal or scoundrel. Early in the 1800s, Americans started using it to refer to workers who refused to support organized efforts on behalf of their trade. A scab should be distinguished from a fink or strikebreaker who is brought into an organization only after a strike begins.

president). The failure of the Boston police strike would inhibit municipal unionization for many decades.

Certainly the most influential single strike in recent decades was the strike of the Professional Air Traffic Controllers Organization (PATCO) in 1981, which resulted in the complete destruction of their union and the dismissal of 11,000 controllers. On July 29, 1981, 95 percent of PATCO's 13,000 members went on strike. In response, the U.S. government cut back scheduled flights and reduced staff at smaller airports. Then it brought supervisors and retired controllers into service and ordered military controllers to civilian stations. Finally, President Ronald Reagan addressed the nation on television. After reminding viewers that it is illegal for federal government employees to strike and that each controller signed an oath asserting that he or she would never strike, he proclaimed: "They are in violation of the law, and if they do not report for work within 48 hours, they have forfeited their jobs and will be terminated." Just over 1,000 controllers reported back. Most thought that the president was bluffing, but he wasn't. The union's assets were frozen by the courts, some PATCO leaders were literally hauled away to jail in chains, and the Department of Transportation started formal proceedings to decertify the union. In late October the Federal Labor Relations Authority formally decertified PATCO—the first time that it had ever done so to any union of government workers. In December PATCO filed for bankruptcy. In the end over 11,000 controllers who stayed on strike lost their jobs permanently.

The strike and subsequent firing of the controllers has had a chilling effect on strikes for the past two decades. If the federal government would fire practically all of the controllers (who must undergo one year of training), there is no doubt that other workers requiring less training would be fired just as fast. Before the PATCO strike, the leaders of the postal workers' unions, facing upcoming contract talks, were making noises about how they did not know if they could "control" the membership. Control here is a code word for a possible illegal wildcat strike—one that breaks out without an appropriate vote. After the PATCO strike, not a word has been heard about "controlling" the postal workers. They and all the other federal unions had been tamed by the only president of the United States who had also once been a union leader. (Reagan was president of the Screen Actors' Guild during the 1950s.)

Summary

The function of a personnel agency is service to line management. Typical services include recruiting, selection, training, evaluation, compensation, discipline, and termination.

Selection is the oldest function of the public personnel administration. Job relatedness is now the main consideration in developing a selection device because the legality of any test hinges on its validity, on its ability to predict job success. Those responsible for the preparation of examinations now have no choice but to develop them on the assumption that they will have to be defended in a court challenge.

The perversion of most civil service merit systems for private, administrative, and especially partisan ends is one of the worst kept, yet least written about, secrets in government. While the vast majority of civil service employees within the merit system enter, perform, and advance on the basis of their own talents and the design of the system, at the same time and within the same system there are other employees who enter the system and advance according to criteria other than those provided for by merit system regulations.

The advent of the civil service commission as a political device was not synonymous with the development of personnel administration as such. The commission impetus was decidedly negative and heavily moralistic. Its goals were to smite out "evil" as personified by the spoils system. Viewed historically and dispassionately, one could argue that considerable good in the guise of executive discretion also got washed away with the evil.

The ultimate goal of the current reinventors of public personnel administration is the expectation that government personnel officers must always remember the customer—that they shift from being reactive processors of paperwork to responsive consultants and advisors.

Public personnel departments have traditionally had the dual function of simultaneously representing management while enforcing and interpreting civil service regulations. This institutionalized degree of conflict over what role personnel should play on what occasion is reaching resolution because public sector unions reject the proposition that personnel management in the public sector has an equal responsibility to employees and to management.

Collective bargaining encompasses both the negotiating process that leads to a contract between labor and management on wages, hours, and other conditions of employment as well as the subsequent administration and interpretation of the signed contract. However, the public sector is incredibly fragmented in terms of collective bargaining. There is no national law on the subject. States and cities vary widely in their practices. Because the law differs so widely, substantial burdens are placed on national labor unions and dispute resolution personnel who work in different jurisdictions.

Key Concepts

civil service A collective term for all nonmilitary employees of a government. Paramilitary organizations, such as police and firefighters, are always included in civil service counts in the United States. Civil service employment is not the same as merit system employment, because all patronage positions (those not covered by merit systems) are included in civil service totals.

civil service reform Efforts to improve the status, integrity, and productivity of the civil service at all levels of government by supplanting the spoils system with the merit system; efforts to improve the management and efficiency of the public service; or the historical events, the movement, leading up to the enactment of the Pendleton Act of 1883.

collective bargaining Bargaining on behalf of a group of employees, as opposed to individual bargaining, in which each worker represents only himself or herself.

impasse resolution A condition that exists during labor-management negotiations when either party feels that no further progress can be made toward a settlement—unless the process of negotiating changes. The most common techniques used to break an impasse are mediation, fact-finding, and arbitration.

management development Any conscious effort on the part of an organization (such as rotational assignments or formal educational experiences) to provide a manager with the skills needed for future duties.

merit system A public sector concept of staffing that implies that no test of party membership is involved in the selection, promotion, or retention of government employees and that a constant effort is made to select the best-qualified individuals available for appointment and advancement.

patronage The power of elected and appointed officials to make partisan appointments to office or to confer contracts, honors, or other benefits on their political supporters. Patronage has always been one of the major tools by which political executives consolidate their power and attempt to control a bureaucracy.

performance appraisal The formal methods by which an organization documents the work performance of its employees. Performance appraisals are typically designed to change dysfunctional work behavior, communicate perceptions of work quality, assess the future potential of employees, and provide a documented record for disciplinary and separation actions.

personnel A collective term for all of the employees of an organization. The word is of military origin—the two basic components of a traditional army being materiel and personnel. *Personnel* is also commonly used to refer to the personnel management function or the organizational unit responsible for administering personnel programs.

position classification The use of formal job descriptions to organize all jobs in a civil service merit system into classes on the basis of duties and responsibilities, for the purposes of delineating authority, establishing chains of command, and providing equitable salary scales.

spoils system The practice of awarding government jobs to one's political supporters, as opposed to awarding them on the basis of merit.

strike A mutual agreement among workers (whether members of a union or not) to a temporary work stoppage to obtain—or to resist—a change in their working conditions.

unions Groups of employees who create a formal organization (the union) to represent their interests before management.

Bibliography

Argyris, Chris. (1964). "T-Groups for Organizational Effectiveness." *Harvard Business Review* (March-April).

Ban, Carolyn, and Norma Riccucci, eds. (1991). *Public Personnel Management*. New York: Longman.

Ingraham, Patricia, and Carolyn Ban, eds. (1984). *Legislating Bureaucratic Change: The Civil Service Reform Act of 1978*. Albany: State University of New York Press.

Hays, Steven W., and Richard C. Kearney, eds. (1995). *Public Personnel Administration: Problems and Prospects*, 3rd ed. Englewood Cliffs, NJ: Prentice Hall.

Kearney, Richard. (1992). *Labor Relations in the Public Sector*, 2nd ed. New York: Marcel Dekker.

Kingsley, J. Donald. (1944). *Representative Bureaucracy: An Interpretation of the British Civil Service*. Yellow Springs, OH: Antioch Press.

Krislov, Samuel. (1967). *The Negro in Federal Employment*. Minneapolis: University of Minnesota Press.

Mosher, Frederick. (1982). *Democracy and the Public Service*, 2nd ed. New York: Oxford University Press.

Mosher, William E., and J. Donald Kingsley. (1936). *Public Personnel Administration*. New York: Harper.

Peters, Charles. (1993). "Tilting at Windmills," *The Washington Monthly* (May).

———. (1994). "Tilting at Windmills," *The Washington Monthly* (November).

Rosenbloom, David H. (1971a). *Federal Equal Employment Opportunity*. New York: Praeger.

———. (1971b). *Federal Service and the Constitution*. Ithaca, NY: Cornell University Press.

Rosenbloom, David H., and Jay Shafritz. (1985). *Essentials of Labor Relations*. Reston, VA: Reston.

Shafritz, Jay M. (1973). *Position Classification: A Behavioral Analysis for the Public Service*. New York: Praeger.

———. (1975). *Personnel Management in Government: The Heritage of Civil Service Reform*. New York: Praeger.

Shafritz, Jay M., Norma Riccucci, David H. Rosenbloom, and Al Hyde. (1992). *Personnel Management in Government*, 4th ed. New York: Marcel Dekker.

Tompkins, Jonathan. (1995). *Human Resource Management in Government.* New York: HarperCollins.

Van Riper, Paul P. (1958). *History of the United States Civil Service.* Evanston, IL: Row, Peterson.

Wurf, Jerry. (1966). "Personnel Opinions," *Public Personnel Review* (January).

Recommended Books

Bissinger, Buzz. (1997). *A Prayer for the City.* New York: Random House. An insider's account of Edward Rendell's first term as mayor of Philadelphia; includes an extensive account of how Rendell tamed the municipal unions and thus brought the city back from the brink of bankruptcy.

Freedman, Anne. (1994). *Patronage: An American Tradition.* Chicago: Nelson-Hall. An engaging historical analysis of the rise and modest fall of political patronage, from the spoils system of the nineteenth century to the most recent Supreme Court decisions curtailing it.

Heclo, Hugh. (1977). *A Government of Strangers: Executive Politics in Washington.* Washington, DC: Brookings Institution. The now-classic analysis of how political appointees and career executives cope with each other in the federal bureaucracy.

Kearney, Richard C. (1992). *Labor Relations in the Public Sector,* 2nd ed. New York: Marcel Dekker. The rules of the game in governmental collective bargaining, at all levels of government.

Mosher, Frederick C. (1982). *Democracy and the Public Service,* 2nd ed. New York: Oxford University Press. The best short history of the U. S. Public Service and the impact that an ever-increasing professionalism has had upon it.

Related Web Sites

American Federation of State, County, and Municipal Employees
http://www.afscme.org/
American Society for Training and Development
http://www.astd.org
Classification and Compensation Society
http://www.classandcomp.org
Federal government jobs
http://www.jobsfed.com/
Federal Mediation and Conciliation Service
http://www.fmcs.gov

International Personnel Management Association
http://www.ipma-hr.org/
National Labor-Management Association
http://www.nlma.org/lbr-link.htm
Public employment statistics
http://www.census.gov/govs/www/apes.html
U.S. National Labor Relations Board
http://www.nlrb.gov
U.S. Office of Personnel Management
http://www.opm.gov/html/topics.htm

11

Social Equity

Keynote: Three Thousand Years of Sexual Harassment

Joseph, the Bible tells us, was sold into slavery by his older brothers for "twenty pieces of silver" (Genesis 37:28). Taken to Egypt by a slave merchant and sold to Potiphar, the captain of Pharaoh's guards, Joseph's talents served his master so well that Potiphar "made him overseer over his house."

Joseph, a natural administrator, was on the fast track, as slavery goes, until his career was derailed by an unfounded claim of sexual harassment. Potiphar's wife "cast her eyes upon Joseph." One day when they were alone in the house, "she caught him by his garment, saying lie with me." Joseph immediately fled, leaving "his garment in her hand."

Poor Joseph. He goes to work one day and the next thing he knows he's running away. But where to? In those days there was no Equal Employment Opportunity Commission to whom Joseph could complain about workplace sexual harassment. Besides, slaves did not have the right to complain about anything anyway—least of all a workplace free of sexual intimidation. While it is bad enough to be harassed, it is worse to be framed and jailed—which is just what happened next to Joseph. Potiphar's wife claimed that Joseph had approached her and ran away when she cried out, leaving his garment behind as evidence. When Potiphar heard this false accusation, "his wrath was kindled." And Joseph was put into prison.

Fortunately, this particular story of sexual harassment has a happy ending. While in prison, Joseph's skills in long-range business forecasting came to the attention of the Pharaoh, who needed a dream interpreted—something about seven thin cows eating seven fat cows. Joseph's warning of a coming famine so impressed the Pharaoh that Joseph began his rise to the top of the Egyptian bureaucracy. It just goes to show that sometimes an ex-convict can be a very effective employee.

More than three thousand years later Joseph's problem with sexual harassment at work arrived on the docket of the U.S. Supreme Court. While too late to help Joseph, the Court ruled in 1986 on a similar case. In *Meritor Savings Bank v. Vinson,* sexual harassment that creates a hostile or abusive work environment, even without economic loss for the person being harassed, was declared illegal—because it was in violation of Title VII of the Civil Rights Act of 1964. (Title VII is that portion of the act that prohibits employment discrimination because of race, color, religion, sex, or national origin.)

This case sought to establish ways by which to judge whether or not sexual harassment exists in any given set of circumstances. Thus the court held that Title VII is violated when the workplace is permeated with discriminatory behavior that is sufficiently severe or pervasive to create a discriminatorily hostile or abusive working environment. The standard laid down by the Court is that of an objectively hostile or abusive environment—one that a reasonable person would find hostile or abusive. Whether an environment is "hostile" or "abusive" can be determined only by looking at all the circumstances: the frequency of the discriminatory conduct, its severity, whether it is physically threatening or humiliating (or only an offensive utterance), and whether it unreasonably interferes with an employee's work performance. The effect on an employee's psychological well-being is also relevant in determining whether the environment is abusive.

But this standard was not detailed or clear enough to provide sufficient guidance to employers and the lower federal courts. So the Supreme Court had to expand upon the 1986 standard in the 1993 case of *Harris v. Forklift Systems.* Teresa Harris worked as a manager at an equipment rental company for more than two years. Throughout Harris's time of employment, the male president of Forklift Systems

Box 11.1

A Reluctant Concurring Opinion

Meritor Savings Bank v. Vinson held that Title VII prohibits sexual harassment that takes the form of a hostile work environment. The Court stated that sexual harassment is actionable if it is sufficiently severe or pervasive "to alter the conditions of [the victim's] employment and create an abusive work environment." Today's opinion elaborates that the challenged conduct must be severe or pervasive enough "to create an objectively hostile or abusive work environment—an environment that a reasonable person would find hostile or abusive."

"Abusive" (or "hostile," which in this context I take to mean the same thing) does not seem to me a very clear standard and I do not think clarity is at all increased by adding the adverb "objectively" or by appealing to a "reasonable person's" notion of what the vague word means. Today's opinion does list a number of factors that contribute to abusiveness, but since it neither says how much of each is necessary (an impossible task) nor identifies any single factor as determinative, it thereby adds little certitude. As a practical matter, today's holding lets virtually unguided juries decide whether sex-related conduct engaged in (or permitted by) an employer is egregious enough to warrant an award of damages. One might say that what constitutes "negligence" (a traditional jury question) is not much more clear and certain than what constitutes "abusiveness." Perhaps so. But the class of plaintiffs seeking to recover for negligence is limited to those who have suffered harm, whereas under this statute "abusiveness" is to be the test of whether legal harm has been suffered, opening more expansive vistas of litigation.

Be that as it may, I know of no alternative to the course the Court today has taken.

SOURCE: Associate Justice Antonin Scalia, concurring opinion, *Harris v. Forklift Systems* (1993). Notes omitted.

NOTE: A concurring opinion is the opinion of a judge who agrees with a decision, but who explains his or her agreement on grounds different from those used by the other judges.

often insulted her because of her gender and often made her the target of unwanted sexual innuendos. For example, he said to Harris on several occasions, in the presence of other employees, "You're a woman, what do you know?" and "We need a man as the rental manager." Again in front of others, he suggested that the two of them "go to the Holiday Inn to negotiate [Harris's] raise." He even asked Harris and other female employees to get coins from his front pants pocket. When Harris complained about this conduct, the company president said he was surprised that Harris was offended, claimed he was only joking, and apologized. He also promised he would stop. Based on this assurance Harris stayed on the job. But a few weeks later the problem began anew. Harris quit, then sued Forklift Systems, claiming that the president's conduct had created an abusive work environment for her because of her gender. The lower federal courts held that the situation had not created an abusive environment. The courts found that the comments would offend any reasonable woman but that they were not "so severe as to be expected to seriously affect [Harris's] psychological well-being."

The Supreme Court agreed to hear this case to resolve the conflict over just what constituted a sexually abusive work environment. Associate Justice Sandra Day O'Connor, in writing the majority opinion of the Court, asserted that Title VII's protections necessarily had to "come into play before the harassing conduct leads to a nervous breakdown." Victims do not have to prove "concrete psychological harm," only that the offending conduct "would seriously affect a reasonable person's psychological well-being." Thus the new standard holds that "so long as the environment would reasonably be perceived, and is perceived, as hostile or abusive, there is no need for it also to be psychologically injurious." In effect, there is no need to wait for it to lead "to a nervous breakdown." O'Connor concluded that "while psychological harm, like any other relevant factor, may be taken into account, no single factor is required" because this is not, and by its nature cannot be, "a mathematically precise test."

The story of the biblical Joseph may be the first recorded instance of on-the-job sexual harassment. More than three millennia later, the issue is still being debated within the courts. Progress has certainly been slow. But the quest for social equity at the office seems to be finally passing into a phase of resolution.

What Is Social Equity?

Social equity is fairness in the delivery of public services; it is egalitarianism in action—the principle that each citizen, regardless of economic resources or personal traits, deserves and has a right to be given equal treatment by the political system. Even though the United States has not lived up to this ideal, has not provided equality to all its men and women throughout its history, it has nevertheless been constantly moving in that direction. Political theorist Jean-Jacques Rousseau warned in *The Social Contract* (1762): "It is precisely because the force of circumstances tends always to destroy equality that the force of legislation must always tend to maintain it." The United States has a long tradition of using legislation to mitigate the "force of circumstances" that so often inhibits equality. For example, in the early nineteenth century, free public schools made education gradually available to all classes. In 1862 the Homestead Act made it possible for any citizen to own 160 acres of public land if he or she would live on it for five years. The Civil War of 1861–1865 can be viewed alternatively as conflict over the nature of intergovernmental relations or a moral crusade to bring "equality" to those in bondage. The twentieth century witnessed an outpouring of legislation that gave new rights to workers, women, and minorities. This has gone so far that social equity, in addition to efficiency, is now a major criterion for evaluating the desirability of any public policy or program.

Associate Justice Sandra Day O'Connor: Crusader against sexual harassment

Associate Justice Antonin Scalia: Reluctant crusader against sexual harassment •

Government organizations have a special obligation to be fair—to pursue social equity both with their employees and the public—because they represent the citizenry. This is in distinct contrast to business organizations, which represent private interests such as stockholders. It is often asserted that corporations have a social responsibility, that they have a moral and ethical duty to contribute to society's well-being—obligations far beyond just seeking a profit in a legal manner. But others, such as economist Milton Friedman, feel that the resolution of social problems is the task of governments, not businesses; that managers who spend money to alleviate social problems act irresponsibly.

Mandating Social Equity

There is a long tradition of government forcing private organizations to better treat their employees. Better treatment was inhibited by social Darwinism, Charles Darwin's (1809–1882) concept of biological evolution applied by others to the development of human social organization and economic policy. American social Darwinism applied Darwin's concepts of "natural selection" and "survival of the fittest" to society in general. Thus, practices such as child labor, the employment of children in a manner detrimental to their health and social development, were justified. Efforts by the labor movement and social reformers to prevent the exploitation of children in the workplace date back well into the nineteenth century. As early as 1842, some states (Connecticut and Massachusetts) legislated a maximum ten-hour workday for children. In 1848, Pennsylvania established a minimum working age of 12 years for factory jobs. But it would be 20 years more before any state had inspectors to enforce child labor laws. And it would not be until the late 1930s that federal laws would outlaw child labor (mainly through the Fair Labor Standards Act of 1938). The practice was so entrenched that earlier federal attempts to outlaw child labor were construed by the Supreme Court as being unconstitutional infringements on the power of the states to regulate conditions in the workplace. So achieving social equity for children was an uphill battle that lasted more than a century because, in large measure, of the social Darwinist belief that the "fit" children would survive and that this was all part of a normal process of "natural selection."

Child labor is just one example of how government regulation has been used to further social equity. The whole thrust of the labor and women's movements that began in the nineteenth century and the post–World War II civil rights movement was to obtain legislation that would equalize the employment and social prospects of unions, women, and minority group members. The fine-tuning of those public policies is an ongoing process. The Supreme Court cases discussed in the keynote dealt with sexual harassment, a variant of sexual discrimination. While it is impossible to predict future cases, it seems certain that the Court will be ruling on the subject well into the next century. The quest for social equity is never-ending. While legislation seeks to cope with gross abuses, the subtleties are left to the courts.

The New Public Administration

By the late 1960s, serious questions were being raised concerning the state of the discipline and profession of public administration. Dwight Waldo, having noted that public administration was "in a time of revolution," called a conference of younger academics in public administration, through the auspices of his position as editor-in-chief of *Public Administration Review* and with funds from the Maxwell School of Syracuse University. Held in 1968 at Syracuse University's Minnowbrook conference site, the event produced papers that were edited by Frank Marini, then managing editor of *Public Administration Review,* and published in 1971 under the title *Toward a New Public Administration: The Minnowbrook Perspective.* The goal of the meeting was to identify what was relevant about public administration and how the discipline had to change to meet the challenges of the 1970s. H. George Frederickson, now a professor at the University of Kansas, contributed a paper, "Toward a New Public Administration," which called for social equity in the performance and delivery of public services.

Frederickson's new public administration called for a proactive administrator with a burning desire for social equity to replace the traditional, impersonal, neutral, gun-for-hire bureaucrat. While this call was heeded by few, it was discussed by many. The basic problem with the new public administration's call for social equity was that it was also a call for insubordination—something that is not lightly tolerated in bureaucracies. **Victor Thompson** immediately attacked the new public administration movement in his aptly titled *Without Sympathy or Enthusiasm* as an effort by left-wing radicals to "steal the popular sovereignty."

Victor Thompson (1912–) One of the most gifted stylists in the literature of public administration. Thompson is best known for dealing deftly with bureaucratic interactions and dysfunctions. In his most influential work, *Modern Organization*, he reminds us that "one must not forget that clients are notoriously insensitive to the needs of bureaucrats."

Thompson need not have worried. All these "radicals" did was talk—and write. From the 1970s to the present day, and still led by Frederickson, they have produced an endless stream of conference papers and scholarly articles urging public administrators to show a greater sensitivity to the forces of change, the needs of clients, and the problem of social equity in service delivery. This has had a positive effect in that now the ethical and equitable treatment of citizens by administrators is at the forefront of concerns in public agencies. Reinforced by changing public attitudes, the reinventing government movement and civil rights laws, the new public administration has triumphed after a quarter century. Now it is unthinkable (as well as illegal), for example, to deny someone welfare benefits because of their race or a job opportunity because of their sex. Social equity today does not have to be so much fought for by young radicals as administered by managers of all ages.

The Challenge of Equality

Equality is an American ideal. In 1776 the Declaration of Independence proclaimed that "all men are created equal, that they are endowed by their Creator with certain unalienable rights." These are rights derived from natural law, which all people have and which cannot be taken away or transferred. Yet the Declaration as well as the subsequent Constitution denied these rights to a large group of residents. Because the Constitution was initially oblivious to the plight of African Americans, Supreme Court Associate Justice **Thurgood Marshall** pointedly rejected the view that Americans should celebrate the Constitution as the source of all that is good in the nation. On the contrary, he said of the founders that "the government they devised was defective from the start, requiring several amendments, a civil war, and momentous social transformation to attain the system of constitutional government, and its respect for individual freedoms and human rights, we hold as fundamental today." Marshall's harsh rhetoric notwithstanding, all discussions of equality in the United States must begin with the issue of race.

Racism

Race can be defined as a large group of people with common characteristics presumed to be transmitted genetically. Which characteristics are properly included has been a subject of debate. They range from physical characteristics that are immediately observable, such as color of hair, skin, and eyes, to the subtler aspects of emotions and aptitudes. Some races even have genetic susceptibility to certain diseases or physical disorders. Rational people of all races are often uncomfortable talking about race. There is a depth of feeling about past injustices that is dangerous to bring to the surface in polite conversation. Yet no subject is more important in administering the public affairs of a multiracial society. The issues must be faced and discussed even if they cannot be immediately resolved.

Thurgood Marshall (1908–1993) The civil rights lawyer who successfully argued the *Brown v. Board of Education* case before the Supreme Court, and who in 1967 was appointed by President Lyndon B. Johnson to be the first African American member of that court.

Up to the middle of the twentieth century, race was used as a way of distinguishing among national groups. This practice is traceable to eighteenth-century distinctions among people according to language. It became a method of attempting to define a hierarchy of races, with the so-called Anglo-Saxons at the top and others arranged along supposedly developmental lines. In recent times, in American political language, race has come to designate issues or attitudes concerning citizens of African origin. Other minority groups are called ethnics. Originally, the term applied only to European ethnics. The term is now more likely to refer to the new ethnics, both those that have long been here and those that are more recent arrivals—for example, the Hispanics and the Vietnamese. Technically, every American except for white Anglo-Saxon Protestants is a member of an ethnic group. And now that they are in the minority, many of them have begun to claim that they are an ethnic group, too. A politician may be said to be practicing ethnic politics when he tells his Irish constituents of his support for a united Ireland, his Jewish constituents of his support for a strong state of Israel, and his Hispanic constituents of his strong support for bilingual education. Ethnic politics does not have to be substantive; sometimes it is nothing more than a "photo opportunity" of the politician eating ethnic food or attending an ethnic cultural festival or wedding.

A racist can be defined as any person or organization that either consciously or unconsciously practices racial **discrimination** against a person on the basis of race (or ethnicity) or supports the supremacy of one race over others. The most notorious of American racist groups has been the **Ku Klux Klan.** But anyone who is insensitive to the feelings of racial minorities and uses racially demeaning language or diction out of genuine ignorance may also be considered racist. Such people might deny they are racist; however, offended minority groups might still perceive them to be so. This is especially true with what is known as stealth racism—racist acts readily apparent to African Americans but virtually invisible to whites. Well-to-do middle class nonwhites are routinely kept under greater surveillance at shopping places, find it difficult to get taxis, are automatically presumed to be dangerous, and are given unequal service in restaurants and airports. Such lack of respect, such affronts to honor, are difficult to deal with by legislation. The Civil Rights Act of 1964 mandated equal access to expensive hotels and restaurants. But it still hurts when an African American guest dressed in a tuxedo is mistaken for a waiter or the valet parking attendant. That's stealth racism.

---

discrimination Bigotry in practice; intolerance toward those who have different beliefs or different religions.

Ku Klux Klan (KKK) The most infamous U.S. terrorist organization; a racist, white supremacist group established in the South following the Civil War. The KKK has a long history of intimidation, beatings, and murders of blacks, as well as other racial and religious minorities. Lynchings are a hallmark of the KKK, as are the burning of crosses, designed to instill fear into the hearts of onlookers. Klansmen traditionally cloak themselves in the anonymity of robes and hide their faces under hoods. Early in this century, the KKK had considerable political power; it dominated politics in a dozen states and counted dozens of congressmen as members. Today, the KKK has only the slightest influence in American politics. Thus it has traveled from the mainstream to the lunatic fringe, from millions of members to a few thousand. In recent years, successful lawsuits brought against the KKK by its victims have dealt the organization severe setbacks.

What distinguishes African Americans from other ethnic Americans is not so much their color—many other groups are nonwhite—but their ancestors, who came to the United States not as the "huddled masses yearning to breathe free," as is engraved on the pedestal of the Statue of Liberty, but as slaves. And slavery has uniquely colored the African American experience down to the present day.

The Bitter Heritage of Slavery

Slavery, which began in colonial times, was addressed, albeit obliquely, in various parts of the Constitution. Article I, Section 2, stated that slaves are to be counted for purposes of congressional appointments as "three fifths" of a person. Article I, Section 9, stated that Congress could not pass any law banning the importation of slaves until 1808 (which it did). Article IV, Section 2, said that persons "held in service"—meaning runaway slaves—who escaped had to be returned. This was upheld by the *Dred Scott v. Sandford* decision of the Supreme Court.

Abraham Lincoln was, even before he became president, the most eloquent spokesman against slavery. He told the Illinois Republican State Convention on June 16, 1858: "'A house divided against itself cannot stand' [the Bible, Mark 3:25]. I believe this government cannot endure, permanently half slave and half free. I do not expect the Union to be dissolved—I do not expect the house to fall—but I do expect it will cease to be divided. It will become all one thing, or all the other." He was right.

In September 1862, President Abraham Lincoln, acting as commander in chief during a time of war, issued the **Emancipation Proclamation,** which became effective on January 1, 1863. The proclamation declared that all people held in slavery "are, and henceforth shall be, free; and the executive government of the United States, including the military and naval authorities thereof, will recognize and maintain the freedom." The Thirteenth Amendment was passed in 1865 to quell the controversy over the constitutionality of the Emancipation Proclamation and to settle the issue of slavery in the United States forever.

Dred Scott v. Sandford (1857) The second case in which the U.S. Supreme Court declared an act of the Congress (the Missouri Compromise) to be unconstitutional (the first was *Marbury v. Madison* in 1803). Dred Scott (1795–1858) was a slave who was taken to a free state in the North. The question before the Court was whether residence in a free state was sufficient basis for declaring Scott a free man. The Supreme Court in a 7 to 2 ruling said no. The chief justice, Roger Brook Taney, wrote in the Court's opinion: "The right of property in a slave is distinctly and expressly affirmed in the Constitution. . . . No word can be found in the Constitution which gives Congress a greater power over slave property or which entitles property of that kind to less protection than property of any other description." While it helped to further entrench the Court's right to judicial review, the Court's holdings—that blacks could not become citizens and that the United States could not prohibit slavery in unsettled territories—did much to make the Civil War inevitable, especially because the decision made a legislative solution to the slavery issue virtually impossible.

Emancipation Proclamation Lincoln showed his cabinet the draft of the proclamation about half a year earlier, on July 22, 1862, but felt that he had to keep it secret until the military situation improved for the North. While the battle of Antietam of September 17, 1862, was essentially a draw, Lincoln considered it enough of a victory to announce the proclamation.

The history of slavery in the United States is still relevant today because it is the underlying basis for African American claims for special treatment. Some argue that reparations are due and point to the Civil Liberties Act of 1988. This law authorized the payment of $20,000 to all living Japanese Americans who were interned by the United States government during World War II. The act authorized a total of $1.25 billion in reparations payments. Of the 120,000 Japanese Americans who were interned, about 70,000 were still alive when the act was passed. But these payments to Japanese Americans went to the still-living victims. There are no direct victims of slavery still living. There is not much sympathy for reparation for slavery when most Americans are not descendants of slave owners but descendants of people who came to the United States after the Civil War—often with little more than the clothes on their backs. Still, the unfinished business of mitigating the heritage of slavery led to the second reconstruction.

From Reconstruction to Second Reconstruction

While the Thirteenth, **Fourteenth** and **Fifteenth Amendments** attempted to settle the issues of slavery and civil rights, the issue of the former slaves remained. After **Reconstruction** many states enacted **Jim Crow** laws, which effectively made African Americans **second-class citizens.**

This second-class status was supported by the Supreme Court in the separate but equal doctrine. In *Plessy v. Ferguson* (1896) the Court held that segregated railroad facilities for African Americans, facilities that were considered equal in quality

Fourteenth Amendment The post–Civil War amendment to the U.S. Constitution that defines citizenship and mandates due process as well as equal protection of the laws for all citizens. Through the due process and equal protection clause of the Fourteenth Amendment, the U.S. Supreme Court has gradually applied (incorporated) most of the protections of the Bill of Rights to the states. The Fourteenth Amendment, which has produced more litigation and court interpretation than any other part of the Constitution, was enacted originally to protect the freed slaves from abrogations of their rights by the southern states.

Fifteenth Amendment The 1870 amendment to the U.S. Constitution that guarantees to all citizens the right to vote regardless of "race, color, or previous condition of servitude." This is the legal source of federal voting rights legislation.

Reconstruction The post–Civil War period when the South was divided into military districts and the states that were formerly part of the Confederacy were brought back into the Union. The official end of Reconstruction was 1876, when the last federal troops were withdrawn.

Jim Crow A name given to any law requiring the segregation of the races. All such statutes are now unconstitutional. But prior to the Civil Rights Act of 1964, many southern states had laws requiring separate drinking fountains, separate rest rooms, separate sections of theaters, and so on for blacks and whites. The name "Jim Crow" comes from a nineteenth-century vaudeville character who was called Jim (a common name) Crow (for a black-colored bird). Thus the name was applied to things having to do with blacks.

second-class citizen A person who does not have all of the civil rights of other citizens. Historically, African Americans were called, and because of segregation and discrimination often considered themselves to be, second-class citizens. But since the civil rights movement and the new laws that flowed from it, there can be no second-class citizens in the United States. Nevertheless, the phrase is still used in various contexts: by minorities who wish to emphasize economic disparities, by women who feel that they have not achieved social equity with men, by prisoners who complain they cannot vote.

to those provided for whites, did not violate the equal protection clause of the Fourteenth Amendment. In a **dissenting opinion** Justice John Marshall Harlan wrote: "We boast of the freedom enjoyed by our people. . . . But it is difficult to reconcile that boast with a state of the law which, practically, puts the brand of servitude and degradation upon a large class of our fellow citizens, our equals before the law. The thin disguise of 'equal' accommodations for passengers in the railroad coaches will not mislead anyone, or atone for the wrong this day done."

More than half a century later the Court overturned the *Plessy* decision and nullified this doctrine when it asserted that separate was "inherently unequal." In *Brown v. Board of Education of Topeka, Kansas* (1954) the Court decided that the separation of children by race and according to law in public schools "generates a feeling of inferiority as to their [the minority group's] status in the community that may affect their hearts and minds in a way unlikely ever to be undone." Consequently, it held that "separate educational facilities are inherently unequal" and therefore violate the equal protection clause of the Fourteenth Amendment. According to Chief Justice Earl Warren, "We come then to the question presented: does segregation of children in public schools solely on the basis of race, even though the physical facilities and other 'tangible' factors may be equal, deprive the children of the minority group of equal educational opportunities? We believe that it does."

This decision, one of the most significant in the century, helped create the environment that would lead to the second reconstruction—the civil rights movement and legislation of the 1960s. The first reconstruction, immediately after the Civil War, gave African Americans their freedom from slavery. But the laws as enforced and customs as practiced did not allow for the full rights of citizens. That came in the 1960s, when public sentiment was aroused and legal action was taken to ensure equal rights for all Americans.

An Administrative Fix for Racism

The problem with the second reconstruction, with its outpouring of equal employment opportunity and civil rights legislation, was that the government formally got into the business of examining people's blood lines. Official race categories were established by the Equal Employment Opportunity Commission (EEOC), which had been created by the Civil Rights Act of 1964. The South once had miscegenation laws, declared unconstitutional in *Loving v. Virginia* (1967). Miscegenation laws meant that if one of your ancestors was African, you could not marry someone whose ancestors were all European. Now, in a reversal of fortune, if one of your ancestors is African you are entitled, under affirmative action provisions of equal opportunity laws, to preferential treatment in employment.

To further this goal, the EEOC has established five racial-ethnic categories for reporting purposes:

---

dissenting opinion The opinion of a judge who disagrees with the decision of a court. On the U.S. Supreme Court, these opinions have sometimes been extremely significant because they have so often established the intellectual framework for subsequent reversals of decisions. Chief Justice Charles Evans Hughes (1862–1948) observed that dissents are "appeals to the brooding spirit of the law, to the intelligence of another day."

A meeting between the two major leaders of the 1960s civil rights movement, Dr. Martin Luther King Jr. (left) and Malcolm X. They became the living symbols of the two extremes of the civil rights movement: King called for civil disobedience to gain voting rights for the disenfranchised, while Malcolm X offered white society a simple choice—"It's either a ballot or a bullet." Both would be dead from assassins' bullets by the end of the decade •

1. *White, not of Hispanic origin:* Those having origins in any of the original peoples of Europe, North Africa, or the Middle East

2. *Black, not of Hispanic origin:* People having origins in any of the black racial groups of Africa

3. *Hispanic:* People of Mexican, Puerto Rican, Cuban, Central, or South American, or other Spanish culture origin, regardless of race

4. *American Indian or Alaskan native:* Those having origins in any of the original peoples of North America and who maintain cultural identification through tribal affiliation or community recognition

5. *Asian or Pacific islander:* Those having origins in any of the original peoples of the Far East, Southeast Asia, the Indian subcontinent, or the Pacific islands. (These areas include China, Japan, Korea, the Philippine Islands, and Samoa.)

These categories are used on the EEO-1 form, the annual report on the sex and minority status of various workforce categories that is required of all employers with 100 or more employees. The report must be filed with the Joint Reporting Committee of the Equal Employment Opportunity Commission and the Office of Federal Contract Compliance within the Department of Labor.

The Supreme Court has also recognized additional race categories that are protected by the federal civil rights laws. In *Shaare Tefila Congregation v. Cobb* (1987), it held that Jews could bring charges of racial discrimination against defendants who were also considered Caucasian. And in *Saint Francis College v. Al-Khazraji* (1987), it held that someone of Arabian ancestry was protected from racial discrimination under the various civil rights statutes.

In addition to employment advantages, recognized minority group members have been granted set-asides—government purchasing and contracting provisions that set aside or allocate a certain percentage of business for minority-owned or female-owned companies. The use of set-asides was upheld by the Supreme Court in *Fullilove v. Klutznick* and *Metro Broadcasting v. FCC* but restricted in *City of Richmond v. J. A. Croson* and *Adarand Constructors v. Pena*. In response to this last decision and to a declining climate of political support for all affirmative action efforts, the Clinton administration announced in 1996 that it was suspending all federal programs that reserve some contracts exclusively for minority- and women-owned companies.

Then in 1998 the Clinton Administration's new policy was announced: minority-owned businesses would be given an advantage when they compete for federal government contracts, but only in industries where survey research shows they do not have a fair share of the overall market. Thus companies controlled by blacks will get preferences in trucking contracts, but not in food manufacturing. Overall, preferences will still be a factor in industries representing about three-quarters of all the money the federal government spends on procurement contracts with small businesses. President Clinton said that the new rules "continue my promise to mend, not end affirmative action."

Equal Employment Opportunity

Equal employment opportunity (EEO) is a concept fraught with political, cultural, and emotional overtones. Generally, it applies to a set of employment procedures and practices that effectively prevent any individual from being adversely excluded from employment opportunities on the basis of race, color, sex, religion, age, national origin, or other factors that cannot lawfully be considered in employing people. While the ideal of EEO is an employment system devoid of both intentional and unintentional discrimination, achieving this ideal may be a political impossibility because of the problem of definition. One person's equal opportunity may be another's institutional racism or institutional sexism. Because of this problem of definition, only the courts have been able to say if, when, and where EEO exists.

Nevertheless, it must always be remembered that EEO laws and programs were created to remedy very real problems of bigotry and sexism—problems that are still with us today. The word that summarizes workplace intolerance toward those who

---

Fullilove v. Klutznick (1980) The Supreme Court case holding that the Congress has the authority to use quotas to remedy past discrimination in government public works programs, reasoning that the Fourteenth Amendment's requirement of equal protection means that groups historically denied this right may be given special treatment.

Metro Broadcasting v. FCC (1990) The Supreme Court case holding that the Federal Communications Commission could use "benign race-conscious measures" to increase minority ownership of broadcast licenses.

City of Richmond v. J. A. Croson (1989) The Supreme Court case holding that a minority set-aside program designed so that 30 percent of city construction contacts went to minority-owned firms was too rigid; it was not justified by past findings of discrimination.

Adarand Constructors v. Pena (1995) The Supreme Court case holding that set-asides could only be used when a minority group has suffered actual discrimination; thus they could only be used as a remedy for past discriminatory practices.

are different is discrimination. In employment, this is the failure to treat equals equally. Whether deliberate or unintentional, any action that has the effect of limiting employment and advancement opportunities because of an individual's sex, race, color, age, national origin, religion, physical handicap, or other irrelevant criteria, is discrimination—and illegal.

Origins of Affirmative Action

It was not until the Kennedy administration that EEO became a central aspect of public personnel administration. Between 1961 and 1965, the civil rights movement reached the pinnacle of its political importance and became a dominant national issue. Indeed, it was a sign of the times when Kennedy declared, "I have dedicated my administration to the cause of equal opportunity in employment by the government." His **Executive Order** 10925 of March 6, 1961, for the first time required that "affirmative action" be used to implement the policy of nondiscrimination in employment by the federal government and its contractors.

Affirmative action first meant the removal of "artificial barriers" to the employment of women and minority group members. Special efforts were made to bring more members of minority groups into the federal service. These included recruitment drives at high schools and colleges heavily attended by minorities. Agencies were encouraged to provide better training opportunities for minority group members.

The Kennedy program was carried forward and expanded by the Johnson administration. The Civil Rights Act of 1964 declared that "it shall be the policy of the United States to ensure equal employment opportunities for Federal employees." It also created the Equal Employment Opportunity Commission to combat discrimination in the private sphere. The coordination of all equal employment activities for federal employees was assigned to the Civil Service Commission.

The continuing rationale for government-sanctioned affirmative action programs was provided by President Lyndon Johnson in a June 4, 1965, speech at Howard University: "You do not take a person who, for years, has been hobbled by chains and liberate him, bring him up to the starting line of a race and then say, 'You are free to compete with the others' and still justly believe you have been completely fair."

The next major development in the evolution of the EEO program came in 1969, when President Nixon issued an executive order requiring agency heads to "establish and maintain an affirmative program of equal employment opportunity." It was also during the Nixon administration, when the federal courts associated affirmative action with specific **goals** and timetables for minority hiring, that the term was altered to include compensatory opportunities for hitherto disadvantaged groups.

---

executive order The principal mode of administrative action on the part of the president of the United States. The power of a president to issue executive orders emanates from the constitutional provision requiring him to "take care that the laws be faithfully executed," the commander-in-chief clause, and express powers vested in him by congressional statutes.

goals Realistic objectives that an organization endeavors to achieve through affirmative action. Quotas, in contrast, restrict employment or development opportunities to members of particular groups by establishing a required number or proportionate representation, which managers are obligated to attain, without regard to equal employment opportunity. To be meaningful, any program of goals or quotas must be associated with a specific timetable—a schedule of when the goals or quotas are to be achieved. Quotas tend to be mandated by courts to remedy patterns of past discrimination.

The Equal Employment Opportunity Act of 1972 solidified the Civil Service Commission's authority in this area and placed the program on a solid statutory basis for the first time. It reaffirmed the traditional policy of nondiscrimination and empowered the commission to enforce its provisions "through appropriate remedies, including reinstatement or hiring of employees with or without back pay . . . and issuing such rules, regulations, orders, and instructions as it deems necessary and appropriate." It also made the commission responsible for the annual review and approval of agency **EEO plans** and for evaluating agency EEO activities. The act also brought state and local governments under the federal EEO umbrella for the first time. The Equal Employment Opportunity Commission (EEOC), hitherto primarily concerned with the private sector, was given equal authority over the nonfederal public sector. In 1979, as part of the overall federal civil service reforms then taking place (see Chapter 10), the enforcement aspects of the federal EEO program were transferred to the EEOC. So after starting out with enforcement authority over just the private sector in 1964, the EEOC by 1979 had been given responsibility for enforcing equal employment opportunity at all levels of government as well.

The Case for Affirmative Action

The case for affirmative action, for special efforts to recruit and advance minorities and women in employment, has always been based on statistics. According to a 1998 report of the President's Commission on Race, the median family income for whites is $47,023 per year, for blacks it is $26,522, and for Hispanics it is $26,179. The home ownership rate for whites is 71.7 percent, for blacks it is 46 percent, and for Hispanics it is 43 percent. While overall life expectancy for whites is 76.1 years; it is 6.6 fewer for blacks. The Department of Labor reports that while blacks are 12.4 percent of the population, they are only 4.2 percent of the doctors, 5 percent of the college professors, 3.7 percent of the engineers, 3.3 percent of the lawyers, and 1.4 percent of the architects. The figures for Hispanics are comparable.

These disparities exist because of continuing patterns of discrimination that are easily traced back to the days of slavery. The only way to overcome and get beyond the **adverse impact** of **systemic discrimination** is to implement a vigorous affirmative action program. To repeal affirmative action and force minorities to compete on the proverbial "level playing field" would only perpetuate the existing patterns of discrimination.

EEO plan An organization's written plan to remedy past discrimination against, or underutilization of, women and minorities. The plan itself usually consists of a statement of goals, timetables for achieving them, and specific program efforts.

adverse impact When a selection process for a particular job or group of jobs results in the selection of members of any racial, ethnic, or gender group at a lower rate than members of other groups, that process is said to have adverse impact. Federal EEO enforcement agencies generally regard a selection rate for any group that is less than four-fifths or 80 percent of the rate for other groups as constituting evidence of adverse impact.

systemic discrimination Use of employment practices (recruiting methods, selection tests, promotion policies, etc.) that have the unintended effect of excluding or limiting the employment prospects of protected-class persons. Because of court interpretations of Title VII of the Civil Rights Act of 1964, all such systemic discrimination, despite its "innocence," must be eliminated where it cannot be shown that such action would place an unreasonable burden on the employer or that such practices cannot be replaced by other practices that would not have such an adverse effect.

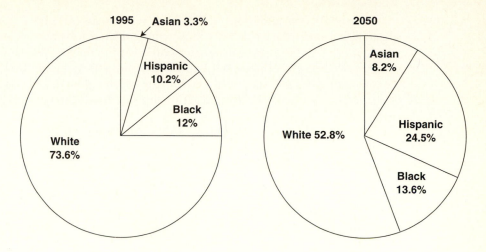

Figure 11.1   A numerical Argument for Diversity: U.S. Population by Race/Ethnicity, 1995 and 2050 (Projected)   SOURCE: U.S. Bureau of the Census, as reported in the *New York Times,* March 14, 1996. Numbers do not add up to 100% because of rounding and because Native Americans are not shown.

Affirmative action offers advantages that go beyond its immediate beneficiaries. As civil rights activist Roger Wilkins wrote: "Racist and sexist whites who are not able to accept the full humanity of other people are themselves badly damaged—morally stunted—people." They, too, are victims of racism and sexism—even if it is their own. Affirmative action programs that bring them into contact with a more diverse group of associates will help liberate them from their own ignorance. They can go from being "morally stunted" to morally elevated.

And the same that can be said of people can be said of organizations. The less damaged they are by racism and sexism, the more productive they will be. This is the effect of diversity management—directing the work of a racially and culturally heterogeneous group of employees to bring a more varied set of perspectives to organizational problems. This variety can translate into greater productivity. Concerns for diversity that started as part of EEO programs are now less a matter of social equity than organizational survival. The simple demographic fact is that whites will be a continuously decreasing part of the national workforce. For large organizations, the future can be summed up in three words: "Diversify or die!"

The Case against Affirmative Action

The case against affirmative action can be simply stated: It is unfair. It negates Dr. Martin Luther King's "dream that my four little children will one day live in a nation where they will not be judged by the color of their skin, but by the content of their character." Well-meaning opponents of affirmative action (as opposed to lunatic fringe racists) favor equal employment opportunity. They hold that race or sexual discrimination is wrong no matter who does it. Racial and sexual preferences in hiring women, blacks, or other ethnic minorities are not only inherently discriminatory, they are also in violation of the Civil Rights Act of 1964, which prohibits discrimination against anybody—even whites.

Despite its best intentions, affirmative action programs have had the effect of stigmatizing minority workers as those who got their jobs not because of their intrinsic merit but because of pressure to fill a formal or informal quota. Thus such programs damage both the self-confidence and self-image of their beneficiaries while creating resentment among those denied such employment opportunities. Minorities who advocate affirmative action are essentially saying, critics charge, that they cannot compete on merit.

Finally, opponents of affirmative action argue that if compensatory benefits are to be provided they should be based on class, not race. Why should a child from a black professional family making more than $100,000 a year be given special educational and employment opportunities when there is greater need for such opportunities by a child from a poor white family with an income close to the national median? Besides, class-based preferences could gain the widespread political support that affirmative action now seems to lack.

Representative Bureaucracy

In 1944 J. Donald Kingsley, coauthor of the first full-scale text on public personnel administration, had published his historical analysis, *Representative Bureaucracy: An Interpretation of the British Civil Service*. In 1967 Samuel Krislov, a constitu-

---

Box 11.2

Why "Affirmative" Action?

At the Texas State Society's inaugural ball [in 1961], Lyndon Johnson, the incoming vice president, was pressing flesh in the receiving line. When a young black lawyer from Detroit named Hobart Taylor Jr. . . . came through the line, Johnson pulled him aside and said he needed something. An executive order banning discriminatory hiring by federal contractors was being drafted for President Kennedy's signature; could Taylor help work on it?

The next day, Taylor holed up in a room at the Willard Hotel with two future Supreme Court justices, Arthur Goldberg and Abe Fortas, to prepare a document with the not-very-catchy title of Executive Order 10925. "I put the word 'affirmative' in there at that time," Taylor later told an interviewer for the archives of the Lyndon Baines Johnson Library. "I was searching for something that would give a sense of positiveness to performance under that executive order, and I was torn between the words 'positive action' and the words 'affirmative action.' . . . And I took 'affirmative action' because it was alliterative."

SOURCE: Nicholas Lemann, "Taking Affirmative Action Apart," *New York Times Magazine*, June 11, 1995.

tional law scholar, expanded upon Kingsley's concept of a governing bureaucracy made up of representative elements from the population being ruled. In *The Negro in Federal Employment*, Krislov examined the advantages of "representation in the sense of personification" and thereby gave a name to the goal for the movement for the fullest expression of civil rights in government employment—representative bureaucracy.

In a subsequent work in 1974, also entitled *Representative Bureaucracy*, Krislov explored the issues of merit systems, personnel selection, and social equity. Krislov asked more directly, how could any bureaucracy have legitimacy and public credibility if it did not represent all sectors of its society? So, thanks in large part to Krislov, the phrase "representative bureaucracy" grew to mean that all social groups have a right to participation in their governing institutions. In recent years, the concept has developed a normative overlay—that all social groups should occupy bureaucratic positions in direct proportion to their numbers in the general population. Today representative bureaucracy is commonly used as a shorthand phrase for the ultimate goal of equal employment opportunity and affirmative action programs.

Reverse Discrimination

Reverse discrimination is a practice generally understood to mean discrimination against white males in conjunction with preferential treatment for women and minorities. The practice had no legal standing in civil rights laws. Indeed, Section 703(j) of Title VII of the Civil Rights Act of 1964 holds that nothing in the title shall be interpreted to permit any employer to "grant preferential treatment to any individual or group on the basis of race, color, religion, sex, or national origin." Yet affirmative action programs necessarily put some white males at a disadvantage that they would not have otherwise had. Reverse discrimination is usually most keenly perceived when affirmative action policies conflict with older policies of granting preferments on the basis of seniority, test scores, and so on.

This has been one of the hottest issues before the Supreme Court over the last two decades. *DeFunis v. Odegaard* was the 1974 case concerning a white male denied admission to law school at the same time minority applicants with lesser academic credentials were accepted. DeFunis challenged the school's action on the grounds that it denied him equal protection of the laws in violation of the Fourteenth Amendment. He was successful in state court and was admitted to the school. On appeal, the school won a reversal. Nevertheless, DeFunis remained in school pending further action by the Supreme Court. As the nation awaited a definitive resolution of the issue of reverse discrimination, the Court sought to avoid the problem. Since DeFunis had completed all but his last quarter of law school and was not in danger of being denied his diploma, a majority of the justices seized upon this fact and declared that the case was moot—beyond the Court's power to render a decision on a hypothetical matter of only potential constitutional substance.

Then in 1978 in *Regents of the University of California v. Allan Bakke* the Court upheld a white applicant's claim that he had been denied equal protection of the law because he was refused admission to the University of California Medical School at Davis when 16 out of the school's 100 class spaces were set aside for minority applicants. The Court ruled that Bakke, whose objective qualifications according to the school's admission criteria were better than those of some of the minority candidates who were admitted, must be admitted to the Davis Medical School as soon as possible; but that the university had the right to take race into account in its admissions criteria. The imprecise nature of taking race into account as one factor among many has created considerable confusion about voluntary affirmative action programs concerning employment. Nonetheless, Bakke was admitted, did graduate, and is now a practicing physician. Ironically, it was these same regents of the University of California who would lead the nation in dismantling affirmative action in higher education. In 1995 it adopted a resolution that: "Effective January 1, 1997, the University of California shall not use race, religion, sex, color, ethnicity or national origin as a criterion for admission to the University or to any program of study."

Then in the 1979 case of *United Steelworkers of America v. Weber et al.* the Court upheld an affirmative action program giving blacks preference in selection of employees for a training program. Justice William Brennan, in delivering the majority opinion of the Court, stated that "the only question before us is the narrow statutory issue of whether Title VII forbids private employers and unions from voluntarily agreeing upon bona fide affirmative action plans that accord racial preferences." The Court concluded that the "Congress did not intend to limit traditional business freedom to such a degree as to prohibit all voluntary, race conscious affirmative action." Brennan went on to add that, because the steelworkers' preferential scheme was legal, it was unnecessary to "define in detail the line of demarcation between permissible and impermissible affirmative action plans."

The practice of reverse discrimination was finally given legal standing when the U.S. Supreme Court, in *Johnson v. Santa Clara County* (1987), upheld an affirmative action plan that promoted a woman ahead of an objectively more qualified man. Critics contended that this turned Title VII's requirement that there be no "preferential treatment" upside down because for the first time the Court sanctioned and gave legal standing to reverse discrimination. This was not illegal sex discrimination because Paul Johnson was not actually harmed. The Court reasoned that he "had no absolute entitlement to the road dispatcher position. Seven of the applicants were classified as qualified and eligible, and the Agency Director was authorized to promote any of the seven. Thus, the denial of the promotion unsettled no legitimate firmly rooted expectation on the part of [Johnson]." While Johnson was denied a promotion, he remained employed with the same salary and seniority, and he remained eligible for other promotions.

Race has always been a hot issue in American politics. But affirmative action policies were tolerated, if not actually supported, by most of the public until a sea change in public opinion began to occur in 1990. That was the year that Republican Senator Jesse Helms of North Carolina, running for reelection against Harvey Gantt, the black mayor of Charlotte, used a notorious television commercial in the last week of the campaign. Over a pair of white hands crumbling a job rejection letter an announcer said: "You needed that job, and you were the best-qualified, but it had to go to a minority because of a racial quota." Helms, who was well behind in the polls, then decisively won reelection. Ever since, politicians—including those who were on record as being in favor of affirmative action, such as Pete Wilson, the governor of California, and Senator Robert Dole of Kansas—have now come out against it. In 1995 Wilson, by executive order, abolished 150 advisory boards that gave state agencies race and gender hiring guidance. His press officer then boasted that Wilson was "the nation's first governor to roll back affirmative action programs." In this same year Senator Dole introduced a bill to end federally sponsored preferences for women and minorities.

Affirmative action is a wedge issue—it drives people apart. Since the 1980s, the Republicans have been quite astute in using the wedge. They branded the Democratic party the champion of special privileges for minorities with gut-turning political commercials about **Willie Horton** and job quotas. This wedge deserves much of the credit for driving traditionally Democratic blue-collar voters into the political arms of the Republicans.

The raw political fact is that affirmative action has lost the support of whites. According to a 1995 *Newsweek* poll, only 25 percent of whites supported it. Appeal was even lower among citizens of Hispanic (22 percent) and Asian (18 percent) origins. When the vast majority of citizens are opposed to reverse discrimination (which to many is just another term for affirmative action), it is absurd to brand them all as racists. True, opposition to affirmative action is a credo of racism. But most who oppose it are not racists; they simply believe that the present EEO program does not further equality, that it will ultimately be found to be unconstitutional, and that while it was once needed to jumpstart black Americans into the economic mainstream, it now—on the whole—does more harm than good.

In 1996 California became the first state to abolish affirmative action when it adopted Proposition 209, a ballot initiative that outlawed racial preferences in education, employment, and public contracts. The most immediate impact was a falling off in minority participation at University of California campuses. While 1997 efforts to repeal affirmative action programs in the city of Houston, Texas, and the state of Florida were defeated in 1998, the state of Washington, by an overwhelming majority, approved a ballot proposition that was almost identical to the affirmative action repeal in California.

Willie Horton The convicted murderer and rapist who did so much to help George Bush become president in 1988 by becoming the symbol of Michael Dukakis's "softness" on crime. In a now famous 30-second television spot, the announcer says over a photo of Bush that Bush believes in the death penalty. Then over a photo of Dukakis he says that Dukakis not only opposed the death penalty but "allowed first-degree murderers to have weekend passes from prison." Then over a mugshot of Willie Horton, a black man, the announcer says "One man was Willie Horton, who murdered a boy in a robbery, stabbing him 19 times. Despite a life sentence, Horton received 10 weekend passes from prison. Horton fled, kidnapped a young couple, stabbing the man and repeatedly raping his girlfriend." Because the spot was produced and run by Americans for Bush, an independent group that was not formally part of the Bush campaign, Bush could and did technically disavow it while at the same time benefitting from its subtle racism.

TABLE 11.1   Affirmative Action: A Chronology

1941	President Franklin D. Roosevelt issues Executive Order 8802, which required (1) that defense contractors not discriminate against any worker because of race, creed, or national origin, and (2) established a Committee on Fair Employment Practice to investigate and remedy violations.
1944	J. Donald Kingsley's *Representative Bureaucracy* develops the concept that all social groups have a right to participate in their governing institutions in proportion to their numbers in the population.
1948	President Harry S. Truman issues Executive Order 9981, which mandated the racial integration in the military and naval forces of the United States and called for an end to racial discrimination in all federal employment.
1961	President John F. Kennedy issues Executive Order 10925, which for the first time required that "affirmative action" be used to implement the policy of nondiscrimination in employment by the federal government and its contractors.
1964	The Civil Rights Act prohibits discrimination on the basis of race, color, religion, sex, or national origin in most private sector employment; creates the Equal Employment Opportunity Commission for enforcement.
1965	President Lyndon B. Johnson issues Executive Order 11246, which required federal government contractors to have affirmative action programs.
1969	President Richard M. Nixon's "Philadelphia Plan" imposes affirmative action quotas on federal building contractors in Philadelphia.
1971	The Supreme Court attacks restrictive credentialism when in *Griggs v. Duke Power Company* it rules that Title VII of the Civil Rights Act of 1964 "proscribes not only overt discrimination but also practices that are discriminatory in operation"; thus, if an employment practice operating to exclude minorities "cannot be shown to be related to job performance, the practice is prohibited."
1972	The Equal Employment Opportunity Act amends Title VII of the Civil Rights Act to include prohibitions on discrimination by public sector employers.
1978	The Supreme Court in *Regents of the University of California v. Bakke* ruled that a white male applicant denied admission to medical school in favor of minorities with lesser objective credentials was discriminated against and had to be admitted; but at the same time the Court held that race was a factor that could be taken into account in admissions decisions.
1979	The Supreme Court in *United Steelworkers of America v. Weber* upheld an affirmative action program giving blacks preference in selection of employees for a training program.
1980	The Supreme Court in *Fullilove v. Klutznick* (1980) held that the Congress has the authority to use quotas to remedy past discrimination in government public works programs.
1984	The Supreme Court in *Fire Fighters Local Union No. 1784 v. Stotts* rules that courts may not interfere with seniority systems to protect newly hired minority employees from layoff.
1987	The practice of reverse discrimination was finally given legal standing when the U.S. Supreme Court, in *Johnson v. Santa Clara County*, upheld an affirmative action plan that promoted a woman ahead of an objectively more qualified man.

TABLE 11.1   Affirmative Action: A Chronology *(continued)*

1989	The Supreme Court in *Wards Cove Packing v. Antonio* puts the burden of proof upon the plaintiff in equal employment opportunity cases.
1991	The Civil Rights Act of 1991 overturns the *Wards Cove* decision.
1995	In reaffirming his administration's support for affirmative action, President Bill Clinton asserts that "affirmative action should not go on forever."
1996	The state of California repeals affirmative action by ballot initiative.
1998	The state of Washington repeals affirmative action by ballot initiative.

Nonracial Discrimination

Equal employment opportunity has been most controversial when race is at issue. However, it is equally illegal to discriminate against someone for reasons of sex, age, or disability.

Sex Discrimination

Sex discrimination is any disparate or unfavorable treatment of a person in an employment situation because of his or her gender. The Civil Rights Act of 1964 (as amended by the Equal Employment Opportunity Act of 1972) makes sex discrimination illegal in most employment, except where a **bona fide occupational qualification** is involved.

Sex discrimination in employment was by no means a significant concern of the civil rights advocates of the early 1960s. Its prohibition only became part of the Civil Rights Act of 1964 because of Congressman Howard "Judge" Smith (1883–1976) of Virginia. As chairman of the House Rules Committee in 1964, Smith was one of the most powerful men in Congress—and as unlikely a hero as the women's movement will ever have. As the leader of the South's fight against civil rights, he added one small word—sex—to prohibitions against discrimination based on race, color, religion, and national origin. He felt confident this amendment would make the proposed law ridiculous and cause its defeat. Smith was an "old style" bigot: to his mind the one thing more ridiculous than equal rights for blacks was equal rights for women.

The "sex discrimination" amendment was opposed by most of the leading liberals in Congress. They saw it as nothing but a ploy to discourage passage of the new civil rights law. The major support for adopting the amendment came from the reactionary southern establishment of the day. There was no discussion of sex discrimination by the Senate. The momentum for a new civil rights law was so great that Smith's addition not only failed to scuttle the bill, but went largely unnoticed. The

---

bona fide occupational qualification (BFOQ) A good-faith exception to EEO provisions; a job requirement that would be discriminatory and illegal were it not necessary for the performance of a particular job. For example, female sex would be a BFOQ for a wet nurse.

Box 11.3

The "Other" Affirmative Action

A young white man . . . was not only troubled but choleric at the very notion that "unqualified minorities" would dare to demand preferential treatment. Why, he wanted to know, couldn't they compete like everyone else? Why should hardworking whites like himself be pushed aside for second-rate affirmative action hires? Why should he be discriminated against in order to accommodate them? His tirade went on for quite awhile. . . .

When the young man paused to catch his breath, I took the occasion to observe that it seemed more than a bit hypocritical of him to rage on about preferential treatment. A person of modest intellect, he had gotten into Harvard largely on the basis of family connections. His first summer internship, with the White House, had been arranged by a family member. His second, with the World Bank, had been similarly arranged. Thanks to his nice internships and Harvard degree, he had been promised a coveted slot in a major company's executive training program. In short, he was already well on his way to a distinguished career—a career made possible by preferential treatment.

My words seemed not to register, and that did not surprise me. Clearly, he had never thought of himself as a beneficiary of special treatment, and no doubt never will. Nor is it likely that either his colleagues or his superiors would be inclined to look down on him as an undeserving incompetent who got ahead on the basis of unfair advantage and was keeping better-qualified people out of work. Yet that assumption is routinely made about black beneficiaries of "affirmative action."

SOURCE: Ellis Cose, *The Rage of a Privileged Class* (New York: HarperCollins, 1993).

legal foundation for the modern women's movement was passed with almost no debate or media attention. Once Smith and his supporters realized the true impact of what they were doing, they sought to withdraw the amendment before the final vote but the then-few female members of Congress stopped this by insisting that it be done by a recorded, as opposed to a voice, vote. The male members did not want to be embarrassed by voting against women, so the amendment remained in the bill.

Although the sex discrimination prohibition was included in the new civil rights law almost in secret, word quickly got out. The new law brought into being the Equal Employment Opportunity Commission to enforce its various provisions. During the first year of the new commission's operation, over one-third of all of the complaints it received dealt with sex discrimination in employment. Typical complaints included inadequate consideration of female applicants for promotion, "help wanted" ads for separate male- and female-labeled jobs, and higher retirement benefits for male workers. All these practices and more were made illegal by Title VII. Over the next three decades, Judge Smith's unintended gift to the nation's women became the judicial reference for countless court cases and out-of-court settlements.

Women, far more than minorities, have been the greatest beneficiaries of affirmative action. Women are now almost a quarter of the medical and legal professions (and more than 40 percent of all medical and law students), more than 30 percent of all natural scientists and 40 percent of all college professors, and about 60 percent of all public officials. While some complain that a **glass ceiling** exists that many women find it difficult to break through, many others are happy to note that it is only a matter of time before it falls down.

Sexual Harassment

When the Civil Rights Act of 1964 prohibited sex discrimination in employment, it would not have occurred to anyone to say or imply that the new law had anything to do with sexual harassment. The phrase "sexual harassment" was not even in the language. Yet today, for all legal purposes, sex discrimination includes sexual harassment—the action of an individual in a position to control or influence the job, career, or grade of another person and who uses such power to gain sexual favors or punish the refusal of such favors. Sexual harassment on the job varies from inappropriate sexual innuendo to coerced sexual relations.

The courts are only gradually giving us a general idea of what behavior should not be permitted on the job. Although there was universal agreement that sexual harassment was bad, there was no agreement as to where the normal give and take between the sexes ended and sexual harassment began. An old maxim of the common law in such situations was that "there is no harm in asking!" But the harm was always there. Countless women left jobs rather than submit to sexual requests. Countless others, out of sheer economic necessity, continued on in humiliation and fear.

Then a few courageous women enlarged the meaning of the law because they were mad enough about unwarranted sexual pressures to "go public" and test their novel interpretation of sex discrimination in federal court. In 1974 Paulette Barnes started the first major case linking sexual harassment to violations of the federal civil rights law. She was an administrative aide in the Environmental Protection Agency when her supervisor began a "campaign to extract sexual favors." This included suggestions that sexual cooperation would advance her career and repeated requests for dates despite her consistent refusals.

After Barnes's supervisor finally gave up hope of seducing her, he initiated an "administrative consolidation" of his office which, as a byproduct, eliminated the need for her job. A federal judge ruled that it was sex discrimination to abolish a woman's job because she refused her male supervisor's sexual advances. The Court of Appeals left no doubt that sexual harassment was sex discrimination when a woman's job "was conditional upon submission to sexual relations—an exaction

---

glass ceiling The unseen barrier through which an organization's highest level positions can be seen but not reached. Women and minorities often perceive that a "glass ceiling" prevents their advancement to the top.

which the superior would not have sought from any male." Consequently, in 1977 Paulette Barnes was awarded $18,000 in damages.

Over the next few years a variety of similar cases were successfully brought to court. They all involved women who had lost their jobs because of sexual harassment. These women were not suing their actual harassers; they were going for the **deep pockets** and suing the organizations that had employed them.

In 1980, after the lower federal courts had decided that sexual harassment was sex discrimination in a variety of cases, the Equal Employment Opportunity Commission issued legally binding rules that defined and prohibited sexual harassment:

> Unwelcome sexual advances, requests for sexual favors, and other verbal or physical contact of a sexual nature constitute sexual harassment when:
>
> 1. submission to such conduct is made either explicitly or implicitly a term or condition of an individual's employment;
> 2. submission to or rejection of such conduct by an individual is used as the basis for employment decisions affecting such individual; or
> 3. such conduct has the purpose or effect of unreasonably interfering with an individual's work performance or creating an intimidating, hostile, or offensive working environment.

Finally, in 1986 the Supreme Court issued its first ruling on sexual harassment. In *Meritor Savings Bank v. Vinson,* it held that a "a violation of Title VII [of the Civil Rights Act of 1964] may be predicated on either of two types of sexual harassment: harassment that involves the conditioning of concrete employment benefits on sexual favors, and harassment that, while not affecting economic benefits, creates a hostile or offensive working environment." The hostile environment standard was expanded upon in *Harris v. Forklift Systems,* discussed in the keynote.

In 1998, the Supreme Court offered further refinements in four sexual harassment cases. In *Oncale v. Sundowner Offshore Services* the Court held that same-sex claims of harassment are permissible. In *Gebser v. Lago Vista Independent School District* the Court held that school districts are not responsible if teachers harassed students when the school administrators did not know about it. In *Faragher v. Boca Raton, Florida* the court held that an employer could be held financially liable for harassment by a supervisor. And in *Burlington Industries v. Ellerth* the Court held that employers were liable for the threatening sexual advances of a supervisor even when the threats are not carried out and the harassed employee suffers no adverse effects.

This odyssey of sexual harassment jurisprudence is also a good example of how the federal courts make public policy—how they can take a piece of legislation and make it into something that nobody ever thought it would be.

Despite the clearly established illegality of it, sexual harassment remains a continuing problem. In 1995 the U.S. Merit Systems Protection Board released a survey, based on a questionnaire sent to 8,000 federal employees, that found that

---

deep pockets A person or organization with enough money to be the most worthwhile target in a lawsuit.

44 percent of women and 19 percent of men said that they had been the victims of "uninvited, unwanted sexual attention." However, most of what was being complained about were the less severe forms of harassment—sexual teasing, jokes, and questionable remarks. A male referring to a female coworker as "honey" or "sweetie" or "doll" is not guilty of criminal sexual assault. But such verbal assaults, if perceived as inappropriate, do constitute sexual harassment, are inappropriate, and may be **actionable**.

Pregnancy Discrimination

A 1978 amendment to Title VII of the Civil Rights Act of 1964 holds that discrimination on the basis of pregnancy, childbirth, or related medical conditions constitutes unlawful sex discrimination. The amendment was enacted in response to the Supreme Court's ruling in *General Electric Co. v. Gilbert* (1976) that an employer's exclusion of pregnancy-related disabilities from its comprehensive disability plan did not violate Title VII.

The amendment asserts that a written or unwritten employment policy or practice that excludes from employment opportunities applicants or employees because of pregnancy, childbirth, or related medical conditions is in **prima facie** violation of Title VII.

Disabilities caused or contributed to by pregnancy, childbirth, or related medical conditions, for all job-related purposes, shall be treated the same as disabilities caused or contributed to by other medical conditions, under any health or disability insurance or sick-leave plan available in connection with employment. Written or unwritten employment policies and practices involving matters such as the commencement and duration of leave, the availability of extensions, the accrual of seniority and other benefits and privileges, reinstatement, and payment under any health or disability insurance or sick leave plan shall be applied to disability due to pregnancy, childbirth, or related medical conditions as they are applied to other disabilities.

While this amendment to Title VII did not require an employer to offer a specific number of weeks of maternity leave, the Family and Medical Leave Act of 1993 requires employers—in both the public and private sectors—with at least 50 workers to allow up to 12 weeks of unpaid leave (for childbirth, care of spouse or parent, new adoption of child, and so on) during a 12-month period for all employees (whether male or female) employed for at least a year.

Age Discrimination

Ageism is discrimination against those who are considered old. During the second presidential debate of the 1984 election, when there had been great speculation about Ronald Reagan's ability to continue to perform as president because of his age, Reagan literally turned the election around when he said, in answer to a question about his age: "I will not make age an issue in this campaign. I am not going to

---

actionable Provides adequate reason for a grievance or lawsuit.
prima facie Latin for at first sight; on the face of it; presumably. Said of a fact that will be considered to be true unless disproved by contrary evidence.

exploit, for political purposes, my opponent's youth and inexperience." Reagan went on to defeat the much younger Walter Mondale in a landslide.

Because not everybody has the Great Communicator's ability to turn the issue of age on its head, the Age Discrimination in Employment Act (ADEA) exists. First passed in 1967 and often amended, this law prohibits employment discrimination on the basis of age and (with certain exceptions) prohibits mandatory retirement. The law applies to all public employers, private employers of 20 or more employees, employment agencies serving covered employers, and labor unions of more than 25 members.

The ADEA prohibits help-wanted advertisements that indicate preference, limitation, specification, or discrimination based on age. For example, terms such as "girl" and "35–55" may not be used because they indicate the exclusion of qualified applicants based on age. Many states also have age discrimination laws or provisions in their fair employment practices laws. Some of these laws parallel the federal law and have no upper limit in protections against age discrimination in employment; others protect workers until they reach 60, 65, or 70 years of age. In 1983 the Supreme Court in *Equal Employment Opportunity Commission v. Wyoming* upheld the federal government's 1974 extension of the Age Discrimination in Employment Act to cover state and local government workers.

Disabilities Discrimination

The federal government has a long history of legislative efforts to provide employment for the disabled. Disabled veterans were the first people formally given employment preference, toward the end of the Civil War. In 1919, just after World War I, employment preferences were extended to the wives of disabled veterans as well. However, it was not until the Vocational Rehabilitation Act of 1973 that federal contractors and subcontractors were required to take affirmative action to seek qualified handicapped individuals for employment. This Act also provided the now accepted definition of a handicapped or disabled individual as any person who:

1. Has a physical or mental impairment that substantially limits one or more of such person's major life activities

2. Has a record of such an impairment

3. Is regarded as having such an impairment

A qualified handicapped individual, according to the act and with respect to employment, is one who with **reasonable accommodation** can perform the essential functions of a job in question.

But it was not until the passage of the Americans with Disabilities Act (ADA) of 1990 that there was a comprehensive federal law to ban discrimination against physically and mentally handicapped individuals in employment, transportation, telecommunications, and public accommodations. All employers with more than 15 workers—not just federal contractors as before—are required to accommodate disabled employees. New buses and trains must be accessible to people in wheelchairs.

---

reasonable accommodation Those steps needed to accommodate a handicapped employee's disability (e.g., adequate workspace for an employee confined to a wheelchair) required of an employer unless such steps would cause the employer undue hardship.

Telephone companies will have to provide hearing- or voice-impaired people with equipment to place and receive calls from ordinary telephones. Renovated or new hotels, stores, and restaurants will have to be wheelchair accessible. Existing barriers must be removed, if that is "readily achievable." Businesses that can demonstrate that these changes would be too costly or disruptive may be exempt from the law.

According to the ADA, "no covered entity shall discriminate against a qualified individual with a disability because of the disability of such individual in regard to job application procedures, the hiring, advancement, or discharge of employees, employee compensation, job training, and other terms, conditions, and privileges of employment." Among those protected by the act are individuals who are in or have successfully completed rehabilitation for drug abuse or alcoholism. However, the act states that "homosexuality and bisexuality are not impairments and as such are not disabilities under this Act." In seeking to limit the applicability of the ADA to those with traditional disabilities the ADA also specifically excludes transvestism, pedophilia, compulsive gambling, kleptomania, and pyromania.

While the U.S. Supreme Court has not ruled that AIDS is a directly-covered disability under the ADA, it has signaled the possibility that it might be. In its decision in *School Board of Nassau County v. Arline* (1987), the Court held that a public school teacher with the contagious disease of tuberculosis was "a handicapped individual" within the meaning of the Rehabilitation Act. Therefore, protection against employment discrimination was provided by the law. This case has been the basis for some lower court rulings that the Rehabilitation Act protects persons with AIDS from employment discrimination. In 1998 the Court offered its first substantial review of the ADA in *Bragdon v. Abbott*. Here it held that people with the H.I.V. infection that leads to AIDS—people with no AIDS symptoms as yet—were protected by the ADA. While the scope of the case was limited, its tone strongly suggested that people with AIDS would also be protected.

The Equal Employment Opportunity Commission, which enforces the provisions of the ADA, requires that an employer may not ask about the existence, nature, or severity of a disability and may not conduct medical examinations until after it makes a conditional job offer to the applicant. This prohibition ensures that an applicant's disability that is not obviously apparent is not considered prior to the assessment of the applicant's nonmedically related qualifications. At this pre-offer stage, employers can ask about an applicant's ability to perform specific job-related functions. After a conditional offer is made, an employer may require medical examinations and may make disability-related inquiries if it does so for all entering employees in the job category. If an examination or inquiry screens out an individual because of disability, the exclusionary criterion must be job-related—and the employer must be able to demonstrate that the essential functions of the job cannot be performed with reasonable accommodation.

Public Administration and Social Equity

All public administrators have an obvious obligation to advance social equity. However, this obligation can be legitimately and honorably interpreted in several ways. First is the obligation to administer the laws they work under in a fair manner. It is hard to believe today that this first obligation was once controversial. Before the passage of the 1960s civil rights legislation—mainly the Civil Rights Act of 1964 and the Voting Rights Act of 1965—minorities and women were routinely denied equitable treatment. For example, when the two female justices of the U.S. Supreme Court—Sandra Day O'Connor and Ruth Bader Ginsberg—graduated from law school, neither could obtain jobs with any major law firm. Today all large employers in the public and private sector are legally obligated to provide equal employment opportunity and legally liable if they don't.

Going the Extra Mile

But it is one thing to simply avoid being in violation of the law; it is another matter altogether to actively seek to foster its spirit. Thus the second way of interpreting obligations to advance social equity is to feel bound to proactively further the cause—to seek to hire and advance a varied workforce. The attitude requires a specific approach: It is not enough to go out and find qualified minorities. You must go out, find them, and then qualify them. This is why the U.S. armed forces have been so much more successful in their affirmative action efforts than the society as a whole. They bring minorities into their organizations as young recruits and nurture them as they grow—just the same as they have been doing with white males for 200 years.

This going the "extra mile" is the spirit of the new public administration. These are not two ends of a continuum, with passive attitudes toward social equity at one end and proactive attitudes at the other. These are different ways of looking at the administrative world and one's responsibilities within it as an individual, as a citizen, and as an administrator.

Inspiring Social Equity

Still there is one other aspect to advancing social equity that is best illustrated by a story. In 1963 George C. Wallace, then governor of Alabama, dramatically stood in the doorway of the University of Alabama to prevent the entry of black students and the desegregation of the university. It was a major media event. Wallace, backed up by the Alabama National Guard, stood waiting at his designated chalk mark on the pavement wearing his TV network microphone. As was arranged, the deputy U.S. attorney general, Nicholas Katzenbach, backed up by 3,000 federal troops, ordered Wallace to allow a black student, Vivian Malone, to enter. After a long-winded speech about federal encroachment on states' rights, Wallace stepped aside and Katzenbach escorted Malone to the university cafeteria.

This incident is a famous aspect of the civil rights movement. Journalist Jacob Weisberg in his *In Defense of Government* adds an element to this well-known story that shows government at its best. After Malone entered the cafeteria, she got her tray of food and sat alone. Almost immediately some white female students joined her. They sought to befriend her, as they would any new student. According to Weisberg, "That's the most powerful part of the story because it is about a change that good government inspired but could not force." Then, as now, governments can go only so far in forcing social equity. But there is no limit to the amount of inspiration it can provide to encourage people to do the right, decent, and honorable thing. This encouragement has a name. It is called moral leadership.

Summary

Social equity is fairness in the delivery of public services; it is egalitarianism in action—the principle that each citizen has a right to be given equal treatment by the political system. Government organizations have a special obligation to be fair because they represent the citizenry.

The history of slavery in the United States is still relevant today because it is the underlying basis for African American claims for special treatment. Equal employment opportunity, created to mitigate the heritage of slavery, is a concept fraught with political, cultural, and emotional overtones. Generally, it applies to employment practices that prevent any individual from being adversely excluded from employment opportunities on the basis of race, color, sex, religion, age, or national origin. The problem with equal employment opportunity programs is that they put the government into the business of examining people's blood lines.

Well-meaning opponents of affirmative action (the means by which EEO is to be achieved) favor equality. They hold that racial and sexual hiring preferences are not only inherently discriminatory, they are also in violation of the Civil Rights Act of 1964, which prohibits discrimination against anybody. Affirmative action has become a wedge issue—an issue that drives people apart. Since the 1980s, the Republicans have been quite astute in using this wedge to brand the Democratic party as the champion of special privileges for minorities.

When the Civil Rights Act of 1964 prohibited sex discrimination in employment, nobody would have said that the new law had anything to do with sexual harassment. Yet today, for all legal purposes, sex discrimination includes sexual harassment. A 1978 amendment to the act holds that discrimination on the basis of pregnancy, childbirth, or related medical conditions also constitutes unlawful sex discrimination.

The federal government has a long history of legislative efforts to provide employment for the disabled. But it was not until the passage of the Americans with Disabilities Act (ADA) of 1990 that there was a comprehensive federal law to ban discrimination against physically and mentally handicapped individuals in employment, transportation, telecommunications, and public accommodations.

Key Concepts

affirmative action A term that first meant the removal of "artificial barriers" to the employment of women and minority group members; now it refers to compensatory opportunities for hitherto disadvantaged groups—specific efforts to recruit, hire, and promote qualified members of disadvantaged groups for the purpose of eliminating the present effects of past discrimination.

child labor Originally, the employment of children in a manner detrimental to their health and social development. Now that the law contains strong child labor prohibitions, the term refers to the employment of children below the legal age limit.

discrimination Bigotry in practice; intolerance toward those who have different beliefs or religions. In employment, the failure to treat equals equally. Any action that has the effect of limiting employment and advancement opportunities because of an individual's sex, race, color, age, national origin, religion, physical handicap, or other irrelevant criteria, is discrimination.

equal employment opportunity Employment practices that prevent any individual from being adversely excluded from employment opportunities on the basis of race, color, sex, religion, age, national origin, or other factors that cannot lawfully be considered in employing people.

new public administration An academic advocacy movement for social equity in the performance and delivery of public services; it called for a proactive administrator with a burning desire for social equity to replace the traditional impersonal and neutral gun-for-hire bureaucrat.

racist Any person or organization that either consciously or unconsciously practices discrimination against another person on the basis of race (or ethnicity) or supports the supremacy of one race over others.

representative bureaucracy The ultimate goal of equal employment opportunity and affirmative action programs.

reverse discrimination Discrimination against white males in conjunction with preferential treatment for women and minorities.

second reconstruction The civil rights movement and legislation of the 1960s. The first reconstruction, immediately after the Civil War, gave blacks their freedom from slavery. But the laws as enforced and customs as practiced did not allow for the full rights of citizens. That came in the 1960s, when public sentiment was aroused and legal action was taken to ensure equal rights for all Americans.

sex discrimination Any disparate or unfavorable treatment of a person in an employment situation because of his or her sex.

sexual harassment The action of an individual (either a supervisor or coworker) in a position to control or influence another's job, career, or grade who uses such power to gain sexual favors or punish the refusal of such favors. Sexual harassment on the job varies from inappropriate sexual innuendo to coerced sexual relations.

Title VII That part of the Civil Rights Act of 1964 that prohibits employment discrimination because of race, color, religion, sex, or national origin and created the Equal Employment Opportunity Commission as its enforcement vehicle.

Bibliography

Bishop, Peter C., and Augustus J. Jones Jr. (1993). "Implementing the Americans with Disabilities Act of 1990," *Public Administration Review* 53 (March-April).

Boller, Harvey R., and Douglas Massengill. (1992). "Public Employers' Obligation to Reasonably Accommodate the Disabled Under the Rehabilitation and Americans with Disabilities Acts," *Public Personnel Management* 21 (Fall).

Cose, Ellis. (1993). *The Rage of a Privileged Class.* New York: HarperCollins.

Frederickson, H. George. (1980). *The New Public Administration.* University, AL: University of Alabama Press.

Henry, William A., III. (1994) *In Defense of Elitism.* New York: Doubleday.

Jamieson, David, and Julie O'Mara. (1991). *Managing Workforce 2000: Gaining the Diversity Advantage.* San Francisco: Jossey-Bass.

Kingsley, J. Donald. (1944). *Representative Bureaucracy: An Interpretation of the British Civil Service.* Yellow Springs, OH: Antioch Press.

Klein, Joe. (1995). "The End of Affirmative Action," *Newsweek,* February 13.

Krislov, Samuel. (1967). *The Negro in Federal Employment.* Minneapolis: University of Minnesota Press.

———. (1974). *Representative Bureaucracy.* Englewood Cliffs, NJ: Prentice Hall.

Marini, Frank, ed. (1971). *Toward a New Public Administration.* San Francisco: Chandler.

Marshall, Thurgood. (1987). "An African-American's Perspective on the Constitution," *Vanderbilt Law Review* 40.

McAllister, Bill. (1995). "The Problem That Won't Go Away: A New Survey Finds Complaints of Sexual Harassment Are Still Widespread in Federal Offices," *The Washington Post National Weekly Edition,* November 20–26.

Pellicciotti, Joseph M. (1991). "Exemptions and Employer Defenses Under the ADEA," *Public Personnel Management* 20 (Summer).

Robinson, Robert K., et al. (1993). "Sexual Harassment in the Workplace: A Review of the Legal Rights and Responsibilities of All Parties," *Public Personnel Management* 19 (Spring).

Sowell, Thomas. (1984). *Civil Rights: Rhetoric or Reality.* New York: William Morrow.

Thomas, R. Roosevelt, Jr. (1990). "From Affirmative Action to Affirming Diversity," *Harvard Business Review* 68 (March-April).

Thompson, Victor A. (1961). *Modern Organization.* New York: Knopf.

———. (1975) *Without Sympathy or Enthusiasm.* University, AL: University of Alabama Press.

Waldo, Dwight. (1968). "Public Administration in a Time of Revolution," *Public Administration Review* 28 (July-August).

Weisberg, Jacob. (1996). *In Defense of Government: The Rise and Fall of Public Trust.* New York: Scribner.

Wilkins, Roger. (1995). "The Case for Affirmative Action," *The Nation* (March 27).

Recommended Books

Arredondo, Patricia. (1996). *Successful Diversity Management Initiatives: A Blueprint for Planning and Implementation.* Thousand Oaks, CA: Sage. A how-to-do-it manual for workforce diversity program implementation; presents a prototype for measuring both qualitative and quantitative results.

Olson, Walter, K. (1997). *The Excuse Factory: How Employment Law Is Paralyzing the American Workplace.* New York: Free Press. A review of the unintended consequences of the Americans With Disabilities Act whereby it has become difficult to fire slacking employees because of the protections the Act offers for those with frivolous physical and mental "problems."

Reese, Laura A., and Karen E. Lindenberg. (1998). *Implementing Sexual Harassment Policy: Challanges for the Public Sector Workforce.* Thousand Oaks, CA: Sage. A review of the problems and opportunities of creating organizational policies for forestalling and dealing with sexual harassment.

Sowell, Thomas. (1990) *Preferential Policies: An International Perspective.* New York: William Morrow. An around-the-world tour of affirmative action policies and practices.

West, Cornel. (1993). *Race Matters.* Boston: Beacon Press. An explanation of how the intellectual frameworks about race used by both blacks and whites impede racial progress and understanding.

Related Web Sites

Affirmative Action and Diversity Project
http://humanitas.ucsb.edu/projects/aa/aa.html

Affirmative Action Manual
http://www.law.ucla.edu/Classes/Archive/CivAA/bible.htm

Americans with Disabilities Act Document Center
http://janweb.icdi.wvu.edu/kinder/

Avoiding sexual harassment claims
hhtp://www.lgu.com/em49.htm

Commission on Civil Rights
http://www.usccr.gov

Federal anti-discrimination laws
http://www.hronline.org/consult/hrtopic/anticisc.html

National Committee on Pay Equity
http://feminist.com/fairpay.htm

Sexual harassment prevention training
http://www.sexual-harassment.com/

U.S. Equal Employment Opportunity Commission
http://www.eeoc.gov

Public Financial Management

Keynote: The Red Ink of Orange County

A default is a failure to pay a debt when due. Unlike the private sector, where a corporate default can result in the end of the corporation and division of all remaining assets, governmental organizations inevitably live on. There is life after default; but often it is a hell of litigation. Just how hellish this can be was illustrated when the specter of default was upon Orange County, California.

Adjacent to Los Angeles, Orange County was known for its orange groves and in recent decades as the home of Disneyland. Among the largest and richest counties in the nation, Orange County was hit hard by the tax revolt, a nationwide grass roots movement heralded by California's 1978 Proposition 13, which decreased or limited the rate of increase possible on property taxes. In a sense, this was a revolt by the middle class against the rising cost of government services. The revolt, it is important to note, was not over the unfairness of the tax burden but over the levels of taxation, especially on real estate, which were increasing dramatically in a period of double-digit inflation. By 1980, the tax revolt movement forced 38 states to reduce or at least stabilize tax rates. In 1990, when California passed Proposition III, which among other things doubled the state gasoline tax over five years to pay for new highways, many analysts hailed this as the end of the "tax revolt." But the damage had already been done. What with new state mandates and rising costs for education, health care, law enforcement, and immigrants (both legal and otherwise), local governments all over California were being fiscally squeezed.

To help out the localities, the state of California relaxed restrictions on the kinds of investments local treasurers could make with public funds. This is when Robert L. Citron, the elected Orange County Treasurer, started his remarkably lucky run of effectively gambling with county funds. The problem with gambling is that when your luck runs out, you lose. And Citron, after seven consecutive elections for, and a quarter century as, the county treasurer, ran out of luck in 1994. He lost more than one and a half billion dollars (yes, billion!) of public money. This was initially hard to believe for the citizens of a county that was so rich. The average household income in 1994 was $57,302, compared to a national average of $38,453. The problem was that the swaggering, freewheeling aggressive business culture of the county—aptly symbolized by the larger-than-life statue of John Wayne in full cowboy regalia that greets visitors to the county's John Wayne Airport—had infected its public finances.

In 1995 Citron pleaded guilty to six felony counts. (He was sentenced to a year in prison and served eight months before his release in 1997.) But he was not embezzling or stealing the missing money. He was just managing an investment pool for the county and more than 180 other localities and agencies. His investors in this mutual fund hybrid were pleased when he gave them returns several percentage points above what treasurers were earning in other counties. He did this by borrowing to buy interest-rate-sensitive derivative securities—essentially "bets" that interest rates would remain stable or go lower. But interest rates rose and he lost $1.7 billion. The loss was so great, the pool of invested funds was so large to begin with, because it was not just Orange County money. But Orange County, being the largest member of the pool, suffered the most. It was forced to cut its budget by more than 40 percent, reduce its workforce by 10 percent (which amounted to 1,500 jobs), and put the John Wayne Airport and its statue up for sale.

There was an explosion of litigation. The other pool members wanted their money back. The bond holders wanted their interest. The county sued the law firm that acted as its bond advisor, several of the brokerage firms that sold it the risky investments, and the accounting firm that should have warned the county about the treasurer's ill-advised investment policies. (By mid-1988 the county had recovered more than $572 million in civil settlements.) The county supervisors figured that with the cuts in jobs and programs and a modest tax increase (that would raise $130 million in new revenue each year) they could cope and eventually repay everybody. So a half a percentage-point increase in the county sales tax (from 7.75 to 8.25 percent) was submitted to the voters. In most states a county can raise taxes on its own. But since the 1978 passage of Proposition 13, California localities can raise taxes only after a referendum vote of the people. Unfortunately, the people were not going to cooperate. In June 1994 the citizens rejected the tax increase by a margin of more than 3 to 2. Shortly after the election, the Standard and Poor's Credit Rating Service declared Orange County to be in default. On December 6, 1994, the county filed for

bankruptcy. The irony here is that the additional interest costs demanded by suspicious creditors will exceed by far this tiny tax increase. The citizens were penny wise and pound foolish. After all, when rating agencies examine a municipality's ability to repay debt, they look at both ability-to-pay and willingness-to-pay. Orange County will get low marks for "willingness" for years to come. And with these low marks will come higher interest rates.

During the Great Depression of the 1930s, Chapter 9 was added to the federal bankruptcy code. Its purpose was to help municipalities fight off paralyzing lawsuits by aggrieved creditors. According to John Peterson, "Up until now, Chapter 9 has remained a curiosity; there had been only about 70 filings since 1980, and they involved very small governments, usually limited-purpose districts, that were hit by some fiscal meteor." Orange County used Chapter 9 to give itself enough of a respite from litigation to

America's icon of fiscal integrity, John Wayne, permanently waiting for a plane at the Orange County Airport. Wayne acted integrity better than he lived it. An accomplished draft dodger during World War II, in the post war period he cynically—and some say in psychological compensation for his ignoble past—became an overt superpatriot. Still the performances in a solid dozen of his films are second to none. For more on Wayne, see the Chapter 6 Keynote ●

make deals with its creditors. According to *New York Times* reporter Joe Mysak, "By filing for Chapter 9 bankruptcy last fall, Orange County did what no other city, town or county—not even New York City in the 1970s—has ever done. It told the holders of its general obligation notes to get in line with the rest of its creditors." When Bruce Bennett, the bankruptcy lawyer representing the county, was asked if he intended to make a specialty of Chapter 9 municipal bankruptcy cases he said: "What the hell are you talking about? These cases aren't supposed to happen."

Finally, in September 1995, the California state legislature helped complete the Orange County bailout. It authorized the county to use hundreds of millions of dollars in earmarked funds to pay creditors. This meant that those millions that were earmarked for highways and mass transit, parks, flood control, beaches and harbors would not be available for those original purposes. But untended parks and polluted beaches are just a small part of the price Orange County citizens will pay for fiscal peace.

The pain of Orange County, like an infectious disease, will be shared with its neighbors. Since investors shy away from the fiscally unstable, all California localities—like it or not, stained by Orange—will be paying higher interest rates than municipal bond issuers in other states. The entire "Golden State" is now more Orange than it ever wanted to be.

The Importance of Public Financial Management

The flow and management of funds is the lifeblood of our system of public administration. No policy, however farsighted, no system of administrative performance, however well crafted, can function unless it is associated with the flow of funds that will make it possible. Like other parts of the story of public administration covered so far, the system of public financial management rests on designs and reforms adopted over many years. Administrators need to understand how that system has been designed, what it is intended to do, what it is capable of doing, and especially what it is not capable of doing. As with the machinery of government and the system of intergovernmental relations, many aspects of the design of the American system of public financial management go back to our deepest political traditions and compacts—to the ideas of the founders at the Constitutional Convention. Others, like the idea of the welfare state, go back only a few generations. Still others, such as the concept of "user pays," are at their height.

Public financial management is a dynamic, living, breathing system with which citizens interact every day. Think of this system as rather like a huge irrigation system, one that gathers rainfall behind large dams, and distributes the flow of water through large and small pipes and channels to many disparate communities, to commercial users, schools and hospitals, to parklands and charities, to businesses and individuals, to seaside areas and deserts. Such a system must be managed and regulated throughout its length, and its consumers must be billed according to some politically acceptable framework. If adequate rain falls, if the dams and pipes do not leak or burst, and if the supplies of water are not diverted or stolen before delivery, the system will become a precondition for life, growth, and even abundance. In one dimension at least, public administrators, as well as concerned citizens, are river wardens on this system. They are all sustained by its flow. And of course, in those very rare cases like the bankruptcy of Orange County in California, they can lose much of their sustenance if the rain does not fall, if the reservoirs are destroyed through sabotage, or if faulty design, incompetence, or greed runs the system dry.

This chapter looks at the many facets of public financial management: how the systems are designed, the strategic objectives of public financial management, how funds are raised in revenue programs, the way yearly allocations are politically fought for and determined in budgetary processes, the way public administrators must manage the downstream flow of funds in program implementation, and the way the function of public financial management interlocks or should interlock with other aspects of public administration.

Six Principles

At the Boston Tea Party in 1773, America's pioneers began to lay down the design of this country's system of public financial management when they cast cargoes of tea into Boston Harbor rather than pay reasonable taxes on them to England. When they shouted their slogan, "No taxation without representation," they were also asserting a cardinal value—a design principle—for the future system of public financial management in America. Taxation and public spending must be voted for; they must have, in effect, the stamp of democratic approval. This had not been the way most governments to that date had operated. States and potentates had levied and extracted taxes as a matter of the exercise of power. Then they kept or spent the money as they chose. America's founders made democratic consent to these things a fundamental design feature. This is why the Constitution requires that all tax legislation must originate in the House of Representatives, the legislative branch most responsive to the popular will.

At the heart of the design of the American system of public financial management are the following six principles:

1. *Democratic consent:* Taxation and spending should not be done without the explicit **consent of the governed**.
2. *Equity:* Governments should be equitable (treat people in similar circumstances similarly) in raising and spending taxes.
3. *Transparency:* What governments do in raising and spending funds should be open to public knowledge and scrutiny.
4. *Probity:* There must be scrupulous honesty in dealing with public funds, of which legislators and administrators are the stewards, not the owners.
5. *Prudence:* These stewards should not take undue risks with public funds.
6. *Accountability:* Those who deal in public funds can and should be regularly called to account for their stewardship through legislative review and audit processes.

---

consent of the governed The notion that the institutions of government must be based on the will of the people.

These normative principles are "shoulds"; but they are all too often breached in real life. Public financial management can be abused. Democratic consent is lacking when government is conducted in secret. Concerns for equity often yield to **pork barrel** favoritism toward areas, clients, or groups. Without transparency, probity, and prudence, the inherent caution so essential to the management of public funds is thrown to the winds. Governments then may incur substantial losses through risky investments or negligence, as in Orange County.

Balanced Budgets

A balanced **budget** is a budget in which receipts are equal to or greater than outlays. A government that has one is financially healthy. The advantages of a balanced budget, not spending more than you take in, are obvious. But there are also advantages to "unbalanced" budgets, those that require public borrowing. The "extra" spending can stimulate the economy during economic downturns and provide needed public works and public support for the less fortunate. But these considerations must be weighed against the danger that large deficits over a significant period can devalue the currency, kindle inflation, and have such a **crowding out** effect on capital markets that an economic depression (or recession) occurs. Note that it is only the federal government that has the option of long-term deficit spending. The states all have constitutional or statutory provisions mandating balanced budgets (at least at the beginning of each year).

A balanced budget amendment to the Constitution is an oft-suggested proposal to force an end to deficit spending by the federal government. Many critics think that this is an exercise in futility because the Congress could easily create any number of mechanisms to meet the letter, but violate the spirit, of any such amendment. Others think that it is absolutely essential because there is no other way the Congress will make the hard decisions needed to get there. In 1995 the House passed a balanced budget amendment bill. The Senate failed to pass it by only one vote. But the budget surpluses that began in 1999 have put this idea "on hold"—for the time being.

The Fiscal Year

Fiscal means having to do with taxation, public revenues, or public debt. The fiscal year is a 12-month accounting period without regard to a calendar year. The fiscal year for the federal government, through fiscal year 1976, began on July 1 and ended on June 30. But the Congress, in part because of the invention of air

---

pork barrel Favoritism by a government in the allocation of benefits or resources; legislation that favors the district of a particular legislator by providing for the funding of public works or other projects (such as post offices or defense contracts) that will bring economic advantage to the district and political favor for the legislator.

budget A financial plan serving as a pattern for and control over future operations—hence, any estimate of future costs or any systematic plan for the utilization of the workforce, material, or other resources.

crowding out The displacement of private investment expenditures by increases in public expenditures financed by the sale of government securities. It is often suggested that, as the federal deficit increases, the money borrowed from the public to pay for it is therefore unavailable for private investment. Such crowding out could thus lead to a recession or worse.

conditioning, increasingly stayed in Washington through the summer. Since it usually waited until the last minute to pass the various appropriations bills, federal agencies increasingly had to depend on **continuing resolutions** for their funding. Finally, Congress realized how silly this was and simply moved the beginning of the new fiscal year to the end of the summer. Since fiscal year 1977, fiscal years for the federal government begin on October 1 and end on September 30. The fiscal year is designated by the calendar year in which it ends (e.g., fiscal year 1996 was the fiscal year ending September 30, 1996).

Not all state and local governments follow the federal example. Most states begin their fiscal year on July 1; but a few use the first day of April, September, or October. Nor is there an international pattern. For example, Brazil, France, and Russia use January 1; Britain and Japan use April 1; and Australia and Kenya use July 1.

Fiscal is also used as an all-purpose adjective to refer to anything to do with government finances. Thus fiscal integrity is a characteristic of a government budget that spends no more than anticipated revenues. A balanced budget has fiscal integrity; a budget with a significant deficit does not. You will be deemed to have fiscal integrity when the person so deeming agrees with your fiscal policies. If that same person disagrees with your policies, you may be deemed so lacking in fiscal responsibility as to be considered fiscally irresponsible.

The Budget Game

In the United States, the budget game is a major preoccupation in politics, occupying the time and energies of thousands of lobbyists, politicians, and officials in the national capital, and fewer but similarly motivated categories of people in state capitals. Why? Because the budget is literally the biggest game in town. As with every game, there are winners and losers, and the stakes are incredibly high.

The Politics of the Budgetary Process

For these reasons, American scholarship in the last 30 years has had a major preoccupation with what Aaron Wildavsky termed the "politics of the budgetary process." We have already discussed many of the structural aspects of the budgetary process—the various theories and approaches used to pursue involvements in formal budget structures and procedures. But budget scholars have indelibly underlined the political sociology and dynamics of budget making in America, to the extent that this subject has in many ways taken center stage.

The emphasis on the "horse trading," the negotiating nature of the budget process as opposed to its formal structure, is the counterpart of Lindblom's emphasis on the "incremental" nature of decision making as opposed to the rational comprehensive model (discussed in Chapter 2). These main currents in the political analysis of budgeting during the past 30 years seem to suggest a decidedly individu-

---

continuing resolution Legislation that provides budget authority for specific ongoing activities when the regular fiscal-year appropriation for such activities has not been enacted by the beginning of the fiscal year. The continuing resolution usually specifies a maximum rate at which the agency may incur an obligation based on the rate of the prior year, the president's budget request, or an appropriation bill passed by either or both houses of the Congress.

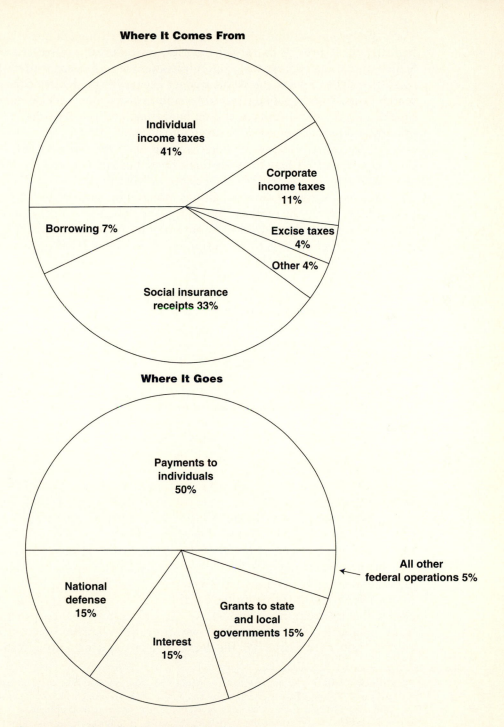

Where It Comes From

Individual income taxes 41%

Corporate income taxes 11%

Excise taxes 4%

Other 4%

Borrowing 7%

Social insurance receipts 33%

Where It Goes

Payments to individuals 50%

All other federal operations 5%

National defense 15%

Grants to state and local governments 15%

Interest 15%

Figure 12.1   The Federal Government's Fiscal Posture

SOURCE: *Budget of the United States*, fiscal year 1998.

Note: Observe how payments to individuals—the entitlements of Social Security, Medicaid and Medicare, and welfare—are half of the federal budget. They were only one-third (33.1 percent) in 1970.

alistic, multicentered decision-making milieu—an environment better studied socio-logically than through its formal theories, procedures, and structures. As **Allen Schick** puts it, "a process that concentrates on the increment is preferable to one that attempts to review the whole budget because it moderates conflict, reduces search costs, stabilizes budgetary roles and expectations, reduces the amount of time that busy officials must spend on budgeting, and increases the likelihood that important political values will be taken into account."

Yet the danger in elevating horse trading to an art and a science is that direction may be lost: We may have the finest horse but nowhere to ride. In his critique of Lindblom's famous article "The Science of Muddling Through," policy analyst Yehezkel Dror spoke of three conditions essential for incrementalist policymaking to be adequate: (1) the results of present policies must be in the main satisfactory; (2) there must be a high degree of continuity in the natures of problems; and (3) there must be a high degree of continuity in the available means for dealing with problems. For Dror, developing countries could not pursue the policies of ousted colonial powers on an incremental basis, nor should the United States in circumstances where changes in values made formerly accepted policies, like segregation, unacceptable. Washington **gridlock**, at least in one dimension, is a feasible outcome of a highly decentralized process of budgeteering in a setting where the institutional separation of powers itself bolsters inertia.

Whatever normative reservations one may have concerning these issues, it is empirically the case that the budget game is played in Washington as an art form, that budgeteers pursue their strategies whether for spending or for tax cuts with the application, strategy, and steely nerve of riverboat gamblers. In fact, the process is rather like the main saloon of a riverboat, with a succession of poker games being played in the same general space amidst a haze of cigarette smoke and poker faces. At one table sit the heads of federal departments and agencies. They play a game based on the formal submission of budget proposals. It is largely a zero sum game—that is, you can win only if someone else loses. For example, if the Department of Defense gains, social programs are likely to lose. Each player seeks to "up the ante" by referring to the dire consequences or risks that will be taken if the latest defense system is not developed, or if flood mitigation public works along the Mississippi River are not undertaken. Lobbyists linger in the background in an area known as **Gucci Gulch**, signing up members of Congress with persuasion or deals. At another table sit congressmen and -women, with one eye on the mirror above them looking for backshooters, the other on the cards being dealt, ever-suspicious that the next card will come from the dealer's sleeve. At the bar, the press corps views the play, forms judgments, and pursues their own strategies and preoccupations for the next day's or next week's issue. On the decks outside, enjoying a little fresh air but still

---

Allen Schick (1934–) A leading chronicler of public budgeting systems. When new budgeting concepts such as PPBS and ZBB became significant to public administration, Schick wrote of their origins and utility; when these same concepts failed in practice, he wrote their obituaries.

gridlock Traffic so bad that virtually no vehicles can move. Its political analogy is a government so divided over issues that no substantial changes can be made in either direction.

Gucci Gulch The hallways outside of the rooms where congressional committees meet; so called because highly paid lobbyists, supposedly wearing expensive Gucci shoes, wait to lobby members of Congress as they enter and exit the committee rooms.

close to the scene of the action, are the members of the conservative and liberal think tanks. They are close enough to have some sense of the play inside the saloon, but it is the imperfect view of camp-followers in any battle. In the steerage below, there are some academic budget theorists, on board for the ride.

The Budget Maximizing Bureaucrat

As in poker, bluff and overstatement are key tactical tools of departments and spending advocates during budget processes. Aware that their bids will be subject to some degree of cutback, bidders build in a protective tactic by providing for cutback in the original level of bid. This is not lying, but playing a tough game in which there are no rewards for losers. The game itself is regulated. There are rules in budget preparation as to the inflation indices that are to be used, the ways in which costs are to be estimated and programs are to be documented. But there are no limits on the ambitions of agency heads who want to maximize their agency budgets and their program's importance. In the often perverted world of government, one may be only as important as the size of one's budget. The bureaucratic battle cry of "mine is bigger than yours" is heard often during the perennial budget wars. This phenomenon is universal. As Sir Humphrey Appleby in the book *The Complete Yes Minister* explains to a British civil service colleague, "we measure success by the size of our staff and our budget. By definition a big department is more successful than a small one."

The misrepresentation of budget estimates is a tool used by both program advocates and program opponents. An executive branch may seek to overestimate or underestimate expenditure or revenue in order to provide an excuse for cost cutting or to minimize the perceived budget deficit. For this reason Congress obtains its own estimates from the **Congressional Budget Office**, which it regards as more reliable than the president's Office of Management and Budget.

The budget game of course consists of two fields of play for politicians: (1) defending your clientele against revenue hikes such as tax increases, and (2) seeking to attract government spending programs that will benefit your clientele. Often the game is played so skillfully that even the categorization of an initiative as revenue or expenditure may serve to conceal its nature. For example, government housing assistance to low-paid workers is categorized as expenditure. Government housing assistance to high-paid workers (tax deductibility of mortgage interest payments) is presented as an exemption on the revenue side. One is a direct expense and one is a **tax expenditure**. How do they differ? Spending on highways is characterized as the provision of necessary **infrastructure**. Spending from general taxation on public transportation is assigned the category "losses." Again, how do they differ?

Congressional Budget Office (CBO) A support agency of the U.S. Congress created in 1974 by the Congressional Budget and Impoundment Act. It provides the Congress with basic budget data and with analyses of alternative fiscal, budgetary, and programmatic policy issues, independent of the executive branch.

tax expenditure The losses of tax revenue attributable to provisions of the federal tax laws that allow a special exclusion, exemption, or deduction from gross income or that provide a special credit, preferential rate of tax, or deferral of tax liability. When an individual or a corporation gets a tax subsidy, the federal government counts it as a tax expenditure.

infrastructure A general term for a jurisdiction's fixed assets, such as bridges, highways, tunnels, and water treatment plants.

TABLE 12.1 Examples of Tax Expenditures

Taxes Not Collected on:	Cost to Federal Government
Home mortgage interest	$54 billion
State and local taxes	$52 billion
Charitable contributions	$25 billion
Social Security benefits	$19 billion
Interest on municipal bonds	$15 billion

SOURCE: *Budget of the United States Government,* fiscal year 1999.

In many respects the interplay between the president and the Congress represents the ultimate showdown in the budget game. After all the convolutions of dealing, trading, and bluffing, the final play is between Congress and the White House, a play heightened in its drama if Congress and president are from opposing parties. Both have budget offices (the CBO and the OMB) to support them in analysis and in repackaging deals into budget options. Both have enormous standing and access to the public through the media. But in the end, the game remains. The president must send his budget to the Congress. The Congress, the more so if hostile, will extensively amend it and return it; the president must decide whether and to what extent to use the veto. Behind the play, horse traders, lobbyists, and pork barrelers continue to trade.

Because of its importance and the way in which it is conducted, the budget game should never be underestimated or ignored by public administrators. At the same time, its centrality should not divert our attention too far from the substantive merits of new and existing policies, rather than the gamesmanship with which funds for them may be sought or denied.

Budgeting Theory and Practice

Budgeting is the single most important decision-making process in public institutions. The budget itself is also a jurisdiction's most important reference document. In their increasingly voluminous formats, budgets simultaneously record policy decision outcomes, cite policy priorities as well as program objectives, and delineate a government's total service effort.

A public budget has four basic dimensions. First, it is a political instrument that allocates scarce public resources among the social and economic needs of the jurisdiction. Second, a budget is a managerial or administrative instrument: it specifies the **ways and means** of providing public programs and services; it establishes the costs of programs and the criteria by which these programs are evaluated for efficiency and effectiveness; it ensures that the programs will be reviewed or evalu-

---

ways and means The methods by which a state gains its funds, supplies, and other necessities. The English House of Commons has had a Committee on Ways and Means at least since 1644. The U.S. House of Representatives has had a Ways and Means Committee since 1795. All national tax legislation must originate in the House Ways and Means Committee.

ated at least once during the budget year or **budget cycle**. Third, a budget is an economic instrument that can direct a jurisdiction's economic growth and development. Certainly at the national level—and to a lesser extent at the state and regional levels—government budgets are the primary instruments for redistributing income, stimulating economic growth, promoting full employment, combating inflation, and maintaining economic stability. Fourth, a budget is an accounting instrument that holds government officials responsible for the expenditure of the funds with which they have been entrusted. Budgets also hold governments accountable in the aggregate. The very concept of a budget implies that there is a ceiling, or a spending limitation, which literally (but theoretically) requires governments to live within their means.

The Taft Commission

Prior to 1900, the processes of public financial management in America lacked overall objectives. A particular need—to build a road, finance a war, or meet the

costs of civil service and military pay—inspired an appropriate allocation by Congress. This century, the growing scale and complexity of government led to calls for budgetary reform. In 1912, the **Taft Commission** recommended a national budgeting system. Writing in 1918, William F. Willoughby (1867–1960), a member of the Taft Commission, outlined developments that were leading to the creation of modern budget systems in state governments. In *The Movement Towards Budgetary Reform in the States*, Willoughby argues that budget reform would involve three major threads: (1) how budgets would advance and provide for popular control; (2) how budgets would enhance legislative

President William Howard Taft displaying his executive profile while thinking about executive budgeting. Taft was the only person to be both president of the United States (1909–1913) and chief justice of the Supreme Court (1921–1930). At 321 pounds, Taft also holds the record as the largest of all presidents. While he was the hand-picked successor of President Theodore Roosevelt, Taft quickly lost Roosevelt's support once in office. Roosevelt found him so unacceptably conservative that both men competed for the Republican nomination in 1912. When Roosevelt won the primaries but lost the nomination to Taft, he ran for president as a "Bull Moose" Progressive. This split the Republican vote and allowed Woodrow Wilson, the Democrat, to win •

---

budget cycle The timed steps of the budget process, which includes preparation, approval, execution, and audit.

Taft Commission The 1912 Commission on Economy and Efficiency, chaired by the president, which called for a national budgetary system. Its recommendations were incorporated into the Budget and Accounting Act of 1921.

and executive cooperation; and (3) how budgets would ensure administrative and management efficiency. Rather prophetic when you consider the topics of some of our everyday headlines: taxpayers' revolts, "Proposition 13" movements, and other forms of expenditure and revenue limitation laws (thread 1: popular control); continued infighting between the executive and legislative branches over budgetary control, deficits, and balanced budgets (thread 2: executive-legislative cooperation); and the effectiveness or lack of it in overburdened budgeting systems in maintaining managerial practices (thread 3: management effectiveness). Finally, in 1921, the Budget and Accounting Act was passed, bringing into being the Bureau of the Budget and the General Accounting Office (GAO), responsible for budgeting and audit respectively. (See Chapter 13 for further details on the GAO.)

At first, budgetary and compliance procedures remained simple, with budgets constructed of "line items" allocating funds to particular expenditure categories in each department—so much for salaries, furniture, paper, and so on. The process of audit was correspondingly simple, emphasizing the examination of the extent to which expenditure had been in compliance with the purposes for which funds were allocated.

The 1930s saw the advent of increasingly larger government domestic programs and concomitant expenditures. Consequently, budgeting became of increasing importance. However, budgetary theory—that is, how to rationally allocate government resources—was woefully inadequate. The emphasis was on process and line-item budgeting, which stressed accountability and control. Performance budgeting (allocating funds for sets of activities), which stressed work measurement, much as scientific management, was increasingly advanced and used as an appropriate management-oriented budgetary process. Nevertheless, there remained little integration of the budgetary process with rational policymaking and decision making. In 1940, **V. O. Key Jr.** wrote an article bemoaning the lack of a budgetary theory. Greatly concerned about the overemphasis on mechanics, he posed what was soon acknowledged as the central question of budgeting: "On what basis shall it be decided to allocate X dollars to activity A instead of activity B?" Key then went on to elaborate on what he felt were the major areas of inquiry that should be researched to develop a budgeting theory. This, along with continuing pressure for even greater increases in the size of government programs, would set the stage for the major advances to come—but they would not be coming until after World War II.

The Influence of Keynes

The British economist **John Maynard Keynes** showed how government spending could be critical in managing an economy, by stimulating demand when resources were underutilized and unemployment was high. His thinking created the notion of budgetary policy as an instrument—in some respects the primary instrument—by

---

V. O. Key Jr. (1908–1963) The political scientist who did pioneering work in developing empirical methods to explore political and administrative behavior.

John Maynard Keynes (1883–1946) The English economist who wrote the most influential book on economics of this century, *The General Theory of Employment, Interest, and Money* (1936). Keynes founded a school of thought known as Keynesian economics, which called for using a government's fiscal and monetary policies to positively influence a capitalistic economy; he also developed the framework of modern macroeconomic theory.

John Maynard Keynes. This was not a modest man. While working on his masterwork (*The General Theory*) in 1935, he wrote to fellow immodest man, playwright George Bernard Shaw: "To understand the state of my mind . . . you have to know that I believe myself to be writing a book on economic theory, which will largely revolutionize—not, I suppose, at once but in the course of the next ten years—the way the world thinks about economic problems." Like Babe Ruth pointing to the far bleachers where he was about to hit a home run, Keynes was right on target •

which a nation could execute **macroeconomic** policy. All U.S. presidents since Franklin D. Roosevelt have used Keynes's theories to, admittedly or unadmittedly, justify deficit spending to stimulate the economy. Even President Richard M. Nixon admitted, "We're all Keynesians now." Keynes observed in his *General Theory* that "practical men, who believe themselves to be quite exempt from any intellectual influences, are usually the slaves of some defunct economist." He even provided the definitive economic forecast when he asserted that "in the long run we are all dead."

Aaron Wildavsky, in successive editions of *The Politics of the Budgetary Process*, highlighted the extent to which budgeting was a political and economic rather than a mechanical process. Later James M. Buchanan and Gordon Tullock of the "public choice" school presented government budgeting as a battle among beneficiaries seeking to capture funds to their own ends. Instead of a lack of budgetary theory, as in 1940, we are now abundantly served with it.

---

macroeconomics The study of the relationships among broad economic trends such as national income, consumer savings and expenditures, capital investment, employment, money supply, prices, government expenditures, and balance of payments. Macroeconomics is especially concerned with government's role in affecting these trends.

Aaron Wildavsky (1930–1993) The author of *The Politics of the Budgetary Process* (1964; 4th ed., 1984), which reveals the tactics public managers use to get their budgets passed and explains why rational attempts to reform the budgetary process have always failed. For this classic work alone, Wildavsky would have earned his place in the pantheon of public administration. However, Wildavsky has also made landmark contributions to the study of the U.S. presidency, policy analysis, and program implementation and evaluation. Because of the volume, quality, and diversity of his work, Wildavsky was one of the nation's most widely read and influential academic analysts of public affairs.

The Objectives of Budgeting

The analysis of economists Richard and Peggy Musgrave in *Public Finance in Theory and Practice* provides a key to the understanding of the objectives of public financial management. They postulate that government revenue raising and spending serve one of the following four objectives:

1. *Allocation:* Ensuring that an appropriate level of funding flows into sectors of the economy where it is required
2. *Distribution:* Ensuring that the balance in public funding between regions, between classes of people in society, between public and private sectors, and between government and business reflects public policy
3. *Stabilization:* Using public spending to stabilize the macroeconomy (or in some cases parts of it) as prescribed by Keynes
4. *Growth:* Using the power of government spending to facilitate economic growth and wealth-creation

When we look at the budget of the national government—or of a state or local government—we can use this perspective for analysis. Is this a budget aimed at supporting growth in the economy? If so, what are its strategies—perhaps a lower tax on business and less government regulation? Is this a budget aimed at distributional objectives? Perhaps it seeks to assist cities and the long-term unemployed? Or it may be designed to stabilize the economic cycle—to stimulate demand during a slump or to moderate it in a boom. There is often disagreement over just how to achieve stated goals. Those who espouse supply-side economics believe that lowering tax rates, especially on marginal income, encourages fresh capital to flow into the economy, which in turn generates jobs, growth, and new tax revenue. Because this concept was adopted by the Reagan administration, it has been popularly called Reaganomics, even though Reagan's actual economic policies were a melange of supply-side thinking, monetarism, old-fashioned conservatism, and even Keynesianism. While economist Arthur Laffer is generally credited with having "discovered" supply-side economics, the underlying premises of it were established almost 200 years ago by Alexander Hamilton in *The Federalist*, No. 21. Hamilton presented this argument:

> It is a signal advantage of taxes . . . that they . . . prescribe their own limit; which cannot be exceeded without defeating the end proposed,—that is, an extension of the revenue. When applied to this object, the saying is as just as it is witty, that, "in political arithmetic, two and two do not always make four." If duties are too high, they lessen the consumption; the collection is eluded; and the product to the treasury is not so great as when they are confined within proper and moderate bounds.

Of course, one person's supply-side economics may be another's **voodoo economics**. Politicians are not always crystal clear in articulating what values and

---

voodoo economics Presidential candidate George Bush's 1980 description of Republican primary opposition candidate Ronald Reagan's economic policy proposals. After joining Reagan as the vice presidential nominee on the 1980 (and the 1984) ticket, Bush thought he had better not say it any more. And he didn't. But the press never let him forget it. When in 1982 he denied ever having said it: "I didn't say it. I challenge anyone to find it," NBC News then showed a videotape of him using the phrase, *Newsweek*, (May 23, 1988). Since then he hasn't denied saying it.

objectives underlie their budgetary strategies. Sometimes when these objectives have crass political motives—tax loopholes for campaign contributors—it is not polite or honorable to publicly admit them. Often, because budgets have grown so enormously complicated and detailed, those who are responsible for them literally do not fully understand the import of what they are doing—budgetarily speaking. Remember that it was David A. Stockman, Reagan's director of the Office of Management and Budget from 1981 to 1985 who, in 1981, confessed to readers of the *Atlantic Monthly* that "None of us really understands what's going on with all these numbers."

The Two Types of Budgets

There are two basic kinds of budgets. The most common, and what most people think of when the word budget comes to mind, is the operating budget. This is a short-term plan for managing the resources necessary to carry out a program. "Short, term" can mean anything from a few weeks to a few years. Usually an operating budget is developed for each fiscal year, with changes made as necessary.

The second kind is the capital budget process that deals with planning for large expenditures for capital items. Capital expenditures should be for long-term investments (such as bridges and buildings), which yield returns for years after they are completed. Capital budgets typically cover five- to ten-year periods and are updated yearly. Items included in capital budgets may be financed through borrowing (including tax-exempt municipal bonds), savings, grants, revenue sharing, special assessments, and so on. A capital budget provides for separating the financing of capital, or investment, expenditures from current, or operating, expenditures. The federal government has never had a capital budget in the sense of financing capital programs separately from current expenditures.

Waves of Innovation in Budget Making

The structure and format of government budgets has been the subject of successive waves of innovation throughout the twentieth century. Why should this be so? Simply because the ultimate statement of what a government stands for and spends is to be found in its budget. The budget is the key focal point of public administration. It places huge power in the hands of those who shape it. To the executive, the bureaucrat, and the "budgeteers" it is of incessant interest because of its timeless potency.

The Executive Budget

The first conceptual breakthrough in budgeting was really the conception that there could be a government budget at all—that is, a single document bringing together in one place the revenue, expenditure, and financing plans of government. Until the twentieth century budgeting in **representative governments** was decidedly

---

representative government A governing system in which a legislature freely chosen by the people exercises substantial power on their behalf.

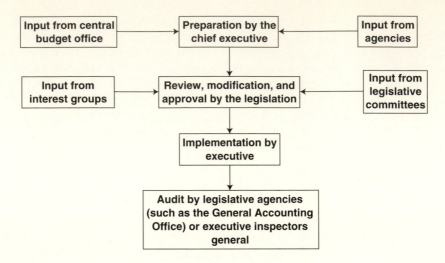

Figure 12.2 The Executive Budget Process

a legislative, not an executive, function. Congressional or state legislative **committees** would appropriate funds for an agency without regard for the other agencies of government. Without overall coordination there was considerable confusion and ample opportunity for both incompetence and corruption. The movement toward an executive (or comprehensive) budget in the United States began in the states and was adopted by the federal government with the Budget and Accounting Act of 1921. Today all state governments except South Carolina use some variation of the executive budget.

An executive budget is both a technical process and a physical thing. First it is the process by which agency requests for appropriations are prepared and submitted to a budget bureau under the chief executive for review, alteration, and consolidation into a single budget document that can be compared to expected revenues and executive priorities before submission to the legislature. Then it becomes a tangible document, the comprehensive budget document for an executive branch of government that a jurisdiction's chief executive submits to a legislature for review, modification, and enactment. The president's budget is the executive budget for a particular fiscal year transmitted to the Congress by the president in accordance with the Budget and Accounting Act of 1921, as amended. Some elements of the budget (such as the estimates for the legislative branch and the judiciary) are required to be included without review by the Office of Management and Budget or approval by the president. After all, the president has no say in the budgets of the other branches of government. It is just convenient to include the comparatively

---

committee A subdivision of a legislature that prepares legislation for action by the respective house or
  that makes investigations as directed by the respective house. Most standing (full) committees are
  divided into subcommittees, which study legislation, hold hearings, and report their recommendations to the full committee. Only the full committee can report legislation for action by the entire
  legislature.

small budgets of other branches in the overall document. The president's budget is the president's "wish list"—his suggestions to Congress. Every president's budget is "dead on arrival" the moment it is formally sent to the **Hill**, since Congress always makes extensive changes. The same considerations apply to state governors. Thus a governor's budget is an executive budget prepared by a state governor.

Be aware that not all of the national budget is open to public scrutiny. The "black budget" is the classified (secret) portion of the federal budget that hides sensitive military and covert projects. According to Tim Weiner in *Blank Check,* "The black budget is a challenge to the open government promised by the Constitution. Today close to a quarter of every dollar in the Pentagon's budget for new weapons is cloaked in blackness. . . . Every dollar spent in secret defies the Framers' intent that the balance sheet of government should be a public document."

Line-Item Budgeting

The line-item budget was the original budget format—each item of expense had a literal line in a ledger book. It classified budgetary accounts according to narrow, detailed objects of expenditure (such as motor vehicles, clerical workers, or reams of paper) used within each particular agency of government, generally without reference to the ultimate purpose or objective served by the expenditure. It was useful as a record of expenditures and the criteria against which audits could measure compliance.

The line-item budget is still widely used. Most local governments use it either as their basic budget format or as a supplement to more sophisticated formats. Because it offers such comprehensive details on proposed expenditures, legislators interested in fine-tuning executive budget recommendations are particularly partial to it because it allows for greater control and oversight.

While the traditional line-item budget was a great step forward, it had a major weakness. It might allow the test to be made as to whether funds had been spent on the purposes for which they had been appropriated, and that truly was (and is) an important test. But it gave no inkling as to how well these appropriations had been spent, whether they had resulted in "value for money."

Performance Budgeting

The concept of performance budgeting, first tried in New York City in the early 1900s, was the first major step beyond the line-item budget. Performance budgeting required a performance measure to be stated alongside each line item, so that elementary calculations of unit cost and efficiency could be made. Line items were grouped, or categorized, in functional terms. For example, a sanitation (trash collection) department's workload could be determined on the basis of the number of houses and businesses served, which made it relatively easy to calculate how much trash is generated each week, month, or year. Using this measure, the efficiency of

---

Hill The U.S. Congress, because it is literally situated on a hill; it is 88 feet above sea level; the White House is 55 feet above sea level. Now there can be no doubt about which is the higher branch of government.

collection could be compared to a base period and a base cost. At this elementary level, comparisons in relative efficiency could be made from year to year, and in concept, between governments (in practice, intergovernmental comparisons required standardized measurement, which usually did not exist).

Performance budgeting, which was in its prime after being officially sanctioned by the Hoover Commission of 1949 (see Chapter 3), stressed using the budget process as a tool for work measurement and efficiency analysis. The heyday of performance budgeting lasted from the 1950s through the 1960s, and even today in some local governments you can still find performance budgets. However, while line-item and performance budgets were helpful in addressing issues of control, compliance, and efficiency, they did not help in the planning dimension, in the identification of global resource allocation to purposes, or in the assessment of effectiveness (that is, the extent to which goals were attained).

Program Budgeting Versus Incrementalism

The next wave of budgetary reform followed hard on the heels of performance budgeting, and essentially met its deficiencies. In 1954, David Novick, an economist with the California-based **RAND Corporation**, proposed "program budgeting"—a form of budgeting that would permit global understanding of expenditure purposes, which consolidated spending into "programs," and which therefore laid foundations for a focus on effectiveness, since the total resources directed to any purpose should now be more readily apparent. Novick defined a program as "the sum of the steps or interdependent activities which enter into the attainment of a specified objective."

If a budget were to comprise large slabs of spending, called programs, directed toward particular objectives, the fragmentation problem common to line-item and performance budgeting would be overcome. Compliance could still be monitored, but the monitoring of efficiency and effectiveness would also be facilitated. And instead of being primarily an instrument of control and management information, the budget would become a planning document, and a document supporting the comparison of alternative expenditures at some meaningful level of aggregation. These were important conceptual breakthroughs.

The team that fashioned program budgeting at the RAND Corporation had an ambitious program, for they proposed not merely a rewrite of budget structure, but a new framework for the analysis of policy and the review of accomplishment. They proposed not just program budgeting but planning-programming-budgeting, a linked system that had elements of forward planning, what they termed "the ana-

---

RAND Corporation   A think tank created by the U.S. Air Force in 1947 and located in Santa Monica, California. The name is an acronym for research and development, and came from Project Rand in which Douglas Aircraft agreed to provide civilian advice to the Air Force about developing new bombers. Separated from Douglas in 1948, the RAND Corporation was located in Santa Monica partly on the grounds that it was better to have a think tank of this kind away from the political pressures of Washington. RAND was concerned with the application of scientific and social scientific methods to the problems of strategy and security in the nuclear age. It became the key institution in the development of civilian expertise on nuclear strategy and remains one of the most important think tanks on national and international security issues.

lytical comparison of alternatives," the allocation of resources in the framework of a multiyear cycle, and budgeting related to broad program groups rather than individual items. The "package" was named PPBS; it was intended "to create a new environment of choice." The document was now no longer about "where we are," but about "Where do we want to go?" It seemed that the theorists were at last making a contribution that had the potential to reshape government budgeting, planning, and resource allocation in a fundamental way.

Budgeting during the 1960s was dominated by PPBS—the planning, programming, budgeting system. First installed in the Defense Department during the Kennedy administration, it seemed to represent the height of rationality for the budget process. According to Schick, the stages of budget reform went from the development of budgetary theory, with its concerns for accountability and control, which were the hallmark of the line-item budget, to performance budgeting, with its emphasis on managerial efficiency, to PPBS, which stressed objectives, planning, and program effectiveness.

In 1965 Lyndon Johnson mandated the use of PPBS for all federal agencies. The application of PPBS, which required among other things that agencies detail program objectives and indicators for evaluation, make five-year expenditure forecasts, and generate numerous special cost-benefit analyses and zero-based reviews of program activities, marked perhaps the zenith of the management systems approach to public administration. Implemented hastily, with insufficient time for understanding, training, and development, the across-the-board implementation of PPBS failed quickly, leaving a platform for cynics and incrementalists to lambaste national initiatives and planning indiscriminately for many years.

PPBS was never without its critics. In 1964, Aaron M. Wildavsky published *The Politics of the Budgetary Process*, his immensely well-received critique of how budgeting was, in reality, an incremental process sharply influenced by political considerations. Incremental budgeting is a method of budget review that focuses on the increments of increase or decrease in the budget of existing programs. Incremental budgeting, which is often called traditional budgeting, is a counter-school of thought to more rational, systems-oriented approaches, such as PPBS or zero-based budgeting. But this old approach nicely takes into account the inherently political nature of the budget process and so will continue to be favored by legislative appropriations committees, if not by budget theorists. As Wildavsky wrote, "The largest determining factor of the size and content of this year's budget is last year's budget." And this is still overwhelmingly true, despite the reinventing government movement and the devolution revolution of the 1990s.

In 1969 Wildavsky wrote a devastating critique of PPBS. Aside from stating flatly that he thought PPBS was unworkable, Wildavsky demonstrated how the planning and analytical functions of PPBS were contradictory to the essential nature of budgeting.

What was once mandatory for all federal agencies and widely adopted by state and local jurisdictions, by the end of the decade was officially "un"-adopted by the federal government and was widely considered to be unusable in its original format. Nevertheless, the influence of PPBS as a major budgeting process remains. Where it is still in use, however, it tends to exist in a hybrid instead of a pure form.

BOX 12.1

No One Can Do PPBS

In a better world, without the vulgar intrusion of political factors (such as the consent of the governed), PPBS would perform its wonders as advertised. Now it is clear that for the narrow purpose of predicting why program budgeting would not work there was no need to mention political problems at all. It would have been sufficient to say that the wholesale introduction of PPBS presented insuperable difficulties of calculation. All the obstacles previously mentioned, such as lack of talent, theory, and data, may be summed up in a single statement: no one knows how to do program budgeting. Another way of putting it would be to say that many know what program budgeting should be like in general, but no one knows what it should be in any particular case. Program budgeting cannot be stated in operational terms. There is no agreement on what the words mean, let alone an ability to show another person what should be done. The reason for the difficulty is that telling an agency to adopt program budgeting means telling it to find better policies and there is no formula for doing that.

SOURCE: Aaron Wildavsky, "Rescuing Policy Analysis from PPBS," *Public Administration Review* (March-April 1969).

Wildavsky, who would later form and be the first dean of the University of California at Berkeley's Graduate School of Public Policy, was greatly influenced by Charles Lindblom, under whom he studied while a doctoral student at Yale. Incremental approaches to budgeting, or what would later be called "traditional budgeting," was the counter-school of thought to the management systems emphasis. The principal contention of the incrementalists (such as Wildavsky and Lindblom) was that budgets are inherently political, and that studying budgeting and budgets is useful because it explains how and what choices (political compromises) have been made. Wildavsky even rebutted V. O. Key's classic question, "On what basis shall it be decided to allocate X dollars to activity A instead of activity B?" as unanswerable and irrelevant. What mattered was that the process of budgeting should facilitate decision making and assist in obtaining consensus about policy goals and program objectives.

TABLE 12.2   The Core Concepts of Public Budgeting

Budget Type	Essential Purpose	Information Displayed	Primary Value
Line-item	Control	Inputs	Legality
Performance	Management	Agency outputs	Efficiency
Program	Planning	Agency missions	Program balance

SOURCE: Adapted from Gerald Garvey, *Public Administration* (New York: St. Martin's Press, 1997).

Zero-Based Budgeting

In 1952 **Verne B. Lewis** continued the quest for the development of a theory of budgeting that Key had sought a dozen years earlier. In his "Toward a Theory of Budgeting," Lewis presented a theory of alternative budgeting. His analysis marked an important link to the PPBS systems of the 1960s and, especially, to the zero-based budgeting systems of the 1970s.

Lewis advocated budget submissions prepared in a manner that would facilitate comparison and demonstrate a range of choices for service and funding levels, and at the same time, have the final choice provide realistic contracts—that is, specific, realistic expectations for the individual program managers. The implied rationale for this process almost seems a restating of Key's classic budgeting equation: for X level of funding, Y level of service can be provided; for $X+1$ funding, $Y+Z$ services, etc.

Alternative budgeting, Lewis's preferred solution, was a means to overcome traditional budgetary review techniques that focus on item-by-item control rather than on scaling levels of program services and goals to varying levels of funding. Lewis, a realist, saw clearly the influence of other factors such as "pride and prejudice, provincialism, and politics" in budgetary decisions. His hope was for the advent of budgeting systems that could overcome these noneconomic and nonrational factors.

The next stage of budget reform after PPBS, zero-based budgeting (ZBB), would fully incorporate Lewis's concept of alternative budgeting. Management consultant Peter A. Phyrr first developed it for Texas Instruments and then for the state of Georgia while Jimmy Carter was governor. In 1976, presidential candidate Carter made the installation of zero-based budgeting a campaign promise, and in 1977, as president, he ordered its adoption by the federal government. The initial reaction to ZBB paralleled the reaction to PPBS in the 1960s, only the downfall of ZBB was even more rapid.

Zero-based budgeting is a budgeting process that is, first and foremost, a rejection of the incremental decision-making model of budgeting. It demands a rejustification of the entire budget submission (from ground zero), whereas incremental budgeting essentially respects the outcomes of previous budgetary decisions (collectively referred to as the budget base) and focuses examination on the margin of change from year to year. So, under ZBB, an agency would have to rank each of its programs according to importance and face the possibility of the least important ones being discontinued.

In large part, ZBB failed because the conditions that had prevailed for most of the previous budgeting systems reforms had changed. In an era of acute resource scarcity, ZBB had little utility because there was little real chance that funding could be provided for any program growth. Critics assaulted ZBB as a fraud; some called it a nonsystem of budgeting. ZBB's fate in the federal government was tied to the Carter presidency. After the inauguration of a new president (Reagan) in 1981, it was quietly rescinded. Still, numerous state and local governments use ZBB techniques or some adaptation of ZBB. Now that the hype has subsided, ZBB remains an important part of public budgeting.

Verne B. Lewis (1913–) A federal budget officer. After retiring from the U.S. Department of Agriculture, he taught public administration at the University of Washington.

BOX 12.2

Visualizing the Budget in the Reagan Administration

[Secretary of Defense Caspar W. Weinberger's] briefing was a masterpiece of ob-fuscation. Incredibly, Weinberger had also brought with him a blown-up cartoon. It showed three soldiers. One was a pygmy who carried no rifle. He represented the Carter budget. The second was a four-eye wimp who looked like Woody Allen, carrying a tiny rifle. That was—me?—the OMB defense budget. Finally, there was G.I. Joe himself, 190 pounds of fighting man, all decked out in helmet and flak jacket and pointing an M-60 machine gun menacingly at—me again? This imposing warrior represented, yes, the Department of Defense budget plan.

It was so intellectually disreputable, so demeaning, that I could hardly bring myself to believe that a Harvard-educated cabinet officer could have brought this to the president of the United States. Did he think the White House was on *Sesame Street*?

SOURCE: David A. Stockman, *The Triumph of Politics* (New York: Harper & Row, 1986).

Contemporary Budget Reform

It is useful to consider three important contemporary budget questions because they remain unanswered and are likely to be so far into the future. Should an integrated national budget and financial statement be created? Can multiyear budgetary cycles be effectively controlled through shorter-term political processes? And, finally, can a budget process with a greater policy focus be created?

Integrated Budgets

The concept of an integrated national budget and financial statement is an important one. No corporation would expect its shareholders to be content with less than an integrated **balance sheet** and operating statement. Yet the rule in government has too often been that the balance sheet is missing and the **operating statement** incomplete. The completion of the operating statement, after all, was the reason why the budget concept itself was originally created—to present a single document integrating at one view what was to be raised and spent. In 1967, the President's Commission on Budget Concepts reaffirmed the need for just such a unified budget, and such a budget was adopted in 1969.

---

balance sheet A summary of the financial worth of an individual or organization broken down by assets (what is owned) and liabilities (what is owed). It is called a balance sheet because total assets balance with, or are equal to, total liabilities plus net worth.

operating statement The detailed financial information that supplements a balance sheet.

A unified budget is one in which receipts and outlays from federal funds and trust funds (such as Social Security) are consolidated. When these two fund groups are consolidated to display budget totals, transactions from one fund group to another (interfund transactions) are deducted to avoid double counting. The fiscal activities of **off-budget federal agencies** are not included in the unified budget. And this is precisely the problem. Because billions and billions of dollars of "off-budget" spending exists outside the unified budget, the budget is not all that "unified" after all. Some expenditures of this type were created to avoid political scrutiny of the costs of new programs, some represent the "black" expenditures of the intelligence community, and some are represented by the budgets of public enterprises whose financial affairs can be excluded from the unified budget if that will help the administration (as it usually does) to understate the total size of government spending. The goal of transparency in public financial administration is a strong argument for reform in this area, with the ultimate goal being an annual consolidated financial statement—both balance sheet and operating statements—which is unified, inclusive, and prepared on independently validated standards as to accounting, estimating, and valuation. Only then can we claim to have a mature budgetary document in line with community expectations and private sector norms.

In principle, the objective of a unified budget is important and should be observed: It is that all revenues and expenditures by government for the budgetary period should be brought into a single document and framework. Only in this manner can democratic control be exerted on a fully informed basis, whereby elected representatives can compare the costs and revenues that make up government activity, and make judgments about alternatives. On the other hand, conflicting principles do apply. Details of secret intelligence operations overseas can hardly be debated during the budget session, lest the lives of operators be put at risk. The commercial latitude critical to public enterprise performance may be jeopardized if excessive detail of public enterprise budget issues is placed in the unified budget, rather than in the separate annual financial and performance reports of the enterprise.

We must be skeptical and suspicious whenever a government seeks to conceal an area of government activity from normal channels of democratic scrutiny; sometimes the reasons for seeking to place a particular category of spending "off budget" may be at odds with the public's right to know. Just because an expenditure item is off-budget, it need not mean that all democratic scrutiny must be forgone. There are several courses that can be taken to provide alternative channels. Security-related issues could be vetted by a special congressional committee. Public enterprise or joint venture results could be covered by separate reports, or covered in supporting appendixes to the main budget documents. All of these options are in use; the key requirements are that no significant area of public spending should evade democratic scrutiny altogether, and that we should be able to rely on the unified budget to furnish the most comprehensive and feasible composite picture of public revenue getting and spending.

---

off-budget federal agencies Agencies, federally owned in whole or in part, whose transactions have been excluded from the budget totals under provisions of law (e.g., the Federal Financing Bank). The fiscal activities of these agencies are presented in an appendix to the federal budget.

Multiyear Budgets

A second long-standing but essentially unresolved issue in budgeting concerns the need of some program areas for multiyear funding—for financing that extends over a number of years. Just as business demands certainty from government as to the rules of the game, so does effective public administration in many areas, from major infrastructure investment to strategic research. Effectively, the federal government uses a multiyear budget for a wide variety of programs, such as transfer payments to the states based on statutory formulas, **entitlement programs**, multiyear **appropriations** for construction projects, and, of course, long-term borrowing authority. Yet, our legislators might argue, if they do not have the opportunity annually to apportion public funds, how can they take an integrated view, and place funds where today's priorities lie?

A strong case can be made for a biennial or triennial budget cycle. The advantages of such a horizon would include a better matching of known funding with the needs of longer-term projects and allocations; an ability for government and business alike to plan with certainty over several years; and the containment of the necessary political wrangling over budget making so that the crescendo of horse trading would occur less frequently. This would thus allow politicians, lobbyists, and bureaucrats more time to do other things—to consider longer-term policies, to engage in in-depth scrutiny of the implementation of programs, and perhaps to concentrate on cooperative rather than adversarial aspects of their responsibilities. But the break with tradition would be severe and the need for new systems significant; the problem of aligning budgetary and electoral timetables would also need to be addressed, and an effective process for midterm revision—whether in the form of the capability to introduce a "minibudget" or one-off revisions—would need to be worked out.

These are complex but not unsolvable problems. And there is ample precedent. Indeed, until relatively recent times biennial budgets were the norm in state government because so many state government legislatures regularly meet only every other year. Indeed, in 1940 only four states (New Jersey, New York, Rhode Island, and South Carolina) even had annual sessions. Some, such as Arkansas, Maine, Montana, Nevada, New Hampshire, North Dakota, and Vermont, still retain biannual budget sessions. But many states with annual sessions have adopted the biennial budget even when they have annual sessions. Vice President Al Gore wrote in the

---

entitlement program Any government program that pays benefits to individuals, organizations, or other governments that meet eligibility requirements set by law. Social Security is the largest federal entitlement program for individuals. Others include farm price supports, Medicare, Medicaid, unemployment insurance, and food stamps. Entitlement programs have great budgetary significance, in that they lock in such a great percentage of the total federal budget each year that changes in the budget can be made only at the margin.

appropriation An act of the U.S. Congress that permits federal agencies to incur obligations and to make payments out of the Treasury for specified purposes. An appropriation usually follows the enactment of authorizing legislation and is the most common form of budget authority, but in some cases the authorizing legislation also provides the budget authority. Appropriations are categorized in a variety of ways, such as by their period of availability (one-year, multiple-year, no-year), the time of congressional action (current, permanent), and the manner of determining the amount of the appropriation (definite, indefinite).

National Performance Review that the federal government "should not have to enact a budget every year. Twenty states adopt budgets for two years. They retain the power to make small adjustments in off years if revenues or expenditures deviate widely from forecasts. As a result, their governors and legislatures have much more time to evaluate programs and develop longer-term plans." While this is a strong argument for reform, it is opposed by all those members of Congress unwilling to concede any additional power to the executive branch—especially if that branch is controlled by someone of another political party.

Financing Public Expenditure

There are three basic elements to public financial management: (1) taxing, (2) spending, and (3) saving. Yes, unlike the federal government, many state and local jurisdictions do not spend all their funds each year. Contingency and "rainy day" accounts are common at the subnational levels. Still, taxing and spending are the essential elements of public finance. And it is a pointless chicken-egg argument as to which comes first. But they eventually have to be reconciled—sort of. Spending must always equal taxing plus borrowing. Because tax revenues tend to be **elastic**, one can only estimate yearly revenues. A booming economy will bring in a surfeit of taxes; a sluggish economy will bring in less revenue than before. This is why budget makers so often paint a rosy scenario—an all-too-optimistic estimate of economic growth and interest-rate levels made by budgeteers so that the estimated deficit will seem less than realistic estimates would suggest. But beware the rosy scenario! If you are a budget maker, it will strain your credibility. If you are a consumer of budgets, it will set you up for a fall. Whether scenarios are rosy, neutral, or harsh, the fact remains that budget making involves the task of matching revenues and expenditures so that government can function in the coming year.

Governments have six principal means of financing their spending requirements. This is something of an advance from biblical times, when revenue from tax collectors and forced seizure of property were the main available strategies. Today, governments must choose from the following:

1. Imposition of a **direct tax**
2. Imposition of an **indirect tax**
3. Collection of revenue by imposing user charges for government customers
4. Obtaining grants from another level of government or an aid agency
5. Making profits from the activities of public enterprises

---

elastic The up-and-down nature of tax revenues; they will increase or decrease depending on overall economic conditions.

direct tax A tax (e.g., an income tax) paid to a government directly by a taxpayer. Article I, Section 9, of the U.S. Constitution holds that "no capitation, or other direct tax shall be laid, unless in proportion to the census or enumeration herein before directed to be taken." This inhibited the enactment of the federal income tax until the Sixteenth Amendment of 1913 changed the Constitution to allow for direct taxation.

indirect tax A tax (e.g., a sales tax) paid to a third party, who in turn pays it to a government.

TABLE 12.3 Landmarks in Federal Budget Practices

1921	The Budget and Accounting Act establishes a Bureau of the Budget in the Department of the Treasury and the General Accounting Office as an audit agency of the Congress.
1939	The Reorganization Act transfers the Bureau of the Budget from the Treasury to the White House.
1950	The Budgeting and Accounting Procedures Act mandates the performance budgeting concepts called for by the Hoover Commission.
1961	The Department of Defense installs a planning programming budgeting system (PPBS).
1965	A PPBS is made mandatory for all federal agencies by the Johnson administration.
1970	The Bureau of the Budget is given more responsibility for managerial oversight and re-named the Office of Management and Budget.
1971	PPBS is formally abandoned in the federal government by the Nixon administration.
1974	Congressional Budget and impoundment Control Act revises the congressional budget process and timetable and creates the Congressional Budget Office.
1977	Zero-based budgeting is required of all federal agencies by the Carter administration.
1981	Zero-based budgeting requirements are rescinded by the Reagan administration. David Stockman, director of the Office of Management and Budget, tells the *Atlantic Monthly* that "none of us really understands what's going on with all these numbers."
1985	The Gramm-Rudman-Hollings Act is signed into law; it seeks to balance the federal budget by mandating across-the-board cuts over a period of years.
1986	The Supreme Court in *Bowsher v. Synar* invalidates certain provisions of the Gramm-Rudman-Hollings Act.
1990	The Budget Enforcement Act amended the Gramm-Rudman-Hollings Act to require that new spending be balanced by new taxes or spending reductions.
	The Credit Reform Act (in response to the savings and loan scandal) tightens require-ments on federal lending and loan guarantees.
	The Chief Financial Officers Act requires federal agencies to create a chief financial officer position to oversee agency finances.
1993	The Government Performance Results Act requires agencies to justify their budget requests on the basis of the results or outcomes to be achieved.
1997	Agencies are required to submit strategic plans, including mission statements and performance goals.
1998	A Government-Wide Performance Plan was first presented with the federal budget.
2000	Agencies must now advise Congress as to how well they met the performance objectives and goals set out in their strategic plans.

6. Borrowing from the public through bonds, or from private lenders through loans

7. Using innovative finance techniques, **public-private partnerships**, franchises, or the licensing of private sector providers

8. Earnings from savings or investments, if any

public-private partnerships Joint efforts on the part of local governments and the business community to plan for, generate public support for, and pay for major social programs or construction projects that will be mutually beneficial.

Each of these methods of raising government revenue involves complex issues of policy, such as incidence (on what group the tax will fall); effectiveness (whether the tax will succeed in yielding the revenue it should); equity (whether it is fair); and administrative ease and cost. If these financing options are still insufficient, governments may turn to privatization, cost cutting, or the termination of programs to reduce the scope of what must be financed.

Taxation

General taxation (or a general property tax in the context of local government) is the most traditional means of financing public services. A tax is a compulsory contribution exacted by a government for public purposes. This does not include employee and employer assessments for retirement and social insurance purposes, which are classified as insurance trust revenue.

Taxes are generally perceived by a public to be legitimate if they are levied by that public's elected representatives. Indeed, one of the causes of, and principal rallying cries for, the American Revolution was that there should be "no taxation without representation" because "taxation without representation is tyranny." Consequently, practically all taxes at all levels of government are now enacted by popularly elected legislatures.

People have been making poignant remarks about taxes since ancient times. For example, the first-century Roman historian Suetonius reported on a complaint presented to the Emperor Vespasian about taxes on the public toilets (in effect, user fees) in Rome. The emperor took a coin that came from this tax, stuck it in the complainer's nose and asked, "Does it smell?" Hardly even waiting for the answer of "no," he continued: "yet it comes from urine." Since then, nothing has been in such bad odor that it could escape taxation. Sometimes tax reform is not as much reform as the addition of new kinds of taxes. New things to tax come about by the inventiveness of fiscal experts or by new technology. A vivid example is presented by James Kendall in his biography of Michael Faraday, one of the pioneers in the development of electricity. When Faraday was first explaining his invention to the British chancellor of the exchequer, he was interrupted with "the impatient inquiry: 'But, after all, what use is it?' Like a flash of lightning came the response: 'Why, sir, there is every probability that you will soon be able to tax it!'" Whether urine or electricity, it is all part of the cosmic, all-encompassing governmental revenue stream.

Taxes are one of the most volatile of political issues. Walter Mondale, in accepting the Democratic party's presidential nomination in 1984, said, "Taxes will go up. And anyone who says they won't is not telling the truth." He lost by a landslide. George Bush in accepting the Republican party's presidential nomination in 1988 said, "Read my lips, no new taxes." He won by a landslide. There is a lesson in this. But Bush's lips did not read true. He raised taxes and this was very much held against him when he futilely sought reelection in 1992.

There are major differences between the federal and state-local revenue systems. The federal system has experienced a trend toward less diversity; over two-thirds of its general revenue is provided by the federal income tax and the several insurance trust funds (such as Social Security). State and local revenue systems, in contrast, depend on a greater variety of revenue sources (such as property taxes, income taxes, sales taxes, user charges, lotteries, and federal grants). While local governments still rely primarily on the property tax, their states—with a few exceptions—rely largely on the state personal income tax. In addition, state sales and business taxes provide a significant source of income. This melange of taxing authorities creates great disparities in the state-local tax burden. A resident of New York may pay hundreds or thousands of dollars in state income taxes, while a resident of Texas—which has no state income tax—pays none. Virginians have to pay more than double the sales taxes paid by Vermonters. There are even greater variations in property taxes. A house in one jurisdiction may be assessed at three times the amount of an identical house in another.

The Ability-to-Pay Principle

Historically the art of taxation has been defined as "So plucking the goose as to obtain the largest amount of feathers with the least possible amount of hissing." While this definition is usually attributed to **Jean-Baptiste Colbert,** efforts to reduce the "hiss" have continued unabated. Two of the classic means of doing this are using the "ability-to-pay" principle or "hiding" the taxes.

The ability-to-pay is the principle of taxation that holds that the tax burden should be distributed according to a person's wealth. It is based on the assumption that, as a person's income increases, the person (whether an individual or a corporation) can and should contribute a larger percentage of income to support government activities. The progressive income tax is based on the ability-to-pay principle.

The personal income tax is based on ability-to-pay, in that the tax rate is applied against income. But income is more than just money; it is any asset that increases one's net worth; and yet income taxes are not necessarily a straight tax on all of one's income in a given year. Remember all those millionaires that the press annually discovers who do not pay any tax on their income? They are able to do this because it is not their total incomes that are subject to taxation, but their adjusted gross incomes. All taxpayers have the right to exclude certain kinds of incomes from their gross incomes for tax purposes. For example, interest from state and local bonds is exempt from federal taxation. Thus, a millionaire whose sole income came from investments in such bonds would pay no federal income tax. (To ensure that such citizens pay at least something, there is now an "alternative minimal tax"—but emphasis is on the minimal.) The taxpayer may also subtract deductions and exemptions from taxable income. Then the taxpayer can deduct a host of expenses, as long as they are allowed by the tax laws: medical care, state and local taxes (if a federal return), home mortgage interest, and charitable contributions. A taxpayer can itemize deductions or take a minimum standard deduction, which is a precalculated weighted average. Progressive tax rates are then applied to the taxable income to determine how much tax is due.

All states but Alaska, Florida, Nevada, South Dakota, Texas, Washington, and Wyoming have personal income taxes, as do many cities. Thus residents of Baltimore, Cleveland, Detroit, New York, and Philadelphia, for example, must pay per-

---

Jean-Baptiste Colbert (1619–1683) King Louis XIV's controller general of finance.

TABLE 12.4 Comparative Tax Rates

Country	Percentage
Denmark	51.6
Sweden	51.0
Finland	47.3
Belgium	46.6
Netherlands	45.9
France	44.1
Austria	42.8
Greece	42.5
Italy	41.7
Norway	41.2
Germany	39.3
Canada	36.1
Spain	35.8
United Kingdom	34.1
Switzerland	33.9
Australia	29.9
Japan	27.8
United States	27.6

SOURCE: Statistical Abstract of the United States (Washington DC: Government Printing Office, 1997).

NOTE: Data represent tax revenues as percentage of gross domestic product. Notice that the United States has one of the lowest overall tax rates in the industrialized world.

sonal income taxes to three different governments: federal, state, and local. With so many taxes at so many levels of government, it is no wonder that **tax avoidance** has become a national pastime rivaling even baseball. The very wealthy J. Pierpont Morgan (1836–1913) provided the intellectual foundation of tax avoidance when he said, "No citizen has a moral obligation to assist in maintaining the government. If Congress insists on making stupid mistakes and passing foolish tax laws, millionaires should not be condemned if they take advantage of them." The Tax Reform Act of 1986, designed to make tax avoidance more difficult by closing many **tax loopholes,** was with good reason informally, cynically, and accurately referred to as the "Tax Accountant's Full Employment Act."

tax avoidance Planning one's personal finances to take advantage of all legal tax breaks, such as deductions and tax shelters.

tax loophole An inconsistency in the tax laws, intentional or unintentional, that allows the avoidance of some taxes. An intentional tax loophole is a tax expenditure. A tax expenditure for one person is often viewed as a loophole by another. Tax loopholes are perfectly legal; but they have an unsavory reputation as the handiwork of special interest lobbyists.

The Flat Tax

An income tax that is flat has no brackets; it charges the same rate to each taxpayer. The concept has been put forward in a variety of proposals for reform of the federal income tax. This has long been advocated by prominent Republicans in the Congress such as Jack Kemp, of New York in the 1980s and Richard Armey of Texas in the 1990s. It even became a major issue in the 1996 presidential race when millionaire publisher Steve Forbes based his campaign for the Republican presidential nomination on it.

The flat tax is attractive in large measure because it is so simple and seemingly fair. Everybody just pays the same percentage of their income. Tax returns could be completed on a postcard. Nevertheless, Democratic party members tend to oppose it because it grossly violates the ability-to-pay principle. A flat tax is inherently regressive in that the poor pay proportionately more than the rich. When the idea became a major issue in the 1996 Republican primary elections, the accounting firm of Price Waterhouse did an analysis reported in *U.S. News & World Report*. They found that a couple with two children and an income of $60,000 would pay 2 percent more if there was a 21 percent flat tax instead of the current system. However, if that same family earned $300,000, they would have an effective tax cut of 31 percent.

Many forces in the economy are natural enemies of a true flat tax. Charitable and religious organizations do not want to lose the deductions that encourage contributions to them. The housing industry is concerned that the loss of the home mortgage interest deduction would depress housing prices. Corporations worry that the elimination of tax deductions for new equipment purchases would hurt profits. And public financial analysts express concern that a flat tax at the oft mentioned rate of 17 percent could not raise enough revenue to run the government.

User Charges

User charges are specific fees that users or consumers of a government service pay to receive that service. For example, a homeowner's water bill, if based upon usage, would be a user charge. Other examples include toll roads and bridges and charges to use public swimming pools. If a sports team plays on a publicly owned field that has been fenced in, gate takings should be the basic source of finance for that operation. Public transportation is a little different. There, some of the costs need to be recovered from riders. But since the existence of public transportation saves government the need to build new freeways, and since the limitation on the resulting number of commuter automobiles lessens air pollution, public transportation also offers obvious advantages. Accordingly, it is customary and proper for publicly owned transportation systems to be financed partly from user charges and partly from taxation. Freeways, because gasoline taxes are used to pay for them, are financed in this manner. Freeways provide some obvious public goods, such as mobility for the car-owning public and a capability for business to truck its products around. But on the other hand, particular freeways do benefit selectively the commuters that are able to access them. These commuters, some argue, should incur a user charge—that is, they should pay a toll—but this is not always politically possible.

While user charges are voluntary in theory, in practice they are often unavoidable. Few citizens consider municipal water and sewer connections among life's little options. Being essential, the charges are in actuality taxes that dare not use their name. Many user charges are more easily avoided. For example, if you do not attend a state university, you do not have to pay their fees—except for your portion of the overall subsidy such institutions receive through general taxation. If you do not hunt or fish, you need not buy a state license to do so. And if you do not build an extension to your house, you need not pay for a local building permit.

User charges are often treated as **earmarked tax** revenue in that the funds they produce may only be used for legislatively determined purposes. Thus charges for hunting and fishing licenses are often earmarked for wildlife conservation programs.

Grants

Grants represent an important category of revenue for state and local governments in the United States, as well as in other federal systems such as Australia and Germany. As we have seen in Chapter 4, Intergovernmental Relations, there are hundreds of federal grant programs, particularly reaching into the areas of health, welfare, and infrastructure (programs involving transportation, water, and sewerage). There are, as well, block grants designed to bolster the financial position of poorer states and regions. The block grants may be automatic, based on population. But when grants are a function of population size, counting people becomes a matter of counting money. Local jurisdictions, especially the big cities, often complain that they are shortchanged in grant money because of a census undercount—the contention that people are missed by the census because they move, are illiterate, or are fearful of filling out government forms, or for other reasons. Because the count is critical for congressional districting and for the funding level of many intergovernmental grant programs, jurisdictions are apt to make an issue of what they consider to be an undercount.

Developing countries often are able to finance significant proportions of their expenditure from international, multilateral, or bilateral aid agencies. In this respect such grant recipients are not unlike states or local governments in the United States in that they usually lack freedom in deciding how grant monies should be spent. Recipient governments are really implementation agencies for the donor. Grants differ from other forms of revenue in that they usually cannot be applied to finance the recipient government's own expenditure program. From the point of view of donor governments, giving a grant to another government may simply be a service delivery alternative to providing the service directly itself, or funding another delivery vehicle, such as a not-for-profit agency. Not surprisingly, the process of seeking, obtaining, and spending grants has become a specialized process, rarely free of scope for misunderstandings, misinterpretations, and bad feelings.

---

earmarked tax A tax whose revenues must, by law, be spent for specific purposes. For example, a state gasoline tax may be earmarked for highway construction.

Profits

Profits from successful public enterprises can and should be a useful part of the revenue streams of governments. In the past, poorly managed public enterprises, or enterprises whose revenue and dividend targets were insufficiently specified by their shareholders, often contributed to the negative rather than the positive side of government finances. In the transportation field, from government-owned airlines down to government-run urban transportation systems, this can still apply. In concept however, public enterprises should return an appropriate dividend and yield to their parent governments. In view of the highly favorable market position, or even monopoly, that many such enterprises enjoy, this is usually possible and is becoming the rule rather than the exception.

Financial Innovations

Innovative funding now comes in many forms. Suppose a government wishes to replace its bus fleet or police headquarters, but does not wish to increase taxes. If it cannot (because of bad credit) or will not (because of policy) borrow, one alternative is leasing. The private sector can be contracted to purchase the facilities provided and lease them back for a recurrent charge to the government. A related category of innovative financing now becoming popular, particularly for road construction schemes in Asia, is "Build-Own-Operate-Transfer" or "BOOT" schemes. Under these schemes, government is able to provide a new facility such as a road without recourse to normal financing. Instead, it enters into a contract with a private corporation or consortium, under which the private concern builds the road and operates it for a set period of years, during which it is entitled to receive tolls, payments from the government, or a combination of both. After this period, the company has recovered its outlay and profits, and the road can be transferred debt-free to the government.

Innovative financing schemes do provide flexibility. While they may step on the toes of established bureaucratic agencies and threaten the jobs of some public sector employees, they can provide for projects to be undertaken sooner than they otherwise would. But they do pose risks. The contracts with which they are undertaken are technical and complex—and frequently secret. The electorate is unlikely to know the detailed terms. Democratic accountability is in danger of being compromised.

The Problem of Debt

Nowhere can the urgency of developing adequate standards of public financial management and reporting be seen more clearly than in the management of debt. The ability to incur debt is in many respects a hallmark of governments. They usually exist, in part, to undertake projects the value of which will last for many generations. This is why Alexander Hamilton wrote in an April 30, 1781, letter to Robert Morris that "A national debt, if it is not excessive, will be to us a national blessing." Of course, there have always been those who disagree with Hamilton's famous sentiment. Andrew Jackson, while a candidate for president, wrote to L. H. Colman on April 26, 1824, that "I am one of those who do not believe that a national debt is a national blessing . . . it is calculated to raise around the administration a moneyed aristocracy dangerous to the liberties of the country." This essential argument continues today among contemporary politicians.

Debt is a way of matching costs with those who benefit from the borrowing, of seeing that future generations pay their share of the costs of roads or buildings we put in place now, of ensuring "intergenerational equity." In the United States, tens of thousands of governments can issue bonds and incur debt. These range from the federal government to the tiniest local governments. The question of public debt is often presented by politicians as a highly emotional issue. They talk in terms of the dollar value of government debt for every man, woman, and child in the community. For example, Newt Gingrich wrote, "If you have a child or grandchild born in 1995, that child can expect to pay $187,000 in extra taxes over his or her lifetime just to pay the interest on the national debt. That comes to about $3,500 every year of the child's working life." Scary, huh? You bet. But Gingrich and company do not mention the corresponding assets—the miles of freeway for every man woman and child, the numbers of school places, the national parks and so on. And of course, politicians seldom attempt, as they well might, to put the question into perspective.

The national debt is the total outstanding debt of a central government. The national debt of the United States was $75 million in 1790. It reached its low point in 1835, when it was a mere $38,000. By 1981, it reached $1 trillion; but by 1986 this doubled to $2 trillion; by 1991 it was about $3 trillion. By 1996 this rose to over $5 trillion. As of late 1998, U.S. Gross Federal Debt stood at $5.5 trillion, about 50 percent of gross domestic product. But whereas the years since 1980 had seen this proportion steadily rise, careful government budgeting and buoyant economic conditions combined to stem the increase, and make it plausible for the General Accounting Office in 1998 to forecast a decrease in the national debt as a proportion of GDP over the next decade. The national debt is often confused with the nation's budget deficit in a given year. The debt is, in effect, the total of all the yearly deficits (borrowing) that have not been repaid, plus accumulated interest. It is President Herbert Hoover who is usually credited with first saying: "Blessed are the young for they shall inherit the national debt."

Deficit financing is a situation in which a government's excess of outlays over receipts for a given period is financed primarily by borrowing from the public. Deficit financing, and especially the general acceptance of it by economic theorists, is largely a twentieth-century phenomenon. Depending on the economist you listen to, a large deficit is either considered a major drag on the economy or a significant stimulus.

Abuse of Public Debt

Borrowing is a tool that has a clear purpose in public administration. It is a tool that in the right circumstances public administrators should use with confidence. It is also a tool notoriously open to abuse. There are six main categories of such abuse:

1. Borrowing to finance operating (or "recurrent") expenditure
2. Borrowing beyond the level of repayments the community can meet

3. Borrowing under poorly structured contracts that leave the borrower no protection against large interest-rate hikes by the lender

4. Borrowing to finance projects that give no return (like public monuments) or are highly speculative (like building facilities to host sporting events the tenure of which cannot be guaranteed)

5. Borrowing where government lacks the administrative capacity to manage or implement projects without major losses

6. Borrowing where there is widespread corruption and where a high proportion of the funds borrowed will be creamed off in payments to corrupt politicians and administrators, rather than applied to the purpose for which the funds were ostensibly borrowed

These risks are compounded by the fact that politicians often view borrowing as politically preferable to imposing higher taxes. Borrowing is virtually invisible to the electorate. If the projects produced by it are impressive, politicians see a painless way of "buying" votes—especially when the proverbial chickens do not come home to roost until a subsequent administration.

Overcoming these problems is not straightforward. There is not a high level of understanding and debate of these issues in the community. It is genuinely hard to assess the masses of confusing data that project boosters disseminate. Democratic oversight through legislative committees is of varying effectiveness. And audit scrutiny is often too late. It is in this context that private credit ratings agencies such as Moody's and Standard and Poor's have come to be important.

Municipal Bonds

A bond is a certificate of indebtedness issued by a borrower to a lender that constitutes a legal obligation to repay the principal of the loan plus accrued interest. Municipal bonds are the debt instruments of subnational governments. This causes some confusion because they appear to refer only to bonds issued by a local government. Yet bonds issued by states, territories, or possessions of the United States, or by any municipality, political subdivision (including cities, counties, school districts, and special districts for fire prevention, water, sewer, irrigation, and other purposes), or public agency or instrumentality (such as an authority or commission) are subsumed under the rubric "municipal bonds." While the interest on municipal bonds is exempt from federal taxes, state and local exemptions may vary. Tax-exempt bonds allow jurisdictions to borrow money at lower than commercial market interest rates. The buyers of the bonds find them attractive because their high marginal tax rates make a tax-free investment more advantageous than a taxable one paying even higher interest.

There are a wide variety of municipal bonds, among them:

1. General obligation bonds, which are backed by the jurisdiction's **full faith and credit** with repayment, usually, from general revenues

---

full faith and credit   The descriptive term for those debt obligations, such as certain bonds, that have first claim upon the resources of the state.

2. Callable bonds, which can be repaid totally or in part prior to the maturity date. For this reason, callable bonds ordinarily carry higher interest rates. Noncallable bonds, on the other hand, may not be repurchased until the date of maturation.

3. Revenue bonds, which are municipal bonds whose repayment and dividends are guaranteed by revenues derived from the facility constructed with the proceeds of the sale of the bonds (e.g., stadium bonds, toll road bonds). As revenue bonds are not pledged against the tax base of the issuing jurisdiction, they are usually not regulated by the same debt limitations imposed by most states on the sale of general obligation bonds. Additionally, revenue bond questions usually do not have to be submitted to the voters for approval, as they do not commit the full faith and credit of the jurisdiction.

4. Industrial development bonds, which are state or local government bonds issued to finance the building of a factory or installation that will be used by a private company. While such bonds are popular as a means of attracting new industry to a community, they are essentially fronts for private borrowing. The Congress, sensing the loss of tax revenue from these fronts, has in recent years put a variety of constraints on their use.

5. Junk bonds, which are issued by a company or government with a poor credit rating; thus it pays higher than normal interest to compensate for the additional risk.

6. Moral obligation bonds, which are state or local government bonds that are backed only by the jurisdiction's promise to repay; they are specifically not backed by a jurisdiction's full faith and credit. Moral obligation bonds often carry a higher interest rate than other municipal bonds, because full faith and credit bonds will always be paid first.

7. Serial bonds, which are sold in such a way that a certain number of them are retired (paid off) each year

8. Term bonds, which all mature (must be paid off) on the same date

The Rating Agencies

The problem of abuse of public debt is critically important for citizens, administrators, and honest politicians. But it is also very important to lending institutions. After all, borrowing is a two-sided activity: There can be no borrowing without some institution agreeing to lend. International financial markets are composed of many thousands of lenders. Their capability of assessing the merits of a project a government wishes to fund by borrowing will vary greatly. Large lenders financing big governments might have an acute idea as to the merits of projects and the creditworthiness of borrowers, but the thousands of smaller governments and smaller lenders may well see each other "through a glass darkly"—that is, very imperfectly indeed.

The New York ratings agencies, Standard and Poor's and Moody's, exist to fill this gap, which they do by rating or assessing the creditworthiness of borrowers (public or private) and assigning them a credit rating—just like those that have long been assigned to individuals and businesses. However, at the scale of borrowing a government undertakes, the difference between a triple A rating and a rating of merely double AA might amount to millions of dollars in loan repayments. Bond rating systems differ, but the highest or most **gilt edge** are triple A; the lowest rating of **investment grade** bonds is triple B. Bonds rated below double B are generally considered speculative or junk. The ratings agencies have independent teams of analysts permanently assigned the task of reassessing ratings, and governments are keen to persuade the agencies of the safety and security offered by their prudent financial management approaches.

The role these agencies have come to play in the financial management of governments is crucial. On the one hand, they are a clearinghouse for information and confidence. No doubt their activities facilitate lending that might not otherwise occur. On the other hand, they are not value-free. By upgrading the ratings of the bonds of governments whose actions accord with their ideology, they impose a value scale on policy decisions throughout the world. It is a value scale that rewards balanced budgets and reductions in government expenditure. It gives a tilt to "the level playing field." And of course, these agencies work in secret and are not subject to any form of democratic accountability. When Standard and Poor's in 1995 rated Detroit triple B, Baltimore A, and Minneapolis triple A, it made judgments that will affect the overall quality of life in those cities for years to come. Minneapolis, because it has the best possible rating, will save millions. It will have more money to spend on police and parks than cities such as Detroit and Baltimore, which will have to spend those "extra" millions on interest.

Local Government Financial Management

If we are sometimes concerned about the difficulty of grasping the full financial picture at federal and state government level, we should be even more concerned about this task at the local government level, where the profusion of jurisdictions and the lack of precise comparability among them makes it very hard to draw conclusions. The 80,000 local governments, school districts, and other government bodies of all types, while created by the states, have many variations among them in how they report, how they budget, what they do, and where their functional and physical boundaries lie.

In the smaller local government units, where functions are bare and relatively unchanging, budgets are relatively simple, and issues can be debated comprehensively by elected part-time local officials. The budget process here provides accountability as well as a forum where the merits of pay raises or new equipment purchases may take place.

In the larger cities, the range of functions undertaken and the complexity of the budgeting process is much greater. Large city governments can reflect fashions in national budgeting, with versions of performance, program, and zero-based bud-

---

gilt edge   A popular term for a stock, bond, or other security with the highest rating (for safety of investment) or for a negotiable instrument with similar safety.

investment grade   Refers to securities that fall into the top four categories, AAA to BBB or Aaa to Baa, for Standard & Poor's and Moody's ratings respectively. Some institutions are required by law to buy only investment-grade issues.

geting being employed. There is often a central budget office that receives and scrutinizes the budget proposals received from department heads. There are usually separate capital budgets in large cities with an extensive process of capital project planning and evaluation.

A distinctive feature of U.S. governmental arrangements is the existence of special-purpose local government bodies, ranging from school districts to regional transportation and port authorities. Budgeting arrangements in these organizations vary. School districts tend to operate in a visible and accountable manner similar to local governments. But infrastructure bodies, such as New York's Triborough Bridge and Tunnel Authority, often resemble public enterprises in which business paradigms dominate and the budget process is more akin to that in the private sector.

Local government budgeting forms an essential part of the process of public financial management in the United States. Though it may seem more visible and accountable than federal or state government in some respects, its budgetary processes are often in equal need of reform. Contemporary blends of performance and program budgeting are common and quite effective at the local government level. On the other hand, there are also many units where the format, procedures, and outcomes are far from clear—hidden from public scrutiny and accountability by the fog imposed by a local political machine. The main difference between federal and state and local budget processes is that the state and local jurisdictions must have balanced budgets each year. The federal government has not had to live with such fiscal inhibitions. After all, Article I, Section 8, of the Constitution gives the Congress the sole right "to coin money." In addition to the income tax (discussed above), state and local governments primarily depend for their income on property, sales, and school taxes.

Property Tax

A property tax is any tax on land and its improvements such as buildings (or on personal property such as automobiles and jewelry). This tax is the mainstay of most local governments; it provides nearly half of the revenues that local governments get from their own sources. To administer a property tax, the tax base must first be defined—that is, as housing and land, automobiles, other assets, etc. An evaluation of the worth of the tax base must then be made—this is the assessment. Finally, a tax rate, usually an amount to be paid per hundred-dollar value of the tax base, is levied. Since the value of the tax base will appreciate or depreciate substantially over time, continuing assessments must be made.

Arguments for the property tax resemble a good news/bad news joke. The good news is that the property tax provides a stable revenue source and has a good track record as a strong revenue raiser. The bad news is that its stability can also be considered inflexibility, as it does not keep pace with income growth. The good news is that, since property is generally unmovable, it is hard to miss and, therefore, provides a visible tax base for relatively unskilled local tax offices to administer. The bad news is that the administration and assessment of property tax is at best erratic and at worst a horrendous mess. The results are that the property tax base tends to erode over time; that the property of the wealthy and the politically influential may be undervalued; that there is a strong incidence effect on newcomers; and that the elderly are increasingly pressed to meet property tax burdens.

Sales Tax

A sales tax is a tax on consumption rather than income. This favorite of many state and local governments calls for a fixed tax rate, ranging from 2 to 9 percent, to be charged on most purchases. A variety of items tend to be excluded from sales taxation—for example, medicine and foods. The major criticism of the sales tax is equity. Sales taxes tend toward regressivity, in that higher-income groups pay a lesser percentage of their income in tax than do lower-income groups. To illustrate, a family of four with an annual income of $8,000 would spend half of that in direct consumption and might pay a 5 percent sales tax of $200, or 2.5 percent of their income. But another family of four with an $80,000 income will have a much lower percentage of direct consumption (say 25 percent) and, although they pay 5 percent on this amount ($1,000), the proportion of their income taken by the sales tax is 1.2 percent—or half that of the lower-income family.

Economic Policy

Isolationism, an option in foreign policy, is most decidedly not a possibility with a government's financial policies. Contemporary financial policies cannot stand alone. They are inherently part of the nation's overall economic policies.

Economic policy, the process by which a nation manages its trade, business, and finances, generally consists of three dimensions: (1) fiscal policy, (2) monetary policy, and (3) those other facets of public policy with economic implications, such as energy policy, farm policy, and labor union policy. The interaction of these dimensions of economic policy is crucial, since none operate in a vacuum. While monetary policy basically exercises control over the quantity and cost (interest rates) of money and credit in the economy, fiscal policy deals with the sizes of budgets, deficits, and taxes. Other policy areas, such as housing policy (also dependent upon interest rates) and programs dependent upon deficit spending, involve aspects of both monetary and fiscal policy, and vice versa. However, their interrelationship does not exist with regard to implementation. Monetary policy, while receiving major inputs from the president and other executive agencies, is the responsibility of the Federal Reserve Board, an independent agency. Fiscal policy, while receiving similar inputs from the Federal Reserve Board, is primarily the responsibility of the president and the Congress. The degree of equality and subsequent share of responsibility varies within a stable range. While a president may wish to spend this or that amount, only the Congress has the constitutional ability to levy taxes (although tax laws, like any others, must be signed or vetoed by the president). Also limiting a president's discretion over economic policy is the fact that so much of it is controlled by prior decisions to fund, for example, welfare, entitlement, and pension programs, which are not easily changed.

Monetary Policy

Monetary policy consists of a government's formal efforts to manage the money in its economy in order to realize specific economic goals. Three basic kinds of monetary policy decisions can be made: (1) decisions about the amount of money in circulation; (2) decisions about the level of interest rates; (3) decisions about the functioning of credit markets and the banking system.

Controlling the amount of money is, of course, the key variable. In 1913, the United States passed into law the Federal Reserve Act, which created a strong central bank, the Federal Reserve. Like most central banks, the **Federal Reserve System** is empowered to control the amount of money in circulation by either creating or canceling dollars. The implementation of money control is achieved through the process of putting up for sale or buying government securities, usually termed **open-market operations**, which means that the Federal Reserve competes with other bidders in the purchasing or selling of securities. The difference is that, when the Federal Reserve buys securities, it pays in the form of new currency in circulation. If it sells some of its securities, it decreases money available, since in effect it absorbs currency held by others. This does not mean, however, that the money stock fluctuates greatly. It steadily increases. It is in the margin of the increase that **money supply** has its impact. Through the use of the two other tools, the Federal Reserve can attempt to affect investments and loans. First, it can change its discount rate—the interest rate it charges other banks for loans of money that these banks can use to make loans. Second, it can change the reserve requirement—the amount of money a bank must have on hand in comparison with the amount of money it may have out on loan.

Fiscal Policy

Fiscal policy consists of the manipulation of government finances by raising or lowering taxes or levels of spending to promote economic stability and growth. Stability and growth must be combined, since stability without growth is stagnation. The use of fiscal policy for economic objectives is a decidedly recent phenomenon. For the greater part of the 200-year history of the United States, fiscal policy was not a factor. The national budgetary policy was premised upon expenditures equaling

---

Federal Reserve System Colloquially known as the Fed, this is in effect the central bank of the United States, created by the Federal Reserve Act of 1913 and charged with administering and making policy for the nation's credit and monetary affairs. Run by a seven-member board of governors appointed by the president (who also appoints their chairman), the system includes 12 Federal Reserve banks, 24 branches, all national banks, and many state banking institutions. Three major monetary tools are available to the Federal Reserve System to control the economy's supply of money and credit: (1) open-market operations, which, through the purchase or sale of government bonds, increase or decrease the availability of dollars to member banks; (2) discount-rate adjustments, which increase or decrease the interest rate charged to member banks for the money they borrow; and (3) reserve requirements, which, through changes in levels of reserve, increase or decrease the number of dollars a bank may make available for loan. Two less significant tools, moral suasion and selective controls over stock purchase margin requirements, are also used to help manage the economy.

open-market operations The purchase and sale in the open market by the Federal Reserve System of various securities, chiefly marketable federal government securities, for the purpose of implementing Federal Reserve monetary policy. Open-market operations, one of the most flexible instruments of monetary policy, affect the reserves of member banks and thus the supply of money and the availability and cost of credit.

money supply The amount of money in the economy.

revenues (a balanced budget). In fact, with the exception of war years, budgeting be-fore the 1900s was primarily an exercise in deciding how to get rid of excess revenues, generated primarily by **tariffs**. This is not to say that modern fiscal policies would not have saved the nation considerable distress from assorted recessions and depressions, but the nineteenth century held that the economy followed a natural order. The first major tampering with the natural order of things came in 1913, with the advent of the federal income tax and the establishment of the Federal Reserve System. The Great Depression of the 1930s, along with the initiation of Social Security and unem-ployment compensation programs, provided the first recognition of the need for a na-tional economic policy. However, legitimization of the goal of a national economic policy came with the passage of the Full Employment Act of 1946. The act not only created a **Council of Economic Advisers** for the president, but it prescribed objectives for economic prosperity and charged the president with ensuring their achievement.

Basically, fiscal policy offers discretionary and built-in courses of action. Dis-cretionary fiscal policy, which involves changing policy, has two major facets: the level of receipts and the level of expenditures. The major fiscal policy actions of re-cent years are replete with tax cuts and temporary reductions. Given the time lags involved in legislating tax changes, it is easy to see why presidents have preferred to wage fiscal policy battles in terms of government spending. The second dimension involves built-in fiscal stabilizers—that is, preset or automatic policy. These are the **transfer payments**, the **progressive tax** rates, and the changing federal budget deficits and surpluses that move automatically to counter economic downturns or to control excessive periods of demand and business activity. For example, as peo-ple are laid off from work in a recessionary period, payments for unemployment compensation mount automatically. This increases the federal budget deficit, which in turn stimulates the economy and moves to offset the economic downswing. If the economy heats up, both regular and overtime wages increase, fueling demand for goods and services and creating inflation. As personal income increases, however, more and more people move into higher tax brackets; the tax structure thus func-tions as an automatic stabilizer by absorbing more personal income and thus re-straining demand for goods and services.

---

tariff A tax imposed on imported products. A duty is distinguished from a tariff solely by the fact that the duty is the actual tax imposed or collected, while the tariff, technically speaking, is the sched-ule of duties. However, in practice the words are often used interchangeably.

Council of Economic Advisers (CEA) The U.S. president's primary source of economic advice. It assists the president in preparing various economic reports, including the annual *Economic Report of the President*. Established in the Executive Office of the President by the Employment Act of 1946, the CEA consists of three economists (one designated chair) appointed by the president, with the ad-vice and consent of the Senate, who formulate proposals to "maintain employment, production, and purchasing power." While council members are now usually professional economists, the Con-gress initially objected to them and preferred practical businessmen.

transfer payments Payments by a government made to individuals who provide no goods or services in return. All of the social welfare programs at all levels of government that provide subsistence in-come support are transfer payment programs. They are often referred to as *entitlement programs* because one becomes entitled to transfer payments if one meets criteria established by the authoriz-ing legislation.

progressive tax Any tax that has people of greater wealth paying a larger percentage in tax than people of lesser means. Income taxes are often progressive.

Summary

Budgeting is the single most important decision-making process in public institutions. The budget itself is also a jurisdiction's most important reference document. In their increasingly voluminous formats, budgets simultaneously record policy decision outcomes, cite policy priorities as well as program objectives, and delineate a government's total service effort.

There are two basic kinds of budgets. The most common is the operating budget—a short-term plan for managing the resources necessary to carry out a program. Usually an operating budget is developed for each fiscal year. The second kind is the capital budget; it deals with planning for large expenditures such as bridges and buildings. Capital budgets typically cover five- to ten-year periods.

An executive budget is both a technical process and a physical thing. First it is the process by which agency requests for appropriations are prepared and submitted to a central budget office for review, alteration, and consolidation. Then it becomes a tangible thing, the comprehensive budget document for an executive branch of government that a jurisdiction's chief executive submits to a legislature for review, modification, and enactment.

General taxation (or a general property tax in the context of local government) is the most traditional means of financing public services. There are major differences between the federal and state-local revenue systems. The federal system has experienced a trend toward less diversity; over two-thirds of its general revenue is provided by the federal income tax and the several insurance trust funds (such as Social Security). State and local revenue systems, in contrast, depend on a greater variety of revenue sources (such as property taxes, income taxes, sales taxes, user charges, lotteries, and federal grants). While local governments still rely primarily on the property tax, their states—with a few exceptions—rely largely on the state personal income tax.

Deficit financing is a situation in which a government's excess of outlays over receipts for a given period is financed primarily by borrowing from the public. Politicians often view borrowing as politically preferable to imposing higher taxes. Borrowing is virtually invisible to the electorate. If the projects produced by it are impressive, politicians see a painless way of "buying" votes—especially when the proverbial chickens do not come home to roost until a subsequent administration.

Economic policy, the process by which a nation manages its trade, business, and finances, generally consists of three dimensions: (1) fiscal policy, (2) monetary policy, and (3) those other facets of public policy with economic implications, such as energy policy, farm policy, and labor union policy. While monetary policy basically exercises control over the quantity and cost (interest rates) of money and credit in the economy, fiscal policy deals with the sizes of budgets, deficits, and taxes.

Key Concepts

budget A financial plan serving as a pattern for and control over future operations; hence, any estimate of future costs or any systematic plan for the utilization of the workforce, material, or other resources.

budget cycle The timed steps of the budget process, which includes preparation, approval, execution, and audit.

budget process The total system a jurisdiction uses to make decisions on government spending needs and how to pay for them. The main difference between federal and state-local budget processes is that the state and local jurisdictions must have balanced budgets each year.

budget surplus The amount by which a government's budget receipts exceed its budget outlays for any given period.

capital budgeting A budget process that deals with planning for large expenditures for capital items such as bridges and buildings.

deficit financing A situation in which a government's excess of outlays over receipts for a given period is financed primarily by borrowing from the public.

executive budget The budget document for an executive branch of government that a jurisdiction's chief executive submits to a legislature for review, modification, and enactment.

incremental budgeting A method of budget review that focuses on the increments of increase or decrease in the budget of existing programs. Incremental budgeting, which is often called traditional budgeting, is a counter-school of thought to more rational, systems-oriented approaches, such as zero-based budgeting.

line-item budget The classification of budgetary accounts according to narrow, detailed objects of expenditure (such as motor vehicles, clerical workers, or reams of paper) used within each particular agency of government, generally without reference to the ultimate purpose or objective served by the expenditure.

national debt The total outstanding debt of a central government.

progressive tax Any tax that has people of greater wealth paying a larger percentage in tax than people of lesser means. Income taxes are often progressive.

regressive tax Any tax that has people with lower incomes paying a higher overall percentage of their income in tax than people of greater income. Sales taxes are examples of regressive taxes.

tax A compulsory contribution exacted by a government for public purposes.

unified budget The present form of the budget of the federal government, in which receipts and outlays from federal funds and trust funds (such as Social Security) are consolidated.

zero-based budgeting A budgeting process that is a rejection of the incremental decision-making model of budgeting. It demands a rejustification of the entire budget submission (from ground zero), whereas incremental budgeting essentially respects the outcomes of previous budgetary decisions (collectively referred to as the budget base) and focuses examination on the margin of change from year to year.

Bibliography

Blais, Andre, and Stephane Dion, eds. (1991). *The Budget-Maximizing Bureaucrat.* Pittsburgh: University of Pittsburgh Press.

Buchanan, James, and Gordon Tullock. (1962). *The Calculus of Consent.* Ann Arbor: University of Michigan Press.

Caiden, Naomi. (1983). "Guidelines to Federal Budget Reform," *Public Budgeting and Finance* 3 (winter).

Dror, Yehezkel. (1964). "Muddling Through—'Science' or Inertia," *Public Administration Review,* 24, No. 3.

Frederickson, H. George. (1995). "Misdiagnosing the Orange County Scandal," *Governing* (April).

Gingrich, Newt. (1995). *To Renew America.* New York: HarperCollins.

Gore, Al. (1993). Report of the National Performance Review, *From Red Tape to Results: Creating a Government that Works Better and Costs Less.* Washington DC: U.S. Government Printing Office.

Grieder, William. (1981). "The Education of David Stockman," *The Atlantic Monthly* (December).

Hyde, Albert C., ed. (1992). *Government Budgeting: Theory, Process, Politics.* Monterey, CA: Brooks-Cole.

Kendall, James. (1955). *Michael Faraday.* London: Farber and Farber.

Key, V. O., Jr., (1940). "The Lack of a Budgetary Theory," *American Political Science Review* (December).

Lemov, Penelope. (1995). "Managing Cash in a Post-Orange County World," *Governing* (May).

Lewis, Verne. (1952). "Toward a Theory of Budgeting," *Public Administration Review* (winter).

Lynch, Thomas D. (1995). *Public Budgeting in America,* 4th ed. Englewood Cliffs, NJ: Prentice Hall.

Lynn, Jonathan, and Antony Jay. (1984). *The Complete Yes Minister.* New York: Harper and Row.

Miranda, Rowan. (1994). "Privatization and the Budget Maximizing Bureaucrat," *Public Productivity and Management Review* (summer).

Musgrave, Richard R., and Peggy B. Musgrave. (1984). *Public Finance in Theory and Practice*, 4th ed. New York: McGraw-Hill.

Mydans, Seth. (1995). "Taxes a Hard Sell in Orange County," *New York Times*, May 8.

Mysak, Joe. (1995). "Winking at Debt," *New York Times*, June 23.

Novick, David. (1968). "The Origin and History of Programming Budgeting," *California Management Review* 11 (fall).

Peterson, John E. (1991). "Is Municipal Bankruptcy an Alternative?" *Governing* (September).

Ratchford, B. U. (1941). *American State Debts.* Durham, NC: Duke University Press.

Phyrr, Peter A. (1977). "The Zero-Base Approach to Government Budgeting," *Public Administration Review* 37 (January-February).

Schick, Allen. (1966). "The Road to PPB: The Stages of Budget Reform," *Public Administration Review* 26 (December).

———. (1973). "A Death in the Bureaucracy: The Demise of Federal PPB," *Public Administration Review* 33 (March-April).

———. (1977). "Budget Gap," *Public Administration Review* (September-October).

———. (1978). "The Road from ZBB," *Public Administration Review* 38 (March-April).

———.(1983). "Incremental Budgeting in a Decremental Age," *Policy Sciences* (September).

Shenk, J. W. (1995). "Hidden Kingdom: Disney's Political Blueprint," *American Prospect* (spring).

Suetonius. (1931). *The Lives of the Twelve Caesars.* New York: Modern Library.

Weiner, Tim. (1990). *Blank Check: The Pentagon's Black Budget.* New York: Warner Books.

Wildavsky, Aaron. (1969). "Rescuing Policy Analysis from PPBS," *Public Administration Review* 29 (March-April).

———. (1984). *The Politics of the Budgetary Process*, 4th edition. Boston: Little, Brown.

Willoughby, William F. (1918). *The Movement Towards Budgetary Reform in the States.* New York: D. Appleton and Company for the Institute of Government Research.

Recommended Books

Blais, Andre, and Stephanie Dion, eds. (1991). *The Budget Maximizing Bureaucrat: Appraisals and Evidence.* Pittsburgh: University of Pittsburgh Press. Everything you need to know about bureaucratic empire builders and how to help them or thwart them.

Bland, Robert L., and Irene S. Rubin. (1997). *Budgeting: A Guide for Local Governments.* Washington, DC: International City/County Management Association. A succinct survey of the theory, obstacles, and practicalities of budgeting at the local level; offers many examples of how budgets are assembled and what municipal budget manuals need to contain.

Mikesell, John L. (1995). *Fiscal Administration: Analysis and Applications for the Public Sector*, 4th ed. Belmont, CA: Wadsworth. The standard text on managing governmental funds.

Wildavsky, Aaron. (1992). *The New Politics of the Budgetary Process*, 2nd ed. New York: HarperCollins. The last update of Wildavsky's *Politics of the Budgetary Process* (initially published in 1964); one of the most influential books in the history of public administration.

Related Web Sites

Congressional Budget Office
http://www.cbo.gov/
Federal Reserve System
http://www.bog.frb.fed.us/
Federation of Tax Administrators
http://www.taxadmin.org/
Government Finance Officers Association
http://www.financenet.gov/gfoa.htm
National Association of State Budget Officers
http://www.nasbo.org

State and local government budgets
http://www.financenet.gov/financenet/state/ stbudget.htm
Treasury Management Association
http://www.tma-net.org/
U.S. Bureau of Public Debt
Http://www.publicdebt.treas.gov
U.S. Office of Management and Budget
http://www.whitehouse.gov/WH/EOP/omb
U.S. Treasury financial manual
http://www.fms.treas.gov/tfm/index.html

13

Auditing, Accounting, and Evaluating

Keynote: Captain Bligh's Program Evaluation of the Mutiny on the *Bounty*

For more than two centuries the ultimate South Seas adventure story has been the tale of the *Bounty* and its mutiny. But this is no tall tale; there really was a mutiny on the *Bounty* in 1787. William Bligh, the captain, and Fletcher Christian, the mutinous officer, were real people. A trio of Hollywood's greatest character actors (Charles Laughton in 1935, Trevor Howard in 1962, Anthony Hopkins in 1983) have played Bligh: first as a sadist, then as an overbearing bureaucrat, and finally as a frustrated corporate climber. They were paired with Christians who were among the greatest romantic leads of their day (Clark Gable, Marlon Brando, and Mel Gibson). The dramatic tension between these two estranged friends is the core of the film, of the mutiny, and of the legend.

Because the *Bounty*'s saga has lent itself so well to novels and movies, readers (and viewers) often forget that this story is a case study in public administration and particularly program evaluation. True, the *Bounty* was a Royal Navy ship, but she was built as a merchant ship, was commanded by an officer (Bligh) with years of experience in merchant ships, and was on a merchant ship's mission. Today, private corporations have the National Aeronautics and Space Administration put satellites in space for them. In the eighteenth century it was the Royal Navy that was on the cutting edge of technological and navigational skill; so it was quite reasonable that they undertake such a "scientific" mission. The navy was only being responsive to the request of influential planters in Jamaica. These West Indian businessmen just wanted a cheap source of fuel for their slaves. Believing that Tahiti, an island in the South Pacific, had a nourishing plant—breadfruit—that could thrive in their climate, they used all their considerable influence to get the navy to do the job for them. Just like today's corporate executives, they lobbied their government to take on their breadfruit research and development costs. Governments, then and now, are happy to accede to such requests in the hope that a relatively small investment would engender substantial economic development and concomitant taxes. The absolute immorality of doing something designed to make slavery a more economically viable institution never occurred to the English colonists, to the Royal Navy, or to the crew of the *Bounty*. While the *Bounty* was not a slave ship, it nevertheless was on a slaver's mission. This mission gave the *Bounty* its name. Originally a merchant ship named *Bethia*, it was rechristened to reflect the king's "bounty" to his West Indian subjects—and their subject slaves.

Bligh was chosen to be the ship's captain because he was a young officer with Captain James Cook when Cook visited Tahiti in 1777. Cook, before he was killed by the local residents of Hawaii, wrote that the breadfruit plant would be excellent food for the slaves of the British-owned West Indian plantations. This is why the Jamaican slave owners lobbied the navy for the voyage. Bligh was one of the very few naval officers in England who had actually been to Tahiti and knew the people there. Besides, Bligh's wife had an uncle who was one of the plantation owners who successfully lobbied the government for the voyage. He then continued his lobbying efforts on Bligh's behalf. While his political sponsor brought Bligh's name to the forefront of consideration, there is no doubt that Bligh was as fully qualified for the command as any officer in England. The *Bounty* command was considered such a choice assignment, one that could really make one's reputation, that Bligh, then a merchant ship captain, accepted the job for a vastly reduced salary (from 500 to 50 pounds a year) and at the rank of lieutenant. So while Bligh was the captain of the *Bounty*, he was only a lieutenant in the Royal Navy. Bligh then chose Christian because he wanted his friend from two earlier voyages to the West Indies along for the ride. Good company can be scarce on the high seas unless you plan for it!

The *Bounty*'s mutiny was in reality a pathetic little affair as mutinies go. While passions ran high, the decks did not run red with blood. The crew totaled 44 but only 12 of them were actually mutineers. Aside from Bligh's bruised ego, nobody was really hurt. No blood was shed and no shots were fired. After much shouting the mutineers put Bligh and 18 other men in a 23-foot lifeboat fully expecting them all to perish. But Bligh, in one of history's most remarkable feats of seamanship, sailed that tiny overloaded craft 3,618 miles to the Dutch colony of Timor, in present-day Indonesia. There he found passage home to England. Had Bligh and his lifeboat colleagues died, there would have been no mutiny in that the world would not have known of it. The *Bounty* would have just been presumed lost at sea—a common enough occurrence in those days.

The mutiny became a cause célèbre because Bligh's account of it, his program evaluation, *The Mutiny on Board HMS* Bounty, was published soon after he returned to England in 1790. It was an instant best-seller, what with its tales of the exotic South Seas and casual sex, betrayal, and a desperate voyage of survival. Adding to the sensationalism was the simple fact that this kind of thing had never happened before in the Royal Navy. Mutiny was a word used for insubordination, for resisting or complaining about orders. But to take over, to steal, one of His Majesty's ships was unthinkable for two reasons. First, under the articles of war, mutiny was punishable by death. Second, there was quite literally no place in the entire world where one could hide from the enormous Royal Navy. Thus Christian and company could only have committed such an act because they were deranged by the allures of Tahiti. Bligh's account, being first, supported the derangement theory and forever defined the terms of the mutiny. He wrote that: "The mutineers had flattered themselves with the hopes of a more happy life among the Otaheiteans (Tahitians), than they could possibly enjoy in England." Bligh's analysis for the underlying causes have been quibbled with and expanded upon but never subsequently refuted:

> The women at Otaheite (Tahiti) are handsome, mild and cheerful in their manners and conversation, possessed of great sensibility, and have sufficient delicacy to make them admired and beloved. The chiefs were so much attached to our people, that they rather encouraged their stay among them. . . . Under these, and many other attendant circumstances, equally desirable, it is now perhaps not so much to be wondered at, though scarcely possible to have been foreseen, that a set of sailors, most of them void of connections, should be led away; especially when, in addition to such powerful inducements, they imagined it in their power to fix themselves in the midst of plenty, on one of the finest islands in the world, where they need not labour, and where the allurements of dissipation are beyond anything that can be conceived.

Bligh knew that there would be a clash of cultures when his normally sexually repressed and especially sex starved crew met the sexually liberated Tahitians. But after a few weeks at most, they would all be back at sea. The problem was that the *Bounty* stayed in Tahiti for almost six months—mainly because Bligh wanted to make sure that the breadfruit shoots had rooted properly so that they would survive the anticipated seven-month voyage to Jamaica. This delay gave the men time to establish extremely strong relationships with the local women.

In his analysis, the "allurements of dissipation" that Bligh only hints at are the prime causes of the mutiny. Bligh saw nothing else amiss. As he wrote, "Had their mutiny been occasioned by any grievances, either real or imaginary, I must have discovered symptoms of their discontent, which would have put me on my guard." Modern audiences of the films about the mutiny often think the crew revolted because of Bligh's harsh discipline and frequent whippings. But this is looking at eighteenth-century management practices with twentieth-century eyes. Lash for lash, Bligh was actually far less harsh than other captains of his era. Statistical analysis of the number and severity of floggings show that Bligh used corporal punishment sparingly. According to historian Sven Wahlroos, "It was not his physical cruelty but, rather, his humiliating tongue—in an era when a man's honor was more important than his life—that contributed heavily to the most famous mutiny of all time." A very strong case can be made that Bligh, far from being too harsh, was too lenient. He allowed the crew almost total freedom to cavort among the Tahitians both on shore and on ship. This is what made it impossible to reassert traditional discipline on the return voyage. But the imagery of the floggings and the pleasure the actors playing Bligh gave to his countenance has made his name a byword for a seagoing martinet.

Bligh was an astute organizational climber. He was not about to let those who would lead a life of dissipation ruin his naval career. Knowing that any officer who loses a ship by mutiny would be court-martialed, he craftily started making his case, writing his program evaluation, while still in the lifeboat. Any court-martial is essentially an evaluation of whether an officer has conducted himself appropriately. Bligh had. But he also knew he had to defend himself before three courts:

1. The formal court-martial, which he had every reason to believe would be a formality that would (and did) exonerate him
2. The informal court of naval opinion, which would determine whether he would ever be given another command
3. The court of public opinion

He won all three at first. He was acquitted by the court-martial; the navy kept promoting him (eventually to admiral) and giving him progressively more responsible assignments; and the public initially considered him to be a great hero. But two years later, during the court-martial of the few mutineers who were captured, new information surfaced that branded him a villain.

Without ever using the phrase, Bligh was a practitioner of the "defensive program evaluation." His assessment of the mutiny prevailed at first because there were no contemporary contradictory evaluations. British Prime Minister Winston Churchill once bragged during World War II that history would look kindly upon his actions because he, as a professional writer, intended to write it. Bligh was no Churchill to be sure; but they both know the advantages of writing the history in which you participated—before the other guy does.

However, Bligh was not completely forthcoming in his analysis. He only told of one of the reasons for the mutiny. According to naval historian Richard Hough, there were two other major contributing factors: Fletcher Christian's tender sensibilities and the fact that Bligh was overwhelmingly detested by everyone on board. Bligh seems to have been unusually obnoxious and bad tempered. He was the worst kind of Theory X manager (see Chapter 6), giving so many orders that they often contradicted each other. When the resulting foul-ups occurred, he tended to blame anyone but himself—and his blame was expressed by language so constantly obscene and insulting that it shocked, yes shocked, sailors who were, as sailors, thoroughly experienced with obscene and insulting language. By constantly impugning the honor and integrity of every sailor and officer on board, he created a situation that when push came to shove—during the mutiny—not a single officer would fight for him. A mutiny must be led by officers for the simple reason that only they knew how to navigate. There would be no point in taking over a ship if you couldn't then go anywhere with it. This is why the focus of the analysis of the mutineers' motivation has been on Christian. The lower deck men encouraged and supported him because they knew he had grievances and they wanted to return to Tahiti. Indeed, Christian, as a gentleman, would have felt obligated to challenge Bligh to a duel because of his verbal abuses, had they been on land.

Bligh was absolutely correct about there being nothing amiss for him to discover. The mutiny was less a plot than a spontaneous outburst. Christian was in despair over his relationship with Bligh. He was effectively suicidal and preparing to jump ship in a makeshift raft when a fellow crew member, noticing his preparations, said the men were "ready for anything." Thus the mutiny began spontaneously because Bligh's treatment of Christian had pushed him over the proverbial edge. What happened on the *Bounty* in 1789 was no different than what seems to happen a few times each year in the U.S. Postal Service—an overbearing supervisor psychologically pushes a mentally delicate clerk too far. So the clerk comes to work one day with a gun and kills the supervisor, a few bystanders, and maybe himself. True, the mutiny was aggravated by the allures of Tahiti, but its underlying cause was less a matter of sadistic perversion than of bad management. The single most significant management blunder was the absence of the squad of marines almost always assigned to naval ships. Marines in all major navies originated not as soldiers to be landed on hostile shores, but as jailers for the sailors. Unfortunately, the *Bounty* was a small ship, less than 90 feet long by 24 feet wide. With a crew of 44 there was simply no room. Many other naval ships visited Tahiti and other friendly Polynesian islands before and after the *Bounty*. They did not suffer a mutiny. But they had marines.

And there was one other contemporary element to the *Bounty* mutiny. One of the most respected accounts of the mutiny, Richard Hough's *Captain Bligh and Mr. Christian*, suggests that its underlying cause was sexual harassment. This suggestion is a mixture of fact and speculation. It was fact that the traditions of the Royal Navy included "rum, sodomy, and the lash." We know that the *Bounty* made ample use of rum and the lash. Because sodomy was a capital offense, it was never lightly discussed. According to Greg Dening, shipmates on Bligh's two earlier voyages with Christian "remarked on Bligh's infatuation with the active, charming young man who had begged—for the experience of it—to join his crew even at no pay, so long as Bligh permitted him 'to mess with the gentlemen.'" It was a fact that Bligh showed extreme favoritism toward Christian—a favoritism which stopped as the return voyage began. The speculation is that the 26-year-old Christian was not the macho romantic portrayed by Hollywood, that he had a homosexual relationship with Bligh before Tahiti, and that he was reluctant to resume it after his Tahitian interlude. And all accounts of the *Bounty*'s odyssey, including Bligh's, agree that Bligh was the only member of the ship's company who did not have a sexual liaison with any of the

Tahitian women. Hough concludes that Bligh's pressure on Christian to resume their previous, not unprecedented, relationship led to the angst that forced Christian over the mental edge. If so, he would not have been the last worker driven crazy by a sexually harassing boss.

A court martial declared that Lieutenant Bligh was personally blameless for the mutiny. He was then promoted to captain and given another ship—this time with marines. He returned to Tahiti for a second cargo of breadfruit plants, which were successfully delivered to Jamaica in 1793. The irony of all this was that even after a successful second voyage, it did not do any good. The West Indian slaves did not like breadfruit and would not eat it. The whole program was a total failure except for the movies that were big hits, the more than 2,500 books published on the adventure, and the still thriving Tahitian tourist industry.

Popular imagery aside, Captain Bligh's adventures conveniently provide modern public managers with five valuable lessons about the politics of program evaluation:

1. *Be first*. Bligh arrived back in England just as promptly as he could. His account of the mutiny, mostly written on his voyage home, was practically ready for the printer. The first evaluation of a major program defines the parameters and sets the tone for the others that inevitably follow. Bligh's assertion that it was lust—and not lashes—that motivated the mutineers has never been completely refuted. Even though many subsequent analyses have shown Bligh's leadership style to be a major contributing factor, his spin on events is still spinning.

2. *Have friendly evaluators*. Your best friend at evaluation time is your own pen—or word processor. Imagine a continuum with yourself at one end and your worst enemy at the other—and everybody else aligned according to their affection for you. Better to have an evaluation written by someone leaning toward you on that continuum. Is arranging for an evaluation to be biased in your favor cheating or simply effective public relations? Hey, we're not talking objective social science here; we are talking management survival. The methodologies naturally differ.

3. *Disseminate your evaluation*. Just as the old adage says that there is no such thing as bad publicity, there is no such thing as too much dissemination of an evaluation. It creates notoriety and fame. In the entertainment business it means that whatever you did, good or bad, someone will hire you or offer you a book contract. There is no way of assaying how much good Bligh's widely disseminated account of the mutiny did him, but this much is for sure: honor after honor and high office after high office came to him. So it probably did a great deal of good. Besides, it proved he could write. To the extent that real life—and especially public administration—is an essay contest, he won. Fletcher Christian lost. His name has become a synonym for a disloyal officer in large part because he never told his side of the story. Had he returned to England and challenged Bligh to a duel of evaluations, he might have been hanged for it—but Bligh's honor would have been at least sullied.

4. *Don't tell all*. Bligh knew more about events leading to the mutiny than he put in his report. He knew he stayed in Tahiti more than necessary. He knew that he had allowed shipboard discipline to become so lax that the decks were filthy and some of the sails had been allowed to rot from neglect. He knew much more

Anthony Hopkins as Captain Bligh at the wheel steering the *Bounty* toward mutiny, with Mel Gibson as Fletcher Christian loyally (for the moment) at his side •

about Christian's motivations and mental state than he admitted. His report did not lie about these things. It was just self-servingly less comprehensive than it could have been. Bligh, no more paranoid than many a manager today, knew he did not have to say bad things about himself because so many of his enemies would be happy to do that for him. And they did. The mutineers and alleged mutineers that were captured in Tahiti and returned in chains for court-martial gave a devastating indictment of Bligh's management style. Only thereafter did Bligh become in the public mind what we still think of as "a Captain Bligh."

5. *Impeach the integrity or methodology of critics—or simply ignore them.* Bligh's court-martial was pro forma. However, while Bligh was off on his two-year second breadfruit-to-Jamaica expedition, the ten members of *Bounty's* crew who were arrested in Tahiti were court-martialed in England. (Christian and the other mutineers fled with the *Bounty* to Pitcairn's Island, where they died, and where their descendants still live.) The crew's account of events on the *Bounty* fleshed out Bligh's earlier evaluation to such an extent that Bligh lost his stature as a national hero. Edward Christian (Fletcher's brother) wrote a stinging rebuttal to Bligh's assessment in *A Short Reply to Captain Bligh's Answer* (1795). Bligh then published a pamphlet attacking his accuser's methodology and facts. Edward Christian then published a rejoinder pamphlet attacking Bligh's attack on him. The attacks by supporters of either side continue to this day.

If you think that the mutiny and the debate it has fostered is ancient history, consider that its essence reoccurs everyday in the United States. The nation is a ship in which we all sail. Indeed, the "ship of state" is a nautical metaphor that has been used since ancient times. All citizens are obligated on the voyage of their lives to obey the shipboard laws. Many people, especially young men the same ages as the *Bounty* crew, "mutiny" by violating the law of the land. They steal. They kill. They rape. The same people who would defend Christian and company offer a similar defense for these new style mutineers—they lived in an oppressive environment and were treated too harshly by those who were "in charge." Those who would defend Bligh, who feel that there can be no excuse for mutiny, today assert that there can be no excuse for breaking the law. To the extent that we as a society refuse to excuse crime and demand longer prison sentences under increasingly harsh conditions, we are all "Captain Blighs." The debate over "the" mutiny is really a debate over the legitimacy of mutiny itself. Fletcher Christian supporters will find ways to rationalize crime, will seek to understand the motivation of the criminals, and will demand more ameliorative programs, such as increased public housing. Captain Bligh supporters see no excuse for crime of any kind anywhere. To those who demand such things as more public housing as a preventative measure, they say that the nation has been on a public housing building boom since the 1980s—only these "public houses" are called jails.

What Is an Audit?

Bligh knew that upon his return to England he would be subject to an audit, a word derived from the Latin word *auditus,* meaning a hearing. The word auditorium retains this original meaning. Bligh's audit, because he was a naval officer, took the form of a court-martial. But even if there had been no mutiny, Bligh's conduct would have been audited—reviewed by his administrative supervisors. Today *audit* is used to refer to any independent examination, any objective assessment of something. In public administration the word audit refers to either of two very common activities:

1. The official examination of a financial report submitted by an individual or organization to determine whether it accurately represents expenditures, deductions, or other allowances determined by laws and regulations
2. The final phase of the government budgetary process, which reviews the operations of an agency, especially its financial transactions, to determine whether the agency has spent its money in accordance with the law, in the most efficient manner, and with desired results

In all cases an audit connotes comparison with some standard. Bligh knew that his behavior would be measured against that of other naval officers. Administrators expect that their performance will be compared to that of other administrators with comparable responsibilities. And financial statements are audited to determine when they are in accord with generally accepted accounting standards. The essence of auditing is measuring something against a good example in order to make a critical, an evaluative, judgment.

Virtually all modern organizations, from a local tennis club to the U.S. government, have auditors whose basic task is to certify that the financial accounts of the organization are correct. Auditing has become a major branch of the **accounting** profession, with complex professional standards and procedures for admission, practice, and reporting. Large accounting firms such as Price Waterhouse and Arthur Andersen are widely known throughout the developed world. In themselves they are multinational organizations of substantial size and complexity. The audit certifications of such firms are attached to the formal financial reports of all major corporations. This independent examination of the financial accounts of organizations is a process designed to establish that they comply both with the law and with national accounting standards. These pictures of an organization's financial position are essential requirements for confident decision making by senior managers, by boards of directors, by investors, and by stockholders.

Multiple Applications

The word audit continues to evolve. Many new applications of the term now exist beside its traditional use for financial reports. Thus it is possible to have a management audit—an independent examination of an organization's management posture (policies, practices, and performance of management within an organization)—or a performance audit or efficiency audit. An audit undertaken within a single organization may seek to combine elements of the financial audit, the efficiency audit, and the management audit. To such global intentions the term "comprehensive audit" is often applied.

The concept of independent audit has not been limited to financial and managerial issues. Many other kinds of independent assessments are also called audits. For example, an environmental audit may seek to examine compliance with environmental laws and sound environmental practices. An energy audit may seek to independently assess how an organization uses or wastes energy. Water or telecommunications audits may do the same to help an individual or organization reduce its utility bills. And a social audit may assess social issues within an organizational context. Audit processes have in common a focus on the present and the immediate past. When the social or environmental effects of a future proposal such as a new airport or highway are examined, they are usually referred to as a social impact, or environmental impact, statement. Logically, we cannot audit something that has not happened, although it is often possible to analyze or predict future impacts.

Independent examinations—audits—of an organization's finances or performance can be conducted internally or externally, by an organization's own staff, or by outsiders from a public (meaning private sector) accounting firm. In government the outsiders could be an independent audit arm of government such as a comptroller general's office. Large organizations are normally subject to both internal and external auditors. An internal audit group, independent of line management and with a reporting line sufficiently high in the organization, may seek to provide management with objective advice quickly so that problems can be identified and rectified before they grow worse. The external auditor not only comes from outside but often reports outside as well—to elected representatives, stockholders, or whoever it is that holds ultimate responsibility for an organization's destiny. Often, an effi-

---

accounting The process of classifying, measuring, and interpreting financial transactions to provide management with information upon which to base economic decisions.

cient internal audit unit can simplify and prepare the ground to make the work of external auditors quicker and more focused. Nevertheless, neither internal nor external auditors alone are likely to be adequate for a large and complex organization—especially in the public sector, where accountability is critically important.

History of Auditing

Government auditing goes back to ancient times. There are records of a Chinese audit function in the eleventh century B.C.E. and in Athens in the fourth century B.C.E. Modern audit in government really developed in the nineteenth century, when the growth of public sector activities became so complex that an independent and objective assessment of financial management became essential. With huge sums of money moving around global empires in the nineteenth century, the opportunities for corruption were effectively limitless. In this context it made financial sense to create strong government audit units with clear links to the top of government. Great Britain created its Office of Comptroller-General in 1857. It had independent links to a Parliamentary Committee of Public Accounts and strong legislative backing to enforce access to accounts and the disclosure of information. The U.S. General Accounting Office was established in 1921. Headed by the Comptroller General of the United States, it is an agency of, and reports directly to, the Congress. However, there were many other examples of government audit in the United States earlier than this. The progressive reform movement early in the twentieth century fought, often quite successfully, for state and local governments to have an appointed civil service commission to curtail patronage abuses as well as an elected **controller/comptroller,** whose job it was to inhibit financial abuses.

The establishment of prestigious and relatively independent national audit organizations like the Comptroller and Auditor-General in Great Britain and the General Accounting Office in the United States helps the audit function to stand above corruption and apart from the political administration of the day. Often the prestige and renown of the individual in charge of an audit office can be important in personifying the integrity and credibility of the office—particularly when (as is inevitable) some of its findings turn out to be unpalatable to the ruling administration.

The General Accounting Office

Today most people assume that it is the president who is responsible for the performance and accountability of the federal bureaucracy. That was certainly not the case in the nineteenth century, when it was assumed that the Congress had the overwhelming responsibility for the national administration. But when Theodore Roosevelt became president in 1901, he led a two-decade-long cry that the president be given greater authority. Finally, after a variety of high level commissions endorsed the notion that the president be given significant administrative responsibility, the

---

controller/comptroller The financial officer of a company or a government agency. For example, the comptroller general of the United States heads the General Accounting Office, which audits government agencies. Normally, a controller has the technical skills of an accountant. The basic functions of the office are to supervise accounting and to make sure that funds are spent for acceptable purposes. The audit function comes afterward; it is a review to see that funds were expended correctly.

Box 13.1

The Athenian Audit

Athenian statesmen were held accountable for expenditures as well as receipts through the public audit, an invention of the ancient Greeks. Established during the preclassical period, the audit had grown out of the gradual democratization of Athenian political institutions. It expressed the governing philosophy of the polis—the reciprocal responsibility and liability of citizen and state. Before being discharged from office at the end of his year of service, an Athenian official was forced to submit to formal public examination. . . . As public information, treasury accounts were chiseled into stone tablets and mounted on public buildings. . . .

An official who would not submit to audit was barred from the courts, prevented from making religious offerings to the gods, and forbidden to travel outside Athens. If his accounts showed discrepancies, the official was brought to trial; if convicted he was fined and forced to restore the amounts in question. If an official did not pay, the state would imprison him and confiscate his property. An office-holder's personal liability for public funds explains why Athenians preferred to use public slaves, rather than free citizens, as clerks. If a discrepancy in the accounts was discovered, a slave could be tortured to elicit a confession, and his superiors could then be exonerated.

SOURCE: Carolyn Webber and Aaron Wildavsky, *A History of Taxation and Expenditure in the Western World* (New York: Simon and Schuster, 1986).

Congress passed the Budget and Accounting Act of 1921. The first half of the act (the "budget") gave in to the reform advocates by creating a Bureau of the Budget in the Department of the Treasury. This new bureau was authorized to prepare an executive budget and was given additional staff to conduct continuing studies of efficiency. So long before the Bureau of the Budget was renamed the Office of Management and Budget in 1970, it had a significant management role.

But the Congress was institutionally suspicious of presidential power. So the second half of the act (the "accounting") created the General Accounting Office (GAO) as a congressional support agency to audit federal government expenditures and to assist the Congress with its legislative oversight responsibilities. Because these two agencies have become so central to the administrative well-being of the federal government, Herbert Emmerich has called their creation "probably the greatest landmark of our administrative history except for the Constitution itself."

The GAO is directed by the comptroller general of the United States, who is appointed by the president with the advice and consent of the Senate for a term of 15 years. While the GAO originally confined itself to auditing financial records to see that funds were properly spent, since the 1960s it has redefined its mission to include overall program evaluation. Its responsibilities include conducting financial

as well as performance audits of all federal government agencies. Indeed, it was always intended that it be so. The 1921 act specifically authorizes the comptroller
general to "make recommendations looking to greater economy or efficiency in
public expenditures." And "all departments and establishments" are required by
the Act to turn over "any books, documents, papers or records" that the comptroller general "or any of his assistants or employees" requests. Long before President
Ronald Reagan popularized the phrase "trust but verify" in regard to nuclear
weapons treaties with the Russians, the Congress was taking this attitude with the
president. Think of the GAO as the "Office of Verification" for the Congress. In a
typical year the GAO completes around 1,000 major reports for the members of
Congress. The mission statement of the General Accounting Office embodies the
ideas of independence and service to Congress, which are central to the GAO's role:

> We seek to achieve honest, efficient management and full accountability throughout
> government. We serve the public interest by providing members of Congress and oth-
> ers who make policy with accurate information, unbiased analysis, and objective
> recommendations on how to use public resources in support of the security and well-
> being of the American people.

Often the information provided by the General Accounting Office is delivered
to Congress in written reports (1,006 in 1997). However, there will also be numerous occasions every year in which the GAO staff provide testimony to congressional
committees (182 times in 1997) or provide formal briefings (149 in 1997). The issues covered may concern conventional financial management. But very often the
scope of reports and briefings goes to matters of vital policy import that Congress
might otherwise not have been aware of. And the breadth of topics the GAO looks
at is vast. As of 1998, the best-seller list of the GAO reports includes:

1. *School Facilities: Conditions of America's Schools*
2. *Information Superhighway: An Overview of Technology Challenges*
3. *Cholesterol Measurement: Test Accuracy and Factors That Influence Cholesterol Levels*
4. *Electric Vehicles: Likely Consequences of U.S. and Other Nations' Programs
   and Policies*
5. *Managing for Results: State Experiences Provide Insights for Federal Management Reform*

The scope of these topics illustrates how far removed a modern national audit
agency is from the kind of green eye-shade, quill pen audit that existed in the past.
These are truly adventures in public administration where the auditor is not
so much a "private" as a "public" detective, and the client not a rich widow but
Uncle Sam himself.

Despite the wide scope of policy and performance investigations the GAO undertakes, financial management remains a central concern. On the revenue side, the
GAO identifies many cases in which government agencies are not pulling in the
money owed. The GAO found out, for example, that the Internal Revenue Service

is less likely to catch high-income people who do not file tax returns than lower income people; and how Medicare contractors were not bothering to recover monies owed by other insurers. On the expenditure side, each year brings new examples of waste identified by the GAO: for example, how Stanford University had overcharged the Office of Naval Research, or how inadequate controls over Department of Defense subcontractors cost the federal government millions of dollars each year.

The GAO, with its 3,800 accountants, lawyers, and engineers, is only the largest government auditing agency in the United States. The GAO is vast both in size and reputation. Its national visibility and reputation for institutional integrity has made it a model for other levels of government. Every major subnational government has its auditors. They range from the elected auditor general of a state government to the local accounting firm retained by a small school board. Indeed, the state level auditor is effectively part of a plural executive, the de facto arrangement of most state governments because most governors share executive authority with other independently elected officers, such as a secretary of state, treasurer, attorney general—or an auditor.

Types of Audit

The GAO in its *Standards for Audit of Governmental Organizations, Programs, Activities, and Functions* maintains that a comprehensive audit program should include the following three types of audit:

1. *Financial and compliance:* Determines (a) whether the financial statements of an audited entity present fairly the financial position and the results of financial operations in accordance with generally accepted accounting principles and (b) whether the entity has complied with laws and regulations that may have a material effect upon the financial statements.

2. *Economy and efficiency:* Determines (a) whether the entity is managing and utilizing its resources (such as personnel, property, space) economically and efficiently, (b) the causes of inefficiencies or uneconomical practices, and (c) whether the entity has complied with laws and regulations concerning matters of economy and efficiency.

3. *Program results:* Determines (a) whether the desired results or benefits established by the legislature or other authorizing body are being achieved and (b) whether the agency has considered alternatives that might yield desired results at a lower cost.

Compliance Audit

The oldest and most traditional form of auditing activity is known as a compliance audit. Here the auditor is looking for the extent to which, in the financial management of an organization, financial inputs have been managed in compliance with the law and accepted standards and conventions for the treatment of accounting information. In the past, a traditional compliance audit was embodied by the annual visit of the auditor to remote parts of the organization, where the auditor would check each entry in financial journals and ledgers, making sure that arithmetic and balances were correct and that no mistakes had been made. At the end of this process, the auditor would certify that the financial records were correct.

The value of this traditional form of audit is clear. Officials dealing with funds could not simply dispose of them as they wished, keeping no records or keeping records that could not be understood. The advent of traditional auditing meant that every public official had to expect and prepare for a regular visit by the auditor, had to keep accounts in a manner officially prescribed (often by regulations), and had to make those records available for the auditor's scrutiny. In some jurisdictions the audit might be accompanied by an inventory of stores and equipment, hence the derisive references at times to the compliance audit as involving the counting of paper clips. In fact, the compliance audit was and remains a powerful primary tool for preventing many types of corruption.

But compliance audits often go beyond financial reviews. Voluntary compliance is the basis of a civil society. No government has the resources to force all of its citizens to comply with all of the criminal and civil laws. Consequently, all governments are more dependent upon compliance than they would ever like to admit. The best single example of massive voluntary compliance is the U.S. federal income tax system, which is essentially administered by self-assessment and voluntary payment. The much dreaded audit by the federal government's tax collecting agency, the **Internal Revenue Service**, is an assessment not just of whether a citizen has paid taxes due, but also whether the taxes were calculated in the appropriate manner.

Compliance auditing is also undertaken by funding agencies to judge whether a grantee is acting (i.e., spending its grant funds) in accordance with the granter's policies or preset guidelines. For example, the aptly named Office of Federal Contract Compliance Programs within the Department of Labor works to ensure (1) that there is no employment discrimination by government contractors because of race, religion, color, sex, or national origin; and (2) that there is affirmative action to employ Vietnam era veterans and handicapped workers.

But compliance auditing is inherently limited. Conceptually it is part of a control system that focuses on the "inputs" or resources used in administration, not the "outputs" or results. An organization might well be able to comply with the letter of the law concerning accounting for public monies, and yet seem to achieve nothing. By the 1960s government auditors at all levels became increasingly discontented with performing such a confined role, of effectively "fiddling while Rome burned," by concentrating only on financial transactions rather than looking at the overall performance of the organization.

Internal Revenue Service (IRS) The federal agency, established in 1862 within the Treasury Department, responsible for administering and enforcing the internal revenue laws, except those relating to alcohol, tobacco, firearms, and explosives (which are the responsibility of the Bureau of Alcohol, Tobacco and Firearms). The IRS mission is to encourage and to achieve the highest possible degree of voluntary compliance with the tax laws and regulations. Basic IRS activities include taxpayer service and education; determination, assessment, and collection of taxes; determination of pension plan qualifications and exempt organization status; and preparation and issuance of rulings and regulations to supplement the provisions of the Internal Revenue Code. The IRS is the largest controller of financial information on private citizens. The potential for abuse of this data and of the tax system is ever present. For example, there were major scandals about using the IRS for political purposes in both the Truman and Nixon administrations.

Performance Audit

The possibility of auditors extending their scope from assessing compliance with the law and regulations to the wider role of assessing efficiency and effectiveness began to be discussed late in the 1960s. By 1972, the General Accounting Office was formally advocating adopting such a wider role. The GAO's enabling legislation had from the beginning given it the legal basis for this expansion of its mission. Efficiency and effectiveness audits are the two steps in the performance audit chain, but in practice they may be telescoped into a single performance or comprehensive audit of the organization.

An efficiency audit compares the activities of an organization with the objectives that have been assigned to it. In a sense, an efficiency audit still entails a compliance notion—though it is now the extent to which the organization has complied with and realized its objectives that is being examined. Such an extension of the auditor's role is compatible with an instrumental view of administration, since it is implementation of the objectives set by political leaders that is being reviewed. They and their constituents want to know how responsive the organization has been to their will, how effective they have been in playing the instruments of state.

When the scope of audit is extended beyond the efficiency of an organization to its effectiveness, attention turns from the extent to which politically set objectives have been achieved to the broader question of whether the objectives themselves were right in the first place. This further extension of scope has been controversial, since it places the auditor firmly in the role of policy evaluator. Is this an appropriate role for an auditor? Does it invite political controversy of a kind that might reflect on the independence of the audit function? If auditors criticize political leaders or suggest that government policies are inappropriate, the audit entity itself could lose the capacity to review programs in a way that will be perceived as not only objective, but above the normal political fray. Effectiveness or performance auditing in government is thus an inherently political activity that must be dressed in apolitical clothes. It must be free of methodological bias as a matter of science at the same time that it is perceived to be free of political bias as a matter of strategy.

Perceived independence from government is undoubtedly an essential requirement for a government auditor to function well. Yet such offices often have built-in potential threats to their independence: They are financed by government, they are sometimes expected in comprehensive audits to examine wide-ranging matters including controversial policies, and they are normally staffed by civil servants who typically feel the need to remain on favorable terms with political leaders to ensure their future career prospects. Thus many political types of policy review are better conducted by agencies other than the traditional audit office—perhaps by a policy review group closely tied to the administration, by consultants or academics, or, if there is a substantial financial management element to the task, a private accounting firm.

The Savings and Loan Scandal

Traditional audit offices function best when they "stick to their knitting" and avoid the adventuresome frontiers of auditing activities. But even when they do just that and do it superbly, it often happens that their political masters ignore their reports.

The savings and loan scandal is a major example of this. The largest financial scandal in American history was brought about by the 1980s loosening of bank regulations and of **oversight** by the federal government. Hundreds of banks (typically savings and loan institutions) failed and the U.S. government was stuck with an estimated $500 billion bill to pay off federally insured depositors. The scandal started with the Garn–St. Germain Depository Institution Decontrol Act of 1982, which allowed for a wider range of investments by savings and loan institutions—including unsecured business loans. At the same time that the law said banks could go beyond traditional conservative home mortgage investments, the Reagan administration dramatically cut the number of federal bank auditors. Thus thousands of bankers, especially those in the South and Southwest, were able to literally loot their own banks because hardly anybody (meaning federal auditors) was looking. Depositors were not concerned because they were largely insured against loss. The Congress had raised the deposit insurance limit to $100,000 (from $40,000) in 1980. The "looting" took the form of sweetheart deals between bankers and unscrupulous business people, land flips (banks selling land back and forth to raise its price), organized crime involvement, and outright incompetence.

The GAO first warned the Congress of the insolvency of 461 savings and loan institutions in 1986. *New Republic* reporter Eric Konigsberg wrote that when GAO investigator Craig Simmons testified about this before the House Committee on Banking, Finance, and Urban Affairs, the "committee members were outraged." But they were not outraged at the facts of the situation, they were outraged at the GAO. Committee Chairman Fernand St. Germain "questioned Simmons' figures and asked of another GAO auditor, William Anderson: 'As the Johnny Mercer song says, Can we accentuate a little positive here?'" This is the attitude that in the end, had Congress ignore the GAO report.

But after another few years and another few dozen GAO reports on corruption in the savings and loan industry, Congress finally took notice and acted. But had they acted on the original 1986 GAO report, they could have saved the nation, quite literally, hundreds of billions (yes, billions!) of dollars.

When the enormous dimensions of the scandal became apparent in late 1988, the Democratically controlled Congress sought to blame the Republican administrations of Presidents Reagan and Bush for their lax supervision of the banking industry. The Republicans sought to lay the blame on the Congress for allowing decontrol in the first place. Only one thing was certain: there was plenty of blame to go around.

However, there was no blame for the GAO. It had, through its various reports, been warning the government about this problem for years—but to no avail. Even the best evaluations of looming disaster are useless if no one reads or acts upon them. In his *Discourses* (1532) Niccolo Machiavelli anticipated just such an eventuality when he wrote, "If you tender your advice with modesty, and the opposition

---

oversight The means by which the U.S. Congress monitors the activities of executive branch agencies to determine if the laws are being faithfully executed. Oversight takes many forms. The most obvious are the annual congressional hearings on agency budget requests, in which agency activities have to be justified to the satisfaction of the Congress.

prevents its adoption, and, owing to someone else's advice being adopted, disaster follows, you will acquire very great glory. And, though you cannot rejoice in the glory that comes from disasters which befall your country or your prince, it at any rate counts for something." So while the GAO got the "glory," the American public still got stuck with a $500 billion bill. At such prices we could do with a little less glory. (While the scandal only cost $150 billion at first, that entire amount had to be borrowed because of the already large annual deficits. The ensuing interest costs brought the scandal's total estimated cost to about $500 billion over 30 years.)

The savings and loan scandal is an example of a government bailout—a government-sponsored rescue of a failing private sector enterprise—even though some of the banks were allowed to fail or forced to merge. The government was stuck with the bill for the scandal because it had guaranteed deposits up to $100,000 each. Astoundingly, the government even voluntarily paid many depositors sums greater than the $100,000 that supposedly was the limit of the insurance. But the federal government is not only in the business of guaranteeing bank desposits through the **FDIC** and other agencies; it also guarantees loans for students, for exports (through the **Export-Import Bank**) and on occasion to private business. A loan guarantee is an agreement by which a government pledges to pay part or all of the loan principal and interest to a lender or holder of a security in the event of default by a third-party borrower. The purpose of a guaranteed loan is to reduce the risk borne by a private lender by shifting all or part of the risk to the government. If it becomes necessary for the government to pay part or all of the loan's principal or interest, the payment is a direct outlay. Otherwise, the guarantee does not directly affect budget outlays. The most famous of all loan guarantees to an individual business is the Chrysler Corporation Loan Guarantee Act of 1979, which authorized the federal government to guarantee up to $1.5 billion in loans to the Chrysler Corporation to prevent the bankruptcy of the company, which would have had widespread negative impacts on the economy. Within four years, Chrysler became profitable again and repaid all of its federally guaranteed loans—seven years ahead of schedule.

Internal Audit

So far we have focused on the audit of governmental programs and activities by external auditors, such as the General Accounting Office. However, line managers are often reluctant to wait until an external examination finds problems in their organi-

---

FDIC The Federal Deposit Insurance Corporation, the federal agency established in 1933 to promote and preserve public confidence in banks and to protect the money supply through provision of insurance coverage for bank deposits. Created by an amendment to the Federal Reserve Act, it was reauthorized by the Federal Deposit Insurance Act of 1950.

Export-Import Bank (Eximbank) An autonomous agency of the U.S. government created by the Export-Import Bank Act of 1945 to facilitate export-import trade. Under various programs, the Eximbank provides export credits and direct loans to foreign buyers and sells insurance and export guarantees to U.S. manufacturers. The bank's funds are derived from stock subscribed by the U.S. Treasury in 1945, the repayment of loans, interest earnings, and loans from the U.S. Treasury and from private banks; it receives no budgetary appropriations. Reversing its initial intention to abolish the bank, the Reagan administration used this agency as an instrument in its efforts to promote international rescue packages for Latin American debtor nations.

Box 13.2

Chrysler's Local Politics

Although I had never been a great friend of big business, I wanted to help Chrysler survive because their crisis boiled down to the loss of jobs, a problem that has always been foremost on my agenda.

When [Lee] Iacocca returned, I said, "Tell me, how many people in my district work for Chrysler or one of its suppliers?"

"I have no idea," he replied.

"Find out," I told him. "That's the key to this thing. And do the same for every district in the country. Make up a list, and have your employees and dealers in each district call and write letters to their own member of Congress. You've heard my famous phrase that all politics is local. A lot of jobs will be lost if Chrysler goes under, and believe me, no member wants to see something like that happen in his district."

Iacocca and his people did a terrific job. By appealing to the local economy of each area, Chrysler was able to put together enough votes to get their loan guarantees.

SOURCE: Tip O'Neill, *Man of the House* (New York: Random House, 1987).

NOTE: O'Neill was the Speaker of the House of Representatives from 1977 to 1987.

---

zations. It is therefore common to find internal audit groups within larger governmental organizations. Such groups need to have a reporting line high in the organization (such as to the chief executive officer or to an audit committee at the highest level). They need adequate clear authority and support as well as resources and the right to enter all parts of an organization. Internal audit functions vary in the tasks they pursue, and the way tasks are assigned to them. Sometimes (especially if the organization is a major cash handler), they may need to have a significant compliance audit role. In other circumstances they can virtually serve as independent troubleshooters, providing early warning to top management of emerging problems. While any such internal audit unit needs to have an **audit program** showing what it intends to focus on, CEO's sometimes give substantial latitude to internal auditors to range free around the organization and to add items to their audit program without top management approval. In this sense they function as an **inspector general**.

---

audit program The detailed steps and procedures to be followed in conducting the audit and preparing the report. A written audit program should be prepared for each audit and it should include such information as the purpose and scope, background information needed to understand the audit objectives, and the entity's mission, definition of unique terms, objectives, and reporting procedures.

inspector general The job title (of military origin) for the administrative head of an inspection or investigative unit of a larger agency.

Internal auditors are always in danger of losing their independence to line management. To ensure that the degree of independence needed for effectiveness is maintained, three key principles need to be observed:

1. Location outside line management
2. A high reporting line for audit results
3. Reasonable latitude in selecting assignments

In smaller organizations, it may be difficult to provide an internal audit function with the resources and credibility to do the job. In the United States this problem has been addressed by a variety of techniques, including the provision of audit services to a number of smaller agencies by the General Services Administration, by cross-servicing between agencies and using state and local government auditors, and through private accounting firms. The concept of internal audit services being independently provided to a number of smaller agencies has been used in a number of countries, including Sweden, Canada, and the United States to ensure that the benefits of independent internal audit are not denied to small agencies.

There is a significant role in the public sector for private accounting firms serving as auditors. Large public corporations, especially those operating under corporations law, normally employ accounting firms in some or all of their audit functions. The General Accounting Office itself, quite appropriately, has been audited by a private accounting firm (Price Waterhouse). There are many occasions when such firms, with their wide networks and expertise, can play an invaluable role in public audit.

However, those who imagine that the whole of government audit can or should be placed in the hands of private accounting firms are in the minority. While public administration remains a large complex and specialized field, with its own framework of accountability leading back to democratically elected representatives, there will remain a need for specialist internal and external audit capacities, such as the General Accounting Office, within government.

Accounting

An important issue underlying any successful traditional or comprehensive audit process is the nature and quality of the underlying financial and performance information kept by the organization. The development of **accounting principles** and practices that lay down procedures for gathering and keeping data in meaningful ways is an absolutely essential foundation for effective management and the auditing of it.

In recent years, accounting standards and procedures, as well as the systems and concepts for the measurement of performance (including performance indicators and benchmarking) in the private and public sectors have moved closer to-

---

accounting principles The basic premises that govern most accounting theory and practice. Accounting principles are validated by general acceptance within the accounting community; they are not immutable in the sense of scientific laws. They arise from common experiences, historical precedents, and formulations of professional bodies and governmental agencies. They change over the years as new techniques, business practices, and laws evolve.

gether. The **Financial Accounting Standards Board** has long been the recognized promulgator of private sector accounting principles. In 1991, GAO, the Office of Management and Budget, and the Treasury Department established the Federal Accounting Standards Advisory Board to make recommendations concerning accounting standards to be followed by government departments and agencies. The resulting standards are jointly issued by the GAO and the OMB. The appointment of a professional government accounting standards body of this kind is common in most developed countries.

Cash Accounting

Traditional systems of government accounting were termed "cash accounting" because they simply sought to control and track the passage of cash funds voted by legislatures as these funds were allocated to and spent by the various departments and agencies. But the growing complexity of modern public administration meant a change of focus from controlling inputs to assessing outputs—the results of public sector work as well. The accounting profession in most countries came to the realization that the cash accounting method was too simplistic. The accrual accounting approach would need to be adopted in the public sector if financial reporting were ever to become comparable with the private sector.

Accrual Accounting

The widespread adoption of **accrual accounting** has been a key measure leading to meaningful reporting, **financial statements**, and asset management in public sector organizations. Accrual accounting allows for true measures of income and expenditures, whether or not the cash payments associated with the earnings and debts have actually taken place. Without an accrual accounting system, costs and obligations can be taken off financial statements, making results and conditions seem better than they are in reality. Under accrual accounting, government organizations can illustrate their financial status with a **balance sheet**, as is done in the private sector. A balance sheet, because it requires assets to be identified and valued, is vital for accountability.

The transition from cash to accrual accounting has not been simple. Controversy has raged over issues such as asset valuation. What is the meaning of attaching values

---

Financial Accounting Standards Board A private organization that sets standards for financial accounting and reporting and promulgates generally accepted accounting principles. Its pronouncements are officially recognized as authoritative by the American Institute of Certified Public Accountants and the Securities and Exchange Commission.

accrual accounting Recording debts owed to and by a company when the debt becomes a legal obligation, which may be before the money is actually paid.

financial statement A summary of the results of operations; what a company or other organization owns and what it owes. It may be in the form of a balance sheet, a profit and loss statement, or an annual report. Sometimes the word is used broadly to include any report in terms of money, even operating reports, but more strictly, it shows the financial status of an organization at a given time.

balance sheet A complete summary of the financial worth of a company, broken down by assets and liabilities. It is called a balance sheet because total assets balance with, or are equal to, total liabilities plus net worth. A corporation's annual balance sheet will show what it owns and owes as of a given day.

Box 13.3

Accounting for the Unquantifiable?

Letter from Charles Babbage to Alfred Lord Tennyson (c. 1850)
[Babbage] extended his demand for statistical accuracy to poetry; it is said that he sent the following letter to Alfred, Lord Tennyson about a couplet in "The Vision of Sin":

> "Every minute dies a man, / Every minute one is born": I need hardly point out to you that this calculation would tend to keep the sum total of the world's population in a state of perpetual equipoise, whereas it is a well-known fact that the said sum total is constantly on the increase. I would therefore take the liberty of suggesting that in the next edition of your excellent poem the erroneous calculation to which I refer should be corrected as follows: "Every one moment dies a man/ And one and a sixteenth is born." I may add that the exact figures are 1.167, but something must, of course, be conceded to the laws of metre.

SOURCE: Philip and Emily Morrison, eds., *Charles Babbage and His Calculating Engines* (New York: Dover 1961).

---

to public assets such as national art collections or national parks when it is inconceivable that such assets could be sold? What return on assets measure should apply to assets such as public monuments that seem to confer no return at all?

Yet despite the many teething problems, modern government accounting statements are usually based on accounting standards that apply accrual accounting concepts to the government context. In the United States, the General Accounting Office (under Title 2 of its Policy and Procedures Manual for the Guidance of Federal Agencies) requires fixed assets to be capitalized (a value assigned) and depreciated. Accrued liabilities such as annual, sick, and other leave must be accounted for and **accounts receivable** must be identified.

Modified Accrual Accounting

While a number of governments worldwide (such as that of New Zealand), have adopted rigorous and comprehensive accrual accounting in the public sector, it is more common in the United States for governments to take a modified approach. Thus modified accrual accounting, which could alternatively be viewed as modified cash accounting, seeks to achieve a matching between revenues raised and costs incurred. However, it may not bring to account long-term liabilities or the adequate valuation and treatment of assets.

---

accounts receivable Money owed to the organization.

Modified accrual accounting, like cash accounting, thus presents an incomplete picture of an organization's position, leaving scope for political opportunists to make political mileage by such tactics as emphasizing liabilities and ignoring debt, a technique that would be much more difficult if an accrual-based comprehensive balance sheet formed part of an annual reporting requirement.

Asset Management

The conceptual move toward accrual accounting has had immense significance in changing the way governments and their political leaders think about public assets. In the days of cash accounting, there was no particular need for government agencies to identify their holdings of land, buildings, and other assets. Today, under the broad concept of asset management, they must systematically program the maintenance of assets throughout their life cycles, to value assets, to look for returns from them, or to have asset disposal programs.

In the private sector, the organizing principle for asset management is the requirement that assets be held in order to generate profits for shareholders. A company that holds assets but does not use them productively is vulnerable to takeover. Some corporations even specialize in taking over other corporations whose assets have been "lazy." They then engage in so-called "asset stripping" to sell idle assets and improve returns to shareholders.

In the public sector, the holding of assets reflects more complex motives. Some assets such as utilities, airlines, or railroads are inherently commercial operations. They, when owned by government, must be managed under commercial criteria. However, most governments also hold some public assets for their intrinsic worth—parks, public buildings, art and archives collections, and so on. To manage these in terms of financial criteria alone would be inappropriate. Accordingly, in order to manage their assets well, governments need to classify their assets according to their functions. Those assets that are intimately associated with the provision of public goods—particular art museums, parks, open space, etc., may need to be classified as "public assets" to which **rate of return** thinking does not apply. Others, held purely for commercial purposes, need to be assessed by commercial management criteria, including return on assets. These issues can become critical when governments face a "fiscal crunch" and there is a legitimate need to reshuffle assets and dispose of what is not essential. At such times governments and their constituents need a realistic approach to identifying which land, buildings, and objects are not negotiable public assets and which are assets that can be sold to help balance the books. For example, while it is unthinkable that the U.S. government would sell off assets such as the Washington Monument or the Lincoln Memorial, there have long been serious discussions about the desirability of selling Amtrak and the Tennessee Valley Authority.

This process of asset stripping is a major aspect of privatization. For example, in the mid-1990s, when Rudolph Giuliani became mayor of New York, he sought to sell a municipal cemetery (valuable because of its many unused gravesites); the commissioners of Allegheny County, Pennsylvania, once sought to sell the county's waste water treatment plant; and Orange County, California, sought to sell its John

---

rate of return A measure of profit as a percentage of money or property value invested.

Wayne Airport. Of course, the most successful government strippers of the last two decades have been the Conservative governments of Margaret Thatcher and John Major in Great Britain. They have privatized an airline, public utilities such as gas, electric, and water works, and countless aspects of public transporation (railroads and bus lines). Of course, the greatest binge of asset stripping in modern times occured in the early 1990s, when the formerly socialist states of Eastern Europe and the former Soviet Union sold off many state-owned enterprises in an effort to jump-start their newly capitalistic economies.

Asset management in all its dimensions has now come to mean something in government. Today, governments ensure that they know what they own, by compiling and maintaining asset registers. In the past, governments and their agencies would simply acquire assets and keep them. There may have been no clear and simple way for an agency to disclose with ease just what it had. Once a list—the asset register—of assets existed, the possibility of having them professionally valued existed. That in turn began to provide the building blocks from which the asset side of a government balance sheet could be constructed. Once inventoried and valued, assets could be managed. Thus the full gamut of management options became more transparently available. How should assets be acquired, maintained, and disposed of? Why were so many public resources tied up in this class of asset? Should a user charge be imposed to reflect that this class of asset is of interest only to a small group in the population, such as campers in parks or hunters in forests? Should divestiture, privatization, or contracting out of this class of asset be considered to improve efficiency or simply to free up funds to use for higher priority programs?

In reverse, a similar logic can be applied to the analysis of public liabilities. What kinds of liabilities does a government or agency hold? What kinds of risks are inherent in these? Was the aggregate level of debt commensurate with the servicing (ability to pay) capability of the government or agency? What alterations could be made to the portfolio of liabilities? Again, the movement toward accrual accounting helps to flush out these questions. The result is that the management of assets and liabilities was properly promoted in importance in the agenda of public financial management.

Financial Reporting

A financial report is a written statement—also called an accountant's certificate, accountant's opinion, or audit report—prepared by an independent accountant or auditor after an audit. It is addressed to the owners, directors, and stockholders of the audited enterprise. The auditor states briefly the nature and the scope of the examination and expresses a professional opinion as to the fairness of the appended financial statement in presenting the firm's financial position and operating results for the specified period. The opinion may be unqualified, or it may contain exceptions, qualifications, or other comments regarding the treatment of particular items, the limitations of the auditing procedures followed, and changes of accounting methods from those used in previous years.

Budget documents need to accompany financial reporting with relevant aggregations of expenditure so that patterns and significance can be seen. The original development of the concept of an executive budget early in the twentieth century, the concepts of performance budgeting in the 1950s, program budgeting in the 1960s, and the unified national budget in the 1970s, were all attempts to shape a national resource allocation document—to provide a framework that would be intelligible and would facilitate the democratic control of expenditure and allocation of funds.

It is important to establish a framework of financial reporting that is intelligible to legislators and citizens alike that is capable of aggregation toward the objective of a unified or "whole of government" financial statement. Private corporations, however large, have long furnished their stockholders with consolidated reports on an accrual accounting basis. A similar accounting framework should be the goal of government as a whole and of each of its constituent agencies. A key problem here is the identification and valuation of public assets and liabilities. This goal is exactly what Harvard student Meredith E. Bagby sought to achieve in the statistical presentation that she titled *The First Annual Report of the United States of America*. She took technical information that was readily available from the federal government and presented it in a user-friendly format. The public's desire for this "easy reading" annual report was so great that this initially self-published report was reprinted and distributed by a major publisher.

Program Evaluation

A program evaluation is the systematic examination of any activity or group of activities undertaken by government to make a determination about their effects, both short and long range. Program evaluation is distinguished from management evaluation (also called organization evaluation) because the latter is limited to a program's internal administrative procedures. While program evaluations use management and organizational data, the main thrust is necessarily on overall program objectives and impact.

Policy Analysis Is Not Program Evaluation

The terms *policy analysis* and *program evaluation* are often confused, often used interchangeably. But they differ. A policy analysis is a set of techniques that seeks to answer the question of what the probable effects of a policy will be before they actually occur. A policy analysis undertaken on a program that is already in effect is more properly called a program evaluation. Nevertheless, the term is used by many to refer to both before- and after-the-fact analyses of public policies. All policy analysis involves the application of systematic research techniques (drawn largely from the social sciences and based on measurements of program effectiveness, quality, cost, and impact) to the formulation, execution, and evaluation of public policy to create a more rational or optimal administrative system. A formal program evaluation effort normally implies that a relationship of "arm's length" independence has been established between the program and those evaluating it. In-house evaluations, however well conducted, are likely to be suspected of special pleading on behalf of the agency concerned.

Of course, program evaluations have always been done by executives, legislators, and their captains. (Remember Bligh!) But as old government programs expanded and new programs were initiated in the 1960s, program evaluations came out of the shadows. By the beginning of the 1970s, it was generally conceded that many of the Great Society programs initiated during the Johnson administration were not working nearly as well as it was originally hoped. As these and other social programs came under increasing criticism, the field of program evaluation gained increasing prominence.

Aaron Wildavsky, in his 1972 *Public Administration Review* article, "The Self-Evaluating Organization," provided an insightful discussion about the difficulties of evaluating public programs in a dynamic political environment. Wildavsky wrote that the "ideal organization would be self-evaluating. It would continuously monitor its own activities so as to determine whether it was meeting its goals or even whether these goals should continue to prevail. When evaluation suggested that a change in goals or programs to achieve them was desirable, these proposals would be taken seriously by top decision makers. They would institute the necessary changes."

But the problem with evaluation, according to Wildavsky, was that no matter how compelling the case for change, change was precisely what evaluation emphasized most and organizations abhorred most. Most public managers, he argued, are hard-pressed to cope with day-to-day operational demands; thus they strive for stability—not constant reorder and reformulation. The costs of change had to be borne, too, and evaluation seldom considered this. Finally, since the most politically feasible organizational strategies would be ones that minimized disruption, managers would tend to resist or ignore evaluation.

Wildavsky's arguments notwithstanding, evaluation would not be denied. In 1967, Edward Suchman of Columbia University published the first major work on evaluation theory, *Evaluative Research*. Suchman's work argued that evaluation was essentially a field of study; that evaluative research and practice can and must be studied in a general context outside of evaluation applications in the various fields of specialization; that evaluation was generic. Generic? Yes. But in whatever context it surfaced, it was also intensely political. Evaluation researcher Carol H. Weiss discovered these four "less legitimate"—meaning wholly political in the worst sense of the word—reasons for evaluation:

1. *Postponement:* The decision makers may be looking for ways to delay a decision. Instead of resorting to the usual ploy of appointing a committee and waiting for its report, they can commission an evaluation study, which takes even longer.

2. *Ducking responsibility:* Sometimes one faction in the program organization is espousing one course of action and another faction is opposing it. The administrators look to evaluation to get them off the hook by producing dispassionate evidence that will make the decision for them. There are cases in which administrators know what the decision will be even before they call in the evaluators, but they want to cloak it in the legitimate trappings of research.

3. *Public relations:* Occasionally, evaluation is seen as a way of self-glorification. Administrators believe that they have a highly successful program and look for a way to make it visible. A good study will fill the bill. Copies of the report, favorable of course, can be sent to boards of trustees, members of legislative

committees, executives of philanthropic foundations who give large sums to successful programs, and other influential people. . . . The program administrators' motives are not, of course, necessarily crooked or selfish. Often, there is a need to justify the program to the people who pay the bills, and they are seeking support for a concept and a project in which they believe. Generating support for existing programs is a common motive for embarking on evaluation.

4. *Fulfilling grant requirements:* Increasingly, the decision to evaluate stems from sources outside the program. Many federal grants for demonstration projects and innovative programs are tagged with an evaluation requirement; for example, all projects for disadvantaged pupils funded under Title I of the Elementary and Secondary Education Act are required to be evaluated. . . . To the operators of a project, the demands of starting up and running the new program take priority. Plagued as they often are by immediate problems of staffing, budgets, logistics, community relations, and all the other trials of pioneers, they tend to neglect the evaluation. They see it mainly as a ritual designed to placate the funding bodies, without any real usefulness to them.

Legislative Program Evaluation

The General Accounting Office, under the leadership of **Elmer Staats**, also helped elevate the general quality and value of program evaluation by setting evaluation standards and working actively to professionalize program evaluation as part of the **expanded scope of auditing**. Many state governments would initiate legislative evaluation commissions based on the GAO idea. Some state legislatures—most notably Hawaii, Wisconsin, and Michigan—have organized separate program evaluation staffs similar to the GAO. Another method used by state legislatures is that of the legislative commission. New York's Legislative Commission on Expenditure Review pioneered with this concept whereby a separate program evaluation staff, under an executive director, reports to the joint leadership of the legislature. New Jersey, Illinois, and Virginia now use variations on this theme. A third format exists whereby the evaluation function is located in a discrete committee that is linked to the several appropriations committees. Connecticut and North Carolina offer examples of this.

In 1976, Colorado, after a major lobbying effort by **Common Cause**, would become the first state to enact a sunset law—the requirement that government agencies and programs have termination dates. Many other jurisdictions subsequently enacted them as well. They require formal evaluations and subsequent affirmative legislation if the agency or program is to continue. Although the purpose of a finite life span of, say, five years is to force evaluation and to toughen legislative oversight, the effect is to subject programs to automatic termination unless the clock is reset. Despite its widespread popularity, such time-bomb evaluation is not without

---

Elmer Staats (1914–) The comptroller general of the United States from 1966 to 1981.
expanded scope of auditing Evaluating the results and effectiveness of a government activity in addition to delving into the traditional financial compliance concerns of auditing.
Common Cause A Washington-based public interest lobby founded in 1970 and devoted to making public officials more accountable to citizens and to improving government performance.

risks. There are limits to the abilities of any legislature's staff to do the kind of thorough evaluation required to make sunset meaningful. And, of course, the political reality is that the evaluation might become a tool of bipartisan infighting. Requiring organizations to submit evaluation data for review and to justify their programs may amount to little more than burying the legislature in an avalanche of insignificant paper—something at which agencies have a demonstrated prowess. Furthermore, some agencies, such as police, prisons, and mental health institutions, will be rightly skeptical of the chances of their programs being shut down. Nevertheless, by the mid-1970s evaluation was a vital and integral part of public administration and remains so today.

Types of Evaluation

There are many types of program evaluation and many perspectives from which it can be undertaken. For example, an *ex ante* evaluation, such as an environmental effects statement, might seek to assess the impacts and outcomes of a program before that program is implemented: Should the outcomes or impacts identified prove problematic, such a study may lead to a program being aborted, or at least significantly modified. A process evaluation may examine aspects of a program's operations while they are in place, and its results may be absorbed directly into the organization's management processes. An *ex post* evaluation, "post-mortem," or "de-briefing" looks at a program or operation after it has been completed, and it has particular relevance when an activity is likely to recur, such as a forest fire emergency, or a serious heat wave like the one in Chicago in 1995 that claimed hundreds of lives. Such studies seek to establish the changes to policy, infrastructure, or operations that would allow a similar circumstance to have more positive results when it next occurs.

Perspectives in program evaluation also vary according to the discipline or paradigm from which they are conducted. Managers will usually think in terms of managerial paradigms and look at the nature and appropriateness of objectives, and the efficiency and effectiveness with which objectives were pursued. Lawyers may stress issues such as authority, compliance, equity, process, and culpability in examining an issue. A political analysis may look at issues of representation and accountability. Clearly, the purpose of undertaking the evaluation must determine the kind of evaluation to be adopted, and the skills required in the evaluation team. Other decisions will include the type of supporting data and research to be used (and the provision of a budget to fund it); the extent to which there will be public hearings or consultations as part of the evaluative process; and whether there are hidden agendas to continue, terminate, or transform the program, which are being worked out.

The zealous evaluator has one cardinal principle: that everything is up for evaluation; there are no exceptions. But many a public manager, while agreeing that most programs are evaluable, will also argue that there are plenty of exceptions. In actuality, it is more a question of degree. Some programs have a high degree of "goal ambiguity"—a quality that can greatly inhibit evaluation. The public sector, because it tends to provide services rather than produce products, has always had

Box 13.4

The Bad News of Program Evaluation

The Book of Exodus in the Bible tells the story of Moses leading the tribes of Israel from bondage in Egypt to the shores of the Red Sea. Looking behind him, he saw the rapidly approaching army of the Egyptians and became naturally concerned. Looking then to the heavens, he called out for assistance. A voice from above promptly answered: "Moses, not to worry, for I have good news and bad news."

Moses replied: "Tell me quickly, for the army grows nearer."

The voice answered: "The good news is that when you raise your staff to the sky, the Red Sea will open, creating a path for your people to cross over in safety. Then the walls of the sea shall come crashing down and destroy the pursuing soldiers."

Moses then said, "Why, that's marvelous; but what's the bad news?"

The voice replied, "The bad news is that you will first have to prepare an environmental impact statement."

more difficulty in defining its output—in measuring its goals. Further complicating matters is the fact that the different functions of government invariably involve different types of evaluation measurement. In evaluating highways we can focus on accidents, injuries, and fatality rates that seemingly represent hard data; the "data" quickly become soft once we move to such functions as parks, mental health, services for the aging, education, and training programs for the unemployed.

Evaluation Standards

Generally speaking, evaluations refer to three standards against which a program can be evaluated: (1) compliance, (2) efficiency, and (3) effectiveness/relevance. These standards indicate the fundamental questions that must be asked of any program.

The first category *compliance*, essentially asks an auditing question: Are government business transactions being conducted in accordance with law? This can be broken down into more specific questions, such as:

1. Were all financial transactions involving the acquisition and expenditure of resources consistent with legislative and administrative authorization/regulation?

2. Are financial records and statements rendered in accord with prescribed accounting standards?

3. Are they accurate and free from fraud?

Most evaluations for ensuring compliance on a regular basis are performed by various audit and control units.

Questions of *efficiency* can be asked: Are government agencies getting optimum productivity out of the resources that they expend? More specific questions can be asked:

1. Is responsibility for specific tasks clearly delegated?
2. Are employees adequately qualified to perform their tasks?
3. Is the waste of resources being avoided?

Efficiency evaluation can also be readily used for comparative analysis; pitting various units, regions, or similar organizations against each other to ascertain who is more efficient and, conversely, who is less. But sometimes this kind of competition can prove counterproductive. For example, Shafritz, Hyde, and Rosenbloom tell the story of a GAO audit of the post office. After a new **postmaster general** sought to foster competition among post offices by generating a list of top offices in productivity, the Postal Service's productivity and mail volume appeared to increase nationwide. After starting at the bottom of the list, the Washington, DC Post Office reported consistently increasing mail volumes and productivity until it ranked at or near the top. The Postal Inspection Service estimated that the total amount of mail handled was inflated over 60 percent. Sometimes the totals were overstated by as much as 110 percent. According to the GAO, these estimates were "supported by hours of videotape records showing individuals reweighing the same mail over and over to inflate volumes and by sworn statements from supervisors and employees admitting record falsification." The GAO concluded that "the most common reasons given by employees for participating in the fabrication were the pressure from higher management to achieve production levels that were unrealistic and a belief that their careers would suffer if these productivity levels were not met." Now "pressure for increased productivity" can be added to the list of all-purpose excuses such as "the devil made me do it" and "the dog ate my homework."

But it has been the third category of questions, those concerning *effectiveness*, that seem to now dominate the program evaluation environment. Questions of effectiveness ask: Is the expenditure of government resources for a specific purpose contributing sufficiently to the achievement of that purpose?" This general question then can in turn be subdivided:

1. Are the various purposes involved in a program compatible?
2. How much of a reduction has there been in the problem?
3. Could the commitment of additional resources to the program have brought about significantly greater advances toward the objectives?
4. What would have happened if the program had not existed?

Despite the close relationship between the effectiveness and the efficiency aspects of a program's operations, they can have an inverse relationship to one another. Thus it is possible to have a program that is relatively inefficient but nevertheless effective (it squanders resources but nevertheless gets the job done) or one

---

postmaster general The chief executive officer of the U.S. Postal Service, appointed by its nine-member board of governors.

that is relatively efficient but ineffective (it may use its resources optimally, but nevertheless has little impact on the problem it was designed to ameliorate).

Management Control: Evaluation in Microcosm

Control is that aspect of management concerned with the comparison of actual versus planned performance as well as the development and implementation of procedures to correct substandard performance. Control, which is inherent to all levels of management, is a feedback process that ideally should report only unexpected situations. This is the essence of management by exception that Moses discovered in Chapter 5. Some management control systems regularly report critical indicators of performance so that management will have advance notice of potential problems.

As we have seen, audits and evaluations provide important perspectives through which managers and elected officials may make evaluative judgments about the efficiency and performance of programs and organizations. However, it is not the only such perspective. On a day-to-day basis, within the organization, the manager must receive continual feedback, make judgments, and exercise corrective and directive control. But Herbert Kaufman has warned that not all feedback is welcome. When organizations are rife with corruption, as is all too often the case with public administration, leaders "may resort to the strategy of discouraging feedback about administrative behavior because they privately approve of the behavior they know they should, according to law and morality, prevent." Such leaders want to be managers but most specifically do not want to appear to be "in control" in case "a pattern of offenses by subordinates is disclosed." They want to be able to make "a credible claim that they, too, were victimized" by their organization's ne'er-do-wells. This is the tactic of the police chief played by Claude Rains in the 1941 movie *Casablanca*. He was "shocked, shocked!" that gambling had been going on (as he pocketed his winnings) in Humphrey Bogart's nightclub.

Management control exists to ensure that managers are made aware on a day-to-day basis of developments within their program or organization, so that a myriad of judgments and corrective actions can be taken. The process can be described as "evaluation in microcosm." As with formal, external evaluation, the manager is likely to have strategic objectives in mind, and to be making progressive but increasingly formed judgments about the extent and rate at which objectives are being achieved. If they are not being achieved, or being achieved too slowly or in the wrong way, the manager will often "exert control" by stepping in and providing program managers with direction. The nature of this direction will reflect management style and the gravity of the position. It may range from a facilitative discussion of available options to a stormy injunction to "shape up or ship out."

Often the audit process focuses on assessing the adequacy of management control systems as a whole. Effective control seeks to ensure that all members of an organization are working together toward organizational objectives. It should provide an early warning system if strategic assumptions are wrong or the environment has changed. An effective management control system will deploy many of the tools of longer-term evaluation; that is, it will involve references to goals and objectives, the selective use of performance standards and performance measures to see whether and how well objectives are being achieved. It will also use informal networks and the **grapevine**, which helps to provide timely information and knowledgeable hunches as to what is happening "in the trenches." A framework of control that is well conceived, uses timely information, and is flexible, can help the program or organization avoid disaster. But if, on the other hand, the system of management control is heavy-handed, based on poor or incomplete information, and excessively rigid, it can frighten out innovation and fail to perform its key task of short-term evaluation and correction. This is what happened with the space shuttle *Challenger* disaster (discussed in Chapter 2).

Evaluation and the Democratic Process

One of the distinguishing features of public administration in democratic societies is the extent to which government is conducted in a "fishbowl." The electorate and elected members of legislatures expect to be able to see clearly how governmental programs and organizations are functioning in "real time" so that policy adjustments and changes in direction can be made—and so that debate can occur about the practicalities of program implementation as well as about the theoretical niceties of policy.

Executive branch internal evaluations, essentially "self" evaluations, are normally incorporated into the management process. More and more budget offices are undertaking this role. Agencies need to be sure that they are accomplishing their objectives, that they are making progress. Of course, this "thirst" for evaluation may be induced from various motives. The noblest is the good management practice of assessing progress in order to focus attention on problem areas so that remedial action can be taken. Equally necessary, though considerably less noble, are program evaluations undertaken for political considerations. A common gambit here is the "defensive program evaluation" whereby possibly controversial programs are evaluated to create, in effect, "good" report cards to show legislative committees or at least to provide some counterarguments against evaluations by others that might produce less favorable results. This is what Captain Bligh instinctively knew he had to do. As a program evaluator, he was far ahead of his time!

The processes of audit and evaluation in government, and indeed many aspects of the exercise of day-to-day management control within public organizations, are no longer conducted in the expectation of secrecy. Rather, the expectation is that decisions and actions are likely to be publicly audited, evaluated, debated, and discussed. "Sunshine laws" exist to this end. Many state and local governments have such laws. The federal government's Sunshine Act of 1977 requires all independent regulatory commissions to give advance notice of the date, time, place, and agenda of their meetings. Closed meetings are allowed if circumstances warrant, but citizens have the right to take agencies to federal court if they feel that closed meetings were not justified. On the whole, this is a healthy development likely to weigh against corruption and incompetence, which fester best in dark places. Yet it must be acknowledged that the weight and extent of accountability, evaluation, and scrutiny does

grapevine The informal means by which organizational members give or receive messages. The expression "heard it through the grapevine" is derived from the practice of stringing early telegraph wires from tree to tree in a vinelike fashion.

impose costs on public administration. These encompass both the direct costs of documenting actions and making information available to inquiries through written or oral testimony, and also the more subtle constraint accountability may impose on spontaneous and flexible decision making. There will be times when administrators take the decision that can best be defended during audit and evaluation, rather than the judgment that is the wisest and best response to a problem.

Despite their imperfections, the systems of audit and evaluation within the public sector form part of the foundations of the public's trust in government. It is the ethical responsibility of public administrators to both improve and facilitate them. After all, as **Alice Rivlin** wrote in her now-classic work, *Systematic Thinking for Social Action*: "Put more simply, to do better, we must have a way of distinguishing better from worse."

Summary

Organizations have auditors whose basic task is to certify that financial accounts are correct. New applications of auditing have evolved beyond this traditional meaning. Thus it is possible to have a management audit, a performance audit, or an efficiency audit. An audit undertaken within a single organization may seek to combine multiple auditing elements. Such efforts are called comprehensive audits.

A comprehensive audit program typically includes three types of audit: (1) financial and compliance, which determines whether the funds were properly spent and whether the law was complied with; (2) economy and efficiency which determines whether resources have been used economically and efficiently; and (3) program results, which determine whether desired results have been achieved. The establishment of relatively independent audit organizations has helped the audit function to stand above corruption and apart from the political administration of the day.

Traditional systems of government accounting were termed "cash accounting" because they simply sought to control and track the flow of cash funds voted by legislatures as these funds were allocated to and spent by agencies. But the growing complexity of modern public administration meant that the cash accounting method was too simplistic. Thus accrual accounting was adopted to create more meaningful reporting and financial statements.

Policy analysis and program evaluation are often confused, and often used interchangeably. But they differ. A policy analysis is a set of techniques that seeks to answer the question of what the probable effects of a policy will be before they actually occur. A policy analysis undertaken on a program that is already in effect is more properly called a program evaluation. Evaluations refer to the standards against which a program can be evaluated—compliance, efficiency, and effectiveness/relevance. These standards indicate the fundamental questions that must be asked of any program.

Alice Rivlin (1931–) The Brookings Institution economist and authority on fiscal policy and program evaluation who became the first director of the U.S. Congressional Budget Office in 1974. During her eight years as head of the CBO, she saw that agency earn a reputation for accurate fiscal and budgetary projections. She became Director of the Office of Management and Budget in 1994 and left to become vice chair of the Federal Reserve Board in 1996.

Key Concepts

assets All money, property, and money-related rights (such as money owed to one) owned by a person or an organization. Capital assets or fixed assets are those things that cannot be turned into cash easily (such as buildings); current assets or liquid assets are those things that can be turned into cash easily (such as cash or goods for sale); and frozen assets are those things that are tied up (for instance, because of a lawsuit).

audit An independent examination, an objective assessment of something; typically the financial reports of an individual or organization to determine whether they accurately represent expenditures and are in compliance with accounting standards and laws.

compliance audit The traditional form of auditing in which the auditor is looking for the extent to which, in the financial management of an organization, funds have been managed in compliance with the law and that accepted standards and conventions for the treatment of accounting information have been used.

evaluation research An attempt to assess specific policy options by conducting experiments, assessing their outcomes, and recommending whether the new concept should be broadly applied.

financial report A written statement—also called an accountant's certificate, accountant's opinion, or audit report—prepared by an independent accountant or auditor after an audit.

General Accounting Office (GAO) A support agency of the U.S. Congress created by the Budget and Accounting Act of 1921 to audit federal government expenditures and to assist the Congress with its legislative oversight responsibilities.

internal audit The function of audit groups within a larger organization. They vary in the tasks they are assigned. Sometimes they have a compliance audit role. In other instances they serve as independent troubleshooters, providing early warning to top management of emerging problems.

management control That aspect of management concerned with the comparison of actual versus planned performance as well as the development and implementation of procedures to correct substandard performance.

performance audit An audit that compares the activities of an organization with the objectives that have been assigned to it.

program evaluation The systematic examination of any activity undertaken by government to make a determination about its effects, both short-term and long-range.

Bibliography

Bagby, Meredith. (1994). *The First Annual Report of the United States of America*. New York: HarperCollins.

Ball, Ian M. (1973). *Pitcairn: Children of Mutiny*. Boston: Little, Brown.

Bligh, William. (1961). *The Mutiny on Board H.M.S. Bounty*. New York: New American Library.

Brown, Judith R. (1984). "Legislative Program Evaluation: Defining a Legislative Service and a Profession," *Public Administration Review* (May-June).

Brown, Richard E., and Ralph Craft. (1980). "Auditing and Public Administration: The Unrealized Partnership," *Public Administration Review* (May-June).

Chelimsky, Eleanor, ed. (1984). *Program Evaluation: Patterns and Directions*. Washington: American Society for Public Administration.

Comptroller General of the United States. (1981). *Standards for Audit of Governmental Organizations, Programs, Activities and Functions*. Washington: General Accounting Office.

Dening, Greg. (1992). *Mr. Bligh's Bad Language: Passion, Power and Theatre on the Bounty*. Cambridge, England: Cambridge University Press.

Emmerich, Herbert. (1971). *Federal Organization and Administrative Management*. University: University of Alabama Press.

Hodge, G. (1993). *Minding Everybody's Business: Performance Management in Public Sector Agencies*. Melbourne, Australia: Montech.

Hough, Richard. (1973). *Captain Bligh and Mr. Christian*. New York: E. P. Dutton.

Hyde, Albert C., and Jay M. Shafritz, eds. (1979). *Program Evaluation in the Public Sector*. New York: Praeger.

Kaufman, Herbert. (1973). *Administrative Feedback: Monitoring Subordinates' Behavior*. Washington, DC: Brookings Institution.

Kearns, Kevin P. (1996). *Managing for Accountability.* San Francisco: Jossey-Bass.

Konigsberg, Eric. (1993). "Waste Watchers," *The New Republic,* April 5.

Morrison, Philip, and Emily Morrison, eds. (1961). *Charles Babbage and His Calculating Engines.* New York: Dover.

Normanton, E. L. (1966). *The Accountability and Audit of Governments.* Manchester, England: University of Manchester.

Rivlin, Alice. (1971). *Systematic Thinking for Social Action.* Washington: Brookings Institution.

Russell, E. W., and G. Macmillan (1994). *Managing Community Assets in Local Government.* Melbourne, Australia: Montech.

Shafritz, Jay M., Albert C. Hyde, and David H. Rosenbloom. (1986). *Personnel Management in Government,* 3rd ed. New York: Marcel Dekker.

Suchman, Edward. (1967). *Evaluative Research.* New York: Russell Sage Foundation.

Wahlroos, Sven. (1989). *Mutiny and Romance in the South Seas: A Companion to the* Bounty *Adventure.* Topsfield, MA: Salem House.

Webber, Carolyn, and Aaron Wildavsky. (1986). *A History of Taxation and Expenditure in the Western World.* New York: Simon and Schuster.

Weiss, Carol H. (1972). *Evaluation Research.* Englewood Cliffs, NJ: Prentice Hall.

Wildavsky, Aaron. (1972). "The Self-Evaluating Organization," *Public Administration Review* 32, No. 5.

Recommended Books

Normanton, E. Leslie. (1966). *The Accountability and Audit of Governments: A Comparative Study.* Manchester, England: University of Manchester Press. The classic study of how governments throughout history and throughout the world have conducted audits.

Sylvia, Ronald, Kathleen Sylvia, and Elizabeth Gunn. (1997). *Program Planning and Evaluation for the Public Manager,* 2nd ed. Prospect Heights, IL: Waveland Press. A systems approach to monitoring and reviewing internal processes as well as conceptualizing outcome evaluations.

Weiss, Carol H. (1997). Evaluation: Methods for Studying Programs and Policies. Englewood Cliffs, NJ: Prentice Hall. A primer on evaluation that deals with both the politics of why and the techniques of how.

Wholey, Joseph S., Harry P. Hatry, and Kathryn E. Newcomer, eds. (1994). *Handbook of Practical Program Evaluation.* San Francisco, CA: Jossey-Bass. A comprehensive reference offering all the how-to "nuts and bolts."

Related Web Sites

Accountant's Home Page
http://www.computercpa.com
American Evaluation Association
http//www.eval.org/
Auditing sites links
http://www.financenet.gov/financenet/start/topic/audit.htm
Evaluation Center
http://www.wmich.edu/evalctr/ess/index.htm
Financial and auditing links
http://www.financenet.gov
Financial statements from government agencies
http://www.financenet.gov/financenet/fed/docs/docsstmt.htm

Government Accounting Standards Board
www.rutgers.edu/Accounting/raw/gasb/gasbhome.html
Government and public accounting site links
http://www.financenet.gov/financenet/start/topic/accnt.htm#govt-
Mutiny on the *Bounty*
http://www.visi.com/~pjlareau//bountyl.html
U.S. General Accounting Office
http://www.gao.gov/reports.htm

14

Honor and Ethics

Keynote: The Blood on Robert McNamara's Hands— and Conscience

Robert S. McNamara offers a clear example of a government official in an ethical quandary. His resolution of it will forevermore be a case study on the ethics of loyalty. The question here is to whom must the official be ultimately loyal—to the administration or to the people? Is a patronage appointee's expected loyalty to a mayor, governor, or president greater or lesser than a competing loyalty to the overall interests of the citizenry?

Before World War II, McNamara taught statistics at the Harvard Business School. During the war, he served honorably and rose to the rank of lieutenant colonel in the U.S. Army Air Corps, where he helped develop statistical control systems. A civilian again in 1946, he joined the Ford Motor Company, rising to become in 1961 its president, the first who was not a Ford family member. It would be only a few months later that President John F. Kennedy would make him secretary of defense. In that position he energetically pursued what was to be by his own admission a futile war in Vietnam. He served as the principal administrative instrument in the deaths of tens of thousands of Americans and more than a million Vietnamese. He consequently was viewed as such a moral and intellectual coward by virtue of his hypocrisy and silence that the *New York Times* in an unusually personal April 12, 1995 editorial damned him as someone "who must not escape the lasting moral condemnation of his countrymen."

How did this man, this Eagle Scout who volunteered for World War II service when he had two legitimate deferments (he was an instructor at an officer training facility—Harvard; and he was a married man with a child), who only wanted to do good in government service end up doing such massive bad—so bad that he was soundly condemned by many on both sides of the issue of whether the war itself was worthy of U. S. involvement? What is undisputed is that McNamara, the archetypal bureaucratic policy analyst and number cruncher, was the architect of American military strategy in Vietnam and the strongest advocate of the war, first for President John F. Kennedy and then, after Kennedy's assassination in 1963, for President Lyndon B. Johnson. In 1964 he even publicly boasted that he was pleased when critics called it "McNamara's War." But gradually, as the war wore on, McNamara became disenchanted with the slaughter; so much so that he began to believe that the war could never be won.

Neil Sheehan wrote in his Pulitzer Prize–winning history of the war, *A Bright Shining Lie* (1988) that by the end of November of 1967 President Johnson would complain that "McNamara's gone dovish on me" and had deteriorated into "an emotional basket case" because of the burdens of the war. Thus "McNamara learned through a press leak of his appointment as the new president of the World Bank." According to Max Cleland, the former head of the Veterans Administration who lost both legs in the war: "McNamara went to the World Bank while a lot of other people went to their graves."

For the next quarter century, McNamara, despite more than a dozen years as head of the World Bank and numerous writings on the inherent evil of nuclear war, was off the public's radar screen. Then in 1995 he published his memoir on the war,

In Retrospect, which brought a firestorm of condemnation on him. The book essentially said that he knew the war was unwinnable long before he left office and that he continued to pour American blood and treasure into a policy rathole out of loyalty to President Johnson. Yet this was well known. For more than two decades, history books by the score acknowledged McNamara's disenchantment. And who was the source for all this information on McNamara's true feelings? Why the man himself! He frequently poured out his anguish to his many influential friends. McNamara's tearful emotions over his role in Vietnam were an open secret. According to David Halberstam, McNamara "carefully fended off (on the record) questions on what he really thought by pointing out that as head of the World Bank, he had no viewpoints, no politics."

The Johnson administration that McNamara served considered support of the war a test of patriotism and loyalty. Those who protested the war even today, are—incorrectly, but nevertheless—seen by their critics as having been disloyal almost to the point of treason. (This accounts in large measure for the harsh feelings that many citizens have toward President Bill Clinton's youthful opposition to the war.) More than a quarter century too late to do any real good, McNamara admitted two explosive things in his book: (1) the Johnson administration did not possess superior knowledge of the situation that was not available to the public (this "you don't know what we know" stance had been used in demanding public deference to their war policies) and (2) that he, the secretary of defense, essentially had agreed with the antiwar protesters that the war was futile and unwinnable. If he had said this at the time he left office if not sooner, it surely would have had a significant effect upon the situation, and could have saved tens of thousands of American lives.

It is hard today to appreciate the deference in which the American public and members of Congress once held executive branch pronouncements about foreign policy and military issues. The modern cynicism and often-expressed attitude that the government, indeed the president, is lying, largely came about because of the lies told during the Vietnam War. If McNamara had rallied the opposition with a timely confession, he could have given political cover to many opinion leaders and officeholders who had doubts but were too fearful to express them. It was literally a matter of life and death. And McNamara chose to sit in his office at the World Bank and let those who were at risk—American soldiers as well as countless Vietnamese—die. There was a time when he could have redeemed his honor—but he let it pass. Colonel David H. Hackworth, one of the most decorated Vietnam veterans, wrote: "He kept his mouth shut and clearly failed in his duty. If he had spoken out in 1967, hundreds of thousands of Americans and Southeast Asians might have escaped death or injury."

The U.S. senator from Arizona, John McCain, was in Hanoi, Vietnam, on a mission to recover the remains of U.S. servicemen when McNamara's book came out. McCain, a Navy pilot who spent seven years as a prisoner of war in Hanoi, said: "I think it's about 25 years too late to save those Americans who would be alive if he hadn't pursued a policy that was doomed to failure. . . . I can only assume that McNamara's doing it now because he's trying to assume some place in history." Many questioned McNamara's motives for the book. Some were angered by the thought that he did it for the money. But he was already wealthy enough that money could not possibly have been a motivator. McNamara's motives can best be compared to those of Lady Macbeth trying to wash the blood off her murderous hands ("Out, damned spot!"). Both had a need to come psychologically clean, had a need to assuage the guilt for all the spilt blood that was their responsibility. ("Who would have thought the old man to have had so much blood in him?") So she went mad ("a mind diseas'd") and he published a *mea culpa*, a public confession, saying that "we were wrong, terribly wrong." Instead of the forgiveness he sought, he got condemned by virtually all sides—and even by the *New York Times*. Those who had protested the war at the time condemned him for not publicly joining their ranks when he first gave them his heart. Those who supported the war condemned him for attacking their strong belief that the war was winnable if only this or that were done. Those who were veterans and families of veterans condemned him for saying in effect that the sacrifices he so often called on them to make were for nothing.

When McNamara was pointedly asked by *Newsweek* (in an April 17, 1995 interview that accompanied an excerpt from his book) whether he put his loyalty to President Johnson over loyalty to the American people, he replied: "I don't think that's the case. We are not a parliamentary government, where ministers can overthrow the prime minister. A minister in our government is there solely as the representative of the president. Therefore, every cabinet officer must do as the president says, or get the hell out. And if he got out, my view is that he cannot attack the president from outside the cabinet, essentially using the power given to him by the president. I recognize this is not a widely accepted view, but I believe it's the correct view—grounded in the Constitution."

However, there is nothing in the Constitution saying that former cabinet secretaries lose their rights as citizens to complain about, indeed "attack," the president they previously served. Indeed, William Jennings Bryan, President Woodrow Wilson's first Secretary of State, resigned in 1915 over Wilson's policy toward Germany. They disagreed on the best way to keep the United States out of the war then raging in Europe. Not only was the policy dispute public at the time, but Bryan continued for months more to attack Wilson's policies at every opportunity. There was much noise and debate about who was correct, but never a hint of a constitutional crisis. But McNamara did not even have to think back to the Wilson administration for an example of a dissenting former cabinet member. His close friend Robert F. Kennedy, to whom he often confessed his misgivings about the war, resigned his position in the Johnson cabinet as attorney general in 1964, then proceeded to criticize Vietnam policy as a senator from New York.

There was no constitutional issue that prevented McNamara from speaking out. So why didn't he? Was he so egocentric that his primary loyalty was to himself, as opposed to the nation, because he wanted to remain a player in the game of power? Or did he, as Colonel Hackworth suggests, "confuse loyalty to his president with a higher loyalty to the country?" As a public official, he was charged with sending fellow citizens to their deaths in a cause he first championed, then believed to be both unworthy and impractical. But despite the Lincolnesque "last full measure of devotion" that he had demanded from thousands of Americans, he was unwilling to risk the sacrifice of his public career in an effort to stop the carnage. This is the essence of his moral cowardice and personal dishonor.

The hypocrisy of the situation is so disturbing because of who McNamara was. He, the master of body count statistics, was the personification of the American war effort. Even those who disagreed with him acknowledged his intellectual brilliance and total command of the farthest nook and cranny of the Pentagon's military establishment. He was the first secretary of defense to have truly bent the brass to his will. Even today he is acknowledged as a public administration reformer who brought a new sense of rationality and management control to defense decision making—especially over budgeting and procurement. He killed so many pending weapons systems that the head of the U.S. Air Force, General Curtis LeMay would, according to Fred Kaplan, ominously ask his friends: "I ask you: would things be much worse if (Soviet Premier) Khrushchev were secretary of defense?" McNamara was so universally acknowledged to be in such total command of the military facts and figures that he, and he alone, could have made a tremendous difference in the course of the war had he had the courage to speak up.

Aside from the vital lessons learned about the limitations of mathematical models and systems analysis as aids in decision making, there are two reasons why McNamara's legacy of deceit is important to modern public administration.

First, McNamara's case offers a clear-cut example of one of the most common ethical quandaries facing public officials at all levels—whether political appointees, as McNamara was, or career civil servants. Who deserves our ultimate loyalty? The individual who, by virtue of a public office, employs us? Or the greater interests of the state? Loyalty is allegiance; but to whom? Mark Twain wrote that "my kind of loyalty was loyalty to one's country, not to its institutions or its office-holders." McNamara's loyalty was bureaucratic—not patriotic. Thus he did not publicly complain about President Johnson's policies. As a good organization man, he did not believe in going over the head of his administrative superior. He silently acquiesced to a policy he knew, and history has proved, to be wrong. This is the kind of loyalty that President Lyndon B. Johnson meant when he told his staff, according to Larry Berman, what he meant by loyalty over Vietnam: "I don't want loyalty. I want *loyalty*. I want him to kiss my ass in Macy's window at high noon and tell me it smells like roses." The strange thing here is that McNamara continued to "smell the roses" long after Johnson was out of office and long after Johnson was dead. It must have been a powerful perfume!

Second, McNamara's most lasting contribution is the cynicism and disaffection so many citizens have toward their governments at all levels in the United States. The Vietnam War made presidential lying to the American public if not normal, then at least an expected part of government. The lying and disinformation machine that McNamara created to "inform" the news media and the American public about the war was continued by and brought into domestic politics and made bipartisan by President Richard M. Nixon. The Nixon administration's lying over the Watergate scandal was just a continuation and extension of Vietnam policy cover-ups. Yet McNamara asserts in his book that one of the reasons he wrote his memoir was that he had "grown sick at heart witnessing the cynicism and even contempt with which so many people view our political institutions and leaders." He should know! It is his legacy to his country—that and all of the names of the dead on the inscribed slabs of the Vietnam War Memorial.

McNamara points the way to victory! •

The Origins and Nature of Honor

Our modern concepts of honor have their origins in ancient Greece and Rome. The classic example of honorable public service was Lucius Quinctius Cincinnatus, the Roman patrician who has become the symbol of republican virtue and personal integrity. In 458 B.C.E., when Rome was threatened with military defeat, Cincinnatus, a farmer, was appointed dictator by the Senate to deal with the emergency. Legend has it that he literally abandoned his plow in mid-field to take command. Within 16 days he defeated the enemy, resigned from the dictatorship, and returned to his plow. Ever since, politicians have been insincerely asserting how much they yearn to give up power and return to the farm, as Cincinnatus did. This is a very strong theme in American political history. Until this century, it was thought politically indecent to publicly lust after political power. Politicians were expected to sit contentedly on their farm, metaphorically behind their plow, until they were called to service.

George Washington is one of the few genuine Cincinnatus figures in world history. Indeed, Lord Byron (George Noel Gordon) in his 1814 *Ode to Napoleon Bonaparte*, called Washington "the Cincinnatus of the West." Garry Wills writes in *Cincinnatus: George Washington and the Enlightenment* (1984): [On December 23, 1783, at the end of the Revolutionary War General George Washington] "spoke what he took to be his last words on the public stage; 'Having now finished the work assigned me, I retire from the great theater of Action . . . I here offer my commission, and take my leave of all the employments of public life.' At that moment, the ancient legend of Cincinnatus—the Roman called from his plow to rescue Rome, and returning to this plow when danger had passed—was resurrected as a fact of modern political life." The example of Cincinnatus is still with us today. It is even unconsciously evoked for a modern public that never heard of the ancient Roman. For example, Ronald Reagan is quoted by E. G. Brown in *Reagan and Reality*: "One thing our founding fathers could not foresee . . . was a nation governed by professional politicians who had a vested interest in getting reelected. They probably envisioned a fellow serving a couple of hitches and then looking forward to getting back to the farm." The modern term limits movement is at its core an effort to legislate Cincinnatus type behavior—to send them back "to the farm." Of course both Cincinnatus and Washington were not merely farmers. They both had major estates with slaves to do the heavy lifting. Modern political leaders not only lack slaves, they do not even have a farm anymore. Having no honorable and luxurious place to which to retreat when recalled from public life, they fight all the stronger to stay in the game.

Shakespeare's Marc Antony was right. We are "all honorable men"—and women. Our culture inculcates us with concepts of honor from childhood. Much of our sense of honor comes from observing the actions of family and neighbors. The rest comes from the media. Many people get their first conscious lessons in honor from movies. Westerns directed by John Ford and others taught Americans the "code of the West." They taught you that one's word was sacrosanct and thus was not given lightly, taught you when an insult was so bad that it warranted violence, and taught you, above all, to protect the weak—all notions from medieval chivalry.

Later, space "westerns" like *Star Trek* and *Star Wars* taught a new generation the intergalactic concept of honor, which, of course, was no different from the medieval concept. Some things have not changed in a thousand years. Thus young people still learn what it means to be honorable by listening to (and watching) the sagas of their culture. *Star Trek* as a transmitter of notions of honor is just a modern version of the eighth-century *Beowulf* or the eleventh-century *Song of Roland*. Those born in the middle of the nineteenth century probably had their first lessons in honor from the novels of Sir Walter Scott (such as *Waverly* or *Ivanhoe*) or Cicero's *On Duties*—which was a reformulation of Aristotle's *Ethics*. The core issues of honor today are no different than in ancient Rome and Greece. Unlike technology of all kinds, the essence of honorable and ethical behavior has remained constant.

Modern thinking of honor, at least in the West, can be traced from Aristotle to medieval chivalry, to aristocratic dueling codes, to the modern concept of the gentleman. Honor has been and remains one of the core influences of human behavior. It is often more important than life itself. The founders of the United States in the last sentence of their 1776 Declaration of Independence stated: "And for the support of this Declaration, with a firm reliance on the Protection of Divine Providence, we mutually pledge to each other our Lives, our Fortunes, and our sacred Honor." Their lives were not sacred. Their fortunes were not sacred. But their honor was.

National Honor

Once reserved for the nobility, honor has since the eighteenth century become increasingly democratized. As absolutist governments declined, national honor (once solely the concern of individual monarchs) became a factor that influenced whole peoples. No less a pragmatist than President Woodrow Wilson in 1916 asserted that: "The nation's honor is dearer than the nation's comfort; yes, than the nation's life itself." Thus a collective democratic citizenry, no less than a defenseless maiden, may espouse the motto "death before dishonor." This notion is more than melodramatic hyperbole. During World War II, the French dishonored themselves by surrendering so quickly to the Germans in the spring of 1940. They were not willing to fight the Nazis in the streets of Paris and see their beautiful city destroyed. But the British, expecting an invasion soon afterward, were willing to sacrifice London. When Winston Churchill told the House of Commons on June 4, 1940, immediately after the Dunkirk evacuation that "we shall defend our island, whatever the cost may be, we shall fight on the beaches, we shall fight on the landing grounds, we shall fight in the fields and in the streets, we shall fight in the hills; we shall never surrender;" he meant exactly that. Indeed, he later wrote in his postwar memoirs, *Their Finest Hour* (1949) that "we were prepared to go to all lengths. I intended to use the slogan, 'you can always take one with you,'" Suicidal? Perhaps. But terribly honorable. When General Charles de Gaulle fled to England rather than surrender, he was asked why he was there. He replied: "I am here to save the honor of France." There is still debate about whether he succeeded or not. At least he tried! Nations and individuals are the same in that some are more honorable than others.

For a concept equally important to the high politics of war and peace and the low politics of interpersonal relations, honor has been given surprisingly little attention. To be sure there are studies of the role of honor in the antebellum South and the code of honor of nineteenth-century gentlemen; but there does not exist a comprehensive analysis of its importance and influence in public, business, military, and personal affairs. However, since the Watergate scandals of the 1970s, a rich vein of ethics literature has been created. Even when these authors hardly use the word honor, they address its core concerns.

Why Honor Precedes Ethics

Honor comes before ethics because a person without honor has no moral compass and does not know which way to turn to be ethical. Honor goes to the essence of public affairs; since ancient times only individuals perceived to be honorable could be trusted with the public's business. Of course, honor always has a context, is always influenced by the prevailing organizational and political culture. Melvin M. Belli, the American attorney, relates a story that illustrates this point. In the early 1950s Belli traveled to Paris to represent his client, movie star Errol Flynn, who had a legal tangle with a French firm over the profits from a movie. When Belli arrived, the French lawyer on the case advised him that there was nothing to worry about: "We have given the judge 200,000 francs and the case is in the bag." When Belli wondered aloud what would happen if the other side were to give the judge

300,000 francs, his French associate became indignant and replied, "But Monsieur, we are dealing with a respectable judge. He is a man of honor. He would not think of taking from *both* sides." This French judge's concept of honor was quite unlike the apocryphal American judge who, after taking bribes from both sides in a dispute, decided to try the case on its merits. Which judge is more ethical?

Dimensions of Honor

Honor has many dimensions. The most obvious and superficial kind is *ex officio*. This is the Latin phrase meaning by virtue of the office. Many people hold positions on boards, commissions, councils, and so on because of another office they occupy. For example, the mayor of a city may be an *ex officio* member of the board of trustees of a university in that city. Thus "honorable" is the form of address used for many public officials, such as judges, mayors, and members of the U.S. Congress. Here honorable does not necessarily imply personal honor or integrity; it merely signifies current (or past) incumbency. Consequently, even after Richard M. Nixon disgraced himself and was forced to resign as president in 1974, he was still formally "The Honorable" in terms of formal address. Other smaller crooks, temporarily in public office, are no less honorable.

Honor is also a function of the outward perception of one's reputation. Reputation in business, whether of an individual or an organization, is a highly valued asset. Indeed, when businesses are sold, they often sell for sums far in excess of their book value because of their intangible **goodwill** or reputation in the community.

Shakespeare often addressed issues of professional reputation and honor. In *Richard II* (Act I, Scene 1) the Duke of Norfolk is accused of treason and responds with this exposition on how mere accusation hurts both reputation and personal honor:

> The purest treasure mortal times afford
> Is spotless reputation: take that away,
> Men are but gilded loam or painted clay.
> A jewel in a ten-times-barr'd-up chest
> Is a bold spirit in a loyal breast.
> Mine honour is my life; both grow in one;
> Take honour from me, and my life is done.

This is the origin of the phrase "spotless reputation." It is also a warning that an attack on someone's honor is also an attack on his or her life—professionally speaking. But outward perception is only one step removed from *ex officio* honor. True honor begins with personal integrity and honesty. It goes beyond Benjamin Franklin's famous admonition from his *Poor Richard's Almanac* that "honesty is the best policy." Think how cynical Franklin's statement is—which seems to have been derived from Cervantes' *Don Quixote* anyway. Honesty is not worthwhile for its own sake; it is simply the optimum policy—one choice from among many. But

---

goodwill The reputation and built-up business of a company. It can be generally valued as what a company would sell for over and above the value of its physical property, money owed to it, and other assets.

true honesty, as opposed to policy honesty, is the essence of a person of honor. Such people act with integrity. This is at the core of honor. Those who have integrity live up to their stated principles, values, and most importantly, their word. A person whose word is his or her bond gives the full faith and credit of his or her whole being to keeping commitments. Sometimes this is almost frivolous, as it was when the legendary Abraham Lincoln walked miles through the snow to return a book by a promised date. But far more often one's word is the coin of the administrative realm. Things happen because one person tells something to another. This integrity of communication is essential for the smooth functioning of organizations which, in essence, are merely information-processing structures. This is why codes of honor (of integrity) first evolved among the military. Because lives, indeed whole battles, depended upon the accuracy of information sent up the chain of command, it was imperative that an ethic of honesty be instilled. This is still true today. If the word of an officer is not known to be good, that officer has lost his or her effectiveness to their superior.

A second but more subtle meaning of integrity is integrated strength or character. A building that holds together is said to have structural integrity. Individuals who have character, as demonstrated by an observable long period of acting with integrity, are said to have **gravitas**, or as the British put it, "bottom"—meaning that they are seated firm enough in their convictions that they are not easily swayed. Thus those who have integrity have a sure sense of right from wrong; they know what their core beliefs are, and what they will or will not do, no matter what the pressure.

Administrators with integrity understand that they have a special moral obligation to the people they serve. They take seriously what John Rohr calls the "regime values" of their jurisdiction. In constitutional systems these values are established by the constitution, whether written, as in the United States, or unwritten, as in the United Kingdom. To a person of honor, an oath to "defend the Constitution of the United States against all enemies, foreign and domestic" is a serious matter. Thus, according to Rohr, the Constitution "is the moral foundation of ethics for bureaucrats." Those senior administrators who gain reputations for being ethical and honorable abide by a new-fashioned *noblesse oblige*. Originally the "nobility obliged" by leading in war, and demonstrated their honor and valor by taking physical risks to prove their courage—to demonstrate on the field of honor (a battlefield) just how honorable they were.

Lacking a traditional nobility, republican governments give leadership roles to senior bureaucrats and elected officials. Once in office, their fellow citizens rightly expect them to take moral and career risks, parallel to the traditional risks of combat, to protect their fellow citizens, to protect the regime, and to protect the constitution. And they must be heroic enough to risk not just their lives, but their livelihoods as well. Louis Brandeis, later to be an associate justice of the U.S. Supreme Court, argued in the 1910 *Glavis-Ballinger* case that public administrators "cannot be worthy of the respect and admiration of the people unless they add to the virtue of obedience some other virtues—virtues of manliness, of truth, of

---

gravitas Intellectual weight. A politician must exhibit a certain degree of gravitas if he or she is to be taken seriously for high office.

courage, of willingness to risk position, of the willingness to risk criticism, of the willingness to risk the misunderstanding that so often comes when people do the heroic thing." It is often said that managers are paid more than workers because they are paid to take risks, to make decisions that can cost them their jobs. Public managers live in an even riskier environment. Not only must they take normal management risks, but they must risk their careers, their reputations, sometimes even their lives, to protect the values of the regime. It is simply a matter of honor.

All too often managers and employees fall from honor—or it may be that they never had it in the first place. Lapses take many forms. The two most common lapses of honor and honesty are corruption and lying.

Corruption in Government

Recurrent **scandals** and instances of official mischief in government, no matter how much they threaten to cost, pose a great threat to the democratic notions of the rule of law. When a public official misuses his or her office for self-gain, then the rule of law no longer obtains and there is, in effect, a return to tyranny. By engaging in such self-aggrandizement, corrupt representatives of the people illegally put themselves above the law. Moreover, a public official's act of wrongdoing is destructive of the claim that in a democracy all individuals are equal. Just like the pig in George Orwell's *Animal Farm* who cannot accept the idea that "all animals are equal," these self-interested officials in effect are saying "but some of us are more equal than others." The porcine imagery continues when you think of them not only feeding at the public trough but "hogging" more than their share.

Bribery

Corruption also undermines economic rights. Consider bribery when it occurs within the competitive process of governmental purchasing. When contracts are awarded illegally by means of bribes, the losing competitors can be said to have had their rights to a fair and impartial bidding process abridged. The public's right to have purchases made in the most efficient and least costly fashion is also subverted.

TABLE 14.1   American Government Officials Convicted of Public Corruption under Federal Law

	1980	1985	1990	1995
Federal officials	131	470	583	438
State officials	51	66	79	61
Local officials	168	221	225	191

SOURCE: *Statistical Abstract of the United States* (Washington, DC: Government Printing Office, 1997).

---

scandal In religion, an offense committed by a holder of high office. The term has been popularized to cover the commission of any action considered a demeaning of the responsibilities of office by the holder of that office.

This kind of corruption makes a mockery of economic considerations. The few that greedily feed at the public trough deny the rights of others to enter a fair system of economic competition.

Of course, viewed systemically, bribery is an important element in any political system. It supplements the salaries of various public officials. This is especially true in societies where public sector salaries are unreasonably low. Some police officers, customs agents, and building inspectors, for example, would be unable to maintain their standard of living if it were not for such informal salary increments. Additionally, such income supplement programs forestall the need for polit-ically unpopular, precipitous tax hikes that would bring the legal wages of such officers up to reasonable levels. Systematic bribery allows business operators, dependent upon the discretionary powers of public officials for their livelihood, to stabilize the relationships essential for the smooth functioning of their businesses. After all, many regulations that govern safety or conditions of business operation may not be universally applicable, reasonably enforceable, or economically feasible. Bribery's occasional exposure by the press serves to foster the political alienation of the electorate, which in turn encourages cynicism and reduces support for the dem-ocratic processes of government. While it is possible to quibble over the particulars of any given instance or noninstance of bribery, its pervasiveness in too many communities is generally not contested except by the most naive or the most corrupt. Bribery is even an important and time-honored tool of foreign policy. Of course, the United States does not have to bribe a foreign government to influence its support on some international issue. It can achieve the same effect by granting or withholding military or economic aid.

For many, the single most important cause of corruption in government is individual greed. Certain personalities tend to have flawed characters that dispose them to engage in illegal activities. This line of reasoning lays blame, then, upon a kind of

Thomas Nast's 1871 caricature of New York City's Boss Tweed became a memorable symbol of political corruption. William Marcy Tweed (1823–1878) controlled a "ring" of officials that systematically looted the city of an estimated $20 million—most notoriously, via a courthouse that cost twice as much to build as the U.S. had recently paid Russia for Alaska. The law finally caught up with Tweed in 1871 and he was jailed. After escaping to Spain for a year, he was caught and returned to New York, where he died in jail awaiting trial •

Box 14.1

The Difference Between Honest Graft and Dishonest Graft

"Everybody is talkin' these days about Tammany men growin' rich on graft, but nobody thinks of drawn' the distinction between honest graft and dishonest graft. There's all the difference in the world between the two. Yes, many of our men have grown rich in politics. I have myself. I've made a big fortune out of the game, and I'm gettin' richer every day, but I've not gone in for dishonest graft—blackmailin' gamblers, saloon-keepers, disorderly people, etc.—and neither has any of the men who have made big fortunes in politics.

There's an honest graft, and I'm an example of how it works. I might sum up the whole thing by sayin': 'I seen my opportunities and I took 'em.'

Just let me explain by examples. My party's in power in the city, and its goin' to undertake a lot of public improvements. Well, I'm tipped off, say, that they're goin' to lay out a new park at a certain place.

I see my opportunity and I take it, I go to that place and I buy up all the land I can in the neighborhood. Then the board of this or that makes its plan public, and there is a rush to get my land, which nobody cared particular for before.

Ain't it perfectly honest to charge a good price and make a profit on my investment and foresight? Of course, it is. Well, that's honest graft."

SOURCE: William Riordon, *Plunkitt of Tammany Hall* (New York: McClure, Phillips, 1905).

---

psychological disorder in which the individual is the sole source of the problem. Others have argued that corruption in government is a much more complex phenomenon. In this view, a mix of variables such as opportunity, risk, organizational culture—and individual susceptibility—is more likely than solitary evil. If the opportunity presents itself, and the risk of getting caught is low, and if the organization does not foster an ethical climate, then chances are fairly good that corruption will occur. James Madison summed up the whole problem more than two centuries ago when he wrote in *The Federalist*, No. 57, that "the aim of every political constitution is, or ought to be, first to obtain for rulers men who possess most wisdom to discern, and most virtue to pursue, the common good of the society; and in the next place, to take the most effectual precautions for keeping them virtuous whilst they continue to hold their public trust."

Watergate

A society's humor is a good indicator of its political corruption. For example, many analysts predicted that President Nixon would eventually be forced from office because of the Watergate scandal once Johnny Carson, the most popular, most mainstream, and most middle-of-the-road of American comedians, started telling jokes

Box 14.2

The Most Famous Solicitation of a Bribe in American History

Daniel Webster, one of the United States Senate's greatest orators in the first half of the nineteenth century, wrote this December 21, 1833, letter to Nicholas Biddle, president of the Second Bank of the United States. The bank was seeking a renewal of its charter, which was vigorously opposed by President Andrew Jackson.

> Sir—Since I have arrived here I have had an application to be concerned professionally against the Bank which I have declined of course, although I believe my retainer has not been renewed, or refreshed as usual. If it be wished that my relation to the Bank should be continued it may be well to send me the usual retainers.

SOURCE: Paul H. Douglas, *Ethics in Government* (Cambridge, MA: Harvard University Press, 1952).

NOTE: According to Douglas, "This letter, which has seldom been surpassed for its essential blackmail, brought the desired result. The retainer was 'refreshed' and Webster girded on the sword of his oratory to do battle for his employer."

on his "Tonight Show" that were premised upon the belief that the president of the United States was dishonest. The jokes were a bellwether because most of the audience—that is most of mainstream America—accepted the premise. Comedians do not lead public opinion, but they certainly reflect it. The same is true today in Russia. *New York Times* columnist Thomas L. Friedman wrote that "corruption reaches right into the leadership." His indicator of this is the often told joke "about a man who drives into Moscow from the countryside and parks his new car right outside the Kremlin's Spassky Gate, in Red Square. A policeman comes along and tells the man, 'Look, you can't park here, this is the gate all our leaders use.' The man answers: 'Don't worry, I locked my car.'"

Lies Big and Little

Lies come in all sizes. A big lie is an untruth so great or so audacious that it is bound to have an effect on public opinion. Both Adolf Hitler in Germany and **Joseph R. McCarthy** in the United States were skillful users of this dishonorable but long-practiced political tactic. Hitler wrote in *Mein Kampf* (1927) that "the great masses of the people will more easily fall victim to a great lie than to a small one." Hitler was

---

Joseph R. McCarthy (1908–1957) The Republican U.S. senator from Wisconsin (1947–1957) whose "red scare" tactics made him the preeminent American demagogue of the 1950s.

TABLE 14.2   Watergate Chronology

1969	January 20	Nixon inaugurated.
1970	July 23	Nixon approves use of illegal methods to gather intelligence on demonstrators and political enemies.
1971	February	Nixon begins secret taping of all Oval Office conversations.
1972	March 30	John Mitchell, head of Nixon's reelection committee, approves plan for illegal entry into and wiretapping of the Democratic National Committee's Watergate headquarters.
	May 27	The first Watergate break-in takes place.
	June 17	The second Watergate break-in occurs; five agents of the Nixon campaign are arrested.
		Nixon's attorney, Herbert Kalmbach, begins making secret payments to Watergate burglars; over a year's time $450,000 in hush money is paid out of campaign contributions.
	August 29	Nixon announces that White House Counsel John W. Dean has conducted an investigation of the Watergate break-in: "I can state categorically that his investigation indicates that no one in the White House staff, no one in this administration, presently employed, was involved in this very bizarre incident. What really hurts is if you try to cover it up." Dean would later testify that he had not heard of his "investigation" until this announcement.
	September 15	Watergate burglars indicted.
	October 10	*Washington Post* reporters Bob Woodward and Carl Bernstein reveal that the Watergate break-in was part of a massive campaign of political spying and sabotage conducted on behalf of the president's reelection and directed by White House and reelection committee officials.
	November 7	Nixon reelected in a landslide; wins every state but Massachusetts. Shortly thereafter bumper stickers appear reading: "Do not blame me: I'm from Massachusetts."
1973	January	Watergate burglars tried and convicted.
	February 7	Senate votes to investigate Watergate and other 1972 campaign abuses.
	March 22	Nixon tells John Mitchell: "I want you all to stonewall it, let them plead the Fifth Amendment, cover-up or anything else, it's save it—same the plan."
	August 30	Nixon announces resignations of White House Chief of Staff H. R. Haldeman; White House Domestic Affairs Advisor John D. Ehrlichman; the Attorney General Richard G. Kleindienst; and the firing of White House Counsel John Dean (who had just reported the cover-up to the Justice Department). Nixon tells the Nation: "We must maintain the integrity of the White House. . . . There can be no whitewash at the White House.
	May 17	Televised Senate Watergate Hearings begin.
	May 18	Archibald Cox named Special Prosecutor.
	June 25	John Dean tells the Senate Watergate committee, "I began by telling the president that there was a cancer growing on the presidency and that if the cancer was not removed . . . the president himself would be killed by it."
	July 16	White House aide Alexander Butterfield reveals existence of White House taping system.

TABLE 14.2 Watergate Chronology (continued)

	July 25	Nixon refuses to release tapes requested by special prosecutor because it would violate executive privilege.
	October 20	Nixon orders the firing of Special Prosecutor Cox.
	October 23	Yielding to public pressure, Nixon agrees to hand over some tapes after "firestorm" of criticism.
	October 30	The House Judiciary Committee begins its impeachment inquiry.
	November 1	Houston lawyer Leon Jaworski is appointed new Special Prosecutor.
1974	March 1	The grand jury indicts seven former White House aides for Watergate cover-up.
	May 24	Special Prosecutor Leon Jaworski appeals to the Supreme Court to rule on his subpoena for more tapes.
	July 24	The Supreme Court in *United States v. Nixon* rules that Nixon must release the tapes.
	July 27	House Judiciary Committee votes for impeachment.
	August 5	Nixon surrenders tapes proving he had approved cover-up from the beginning.
	August 9	Nixon resigns.
	September 8	Nixon is pardoned by his successor, President Gerald R. Ford.

such a constant and proficient liar that he has become as famous for his lying as for his epic evil. Yet he was right about one thing: "something of even the most insolent lie will always remain and stick." So even today, after he has become the personification, the icon, of evil in the modern world, some perverted souls still believe his lies.

On a far smaller but no less morally deplorable scale were the lies of McCarthy. He first came to national prominence after a February 9, 1950, speech in Wheeling, West Virginia, in which he held up a piece of paper and told the audience: "I have here in my hand a list of 205 persons that were known to the secretary of state as being members of the Communist party and who nevertheless are still working and shaping policy of the State Department." These were typical of the kind of reckless charges for which McCarthy became famous. Typical also is the fact that McCarthy did not provide supporting evidence. McCarthy grew so reckless with his accusations that in 1954 he became one of the few senators in American history to be formally **censured** by the U.S. Senate for the fact that he "tended to bring the Senate into dishonor and disrepute." Now wait a minute you say! How can the lies of a second-rate politician like McCarthy be compared to Hitler? McCarthy did not kill anybody. Or did he? He led

---

censure A vote by a legislature reprimanding one of its members. It is a disciplinary action short of expulsion and more serious than a formal reprimand. Article I, Section 5 of the Constitution provides that "Each house may . . . punish its own members for disorderly behavior, and with the concurrence of two-thirds, expel a member." In the U.S. Congress expulsion has been rare. In recent decades formal censure has only involved about a dozen members—typically on charges of financial or sexual misconduct. Recently the Senate has taken to using the word "denouncement" instead of censure, but it means the same thing.

The Watergate Complex in Washington, DC. The Watergate once again became the center of an American political scandal in 1998 when Monica Lewinsky, the young woman with whom President Clinton had "an inappropriate relationship" resided there with her mother—who was also younger than the president. The affair was given
a small-town flavor when it turned out the Lewinskys' next door neighbor at the Watergate was Bob Dole, the
former senator from Kansas who was Clinton's Republican opposition in the 1996 presidential election •

the Republican party **red-baiting** of the Democratic party under President Harry S.
Truman for being soft on Communism both domestically and internationally. When
the Chinese Communists under Mao Zedong, after a 20-year civil war, finally ousted
the nationalist regime of Chiang Kai-shek in 1949, McCarthy accused the Democrats
of being "traitors" for having "lost" China to the Communists—as if China was
"ours" to lose. This so changed the political climate that Democratic administrations
fought wars in Korea and Vietnam in part not to be accused of being too soft. As the
retired President Lyndon B. Johnson told Doris Kearns: "I knew that Harry Truman
and Dean Acheson had lost their effectiveness from the day that the Communists took
over in China. I believed that the loss of China had played a large role in the rise of Joe
McCarthy. And I knew that all these problems, taken together, were chickenshit compared with what might happen if we lost Vietnam." So McCarthy's lies, while not as
lethal as Hitler's, nevertheless had severe consequences. Lies kill!

---

red-baiting Accusing someone, usually falsely and often a political opponent, of being a Communist or
being supportive of Communist policies. Since World War II this has been an oft-used tactic in political campaigns. One of the most famous instances of red-baiting occurred during the 1950 race
for the U.S. Senate from California. Richard M. Nixon won by accusing his opponent, Helen
Gahagan Douglas, of being "pink down to her underwear," and she never recovered.

President Richard Nixon takes time out from subverting the U.S. Constitution (he had already approved illegal methods to gather information on his political enemies) to meet with Elvis Presley in the Oval Office on December 21, 1970. Elvis had a keen interest in public administration and came to offer his services to the country as a part-time, volunteer, federal narcotics agent. After all, few people had more experience with narcotics abuse. Not realizing the irony in this, Nixon was only too pleased to give the even-then drug-saturated singer (who was destined to die of drug abuse) the badge and credentials of a special agent of the Bureau of Narcotics and Dangerous Drugs. Elvis was a strong supporter of the administration, who had publicly criticized anti-Vietnam War entertainers such as the Smothers Brothers and Jane Fonda. He wanted the credentials so that he would have more credibility as a kind of ambassador to troubled young people. But alas, the only troubled young people with whom he met were teenage girls who had agendas other than politics•

Lying for Your Country

The public officials who have the greatest reputation for lying are ambassadors—the highest ranking of all diplomats, sent as the personal representatives of one head of state to another. Sir Henry Wotton (1568–1639), Queen Elizabeth I's ambassador to Venice, was the first of many wits to write that "an ambassador is an honest man sent to lie abroad for the commonwealth." Often ambassadors are not trusted to lie well enough, so their governments purposely misinform them to ensure that their false representations will seem all the more sincere. Thus the Japanese ambassador to the United States in 1941 did not know of the impending Pearl Harbor attack; the German ambassador to the Soviet Union in 1941 was not told of the coming invasion, and the U.S. ambassador to the United Nations in 1961, Adlai Stevenson, was not told of the Bay of Pigs landing.

If lying politicians have a patron saint, it must be Niccolo Machiavelli, who wrote in *The Prince* (1532) that "it is necessary that the prince should know how to color his nature well, and how to be a great hypocrite and dissembler. For men are so simple, and yield so much to immediate necessity, that the deceiver will never lack dupes." Machiavelli's ideal prince would not be a traditional man of honor; his word would not be his bond. Machiavelli's advice was "not to keep faith when by so doing it would be against his interest, and when the reasons which made him bind himself no longer exist." This was the kind of thing that made people suspect that Machiavelli was not only not a gentleman, but not fit reading for gentlemen as well. A true gentleman had to absolutely keep his word. Not to do so would "prove" that he was not a gentleman—and that he was without honor. Thus lying became as unforgivable an act of moral courage as cowardice was of physical courage. Of course, only if you got caught!

When is it acceptable to tell a lie, not for personal benefit, but for a perceived public good? This question has been a subject of discussion and analysis by students of government since ancient times. The ancient Greek philosopher Plato asserts in his *Republic* that the guardians of a society may put forth untruths, royal lies, necessary to maintain social order: "The rulers of the State are the only ones who should have the privilege of lying, either at home or abroad; they may be allowed to lie for the good of the state." Plato's noble lie was simply a poetic or allegorical way of telling ordinary people difficult truths. It is absolutely incompatible with the big lie of fascist propaganda or red-baiting demagogues.

The Dirty Hands Dilemma

When do desirable public ends justify the lying means? When is doing evil acceptable to produce a greater political good? The dirty hands dilemma is a graphic phrase for this problem. Public officials dirty their hands when they commit an act generally considered to be a wrong to further the common good. This is a dilemma in the sense that doing bad seems to lead to something good. Thus public officials need to decide if they are willing to engage in wrongdoing for the sake of a perceived good deed. Of course as a general rule they are prohibited from engaging in wrongdoing. Thus the dirty hands dilemma is the product of a tension between perceived professional obligations and long-standing moral obligations that are the standards of everyday life.

Machiavelli did not see this as a problem at all. He held that the rules of morality in everyday life should not be applied to the acts of public officials when they are carrying out their professional roles and responsibilities to further the common good. As Machiavelli expressed it in *The Discourses*, "When the act accuses, the result excuses." But can we divorce the person from his or her administrative role? If any moral judgment is to be made, it must be made about the office or the governmental unit in which the official is housed. We should not apply the ordinary standards of right and wrong to the extraordinary situation of a person who is acting only as a bureaucratic functionary. Others argue that it is a mistake to confuse the role of public official with the person who temporarily holds that role; moral rules are still applicable to the acts of the person who commits wrongs, whether that person be a public official or not. One cannot use one's position in an organization as an excuse to be exempted from basic morality. Wrongdoing is wrongdoing, no matter what the context. Public officials must be held accountable for their unethical acts, even if those acts were done in the name of the common good and performed by someone claiming to be a professional or a mere functionary.

There can be little doubt that the most common form of the dirty hands dilemma in public administration is lying. Lying can take many forms—direct falsehoods, exaggerations, omissions, evasions, deceptions, duplicity, and so on. There are few who would be so naive as to claim that the art of politics and the practice of governance are free from any of these moral shortcomings.

Do public officials have a special obligation to tell the truth? Do their offices permit them special excuses to depart from truth-telling? It can be argued that since knowledge is the cornerstone of democracy, an informed public is a prerequisite for a democratic government. Hence, citizens have an inherent right to know the truth of public issues so that they can make intelligent decisions as voters and constituents. When public officials decide to dirty their hands whether by direct falsehood, omission, evasion, and so on, then they are abridging the public's right to know. There is, on this account then, a special obligation for public officials to tell the truth, based upon this inherent need of democracy. McNamara is a leading example of this. The democratic process would have been better served had he told the public the truth as he saw it about the Vietnam War. While technically not a public official, the First Lady of the United States effectively functions as one. Thus it was a serious matter when the *New York Times* columnist William Safire wrote in 1996 that Hilary Rodham Clinton was a "congenital liar." Because this was tantamount to saying that the White House was subverting democracy on a regular basis, the response was immediate. President Clinton had his press secretary announce that, but for being president, he would punch Mr. Safire in the nose. Safire, nose unbloodied, stood his ground.

On the other hand, it also can be argued that public officials in a democracy may be excused at times from the general obligation of truth-telling. There may be dire situations or times of crises that threaten the government and its people; under such conditions it may be permissible for a public official to deceive the public for its own good. In other words, when public officials take their oaths of office, they are sworn to do everything in their power to ensure the survival of the government and the safety of the public. It is the very nature of public office, then, that excuses the public official who lies for the public good because the public good is essentially what the official is required to protect. If such protection in times of war or crises entails that officials engage in deception, then so be it. They are only fulfilling the responsibilities of their office. The argument for excusing lies by officials has a long history. The first instance of it appears in Plato's *Republic*, in which the term "royal lie"—referring to lies for the public good—was first coined.

This line of reasoning about excusing public officials who lie for the public good leads directly to the core question about lying in public administration— namely, are such lies justifiable? Again, there is no doubt that lying in government is an activity that appears widespread. But the underlying question remains: Are these instances of duplicity justifiable, and if so, what are the conditions under which they are justifiable? If we can identify these conditions, then we may be in a better position to decide if the public's right to know has been abridged or if an official's act of lying might be excused.

Lying About Sex

When essayist Charles Dudley Warner (1829–1900)wrote in 1871 that "politics makes strange bedfellows," he was referring to the fact that political necessity so often forces unlikely pairs to work together for a common goal—not that politicians must necessarily end up in bed with strangers. Yet those who have a passion for politics all too often have a problem with their passions. American presidents are no exceptions. The multitudinous, miscellaneous trystings of Presidents John F. Kennedy and Lyndon B. Johnson are only the most recent examples that have been thoroughly documented by historians. Johnson even felt competitive with the deceased Kennedy about this. According to biographer Robert Dalleck, Johnson as president bragged that "I had more women by accident than he [Kennedy] ever had by design." President Bill Clinton is unique only in that he has been forced to admit to such infidelities while in office.

Until recently, lies about the sexual activities of consenting adults would not have been of concern to a textbook on public administration. But President Clinton changed that in 1998 when he told one lie after another about his Oval Office encounters with Monica Lewinsky, the White House intern with whom he eventually admitted having a relationship "that was not appropriate." And none of this would have come to public attention, no lies would have publicly been told, except for the involvement of the U.S. Supreme Court.

In what could turn out to be one of the most important modern Supreme Court decisions about the presidency, the Supreme Court ruled in 1998 (*William Jefferson Clinton v. Paula Corbin Jones*) that a sitting president could be sued by a private citizen seeking money damages in a civil suit for conduct alleged to have occurred before the president took office. Jones claimed that she was sexually harassed by Clinton while he served as governor of Arkansas years earlier. President Clinton urged the Court to delay the suit until he left office, claiming that the chief executive should not be burdened and distracted by having to defend against civil suits, except in far more exceptional circumstances.

Writing for the majority, Justice John Paul Stevens rejected Clinton's argument and concluded that that it would be highly unlikely that allowing the Jones case to proceed would generate a flood of other suits against this or other presidents and, in any event, Stevens noted, the lower court judge could always defer such a case when it appears that to proceed would hamper a president's ability to do his job. What neither the members of the Court, nor the public, knew at the time was that President Clinton's testimony about Monica Lewinsky in a sworn deposition in the Jones case would set off a political firestorm powerful enough to threaten Clinton's presidency. Whether the Supreme Court's decision to permit civil actions against sitting presidents will result in future political and legal battles for presidents cannot be known. It is possible that the ever-present existence of powerful and well-funded political opponents anxious to "trap" presidents in sworn statements in civil suits was underestimated by the Court.

While Lewinsky's passion for President Clinton has been amply documented, she certainly seems to have lacked the "passion for anonymity" that the Brownlow Committee's prescribed for White House assistants (see Chapter 3)—a passion that more mature presidential inamoratas have demonstrated by their silence. Because Lewinsky told so many people about her affair with Clinton, which began in 1995 when she was a 22-year-old, unpaid White House intern, evidence began to appear that she lied in her sworn statement in the Jones case. Jones's lawyers had sought her statement to bolster their contention that Clinton was a persistent and consistent philanderer.

When audio tapes of Lewinsky's telephone conversations about the affair with her "friend" Linda Tripp surfaced early in 1998, two things happened: (1) a special prosecutor (Ken Starr) who had earlier been authorized by Congress to investigate alleged illegalities by the Clintons in other matters, sought and gained the permission of the Clinton-appointed attorney general to expand the investigation into possible perjury by the president in his Jones statements; and (2) the president emphatically denied having had sexual relations with Lewinsky, many times before many audiences. There is little doubt that he would have continued to lie about the affair had not physical evidence become available that supported Lewinsky's testimony to a grand jury that both she and the president lied in their Jones case depositions. The evidence was a dress of Lewinsky's that was stained with presidential semen. Prior to the announcement of the existence of the physical evidence, the White House spin on the story was that Lewinsky was delusional about having an affair with the president—that she was just a politically star-struck kid who had lost a firm grasp on reality. But after the DNA of the dress stain was compared with freshly sampled presidential DNA, all doubts were over. After lying about this for seven months, the president, knowing of the DNA evidence of his lying, confessed before the grand jury, and then to the nation in a televised address, that he had had an "inappropriate relationship" with Lewinsky.

What got the president into legal trouble was not his multiple infidelities, but the allegations of perjury about them. The party line from the White House after the confession was that since this whole scandal was about sex, it didn't rise to an impeachable offense. As with Watergate, it was not so much the initial "crime" as it was the cover-up—the lies—that forced Nixon from office and brought Clinton to impeachment. While some make the claim that lying about sex between consenting adults is only good manners, such matters are different affairs entirely once the parties have sworn to a grand jury to tell "the truth, the whole truth, and nothing but the truth." What does it say about the American legal system if the president of the United States is held exempt from that legal obligation—the violation of which has landed many of his fellow citizens in federal prison? This question was so troubling and Clinton's behavior was considered so reckless that in the fall of 1998 the House of Representatives impeached him for perjury and obstruction of justice. Clinton was tried by the Senate early in 1999 and was acquitted because there was nowhere near the constitutionally required two-thirds vote needed for his removal from office. Clinton remained president because many senators who believed he was guilty as charged felt that lying about sex was too petty a reason to remove a president.

Conflicts of Responsibilities

What is an administrator to do when he or she experiences a basic conflict in duties, obligations and/or loyalties? One way to visualize the conflicts of responsibilities that plague public administrators is to use the technique of stakeholder analysis. A stakeholder is any individual or group that might be affected by the outcome of something. All decisions have their stakeholders. The responsible public decision maker seeks to obtain the maximum possible stakeholder satisfaction. He or she wants everybody to be happy. But how does a decision maker provide for the universal happiness of stakeholders? To answer this question, we must first identify the various stakeholders. This is especially important in public administration because, in conducting the public's business, the decision maker is inherently a representative expected to safeguard the fundamental concepts of justice, equality, and the inviolability of individual rights. Public administration is unique in this respect because the governmental decision-making process is by definition, as Mr. Lincoln said, "of the people, for the people, and by the people." That's what the "public" in public administration automatically implies. All citizens have at least an indirect stake in the decision making of public officials. It is their responsibility to ensure that a majority of the people are at least content, if not happy, with each administrative decision that they make.

Stakeholders

The public manager whose task it is to devise an acceptable policy on any given issue is confronted by multiple groups, each having its own concerns that must be considered. Public policymaking is often a matter of negotiating with various constituencies and seeking to reconcile their conflicting views of the public manager's responsibilities in making policy. Some stakeholder groups are obvious and some are far from obvious. Most obvious are established public interest groups that continuously let their interests be heard by policymakers. They lobby public administrators, spend money to influence public opinion, offer expert testimony at public hearings, collect signatures for a **referendum**, and so on. Client groups are also obvious stakeholders. Public policy is often made with reference to client groups within an administrative area. For example, the Veterans Administration makes policy about veterans, welfare agencies about those who are poor, Agricultural Departments about farmers, and so on. Other more obvious stakeholders include the public manager's peers, supervisors, and subordinates. The administrative agency in which the public manager is located will be affected by the outcome of the policymaking process, since it is its organizational structure that must implement the new policy. Among the less obvious stakeholders are the media, the court system, legislative bodies, executives, and a multitude of professional associations. Each of these groups makes a genuine, if sometimes indirect, claim on the attention of public policymakers.

Stakeholder analysis illustrates the first kind of dilemma that typically confronts public administrators. Because there are so many legitimate stakeholders, administrators must attend to the needs of each of them. Thus there is an inherent conflict of responsibility that administrators must face. The pressures of competing claims is unrelenting. Nevertheless, the public administrators must reach decisions that can on the whole satisfy the stakeholders. This conflict of responsibility, this

---

referendum A procedure for submitting proposed laws or state constitutional amendments to the voters for ratification. A petition signed by an appropriate percentage of the voters can force a newly passed law onto the ballot, or the law could be put on the ballot by the recommendation of the legislature. While only a minority of the states provide for statutory referenda, practically all states require them for constitutional amendments. Local governments also use the referendum, especially when the law requires that certain issues, such as capital project borrowing, must be submitted to the voters via referenda.

Box 14.3

The Most Famous Myth of Not Lying in American History

When George [Washington] was about six years old, he was made the wealthy master of a hatchet! of which, like most little boys, he was immoderately fond, and was constantly going about chopping every thing that came in his way. One day, in the garden, where he often amused himself hacking his mother's pea-sticks, he unluckily tried the edge of his hatchet on the body of a beautiful young English cherry-tree. . . . The next morning the old gentleman finding out what had befallen his tree, which, by the by, was a great favorite, came into the house, and with much warmth asked for the mischievous author. Nobody could tell him any thing about it. Presently George and his hatchet made their appearance. "George," said his father, "do you know who killed that beautiful little cherry-tree yonder in the garden?" This was a tough question; and George staggered under it for a moment; but quickly recovered himself: and looking at his father, with the sweet face of youth brightened with the inexpressible charm of all-conquering truth, he bravely cried out, "I can't tell a lie, Pa; you know I can't tell a lie. I did cut it with my hatchet."

SOURCE: Mason L. "Parson" Weems (1759–1825), *The Life of George Washington* (1809).

NOTE: This most famous of all stories of Washington is false; Weems's biography has long been denounced by serious historians. Nevertheless, this story has had such resonance because it so reflects the actual character of Washington—a man who in life was generally considered to represent the very essence of republican virtue.

---

dilemma, is too often an obstacle to the effective and ethical discharge of the duties of public administrators.

Administrative Ethics

Dennis F. Thompson has raised the radical and fundamental question of whether there is such a thing as administrative ethics at all. According to Thompson, there are two commonly accepted administrative theories that undercut the possibility of ethics in government. The "ethic of neutrality" holds that administrators make their decisions on behalf of others and must remain morally neutral in doing so, if representative government is to work at all. But if administrators are indeed morally neutral when they make representative decisions, then it is not possible to hold them ethically accountable. Likewise, the "ethic of structure" claims that organizations and not individuals are responsible for the design, development, and implementation of public policies. Hence we cannot and should not cast moral judgments about government officials, who merely find themselves somewhere in that structure.

Now, if either of these two theories were to hold sway, then it would seem to follow that administrative accountability for individuals does not exist. Administrators would not be liable for their actions. Administrative ethics that would seek to make moral judgments of those actions would be an impossibility. Thompson asserts that we "are forced to accept neither an ethic of neutrality that would suppress independent moral judgment, nor an ethic of structure that would ignore individual moral agency in organizations." Not only do we have the right to continue as moral agents but we have a positive duty, all of us, not to do harm—not to violate the law. The "Nuremberg defense" is the often used excuse of those caught performing illegal acts for their political or military superiors: "I was only following orders." The term and the tactic comes from war crimes trials in Nuremberg, Germany, of top Nazi leaders in the aftermath of World War II. The fallacy of this defense is that no soldier (or civilian employee) can be required to obey manifestly illegal orders. Indeed, as was even shown in the **My Lai** massacre during the Vietnam War, a soldier (or civilian employee) has a positive obligation to disobey such orders. Fortunately, few officials have to suffer angst over war crimes. But what about fixing traffic tickets, forcing a tax audit on someone, or pressuring employees to buy tickets to political dinners? Same issue, smaller stakes!

Hierarchy of Ethics

The public administrator is frequently adrift in a sea of competing duties and obligations. Here, it is not so much a matter of stakeholder conflicts as it is a matter of recognizing that there are differing kinds of conflicting responsibilities. This kind of conflict occurs when an individual is called upon to perform mutually exclusive acts by parties having legitimate "holds" on him/her. For example, a rising young manager may not make it to the "big" meeting if he must at that moment rush his child to the hospital for an emergency appendectomy. When such conflicts arise, most individuals invoke a hierarchy of role obligation that gives some roles precedence over others. To most fathers, their child's life would be more important than a business meeting—no matter how "big." Real life is not always so unambiguous, however, and role conflict is a common dilemma in the world of work.

The Four Levels of Ethics

In public administration there is a hierarchy of levels of ethics, each of which has its own set of responsibilities. First, there is personal morality—the basic sense of right and wrong. This is a function of our past and is dependent upon factors such as parental influences, religious beliefs, cultural and social mores, and one's own personal experiences.

Second in the hierarchy is professional ethics. Public administrators increasingly recognize a set of professional norms and rules that obligate them to act in certain "professional" ways. Such guidelines are codified by professional associations such

---

My Lai The South Vietnamese village wherein more than several hundred old men, women, and children were murdered in 1968 by a U.S. Army unit commanded by Lieutenant William Calley Jr. Despite complaints by several soldiers, the U.S. Army sought to ignore or cover up this atrocity until congressional inquiries and press reports forced a comprehensive investigation that led to Calley's court-martial.

as the American Society for Public Administration and the International City Management Association. However, occupations such as law and medicine, while operating within public administration, also have their own independent professional codes.

A third level of ethics is organizational. Every organization has an environment or culture that includes both formal and informal rules of ethical conduct. Public organizations typically have many such rules. Public laws, executive orders, and agency rules and regulations all can be taken as formal organizational norms for ethical behavior.

Finally, there are social ethics. The requirements of social ethics oblige members of a given society to act in ways that both protect individuals and further the progress of the group as a whole. Social ethics are formal to the extent that they can be found in the laws of a given society, informal to the extent that they are part of an individual's social conscience.

The Iran-Contra Affair

To illustrate the conflicting nature of responsibility and different levels of ethical obligations, let's consider the Iran-Contra affair in general and the actions of Oliver North in particular.

The Iran-Contra scandal arose in the fall of 1986, when it was revealed that the Reagan administration had secretly sold arms to the government of Iran (so Iran would use its **good offices** to gain the release of American hostages in Lebanon) at higher than normal prices and used the "profits" to fund the **Contras** in Nicaragua. The controversy grew into a scandal because it was illegal to sell arms to Iran, illegal to fund the Contras beyond limits set by the Congress, and against the expressed policy of the United States to negotiate for, let alone trade arms for, the release of hostages. Because the Iran-Contra operation was undertaken primarily by the National Security Council without the formal approval of the departments of Defense and State, the affair called into question the coherence of the Reagan administration's foreign policy.

As the major operative in the scheme, Lieutenant Colonel Oliver North of the U.S. Marine Corps, assigned to the White House National Security Council, serves as a case study in the conflict of responsibility. North has admitted that he found it necessary to lie to Congress about the Iran-Contra arms deal in order to further what he called national security goals. Thus, by overseeing the illegal sales of arms to Iran and channeling profits from the transactions to the Contras in violation of the law, North reached a decision that one set of responsibilities was higher than another. He justified his lies to Congress as necessary for national security. North violated the formal rules of organizational ethics and social ethics in illegally supplying military aid to the Contras and in lying to Congress to cover it up. However,

---

good offices The disinterested use of one's official position, one's office, to help others settle their differences; an offer to mediate a dispute.

Contras The U.S.-backed "democratic resistance movement" in Nicaragua. The Contras opposed the Communist Sandinista government. They disbanded in 1990 after the democratically-elected government replaced the Sandinista regime.

he argued that he upheld his own personal morality and sense of duty to the country by acting as he did. Caught between his own interpretation of what is right and wrong on the personal level and that which his organization and society had deemed to be right and wrong, North chose the former over the latter. For many, he was a hero for doing so. Yet for many others, his actions were criminal and unconstitutional.

The Higher Law Defense

When North's secretary, Fawn Hall, was called to testify during the 1987 congressional hearings on the scandal she asserted, "I felt uneasy but sometimes, like I said before, I believed in Colonel North and there was a very solid and very valid reason he must have been doing this for and sometimes you have to go above the written law, I believe." In her pedestrian way Ms. Hall defended North by asserting the ancient idea of a higher law—the notion that no matter what the laws of a state are, there remains a higher law, to which a person has an even greater obligation.

A higher law is often appealed to by those who wish to attack an existing law or practice that courts or legislators are unlikely or unwilling to change. In a famous speech in the Senate on March 11, 1850, William Henry Seward of New York argued against slavery by asserting that "there is a higher law than the Constitution which regulates our authority." Martyrs throughout the ages have asserted a higher law in defiance of the state, thus earning their martyrdom. The classic presentation of this concept is in Sophocles' fourth century B.C.E. play *Antigone*, in which the heroine defies the king, asserts a higher law as her justification, and "forces" the king to have her killed. Because the courts of any state will only enforce the law of the land, appealing to a higher law is always chancy business. Examples of Americans who have appealed to a higher law and wound up in jail as a result are Henry David Thoreau, Martin Luther King Jr., and Vietnam War resisters. Oliver North was convicted and would have gone to jail except that his conviction was overturned on a legal technicality. Thus he had all the glory of being a martyr with none of the pain of serving a prison sentence.

Box 14.4

Thomas Jefferson on Higher Law

A strict observance of the written laws is doubtless one of the high duties of a good citizen, but it is not the highest. The laws of necessity, of self-preservation, of saving our country when in danger, are of higher obligation. To lose our country by a scrupulous adherence to written law, would be to lose the law itself, with life, liberty, property and all those who are enjoying them with us; thus absurdly sacrificing the end to the means.

SOURCE: Thomas Jefferson, letter to John B. Colvin, September 20, 1810.

As the North case suggests, responsibilities can conflict because there are multiple levels of ethics and morality, each with its own set of obligations and duties. One of the most difficult aspects of being a public administrator is managing the conflict of responsibilities between the competing claims of stakeholders and the varying levels of ethics.

Whistleblowing

Whistleblowing refers to what happens when an employee decides that obligations to society come before obligations to an organization. Thus a whistleblower is an individual who believes the public interest overrides the interests of his/her organization and publicly blows the whistle on—exposes—corrupt, illegal, fraudulent, or harmful activity. Whistleblowers in our society are not well received. Children have long been taught not to be "squealers." Whistleblowers run the risk of being ostracized by their coworkers, losing their jobs, and being blacklisted in their field. The two most famous whistleblowers in recent decades were A. Ernest Fitzgerald and Daniel Ellsberg.

Fitzgerald was the GS-17 deputy for Management Systems in the Office of the Assistant Secretary of the Air Force who in 1968 testified before a congressional committee about **cost overruns** on the Air Force's giant C-5A military cargo plane. The Air Force, which had not acknowledged the cost overruns, stripped him of his primary duties of overseeing cost reports on the major weapons systems and assigned him to essentially clerical tasks. A year later, the Air Force reorganized Fitzgerald's office and abolished his job. Fitzgerald appealed the Air Force action. After almost four years of litigation, Fitzgerald was reinstated to his original civil service position and given back pay.

The Pentagon Papers

The Pentagon Papers were an unedited and unexpurgated record of the step-by-step judgments that brought American involvement in Vietnam to its peak point by the end of the Johnson administration. A historian's dream because of the raw data involved, this essentially shapeless body of material was destined to become a cause célèbre when 47 volumes of these secret documents were leaked in 1971 to the *New York Times* and the *Washington Post* by Daniel Ellsberg, a former Defense Department employee. The Nixon administration got an injunction to prevent their publication, but in the case of *New York Times v. United States* (1971), the Supreme Court dissolved the injunction and the papers were published beginning on June 13, 1971. Ellsberg was then charged with espionage, but the case was dismissed when it was

---

cost overruns A situation in the procurement of big-ticket, usually defense, items such as tanks and fighter planes when the cost to the government is greater than originally planned. Cost overruns, usually due to a change in contract specifications requested by the government or to the need to respond to the latest technology, are the butt of countless jokes because the overruns have sometimes been enormous and occasioned by corruption. One example from comedian Jay Leno appeared in the *New York Times Magazine* on February 26, 1989. "President Bush is starting to get tough. Last week he said he would not tolerate cost overruns from defense contractors. So from now on if the Pentagon wants to get sophisticated weapons, they're going to have to go down and buy 'em at the gun shop like everybody else."

shown that the Nixon administration authorized a burglary to steal Ellsberg's medical records from his psychiatrist's office. The then-chairman of the Senate Foreign Relations Committee, J. William Fulbright, said of the papers: "Most of the material should not have been secret in the first place. . . . I still do not see the harm that came from it, other than the fact that there is involved a violation of the law. . . . I can disapprove of the leaking of documents, but at the same time I disapprove just as heartily of the abuse of the classification power." Ellsberg wanted the truth about U.S. policy in Vietnam to be revealed to the American public. Thus he was willing to risk jail to expose the incompetence he believed existed at the highest levels. Ironically, the papers were created in the first place at the instigation of Robert McNamara.

The Fitzgerald and Ellsberg affairs triggered a great deal of discussion in the media and the government about the need to protect whistleblowers. This eventually led to the Civil Service Reform Act of 1978, which included unlawful retaliation against whistleblowers on its list of prohibited personnel practices. The act defined whistleblowing as revealing illegal actions, mismanagement, waste of funds, abuse of authority, or danger to the public's health or safety. The act was the culmination of a 20-year history of encouraging public disclosure. In 1958 Congress passed a Code of Ethics of Government Service, which exhorted federal employees to expose corruption and to place loyalty to the highest moral principles above loyalty to their agencies. The impact of this was negligible. The Freedom of Information Act of 1966 provides for public availability of information unless the information falls within one of the specific categories exempt from public disclosure. Exempt records are those whose disclosure would impair rights of privacy or national security.

Virtually all agencies of the executive branch of the federal government have issued regulations to implement the Freedom of Information Act. These regulations inform the public where certain types of information may be readily obtained, how other information may be obtained on request, and what internal agency appeals are available if the request for information is refused. (To locate specific agency regulations pertaining to freedom of information, consult the *Code of Federal Regulations* index under Information Availability.) The Freedom of Information Act provided would-be whistleblowers with a statutory justification for exposing misconduct. After all, such disclosures were vindications of the public's right to know. Two years later, in 1968, the U.S. Supreme Court gave whistleblowers some constitutional support. The Court held in *Pickering v. Board of Education* that when public employees' rights to freedom of speech are in question, the special duties and obligations of public employees cannot be ignored; the proper test is whether the government's interest in limiting public employees' "opportunities to contribute to public debate is . . . significantly greater than its interest in limiting a similar contribution by any member of the general public."

Protecting Whistleblowers

But Congress recognized that to fully encourage employees to disclose information about illegal and wasteful activities, something more would have to be done to make employees feel safe from retaliation. There were only a few anti-retaliation statutes in effect—limited laws that made it illegal to retaliate against employees for such things as testifying before Congress or for assisting in civil rights investigations. To provide comparable protection to whistleblowers, the Civil Service Reform Act of 1978 created the Merit Systems Protection Board and empowered it to reverse the removal, demotion, or suspension of employees who had been the victim of retaliation. In addition, the act authorized an Office of Special Counsel to prosecute any official responsible for acts of unlawful retaliation.

Since 1978, whistleblowing protections have grown considerably. Following the federal example, at least 34 states have enacted various provisions protecting their employees against retaliation for making disclosures. And state courts often have found it unlawful, even without the existence of statutory protections, for an employer to terminate someone who has made a disclosure that serves the public interest. Congress itself has also enacted over 25 additional laws that provide additional whistleblowing protections for specific kinds of disclosures, such as disclosures of violations of the Occupational Safety and Health Act. In addition, Congress strengthened and improved the protections contained in the Reform Act by enacting the Whistleblower Protection Act of 1989. This allows federal employees to appeal to the Merit Systems Protection Board to seek redress for alleged acts of retaliation involving previously nonappealable personnel actions, such as undesirable reassignments and poor performance ratings.

But despite the existence of so many whistleblowing laws, whistleblowing is not primarily a legal matter. The existence of legal protections alone will not encourage employees to disclose much information. Surveys by the Merit Systems Protection Board "have consistently demonstrated that employees will be willing to share information about fraud, waste, and abuse only when they feel that someone will be receptive to the information they share and will help to correct the problems which they've identified." Of course, the most famous whistleblower in American history would have been Robert McNamara—if only he had not been 25 years too late.

As an additional encouragement to whistleblowers, Congress passed the False Claims Act of 1986. This encourages both public employees and private citizens to report the misuse of public funds by government contractors. Such whistleblowers can collect up to 25 percent of money that the federal government may eventually recover. This act has allowed the federal government to salvage hundreds of millions of dollars. The record payment to a whistleblower was $7.5 million, earned by an employee of the federal Defense Contract Audit Agency in 1992. (Sometimes it can really pay to blow the whistle!)

Codes of Honor, Conduct, and Ethics

It was a code of honor that forced Alexander Hamilton, one of the authors of *The Federalist* and the first U.S. Secretary of the Treasury, to face Aaron Burr, then the vice president of the United States, in an 1803 duel (pistols at ten paces) that ended with Hamilton's death. Duelists have often been occupants of the White House. Andrew Jackson was notorious for it—though not as president. Today disagreements that once would have warranted duels are decided in the courts or the tabloids. Dueling over honor has not subsided; it has only taken new forms. The one constant factor in affairs of honor, as the McNamara case demonstrates, is that they are still often matters of life and death.

The New Face of Dueling

Dueling has never abated. It has only taken on new forms, adapted to new circumstances and new technology. In the classic 1955 film *Rebel Without a Cause*, James Dean is challenged to a duel. The weapons are automobiles. He and the challenger drive the cars at high speed toward a cliff. The first one to jump free is "chicken." Afterwards, Dean explains what happened to his father: "Dad, I said it was matter of honor, remember? They called me chicken. You know, chicken? I had to go 'cause if I did not I'd never be able to face those kids again. I got in one of those cars, and Buzz, that—Buzz, one of those kids—he got in the other car, and we had to drive fast and then jump, see, before the car came to the end of this bluff, and I got out okay, but Buzz did not and got killed."

Dueling by hotheaded teenage boys is the stuff of daily newspaper headlines. Teenage gang members, who once would have fought with fists or knives, now have cheap pistols or automatic weapons. A disrespectful comment or even a "look" is, as a matter of honor all too often repaid with rapid fire. Those who do not act in accordance with gang codes of behavior suffer the consequences. Not all who kill for honor are gentlemen; but no one can be a gentleman if he is not prepared to die for honor.

Honorable Behavior

We still expect that leaders will act honorably—meaning responsibly—and disdain them when they do not. Almost everybody has heard of the 1912 *Titanic* disaster, in which many of the richest men in the world quietly went to their deaths when they could have taken the places of women and children in the lifeboats. The *Titanic* followed the tradition of the "Birkenhead Drill." When a British ship, the *HMS Birkenhead*, was sinking in 1852, the captain asked the men to "stand fast" so that the women and children could have the lifeboats. Over 400 men, including the captain, drowned. Ever since, "women and children first" has been the informal law of the sea because no man of honor could dispute it. And a ship's captain, responsible for all souls on board was, as a matter of honor, traditionally expected to be the last one off of his sinking ship. Thus the world was appalled when Captain Yiannis Avranas was among the first to abandon his sinking Greek cruise ship, the *Oceanos*, off the coast of South Africa in 1991. Hundreds of passengers, many elderly, were left to shift for themselves. (The South African military eventually rescued everyone with helicopters.) As Captain Yiannis cravenly told reporters who asked him why he left his ship so soon, "When I order abandon ship, it does not matter what time I leave. Abandon is for everybody. If some people like to stay, they can stay." But his cowardly act was not morally different from the executive who arranges a golden parachute for himself while hundreds of employees who depended upon his leadership are left with pink slips barren of financial windfalls. McNamara's dishonor was similar. He bailed out of the sinking ship of the Vietnam War, leaving thousands upon thousands of his country's children, eighteen- and nineteen-year-old drafted boys, to die. Leadership, as Shakespeare said of ambition, "should be made of sterner stuff."

Codes of honor have their origins in ancient precepts about how a person should behave in the face of danger, when confronted with temptation or before authority figures. Much of what are still considered important elements of honorable behavior is contained in the Bible's Ten Commandments. Thus it is still honorable behavior to not kill, not steal, not bear false witness, and not covet thy neighbor's wife. As life grew more complicated, codes evolved for occupations as varied as clerics, masons, and warriors. The latter is both the most famous and most important because those who feel a sense of traditional honor in their breasts today ultimately derive these emotions from medieval knights, eighteenth-century military and naval officers, and nineteenth-century British gentlemen.

But the honor of knights and gentlemen was highly stratified. Remember they were gentlemen in the first place not because they were "gentle" (with women and horses!) but because of their genetic origin (Latin *gentilis*, "of a clan"), because of their breeding. Even today polite people, those who ape upper-class manners, are called "well bred"—as if they were! Gentlemen were bound to act honorably only toward others in their own class. Consequently, if an ordinary citizen, having taken a dislike to Alexander Hamilton's face, had challenged him to a duel, he would not have been obliged to accept. There would have been no dishonor in declining. But a gentleman had always to defend his name, his reputation, his honor before members of his own class. According to Robin Gilmour, traditional honor to a gentleman "meant paying one's gambling debts, but not the tradesman's bill; deceiving a husband, if need be, but not cheating him at cards; insulting a servant with impunity, but one's equals only at the risk of a duel. The testing ground for one's courage, and therefore the justification for the whole bizarre code, was the gentleman's readiness to defend his honour with his life."

The Common Law

But how were the aristocratic gentlemen rulers to induce the lower classes to behave themselves? Religion, Marx's "opium of the people," helped—still helps. But the common law was even more effective. As George Savile, the Marquis of Halifax, said in his seventeenth-century theory of deterrence: "Men are not hanged for stealing horses, but that horses may not be stolen." Deterrence, which seems to have worked well as a matter of nuclear defense policy, has had a poorer record of success in the domestic arena: Some people will violate the law no matter how severe the penalties. A classic example of a sentence designed to have a deterrent effect concerned Alfred E. Packer, who had murdered and eaten five companions during an 1873 Colorado blizzard. Packer's cannibalism was tainted with politics. So the judge at Packer's trial, M. B. Gerry, said: "Stand up, you man-eating son-of-a-bitch, and receive your sentence! There were seven Democrats in Hinsdale County, but you, you voracious, man-eating son-of-a-bitch, you ate five of them. I sentence you to be hanged by the neck until you're dead, dead, dead, as a warning against reducing the Democratic population of the state." *American Heritage* (October 1977) reports that while the judge's outburst "was probably apocryphal," Packer was hanged. In the early 1980s the students of the University of Colorado at Boulder renamed their school cafeteria "The Alfred E. Packer Memorial Grill" in honor of one of the state's most famous gourmet diners.

The common law was good enough for the common people. Those in special service, such as the army and navy, needed additional information to guide their behavior in extraordinary circumstances. Thus codes of conduct were first developed for enlisted men. The first such codes were articles of war that told soldiers what they could and could not do once they took the **king's shilling**. For example, they could not refuse an order or strike an officer. Violators were usually punished with the amputation of a limb or death. George Washington drew up the first articles of war for the American Army during the Revolutionary War. The U.S. military abandoned its articles of war only in 1950, when they were superseded by the Uniform Code of Military Justice.

Standards of Conduct

Many civilian government agencies now have standards of conduct, formal guidelines, for ethical behavior. Their objective is to ensure that employees refrain from using their official positions for private gain. Typically, a variety of prohibited activities seek to ensure that employees conduct themselves in a manner that would not offer the slightest suggestion they will extract private advantage from public employment. All too frequently, standards of conduct are used to say the obvious. For example, the British Cabinet Office created a document meant to be helpful to new cabinet ministers. Paragraph 55 of "Questions of Procedure for Ministers" offers the unsurprising advice that ministers "have a duty to refrain from asking or instructing civil servants to do things they should not do." Standards are often part of a state's formal legal code; thus violations can carry severe penalties—though never as draconian as articles of war. For example, the honest graft described by George Washington Plunkitt earlier in this chapter is now illegal in most jurisdictions in the United States. But since it was once both legal and quite common, we can surmise that ethical progress is being made.

While standards of conduct are always related to a specific organization, codes of ethics are wide in scope and encompass a whole profession or occupational category. A code of ethics is a statement of professional standards of conduct to which the practitioners of a profession say they subscribe. Ethical codes have a long lineage. The Physician's Oath of Hippocrates in ancient Greece whereby healers vow to "never administer a poison" and to "never divulge . . . secrets" is certainly the best known. But the Athenian Oath is the most ancient oath of civic duty. Designed for the young Athenian men of 18 who were about to be admitted to citizenship and subjected to military training, it was once a common part of **civics** education in the Western world. It is still a good oath for public administration and all community leaders:

> We will never bring disgrace to this our city
> by any act of dishonesty or cowardice,
> nor ever desert our suffering comrades in the ranks;
>
> We will fight for the ideals and the sacred things of the city,
> both alone and with many;
>
> We will revere and obey the city's laws and
> do our best to incite to a like respect and reverence
> those who are prone to annul or set them at naught;

---

king's shilling The coin given to new recruits as a token of their enrollment in "the King's service." Those who have "taken the King's shilling" have formally signed on and have an obligation to be loyal.
civics That part of political science dealing with the rights and responsibilities of citizenship.

We will strive unceasingly to quicken
the public sense of public duty;

That thus, in all these ways, we will transmit this city
not only not less, but greater, better and more beautiful
than it was transmitted to us.

Codes of ethics are usually not legally binding, so they may not be taken too seriously as constraints on behavior. They sometimes become significant factors in political campaigns when questionable behavior by one side or the other is attacked or defended as being within or without a professional code. Professional groups also hide behind codes as a way of protecting (or criticizing) a member subject to public attack. President Ronald Reagan took the attitude "that people should not require a code of ethics if they're going to be in government. They should be determined, themselves, that their conduct is going to be beyond reproach." Nevertheless, the problem remains that some people need help in determining just what constitutes ethical behavior. So codes are useful; but standards have the kind of teeth that can put you in jail.

Summary

Our modern concepts of honor can be traced from Aristotle to medieval chivalry, to aristocratic dueling codes, to the modern concept of the gentleman. Honor remains one of the core influences of human behavior, often more important than life itself.

Honor comes before ethics because a person without honor has no moral compass and does not know which way to turn to be ethical. Honor goes to the essence of public affairs; since ancient times only individuals perceived to be honorable could be trusted with the public's business.

Recurrent government scandals, no matter how much they cost, pose a great threat to the democratic notions of the rule of law. When a public official misuses his or her office for self-gain, then the rule of law no longer obtains and there is, in effect, a return to tyranny.

Do public officials have a special obligation to tell the truth or do their offices permit them special excuses to depart from truth-telling? Since knowledge is the cornerstone of democracy, an informed public is a prerequisite for a democratic government. Hence, citizens have an inherent right to know the truth of public issues. On the other hand, there may be times of crises when it may be permissible for a public official to deceive the public for its own good.

In public administration there is a hierarchy of levels of ethics: personal morality, professional ethics, organizational ethics, and social ethics. This last level obliges members of a given society to act in ways that both protect individuals and further the progress of the group as a whole.

Codes of honor have their origins in ancient precepts about how a person should behave in the face of danger, when confronted with temptation or before authority figures. Many civilian government agencies now have parallel standards of conduct, formal guidelines for ethical behavior, which seek to ensure that employees refrain from using their official positions for private gain.

Key Concepts

big lie An untruth so great or so audacious that it is bound to have an effect on public opinion.

bribery The giving or offering of anything of value with intent to unlawfully influence an official in the discharge of duties; a public official's receiving or asking of anything of value with the intent to be unlawfully influenced.

code of ethics A statement of professional standards of conduct to which the practitioners of a profession say they subscribe. Codes of ethics are usually not legally binding, so they may not be taken too seriously as constraints on behavior.

common law The totality of judge-made laws that initially developed in England and continued to evolve in the United States. Whenever this kind of law—which is based on custom, culture, habit, and previous judicial decisions—proved inadequate, it was supplanted by statutory laws made by legislatures. But the common law tradition, based upon precedent, is still the foundation of the American legal system, even though much of what was originally common law has been converted into statutes over the years.

corruption The unauthorized use of public office for private gain. The most common forms of corruption are bribery, extortion, and the misuse of inside information.

dirty hands dilemma A graphic phrase for the tendency of public officials to commit an act generally considered to be a wrong to further the common good. This is a dilemma in the sense that doing bad seems to lead to something good.

higher law The notion that no matter what the laws of a state are, there remains a higher law, to which a person has an even greater obligation. A higher law is often appealed to by those who wish to attack an existing law or practice that courts or legislators are unlikely or unwilling to change.

honor The internalized moral compass by which individuals ascertain correct behavior in public and private life; the perception by others of one's reputation for integrity.

integrity The core of honor. Those who have integrity live up to their stated principles, values, and most importantly, their word. A person whose word is his or her bond gives the full faith and credit of his or her whole being to keeping commitments.

stakeholder Any individual or group that might be affected by the outcome of something. All decisions have their stakeholders. The responsible public decision maker seeks to obtain the maximum possible stakeholder satisfaction.

standards of conduct A compendium of ethical norms promulgated by an organization to guide the behavior of its members. Many government agencies have formal codes (or standards) of conduct for their employees.

Watergate The scandal that led to the resignation of President Richard M. Nixon. Watergate itself is a hotel-office-apartment complex in Washington, DC. When individuals associated with the Committee to Reelect the President were caught breaking into the Democratic National Committee Headquarters (then located in the Watergate complex) in 1972, the resulting cover-up and national trauma was condensed into one word—Watergate. The term has grown to refer to any political crime or instance of bureaucratic corruption that undermines confidence in governing institutions.

whistleblower An individual who believes the public interest overrides the interests of his or her organization and publicly blows the whistle on—meaning exposes—corrupt, illegal, fraudulent, or harmful activity.

Bibliography

Berman, Larry. (1982). *Planning a Tragedy: The Americanization of the War in Vietnam.* New York: Norton.

Belli, Melvin M. (1973). Review of *The Finest Judges Money Can Buy* by Charles Ashman in the *New York Times Book Review,* November 18.

———. (1976). *My Life on Trial.* New York: Morrow.

Brown, E. G. (1970). *Reagan and Reality.* New York: Praeger.

Chandler, Ralph Clark. (1983). "The Problem of Moral Reasoning in American Public Administration:

The Case for a Code of Ethics," *Public Administration Review* 43 (January-February).

Dallek, Robert. (1998). *Flawed Giant: Lyndon Johnson and His Times*. New York: Oxford University Press.

Gilmour, Robin. (1981). *The Idea of the Gentleman in the Victorian Novel*. London: George Allen and Unwin.

Halberstam, David. (1972). *The Best and the Brightest*. New York: Random House.

Jos, Philip H., Mark E. Tompkins, and Steven W. Hays. (1989). "In Praise of Difficult People: A Portrait of the Committed Whistleblower," *Public Administration Review* 49 (November-December).

Kaplan, Fred. (1983). *The Wizards of Armageddon*. New York: Simon and Schuster.

Kearns, Doris. (1976). *Lyndon Johnson and the American Dream*. New York: Harper and Row.

Madsen, Peter, and Jay M. Shafritz, eds. (1992). *Essentials of Government Ethics*. New York: Meridian Books.

Miceli, Marcia, and Janet Near. (1992). *Blowing the Whistle*. New York: Lexington Books.

Miller, Merle. (1973). *Plain Speaking: An Oral Biography of Harry S. Truman*. New York: Berkeley.

Orwell, George. (1946). *Animal Farm*. New York: Harcourt, Brace.

Rohr, John. (1986). *Ethics for Bureaucrats*, 2nd ed. New York: Marcel Dekker.

Steffens, Lincoln. (1904). *The Shame of the Cities*. New York: Sagamore Press.

Stevenson, Richard. (1992). "U.S. Judge Orders $7.5 Million Award to Whistleblower," *New York Times*, July 7.

Thompson, Dennis F. (1985). "The Possibility of Administrative Ethics," *Public Administration Review* (September-October).

Twain, Mark. (1899). *A Connecticut Yankee in King Arthur's Court*. New York: Harper.

Williams, Charles. (1993). *The Last Great Frenchman*. New York: Little, Brown.

Wills, Garry. (1984). *Cincinnatus: George Washington and the Enlightenment*. New York: Doubleday.

Recommended Books

Adams, Guy B., and Danny L. Balfour. (1998). *Unmaking Administrative Evil*.

Thousand Oaks, CA: Sage. Finally, a book that seeks out the evil that lurks within government bureaucracies; explains how ordinary people doing their normal professional duties can take part in evil without even being aware of it.

Emery, Fred. (1994). *Watergate: The Corruption of American Politics and the Fall of Richard Nixon*. New York: Random House. A history of the scandal that forced a president to resign in disgrace.

Madsen, Peter, and Jay M. Shafritz. (1992). *Essentials of Government Ethics*. New York: New American Library. A collection of writings on government ethics from ancient times to the present.

McMaster, H. R. (1997). *Dereliction of Duty: Lyndon Johnson, Robert McNamara, the Joint Chiefs of Staff, and the Lies that Led to Vietnam*. New York: HarperCollins. The history of the lies and dishonor of America's top military and civilian leadership during the Vietnam War.

Rohr, John A. (1989). *Ethics for Bureaucrats: An Essay on Law and Values*. New York: Marcel Dekker. The original presentation of the concept of regime values, which holds that the most fundamental principles of a polity—such as its constitution—should be the primary guide to ethical behavior.

Van Wart, Montgomery. (1998). *Changing Public Sector Values*. Hamden, CT: Garland Publishing. A values approach to public sector ethics; examines values from the individual administrator's perspective, from the cultural framework, and from the functional standpoint.

Related Web Sites

Center for the Study of Ethics
http://www.iit.edu/departments/csep
Centre for Applied Ethics
http://www.ethics.ubc.ca/resources/business/
Institute for Business and Professional Ethics
http://www.depaul.edu/ethics/contents.html
New York Times Web page on Watergate
http://www.nytimes.com/library/cyber/week/061797watergate.html

Online Journal of Ethics
http://www.condor.depaul.edu/ethics/ethgl.html
U.S. Office of Government Ethics
http://www.usoge.gov/index.html

Glossary

accountability The extent to which one must answer to higher authority—legal or organizational—for one's actions in society at large or within one's particular organizational position.

administration The management and direction of the affairs of governments and institutions; a collective term for all policymaking officials of a government; the execution and implementation of public policy.

administrative doctrine The rules, procedures, and ways of doing things that reflect the basic values of an organization.

affirmative action A term that first meant the removal of "artificial barriers" to the employment of women and minority group members; now it refers to compensatory opportunities for hitherto disadvantaged groups—specific efforts to recruit, hire, and promote qualified members of disadvantaged groups for the purpose of eliminating the present effects of past discrimination.

agenda setting The process by which ideas or issues bubble up through the various political channels to wind up for consideration by a political institution such as a legislature or court.

assets All money, property, and money-related rights (such as money owed to one) owned by a person or an organization. Capital assets or fixed assets are those things that cannot be turned into cash easily (such as buildings); current assets or liquid assets are those things that can be turned into cash easily (such as cash or goods for sale); and frozen assets are those things that are tied up (for instance, because of a lawsuit).

audit An independent examination, an objective assessment of something; typically the financial reports of an individual or organization to determine whether they accurately represent expenditures and are in compliance with accounting standards and laws.

big lie An untruth so great or so audacious that it is bound to have an effect on public opinion.

block grant A grant distributed in accordance with a statutory formula for use in a variety of activities within a broad functional area, largely at the recipient's discretion.

bribery The giving or offering of anything of value with intent to unlawfully influence an official in the discharge of duties; a public official's receiving or asking of anything of value with the intent to be unlawfully influenced.

Brownlow Committee A committee appointed by President Franklin D. Roosevelt in 1936 for the purpose of diagnosing the staffing needs of the president and making appropriate recommendations for the reorganization of the executive branch.

budget A financial plan serving as a pattern for and control over future operations; hence, any estimate of future costs or any systematic plan for the utilization of the workforce, material, or other resources.

budget cycle The timed steps of the budget process, which includes preparation, approval, execution, and audit.

budget process The total system a jurisdiction uses to make decisions on government spending needs and how to pay for them. The main difference between federal and state and local budget processes is that the state and local jurisdictions must have balanced budgets each year.

budget surplus The amount by which a government's budget receipts exceed its budget outlays for any given period.

bureau movement The efforts of progressive reformers early in the twentieth century to apply scientific methods to municipal problems. Their efforts led to the creation of research bureaus, which in turn created the academic field of public administration.

bureaucracy The totality of government officers; all of a government's employees; a general invective to refer to any inefficient organization encumbered by red tape or a specific set of structural arrangements.

bureaucrat bashing Either justified criticism or inappropriate condemnation of public employees.

bureaucratic dysfunctions The pathological elements of bureaucratic structures that often make them inefficient in operation; the pressures on workers to conform that causes them to adhere to rules as an end rather than a means.

bureaucratic impersonality The dehumanizing consequences of formal organizational structures eliminating personal and emotional consideration from organizational life so that the individual bureaucrat functions only as a cog in an ever-moving machine.

cabinet The heads of the executive departments of a jurisdiction who report to and advise its chief executive; examples would include the president's cabinet, the governor's cabinet, and the mayor's cabinet.

cabinet government The British system, whereby the cabinet as a whole, rather than only the prime minister who heads it, is considered the executive, and the cabinet is collectively responsible to the parliament for its performance. In addition, the cabinet ministers are typically drawn from among the majority party's members in Parliament, whereas in the United States the cabinet secretaries are only from the executive branch.

capital budgeting A budget process that deals with planning for large expenditures for capital items such as bridges and buildings.

casework The services performed by legislators and their staffs at the request of and on behalf of constituents.

categorical grant A grant that can be used only for specific, narrowly defined activities—for example, to construct an interstate highway.

charisma Leadership based on the compelling personality of the leader rather than upon formal position. The word *charisma* is derived from the Greek word for divine grace. The concept was first developed by Max Weber, who distinguished charismatic authority from both the traditional authority of a monarch and the legal authority given to someone by law.

child labor Originally, the employment of children in a manner detrimental to their health and social development. Now that the law contains strong child labor prohibitions, the term refers to the employment of children below the legal age limit.

civil service A collective term for all nonmilitary employees of a government. Paramilitary organizations, such as police and firefighters, are always included in civil service counts in the United States. Civil service employment is not the same as merit system employment, because all patronage positions (those not covered by merit systems) are included in civil service totals.

civil service reform Efforts to improve the status, integrity, and productivity of the civil service at all levels of government by supplanting the spoils system with the merit system; efforts to improve the management and efficiency of the public service; or the historical events, the movement, leading up to the enactment of the Pendleton Act of 1883.

classical theory The original theory about organizations that closely resembles military structures.

code of ethics A statement of professional standards of conduct to which the practitioners of a profession say they subscribe. Codes of ethics are usually not legally binding, so they may not be taken too seriously as constraints on behavior.

collective bargaining Bargaining on behalf of a group of employees, as opposed to individual bargaining, in which each worker represents only himself or herself.

common law The totality of judge-made laws that initially developed in England and continued to evolve in the United States. Whenever this kind of law—which is based on custom, culture, habit, and previous judicial decisions—proved inadequate, it was supplanted by statutory laws made by legislatures. But the common law tradition, based upon precedent, is still the foundation of the American legal system, even though much of what was originally common law has been converted into statutes over the years.

compliance audit The traditional form of auditing, in which the auditor is looking for the extent to which, in the financial management of an organization, funds have been managed in compliance with the law, and to which accepted standards and conventions for the treatment of accounting information have been used.

congressional oversight The total means by which the U.S. Congress monitors the activities of executive branch agencies to determine if the laws are being faithfully executed.

constitutional architecture The administrative arrangements created by a government's constitution—from the separation of powers to the requirement that specific departments be created or services performed.

contingency theory An approach to leadership asserting that leadership styles will vary in their effects in different situations. The situation (not traits or styles themselves) determines whether a leadership style or a particular leader will be effective.

corruption The unauthorized use of public office for private gain. The most common forms of corruption are bribery, extortion, and the misuse of inside information.

council of government (COG) An organization of cooperating local governments seeking a regional approach to planning, development, transportation, environment, and other issues.

deficit financing A situation in which a government's excess of outlays over receipts for a given period is financed primarily by borrowing from the public.

devolution The transfer of power from a central to a local authority.

Dillon's rule The criteria developed by state courts to determine the nature and extent of powers granted to local governments.

dirty hands dilemma A graphic phrase for the tendency of public officials to commit an act generally considered to be a wrong to further the common good. This is a dilemma in the sense that doing bad seems to lead to something good.

discrimination Bigotry in practice; intolerance toward those who have different beliefs or religions. In employment, the failure to treat equals equally. Any action that has the effect of limiting employment and advancement opportunities because of an individual's sex, race, color, age, national origin, religion, physical handicap, or other irrelevant criteria, is discrimination.

empowerment Giving a person or organization the formal authority to do something.

equal employment opportunity Employment practices that prevent any individual from being adversely excluded from employment opportunities on the basis of race, color, sex, religion, age, national origin, or other factors that cannot lawfully be considered in employing people.

evaluation research An attempt to assess specific policy options by conducting experiments, assessing their outcomes, and recommending whether the new concept should be broadly applied.

executive branch In a government with separation of powers, that part that is responsible for applying or administering the law. Thus a president, governor, or mayor and their respective supporting bureaucracies are the executive branches of their respective jurisdictions. But not all of the federal bureaucracy is part of the executive branch. Some agencies, such as the General Accounting Office, are directly responsible to Congress. Others, such as the Federal Trade Commission (and other regulatory agencies), have been held by the Supreme Court not to be part of the executive branch.

executive branch The part of a government responsible for applying or administering the law. Thus a president, governor, or mayor and their supporting bureaucracies are the executive branches of their respective jurisdictions.

executive budget The budget document for an executive branch of government that a jurisdiction's chief executive submits to a legislature for review, modification, and enactment.

Executive Office of the President (EOP) The umbrella office consisting of the top presidential staff agencies that provide the president help and advice in carrying out his major responsibilities. The EOP was created by President Franklin D. Roosevelt under the authority of the Reorganization Act of 1939. Since then, presidents have used executive orders, reorganization plans, and legislative initiatives to reorganize, expand, or contract the EOP.

federalism A system of governance in which a national, overarching government shares power with subnational or state governments.

federalism, cooperative The notion that the national, state, and local governments are cooperating, interacting agents, jointly working to solve common problems, rather than conflicting, sometimes hostile competitors, pursuing similar or possibly conflicting ends.

federalism, dual The nineteenth-century concept, now no longer operational, that the functions and responsibilities of the federal and state governments were theoretically distinguished and functionally separate from each other.

federalism, marble-cake The concept that the cooperative relations among the varying levels of government result in an intermingling of activities; in contrast to the more traditional view of layer-cake federalism, which holds that the three levels of government are totally or almost totally separate.

Federalism, New The Republican efforts begun during the Nixon administration to decentralize governmental functions by returning power and responsibility to the states. This trend was continued in the 1980s by the Reagan administration and culminated in the 1990s movement toward devolution.

federalism, picket-fence The concept that bureaucratic specialists at the various levels of government (along with clientele groups) exercise considerable power over the nature of intergovernmental programs.

financial report A written statement—also called an accountant's certificate, accountant's opinion, or audit report—prepared by an independent accountant or auditor after an audit.

fiscal federalism The financial relations between and among units of government in a federal system. The theory of fiscal federalism, or multi-unit government finance, is one part of the branch of applied economics known as public finance.

General Accounting Office (GAO) A support agency of the U.S. Congress created by the Budget and Accounting Act of 1921 to audit federal government expenditures and to assist the Congress with its legislative oversight responsibilities.

Grace Commission An attempt made by the Reagan administration to have business leaders study and reform the federal government; much was studied, little was reformed.

grant An intergovernmental transfer of funds (or other assets). Since the New Deal, state and local governments have become increasingly dependent upon federal grants for an almost infinite variety of programs.

group cohesion The shared beliefs, values, and assumptions of a group that allows it to function as a team.

group dynamics The subfield of organization behavior concerned with the nature of groups, how they develop, and how they interrelate with individuals and other groups.

Hawthorne experiments The late 1920s and early 1930s management studies undertaken at the Hawthorne Works of the Western Electric Company near Chicago. Conducted by Elton Mayo and his associates from the Harvard Business School, they became the most famous management experiments ever reported.

higher law The notion that no matter what the laws of a state are, there remains a higher law, to which a person has an even greater obligation. A higher law is often appealed to by those who wish to attack an existing law or practice that courts or legislators are unlikely or unwilling to change.

honor The internalized moral compass by which individuals ascertain correct behavior in public and private life; the perception by others of one's reputation for integrity.

Hoover Commissions The post–World War II efforts to reorganize the federal government.

impasse resolution A condition that exists during labor-management negotiations when either party feels that no further progress can be made toward a settlement—unless the process of negotiating changes. The most common techniques used to break an impasse are mediation, fact finding, and arbitration.

implementation Putting a government program into effect; the total process of translating a legal mandate, whether an executive order or an enacted statute, into appropriate program directives and structures that provide services or create goods.

incremental budgeting A method of budget review that focuses on the increments of increase or decrease in the budget of existing programs. Incremental budgeting, which is often called traditional budgeting, is a counter school of thought to more rational, systems-oriented approaches, such as zero-based budgeting.

incremental decision making model A view of the public policymaking process that assumes that small decisions made at the margins of problems are the usual reality of change.

integrity The core of honor. Those who have integrity live up to their stated principles, values, and most importantly, their word. A person whose word is his or her bond gives the full faith and credit of his or her whole being to keeping commitments.

intergovernmental relations The complex network of interrelationships among governments; the political, fiscal, programmatic, and administrative processes by which higher units of government share revenues and other resources with lower units of government, generally accompanied by special conditions that the lower units must satisfy as prerequisites to receiving the assistance.

internal audit The function of audit groups within a larger organization. They vary in the tasks they are assigned. Sometimes they have a compliance audit role. In other instances they serve as independent troubleshooters, providing early warning to top management of emerging problems.

leadership The exercise of authority, whether formal or informal, in directing and coordinating the work of others.

learning organization Peter Senge's term for organizations in which new patterns of thinking are nurtured, and where people are continually learning together to improve both the organization and their personal lives.

line-item budget The classification of budgetary accounts according to narrow, detailed objects of expenditure (such as motor vehicles, clerical workers, or reams of paper) used within each particular agency of government, generally without reference to the ultimate purpose or objective served by the expenditure.

management A word that refers both to the people responsible for running an organization and to the running process itself; the use of numerous resources (such as employees and machines) to accomplish an organizational goal.

management control That aspect of management concerned with the comparison of actual versus planned performance as well as the development and implementation of procedures to correct substandard performance.

management development Any conscious effort on the part of an organization, such as rotational assignments or formal educational experiences, to provide a manager with the skills needed for future duties.

managerial revolution James Burham's concept that as control of large businesses moved from the original owners to professional managers, society's new governing class would be not the traditional possessors of wealth—but those who have the professional expertise to manage, to lead, large organizations.

managerialism An entrepreneurial approach to public management that emphasizes management rights and a reinvigorated scientific management.

mandating One level of government requiring another to offer—and/or pay for—a program as a matter of law or as a prerequisite to partial or full funding for either the program in question or other programs.

merit system A public sector concept of staffing that implies that no test of party membership is involved in the selection, promotion, or retention of government employees and that a constant effort is made to select the best qualified individuals available for appointment and advancement.

micromanagement A pejorative term for supervising too closely. Any manager may be guilty of micromanagement for refusing to allow subordinates to have any real authority or responsibility, thereby ensuring that subordinates can neither function as, or grow into, effective managers. Also used to refer to interference by legislators with the minutiae of administration for the benefit of their constituents.

moral leadership Leading people in specific directions of action and thought based on morals and decency.

motivation An amalgam of all of the factors in one's working environment that foster (positively or negatively) productive efforts.

national debt The total outstanding debt of a central government.

needs hierarchy Five sets of goals or basic needs arranged in a hierarchy of prepotency: physiological needs (food, water, shelter, etc.), safety needs, love or affiliation needs, esteem needs, and the final need for self-actualization.

neoclassical theory Theoretical perspectives that revise, expand, and/or are critical of classical organization theory.

new public administration An academic advocacy movement for social equity in the performance and delivery of public services; it called for a proactive administrator with a burning desire for social equity to replace the traditional impersonal and neutral gun-for-hire bureaucrat.

new public management A disparate group of structural reforms and informal management initiatives that reflects the doctrine of managerialism in the public sector.

nonprofit organization, An organization created and operated for public or societal purposes (such as alleviation of poverty) rather than private benefit purposes (such as return on shareholders' investments).

objective A short-term goal; something that must be achieved on the way to a larger overall achievement.

organization A group of people who jointly work to achieve at least one common goal.

organization development An approach or strategy for increasing organizational effectiveness. As a process it has no value biases, but it is usually associated with the idea that effectiveness is found by integrating the individual's desire for growth with organizational goals.

organization theory A set of propositions that seeks to explain or predict how groups and individuals behave in differing organizational arrangements.

organizational culture The culture that exists within an organization; a parallel but smaller version of a societal culture.

paradigm An intellectual model for a situation or condition.

patronage The power of elected and appointed officials to make partisan appointments to office or to confer contracts, honors, or other benefits on their political supporters. Patronage has always been one of the major tools by which political executives consolidate their power and attempt to control a bureaucracy.

performance appraisal The formal methods by which an organization documents the work performance of its employees. Performance appraisals are typically designed to change dysfunctional work behavior, communicate perceptions of work quality, assess the future potential of employees, and provide a documented record for disciplinary and separation actions.

performance audit An audit that compares the activities of an organization with the objectives that have been assigned to it.

performance management The systematic integration of an organization's efforts to achieve its objectives.

personnel A collective term for all of the employees of an organization. The word is of military origin—the two basic components of a traditional army being materiel and personnel. Personnel is also commonly used to refer to the personnel management function or the organizational unit responsible for administering personnel programs.

planning horizon The time frame during which the objectives of a strategic plan are to be achieved.

pluralism A theory of government that attempts to reaffirm the democratic character of society by asserting that open, multiple, competing, and responsive groups preserve traditional democratic values in a mass industrial state. Pluralism assumes that power will shift from group to group as elements in the mass public transfer their allegiance in response to their perceptions of their individual interests.

political culture That part of the overall societal culture that determines a community's attitudes toward the quality, style, and vigor of its political processes and government operations.

POSDCORB The mnemonic device invented by Luther Gulick in 1937 to call attention to the various functional elements of the work of a chief executive.

position classification The use of formal job descriptions to organize all jobs in a civil service merit system into classes on the basis of duties and responsibilities, for the purposes of delineating authority, establishing chains of command, and providing equitable salary scales.

postbureaucratic organization Constantly changing temporary organizational systems; task forces composed of groups of relative strangers with diverse skills created in response to a special problem, as opposed to continuing need.

postmodernism The belief that constant change is a new fact of life for large organizations that are living on the edge, on the boundary, between order and chaos.

principles of management Fundamental truths or working hypotheses that serve as guidelines to management thinking and action.

privatization The process of returning to the private sector property or functions previously owned or performed by government.

productivity A measured relationship between the quantity (and quality) of results produced and the quantity of resources required for production. Productivity is, in essence, a measure of the work efficiency of an individual, a work unit, or a whole organization.

professional A member of an occupation requiring specialized knowledge that can be gained only after intensive preparation. Professional occupations tend to possess three features: a body of academic and practical knowledge that is applied to the service of society, a standard of success theoretically measured by serving the needs of society rather than seeking purely personal gain, and a system of control over the professional practice.

program evaluation The systematic examination of any activity undertaken by government to make a determination about its effects, both short-term and long-range.

progressive tax Any tax that has people of greater wealth paying a larger percentage in tax than people of lesser means. Income taxes are often progressive.

public administration Whatever governments do, for good or ill. It is public administration's political context that makes it public—that distinguishes it from private or business administration.

public interest The universal label in which political actors wrap the policies and programs that they advocate.

public policy Decision making by government. Governments are constantly concerned about what they should or should not do. And whatever they do or do not do is public policy.

public program All those activities designed to implement a public policy; often this calls for the creation of organizations, public agencies, and bureaus.

racist Any person or organization that either consciously or unconsciously practices discrimination against another person on the basis of race (or ethnicity) or supports the supremacy of one race over others.

rational decision making model A view of the public policymaking process that assumes complete information and a systematic, logical, and comprehensive approach to change.

red tape The ribbon that was once used to bind government documents; the term now stands as the symbol of excessive official formality and overattention to prescribed routines.

reengineering The fundamental rethinking and redesign of organizational processes to achieve significant improvements in critical measures of performance, such as costs or quality of services.

regressive tax Any tax that has people with lower incomes paying a higher overall percentage of their income in tax than people of greater income. Sales taxes are examples of regressive taxes.

regulation The totality of government controls on the social and economic activities of its citizens; the rule-making process of those administrative agencies charged with the official interpretation of laws.

regulatory commission An independent agency created by a government to regulate some aspect of economic life.

reinventing government The latest manifestation of the progressive tradition of continuously improving government—this time with an emphasis on privatization.

representative bureaucracy The ultimate goal of equal employment opportunity and affirmative action programs.

republic A form of government in which sovereignty resides in the people who elect agents to represent them in political decision making.

reverse discrimination Discrimination against white males in conjunction with preferential treatment for women and minorities.

rule of law A governing system in which the highest authority is a body of law that applies equally to all (as opposed to the traditional "rule of men," in which the personal whim of those in power can decide any issue).

scientific management A systematic approach to managing that seeks the "one best way" of accomplishing any given task by discovering the fastest, most efficient, and least fatiguing production methods.

second reconstruction The civil rights movement and legislation of the 1960s. The first reconstruction, immediately after the Civil War, gave blacks their freedom from slavery. But the laws as enforced and customs as practiced did not allow for the full rights of citizens. That came in the 1960s, when public sentiment was aroused and legal action was taken to ensure equal rights for all Americans.

self-directed work team A work group that will accept responsibility for their processes and products—as well as for the behavior of other group members.

separation of powers The allocation of powers among the three branches of government so that they are a check upon each other. This separation, in theory, makes a tyrannical concentration of power impossible.

sex discrimination Any disparate or unfavorable treatment of a person in an employment situation because of his or her sex.

sexual harassment The action of an individual in a position to control or influence another's job, career, or grade who uses such power to gain sexual favors or punish the refusal of such favors. Sexual harassment on the job varies from inappropriate sexual innuendo to coerced sexual relations.

spoils system The practice of awarding government jobs to one's political supporters, as opposed to awarding them on the basis of merit.

stakeholder Any individual or group that might be affected by the outcome of something. All decisions have their stakeholders. The responsible public decision maker seeks to obtain the maximum possible stakeholder satisfaction.

standards of conduct A compendium of ethical norms promulgated by an organization to guide the behavior of its members. Many government agencies have formal codes (or standards) of conduct for their employees.

strategic management A philosophy of management that links strategic planning with day-to-day decision making. Strategic management seeks a fit between an organization's external and internal environments.

strategic plan The formal document that presents the ways and means by which a strategic goal will be achieved.

strategic planning The set of processes used by an organization to assess the strategic situation and develop strategy for the future.

strategy The overall conduct of a major enterprise to achieve long-term goals; the pattern to be found in a series of organizational decisions.

strike A mutual agreement among workers (whether members of a union or not) to a temporary work stoppage to obtain—or to resist—a change in their working conditions.

SWOT analysis A review of an organization's Strengths, Weaknesses, Opportunities, and Threats. This technique is widely used to examine the viability of strategic plans.

systems theory A view of an organization as a complex set of dynamically intertwined and interconnected elements, including its inputs, processes, outputs, feedback loops, and the environment in which it operates and with which it continuously interacts.

tactics The short-term immediate decisions that, in their totality, lead to the achievement of strategic goals.

tax A compulsory contribution exacted by a government for public purposes.

technocracy A contraction of "technical" and "bureaucracy," which refers to the high-tech organizational environments of the postmodern world.

Theory X The assumptions that the average human being has an inherent dislike of work; that most people must be threatened to get them to put forth adequate effort; and that people prefer to be directed and to avoid responsibility.

Theory Y The assumptions that work is as natural as play, that workers can exercise self-direction and self-control, and that imagination, ingenuity, and creativity are widespread.

Title VII That part of the Civil Rights Act of 1964 that prohibits employment discrimination because of race, color, religion, sex, or national origin and that created the Equal Employment Opportunity Commission as its enforcement vehicle.

total quality management (TQM) A phrase for quality control in its most expanded sense of a total and continuing concern for quality in the production of goods and services.

trait theory An approach to leadership that assumes leaders possess traits that make them fundamentally different from followers. Advocates of trait theory believe that some people have unique leadership characteristics and qualities that enable them to assume responsibilities not everyone can execute. Therefore they are "born" leaders.

transformational leadership Leadership that strives to change organizational culture and directions. It reflects the ability of a leader to develop a values-based vision for the organization, to convert the vision into reality, and to maintain it over time.

unified budget The present form of the budget of the federal government, in which receipts and outlays from federal funds and trust funds (such as Social Security) are consolidated.

unions Groups of employees who create a formal organization (the union) to represent their interests before management.

vision A view of an organization's future. The purpose of strategic management is to make such a vision a reality.

vision statement The identification of objectives to be achieved in the future.

Watergate The scandal that led to the resignation of President Richard M. Nixon. Watergate itself is a hotel-office-apartment complex in Washington, D.C. When individuals associated with the Committee to Reelect the President were caught breaking into the Democratic National Committee Headquarters (then located in the Watergate complex) in 1972, the resulting cover-up and national trauma was condensed into one word—Watergate. The suffix "-gate" has grown to refer to any political crime or instance of bureaucratic corruption that undermines confidence in governing institutions.

whistleblower An individual who believes the public interest overrides the interests of his or her organization and publicly blows the whistle on—meaning exposes—corrupt, illegal, fraudulent, or harmful activity.

zero-based budgeting A budgeting process that is a rejection of the incremental decision making model of budgeting. It demands a rejustification of the entire budget submission (from ground zero), whereas incremental budgeting essentially respects the outcomes of previous budgetary decisions (collectively referred to as the budget base) and focuses examination on the margin of change from year to year.

Appendix:
Additional Sources

Chapter 1
"Oh my God . . ."   Clive Irving, ed., *In Their Name* (1995)
"This is state of . . ."   Ibid.
"Last night I just thought . . ."   Buzz Bissinger, *A Prayer for the City* (1997)
"snow buttons"   *U. S. News and World Report,* January 17, 1994

Chapter 2
"Just what is it . . ."   Speech of January 29, 1916
"Remember, democracy . . ."   Letter to John Taylor, April 15, 1814
". . . that my oath . . ."   Letter to A. G. Hodges, April 4, 1864

Chapter 3
". . . are supervisors in California, judges in . . ."   *Governing* (May 1989)

Chapter 4
"What the judges say . . ."   Hughes speech, May 3, 1907
"States are not colonies . . ."   *The Economist,* November 26, 1984
"On bended knee . . ."   Ibid.
"We do not want to be in the importing . . ."   *Washington Post National Weekly,*
    September 18–24, 1995

Chapter 5
"I found Rome . . ."   Michael Grant, *The Founders of the Ancient World* (1991)
"No rule of war . . ."   *Military Maxims* (1827)
"With 2,000 years . . ."   Norman F. Dixon, *On the Psychology of Military
    Incompetence* (1976)
"There is nothing so practical . . ."   Alfred J. Marrow, *The Practical Theorist:
    The Life and Work of Kurt Lewis* (1969)

Chapter 6
". . . the giant power wielded . . ."   H. Balzac, *Bureaucracy* (1901)

Chapter 7

". . . if Congress . . . passed a law . . ."   C. G. Dawes, *The First Year of the Budget of the United States* (1923)

". . . every revolution evaporates . . ."   Kafka quoted in *Newsweek*, October 14, 1968

". . . clocks look bureaucratic . . ."   *Newsweek*, October 31, 1994

"All at once, five postal . . ."   *New York Times*, June 6, 1993

Chapter 8

". . . the public be damned"   Remark to reporter on October 8, 1882

Chapter 9

"Federal Centers for Disease Control . . ."   *New York Times*, July 10, 1995

"The Presidency is not merely an . . ."   *New York Times*, September 11, 1932

"This brand is cynically . . ."   *Washington Post National Weekly,* February 5–11, 1990

". . . each year the military spends . . ."   *U. S. News and World Report,* May 24, 1993

Chapter 11

"Effective January 1, 1997, the University . . ."   *New York Times,* July 22, 1995

". . . the nation's first governor . . ."   *Pittsburgh Post Gazette,* June 2, 1995

Chapter 12

"What the hell . . ."   *New York Times,* December 18, 1994

"No citizen has a moral obligation . . ."   *New York Times,* April 16, 1995

Chapter 14

"McNamara went to the World Bank . . ."   *New York Times,* April 15, 1995

"He kept his mouth shut . . ."   *Newsweek,* April 24, 1995

"I think it's about 25 years . . ."   *New York Times,* April 15, 1995

"The nation's honor . . ."   Speech in Cleveland, January 29, 1916

". . . about a man who drives into Moscow . . ."   *New York Times,* May 3, 1995

"Most of the material should not have been secret . . ."   *Christian Science Monitor,* July 18, 1973

"When I order abandon ship . . ."   *Time,* August 19, 1991

"Stand up, you man-eating . . ."   *American Heritage,* October 1977

". . . have a duty to refrain . . ."   *Times* (London), April 15, 1993

". . . that people shouldn't require . . . ."   *U.S. News and World Report,* January 19, 1981

Photo Credits

Index

Page numbers in italics indicate figures.

1954
- Peter Drucker's book, *The Practice of Management,* popularizes the concept of management by objectives.
- The Supreme Court, in *Brown v. Board of Education,* holds that racially separate educational facilities are inherently unequal and therefore violate the equal protection clause of the Fourteenth Amendment.
- Senator Joseph McCarthy (and in effect McCarthyism) censured by the U.S. Senate.
- Lakewood, California, pioneers the service contract, whereby a small jurisdiction buys government services from a neighboring large jurisdiction.

1955
- The Second Hoover Commission recommends the curtailment and abolition of federal government activities that are competitive with private enterprise.
- Department of Health, Education and Welfare (HEW) created.
- AFL-CIO is formed by the merger of the American Federation of Labor and the Congress of Industrial Organization.

1957
- C. Northcote Parkinson discovers his law that "work expands so as to fill the time available for its completion."
- Chris Argyris asserts in *Personality and Organization* that there is an inherent conflict between the personality of a mature adult and the needs of modern organizations.
- Douglas M. McGregor's article, "The Human Side of Enterprise," distills the contending traditional (authoritarian) and humanistic managerial philosophies into Theory X and Theory Y.

1958
- NASA created.

1959
- New York City is the first major city to allow collective bargaining with its employees.
- Wisconsin is the first state to enact a comprehensive law governing public sector labor relations.
- The Advisory Commission on Intergovernmental Relations is established.
- Charles A. Lindblom's "The Science of 'Muddling Through'" rejects the rational model of decisionmaking in favor of incrementalism.
- Herzberg, Mausner, and Snyderman's *The Motivation to Work* puts forth the motivation-hygiene theory.

1960
- Richard Neustadt's *Presidential Power* asserts that the president's (or any executive's) essential power is that of persuasion.

1961
- President Dwight D. Eisenhower in his farewell address warns of "the military-industrial complex."
- President John F. Kennedy's Executive Order 10925 requires that "affirmative action" be used in employment.
- The Peace Corps is established.
- Alan B. Shepard becomes the first American astronaut to fly in space.
- The Rand Corporation helps the Department of Defense install PPBS.

1962
- President John F. Kennedy issues Executive Order 10988, which encourages the unionization of federal workers.

1963
- During the "March on Washington," Martin Luther King Jr. delivers his "I have a dream" speech.
- President John F. Kennedy is assassinated; Vice President Lyndon B. Johnson becomes president.

1964
- The Civil Rights Act prohibits discrimination in private sector employment and public accommodation.
- Aaron Wildavsky publishes *The Politics of the Budgetary Process,* which becomes the classic analysis of the tactics public managers use to get budgets passed.
- The Economic Opportunity Act becomes the anchor of President Lyndon B. Johnson's "war on poverty" and other Great Society programs.

1965
- PPBS made mandatory for all federal agencies.
- The Department of Housing and Urban Development established.
- Medicare is created through amendments to the Social Security Act.

1966
- The Freedom of Information Act allows greater access to federal agency files.
- Morton Grodzins in *The American System* asserts that the federal system is more like a marble cake than a layer cake.

1967
- Age Discrimination in Employment Act passed.
- The National Academy of Public Administration is organized; its first members will be all of the living past presidents of the American Society for Public Administration.
- Edward A. Suchman's *Evaluative Research* asserts that evaluation is a generic field of study.
- Terry Sanford in *Storm Over the States* develops the concept of "picket-fence federalism," which holds that bureaucratic specialists at the various governmental levels exercise considerable power over the nature of intergovernmental programs.

1968
- "Younger" public administration scholars meeting at Syracuse University's Minnowbrook conference site call for a "new public administration" that would emphasize social equity.
- Martin Luther King Jr. is assassinated.
- Robert F. Kennedy is assassinated.
- Richard M. Nixon is elected president.

1969
- Laurence J. Peter promulgates his principle that "in a hierarchy every employee tends to rise to his level of incompetence."
- Theodore Lowi's *The End of Liberalism* attacks interest group pluralism for paralyzing the policymaking process.
- Neil Armstrong, an American astronaut, becomes the first man to walk on the moon.

1970
- The Bureau of the Budget is given more responsibility for managerial oversight and renamed the Office of Management and Budget.
- Postal Reorganization Act creates the U.S. Postal Service as a public corporation within the executive branch.
- Hawaii becomes the first state to allow state and local government employees the right to strike.
- Environmental Protection Agency established.

1971
- The Supreme Court attacks restrictive credentialism in *Griggs v. Duke Power Company.*
- PPBS formally abandoned in the federal government by the Nixon administration.